THEY LIVED TO TELL
THE TALE

THEY LIVED TO TELL
THE TALE

PUBLISHED BY
READER'S DIGEST ASSOCIATION LTD
LONDON · NEW YORK · SYDNEY · MONTREAL

CONTENTS

INTRODUCTION

Life is not predictable. It can become terrible and frightening with the suddenness and randomness of a bolt of lightning. A storm descends, a boat overturns, a plane crashes, a ferocious animal attacks out of nowhere, a terrorist unleashes a bomb, or a child is simply washed into the sea. *They Lived to Tell the Tale* celebrates the superhuman acts of bravery and self-preservation that can be unleashed by the overwhelming urge to survive that such events trigger.

Captured in this book are 51 remarkable dramas that have all happened in real life, starring men, women and children who have lived through incredible trials of endurance, battled with the elements and achieved great feats in adversity. There are many heroes here and they are people you are glad to know exist.

It could happen to anyone

The stories travel the world, from the Alps to the Andes, Iraq to Utah, the Amazon jungle to Tiananmen Square, and even into space. Each narrative is guaranteed to keep you gripped. From Ernest Shackleton's epic 1,290km (800 mile) voyage in a flimsy lifeboat through mountainous Antarctic seas, to the prisoner of war who survived inhuman torture but forgave his torturer, to the office worker who unhesitatingly risked his life to save a stranger's in the maelstrom of 9/11, you are right there: freezing cold, exhausted, drenched in spray, or lying broken-bodied in a bamboo hut in the stifling heat of the Burmese jungle, or descending the stairwell of a skyscraper close to collapse in the confusion of billowing smoke and pitch darkness.

What would you do in the same situation? Would you hold out? Would you find inner resources to cope? We may never be tested so severely — but we can learn from those who have. Nelson Mandela tells us of his 27 years in prison, many of them on the infamous Robben Island. Somehow he kept his hope and humanity, and emerged without bitterness to build a new country. Mandela had been arrested several times, so he might have been able to prepare himself. But young British estate agent Stephanie Slater had no such warnings. On a morning like any other, while simply doing her job, she was kidnapped, raped and imprisoned in a coffin-sized box. Her extraordinary fortitude during and after her eight-day nightmare is both inspiring and humbling.

Not what they bargained for

There are those highly trained and expert in their field, though, who have to expect the unexpected and cope with it. Cosmonaut Alexei Leonov was the first man to walk in space — but no one had foreseen that the over-inflation of his space suit would make it impossible for him to get back into the capsule. Surgeon Angus Wallace put up his hand when the captain asked 'Is there a doctor on the flight?' and

> **I saw the jaws of a 15ft tiger shark** cover the top of my board and my left arm. Then I watched in shock as the water around me turned bright red. My left arm was gone almost to the armpit.
> **Bethany Hamilton, OUT OF THE BLUE**

improvised enough equipment to perform an emergency operation that saved the life of a fellow passenger.

Then there are the risk-takers, pitting themselves against nature and the elements. Mountaineers and climbers are a breed apart – they crave challenge and may go where no rescue team could ever reach them. They know that if they get into trouble, they can only rely on themselves. Even the best-planned expedition can go wrong, and then the key to survival is the adventurer's mental fitness. Joe Simpson plunged down a crevasse in the Andes, and his partner thought he was dead. Yet, despite a shattered knee and ankle, Joe found a way out, and then crawled for three agonising days to reach base camp. When canyoneer Aron Ralston ventured into the remote Utah desert and found himself trapped when a boulder fell on to his hand, he knew no one could possibly find him. He had to do the unthinkable – amputate his own arm, with a penknife.

For journalists and camera crew, committed to bringing us our news, their next job may be to report on the latest armed conflict. They learn not to take unnecessary risks, rely heavily on local guides and fixers, and develop an instinct for danger. Yet theirs is an increasingly perilous job. Hear from Kate Adie what happened when she had to dodge the tanks in Tiananmen Square, and from John Simpson how he survived 'friendly fire' in northern Iraq.

A policeman went for the tape in my hand. I kicked him in the groin, punched the second with my left hand and body-charged the third. I'm no fighter, but surprise and a sense of outrage are enough.
Kate Adie, DODGING TANKS AND BULLETS

Beyond the call of duty
How often do we read grumblings in the media about a lack of suitable role models in modern society? But there are, among us, ordinary people doing extraordinary things – unexpected heroes. Faced with an emergency, they have responded instinctively, courageously. Like Cornish hotel owner Nick Leeds, who jumped into a raging sea to rescue his son. Then there are those who will risk their lives to save even a complete stranger. A man like fireman Royd Kennedy, who entered a deadly ring of burning fuel to comfort a child trapped beneath the wheels of a blazing fuel tanker in New Zealand.

The end of the adventure is seldom the end of the story. Some of our heroes have slipped back into normal, everyday life, but many have been profoundly affected by what they endured. We have found out what happened to them next – with some surprising discoveries. Ex-steelworker Ted Edwards followed up his solo Saharan trek with the first solo walk across Iceland, and then tried to join the NASA and Soviet space programmes. Soldier George Millar, who repeatedly cheated death to sabotage German supply lines with the French Resistance in the Second World War, ended his days quietly as a gentleman farmer in Dorset. Kosovan girl Saranda Bogujevci, who witnessed the massacre of many family members, is now settled in Manchester and looking ahead to a photography career. Without exception, their lives have been shaped and changed by their experiences. And without doubt, their stories will leave you moved, shocked, amazed, even outraged, but ultimately uplifted by the power of the human spirit to triumph over the worst of circumstances. ■

A SMALL BAND of scientists was investigating Galeras, a Colombian volcano, dormant for 40 years. The vital signs were good, but as volcanologist Stanley Williams led a group to the summit, Galeras began to shake ominously. Was the sleeping giant about to erupt?

ON THE BACK OF THE BEAST

For 40 years the great volcano had slumbered, before stirring to snort out ash, boulders and gas. Now Galeras was quiet again, and seismic activity was low: a good time, it seemed, for our small band of scientists to climb the mountain and explore the crater. But as we reached the summit, tentacles of superheated gas were rushing up inside the volcano. A cascade of rocks would be our only warning: Galeras was about to erupt.

Our caravan of Jeeps left for the mountain at around 8am. The temperature was in the 40s, and thick clouds drifted slowly across the peaks. Soon we were passing the corn and potato fields at the base.

About 100 scientists had come to Pasto, Colombia, for the conference I was sponsoring to study the volcano. It was our third day, January 14, 1993, and several groups were heading out on field trips to Galeras. Marta Calvache, my prize graduate student, was leading one group, and I another.

At the moment, Galeras seemed relatively quiet. Only faint tremors were occasionally recorded by the local observatory. And the volcano was releasing a minuscule amount of sulphur dioxide, another encouraging sign. As a rule, the less gas, the less active the magma.

But after a long career studying volcanoes, I knew these readings could change suddenly. Over the past 500 years, Galeras had erupted nearly 30 times. That there were no recorded deaths in these earlier events was due to serendipity and lower population numbers. Now some 300,000 people lived in the area. By studying the mountain we hoped to be better able to forecast future eruptions – and possibly save people's lives.

The local indigenous population had long referred to Galeras as Urcunina, the Fire Mountain. But to 19th-century Spanish colonialists, the clouds that formed over the volcano resembled sails, and its long, gentle slope looked like a ship's hull. So they rechristened it Galeras, from the Spanish word *galera* – a boat with large, open sails.

Driving through the countryside, we passed a landscape that was typical of the higher altitudes of the Andes. A few pines grew on the lower slopes, but as we rose the vegetation became scrubbier.

A pact with the beast *The people of Pasto, in the shadow of Galeras, live at the mercy of the volcano. In return, they reap the agricultural benefits of the mineral-rich volcanic soil.*

We sped by white stucco farmhouses on a dirt road. About 820m (2,700ft) from the summit, we entered a national park where the mountainside was thick with frailejón, a succulent plant with silvery green leaves and vivid yellow flowers.

After bouncing through deep, muddy holes, our caravan reached the top of the mountain at around 9.30am. We were actually on the rim of an old volcano that had collapsed long ago, leaving a horseshoe-shaped amphitheatre that opened to the west.

In the middle, rising more than 90m (300ft) above the amphitheatre floor, was the current cone of Galeras. In the centre of the cone was a crater about 350m (1,150ft) wide and 76m (250ft) deep.

A Colombian TV reporter approached Patty Mothes, who had come with her husband, Pete Hall, from Quito, where they were studying Ecuador's many active volcanoes. The reporter asked, 'Is there a possibility of an eruption in the next five years?'

To 19th-century Spanish colonialists, the clouds that formed over the volcano resembled sails, and its long, gentle slope looked like a ship's hull. So they rechristened it Galeras, meaning a boat with large, open sails.

'That's the purpose of what we're doing now – to understand the volcano's activity,' Patty replied in Spanish. 'There is no volcanologist who can say if the volcano is going to erupt next week or in five years. At this time the signs we are receiving indicate it is calm.'

'But,' she added, 'you always have to be watchful.'

Preparing to climb

Standing at the police post – an ideal spot from which to survey the countryside, which is probably why the police had chosen the site – we could gaze about half a kilometre down to the active volcano. The crater lip was some 150m (500ft) lower than where we stood on the top of the amphitheatre wall.

To get to the crater, we had to descend about 245m (800ft) down the side of the old volcano, then cross the amphitheatre floor before reaching the cone, a scree slope that rose up at about a 40-degree angle.

As we made preparations to move to the lip of the scarp above Galeras, our 16-person group paused to check on the gear we were carrying.

My outfit included tough leather hiking boots, a turtleneck, a chamois shirt and a fleece jacket. I had a rock hammer with me, and a knife and compass attached to a wide brown belt on my waist. In a backpack I carried a Gore-Tex jacket, rain trousers, leather gloves (for scrambling over rocks), a lightweight blanket, some candy bars, water and sunscreen, a camera and, perhaps most important, a flashlight. One has to prepare for getting lost on a volcano; that could mean spending the night at over 4,000m (14,000ft).

Two team members, an American, Andy Adams, and a Guatemalan chemical engineer, Alfredo René Roldán Manzo, wore hard hats. Adams also had on an insulated jumpsuit. None of the rest of us was wearing such protective clothing, deciding that good boots and warm layers were enough. Many of us had respirators, however, to protect us against sulphurous gases.

I would be overseeing the group's foray to the crater. Assisting me was José Arlés Zapata Granada, one of my closest associates at INGEOMINAS, the

Geological Survey of Colombia. Wearing a bright yellow parka, José Arlés was a good-looking, baby-faced 35-year-old with large dark eyes and black hair.

As a young geology student, José Arlés had lost nearly a dozen classmates in a mudflow when the nearby volcano of Nevado del Ruiz erupted in 1985. This catastrophe claimed the lives of more than 23,000 residents of Armero, the town below the mountain. For José Arlés, Marta Calvache and an entire generation of Colombian geologists, this was a formative event.

Hired by the Colombian Geological Survey after graduation, José Arlés had a terrific wife and a rewarding job. He was a rising star in his field. I was glad to have him with me.

I was also happy to be joined by Geoff Brown, a lanky Yorkshireman in his late 40s, who had done pioneering work on the magmatic 'plumbing systems' of volcanoes. Geoff would carry a gravimeter. One hundred million times more sensitive than a grocer's scale, this instrument can gauge the forces of gravity within a mountain as it heaves under the power of rising, molten rock. Geoff was trying to map the innards of Galeras, to determine if magma was on the move or if an eruption was likely.

Unusual readings

I was eager to begin work. Whenever I walk onto a volcano, a clock is ticking in my head. I'm not counting down towards a feared eruption, but am always aware that volcanoes are unpredictable places and the sooner I clear out the better. Also, fog and clouds can quickly gather over a mountain, greatly increasing the likelihood of becoming disoriented or stumbling over a cliff.

The group moved slowly, but eventually we reached the floor of the amphitheatre and began to ascend the volcano's cone.

As we made our way upwards, I talked with my Russian friend Igor Menyailov. A leading specialist in what gases tell us about a volcano's behaviour, Igor had a superb geochemical pedigree. Both of his parents were renowned Soviet volcanologists, and his mother had reportedly climbed one of the country's highest volcanoes while pregnant with him.

In addition, his wife, Lyudmila, was a fellow scientist. And now their daughter, Irina, was also a budding volcanologist. Igor and I chatted about Irina coming to study with me at Arizona State University.

We soon reached a volcanic gas vent, called a fumarole, which was a complete assault on our senses. Its 'whooshing' sound fell somewhere between the roar of the ocean and the howl of a jet engine. The vapour hit us in the face and filled our mouths with an acrid taste of burnt matches. The rocks around the vent were encrusted with bright yellow sulphur.

We probably reached this vent at around 11am. For the next 2 hours or so my colleagues came and went in the clouds, checking the vital signs of Galeras. From deep inside the earth, gases streamed out of the vent at 225°C (440°F) and bubbled as a solution into Igor's new double-chambered collection bottle.

Taken over time, these samples would show how much sulphur was present and in what forms, helping to reveal the volcano's secrets. Was the magma rising? Was an eruption imminent?

Alfredo René Roldán Manzo

Stanley Williams

Néstor García

José Arlés Zapata Granada

Fabio Garcia

Igor Menyailov

The final picture *Members of the team smile for the camera in what was for some to be their last photograph together. Of the six, only Manzo, Williams and Fabio García survived the ordeal in the mouth of Galeras.*

At one point I noticed that Andy Adams was looking tired and winded. I suggested that he and Alfredo Roldán head down the cone and begin the taxing climb back up the face of the amphitheatre. They left at about noon.

Meanwhile, Igor and Marta Calvache's Colombian colleague, Néstor García, had descended into the throat of Galeras.

A geochemist by training, Néstor was a true volcano lover. He was in the process of studying volcanic gases, and had told me how excited he was to work with someone of Igor's renown.

Now the two crouched low to avoid being incinerated by the scorching gases whooshing out of the crater's vents, as Igor continued his sampling.

The Russian looked content, smiling, swivelling his head away from the shifting gas clouds as he talked with Néstor.

At around 1pm I stood with several others on the crater's lip, gazing into the steaming pit. As with most explosive volcanoes, there was no cauldron of lava. It was a moonscape, pocked with fumaroles.

I felt it was time to begin wrapping up our work and get off the mountain. Just then Geoff Brown came to me with his gravimeter.

He mentioned that he had been getting some strange readings on his machine – showing rapid fluctuations in gravity. He suspected that the gravimeter had been damaged on an earlier research trip, and said he'd check on it later. He didn't seem concerned, and neither was I.

An ominous shaking

As we were finishing up, Marta Calvache and her colleagues were gathering on the outer slope of the mountain at about 3,600m (12,000ft). Galeras was a thing of beauty, to be sure, but also an object of study. A lump of volcanic deposit could be read like the rings of a tree.

So at around 1.30pm Marta had roused the group from a lunch break and was busy explaining the mysteries of the mountain to them.

At about the same time, I decided we should leave. We'd been on Galeras for more than 3 hours. I yelled to Igor down in the crater that it was time to clear out. 'How are the samples?' I added at the top of my voice.

'Good,' he yelled back, smiling.

Later, many people remembered Igor's smile. 'He and Néstor looked really happy,' recalled one team member. 'They shouted to us that they would rest a minute, and then they would go.'

Standing next to me on the crater rim was José Arlés, checking in regularly by radio with the observatory in Pasto. As we stood together on the cone, I was reassured by his radio communications. Time and again, staff members there told us that the six seismic stations around Galeras showed no hint of unusual activity.

While I was trying to round up my fellow researchers, three men materialised out of the clouds, one middle-aged and two in their late teens. The older man was courteous and intensely curious about the volcano and the work being done by the men in the crater. I tried to be polite, but my answers were brusque. I was much more concerned about getting my group off Galeras.

Subsequently, I learned who these tourists were. The man was a 45-year-old official from a local school with two 18-year-olds: his son and a friend. They had come hoping to talk with the scientists and learn about Galeras.

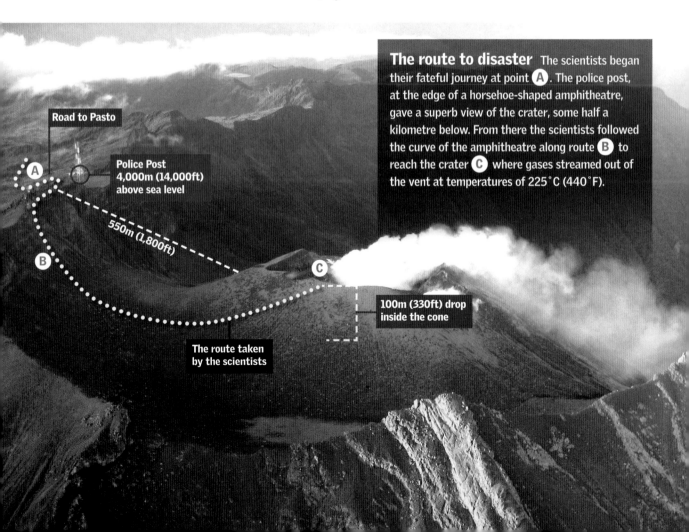

Road to Pasto

Police Post
4,000m (14,000ft)
above sea level

550m (1,800ft)

100m (330ft) drop
inside the cone

The route taken
by the scientists

The route to disaster The scientists began their fateful journey at point **A**. The police post, at the edge of a horsehoe-shaped amphitheatre, gave a superb view of the crater, some half a kilometre below. From there the scientists followed the curve of the amphitheatre along route **B** to reach the crater **C** where gases streamed out of the vent at temperatures of 225°C (440°F).

The time was now between 1.35 and 1.40pm. We all began walking off the volcano. Igor and Néstor García were still in the crater, but were preparing to leave. Rocks began tumbling off the inside wall of the crater – a common occurrence that at first aroused no concern in me.

But soon a cascade of stones and boulders rained onto the floor of the volcano, and I felt it shake ominously.

Alarmed, I recall shouting, 'Hurry up! Get out!' in English and in Spanish.

I turned to run down the scree-covered flank of the cone. The air was rent by a sound like a thunderclap or a sonic boom. Immediately afterwards, I heard a deafening 'craaack', the sound of the earth's crust snapping as Galeras began to disgorge its deadly contents.

Then a rock hit me. It was as if someone had taken a swing at my head with a baseball bat. I was knocked a few feet sideways and crumpled to the flanks of Galeras.

It's been said that time slows down in a disaster. For me, in the opening moments of the eruption, everything seemed to move at warp speed. The crater was roaring, the mountain throbbing, and the air around me crackling with volcanic shrapnel. Racing frantically, overloaded by sensations and emotions, my mind seemed to blow a fuse.

Then a rock hit me. It was as if someone had taken a swing at my head with a baseball bat. I was knocked a few feet sideways and crumpled to the flanks of Galeras. Stunned, I lay on the slope for a minute, my head ringing, the air filled with the bellowing of the eruption and the 'Zzzzip! Zzzzip! Zzzzip!' of incandescent chunks of Galeras whizzing past.

Bomblets from the volcano, many of them more than a metre in diameter, shattered when they hit the earth, flinging out fragments of red-hot hissing shrapnel.

I had made it no more than 20m (60ft) below the crater's lip. Pulling myself to my feet, I looked to the side and noticed, just a few yards away, a vivid patch of yellow against the lead-grey flank of the volcano. It was José Arlés Zapata, and it was obvious that he was dead. His head was bloody, his body contorted. His radio lay smashed beside him. Not far from José Arlés, the three tourists were splayed across the field of scree. Bloodied and disfigured, they, too, were clearly dead.

Determined to survive

Stumbling down the 40-degree slope, I was pelted by rocks, several slamming into my backpack, which was by now on fire. I managed to run a few more yards before a barrage of rocks cut me off at the legs, knocking me to the ground.

Rolling on my side, I looked down. A bone protruded from my lower left leg, poking through my smouldering trousers. Another projectile had almost severed my right foot at the ankle. Staring at my legs, I thought it odd that I didn't feel more pain.

I had no idea what might be coming out of the volcano next, so I was hell-bent on getting clear of the cone. All I wanted to do was run.

I tried to pull myself up, but in seconds I fell on my face once more. This time I knew I was down for good. I lay there, my foot bleeding steadily, but my wounds scarcely hurt. I noticed, though, that my back, arms and legs had been burned by the fiery rocks that had pelted me.

No longer able to walk, I dragged myself several yards across the mountainside to the shelter of a boulder. My trousers and jacket were on fire. The largest blaze was on my back, where my backpack was consumed by flames; I tore off the pack and rolled around to extinguish the fire.

I wasn't aware that the rock – or rocks – which hit me in the head had also broken my jaw, destroyed the hearing in my left ear, and caused the retinas in both eyes to become partially detached. I also didn't realise that the rocks which had smashed into my spine had caused hairline fractures in two vertebrae – injuries that could have been far worse, even crippling, had I not been wearing the backpack.

With the boulder shielding me from the volcano's horizontal projectiles, I turned onto my back and scanned the sky for falling objects. This was a difficult task, especially as my glasses had been shattered.

I saw superheated rocks glowing red, orange and white, and ranging in size from a marble to a softball. As they whistled out of the sky, I tried to roll out of their way.

At that point, Galeras seemed to me as if it were alive, a large beast that was toying with me. Unable to move, I was at the volcano's mercy.

Eventually the eruption slowed, until only gravel-size particles rattled down. Then, strangely, it began to rain, almost as if the blast had altered the climate in this corner of the Andes. Drizzle mingled with the ashes, coating me with a grey paste.

Exhausted, I put my head down on the craggy slope. I couldn't believe Galeras had erupted. José Arlés had been in frequent contact with the observatory, and no one had detected ominous seismic activity.

Now José Arlés lay just a few yards away, dead, and when I thought of Igor and Néstor in the crater I was overwhelmed with grief and confusion. How could they have survived? And what about Geoff Brown? How could anyone have made it out alive?

Galeras was still chuffing, still sending a column of ash into the sky. Every few minutes I cried out. I yelled to see if anyone else was alive. I yelled for help. I yelled because that was all I could do, and because the sound of my own voice offered a certain reassurance that I was still there and that I hadn't given up. No one replied.

Rain had penetrated the many holes in my jacket and trousers, and I was chilled to the bone. As I lay there behind the boulder, I became less worried about a second eruption. But I feared I was going into shock and was terrified of being left on the volcano after dark. Over and over I told myself I had to remain conscious. Twisting my head towards the crater, all I could see was the black pillar of ash towering into the clouds.

As the volcano's tremors subsided, my relief was tempered by indescribable fatigue. Stay awake, I kept telling myself. Stay awake.

My mind repeatedly returned to the blast and the fates of my friends. How could this have happened? How could some of the world's top volcanologists not have seen signs that Galeras – the very volcano we had come to study – was about to blow?

I thought about my family – my wife, Lynda, my seven-year-old daughter, Christine, and five-year-old son, Nick – back in Phoenix, and began to cry. To die on Galeras, I thought, would be to fail them. Somehow I had to make it off the mountain.

It was now 3pm. I knew that at our equatorial latitude it would get dark swiftly at around 6pm. The rescue teams had 3 hours to find me and any other survivors. But would the rescuers hesitate to descend onto this volcano that looked far from spent? As I fretted over who might show up, and when, the answer soon came to me. Marta.

Into the heart of danger

Far from the cone, Marta Calvache was on the mountain's outer flank when Galeras blew. She knew right away that it was an eruption.

Patty Mothes, who was with her and who has probably spent more time on Andean volcanoes than any other American except her husband, thought at first that the explosion might be the sound of a jet fighter. But when pumice and ash began falling, she knew what had happened.

As the scientists in their group started bolting in all directions, Marta and Patty both instantly thought of the danger of a pyroclastic flow. This is a deadly avalanche of gas, ash, pumice and hot lava blocks that can spew from a volcano at over 160km/h (100mph). With no sign of one, gradually the general panic subsided, replaced by concern for the men in the crater.

Marta led the scientists to the Jeeps, about a kilometre or so down the trail. 'I told the people, "You go to Pasto and I will go see what happened,"' she recalled later. 'Patty said, "No, I'll go with you."'

The two women sped up the mountain in their Jeep, ploughing through puddles and bouncing over boulders on the abysmal road. As they negotiated the sharp turns, several vehicles came racing down the mountain, filled with panicked national park employees and tourists fleeing the eruption. An army truck rumbled down the road and Marta waved it to a stop. Knowing they would need help rescuing survivors, Marta and Patty persuaded two soldiers to get in their Jeep.

Pulling in behind the police post on the amphitheatre rim, the women confronted a grim scene. Volcanic bombs had smashed the windows of one vehicle and knocked holes in the post's roof and walls.

White-hot angular rocks littered the ground. Patty spat on one and it hissed back at her. The volcano still thrummed and emitted an eerie sound, like the howl of a strong wind. When the swirling clouds over the ridge occasionally parted, Marta and Patty glimpsed a column of vapour and ash emanating from the crater in the amphitheatre below them.

Several members of the team that had gone onto the volcano had made it to the police post, including Andy Adams, Alfredo Roldán and the American geologist Mike Conway. Mike looked awful, bloodied and ash-covered, his clothing burned.

Another team member, the Ecuadorean geochemist Luis LeMarie, made it about two-thirds of the way up the scarp. Unable to climb higher because

The life-saving science of volcanology

HOT WORK An American Geological Survey volcanologist surveys lava from Kilauea, on the Hawaiian Islands, flowing into the Pacific Ocean below him.

THE ANCIENT AZTECS, in awe of volcanoes, placed their faith in dreamers known as *tiemperos* (weather men), who could sense an imminent eruption. In a state of trance, the *tiemperos* would contact the spirit of a volcano to ask if it was about to vent its wrath. Modern science does things differently.

Volcanology is a new, increasingly sophisticated science, which can save countless lives. (Some 500 million people live in the shadow of the world's 1,500 or so active volcanoes.) In 1991, volcanologists detected tremors in Mount Pinatubo in the Philippines, and, as the volcano started coughing up clouds of ash, the government ordered the evacuation of 60,000 people ahead of an eruption. In the same year, an American geophysicist accurately predicted the eruption of the Colima volcano in Mexico.

Usually, before it blows its top, a volcano will give warnings. As with Pinatubo, there will be seismic activity (quakes and tremors), which may be picked up by seismometers. Other devices, such as tiltmeters and geodimeters, can detect the subtle shifting and swelling of a volcano, and global positioning satellite technology can measure the minute expansion of the flanks of a mountain. Correlation spectrometers measure increasing levels of sulphur dioxide, while remote infrared technology measures the radiative temperature of surfaces around a volcano.

Because it is not possible to make close study of an erupting volcano, most field work is done on dead or dormant volcanoes, and volcanologists spend much of their time in laboratories, analysing rock samples, or at a computer, modelling aspects of eruptions.

Volcanic harmony

When a volcano reawakens, there are also acoustic signals. Before Piton de la Fournaise erupted on Réunion Island in 2006/7, scientists detected changes in the low-frequency seismic waves of the ocean hitting the seabed. Again, locals were evacuated.

In Italy, researchers have developed a technique in which software translates the seismic waves that travel through the earth into music audible to the human ear. Music pattern-recognition software – previously used to detect copyright fraud – is used to search for patterns in the sound.

So do volatile volcanoes all sing in harmony? And was it to this that the entranced *tiemperos* harkened: the spirit of the volcano, singing?

of broken legs and a broken clavicle, he was half-carried and dragged the rest of the way by a rescuer.

Perched atop the scarp, Marta and Patty strained to see or hear signs of life in the amphitheatre. 'I heard Stan saying, "Help me! Help me!"', Patty recalled later. 'It sent a chill through me. I could tell he was really bad off because of his voice. And I yelled out, "Yeah, we're coming, Stan! We're coming!"'

A handful of policemen and Colombian survey employees gathered on the scene to assist in the rescue effort. Marta spoke by radio with the observatory in Pasto. A volcanologist there warned her that the volcano was being rocked by earthquake activity. Everyone should get out immediately, he advised.

But Marta, determined that no survivors would be left on Galeras, brushed aside the warning. She, Patty and half a dozen others began backing down the slope, holding on to a climbing rope permanently anchored into the rock.

Towards the lower fringes of the slope, Marta and Patty found another team member, Andy Macfarlane. He had a hairline skull fracture and burns on his hands, arms and legs. Though his injuries were far from life-threatening, Macfarlane was going into shock. Some more rescue workers arrived with a metal stretcher, attached a rope to it and hauled him up.

Marta and Patty now clambered back down the scarp in search of me and any other survivors. They were joined by several other Colombian survey workers.

Reaching the cone, the rescuers split up. They could no longer hear me yelling for help. Fresh ash had covered everything in a thin blanket of grey, and large boulders – some old, some new and white-hot – made finding a prone body much more difficult.

One distraught worker ran to Marta. He had just found the corpse of his friend, José Arlés. As he started to tell Marta about it, she looked to the side and spied an ash-covered figure lying crossways on the flank of the volcano. It was me.

I was in frightful shape – sprawled on my side, caked in ash and blood, wet from the rain, bones protruding from my burned clothes, my jaw hanging slackly. I remember very little about being found, and recall that once the sense of relief passed, I began to feel the cold and pain all the more intensely.

Patty Mothes arrived, which I scarcely recollect. She said, 'Stanley, it's Patty and Marta. We're here to help you.'

She remembers me muttering, 'I want to see Lynda, I want to see my children, I want to live.' At times I seemed coherent, at times I was out of it.

One rescuer used a piece of a foam cooler to fashion a splint that he tied to my lower right leg with shoelaces. Then two of the men helped Patty and Marta lift me onto a stretcher they had carried down from the police post.

Picking me up, they trudged across the broken terrain. At the bottom of the scarp, more rescuers, including Red Cross workers, arrived with an aluminium mountaineering stretcher. They transferred me to the new litter and began the arduous ascent up the amphitheatre wall.

Then Patty, Marta and several INGEOMINAS workers fanned out on

The volcano was being rocked by earthquake activity. Everyone should get out immediately. Marta brushed aside the warning.

the cone looking for other survivors. One stopped at the body of José Arlés and wept at the sight of his colleague. The group also found the three tourists, all plainly dead.

The volcano rumbled like a giant pair of bellows, and the rescuers dashed across the flanks, wondering if Galeras might blow again. Nevertheless, the women continued searching. Patty climbed to the top of the cone, where she was completely exposed to the volcano. Even a tiny cough from Galeras could have killed her. Still she continued to look frantically around for signs of life, for bodies, but the landscape was nothing but steaming hot boulders, scree and ash.

Only one more body would ever be found. Searchers discovered it two days later where it had been flung over 450m (1,500ft) by the force of the blast. But no trace of the others, including Igor Menyailov, Néstor García and Geoff Brown, was ever found. Horrific as their deaths were, there was one measure of comfort for us: the end was instantaneous.

Sometime around 5pm, more than 3 hours after the eruption and with an hour of daylight remaining, a crowd of workers on the top of the scarp finally grabbed my stretcher and deposited me onto safe ground.

Amid the hubbub and shouts of rescuers, I felt a vague sense of relief. But mostly I was cold, colder than I'd ever been in my life.

Rescuers loaded me on board an army helicopter. The sensation of hot air enveloping me was one of the most sublime feelings I've ever experienced.

The helicopter was too small for Marta and Patty to ride with me. So they remained standing on the ridge atop Galeras, watching as the helicopter lifted off and banked towards Pasto, some 1,500m (5,000ft) below.

Luck on my side

As I look back on that day, I am amazed at the good fortune that helped me to survive. I still have no idea how I managed to escape with a skull fracture while two of the tourists and José Arlés – who were so close to me on the volcano – all suffered lethal head injuries.

The second stroke of luck came at the hospital. As it turned out, I badly needed a neurosurgeon, and just eight days before the eruption, a highly competent specialist, Dr Porfirio Muñoz Bermeo, had reported for duty at this provincial hospital in Pasto.

Dr Muñoz could see that a quarter-size section of my head above the left ear had been staved in. A scan showed that skull fragments driven into my brain had only narrowly missed the sigmoid sinus, an area of about one square centimetre that drains venous blood from the brain. Had that been cut, I would have bled to death on Galeras in a matter of minutes.

Dr Muñoz operated on me for 3 hours. Although he was confident that I would survive my injuries, he was not sure of the long-term damage.

My wife, alarmed by calls from Colombia bringing progressively worse news, made hasty arrangements to fly down.

Two days later Lynda was led into the room where I lay, expecting to see me in pretty bad shape. Instead, she found me smiling and talking coherently with the nurses in Spanish.

Walking to my bedside, she leaned over and hugged me, and we both began to cry. I remember looking into her green eyes and being flooded with feelings of love, relief and hope.

I talked almost nonstop, much to Lynda's relief. But then she noticed I was mixing up words, repeating myself. In fact, after Galeras my recovery would be long and difficult. For now, though, we both took comfort in the fact that I was alive and we were heading home.

Painful lessons

Over the next two years, I would undergo 17 operations designed to return me to a semblance of my former self.

The nonstop tinkering with my body left me with a few quiet moments, but when they came I was haunted by the thought that Igor, Geoff, Néstor, José Arlés and the others had died in the eruption. I missed my friends, and felt terribly for their families.

As I struggled to accept the deaths of my colleagues, I was consoled by letters and visits from friends and fellow scientists. Geoff Brown's widow, Evelyn, wrote my wife a touching note two weeks after the eruption:

Where are they now?

IT WAS WHEN HE STARTED TO WRITE HIS BOOK, *Surviving Galeras*, in 1999 and 2000, that Stanley Williams began to realise quite how many difficulties and disabilities he had in relation to his severe brain injury – to realise, indeed, that a part of him had not survived. 'In the first years, I refused to acknowledge that I had any problems. Then, in 1994, I had a seizure, and was given the standard anti-seizure medication, which was exactly wrong to give to me, because it is known to make people more irritable or agitated. I was already a very energetic and easily annoyed person, and people writing about me in those days naturally portrayed me as this cranky guy who couldn't get along with anyone.'

Eventually, recognising that he needed help, he hired a lawyer to argue that his insurance company should send him on a neurological rehabilitation programme. Ten years after the eruption, a judge agreed.

In the meantime, he had been having many physical and emotional problems. 'With TBI (traumatic brain injury), you lose your inhibitions, so I cry too easily, and yell and swear too much, and you're supposed to get divorced, or suicidal, or to lose your job or "all of the above".' He didn't commit suicide, or lose his job as Professor of Volcanology at Arizona State University, but he did get divorced from Lynda.

The rehabilitation, which he went through in 2003, proved tough but therapeutic. One thing that emerged in the process was the fact that Stanley can no longer multitask, and he still has to take 19 pills a day, though his medication is in balance. Today, though, he frequently prefaces his speech with the words, 'I'm lucky'.

Such has been his progress that, in 2005, he and Lynda got back together, and in 2007, their son, Nick, by then 17, was a witness at their second wedding. The family has a way of understanding him like no one else. 'At the time of Galeras, Nick was not yet five, and Christine was seven, so they've basically grown up with the me of the current variety. It's entertaining at times how I make terrible, frequent errors in speech. I'll say something that makes no sense whatsoever, but they are able to figure it out, and we wind up laughing about it.'

'Please reassure [Stan] that he must not yield to any sense of guilt on Geoff's behalf. Geoff was a gambler. The accident was nobody's fault except good old nature. We may think we are learning to control or manipulate geological hazards, but the earth has a mind of its own.'

Others had a harder time accepting the tragedy. When I went to see Igor's widow long afterwards, the visit started pleasantly enough, if sadly, in her Moscow apartment. Before leaving, I felt compelled to explain what had happened on Galeras and why we had been unable to foresee the eruption. It was then that Lyudmila's anger at me surfaced.

'Do you think Igor and I would have dared invite people to the volcano without knowing what condition it was in? There had to have been signs. You just missed them, that's all.'

I kept quiet, and Lyudmila cooled off. She blamed me, but, like many Russians, she also had a deeply mystical streak and thought that perhaps the gods had punished her and Igor for their overconfidence on volcanoes.

Others also believed we hadn't done enough to protect ourselves. Andy Adams returned home certain that his hard hat had saved his life and made suggestions to a panel drafting safety guidelines for volcanologists. These included wearing hard hats and protective clothing. The new rules were approved by the International Association of Volcanology and Chemistry of the Earth's Interior.

Since the disaster, Marta and I have remained good friends. Once, she told me that the hardest thing about the eruption was the loss of her close friends José Arlés Zapata and Néstor García. Since then, Marta and her observatory staff have carried on the men's work, learning a great deal about Galeras's seismic rumblings and emissions of gases.

The results of our ill-fated conference and subsequent studies filled an entire volume of the *Journal of Volcanology and Geothermal Research* in May 1997. Thanks to the work of Marta and other Colombian and American scientists, we have got much closer to being able to forecast when volcanoes will blow.

Was this progress worth the lives of Igor Menyailov, Geoff Brown, José Arlés Zapata, Néstor García and the others? Of course not. But did they die in vain? This was a question put to me by José Arlés's wife, Monica, when I visited her in 1999. I assured her that his contributions had taught us much about the volcano and its behaviour.

For José's wife and for all of us, the tragedy has left lasting scars. Six years after the eruption I stood again at the crater's rim on Galeras and scarcely recognised the blasted grey pit spread out before me. The ledge on which Igor and Néstor had knelt and sampled gases had disappeared. The western rim of the crater, where Geoff Brown and two others had stood, was partially blown away by the eruption.

As I gazed into the crater, I was struck by how tiny, in a geological sense, the eruption had been. It had been a mere hiccup, a blast so small that geologists decades hence will find no sign of it.

Yet its power, to those of us who lived through it, was staggering. It killed nine people, injured half a dozen others and nearly killed me. And it continues to ripple like a fault line through the lives of dozens of people. ■

A **WHIRLWIND ROMANCE** in Hong Kong had left Paula Dixon dreaming of a fresh start. Now, as she lay close to death on her return flight to the UK, her life was in the hands of one man. But high in the air, Professor Wallace did not have the necessary medical equipment to perform the life-saving surgery she so desperately required.

SURGERY AT 28,000 FEET

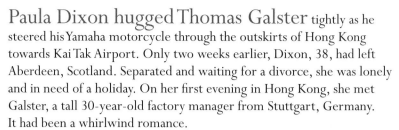

Paula Dixon hugged Thomas Galster tightly as he steered his Yamaha motorcycle through the outskirts of Hong Kong towards Kai Tak Airport. Only two weeks earlier, Dixon, 38, had left Aberdeen, Scotland. Separated and waiting for a divorce, she was lonely and in need of a holiday. On her first evening in Hong Kong, she met Galster, a tall 30-year-old factory manager from Stuttgart, Germany. It had been a whirlwind romance.

Three days before her trip was over, Galster asked her to marry him. 'You're joking!' Dixon responded.

'I've been looking for you all my life,' he said.

She hugged him ecstatically. 'The answer's yes!'

Now, as they rode slowly through the balmy twilight, Dixon was already dreaming about starting a new life. Suddenly a blue car pulled out from a side road. As Galster braked hard, the motorcycle hit the car's door. Dixon catapulted forward, slammed onto the car's boot and slid to the road.

Dazed, the dark-haired woman struggled to her feet. Galster ran to her. 'Are you hurt?' he asked.

'Just a scratch,' she said shakily. Her left forearm had a bleeding 8cm (3in) graze. 'What about you?'

'I'm okay – but I'm taking you to the hospital,' he replied.

Dixon shook her head. 'It's not that bad,' she said. 'I want to get to the plane. Please, darling, just take me to the airport.'

Panic in the air

At the check-in desk, Barbara Murray waited impatiently beside a trolley piled high with luggage. Why was Paula so late? The two long-time friends had come on this trip together. Check-in for their return flight, British Airways 032, would close in 15 minutes.

Finally Dixon arrived, looking pale. 'We were knocked off the bike,' she said, showing Murray her bruised arm.

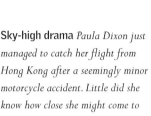

Sky-high drama *Paula Dixon just managed to catch her flight from Hong Kong after a seemingly minor motorcycle accident. Little did she know how close she might come to death on the plane.*

'You ought to get it looked at,' her friend told her.

'No,' Dixon said. 'The sooner I get home, the sooner I'll be back.' She embraced Galster and, with a final wave, the women passed through passport control.

The huge Boeing 747, carrying 331 passengers, would take nearly 15 hours to reach London. Dixon and Murray had the four middle seats in Row 53, at the very back, to themselves. Dixon stopped a flight attendant and asked for some painkillers. 'Could I also have something to clean my arm?'

'I think it needs more than that,' said the attendant, seeing the gash. Moments later, an announcement went out over the PA system: 'If there is a doctor on board, would you please make yourself known to a member of the cabin crew?'

Tom Wong, in economy class, snapped open his seat belt. The slim 26-year-old in blue jeans looked like a student. But Wong was a newly qualified doctor, heading back to his job at a hospital in Scotland.

Upstairs, in business class, another hand went up. 'Can I help?' Angus Wallace asked. The burly 46-year-old Scot, a professor of orthopaedics and accident surgery in Nottingham, England, had been in Hong Kong quizzing medical students. He had planned to spend the flight reading medical papers.

Instead, the surgeon made his way to the back of the plane, where Wong was already examining Paula Dixon. The younger doctor stepped aside for the professor.

Stooping, Wallace gently pressed Dixon's bruised forearm. The woman winced, but her colour was fine and she had no other complaints. Even if the arm was fractured, the doctor decided, she could continue on the flight.

When Wallace returned with a syringe, Dixon was worse. Her colour was blue, and her breathing shallow and rapid.

At 10.30pm, the 747 blasted down the runway and lifted into the night. When the 'fasten seat belt' sign was switched off, Wallace looked through the plane's medical kit and found a splint and bandages. He and Wong returned to Row 53. Deftly, Wallace cradled the splint around Dixon's elbow, and Wong wrapped her arm in bandages. 'That should hold you,' Wallace said.

'You're spoiling me,' Dixon replied, thanking them.

Well after midnight, Hong Kong time, Dixon was still awake. Her injured arm ached only a little, but the altitude had made her feet swell. She leaned forward to unlace her boots.

Angus Wallace couldn't imagine what the problem might be when a flight attendant asked him to look at the passenger he had treated a couple of hours before. 'What's the matter?' he asked Dixon.

'My chest,' she said, panting. Wallace pressed his fingers against her ribs. 'Why didn't you tell me about this before?'

'It wasn't sore then,' she said.

'I think you've fractured some ribs.' Turning to Sammy Burleton, the cabin services director, he said, 'We'll give her a painkiller. Would you open the medical kit?'

But when Wallace returned with a syringe, Dixon was worse. Her colour was blue, and her breathing shallow and rapid. He tried to listen to

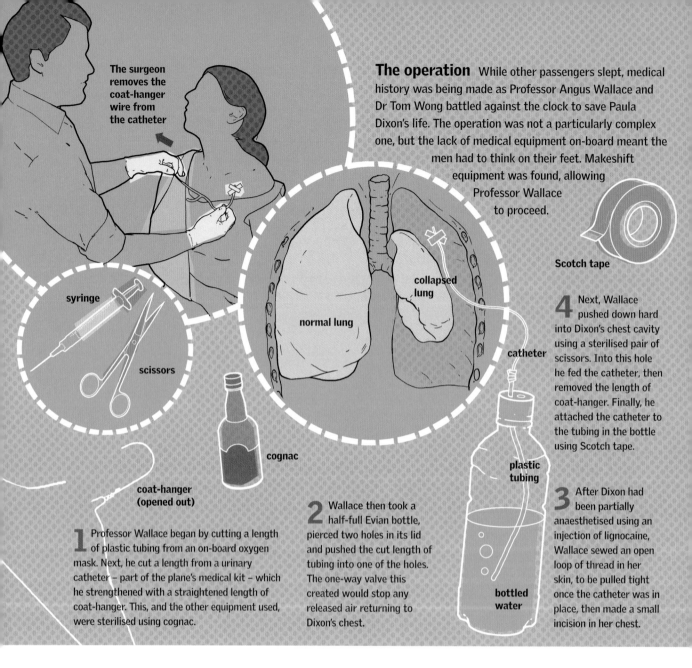

The surgeon removes the coat-hanger wire from the catheter

The operation While other passengers slept, medical history was being made as Professor Angus Wallace and Dr Tom Wong battled against the clock to save Paula Dixon's life. The operation was not a particularly complex one, but the lack of medical equipment on-board meant the men had to think on their feet. Makeshift equipment was found, allowing Professor Wallace to proceed.

Scotch tape

syringe

scissors

normal lung

collapsed lung

catheter

4 Next, Wallace pushed down hard into Dixon's chest cavity using a sterilised pair of scissors. Into this hole he fed the catheter, then removed the length of coat-hanger. Finally, he attached the catheter to the tubing in the bottle using Scotch tape.

cognac

plastic tubing

bottled water

coat-hanger (opened out)

1 Professor Wallace began by cutting a length of plastic tubing from an on-board oxygen mask. Next, he cut a length from a urinary catheter – part of the plane's medical kit – which he strengthened with a straightened length of coat-hanger. This, and the other equipment used, were sterilised using cognac.

2 Wallace then took a half-full Evian bottle, pierced two holes in its lid and pushed the cut length of tubing into one of the holes. The one-way valve this created would stop any released air returning to Dixon's chest.

3 After Dixon had been partially anaesthetised using an injection of lignocaine, Wallace sewed an open loop of thread in her skin, to be pulled tight once the catheter was in place, then made a small incision in her chest.

her chest with a stethoscope but could hear nothing over the roar of the engines. Then he pressed his fingers against her neck and was horrified.

Dixon's trachea – the windpipe – had moved to the right. It can't be. Wallace pressed again. No doubt about it.

Wong was awakened and asked to come to the galley. 'Tom, I want your opinion,' Wallace said. Wong confirmed that Dixon was having difficulty breathing. Wallace suspected that the left lung was collapsing.

'I need to talk with the captain,' Wallace said. In the cockpit he perched on the jump seat behind Capt. Barrie Hattam and explained the problem. 'A broken rib must have punctured her left lung.' Dixon needed an operation. 'How soon can we land the plane?'

'New Delhi's our best bet,' Hattam said. 'We could be on the ground in an hour and a half.'

'Forget it,' Wallace replied. She could die in less than an hour, he thought, then said, 'I'll have to take action myself.'

Each time Dixon breathed out, a little more air leaked through the hole in her left lung into her chest cavity. The bubble of air building up there was compressing her damaged lung, deflating it. The more she struggled for breath, the bigger the bubble grew. When the left lung was fully deflated, the second lung would start to go. Gasping in agony, Dixon would suffocate. She had, Wallace gauged, about 45 minutes.

In a hospital, relieving the problem was a routine procedure: a hollow needle would be inserted into the chest cavity, allowing the air to escape. Here, Wallace would have to improvise. 'I need some kind of tubing,' he told the cabin crew. 'What have we got?'

A drinking straw? 'Too weak,' Wallace thought. Then a flight attendant brought the oxygen mask used in safety demonstrations. Wallace's eyes lit up, and he snipped off a length of its plastic tubing.

Overcoming all hurdles

In the bottom of the medical kit he found a urinary catheter – a thin tube designed for insertion into the bladder. One end was sealed, like the bottom of a bottle, but its last inch or so was perforated with tiny holes to allow liquid to enter the tube and flow out. 'So could air,' Wallace thought.

'This will work, but it's too floppy,' he said. 'I need something rigid to go in the centre of the tube so I can push it into the chest.'

A flight attendant found a wire coat-hanger. Wallace untwisted the hooked end and straightened out the hanger. Measuring it against the catheter, he bent the wire back and forth until it broke into a length – about 45cm (18in) – a little longer than the tube.

The wire had to be sterilised. Someone produced a bottle of Courvoisier XO Imperial cognac – 40 per cent alcohol. Wallace nodded quickly. Cleaning the wire, he laid it on a tray that Burleton had covered with a white cloth. Then he disinfected the tubing from the oxygen mask and finished by splashing cognac over the scissors.

Wallace knew he needed a one-way valve to trap the released air and prevent it from going back into Dixon's chest. Opening a small bottle of Evian water, he pierced two holes in its plastic cap. Next, he drank half the water, replaced the cap and threaded the piece of oxygen tubing through one hole, leaving the other open. 'That's our valve,' he said, putting it on the tray.

Rubber gloves, scalpel, swabs and sutures were in the medical kit. Burleton also produced a roll of Scotch tape from her cabin bag.

The last hurdle was the anaesthetic. The medical kit held lignocaine, a powerful drug used in cases of cardiac arrest. Wallace knew it could also serve as a local anaesthetic – but how much could safely be given?

'Wait a minute,' said Wong. 'I've got a *BNF*.' He hurried to retrieve the book from his hand luggage. The *British National Formulary* lists every known drug. Wong quickly thumbed to 'lignocaine' and in a moment worked out the right dose.

'Good,' Wallace said, drawing off that amount into a syringe. He checked his watch. Fifteen precious minutes had sped by – not much time left.

The flight attendants had made an operating theatre by taping curtains and blankets round Row 53 and flipping on the reading lights. Dixon sat up in her seat, her face covered with beads of sweat. Breathing shallowly, she felt as if she were drowning.

'You've got a collapsed lung, and I have to operate,' Wallace told her. 'You're not in a fit state to give consent,' he added, inviting no argument. 'So I'm just going to do it.'

Dixon took the measure of this man. 'What are you waiting for, doctor?' she gasped, managing a weak grin.

Squeezing between the seats, Wallace faced his patient and pushed anxiety out of his mind. If he punctured one of the arteries that lie beneath each rib, Dixon could bleed to death in minutes. 'I could be up on a manslaughter charge by morning,' he thought. 'But if I don't do something, she'll die anyway.'

Dixon groaned loudly and grimaced in agony. She tried to focus on reasons to survive. Her three grown children. Galster. I am coming back to you. I am, I am.

Placing sterile hand towels over her chest, Wallace tore open a surgical wipe to clean the skin. Next he injected the anaesthetic. It would numb only half the thickness of her chest wall, but that was all he could do.

The insertion point would be between the second and third ribs. Wallace threaded a curved suture needle and quickly flicked it in and out of the skin. He tied the thread in an open loop, like a purse string, ready to be drawn tight around the tube later. With the scalpel he made a small incision – barely half a centimetre – where the drain was to go.

Now came the critical moment. Gripping surgical scissors like a screwdriver, Wallace put his right knee on the edge of the seat beside Dixon. The chances of hitting an artery were 10 per cent, he calculated. But an arterial wall is tough and rounded. He hoped the scissors would be blunt enough to push it aside. Positioning the closed point of the scissors in the incision, Wallace pushed down.

As the steel cut through the muscle and tissue into her chest, Dixon felt as if she were being skewered on a meat hook. Her chin jerked upwards and she shuddered. Wallace then twisted the scissor blades 90 degrees to widen the hole. The scissors were 5cm (2in) into the chest cavity. As Wallace drew them out, Wong quickly passed him the wire-reinforced catheter. Wallace positioned it in the hole he'd made and thrust downwards.

Dixon groaned loudly and grimaced in agony. She tried to focus on reasons to survive. Her three grown children. Galster. I am coming back to you. I am, I am.

Wallace pulled the coat-hanger out of the catheter, leaving the tube in her chest. 'Be brave, lassie,' he said.

Hurrying now, he connected the catheter to the oxygen tube that was threaded into the Evian bottle. Then he drew the purse-string suture tight, sealing the skin against the catheter to make the hole airtight.

In a moment Burleton exclaimed, 'You've got bubbles! Is that what you want?' From the end of the tube in the water, bubbles were streaming forth.

'That's exactly what I want,' Wallace replied. He glanced at Wong. 'Is there blood in the water?'

'No blood,' Wong answered, grinning. 'Well done, Prof!'

Wallace adroitly put another stitch around the tube to hold it in place on Dixon's chest. Where the two tubes joined, he sealed them with Scotch tape. At last he looked up at his patient. Her colour was returning, and she gave him a wan smile.

Theatrically, Burleton wiped Wallace's brow like a practised nurse. The doctor joined in the laughter. After making sure that Dixon was stable, he walked forward, past dozing passengers. Their 747 was now piercing the night sky at 925km/h (575mph), 8,500m (28,000ft) over India.

Reaching the galley, Wallace spotted the cognac he'd used to disinfect the instruments. Weak with relief, he picked up the bottle and took a gulp.

Just before landing at 5.15am at Heathrow Airport, Wallace checked Dixon one last time, finding her cheerful and composed. 'Thank you, doctor,' she said, planting a grateful kiss on his cheek. Then he shook hands with Wong. Neither spoke of the medical history they had made. It was the first time a collapsed lung had been operated on in midair.

Two weeks later, completely recovered, Paula Dixon flew back to Thomas Galster in Hong Kong. Shortly after she arrived, he gave her an engagement ring. ■

What happened next?

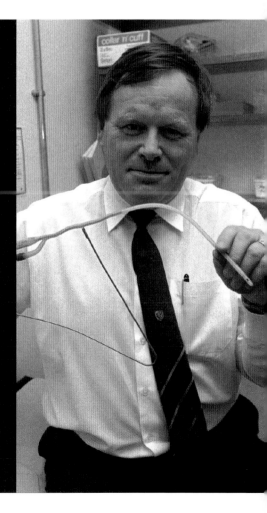

TWO DAYS AFTER returning to the UK from his trip to Hong Kong, Professor Angus Wallace was woken at 5am by a call from an Australian newspaper, and found himself, to his embarrassment, at the centre of a media storm.

By his swift and professional actions, and with makeshift 'equipment', he had saved Paula Dixon's life, and pressing questions were now being asked about the adequacy of in-flight emergency kits and cabin-crew training. 'I was invited to become a consultant to the company that makes medical kits for British Airways,' recalls Professor Wallace, 'and I was involved for the next four years in giving them advice. I also went to a number of airlines and asked for details of the medical kits they had on-board. We did a comparison of the kits. Some were very poor indeed. I produced a research paper on training and equipment for in-flight emergencies, which I presented in Atlanta, Georgia, in 1995. I said at that meeting, "If anyone here has a relative who dies on an aircraft because of lack of emergency equipment, or lack of medical support, I am very happy to be an expert witness and to act for you." That caused an absolute sensation.

'I was then approached by the union leader for cabin crew in Europe, who said would I come and join a European round table on cabin safety and the rescue role of cabin crews.' At the discussion, in Brussels in 1996, Professor Wallace had the sinking feeling that any harmonisation of standards among EU countries would be a levelling down.

Things have improved, though. 'I think cabin crew are better trained than they were, and the standard is more uniform across the board.'

A LONG WAY TO FREEDOM

HE HAD FIRST HEARD about the windswept Robben Island as a child, of how a Xhosa king jailed there had drowned in icy waters trying to escape. Now, anti-apartheid activist and lawyer Nelson Mandela was facing life there behind bars.

On Thursday, June 11, 1964, we reassembled in the Palace of Justice in Pretoria for the verdict. We were alleged to have recruited persons for sabotage and guerrilla warfare for the purpose of starting a revolution; we had allegedly conspired to aid foreign military units to invade the republic in order to support a communist revolution; and we had received funds from foreign countries for this purpose. Judge Quartus de Wet, who sat in flowing red robes beneath a wooden canopy, wasted no time in getting down to business. He spoke in low, rapid tones and pronounced each of the main accused guilty on all counts.

'I do not propose to deal with the question of sentence today,' de Wet said. 'The State and the defence will be given opportunities to make any submission they want tomorrow.'

That night, after discussions among ourselves, Walter Sisulu, Govan Mbeki and I informed defence counsel that whatever sentences we received – even the death sentence – we would not appeal. Our message was that no sacrifice was too great in the struggle for freedom.

On Friday, June 12, we entered court for the last time. Nearly a year had passed since our arrests. The spectators' gallery was full and it was standing room only for the press. I waved hello to my wife Winnie and my mother. It was heartening to see them there, my mother having come all the way from the Transkei. Her support never wavered. Winnie was equally stalwart, and her strength gave me strength.

De Wet nodded for us to rise. His face was very pale, and he was breathing heavily. He began to speak. 'The main crime of which the accused have been convicted is in essence one of high treason. The State has decided not to charge the crime in this form. Bearing this in mind, I have decided not to impose the supreme penalty, which in a case like this would usually be the proper penalty, but consistent with my duty that is the only leniency which I can show. The sentence in the case of all the accused will be one of life imprisonment.'

I turned and smiled broadly at the gallery, searching out Winnie's face and that of my mother, but it was extremely confused in the court, with people shouting and the police pushing back the crowd, and I could not see them. Our police guardians began to hustle us out of the dock and towards the door leading underground.

I looked again for Winnie's face, but I was not able to see her before I ducked through the door leading to the cells below.

Life behind bars

Robben Island, which lies off the coast of Cape Town, had changed since I had been there for a fortnight's stay in 1963. Then the place seemed more like an undisciplined experiment than a fully fledged prison. One year later it was without question the harshest, most iron-fisted outpost in the South African penal system. Gone were the Coloured warders who had supplied sympathy. Now the warders were white and overwhelmingly Afrikaans-speaking, and they demanded a master-servant relationship.

On my first visit I had arrived by ferry and was met by burly white warders shouting, '*Dis die eiland! Hier julle gaan vrek!*' ('This is the island!

No escape *Nelson Mandela's stark prison cell (below) had no running water. He endured almost two decades of harsh treatment at Robben Island Maximum-Security Prison (opposite, top). His work detail there included repairing prison-issue clothing (opposite, bottom).*

Here you will die!') The guards started screaming, '*Haak! Haak!*' The word *haak* means 'move' in Afrikaans, but it is customarily reserved for cattle.

This time all seven of us – Walter Sisulu, Raymond Mhlaba, Govan Mbeki, Ahmed Kathrada, Andrew Mlangeni, Elias Motsoaledi and I – were kept in a separate maximum-security structure for political prisoners. It was a one-storey rectangular stone fortress with a cement courtyard in the centre, about 30 x 9m (100 x 30ft). It had cells on three of the four sides. The fourth side was a 6m (20ft) high wall with a catwalk patrolled by guards with German shepherds.

We each had our small damp cell on the easternmost side of the quadrangle. When I lay down, I could feel the wall with my feet while my head grazed the concrete on the other side. Each cell had a white card posted outside with our name and prison service number. Mine read 'N. MANDELA 466/64', which meant I was the 466th prisoner admitted to the island in 1964. I was 46 years old, a political prisoner with a life sentence, and that small cramped space was to be my home for I knew not how long.

Our life soon settled into a pattern. Prison life is about routine: each day like the one before, each week like the one before it. Timepieces of any kind were barred, so we never knew precisely what time it was. We were dependent on warders' whistles and shouts. One had to make an effort to recall what day it was. I made a calendar on the wall of my cell. Losing a sense of time is an easy way to lose one's grip and even one's sanity.

Prison is designed to break one's spirit and destroy one's resolve. The authorities attempt to exploit every weakness, demolish every initiative, stamp out that spark which makes each of us who we are. It would be very hard for one man alone to resist. But the authorities' greatest mistake was keeping us together, for together our determination was reinforced. The

Spirit-breaking labour *Men at Robben Island Prison carry out their daily work, watched over by warders. Those at the front are breaking up large rocks, while the men in the back row sit mending prison clothes.*

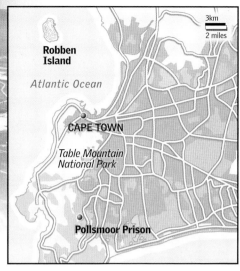

stronger ones raised up the weaker ones, and both became stronger in the process. I knew I would not give up the fight. I was in a smaller arena, but the racism and repression were the same. This assured that I would survive, for any man or institution that tries to rob me of my dignity will lose because I will not part with it at any price.

We were woken at 5.30 each morning by the night warder, who clanged a bell and yelled, '*Word wakker!*' ('Wake up!'). By 6.45 we were meant to have cleaned our cells and rolled up our mats and blankets. We had no running water in our cells, and, instead of toilets, we had iron sanitary buckets known as 'ballies'. The ballies had concave porcelain lids that could contain water, with which we were meant to wash. We were then let out of our cells to empty our ballies and cleanse them in the sinks at the end of the hallway. The only pleasant thing about cleaning them was that this was the one moment in those early days when one could have a whispered word with our colleagues.

A breakfast of mealie pap [grain] porridge was delivered to our cells. In addition, we received a mug of what was described as coffee, but which was in fact ground-up maize, baked until it was black, then brewed with hot water.

In the midst of breakfast our guards would yell, '*Val in!*' ('Fall in!') and we would stand outside our cells for inspection. Each prisoner was required to make his cell tidy, to button his khaki jacket properly, and to doff his hat as the warder walked by. Otherwise we were punished either with solitary confinement or with the loss of meals.

A visitor

After inspection we would begin work. A load of stones about the size of volleyballs was dumped each morning by the entrance to the courtyard. Using wheelbarrows we moved them to the centre of the yard. Our job was to crush the stones into gravel using hammers. We sat cross-legged on the ground in four rows and placed the stones in a thick rubber ring that had once been part of a tyre. The ring was meant to catch flying chips of stone, but we also wore makeshift wire masks to protect our eyes.

Warders walked among us to enforce silence. The work was tedious and difficult, demanding enough to make all our muscles ache. At noon the bell

Off limits *Robben Island (top left) is no longer a prison but a World Heritage Site and museum. The island is close to the city of Cape Town, home also to Pollsmoor Prison, where Mandela was taken in 1982 – but a long way from his Transkei homeland in the Eastern Cape.*

would clang and a drum of food would be wheeled in. For lunch we often received *phuzamandla*, which means 'drink of strength', a powder made from mealies and a bit of yeast. It is meant to be stirred into water or milk and can be tasty, but we were given so little powder that it barely coloured the water.

After lunch we worked again until 4pm, when the guards blew shrill whistles. We were then permitted half an hour to clean up. The bathroom at the end of our corridor had two sea-water showers, a salt-water tap and three large metal buckets for bathtubs. We would stand or squat in these buckets, soaping ourselves with the brackish water, rinsing off the dust.

Precisely at 4.30pm a loud knock would come on the wooden floor at the end of our corridor: supper was delivered. The warder would dish out food and we would eat it in our cells. We again received mealie pap porridge,

The apartheid years

'THE HISTORY OF THE AFRIKANER reveals a determination and a definiteness of purpose which make one feel that Afrikanerdom is not the work of man but a creation of God. We have a Divine right to be Afrikaners. Our history is the highest work of art of the Architect of the centuries.' So spoke Daniel François Malan, a preacher in the Dutch Reformed Church, Prime Minister of South Africa from 1948 to 1954, and one of the principal architects of apartheid.

Not that segregation was anything new. In the 19th century, British colonial rulers had introduced 'pass laws' in the Cape Colony and Natal to restrict the movement of blacks. From 1910, a welter of legislation increasingly deprived the black majority of South Africa of basic rights and confined them to reservations on under a tenth of the country's territory. In response, the African National Congress (ANC) and other resistance groups formed. At first these movements were ineffectual, but after the Second World War the struggle intensified, and jittery whites voted in the right-wing National Party under the zealous Malan, who was determined to tackle the 'black menace'.

Marriage between different racial groups was banned. Segregation was enforced in public buildings, on public transport and in education: black children received very basic schooling, learning only kitchen and garden skills.

Malan was succeeded by J.G. Strijdom, and he, in turn, in 1958, by H.F. Verwoerd, who declared the black reservations semi-autonomous homelands – by which means the government washed its hands of responsibility for their financial and social problems.

Inevitably, black resistance had been growing, with the ANC taking a lead. Mass protests were staged, and a government ban on opposition groups drove them underground. On June 16, 1976, there was an uprising of black youths in Soweto. When the guns were turned upon them, the ANC struggle became militant and South Africa became a fully blown police state.

The country meanwhile was in straits, after years of economic sanctions. In 1989, President F.W. de Klerk acknowledged that apartheid had failed, and in 1990 he lifted the ban on the ANC.

sometimes with the odd carrot or beetroot thrown in. Every other day we received a small piece of meat. At 8pm the night warder walked up and down the corridor, ordering us to go to sleep. No cry of 'lights out' was ever given, because the single mesh-covered bulb in my cell burned day and night.

During the first few months, I received one letter from Winnie, but it was so heavily censored that not much more was left than the salutation. The island's censors would black out the offending passages in ink. But when they realised we could wash away the ink and see what was underneath, they began to use razors to slice out whole paragraphs. They seemed to relish delivering letters in tatters.

At the end of August, after I had been on the island less than three months, I was informed that I would have a visitor the following day. In the visitors' office I took a seat before a small, square piece of glass in a cubicle. I waited with some anxiety, and suddenly, filling out the glass on the other side of the window was Winnie's lovely face. It was tremendously frustrating not to be able to touch my wife, to speak tenderly to her, to have a private moment together. I could see immediately that she was under tremendous strain. Just getting to the island was difficult, and added to that were the undoubted indignities of the warders and the impersonality of the contact.

Winnie had recently been fired from her job at the child-welfare office because of a second banning order, restricting her movements, and her office had been searched by the police. The banning and harassment of my wife greatly troubled me. I could not look after her and the children, and the state was making it difficult for her to look after herself.

Our conversation was awkward at first, made no easier by the presence of two warders standing directly behind her and three behind me. Regulations dictated that conversation could involve family matters only. I enquired about all the children, my mother and sisters and Winnie's own family.

Suddenly I heard the warder behind me say, 'Time up! Time up!' I turned and looked at him with incredulity. It seemed impossible that half an hour had passed. Winnie and I were hustled from our chairs and we waved a quick farewell. I felt like lingering, just to retain a sense of Winnie's presence, but I would not let my warders see such emotion. I walked back to my cell, reviewing in my head what we had talked about. As it turned out, my wife was not able to visit me again for another two years.

Solitary confinement

At weekends during our first year on the island, we were kept inside our section all day except for half an hour of exercise. One Saturday, after returning from exercise in the courtyard, I noticed a warder had left a newspaper on a bench. Newspapers were more valuable to prisoners than gold or diamonds. We were not allowed any news at all, and we craved it.

I looked in both directions, then I plucked the newspaper off the bench and slipped it into my shirt. Normally I would have hidden it and read it after bedtime. But I was so eager for news that I opened it in my cell immediately.

I was so engrossed that I had not heard any footsteps. Suddenly an officer and two other warders appeared. 'Mandela,' the officer said, 'we are charging you with possession of contraband, and you will pay for this.'

Within a day or two a magistrate was brought from Cape Town and I was taken to a room that was used as the island's court. I offered no defence and I was sentenced to three days in isolation and deprivation of meals.

The first day in isolation was always the most painful. I found that by the second day I had more or less adjusted to the absence of food, and the third day passed without much craving at all. Such deprivation was not uncommon among Africans in everyday life. I myself had gone without food for days at a time in my early years in Johannesburg.

In solitary confinement you begin to question everything. Did I make the right decision? Was my sacrifice worth it? There is no distraction from these haunting questions. But I have found that you can bear the unbearable if you can keep your spirits strong. Strong convictions are the secret of surviving deprivation; your spirit can be full even when your stomach is empty.

By 1966 the warders had adopted a laissez-faire attitude. We could talk as much as we wanted about every subject under the sun as long as we worked. This relaxation of iron-fisted discipline proved to be short-lived. One morning in September 1966 a prisoner wheeling a drum of food towards us whispered, 'Verwoerd is dead.' We looked at each other in disbelief. An obscure white parliamentary messenger had stabbed the Prime Minister.

The following day the authorities began a crackdown against political prisoners, as though we had held the knife that stabbed Verwoerd. The punishment was a renewal of the harsh atmosphere that had prevailed upon our arrival on the island. Van Rensburg, a big, clumsy, brutish warder, who had a small swastika tattooed on his wrist, was put in charge of us at the lime quarry where we now worked. His job was to make our lives as wretched as possible, and he pursued that goal with great enthusiasm. Each day over the next few months he charged one of us for insubordination or malingering. It was a policy of selective intimidation. When we were trudging back to our cells, van Rensburg would read names from a list, saying, 'I want to see you immediately in front of the head of the prison.'

The island's administrative court began working overtime. In response, three of us formed a legal committee to advise our comrades about how to conduct themselves before the magistrates. Van Rensburg was not a clever fellow, and while he could lord it over us at the quarry, we could outwit him in court. The charge would be read by the presiding magistrate. 'Malingering at the quarry,' he might say, at which van Rensburg would look smug. After a charge was read in full, I always advised my colleagues to do one thing and one thing only: ask the court for 'further particulars'. This was one's right as a defendant, and though the request was to become a regular occurrence, van Rensburg would almost always be stumped. Court would then have to be adjourned while he went out to gather 'further particulars'.

Two grievous losses

Time may seem to stand still for those of us in prison, but it did not halt for those outside. I was reminded of this when I was visited by my mother in the spring of 1968. I had not seen her since the end of my trial in 1964 and she suddenly seemed very old. She had journeyed all the way from the Transkei, accompanied by my son Makgatho, my daughter Makaziwe and

In solitary confinement you begin to question everything. Did I make the right decision? Was my sacrifice worth it? There is no distraction from these haunting questions. But I have found that you can bear the unbearable if you can keep your spirits strong.

my sister, Mabel. Because I had four visitors and they had come a great distance, the authorities extended the visiting time to 45 minutes.

I had not seen my son and daughter since before the trial. They had become adults, growing up without me. I looked at them with amazement and pride. I spoke to them about my desire for them both to pursue further schooling, and I asked Mabel about relatives in the Transkei. The time passed far too quickly. As with most visits, the greatest pleasure often lies in the recollection, but this time I could not stop worrying about my mother. I feared that it would be the last time I would ever see her.

Several weeks later I received a telegram from Makgatho informing me that my mother had died of a heart attack. It added to my grief that I was not able to bury her, which was my responsibility as her eldest child and only son.

The following year – with Winnie under house arrest and not allowed to visit me – I experienced another grievous loss. On a cold morning in July 1969 I received a telegram from Makgatho, only a sentence long. He informed me that his older brother, my first son, Thembi, had been killed in a car accident. Thembi was then 23 years old, the father of two small children.

I do not have words to express the sorrow I felt. I returned to my cell and lay on my bed. I do not know how long I stayed there, but I did not emerge for dinner. Some of the men looked in, but I said nothing. Finally, Walter Sisulu came to me, and I handed him the telegram. He said nothing, only held my hand. There is nothing that one man can say to another at such a time.

I asked for permission to attend my son's funeral, but it was denied. All I was permitted to do was write a letter to Thembi's mother, Evelyn, my first wife, in which I did my best to tell her that I shared her suffering.

I thought back to one afternoon when Thembi was a boy and came to visit me at a safe house that I used for secret ANC work. He was wearing an old jacket of mine that came to his knees. When we said goodbye, he stood up tall, as if already grown, and said, 'I will look after the family while you are gone.'

Single purpose *Black people unite in Cape Town on September 4, 1976. They were protesting about the violence used by riot police against those who took part in the Soweto riots the previous month.*

Brutish behaviour

The graph of improvement in prison was never steady. We had been through several commanding officers by the end of 1970, when Colonel Piet Badenhorst came to the island. He was reputed to be one of the most brutal officers in the entire prison service. His appointment indicated one thing: the government believed our life was too lax and a strong hand was needed.

We felt the effects of Badenhorst's regime before we ever saw him. Our old warders were replaced by younger, coarser men whose job was to harass and demoralise us. Within days of Badenhorst's appointment our cells were raided and searched: books and papers were confiscated. Meals were suspended without warning. The answer to every question was no. Complaints were ignored. Visits were cancelled without explanation.

We were determined not to let Badenhorst put us back into the Stone Age of prison conditions. We smuggled messages to our people on the outside to agitate for his dismissal. These efforts finally produced a response.

A troika of judges came to the island and I explained that I had been selected to represent the prisoners. I recounted a recent assault but Badenhorst interjected, 'Did you actually witness this assault?' I replied calmly that I had not. He wagged his finger in my face. 'Be careful, Mandela,' he said. 'If you talk about things you haven't seen, you will get yourself in trouble. You know what I mean.'

I turned to the judges, 'If he can threaten me here, in your presence, you can imagine what he does when you are not here.' One of the judges turned to the others and said, 'The prisoner is quite right.'

Within three months we heard that Badenhorst was to be transferred. A few days before his departure I was called to the main office. 'I just want to wish you people good luck,' he said. I was amazed. He spoke like a human being, and I thanked him. Ultimately Badenhorst was not evil; his inhumanity had been foisted on him by an inhuman system. He behaved like a brute because he was rewarded for brutish behaviour.

Colonel Willemse succeeded as commanding officer and while obviously not a progressive man, he was courteous and reasonable. One morning, instead of walking to the quarry, we were ordered into a truck; 15 minutes later, there in front of us was the Indian Ocean and, in the distance, winking in the sunshine, the glass towers of Cape Town. The senior officer explained that we had been brought to the shore to collect seaweed, which was to be dried and shipped to Japan to be used as a condiment and as fertiliser.

The atmosphere at the shore was more relaxed than at the quarry and we ate well there. Each morning we would take a large drum of fresh water, which we would use to make a kind of Robben Island seafood stew. We would pick up clams and mussels and catch crayfish. When it was ready the warders would join us for a picnic lunch. One day our newest commanding officer, Lieutenant Terblanche, made a surprise visit. He looked inside the drum, then speared a mussel, ate it and pronounced it 'Smaaklik' – Afrikaans for 'tasty'.

Turning point *More than 100 people were killed and 1,000 injured as South African authorities put down student riots in Soweto in 1976. The uprising, against the decision to force schools to teach in Afrikaans, was to be a turning point in the struggle of black South Africans.*

Changes afoot

In June 1976 we began to hear vague reports of a great uprising. The whispers were improbable: the youth of Soweto had overthrown the military. It was only when the first prisoners who had been involved began to arrive on Robben Island in September that we learned what had truly happened. On June 16, 15,000 schoolchildren had gathered in Soweto to protest at the government's ruling that all secondary schools must teach in Afrikaans. A detachment of police had opened fire without warning, killing a 13-year-old boy and many others. Chaos ensued, with hundreds of children wounded.

The events of that day triggered riots and violence across the country. Suddenly, the young people of South Africa were fired with the spirit of protest and rebellion. In their anxiousness to deal with these young lions, the authorities more or less let us fend for ourselves. We were in the second year of a go-slow strike, demanding a complete end to all manual labour and the right to do something useful with our days, like studying or learning a trade. In early 1977 the authorities capitulated.

In 1978, after we had spent almost 15 years agitating for the right to receive news, the authorities started their own news service over the prison's intercom system. The broadcasts consisted of what was good news for the government and bad news for its opponents, but we were glad to have it. We prided ourselves on being able to read between the lines of the broadcasts.

Finally, in 1980, we were granted the right to buy newspapers. This was another victory but, as always, it contained a catch. The newspapers were *Cape Times* and *Die Burger*, both conservative. Prison censors still went through them every day with scissors, clipping articles they deemed unsafe for us to see.

One story I was certainly not able to read was in the *Johannesburg Sunday Post* in March 1980. The headline was FREE MANDELA!

The campaign for our release rekindled our hopes and as we entered the new decade my hopes for a democratic non-racial South Africa rose. Then in March 1982 I was told by the commanding officer that he had received instructions from Pretoria that I was to be transferred off the island immediately. He then went to the cells of Walter, Andrew Mlangeni and Raymond Mhlaba and gave them the same order.

Everything I had accumulated in nearly two decades could fit into a few boxes. We packed in little more than half an hour – we had no time to say a proper goodbye to our comrades of many years – and within an hour we were on board the ferry headed for Cape Town. I looked back at the island as the light was fading. A man can get used to anything, and I had grown used to Robben Island. While it was never a home, it had become a place where I felt comfortable. I had no idea what to look forward to.

At the docks, surrounded by armed guards, we were hustled into a windowless truck. The four of us sat in the dark while the truck drove for more than an hour. Eventually we slowed down, passed through various checkpoints and finally came to a stop. The back doors swung open and in the dark we were marched up concrete steps into another security facility.

Pollsmoor Maximum-Security Prison is located on the edge of a prosperous white suburb amid the strikingly beautiful scenery of the Cape. Pollsmoor had a modern face but a primitive heart. The four of us

The events of that day triggered riots and violence across the country. Suddenly, the young people of South Africa were fired with the spirit of protest and rebellion.

were isolated from the general prisoners and given what was in effect the prison's penthouse: a spacious room, about 15 x 9m (50 x 30ft), on the topmost floor. There was a separate section with a toilet, two basins and two showers, and there were four proper beds – a great luxury for men who had spent much of the past 18 years sleeping on thin mats on a stone floor. Compared to Robben Island, we were in a five-star hotel.

We also had a radio and newspapers. We could see the liberation struggle was intensifying. The anti-apartheid movement had captured the attention of the world. In 1984 Bishop Desmond Tutu was awarded the Nobel Peace Prize. The South African Government was under growing international pressure as nations across the globe began to impose economic sanctions.

In May 1984 there was one consolation that seemed to make up for our small discomforts. I had a visit from Winnie, our daughter Zeni and her youngest daughter. Instead of taking me to the normal room where we spoke through glass, I was ushered into a separate room, with no dividers at all.

Soon Winnie and I were in each other's arms. It was a moment I had dreamed about a thousand times. We were still and silent, except for the sound of our hearts pounding against our ribs. I did not want to let go of her at all. It had been 21 years since I had even touched my wife's hand. ∎

What happened next?

IN 1985, NELSON MANDELA was diagnosed with an enlarged prostate and sent for surgery. On his return to Pollsmoor he was separated from his comrades and given three damp, musty rooms with space to study and exercise. Here, President P.W. Botha offered him his freedom if he would renounce the armed struggle. 'What freedom am I being offered, while the organisation of the people remains banned?' responded Mandela, adding that only free men could negotiate; a prisoner could not enter into contracts.

Over the next four years, a series of 'talks about talks' produced little real progress. Meanwhile, in 1988, Mandela contracted tuberculosis

SALUTE TO THE WORLD Nelson and Winnie Mandela greet well-wishers after his release from Victor Verster Prison.

and spent six weeks in hospital, before being moved to a clinic, where he was the first black patient.

This time, on his discharge, he was removed to the relative luxury of a cottage with its own swimming pool within Victor Verster Prison – a low-security halfway house on the road to freedom.

In early 1990, P.W. Botha stood down, to be succeeded as president by the pragmatic F.W. de Klerk, who lifted the ban on the ANC and announced that Mandela would soon be released. On February 10, 1990, Mandela was summoned to a meeting, at which de Klerk informed him he would be freed the next day.

With his customary grace and dignity, on the day that he left prison, after 27 years' confinement, Mandela declared his commitment to peace and reconciliation with the country's white minority, while warning that the struggle was not yet over. The main aim, he said, was to bring peace to the black majority, who must have the right to vote in national and local elections.

On April 27, 1994, black South Africans exercised that right. The ANC won 62 per cent of the vote, and on May 10, Nelson Mandela was inaugurated as the country's first black president, with F.W. de Klerk as his deputy in the Government of National Unity.

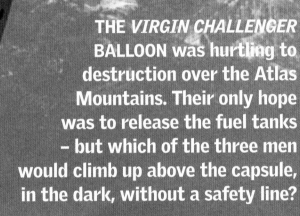

THE *VIRGIN CHALLENGER* BALLOON was hurtling to destruction over the Atlas Mountains. Their only hope was to release the fuel tanks – but which of the three men would climb up above the capsule, in the dark, without a safety line?

LOSING HEIGHT!

BRANSON: HE'S SAVED MY LIFE

Balloon pilot climbs out on to capsule to stop terrifying plunge to earth

Alex Ritchie stood in the evening shadows at Marrakech Airport and watched nervously as 16 enormous steel hawsers took the strain of a billowing white balloon. It would take 31,150m³ (1.1 million cu ft) of helium gas to inflate *Virgin Global Challenger* to her full 60m (195ft) height, ready for her attempt on aviation's last great record: the first nonstop circumnavigation of the globe by balloon.

Ritchie, a small, bespectacled 52-year-old mechanical engineer, had designed the aircraft-style pressurisation system of the 3.3 x 3m (11 x 10ft) capsule. It would allow the three-man crew – balloon manufacturer and former Swedish Air Force pilot Per Lindstrand, Irish millionaire and skydiver Rory McCarthy, and Richard Branson, boss of the Virgin commercial group – to fly at up to 12,200m (40,000ft).

For 48 hours, Ritchie had been working round the clock to prepare the world's biggest helium balloon for her maiden flight the next day. Lindstrand, 48 and one of the world's most experienced balloonists, was worried about the weather. Twice winds gusting off the Atlas Mountains had almost torn the £3 million canopy from her moorings. But Branson, aware that two other record-seeking balloons were about to launch, wanted to be first in the air.

Like both of the other contenders, *Challenger* was a gas-and-air canopy. The sealed bubble at its cap was filled with lighter-than-air helium. Under it was a cone-shaped area of air that could be heated by three propane gas burners on the capsule roof.

By day the sun would heat the helium, making the balloon expand, rise and then stay at cruising altitude. At night the crew would maintain the temperature by firing the burners.

But nobody had ever flown a helium balloon as big as this. Alex Ritchie was not alone in asking himself: will she actually fly?

All systems go *As the three men prepared for their epic balloon flight little did they know the difficult decisions that lay ahead. For one man, Alex Ritchie (left), it would involve a terrifying skywalk in the dark. Teammates Richard Branson (centre) and Per Lindstrand (right) could only hope and wait.*

Having worked on Lindstrand and Branson's previous record flights, Ritchie well knew the slim frontier between disaster and triumph. In 1987 *Atlantic Flyer* gouged a furrow through Ulster before ditching in the sea off Scotland to complete the first hot-air balloon crossing of the Atlantic. And in 1991 they had a fire on-board during the first hot-air Pacific crossing.

At 8pm, with the vast canopy hitched to the capsule and ready for take-off, Ritchie saw an agitated Lindstrand walking towards him. 'Alex, you'd better get some rest,' the pilot said. 'Rory doesn't look well.'

McCarthy had a chest infection. And months before, Ritchie had promised Lindstrand that he would step in if a crewman had to drop out at the last minute. 'Still, Rory's tough,' he reassured himself. 'He'll make it.'

At 6am on launch day, January 7, 1997, the phone rang at Ritchie's hotel bedside. It was Branson. 'Can you come down and have a chat?'

In Branson's suite, Ritchie found the Virgin boss with a dejected McCarthy and project doctor Tim Evans. McCarthy had developed pneumonia and was too ill to fly. But weather conditions meant they had to take off that day or abort the attempt.

'Let's have a look at you,' said Evans to Ritchie. After a quick once-over he nodded. 'Better find some overalls.'

Hurrying from the room, Ritchie heard Branson's wife, Joan, who was implacably opposed to the project, ask Evans, 'Have you had a look at Richard's head yet?'

Ritchie phoned his wife, Jill, a primary-school teacher, at their home near Harwich, Essex. Then, clad in red overalls and an ill-fitting borrowed helmet, he posed for the cameras with his fellow aviators. 'Things couldn't be looking better,' Branson told journalists before sprinting over to his wife and children. His 11-year-old son Sam clung to him. 'Daddy!' he sobbed. 'Please don't go.'

An exhilarating start

The three men pulled themselves into the capsule, up through the honeycombed storage and sleeping areas in its base. Three airline chairs faced outwards, but the view from the four small windows was obscured by the six 2.5m (8ft) high propane tanks, disguised as Virgin drinks cans, fixed outside.

As Branson checked the video cameras on which he would film the trip, pilot Lindstrand ran through the final checks with the ground crew.

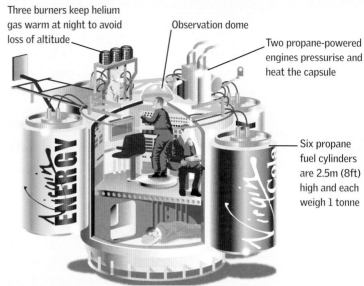

Three burners keep helium gas warm at night to avoid loss of altitude

Observation dome

Two propane-powered engines pressurise and heat the capsule

Six propane fuel cylinders are 2.5m (8ft) high and each weigh 1 tonne

Balloon nerve centre *Challenger's* capsule was made from aluminium and covered with 10-13cm (4-5in) of Styrene foam for insulation and protection. The cramped structure performed two functions for the three balloonists – a control room, on the upper deck, and a living area, on the lower deck, with sleeping quarters, an airline-style toilet and storage areas.

Surrounded by dials, computers and printers, he would communicate with the world below via radio, satellite and the internet.

Ritchie was tense as he fumbled with his seat straps. He had never been in a balloon like this. Still, there was no time to worry about being blown along at a height of almost 10km (6 miles) in a craft the size of a garden shed.

Lindstrand called the control tower: 'Request take-off clearance.' Berber horsemen waved their rifles in the air; dancers and musicians in Moroccan national costume swayed on the tarmac. At 11.19 Greenwich Mean Time there was an almighty crack as explosive charges severed the anchoring cables. *Challenger* soared into a vivid blue sky.

At 3,000m (10,000ft) above a panorama of snowy mountains, Ritchie's fear turned to exhilaration. He gazed through the perspex observation dome at the canopy's gaping mouth and thought, 'It's great to be alive.'

An hour after take-off, Branson was talking into the video camera: 'We've settled down at 29,750ft; exactly what we'd been told we would do.'

Falling from the sky

For the first 24 hours they would fly over the Atlas Mountains into Algeria, then on over Libya to Egypt. There they would hitch a ride on the high-altitude winds known as jet streams that circle the earth at speeds rising to 480km/h (300mph) or more. These would blow them across the Middle East to northern India, China, over the Pacific to North America, then back to Europe and into the record books after 18 days and more than 38,000km (24,000 miles).

Five hours into the flight, the satellite communications printer spewed a message from project control. Lindstrand read it and, without a word, passed it over his shoulder to Ritchie. 'Be advised,' it stated tersely, 'the Tema locks have been left accidentally on.'

These safety locks were on the quick-release couplings that connected the two hoses on each fuel tank to the capsule. The tanks had a vital safety function. If the balloon started to lose altitude fast, Lindstrand could jettison them as ballast by firing explosive cable cutters.

But with the Tema locks still on, he would be powerless to stop *Challenger* should she start to plummet towards the earth. Although they were in no immediate danger, it was potentially a major problem. And with 3,500m (12,000ft) mountains below, they could not land to clear the locks.

Lindstrand remained confident. 'There is a way to keep our world-record hopes alive,' he assured the other two. As the air cooled at nightfall, the balloon would drop naturally to roughly 3,000m (10,000ft) over lower peaks, where they could depressurise the capsule. 'Then one of us can climb out and release the locks. Once the sun is out, we'll go up again and we won't have lost much time or wasted any helium.'

But who would do the hazardous skywalk? Both Lindstrand and Ritchie knew how to free the locks. Only Lindstrand knew how to fly the balloon. It would have to be Ritchie.

By 4.55 the sun was setting and the big balloon began to lose height. Inside the dark capsule, they were like a submarine crew, relying on dials and digital displays. Then Ritchie drew Lindstrand's attention to the

The capsule was caught in a rotor: a Ferris wheel of wind which can suck a balloon straight into the ground.

rate-of-climb pointer. Instead of falling slowly from horizontal, it was shooting up and plunging down again, with each dive deeper than the last.

'We're not supposed to be going down this fast!' Lindstrand exclaimed. The capsule was caught in a rotor: a Ferris wheel of wind found in the lee of mountains, which can suck a balloon straight into the ground.

Challenger was falling out of the sky at 600m (2,000ft) a minute – and they couldn't release the tanks.

'We've got to get rid of some weight,' Ritchie shouted. He jumped down to the hold and started dropping sock-sized bags of lead-shot ballast through the airlock. But *Challenger* was out of control.

Branson knew that something big would have to go to halt her descent. At 3,000m (10,000ft) he released the two pressurisation valves on the main cabin hatch and ripped off the door. Ritchie began throwing boxes up to him. 'Seven and a half kilos, 15 kilos,' he called to Lindstrand as Branson hurled out their water, engine oil and other supplies.

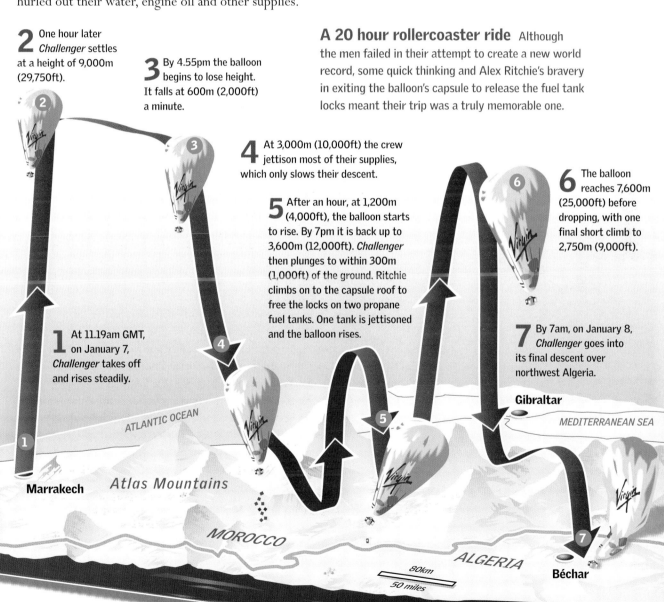

2 One hour later *Challenger* settles at a height of 9,000m (29,750ft).

3 By 4.55pm the balloon begins to lose height. It falls at 600m (2,000ft) a minute.

A 20 hour rollercoaster ride Although the men failed in their attempt to create a new world record, some quick thinking and Alex Ritchie's bravery in exiting the balloon's capsule to release the fuel tank locks meant their trip was a truly memorable one.

4 At 3,000m (10,000ft) the crew jettison most of their supplies, which only slows their descent.

5 After an hour, at 1,200m (4,000ft), the balloon starts to rise. By 7pm it is back up to 3,600m (12,000ft). *Challenger* then plunges to within 300m (1,000ft) of the ground. Ritchie climbs on to the capsule roof to free the locks on two propane fuel tanks. One tank is jettisoned and the balloon rises.

6 The balloon reaches 7,600m (25,000ft) before dropping, with one final short climb to 2,750m (9,000ft).

1 At 11.19am GMT, on January 7, *Challenger* takes off and rises steadily.

7 By 7am, on January 8, *Challenger* goes into its final descent over northwest Algeria.

ATLANTIC OCEAN

Gibraltar

MEDITERRANEAN SEA

Marrakech

Atlas Mountains

MOROCCO

ALGERIA

80km
50 miles

Béchar

The rate of fall slowed to 120m (400ft) a minute. It wasn't enough. In the next hour the two sweating men jettisoned three-quarters of a tonne of supplies, until all they had left was some water and two bottles of champagne.

Challenger had plunged nearly 8,000m (26,000ft). At last, at 1,200m (4,000ft), Lindstrand shouted, 'Yes! We're going up!'

By 7pm *Challenger* was back up to 3,600m (12,000ft). Branson told himself, 'If you get out of this alive, for God's sake don't do it again.'

The respite lasted just 10 minutes. Then the rate-of-climb needle once more swung to zero. *Challenger* was caught in a second rotor, plunging down and down as though drowning in a tempestuous sea.

Alex Ritchie had no time to waste on fear. He slid back the catches on the observation dome and hauled himself up and out.

Lindstrand looked at his watch. They had just crashed through 1,800m (6,000ft). Alex had only 5 minutes to free those locks.

A dangerous job

Out on the roof, roughly 2.1m (7ft) wide, the temperature was at freezing point. Ritchie was wearing a parachute, but if he was thrown off it would never open in time. He lashed himself to the superstructure with some strong nylon webbing. On his hands and knees, in darkness, he felt his way through a thicket of aerials and engine parts towards the edge of the roof.

Suddenly there was no more roof to feel. 'The top of tank one should be about 23cm (9in) beneath me,' he thought. Flat on his stomach, Ritchie stretched. His fingertips touched the bobble of steel. Below him, getting ever closer, the Atlas peaks lay waiting like sharks' teeth.

We're safe *Richard Branson speaks on his satphone from the Algerian desert, beside one of* Challenger's *giant propane gas tanks, designed to resemble Virgin drinks cans. It was a problem with the locks on these fuel tanks that necessitated Alex Ritchie's venture out of the balloon's capsule.*

He stretched farther, managing to grip one of the circular 1cm long safety catches and pushed it down. It was incredibly stiff. Jaws clenched, he pushed until he had moved it as far as it would go, then turned it until he felt it click. The first one was free. He scrabbled for its twin. This one moved much more easily.

Lindstrand looked again at his watch. Ritchie had been gone 2 minutes. The balloon was still falling.

Above them, Ritchie's mind began playing tricks. 'Did I really open the first lock? Maybe I closed it!' He went back and repeated what he had done until he was sure he had freed both locks. Then he clambered above tank two and freed its couplings.

Lowering himself back into the capsule, he nodded at Lindstrand. The Swede pressed an orange button. Instantly there was a bang, and the capsule lurched. Outside, tank one tumbled into the night.

The three men stared at the dial. The pointer

twitched, then began creeping upwards. Ritchie had done it! *Challenger* was climbing. They had missed death by just 300m (1,000ft).

At 2,400m (8,000ft), the mood in the capsule had lightened. 'I may be gone some time,' Ritchie joked as he went out again to release the couplings on the other four tanks. He returned in 10 minutes. By 9pm the capsule was repressurised and *Challenger* was rising through 4,000m (13,000ft), out of harm's way.

By now, though, they knew their record attempt was over. Lindstrand fired the burners. He would gain enough height to clear any remaining mountains and land in the Sahara desert next morning.

Suddenly *Challenger* went out of control once more, soaring towards the stratosphere. Four thousand metres. Five thousand.

At 7,600m (25,000ft), Branson recorded on camera: 'She's leaking propane.' The leak, on top of the dropped tank and their jettisoned supplies, meant they had now lost too much weight. 'She'll keep rising until she pops,' thought the Virgin boss glumly.

But this time the chill of night did its work and cooled the balloon. *Challenger* began to fall again. By 7am Lindstrand was into his final descent over northwest Algeria.

Air traffic control in Algiers was guiding him into a safe site, but the five remaining tanks were blocking his view. He needed another pair of eyes. 'Alex?' he said.

'Roof?' shrugged Ritchie.

At 900m (3,000ft), Ritchie climbed onto the roof for the third time. The sun was rising and there was a pink glow across more than a thousand kilometres of desert. 'Absolutely superb,' he thought as he took photographs.

Ritchie had been puzzled by a series of black dots described as 'monuments' on the map. At 300m (1,000ft) he saw them.

'Per, it looks like Arizona out here,' Ritchie called down. As he guided Lindstrand through rock formations the size of office blocks, he realised: 'If we'd come down at night, we would have smashed into these.'

Safely through, Lindstrand thought, 'That's got to be the last hazard.'

'Per!' It was Ritchie again. 'There's a power line ahead!'

'What do you mean, a power line? This is a desert!'

'Concrete pylons about half a mile away!' Ritchie confirmed.

Lindstrand ordered Ritchie back inside. He had just buckled himself into his seat when the capsule hit the ground with the impact of a slow-lane shunt. After 20 hours and barely 640km (400 miles), their adventure was over.

As they opened the champagne, Alex Ritchie finally allowed himself a long, deep sigh of relief.

After their rescue by the local militia and air force, Richard Branson paid tribute to Ritchie's courage. Alex brushed aside the compliments, saying he had done only what anybody would do. His wife Jill disagreed. 'It's not something most people would do,' she insisted, 'but I've always known that I didn't have an ordinary husband.'

Some time later, the Association of Retired and Persons Over Fifty presented Alex with a British Gold Hero Award for his bravery. ■

Ordeal over *Alex Ritchie (left) and Richard Branson (right) return home. Branson praised Ritchie's bravery, saying, 'It was a twist of fate that Alex was even there and that he knew how to release the tanks. Without him, there's no way we'd have come back.'*

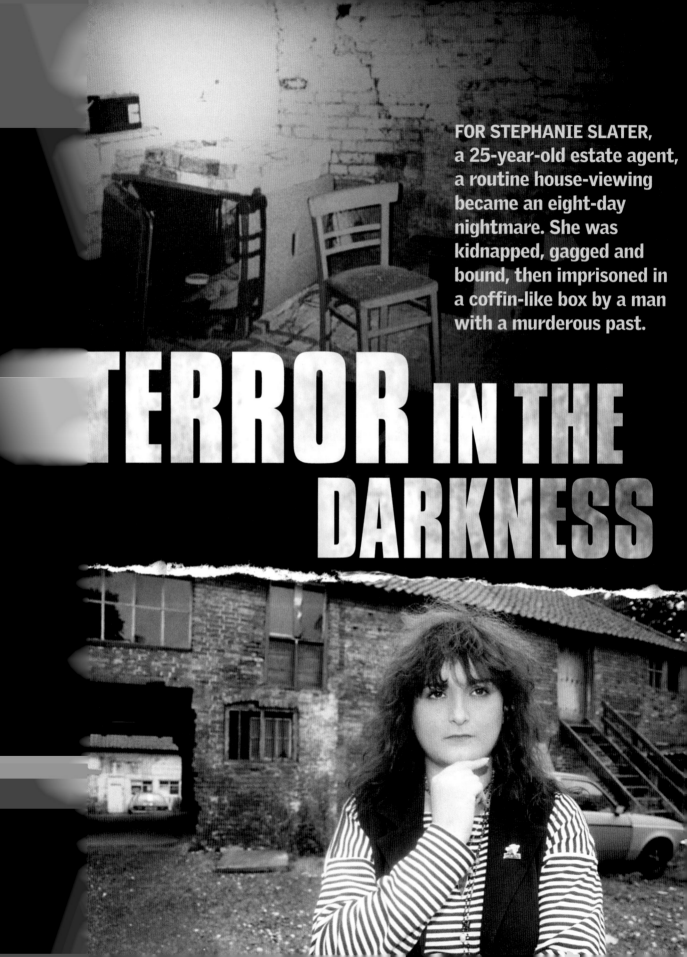

FOR STEPHANIE SLATER, a 25-year-old estate agent, a routine house-viewing became an eight-day nightmare. She was kidnapped, gagged and bound, then imprisoned in a coffin-like box by a man with a murderous past.

TERROR IN THE DARKNESS

There was nothing unusual about him. On this bitterly cold Wednesday, January 22, 1992, he was just the prospective buyer of the house in Turnberry Road, on sale with Shipways, the estate agent where I worked.

I parked my car outside the house. 'Mr Southall?'

He nodded and muttered, 'Yes.'

As we looked round the ground-floor rooms, I put his age at between 40 and 55. He was of medium to stocky build, only about 2 inches taller than me, which would make him 5ft 8in, and he wore heavy-rimmed glasses. I noticed a faint smell of industrial oil about him. When he asked me about the house, I realised he wasn't from the Birmingham area. He had a softer, northern accent, which I could not place – Yorkshire or Lancashire, perhaps.

Upstairs in the bathroom, he pointed to something just above the bath. 'What's that?' he asked. I went up close to see what it was. 'A little hook,' I said. 'Probably to hang your flannel on.'

The smile on my face froze as I turned to face him. Physically, he had completely changed. He was somehow bigger. He was filled with snarling anger, brandishing a knife with a 9in blade in one hand and a long flat chisel, or file, in the other.

I stared at him in total astonishment as he waved the dangerous-looking weapons in the air. With my gloved hands, I tried to wrest the knife from his grip but it was useless. I began screaming, then glanced at the bathroom window. It was double-glazed. Nobody outside would hear me.

He pushed against me until I fell across the top of the bath, his knife pressed against my throat. There was no way I could overpower this man. 'Don't kill me,' I pleaded.

'Shut up!' he shouted.

Years earlier I had read that if you are attacked, it is important to stay calm and cooperative. Don't panic or it will make your assailant panic too and he may harm you even more. Try to establish some sort of relationship with him; remind him you are human.

He took a piece of what looked like washing line from his pocket and bound my hands one over the other. Then he put a pair of dark glasses on my face. I could hardly see a thing. I was breathless with fear: he was going to rape me, or kill me, or both. My heart was thumping crazily, the blood pounding through my head. Perhaps I could beg for my freedom. 'Don't look at me!' he yelled.

He positioned himself behind me. 'We're going downstairs.' He put a hand on each of my shoulders to steer me. The glasses kept slipping down my nose, so he used a strip of my scarf to blindfold me tightly. He told me to open my mouth and placed a rolled-up piece of fabric with an unpleasant bitty texture on my tongue. He then tied a strip of cloth over my mouth as a double gag.

Living nightmare Stephanie Slater bravely revisits the workshop (opposite, below) where she was forced to sleep night after night in a bizarre wheelie-bin coffin (reconstructed opposite, above). The public learned of her terrifying ordeal in the London Evening Standard on January 30, 1992 (below).

Estate agent freed after £175,000 ransom is paid

KIDNAP WOMAN HELD 8 DAYS

ESTATE agent Stephanie Slater today ran weeping into the arms of her mother after eight terrifying days being held by a kidnapper who had posed as a house-hunter.

But despite a police operation involving 1000 officers and 500 cars, the kidnapper got clean away in the early hours of this morning with a ransom of £175,000.
In a kidnapping sting

Kidnapper outwits police: Pages 2 and 3
Echoes of Suzy Lamplugh case: Page 9

kidnapper rang her office, demanding the ransom and threatening to kill her if the police were informed.

But the estate agents, Shipways, immediately contacted West Midlands police, who launched operation Kaftan and maintained a total news blackout with the co-operation of newspapers and broadcasters

Next, with what I believe was another piece of washing line, he encircled my legs once, below my knees. I could just about walk, but not run. He guided me to my feet – 'Keep walking and keep quiet' – unlocked the French windows in the lounge and pushed me along the garden path. I walked as slowly as he would allow, hoping against hope we would be seen. It must have been about 11am – surely someone was looking out of their back window? This couldn't happen in broad daylight. Surely someone must come to my rescue? But no one did.

Before I realised it, we were inside number 153's garage. 'There's a car. Get in.' He manoeuvred me into the front passenger seat, which was reclined almost horizontally, and tied me down with rope under my chin, and covered me with coats and a blanket. I felt absolute panic. What sort of weirdo was I dealing with to truss me up like this?

I tried to memorise every right or left turn, every stop at what I imagined must be traffic lights or zebra crossings; when I got away from this crazy man, I wanted to explain, in detail, where he had taken me. But by the time the route became less congested, and we were travelling at what felt like around 40 miles an hour, I had lost my sense of direction.

Eventually we pulled into what I think was a large, open-air car park. I could hear traffic in the distance. He removed my gags. The blindfold remained in place.

'You've probably realised that you have been kidnapped,' he said. Kidnapped? His words didn't make a lot of sense to me. You had to be rich to be kidnapped, but Mum and Dad had no money to pay a ransom. My Dad was a coach fitter and Mum worked in the local supermarket. He was definitely on the wrong track.

'We are going to make a tape to send to your boss,' he told me, and asked me my name. 'You can call me Bob,' he continued. I wasn't allowed to sit up. I simply turned my head towards the microphone Bob held at my mouth.

'Repeat after me,' he instructed. 'It's 11.45am. This is Stephanie Slater.' I was so anxious to get it right and not make him angry again that I paid hardly any attention to the actual words, but I remember saying, 'I'm OK and unharmed, and providing these instructions are carried out I will be released.'

Bob put the tape in an envelope, re-gagged me and opened the car door. 'I'm going to post this and make a phone call. I won't be long.'

Start of the terror *Policemen guard the house at 153 Turnberry Road, Birmingham, where Stephanie's kidnapping began. Michael Sams lured her to this ordinary house by posing as a potential buyer.*

All I could think about was the hopelessness of my plight. Nobody had seen me, nobody was coming to my aid. My hands were shaking uncontrollably, my stomach turning over.

Terror and torture

Bob returned and we continued our journey along what seemed to be open roads or dual carriageways. It must have been about 6pm, and dark, when I was aware of the car slowing down, turning left along a bumpy track and stopping. Bob switched off the engine. 'We're here.'

I heard the crunch of gravel as he walked away. Then came the grating, scraping sound of a large metal door being pulled open along metal runners. Bob untied the ropes preventing me from moving. 'Swing your legs out,' he ordered, 'and stand up.'

He propelled me slowly into the building; it gave the impression of being totally deserted and I felt stone or brick beneath my feet. He sat me down on a hard, straight-backed wooden chair, then secured handcuffs around my wrists and ankles, and tied my arms and body to the chair with rope. I wondered whether this was it; he could do whatever he wanted to me now. I wanted to speak, to break the moment, but I was simply too frightened to say anything.

'Are you hungry?' he asked, unfastening my gags, brisk and business-like. 'Do you like fish and chips?'

The last thing on my mind was food, but I told him I liked chips.

'I'll go and get you some. While I'm gone don't make a sound. You can't get out of here and nobody can get in unless they break the door down.'

Rigid with fear, I heard him open and close the sliding door. I wondered what was happening at Shipways now. They must have told my Mum and Dad, but nobody would know where to begin looking for me.

Bob's telephone call had been to Kevin Watts, manager of the Shipways estate agency. Bob said he'd kidnapped Stephanie for a ransom, and a taped message from her was in the post. Ignoring the kidnapper's warning, Watts called West Midlands Police.

At 2.40pm the police asked for a media blackout because of the danger to Stephanie's life. Only six months earlier, 18-year-old Julie Dart had been abducted in Leeds. Ten days later, her naked body was found in a field near Grantham, Lincolnshire, after she had been beaten over the head and strangled. Police suspected her killer could be Stephanie's kidnapper.

Bob came back and without a word untied me from the chair. He removed my gags but left in place the handcuffs on my wrists and ankles, and the blindfold. I heard him tear open the paper that contained the chips.

Evil intent *Police produced an artist's impression of Michael Sams (above). The resemblance to the real Sams (left) is clear.*

I only managed about five – they tasted foul. He handed me a cup of hot, sweet tea, which I held between my handcuffed hands and sipped gratefully.

'It's time we got you out of those clothes,' he said. 'I've got some here for you to wear.'

He took off both sets of handcuffs and helped me remove my coat, jacket and blouse, my knee-length boots, corduroy skirt and underwear.

I felt horribly exposed standing there naked and blindfolded. He clamped the handcuffs back on my wrists. Then he began to touch and rub me as I stood motionless, frozen with fear – not the fear of the unknown I had endured since the morning, but dread of the inevitable. His voice coarser now, he instructed me to get down on a mattress on the floor, and lie with my hands above my head. It sounded as if he was getting undressed.

Whatever happened, I must not make him angry with me. My body and my mind split into separate entities. My body could feel him moving over me, humping and grunting, and feel the intense pain of him savagely biting my breasts, but my mind was completely empty of thought. I didn't even register disgust as he slobbered all over my mouth. I cut out.

'I hope you're not claustrophobic,' he said when I was dressed. I told him I wasn't. 'Good,' he replied, 'because I'm going to put you in a box within a box and that will be where you sleep.'

When it was over he said, 'You don't have to worry about catching AIDS, because I was wearing something.'

He pulled me up off the mattress and handed me my own underclothes, plus an old, over-large pair of denim jeans and two jumpers. Before returning my boots, he gave me a pair of socks.

'I hope you're not claustrophobic,' he said when I was dressed. I told him I wasn't. 'Good,' he replied, 'because I'm going to put you in a box within a box and that will be where you sleep.'

First he manoeuvred me behind the mattress to a bucket, and told me I could use it once in the morning and once at night. He handcuffed my ankles and I had to lie on the mattress and shuffle on my back into a coffin-like wooden box, as if I were getting into a sleeping bag. The box encased me up to my armpits and was too small for me to lie down properly; my hips got tightly wedged and my legs were jammed in at an angle. It was inside what I later discovered to be a plastic wheelie bin lying on its side and with the bottom cut out. The bin didn't rock at all; it was clearly secured to the ground.

As soon as I was in the box, he tied my handcuffed wrists to a metal bar in front of my face. 'Don't pull on the bar, because there are boulders above you. You'll bring them down and crush yourself.'

I could feel a wire running the length of the coffin. 'That,' he explained, 'is attached to electrodes. If you move you will get an electric shock. In fact, don't move at all. I'm going to close the bin lid, but there are air holes in it, so you won't suffocate. See you in the morning, then.' He sounded almost jaunty.

I would never be able to breathe in here. I sucked in air desperately. My heart lurched and I felt a sob rise in my throat and break silently against the gag. Please, please don't let this happen to me.

But he was already securing the bin lid with bolts. Then I heard him drive off.

I lay and listened intently to the silence, terrified that he might have crept back, but he had definitely gone. It was so cold in the box that every inch of my body ached, so dark that the blackness was almost a solid shape in front of my eyes. My breasts stung painfully from his repeated biting. I felt like crying, but I didn't. I knew that to get through this ordeal, I had to be strong.

The horrible thought entered my mind that perhaps Bob's kidnap story was just a ploy to keep me quiet. He might have plans to keep me as a captive sex toy. And what was to stop him killing me when he had finished with me?

At the worst point of the night, something strange and mystical happened. Suddenly, from what looked like the distance, I saw a speck of light. It gradually came closer, moving into focus, until I recognised it as the picture of Christ's face I had seen in Godshill Parish Church on the Isle of Wight.

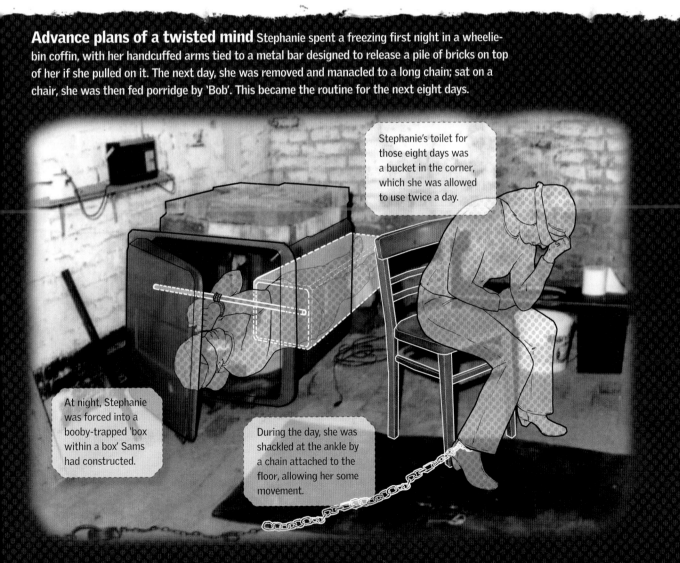

Advance plans of a twisted mind Stephanie spent a freezing first night in a wheelie-bin coffin, with her handcuffed arms tied to a metal bar designed to release a pile of bricks on top of her if she pulled on it. The next day, she was removed and manacled to a long chain; sat on a chair, she was then fed porridge by 'Bob'. This became the routine for the next eight days.

Stephanie's toilet for those eight days was a bucket in the corner, which she was allowed to use twice a day.

At night, Stephanie was forced into a booby-trapped 'box within a box' Sams had constructed.

During the day, she was shackled at the ankle by a chain attached to the floor, allowing her some movement.

People will interpret my 'vision' in different ways. It seems probable that this portrait of Christ on his way to Calvary had such a mesmerising effect on me when I first saw it that I recalled it in an unprecedented moment of mental and spiritual anguish. I knew it was a picture – I didn't think it was Christ visiting me – but the disembodied face was beautiful, real and warm.

Miraculously, my feelings of cold and pain vanished; I was filled with tranquillity. Then the vision faded into the distance, and I fell asleep.

Police found Bob's envelope addressed to Watts at Birmingham's main sorting office shortly before 7am the next morning. It contained Stephanie's cassette, plus a ransom demand for £175,000. Her message said that Kevin Watts had to be the courier.

Talking to 'Bob'

The temperature that night, I later learned, fell to nearly -4°C. I woke up, wedged into the torture chamber, feeling as if I were lying in snow.

I was convinced I was in some sort of workshop (the smell of oil I had noticed around Bob at Turnberry Road was stronger here), so I reckoned there must be metal objects around. On Bob's return I would get him to untie my hands, then pick something up and clobber him with it. But when I heard Bob walk up to the bin, draw back the bolts and say gruffly, 'Out you come!' all ideas of escape vanished. I couldn't move, let alone struggle for freedom. My arms, suspended above my face all night, were completely numb. They fell on my chest like lead weights. He had to drag me out of the box.

After he had removed the gag he made me a mug of tea, but I couldn't hold it. He rubbed my elbows and inner forearms gently to ease the pain.

'Is that any better?' he asked.

'Yes, thank you,' I replied.

'Don't thank me!' he snapped angrily. 'You've got nothing to thank me for.'

'No, I don't suppose I have, you bastard,' I thought, but as a child I had been taught to be polite – and by remaining polite, and communicative, I might just be able to convince this man of my humanity and in that way save my life.

The temperature that night, I later learned, fell to nearly -4°C. I woke up, wedged into the torture chamber, feeling as if I were lying in snow.

Bob had turned on some kind of electric heater. He cooked some porridge – I heard the short 'ping' of a microwave – and fed me with a spoon. My hands were now free of the handcuffs, but I was still unable to move them. The porridge was lumpy but hot, and I was hungry. I ate it all. He placed a fresh mug of tea in my hands and guided it towards my lips.

Next, he unfastened the handcuffs from around my boots and fixed a manacle attached to a chain on my right ankle. The chain was long enough to let me move between the box, the chair, the mattress and my makeshift toilet.

Then he told me of the £175,000 ransom. He assured me I'd be home within a week if I behaved myself – which included keeping my blindfold on at all times, doing as I was told, and not attempting to shout, scream or escape. He put the hated roll of bitty material back into my mouth and secured it with a strip of 3in sticky tape of some sort. 'I've got work to do. Lie down, keep still and be quiet.' He covered me with a lightweight blanket and walked away.

I lay there, worrying. Mum had always suffered with her nerves; although Dad would be a source of strength and support, what would this do to her? And I now had two other worries. What if Shipways decided not to pay the £175,000? It was a lot of money and I had been with them for only a month.

Several times during the day I heard people talking to Bob, then the ring of what sounded like an old-fashioned till, followed by silence. Obviously I was being held in the back of a shop or a garage of some kind. Bob's radio, tuned to Radio Two, played all the time. I pricked up my ears at the pre-news jingle, but the bulletins were about world politics and aircraft disasters; it seemed that the disappearance of a 25-year-old estate agent in Birmingham didn't warrant a mention.

When he reappeared with more chips he was in a mood to talk. 'So, Stephanie Slater, tell me about yourself. I can't tell you about me, but we can talk about you.'

Here was a conversation opportunity. 'I've lived in Great Barr all my life,' I began. 'I'm adopted, actually.'

'Oh no, don't say that!' He sounded distressed.

I was taken aback, and assured him, 'I have a smashing Mum and Dad. They couldn't have children, so they adopted me when I was six months old.'

'I would have liked children,' he said, but didn't elaborate, so neither did I.

We chatted about my job; I had worked for seven years in the West Midlands as an estate agency sales negotiator before joining Shipways. We also talked about my social life. 'I have a boyfriend, David. He's a good laugh – we get on well. I have quite a lot of other friends and regularly on a Friday a group of us meet in my local pub for a drink.'

'I don't go into pubs,' he replied sourly. 'I think it's time you went back in the box.' The prospect filled me with dread, but as I eased my way into the box I realised that he had reduced its size. It now stretched only from the top of my thighs to my feet, leaving my upper body free. He had even provided me with a duvet in addition to the blanket.

'It's much better – thanks a lot.' I didn't attempt to keep the gratitude out of my voice. After what I had endured the previous night, the box felt almost luxurious, though I still experienced a momentary panic as I heard him shut the wheelie-bin lid and shoot the bolts.

A promise

Bob had his caring side. But he enjoyed seeing me frightened. On the Friday morning, I was sitting on the chair after my porridge-and-tea breakfast when he announced, 'I'll have to get rid of that bin.' Ever alert to a conversational opening, I said keenly, 'Which bin?'

Paid in full *When Kevin Watts handed over the £175,000 ransom money, Sams was true to his word and released Stephanie.*

Safety measures for lone workers

IN FEBRUARY 2008, in Saanich, British Columbia, 24-year-old estate agent Lindsay Buziak was stabbed to death in the bedroom of a house she had been scheduled to show to an alleged prospective buyer. Earlier that day she had received a call from a woman requesting a viewing. Later, she took a call from a man who said that he would be meeting her alone at the property. Something about the proposition unnerved Lindsay. She asked her boyfriend, also an estate agent, to check on her later at the house. Just the same, she went along – and met her death.

Such a scenario is the despair of the Suzy Lamplugh Trust, the UK's national charity for personal safety. The Trust was set up in memory of British estate agent Suzy Lamplugh, who vanished in July 1986 after going to keep an appointment with a 'Mr Kipper'.

'Such things do still happen,' says Trust press officer Jo Walker, 'although I think it's a lot better in the UK today.' An entire industry has grown up in response to the fear, and the real, though rare, occurrence of attack and kidnap, with the latest technologies offering sophisticated safety systems for lone workers. There are also, says Jo Walker, a few elementary and common-sense practices that can be followed for almost no cost and by anyone, not just estate agents.

'Although there are still agents who will agree to meet a client at a property, taking only a mobile phone number, a conscientious agency will insist on taking a work phone number, and then calling to verify it.' Walker also draws attention to some estate agents' brochures that show photographs of the individual agents to be contacted about particular properties. A criminal, disturbed or psychopathic person, reviewing these portraits, is thereby given assurance

SAFETY FIRST Diana Lamplugh founded the Suzy Lamplugh Trust after her daughter was abducted. The Trust promotes awareness of personal safety issues for all.

that the agent of his choosing will show up at a given address – probably alone.

The Trust works closely with the National Association of Estate Agents, which issues safety guidelines to its members. 'It's just about being very cautious,' says Ruth Lilley for the Association. As well as verifying phone numbers, for instance, it is also often possible to verify an address.

Lone workers should trust their instincts and, if they have the slightest cause for concern, have an excuse ready and rehearsed – for instance, that they suddenly feel unwell. Lilley adds, 'An agent might say, "I've brought the wrong key." And it's always best to have a coded distress signal. Instead of shouting "Help!" down the phone, or trying to dial 999, you might call the office and say, "Please ring my mum and tell her I'm going to be late." Also, always check in with the office after an appointment. If they don't hear from you when they expect to, they'll know something is wrong.'

These precautions apply as much to men as they do to women – after all, young men are at the highest risk of violent assault, and a lone male estate agent is every bit as vulnerable as a female is to attack.

'In the end, it's about trusting your gut,' says Ruth Lilley. 'If you have concerns, go back to the office, or ring and ask for someone to come round with you.'

'The other wheelie bin in the corner over there. We planned to wheel you out in it and then get rid of your body.'

I was crushed. Until this moment he had never admitted that killing me was ever a consideration. Bob sniggered. 'My heart sank when I saw you at the house. I said to myself, "Oh no, she's too big – she'll never fit into that bin." But it doesn't matter now, because we won't be needing it, will we?'

'You aren't going to kill me, are you, Bob?'

'I promise – there will be no hurting and no killing.'

I lay in the semi-darkness for most of that day, as Radio Two droned on in the background. Had Bob really intended to allay my fear of being murdered by telling me he intended to get rid of the bin? Eventually I decided that his motive for mentioning it could only have been to stop me from becoming complacent, to remind me who was in charge – as if I would forget.

I thought, too, about my friends and about Mum and Dad, who, despite our disagreements over the years, had always been there for me, offering love and support. Thinking about home made me feel very down.

The days followed a pattern. Bob would get me out of the box in the morning, give me porridge and tea for breakfast, provide me with a bowl of hot water in which to wash, and hold my hands while I did a couple of minutes' running on the spot to ease my stiffened legs. His hands were square and his small, fat fingers were hairy on the back.

Saturday, the fourth day of my kidnap, didn't seem as busy as the previous days; hardly anyone came into the workshop and Bob seemed happy to chat. I felt he enjoyed talking, and that there was something lonely about him.

I tried very hard to appear relaxed, but despite conversations that might have seemed almost light-hearted, the thought of death was never out of my mind for long. I never – not ever – felt less than terrified about what he might do to me.

On Sunday, he came in and said, 'We are going to make a tape to play to your Mum and Dad.' He sat me on the chair, held the microphone towards my mouth and told me to repeat after him:

'Hello, it's Stephanie. They have allowed me to send a message to you, just to let you know that I am all right and unharmed. I hear that West Bromwich Albion lost yesterday to Swansea 3–2.' (This would convince them the tape was a new one, proving I was still alive.) 'I want you to know that I love you. I'm not to say too much, but whatever the outcome, I'll always love you.'

After I had made the tape, which Bob explained was intended to keep everyone on their toes, he put me back in the box and went out to use a telephone. During the few hours he was gone, I could think of nothing except what might be happening at home, which made me very tearful. When he returned, I sat on the chair while he prepared a mug of tomato soup for me and asked him, 'What did they say?'

'They didn't say anything. I didn't give them a chance. When a bloke answered the phone I made sure it were your Dad and then I played him the tape. Once it had finished I put the phone down.'

I couldn't summon the necessary reserves to be chatty and entertaining that evening. 'Come on, eat up,' Bob urged me, but I had no appetite.

'I'm just not hungry today, sorry,' I told him, forcing a smile. I was teetering on an emotional tightrope, desperately trying to keep my sanity.

As the days passed, police hopes for Stephanie's safe return diminished. Her distraught parents could do nothing but wait. On Tuesday, Kevin Watts confirmed that the ransom money, put up by Shipways' parent company, was ready.

Hugging a killer

Once Bob said in a joky tone, 'I've enjoyed looking after you. Are you sure you don't want to stay on a bit, have another week here?'

I managed to force a smile. 'Thanks, but no. That's an offer I will have to decline.' Bob laughed to himself.

Then later he said, 'When you are released the police will question you. They will want to know everything you remember.'

'I won't say anything,' I lied, knowing full well that if I made it the police would have all the help I could give them. I wanted Bob caught and punished. 'There isn't really much I can tell the police.'

'Will you tell them about, you know, that?' He meant the rape.

I shook my head.

'Not that it were much.'

I could hardly believe my ears. How can rape not amount to much? Silent tears poured down my face. All the fear and horror of that first night, my overwhelming feelings of humiliation and degradation, could not be dismissed so easily. But I told him, 'I won't say anything about it.'

'I would deny it, anyway,' he snapped.

His tone softened. 'After all this is finished, go back to your job and get on with your life. Don't let this ruin things for you.'

I could tell he was standing directly in front of me. As I stood up, the chain around my ankle rattled. I was desperate for reassurance and some form of human contact, even from him. 'Can I give you a hug?' I asked.

'What?' He sounded incredulous. I pulled him into my arms. 'I am going home, aren't I? Please say I am!'

'Aye, it will be all right,' he said.

For a split second my cheek touched his and I noticed he wasn't wearing glasses. 'I must remember that,' I thought.

On Wednesday we were finishing breakfast when Bob suddenly said, to my astonishment, 'It would be nice to have a photograph of you. Something to remember you by. Sit on the mattress and take your blindfold off – but don't open your eyes.'

I did as he asked and attempted a watery smile. I was aware of a flash, and within seconds he was helping me replace the blindfold.

He told me I had to go back into the box. Today being 'the big day', he had a lot to do, including a phone call to make. He handed me the plastic-tray toilet, five chocolate wafer bars and a can of lemonade. At around midday he turned the radio down and spoke to me through the bolted bin lid, 'I'm going to pick up the money. I won't be back until 9 o'clock tonight.'

'Drive carefully.' I could hear the anxiety in my voice. Bob replied, 'Don't worry, I've got a note in my wallet. If anything happens to me — a traffic accident or something — the note will be found explaining all about you and you will be rescued. I'm off.'

I prayed that day as I have never prayed before.

The drop

I lay in the darkness. My thoughts were almost constantly with Bob. I hoped that his mad scheme was going to succeed; in an odd sort of way I was on his side. If everything went according to plan, he would collect the money and take me home. If it didn't — well, I didn't want to think about that.

'Hello, it's Stephanie. They have allowed me to send a message to you, just to let you know that I am all right and unharmed. I hear that West Bromwich Albion lost yesterday to Swansea 3–2.'

At 3.30pm, Bob telephoned Kevin Watts at Shipways and told him to go to a payphone in Glossop railway station, Derbyshire. After following an elaborate trail, designed to shake off police pursuit, and driving more than 160 circuitous kilometres (100 miles), Watts arrived at a railway bridge near Barnsley, Yorkshire. As instructed, he put the ransom money in a wooden drawer balanced on the bridge parapet. Some 25m (80ft) below, the kidnapper tugged at a line attached to the drawer handle and the cash tumbled down to him.

Teams of police officers were positioned in surrounding fields and on nearby roads. But at the last moment, contact between the police and Kevin's radio failed, although Kevin was not aware of this. Rather than alert the kidnapper to the police presence and risk him eluding them in the fog and eventually harming Stephanie, the operation was called off. The kidnapper escaped with the money.

By 9.15pm I had finished the last chocolate finger and there was no sign of Bob. I tried to speak calmly to myself. It was January: the roads might be icy. By 9.30pm I could feel my panic mounting.

When the 10pm news ended, I was completely frantic. Something serious must have happened to Bob. 'He's not coming back and I'm going to die here.' I spoke the words out loud.

I began banging on the lid of the bin — lifting my arms up and behind, as I lay on my back, thumping as hard as I could. If Bob came back and heard me he might easily kill me for trying to escape, but the fear of being left in

In the media spotlight *Soon after her release, Stephanie summoned up the courage to appear alongside her parents at a police press conference and speak about her ordeal.*

the bin to rot was even greater than my fear of Bob.

I lay back panting. 'I'm not going to starve to death here,' I decided, 'not after all these horrifying days.' I would suffocate myself instead.

I pulled the duvet right up and pressed the soft fabric into my face, trying to hold my breath, but it was futile. I didn't want to die.

I was crying by now, huge sobs of despair. All the control I had worked at maintaining since Turnberry Road was suddenly no longer there. I was an emotional wreck.

In a frenzy, I kept pressing the emergency light switch Bob had given me, but nobody was out there. God knows how long it would take anyone to find me, dead in this box, my only communication with the outside world a little red light shining in a deserted workshop miles from anywhere.

I was determined to commit suicide properly this time. I wrapped myself up in the duvet and pressed it tightly against my mouth and nose. But much as I wanted to lose consciousness, I couldn't prevent myself turning away to gasp for air.

Nightmare ride

At about 10.30pm I heard a car in the distance and my heart began to race. 'Oh God, let it be him!' A light then came on in the workshop and I put my blindfold back in position.

Bob opened the wheelie bin to find me in a state of collapse, unable to stand up without his support. I was crying and shaking in my distress. 'Can I go home now?'

'Sshh, calm down.' He got me to change into the clothes I came in and walked me slowly towards the door. The fog-laden night air was numbingly cold but wonderfully sweet and clean.

Still blindfolded, but this time without handcuffs or ropes, I set off with Bob in the car.

'I've decided to drive you as near home as I can,' Bob told me. 'We don't want anybody getting hold of you on a night like this, do we?' I thought, 'Like somebody who will rape me and keep me a prisoner in a box for eight days?'

At about 1.30am we approached the top of my road, Newton Gardens. 'You can take your blindfold off but keep your eyes shut.' The car pulled up. With my heart in my mouth I heard Bob make his final speech: 'None of this was your fault. I'm really sorry it had to be you. I want you to get out and stand there. Do not look back at the car.'

I felt him lean over and open the car door. All the time I kept my eyes tightly closed, scared that at this last critical moment I might glimpse him and blow everything.

'Give me a kiss,' he said. I quickly turned and with repulsion granted his request.

I got out, waited for him to drive off, then opened my eyes and stumbled up to the front door, hurling myself at it, banging on the knocker and ringing the bell.

Within seconds my Dad pulled me into the house, repeating as he kissed me, 'It's all right, it's all over now.' He yelled upstairs to where Mum was waiting, 'It's our Stephanie! She's home!' ■

Where are they now?

AT THE TIME that Stephanie was abducted, she was a happy, balanced 25-year-old with every prospect of happiness, marriage and children.

Michael Sams destroyed all that. He advised her to go back to her normal life, but that was never likely to be possible.

Sams was on the run for three weeks before he was caught by the police. His capture came after the BBC TV programme *Crimewatch* played a tape with his voice, which his ex-wife recognised. He remains in prison to this day.

Despite the relief of her safe homecoming, Stephanie struggled to get back on track. Although she did try to return to work, she found she could not cope. In time, she moved with a friend, Stacey Kettner, to live on the Isle of Wight, where she had spent many happy family holidays, but she said there persisted 'a strange feeling of not being a hundred per cent in touch, not a real part of what was going on. I was a different person.' She moved four times, changing her name to Phoenix (Phoe) Rhiannon.

On her 40th birthday, she reflected in the press on 15 years spent 'in limbo'. By this time, she was living in converted stables, surrounded by pets – dogs, birds and her cat, Twiglet. On previous anniversaries she had found herself quiet and reflective, but with the 15th there came tears and panic. She had written a book, helped to make a documentary about her ordeal, given talks to police officers about how to handle kidnappers, but the feeling persisted, 'What the hell have I done with my life?'

What she *is* doing these days is reaching out to others through a website, which she decided to launch 'having been asked on numerous occasions by police officers, victims of crime and members of the criminal justice system to provide "something to click on".' Her trauma, she says, 'will always be a part of me. But I'm not ashamed and do not run away from it. I want to use it positively. Everyone always remembers the criminal – but you don't often remember the victim.'

There is a curious postscript to the story. In the last night that she spent in her cramped box, Stephanie dreamed she was in a medieval village, watched by a man in jester's costume, whom she recognised as the British comedian Frankie Howerd. 'Oh, no, you're not going to die,' he reassured her. 'You're going to be just fine. I'm going to die this year, but don't worry about me, my dear, you'll be all right, and that's all that matters.'

Not three months later, on April 19, Howerd did indeed die, aged 76.

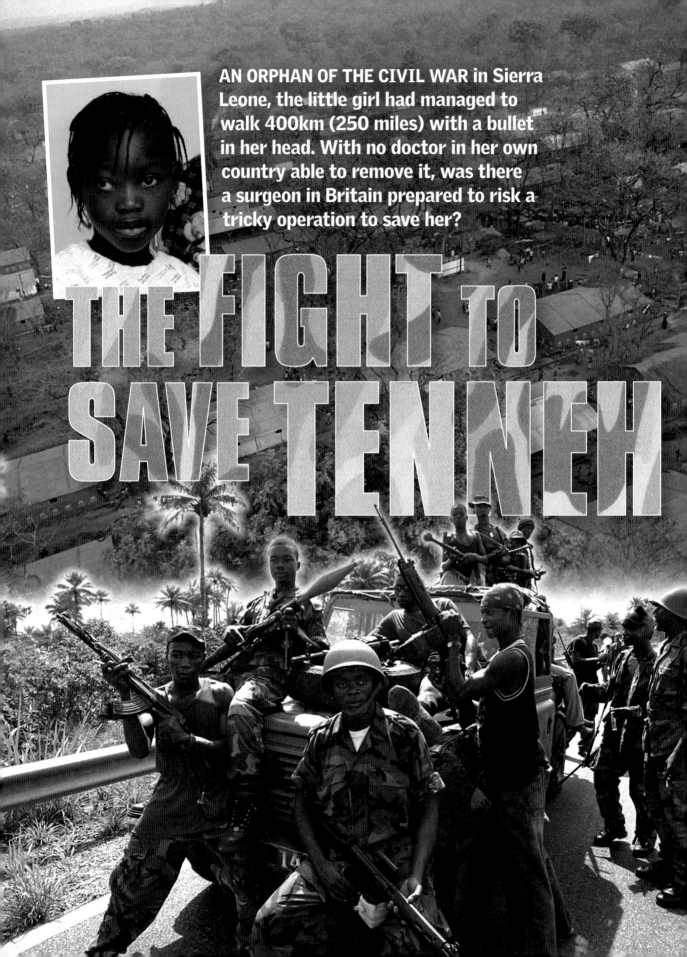

AN ORPHAN OF THE CIVIL WAR in Sierra Leone, the little girl had managed to walk 400km (250 miles) with a bullet in her head. With no doctor in her own country able to remove it, was there a surgeon in Britain prepared to risk a tricky operation to save her?

THE FIGHT TO SAVE TENNEH

A vicious civil war was raging throughout southern Sierra Leone in early 1995 as Malomoh Cole, a 29-year-old mining engineer, fled northwards with his heavily pregnant wife, Mariama. His one thought was to escape the anti-government rebels who descended on villages with AK-47 assault rifles, rocket grenades and machetes, intent on butchering men, women and children they considered loyal to the government.

As the couple prepared to spend the night in a derelict farmhouse, they heard the sound of crying. Outside in the fading light, they found a little girl of about four curled up in the grass, sobbing piteously. In the distance, smoke still rose from the thatched, clay-walled huts of a village that had been torched.

Clearly traumatised, the child wouldn't speak, not even to tell them her name. But she ravenously shared in their meal of cassava and rice, before crying long into the night.

Next morning, she clung silently to them as they resumed the trek north towards the capital, Freetown. The Coles could only guess at what she had endured: perhaps the massacre of her own family. Malomoh decided to call her Tenneh, meaning 'God has provided', after his mother.

Four days later, Malomoh had just started making an evening fire when his head jerked up at the sound of nearby gunfire: AK-47s. Suddenly, Tenneh fell to the ground screaming. Blood oozed from the top of her head. Malomoh dressed the wound as best he could. Because the little girl had not been killed outright, he assumed that she had been hit by a stone thrown up by the firing.

Blinded in the attack

The next day, with Malomoh carrying Tenneh, they made their way to a nearby village. There, Mariama gave birth to a boy, who lived only a few hours. Then the distraught couple noticed that Tenneh's condition had worsened. Often, she cried out with pain. She was becoming feverish and listless, her right eye flickering alarmingly.

Malomoh knew he had to seek medical help. 'God has sent us this child,' he thought. 'We must take care of her.' He decided to surrender to the rebel troops in Moriba, where he knew there was a clinic at the local mine. It would put his own life at risk, but he saw no other choice.

At first, the rebels suspected a trap. 'You're a government soldier,' they yelled. 'A spy.' They beat Malomoh and threatened to shoot him and Tenneh. 'I have come to you only to save this child,' he kept insisting. Eventually, he convinced them.

His captors ordered a nurse to care for Tenneh and at last the head wound, encrusted with blood, was properly dressed. Slowly it began to heal. As darkness fell on their fourth day of captivity, Malomoh hoisted the little girl into his arms. Then they melted away into the bush to rejoin Mariama.

They hurried on north, avoiding all roads for fear of being caught. It was a gruelling journey, yet Tenneh never complained. She had begun to talk to the Coles in Mende, the local dialect, but never about her life before they found her. Occasionally she rewarded them with a shy smile.

Alert and observant, she helped to forage in the lush vegetation for cassava, mangoes, kola nuts, anything edible. But Malomoh noticed

As the couple prepared to spend the night in a derelict farmhouse, they heard the sound of crying. Outside they found a little girl of about four curled up in the grass, sobbing piteously.

something different in the way she turned her head. Then he realised Tenneh was now blind in one eye.

After walking some 400km (250 miles) in three months, they reached Freetown in April 1995, with thousands of other refugees. They ended up in a disease-ridden camp called the Brickworks: there, 5,000 people were crammed into the semi-gloom of a disused brick factory.

Offers of help

Jobless and homeless, Malomoh worried about Tenneh not receiving the food and medical treatment she needed. Then he heard that aid officials from HANCI (Help a Needy Child International) were working their way through the camp, registering the orphans of war. It was agreed that Tenneh would move to an orphanage being set up by a British charity in Makeni, 200km (125 miles) east of Freetown.

No sooner had she transferred there in December 1995 than life struck another cruel blow. Tenneh became delirious and confused. After ten days of high fever it was clear that she had lost much of her hearing. And her right eye was still swollen and pushed out to one side.

Tenneh was sent to the Connaught hospital in Freetown. There an X-ray revealed something scarcely credible: the outline of a bullet lodged behind her right eye. She must have been carrying it in her head for a full year. If it was not removed soon, it was likely to set off an infection that could prove fatal. But there was no surgeon in Sierra Leone with the experience or facilities to operate.

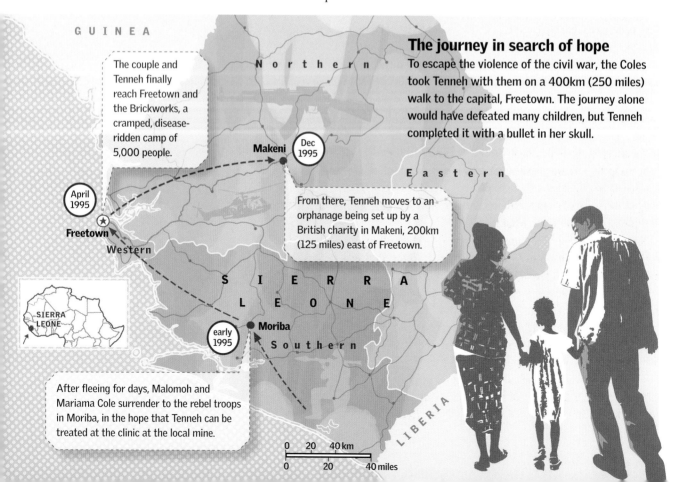

GUINEA

Northern

The couple and Tenneh finally reach Freetown and the Brickworks, a cramped, disease-ridden camp of 5,000 people.

Makeni Dec 1995

Eastern

The journey in search of hope

To escape the violence of the civil war, the Coles took Tenneh with them on a 400km (250 miles) walk to the capital, Freetown. The journey alone would have defeated many children, but Tenneh completed it with a bullet in her skull.

April 1995

Freetown

Western

From there, Tenneh moves to an orphanage being set up by a British charity in Makeni, 200km (125 miles) east of Freetown.

SIERRA LEONE

SIERRA LEONE

Moriba

early 1995

Southern

LIBERIA

After fleeing for days, Malomoh and Mariama Cole surrender to the rebel troops in Moriba, in the hope that Tenneh can be treated at the clinic at the local mine.

0   20   40 km

0   20   40 miles

HANCI's president, Dr Roland Kargbo, who had taken a keen interest in Tenneh, refused to give up. He kept remembering a British couple, the Cooks, who had helped to set up the Makeni orphanage through their charity, Hope and Homes for Children. Surely they could help?

Late on a Friday afternoon in April 1996, Caroline Cook took a call from Sierra Leone at her home in rural Wiltshire. At first she didn't see how she could get involved. 'Bringing children to Britain has never been part of our charity's remit,' she thought. But Kargbo explained that Tenneh would die unless the bullet was removed. 'You are our last hope,' he concluded. After a brief pause Caroline said, 'I'll talk to my husband.'

She already knew how he would react. A former colonel who had commanded the British contingent of the UN Protection Force in Croatia, Mark Cook had been drawn into international aid work after seeing 65 terrified youngsters who had sheltered from Serbian bombardment in the ruins of their gutted orphanage.

Cook had promised to help them. He'd resigned his commission, set up Hope and Homes for Children and, together with Caroline, had raised more than a million pounds to rebuild children's homes in Croatia, Sarajevo and Albania.

When Caroline contacted Mark in Sarajevo, he immediately said, 'Of course we'll help. Or we'll find someone who can.'

Several days later, thanks to the efforts of a friend in Norwich, Norfolk – James Ruddy, deputy editor of the *Eastern Daily Press* – consultants at the nearby Norfolk and Norwich Hospital were being asked to examine some X-rays flown in from Sierra Leone. They showed a child's skull and the perfect outline of a bullet. 'Can we do anything to help this little girl?' asked administrator Richard Drew.

Among the doctors crowding round was maxillofacial consultant Geoffrey Cheney. Over 40 years, the stocky surgeon had rebuilt faces ravaged by disease, road accidents and gunshot wounds. But he had rarely seen pictures of such potential menace.

Surgically, it would be possible to remove the bullet. But at what risk? At the back of his mind lurked the cardinal rule for all doctors: first, do no harm. Finally he told Drew, 'The best thing would be to get the little girl over here to see if surgery could help her.' To keep costs down, the hospital offered its services free.

Studying the X-rays again, he mused: even if the bullet hadn't killed the child outright, you would expect infection to have done so. How could she have survived for so long?

Three weeks later, Mark and Caroline Cook flew out to Sierra Leone to collect Tenneh. Gazing out of the aircraft window, Mark wondered, 'What will Tenneh be like? She has endured so much in her short life.'

A devastating picture *Tenneh's X-ray revealed just how much danger the little girl was in: a bullet was wedged perilously close to her right eye.*

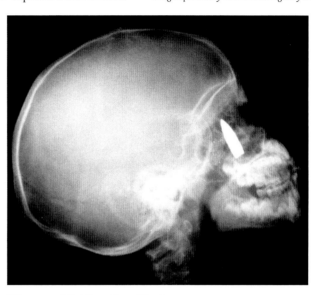

Even if the bullet hadn't killed the child outright, you would expect infection to have done so. How could she have survived so long?

His mind went back to his first visit to the country the previous year. The tall, fair-haired 52-year-old had actually been to the teeming Brickworks refugee camp where Tenneh had once lived. As he'd stepped into its stifling stench, they were laying out the body of a woman who had died of cholera. Each day, dozens succumbed to disease and malnutrition. Even more harrowing were the groups of young orphans, desperate for adult affection, who'd clung to Cook as he'd toured the camp. The memory had stayed with him.

Landing outside Freetown, Mark and Caroline travelled by truck to the Makeni orphanage. As they arrived, the children crowded round excitedly, singing songs. Tenneh Cole hung back, keeping close to her friend, Amie, solemnly appraising them with her one good eye.

A tense operation

Locked by deafness into her own private world, she was a reserved, self-contained little girl. The Cooks noticed that she often sat on her own while the others danced and sang. But in the tilt of her chin, Mark noted the determination of a true survivor.

When it was time to leave for Britain, Tenneh happily accompanied them – two white adults, almost strangers – on the next unknown phase of her life. On the plane, she nestled close to Caroline to explore the contents of her handbag. Preferring the meat in Mark's meal to her own fish, she cast him a hopeful glance then deftly scooped the meat from his tray. That done, she shovelled forkfuls of her fish into Mark's mouth. He knew then that he had been accepted.

Tenneh settled into the children's unit of the Norfolk and Norwich Hospital with equal aplomb. She would help to push the food trolley through the ward, or assist with the bed-making.

While the other sick children had their parents to help to care for them, Tenneh shadowed staff nurse Helen Shorten. She would sit happily on her lap during reports at the start of the nurse's shift, and hold her hand as she did her ward round.

After more X-rays and a brain scan, Geoffrey Cheney decided that he should operate. The bullet was resting on its base, a third in the sinus and two-thirds behind the right eye. Before it could be removed, the bullet

Tenneh's amazing escape *People the world over wanted to read the story of this astonishing child, who carried a bullet inside her head for over a year without anyone realising it was there.*

Time bomb in a little girl's head

DOCTORS REMOVE BULLET WHICH COULD HAVE KILLED AFRICAN ORPHAN

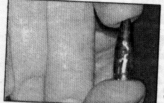

HIS is the 'time bomb' British
urgeons removed yesterday from
ae head of a young African
phan.

They operated on five-year-old Ten-
h Cole because there was a signifi-
nt risk of her dying through a brain
ection.

delicate two-and-a-half hour opera-
n to remove the bullet from behind
right eye was carried out at the Nor-
k and Norwich Hospital in Norwich.
eoffrey Cheney, who led the surgi-
team, said there was already

Left: The bullet removed from Tenneh.

Right: The five-year-old with Caroline Cook last week

Orphans of Sierra Leone

No one can say precisely how many thousands of orphaned and displaced children there are in the country. Mark Cook's charity has reintegrated more than 500 children into their extended families or their communities, and is providing education and training to ensure that they have a real chance of a future. But this is a tiny fragment of the picture. 'Still,'

AT THE TIME OF ITS INDEPENDENCE from Britain in 1961, Sierra Leone was one of the wealthiest countries in West Africa, broadly self-sufficient, an exporter of rice, gold, diamonds and iron. It had an effective educational system, two universities, and rail and road networks. Now the infrastructure is in ruins. What was not destroyed by 30 years of greed and corruption has been wrecked by a decade of civil war. Decent sanitation is a distant memory, and diseases such as cholera and HIV/AIDS are rife. Thousands of child soldiers, pressed into service and high on drugs, were among the perpetrators of appalling mutilations.

Viewed from a distance, the problems might seem insurmountable. 'And yet,' says Mark Cook of Hope and Homes for Children, 'what is amazing is that, when you go there, you don't get any feeling of depression. You might get depressed yourself, but the people are happy; they smile though they have nothing. The children sing.'

he insists, 'now is a time for looking forward. Peace has come, things are beginning to work, roads are being built, schools have reopened. People seem to respect the new president. Let's just hope it continues, because it is a beautiful country.'

In 2008, the headmaster of Wellington College in Crowthorne, Berkshire, pledged support to Hope and Homes for Children. A century and a half after it was founded for the orphans of British army officers, the college launched a drive to raise a minimum of £150,000 in funding for the orphaned children.

With two teachers and four pupils from the college, Mark Cook travelled to Freetown; afterwards they praised the work being done in the country, also commending the wonderful indigenous staff, and impressive HANCI founder, Dr Roland Kargbo. 'Having never been to Africa,' wrote one teacher, 'I expected misery and despair, but found only hope and optimism.'

would somehow have to be tilted through 90 degrees, from its almost vertical position.

At 8.30 on a May morning, Tenneh was carried into theatre in Helen Shorten's arms. With the child anaesthetised, Cheney's first approach towards the bullet was through the roof of her mouth. Drilling gently into the bone, he skirted carefully past her second teeth, which had not yet come through. After 20 minutes, Cheney's team huddled at his shoulder to peer at the bullet's base — a circle of ugly, blackish metal. Delicately, Cheney tugged at it with a pair of forceps. It wouldn't budge.

Next, he made an incision in Tenneh's cheek, just below her right eye. Lifting up the floor of the eye, and the soft tissue round it, he tried jiggling the bullet with his forceps. Still it was stuck fast. He would have to try a more radical approach.

Underneath the eye, he cut out a narrow sliver of bone, about 1.3cm (0.5in) in length. Then he had to separate the infra-orbital nerve that ran like a white bootlace through it. Cutting along the nerve channel with a fine drill, he teased out the nerve. At last, he could get at the bullet with his forceps and turn it flat. The tense silence of the operating theatre was broken as he finally held the black metal object aloft. 'There it is,' he declared with satisfaction. Mercifully, the bleeding he'd feared had not occurred. But he could now see a mass of chronic infection around and behind the eye. Cautiously, he began poking and pulling at the greyish-black tissue, which simply broke away as his forceps played over it.

Eventually, when he had removed some 80 per cent of the infected tissue, he called a halt. Intravenous antibiotics would take care of any lingering infection. Deftly, he replaced the wedge of bone in Tenneh's face. On top of it, he fixed a curved titanium plate with five tiny screws to hold the bone in place and help to re-form the damaged margin of the eye. At 10.45am, the surgery was complete. Luckily, there was no sign of brain damage and in time the stitches under Tenneh's eye would fade to a faint scar.

Just two days after the operation, Tenneh was again busily helping the nurses, as observant and imitative as ever. ■

Where are they now?

ALTHOUGH IT SEEMED THAT TENNEH had reached a place of love and safety in Makeni, it was not until 2002 that the civil war in Sierra Leone was brought to an end. Today, as the country struggles to rebuild itself, Tenneh has security.

Sadly, she is completely deaf: no hearing aid will help. She does, though, continue to learn lip-reading and sign language, attending a restored boarding school that was wrecked by rebels. In school holidays, she returns to the Makeni home she shares with her fellow orphans; they are as close as sisters after growing up together in a strife-torn land. She is bright and popular, and loving with younger children, but it is her future that concerns those who watch over her. As Mark Cook warns, it is all too common for vulnerable Sierra Leonean girls to drift into prostitution just to buy food.

In the absence of a birth certificate, no one can be sure of Tenneh's age, but she seems young for her presumed years. She has, after all, lived through unimaginable trauma, loss and physical injury, and inevitably her deafness holds her back.

Still, her future is not bleak. Thanks to the publicity surrounding her case, people were moved to send donations, and a sum of money is being held in trust for her. If, as seems likely, the funds cannot be used for an operation to restore some hearing, they will help to set her up in a small enterprise – a market stall, say, or a hairdressing business.

The self-effacing Geoffrey Cheney, who performed such delicate surgery, never understood what all the fuss was about, remarking that there could not have been much other news on that particular day. He died of a stroke on May 13, 2008, aged 72.

70

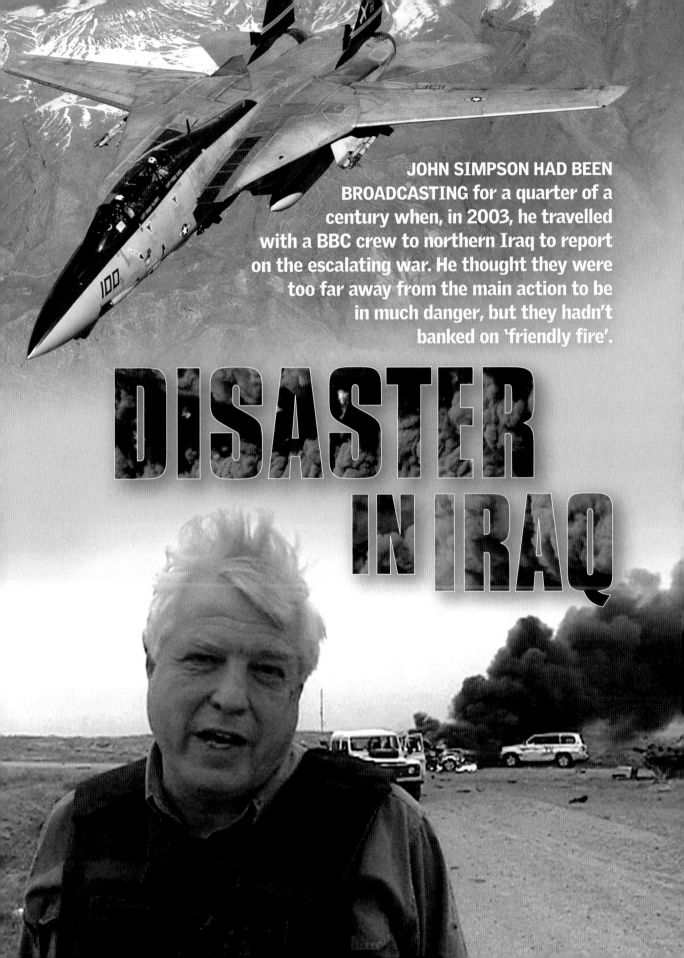

JOHN SIMPSON HAD BEEN BROADCASTING for a quarter of a century when, in 2003, he travelled with a BBC crew to northern Iraq to report on the escalating war. He thought they were too far away from the main action to be in much danger, but they hadn't banked on 'friendly fire'.

DISASTER IN IRAQ

In the thick of it *At great personal risk, John Simpson (previous page, bottom) does a piece 'to camera', describing events in the US 'friendly fire' attack on the convoy in which he was travelling. The bomb was dropped by a US Navy F-14 Tomcat jet (previous page, above).*

Allies *Soldiers from the US special forces discuss tactics with Kurdish Pesh Merga troops in northern Iraq during the Iraq War.*

There were seven of us. Tom Giles was directing a film about our war. Oggy was the producer. Dragan was a friend of mine from Belgrade, who fixed things and did some of the filming. Fred was the cameraman. Craig was our security adviser. Kamaran, who came from the town where we were based, was our translator, a charming and likeable young Iraqi of 25.

For more than two weeks we had been moving forward with the Kurdish forces from one front line to another, as the Iraqis pulled back. It was exciting and sometimes dangerous, but it was nothing like as spectacular as the action to the south of us. The previous evening, Saturday, April 5, 2003, as the Americans carved their way through Baghdad, my team and I found ourselves in the small village of Shemamer, northwest of Kirkuk. The Iraqi front line was less than a kilometre away and the 50 Kurdish Pesh Merga troops (armed Kurdish fighters) in the village had the support of eight American special forces soldiers. They kept themselves to themselves, and we were careful not to film them, but we had access to all sort of things they might want, especially satellite phones. The next day was clearly going to be an important one, and we needed to keep close to them.

At about 7am everyone was starting to stir. I strolled around the village, which until the day before had been occupied by the Iraqis. Kamaran came with me, translating the signs and notices and pointing out the big portrait of Saddam Hussein; there wasn't even a bullet mark on the face.

Was the work all right? I asked. He had been talking to the other translators, he said, and they had told him to ask for more money. I promised to see if we could afford some more. But did he want to continue?

We stopped and faced each other as they sun came up over the distant hillside and I felt its warmth. Kamaran's pleasant open face with its Mexican-style moustache was immobile for a moment, as he thought about it.

'Yes, I want to continue, Mr John. But I have many costs, and I have to pay for my mother and sisters.'

'Do they know the work you are doing?'

'No, they think I stay in the hotel and translate the newspapers. It is easier that way.'

'So – no other problems?'

'No Mr John. I like adventures.'

I smiled at him; he grinned back, the sun lighting his face.

'Flak jacket time'

There was shouting down the road, and the sound of vehicles starting up. In the usual haphazard fashion, another advance was beginning. The Iraqis had pulled back during the night. We headed to the village of Hamweira, passing a column of burnt-out Iraqi vehicles destroyed by American aircraft.

In Hamweira itself someone was raising the Kurdish flag in place of the Iraqi one, and others were going round shooting up pictures of Saddam.

I walked up and down the main street dictating copy to London into my phone and answering the questions of the presenters in various BBC radio and television studios. They didn't sound very interested.

We heard that the nearby town of Dibarjan had been captured by the Kurds. It lay between Mosul and Kirkuk, and seemed a good jumping-off place for the Kurds to attack either city. We had watched and filmed the road leading to Dibarjan many times in the past. It made an evocative sight, running off in the heat haze into the heart of enemy territory and I had often wondered if we would ever travel down it. Now we could.

It was eerie. The road was entirely empty, and we had no knowledge of what might lie ahead. There were occasional loud explosions coming from somewhere, but it was hard to know where. Our car, containing Fred, Kamaran and me, was in the lead, and Fred and I were becoming less and less certain about carrying on. At that moment there was a roar of engines behind us in the distance, and a cloud of dust. Our driver pulled over.

There must have been 16 of them: big Land Cruisers, new and still quite shiny. The first couple bore big KDP (Kurdistan Democratic Party) flags, and after the Kurdish part of the convoy had passed there were several American vehicles with big Stars and Stripes carrying special forces soldiers.

'It's Waji,' said Kamaran.

Waji Barzani was an impressive character: the younger brother of the KDP president, and the leader of the Pesh Merga's special forces. We had interviewed him a couple of days before. This was a very high-level group indeed, and it would be excellent for us to stick with them.

Our driver slotted in behind them. The dust welled up all around us. Ahead of us lay a ridge, and the Kurdish and American vehicles were stopping there. I noticed two American planes circling overhead.

'Flak jacket time,' I said.

The convoy had stopped at a crossroads on the top of the hill, and Waji Barzani and his man were standing there looking down into the valley beyond. Someone was pointing towards a couple of Iraqi tanks about a mile away, and I realised then that the thin column of black smoke that was still hanging in the air a few hundred metres behind us had come from a shell fired by one of the tanks. The American special forces vehicles were drawn up alongside each other close by, each flying a gigantic Stars and Stripes. A little way ahead of us, down the road, several American armoured personnel carriers had also stopped. They too carried vast flags.

The rest of the vehicles in the convoy, a dozen or so, all displayed big panels of orange material on their roofs, clearly visible from the air. Our vehicles had them too. If you were a pilot flying reasonably low you could not have glanced at the scene on the ground and mistaken us for an enemy. I heard a radio crackling; one of the Americans was calling in an air strike against the tanks. By chance, there was a wrecked Iraqi tank lying beside the crossroads. It's not impossible that the presence of this tank, when an attack was being requested on another tank nearby, caused the disaster that followed.

An ancient land *Iraq, formerly known as Mesopotamia, is mostly landlocked, with just a thin strip of coastline in the southeast. John Simpson's team were in the north of the country at the time of the attack, away from much of the main war action in the south. The incident occurred on the way to Dibarjan, between Mosul and Kirkuk.*

Journalists in the firing line

IRAQ HAS PROVED to be a hazardous place for journalists and media support workers since the start of the US-led intervention in March 2003. In the first 2½ years of Operation Iraqi Freedom, more media personnel were killed than in the entire Vietnam War, according to a report by the *American Journalism Review*.

American firepower – so-called 'friendly fire' – was second only to death at the hands of insurgents as the cause of media fatalities. In January 2006, the New York-based Committee to Protect Journalists attributed the deaths of 13 journalists and two media assistants to US forces.

One of the victims of this tragic situation was the highly experienced British correspondent Terry Lloyd. Lloyd met his death in March 2003 while reporting for the British commercial news broadcaster ITV News, after US tanks opened fire on the news crew. His team had been heading towards Basra when they came into contact with a group of Iraqi soldiers, who appeared to wish to surrender. Lloyd was 50 and married with two children. He had just celebrated 20 years with the British TV news provider ITN, and was ITV News's longest-serving reporter. He was the first correspondent to be killed in ITN's 48 years.

A statement issued by ITN after Lloyd's death read, 'Coalition forces had seen a number of Iraqi "irregulars" operating in the area. When they saw four vehicles going down a road in the same direction, and saw that one of them contained armed Iraqi soldiers, they took this group of vehicles to be a group of irregulars. We assume that is why they opened fire.'

In March 2009, the Paris-based press-freedom organisation *Reporters Sans Frontières* (Reporters Without Borders) stated that 'a total of 223 journalists and media assistants had been killed in the six years of fighting.' The vast majority of journalists killed have been Iraqi.

FINAL REPORT On March 22, 2003, Terry Lloyd filed his report en route to the Iraqi port of Basra. Shortly after, he was killed by 'friendly fire'.

'Call your bloody friends off'

The two US Navy F-14s were flying very low, at about 300m (1,000ft). Fred wanted to film them as we were standing near the group around Waji Barzani, and called out to Tom Giles that he needed his tripod to film the planes. 'OK, tripod,' Tom shouted, and he and Craig headed back to our vehicles.

I was aware of Fred standing quite close to me, and Kamaran a couple of metres away. Dragan was also there somewhere; he said something too, which I couldn't hear. The noise of the planes overhead was too loud.

Just as Tom was getting the tripod out of the vehicle, his phone rang. It was his birthday, and his mother was calling to wish him many happy returns. He thanked her, then held the phone up in the air so she could hear the noise the planes were making. As she listened, there was a huge whistling roar at the other end of the phone, followed by a terrible explosion. For an instant she must have thought that Tom was dead, but then she heard his voice swearing. He had forgotten she was there, and was blundering around in the smoke that was rising from the centre of the crossroads, still holding the phone. Car alarms were going off, and all around there were screams and groans of injured and dying men.

Twenty metres away, on the other side of the parked cars, Fred and I both saw the bomb as it landed. I found it hard afterwards to credit my senses, but when I checked what I had seen with Fred I realised it was true. There was an immense downward force, hitting the ground at an acute angle, and I had the impression of something white and red. Later in 2003, Tom Giles and I were given a reluctant briefing by the Pentagon about the attack. We were told it had been a 1,000lb bomb. The angle of its detonation was so acute that anyone standing outside the vector (the main area of impact) of its blast had a chance of surviving. Most of my team and I were between 9 and 11m (10 and 12yd) away.

Fourteen pieces of shrapnel hit me altogether, and I was knocked to the ground. Most were pretty small, but two the size of bullets were big enough to have killed me. One lodged in my left hip, the other stuck in the plastic plate of my flak jacket right over the spine. I was wearing a pair of trousers that unzip to turn into shorts; the left leg section was entirely blasted off its zip by the explosion, leaving my leg naked and bleeding.

I lost consciousness for an instant, then felt myself being pulled up. Dragan, instead of running for shelter, had come back to help me, thinking the plane might drop a second bomb. People have won medals for less. He ran across the grass, pulling me along. The roar of the explosion was still in my ears, but I slowly realised it was worse than that: my left eardrum seemed to have gone.

Ahead of us, Fred was kneeling behind a small hillock, his glasses and face entirely covered with thick, viscous blood. It was a shocking sight.

'Is my eye OK?' he kept asking. Dragan told him it was fine, though neither of us thought it could be.

'We've got to film this,' I shouted above the racket. There were small explosions too, which I couldn't understand. The two planes still circled overhead.

'Call your bloody friends off,' I shouted at the Americans on the ground; they had already done so.

Fred switched his camera on. A large drop of blood landed on it, and he had to wipe it off with a bloody finger a second or so later. The blood on the lens summed up the entire appalling business.

In circumstances like these, it is often easier to do what you know best. Fred and Dragan behaved with great calmness and courage, and I found myself trying to work out what we needed to make this into a proper television news report.

Fred and I peered over the lip of our defensive position. Almost all the Land Cruisers were on fire.

Tell them to go! Tell them it's us! Tell them it's us!

JOHN SIMPSON'S CRY TO U.S. CHIEFS

Before the attack *Some of John Simpson's team pose for a photograph in Arbil, northern Iraq. Seen here from left to right are Commander Nariman of the Kurdish forces alongside Dragan Petrovic, Oggy Boytchev, Craig Summers, Fred Scott, Tom Giles and John Simpson.*

19.03

Unexpected carnage *All hell broke loose when US forces fired on John Simpson and his crew, forcing them to flee to safety.*

That afternoon, after our injuries had been treated, we went to see Kamaran's mother. Tom's jeans and shoes were still soaked in her son's blood.

The vehicles were packed with ammunition and rocket-propelled grenades, and as the fire got to them they exploded in every direction. As Fred filmed, a grenade flew just inches over our heads.

I went off to find the others, but apart from Dragan I couldn't see anyone else. There was screaming from close by, and a man staggered past me with his arms full of his intestines, gleaming and salmon-pink in the sunlight. He looked around for a place to sit down and collapsed there. The next time I looked he was dead. Nearby a man was burning to death. There was nothing I could do to save him. The stench made me gag, and I stumbled away.

I stared at the inferno where the cars were burning and tried to tell myself that Tom and the others were there somewhere, but I couldn't see them. I stopped myself thinking what might have happened to them.

'We should do a piece to camera,' I said when the bullets and rockets seemed to have died down a little.

We stood out gingerly in the open, with the cars blazing away, but at that moment Craig staggered through the smoke. 'Kamaran? Where's Kamaran?'

'Is Tom OK?' I bellowed, then Tom appeared through the smoke.

I dialled the BBC in London and got through to Traffic, the department that takes in all foreign reports and distributes them to the right programmes. There was quite a wait, and I felt very vulnerable out in the open. 'I'm going to die here,' I thought, 'because someone can't take a decision quickly enough.'

'Put me on the f—— air,' I shouted, then immediately felt bad about it. It wasn't the Traffic manager's fault. 'Sorry,' I mumbled.

Soon a studio presenter was asking me sensible and thoughtful questions; I realised I was much too worked up and would have to quieten down a little.

'Well, it's been a bit of a disaster,' I replied, before realising it was important not to downplay what was happening too much. 'It was an American plane that dropped the bomb right beside us. I saw it land about 10, 12 yards away, I think. This is just a scene from hell here … There are bits of bodies on the ground. This is a really bad own goal by the Americans.'

While I was talking, an American soldier came up to me. In my confused state, I got the idea that he was going to try to stop me reporting the news of an American disaster. 'Shut up, I'm broadcasting,' I shouted at him.

He took it well, and explained he just wanted to help because he could see I was bleeding from the head. I let him look at me while I talked to London.

They had found Kamaran. The blast must have flung his considerable weight onto a bank of earth 4m (13ft) or more from where he and I had stood. One foot seemed to have been mostly blown off, and they were trying to put a tourniquet round his thigh and give him an intravenous injection.

Death isn't a neat, convenient thing. Kamaran, horribly shocked by what had happened and traumatised by his massive injuries, fought off his helpers with all his weight and strength, while the blood that might have saved his life pumped out of him even faster. Sometimes he called out Tom's name, recognising his face among all the others bending over him.

'It's Tom here. You'll be all right.' But Tom could see he wouldn't last much longer. I badly wanted to stay; it was my fault Kamaran was there. But the American medics were round him, and Tom was with him. I had to do a piece to camera while the full force of this terrible business was still going on.

'Why was he there?'

They managed to lift Kamaran onto a flatbed truck. He was still alive, but only just. After a kilometre they met an ambulance, and the medics pronounced him dead. I felt angry. All the rest of us had survived with only the most superficial wounds – Fred's injury turned out to be a flesh wound. Even our bags and equipment had been rescued unharmed. With 18 people killed around us and 45 wounded, we had had an extraordinary escape.

Yet Kamaran had escaped nothing. That afternoon, after our injuries had been treated, we went to see Kamaran's mother. Tom's jeans and shoes were still soaked in her son's blood. I had thought she might rail at me and accuse me of killing him. She asked only why it had happened. 'He told me he never went to the front line; why was he there?' And 'How could the Americans not know they were attacking you?' These were questions I couldn't answer.

That night I slept heavily and without dreaming, but in the morning I turned on the TV and found that BBC World was running our report. I watched the pictures of Kamaran being loaded onto the back of the truck, and found the tears running down my face. Staring at the screen I could only say over and over again, 'I'm so sorry. I'm so very, very sorry.' ∎

Where are they now?

JOHN SIMPSON, CBE, joined the BBC in 1966 as a trainee sub-editor. Forty years later, having served as World Affairs Editor since 1988, he had reported from 120 countries and interviewed more than 150 monarchs and heads of state.

He has seen, at first hand, history unfolding: the revolution in Iran, the fall of Communism in Eastern Europe and in Russia, the brutal events around Tiananmen Square, the Gulf War, the war in Bosnia, the end of Apartheid in South Africa, the fighting against the Taliban in Afghanistan, and the protracted, bloody struggles in Iraq.

Back in Iraq in 2007, he reported from Baghdad, on a city where 'the common feeling ... is a kind of slow-burning, gloomy anger', where the rattle of gunfire could still be heard, and where, at the city hospital in one day, he saw six bodies brought in. All had been tortured. One had had his feet sawn off. 'It was just a normal morning,' remarked Simpson. 'One day,' he said, 'Iraq will become once more a vibrant, effective country – but it will not happen for a while.'

As though he had not experienced enough risk in his career, for a three-part TV series, *Top Dogs: Adventures in War, Sea and Ice*, aired in spring 2009, Simpson (below, right) teamed up with polar explorer Sir Ranulph Fiennes (below, left) and solo yachtsman Sir Robin Knox-Johnston (below, centre), to take part in death-defying adventures, as each man introduced the others to their personal challenges. Fiennes led Simpson and Knox-Johnston around the freezing Arctic. With Knox-Johnston, Fiennes and Simpson sailed around stormy Cape Horn. And Simpson took his two companions to Afghanistan to instruct them in the art of war reporting.

In the Arctic, Simpson had to be evacuated with frostbite, while Fiennes suffered seasickness in a boat rocked by waves the size of houses. And the three men confronted terror when they learned that the Taliban had organised an ambush for them. They lived to tell the tale.

John Simpson has two daughters from his first marriage, and in 2006 had a son, Rafe, with his second wife.

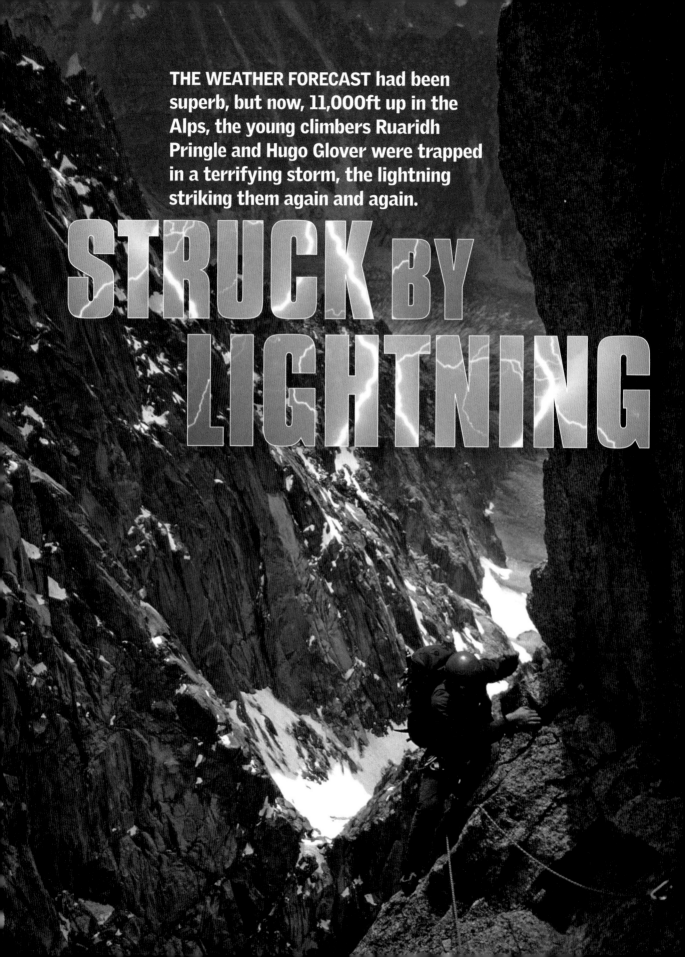

THE WEATHER FORECAST had been superb, but now, 11,000ft up in the Alps, the young climbers Ruaridh Pringle and Hugo Glover were trapped in a terrifying storm, the lightning striking them again and again.

STRUCK BY LIGHTNING

Balanced on the tiny Alpine ledge

with my climbing companion, Hugo Glover, I'd known for a couple of hours that we were in serious trouble. Beside me, Hugo dangled wretchedly from his harness in the freezing rain. He was behaving oddly.

'Hugo? You okay?'

I had to repeat the question. Puzzlement crept over his white, waxy face.

'I keep thinking I'm abseiling.'

It seemed a bizarre response. Why would Hugo think he was descending ropes, when clearly he wasn't? The mist seemed to be brightening, the rain easing. The Japanese climbers sheltering nearby were showing signs of movement. Hoping the weather might soon be safe enough for us to climb again, I tied a figure of eight in the rope Hugo would need for ascending the difficult crack above us, and passed it to him.

'Here, tie on.'

I'd hoped the task might distract him from our situation, but after watching him fumble with the rope, something made me check what he'd done.

'Hugo …? You've just duplicated the first knot!' He had been about to release himself from the anchor he was hanging from, with nothing else holding him to the cliff.

'Always thorough, me,' he slurred. Horrified, I grabbed his shoulders.

'Tell me exactly how you feel.'

His eyes were dull, wandering. 'Dunno.'

I'd been mountaineering long enough to recognise severe hypothermia. His speech was slow and muddled. He was *convinced* he was abseiling. His skin felt corpse-like; he couldn't feel his limbs. I thought he couldn't be far from unconsciousness.

We were at an altitude of 3,350m (11,000ft), two-thirds of the way up the legendary Bonatti Pillar on the southwest face of the 3,733m (12,247ft) Petit Dru – a sheer granite obelisk in the French Alps. I couldn't know that this was the start of the worst storm in the Alps for 27 years.

Already I couldn't see how Hugo would get off the mountain alive.

Heading for the Bonatti Pillar

We'd met ten days earlier at a campsite near the town of Chamonix – a popular haunt for British climbers. At 26 I'd more experience than 19-year-old Hugo, particularly on snow and ice, while he'd climbed technically harder routes on rock. He'd just left London following his A-levels for his first season of Alpine climbing.

Majestic scenery *Hugo Glover sits in the sunlight beneath the awe-inspiring Bonatti Pillar before the ill-fated climb. On the right is the jagged Flammes de Pierre.*

Steady progress *Hugo climbing halfway up the Bonatti Pillar (opposite), with the Mer de Glace below, shortly before the terrible storm hit.*

At a stocky 5ft 7in, he proved irrepressibly cheerful and a fine, level-headed climber. We made a good team, and, over the following week in the granite spires above Chamonix, climbed routes more difficult than either of us had climbed before.

Feeling fit and prepared, we found our thoughts turning to the Bonatti Pillar: a granite column over 600m (2,000ft) high, up which snakes one of Europe's most famous rock-climbs. Its base is reached by abseiling: all logical lines of access or retreat made lethal by constant rockfall. Once the abseil ropes are pulled down, escape requires climbing the Pillar almost to the peak of the Petit Dru, then descending a blade-thin ridge called the Flammes de Pierre, from which steep slopes and a glacier lead to a mountain hut. The mountain is also a magnet for unpredictable electrical storms, so this is a climb where safety lies in speed. This means travelling light, carrying minimal emergency clothing and equipment.

We agreed we wouldn't go near the Pillar without a week's perfect weather forecast.

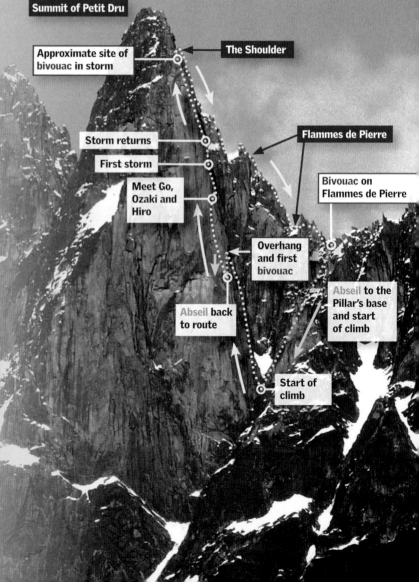

At the mercy of nature Ruaridh and Hugo set out from the Charpoua Hut on Saturday, July 20, 1995, and bivouacked the following night on the Flammes de Pierre. From there, they abseiled 240m (800ft) next morning to the base of the Bonatti Pillar. Committed to the climb now because of no safe escape routes, they intended to climb to near the summit of Petit Dru before descending the Flammes de Pierre: the simplest safe retreat. The first hurdle they encountered was 240m (800ft) up the Pillar when they went off-route and met an impassable overhang. After retracing their steps, they relocated the route and were overtaken by the three Japanese climbers; the two groups climbed on each others' heels until the first storm hit. With Hugo hypothermic, after a brief lull in the weather they continued together until forced to shelter just before reaching The Shoulder, near the peak of the Petit Dru. There they were repeatedly hit by lightning for 12 hours. When the storm abated, they continued to The Shoulder, before descending the Flammes de Pierre, eventually reaching the Charpoua Hut.

Summit of Petit Dru

Approximate site of bivouac in storm

The Shoulder

Storm returns

Flammes de Pierre

First storm

Meet Go, Ozaki and Hiro

Bivouac on Flammes de Pierre

Overhang and first bivouac

Abseil to the Pillar's base and start of climb

Abseil back to route

Start of climb

On Saturday, July 20, it finally came, and we trekked up to the Charpoua Alpine Hut at 2,835m (9,300ft). The following evening we bivouacked on a 60cm (2ft) ledge 490m (1,600ft) above the hut on the crest of the Flammes de Pierre, from which we'd begin the 240m (800ft) abseil to the Pillar next morning. The view was breathtaking: rows of jagged peaks silhouetted against bands of sunset-pink, with the pillar towering crimson against the stars. Hugo was almost in tears, 'I can't believe I'm actually up here.'

At 4am, we stumbled from sleeping bags, cached spare equipment under rocks in waterproof bags, and abseiled into darkness to start the climb.

Eight hundred feet up the Pillar, we found our way blocked by an impassable overhang. We abseiled back to the Pillar's base, but could find no alternative route matching our guidebook's description. Back at our previous high point, legs jammed into a single sleeping bag and bivouac bag, we spent an uncomfortable, cold night perched on a flake of rock.

Safe and secure *Hugo pictured at the Flammes de Pierre bivouac the night before he and Ruaridh abseiled to the foot of the Bonatti Pillar to start their ascent of the Petit Dru.*

Darkness closing in

At first light, with Hugo again attacking the overhang, I spotted climbers moving quickly to our left. 'That has to be the route!' I called out. After a long diagonal abseil to where they'd been, everything made sense. Moderately difficult rock, steep and often unstable, led to a big ledge where we ate most of our remaining rations. The rough granite had shredded Hugo's windproof trousers, baring his legs. We were overtaken at midday by three Japanese climbers, who introduced themselves as Go, Hiro and Ozaki.

To my alarm, big cauliflower clouds were boiling up. Westwards, Mont Blanc wore an ominous cloud-cap. Distant foothills were dim shapes. The unthinkable was happening: bad weather would hit us long before we could escape the Pillar.

Darkness swallowed the valley in huge gulps. Thunder boomed, growing closer. A gusting wind rose and the rain began. Roped to the cliff, feet perched on a crack in the rock, Hugo and I wrestled my thrashing bivouac bag over our heads. We were soon soaked.

An hour and a half later, with a third of the climb still to come, Hugo delirious, and the storm easing, I had decisions to make. With things getting serious I'd already suggested to the Japanese that we climb together, with one person climbing ahead protected by the second, while the third used further ropes to bring up the last two. With route-finding slowing whichever party was ahead, we'd been in each other's way. I reasoned we'd climb faster and more safely as a group.

Now Hugo would die if we didn't get moving and off the mountain – but even if I hauled him upwards, he was in no condition to use our ropes to protect me as I climbed the crack directly overhead: the technical crux of the route. And rescue was no option. Days might pass before the weather allowed helicopters near.

I explained his condition to the others. To my relief, despite little shared language, they understood. As Go climbed above us, fixing devices in the

Lightning safety

WHEN A STORM IS APPROACHING, once you can hear the thunder, you're close enough to be in danger. If you're in the open, try to get down from exposed ridges or peaks, or any tall objects.

• DON'T take shelter under a rocky overhang or in a shallow cave, because they create spark gaps across which lightning can arc on its way to earth.

• DON'T lie down, as the more contact points your body has with the ground, the greater the chance of a current using you to bridge a gap.

• If you're in town, get into an enclosed building, car or bus; AVOID bus shelters and porches.

If you're struck by lightning, it is likely to 'flash' all over you and may blow off your clothes, but there will be few, if any, signs of injury. The main cause of immediate death is cardiac or cardiopulmonary arrest, but 80 per cent of people hit by lightning survive.

SURVIVAL TIPS In an exposed location, squat close to the ground with your hands on your knees and your head tucked between them. Fold a waterproof garment and put it under your feet to increase insulation between your feet and the ground. Place all metal objects, such as cameras and poles, away from you.

rock for protection and footholds, I fed Hugo water and my remaining chocolate, making him wear my balaclava and bin-bag rucksack liner as a cagoule. Confused, he shredded it. 'Hugo!' I rubbed his arms and legs to get the circulation back. I suspected this was ultimately chilling him, but without working limbs he would never climb anything.

'Hugo, you've got to keep moving.' No response. 'Listen. You must warm yourself up. Move your legs.' A feeble rocking started. '*Hard*, dammit. If you don't warm up, and stay warm until we get off this mountain, you will die. Understand?'

The rocking became more vigorous. 'Move your arms. Get angry! Punch.' I rubbed his torso and thighs until breathless. 'Any warmer?'

'Think so … Numb level's going back down my legs.'

I rubbed his legs until I felt faint, then turned back to his body. 'How about your body? Tell any difference?'

A pause. 'Cold… but better.' I began breathing again. Hugo still felt icy, but the rain was tailing off. '*If I can just keep him going until he dries …*'

As Hiro and Ozaki began climbing, I emptied Hugo's rucksack into mine. Soon it was our turn. 'Can't do it,' Hugo mumbled. 'Legs won't work.'

'Get angry!' I ordered, just behind. 'You hate this climb. Give it hell!'

With an incredible effort, Hugo propelled himself upwards. Though exhausted, hypothermic, and climbing a strenuous, soaking and vertigo-inducing overhang after two days of scant food and sleep, he was soon progressing steadily.

Soon, though, there was a familiar distant boom. Then more, growing louder. The second storm exploded on us in a chaos of water and noise. I'd expected Go to climb ahead, leaving Hiro or Ozaki to bring up Hugo and me, but instead he'd brought us all up together. Things went faster after that, but the climbing – up vertical, icy waterfalls in hurricanes of blinding spray – seemed endless.

As I thought we *must* be near our point of descent, we scrambled into a tiny walled niche beneath an overhang, stripping off metal gear that could attract lightning. Discussion was unnecessary. Our Japanese friends hustled us inside their little bivouac shelter. At the niche's open corner, I jammed Hugo between myself and Ozaki, hugging him to try to preserve what heat he had left. Sat on rucksacks, we squeezed as best we could into our saturated sleeping bag.

The shelter thrashed. Spray deluged through nylon I was amazed hadn't already torn. Hugo was still too cold to shiver. I asked how he was.

'Not warm. But OK.'

Of more pressing concern was the assault of nearby thunder. I'd read warnings of caves in lightning storms. Acting like the gap in a spark plug, they've caused numerous deaths. But cracks – which we'd need for purchase and protection – are favoured by lightning too. Near the tip of a 900m (3,000ft) lightning conductor in a storm, there simply was no safe place.

Lightning strikes

Ozaki produced a stove and a bowl of welcome soup. Later, there was an ear-splitting crack, and everything turned blinding white. Then the niche was full of screaming – some of which I realised came from me. Then everyone was staring round with popping eyes in the dim headtorch-light, as what had happened sank in.

We'd survived a lightning strike.

It seemed unbelievable. And I didn't know if it meant more strikes were likely. We flinched at every crack of thunder until the anticipation grew exhausting.

Then the niche detonated once more, and an exploding sensation tore up from the soles of my feet, seeming to exit my back. I was screaming again. My right leg felt like it was being crushed. Others were also screaming. Pain faded to numbness; groans to brittle titters, before the niche exploded in light once more and the screaming resumed.

I began counting electrocutions to distract myself. After five, the bivouac stank of burning, and the scorched-rubber musk of humans who expect to die at any second. On the sixth, the charge ripping through my body was so strong that I passed out.

Trapped by the roof in an excruciating foetal position, I thought, '*Should we try to find somewhere safer?*' Doubtful. None of us, let alone Hugo, would survive long in the open, even if the wind didn't claw us from the mountain. And a lightning strike while climbing seemed guaranteed to be fatal. With a pang I wondered if, but for Hugo's hypothermia, Go, Hiro and Ozaki could have escaped the storm's worst. At best, though, it seemed likely they'd have got trapped on the even more exposed Flammes de Pierre.

I began counting electrocutions to distract myself. After five, the bivouac stank of burning, and the scorched-rubber musk of humans who expect to die at any second.

On top of the world *Hugo captured on the ascent to the Flammes de Pierre, looking out towards the Mont Blanc massif.*

Another strobe-image of terrified, bloodshot eyes. *Ten.* This time my knees felt as if they were being torn off. We waited, impotently, half-expecting each next strike to be fatal. Sometimes minutes separated them. Sometimes hours.

The storm raged into murky daylight. In 12 hours, we'd been electrocuted 17 times.

Then at 10.30am, after half an hour without thunder, we got ready to climb within seconds. The rocks had frozen. Climbing with gloves proved impossible, but grasping ice beneath streams of water stopped the circulation in my hands, inflicting agony whenever I tried warming them. I was finding it very difficult to work the ropes. It was Hugo's turn to urge me on.

At last we were on the traverse. More climbing, a tricky sideways abseil ... Then the pinnacles of the Flammes de Pierre, abseiling towards our first bivouac.

But the storm wasn't to let us off so easily. Thunder resumed. This was the worst possible place to be caught by lightning, and we worked frantically; my fingers hideously swollen with frostnip – one stage short of frostbite. Another flash. Electricity ripped up my arms from the rope I was hauling down. I regained consciousness somehow still on my feet.

The ridge consumed 4 more hours, during which I was electrocuted twice more: 20 in total. By late afternoon, Hugo was shivering violently. Back at our bivouac, the Japanese clambered down into the clouds. Having retrieved our cached belongings, we decided to keep abseiling. With an end in sight and our judgment skewed by exhaustion, this straightforward final descent was when a slip was likeliest.

Against the odds *Amazingly, the men, now safely within the Charpoua Hut, survived numerous lightning strikes. Left to right: Go, Ozaki, Hugo, Hiro and Ruaridh.*

We regained the glacier to find the snow-bridge we'd crossed previously had collapsed, forcing a long detour uphill over unstable, melting ice. As we staggered onto the rocks leading back to the Charpoua Hut, Hugo shook my hand. 'Not much left that can happen to us now,' he said.

Minutes later, blizzards of hailstones made us crawl the final 450m (500yd), blinded. It was almost funny.

We shuffled inside, astonishing the warden. Next day, as I hiked back to the flooded Chamonix Valley to reassure disbelieving friends, seven parties were rescued by helicopter from the Petit Dru.

Reflection

Back home near Edinburgh, my doctor assured me the numbness in my fingers and leg should fade. 'Though,' he added, 'I've not had many patients struck by lightning.' He didn't warn me about the nightmares.

I've been asked if Hugo or I regret our ordeal. It's a question neither of us can answer directly. What happened was a result of extraordinary luck – both bad and good. When things got out of control we stayed calm, and did most things right. Hugo's resilience was extraordinary, as was the selflessness and sheer stoic competence of Go, Hiro and Ozaki, to whom Hugo almost certainly owes his life.

But it's eerie to consider how things could have been, and what our survival owes to chance. The night we were fighting for our lives, a man at a Chamonix cable-car station was killed by lightning. Three others died in mountains nearby. Why them, and not us?

Especially when climbing, I'm aware more than ever that life is precious, unpredictable and to be savoured. ■

Where are they now?

WHEN RUARIDH PRINGLE came down from the Bonatti Pillar he felt exhilarated and deeply relieved that all five of them had escaped. 'We'd lived through something extraordinary,' he recalls, 'and miraculously emerged unscathed. For a while, at least, the world seemed a sweeter, more vivid place.' Even when the nightmares began a month later – he would start up in bed, finding his room transformed into that mountain niche – his enthusiasm for mountaineering remained.

In 1998, though, when he travelled to Pakistan's Karakoram to climb near the infamous peak of K2, despite some magical experiences, he was dismayed by 'the whole mountaineering circus' that the sport, for him, was becoming. 'I saw people behaving in ways I found disgusting. I think perspectives get skewed by the enormous commitment of effort and money required by expeditions. Some people seem to cease seeing those around them, including porters, as human beings. For me, mountaineering was about being in amazing, wild, ethereally beautiful places with people whose company I enjoyed, and that became increasingly hard to hold onto when I got into the commercial side of it.'

A close call in New Zealand in 2000 unsettled him. Hurrying to descend a slippery mountainside, with night and uncertain weather approaching, he had made a mistake clipping onto his ropes, abseiling down a cliff on what transpired to be a very tenuous thread. 'When I reached the bottom and saw what had supported my weight, I had a bit of a wobbly. I thought I didn't deserve to be alive. You're always balancing competing factors in the mountains, and safety often means sacrificing security for speed. Unless you're superhuman, it makes lapses of judgment inevitable, and I think it was the realisation of this that rattled me more than the incident itself.'

Global warming had an impact too. 'I used to do a lot of winter climbing in the Scottish Highlands, which was what I enjoyed most. When I started you could climb from September through to May or June – but now if the mountains properly freeze, which is rare, a southwesterly wind comes in and melts everything off. It means more people than ever trying to climb too few routes in marginal conditions. I was climbing on Creag Meagaidh in the Central Highlands; near the top I was horrified to find more than 14 people queueing below the final part. Somebody started talking to me, and someone above knocked down a typewriter-sized piece of ice that flattened his head. I had to grab him before he fell off. I thought he would die – he'd a 'blown' pupil indicating brain haemorrhaging – but someone had a mobile phone, and a helicopter team came within 90 minutes, and took him to intensive care.'

Discouraging experiences like these, as well as a shoulder problem, have led Ruaridh reluctantly to give up climbing, though he still loves hillwalking. A photographer and writer, he is the author of *Hill Walks: Glencoe and Lochaber* (The Stationery Office Ltd or TSO). With cellist Seylan Baxter he has also formed Tattie Jam – a duo playing 'mainly Scottish folk music with a contemporary spin'.

HE BEAT CANCER

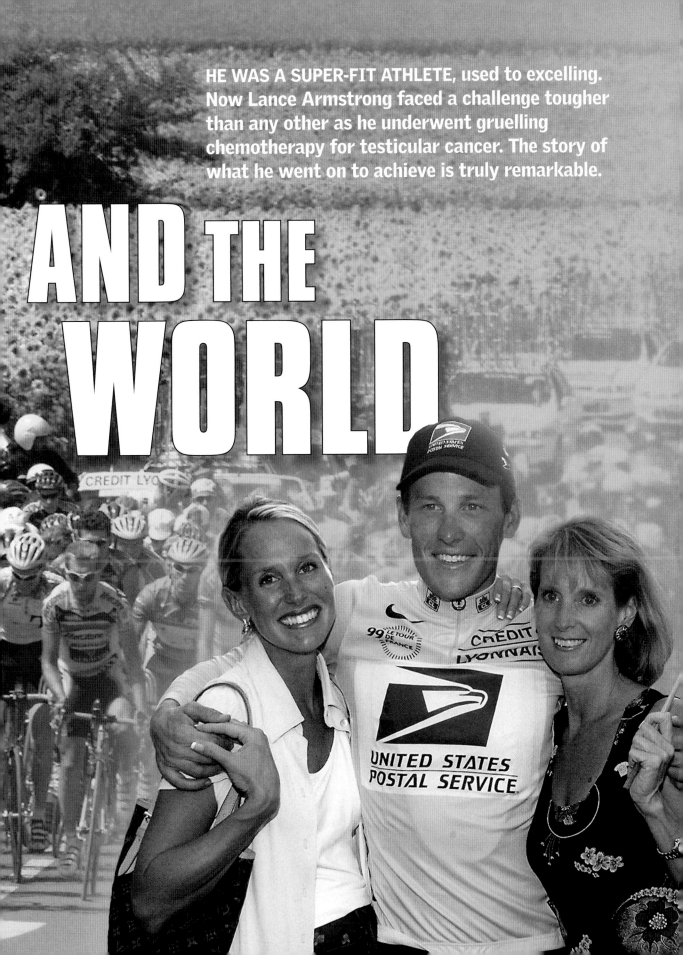

HE WAS A SUPER-FIT ATHLETE, used to excelling. Now Lance Armstrong faced a challenge tougher than any other as he underwent gruelling chemotherapy for testicular cancer. The story of what he went on to achieve is truly remarkable.

AND THE WORLD

In the saddle *Lance Armstrong looks at home on the bike he received for his 8th birthday, on September 18, 1979.*

Agony and ecstasy *Lance had to endure some low moments during his treatment at Indiana University School of Medicine Hospital in 1996 (previous page, top left). Three years later he triumphed in the 1999 Tour de France, a victory he was able to celebrate with his then-wife Kristin and mother, Linda (previous page, bottom right).*

Your past shapes you, whether you like it or not. I never had a real father, but I never sat around wishing for one either. My mother was 17 when she had me and from day one everyone told her we wouldn't amount to anything. But she believed differently.

Athletes don't have much use for poking around in their childhoods because introspection doesn't get you anywhere in a race. That said, it's all fuel for the fire. The old wounds and long-ago slights become the stuff of competitive energy. Back then I was just a kid with about four chips on his shoulder, thinking, 'Maybe if I ride my bike on this road long enough it will take me out of here.'

In Plano, Texas, if you weren't a football player you didn't exist. I tried to play, but when it came to anything involving a ball, I was no good. I was determined to find something I could succeed at. When I was about 13, I saw a flyer for a competition called IronKids, a junior triathlon that combined biking, swimming and running – all the things I was good at – so I signed up.

I won by a lot, without even training. Not long after, there was another triathlon in Houston. I won that too. I came back full of self-confidence. I was better at triathlons than any kid in the whole state. I liked the feeling.

I was discovering that if it was a matter of gritting my teeth and outlasting everybody else, I won. In a straight-ahead, long-distance race, I could beat anybody.

If it was a suffer-fest, I was good at it.

Metaphor for life

When I was 15, I entered the 1987 President's Triathlon against a field of experienced older athletes. I finished 32nd, shocking the other competitors, who couldn't believe a 15-year-old had held up. The next year I finished 5th.

Triathlons paid good money. All of a sudden I had a wallet full of first-place cheques. If it sounds like it came easy, it didn't. In one of the first pro triathlons I entered, I completely ran out of energy. I was first out of the water and first off the bike, but in the middle of the run I nearly collapsed. My mother found me struggling along.

'I'm totally gone,' I said.

'All right,' she said. 'But you can't quit. Even if you have to walk to the finish line.'

I walked to the finish line.

By now my mother and I realised I had a future as an athlete. I got a call from Chris Carmichael, the new director of the US national cycling team. Chris had heard about my reputation: I was super-strong but I didn't understand a lot about tactics. Chris told me the sport was stagnant in the USA and he was seeking fresh kids to rejuvenate it. How would I like to go to Europe?

When I left home at 18, my idea of a race was to leap on and start pedalling. In my first big international race I did everything my coach told me *not* to do. It was at the 1990 amateur World Championships, a 115 mile road race over a tough course. To make matters more difficult, it happened to be a sweltering day.

Chris gave me strict instructions to hang back in the pack. The smart thing to do was to conserve my energy. On the first lap I did what he told me, but then I couldn't help myself. On the second lap, I took the lead. I streaked past Chris. He had his arms spread wide, as if to say, 'What are you doing?'

I proceeded to build a lead of about a minute and a half. I was feeling pretty good about myself when the heat started to get to me. Next thing I knew, 30 guys joined me. I tried to keep riding at the front but, sapped by the heat, I finished 11th.

Still, it was the best American finish in the history of the race and Chris congratulated me, then he added, 'Of course, if you had known what you were doing, you'd have been in the medals.'

I had to learn how to race. That first year I must have spent 200 days riding around Europe. I learned about the peloton – the massive pack of riders that makes up the main body of the race. To the spectator it seems like a blur, but that colourful blur is rife with contact, the clashing of handlebars, elbows and knees, and it's full of intrigue.

The politics could be confusing to a young rider. I was a member of two different teams: internationally, I raced for the national team under Chris, but domestically I competed for Subaru-Montgomery. In 1991 our US team entered the Settimana Bergamasca, a pro-am ten day ride through northern Italy; some of the best cyclists in the world would be there. No American had ever won it, but we felt we just might pull it off.

Early in the race, a Subaru-Montgomery rider and friend, Nate Rees, took the lead. I moved into second. It seemed like the best of both worlds to have the two of us riding at the front. But the Subaru-Montgomery team director was not happy. He told me straight out I was obliged to let Nate win.

The next day I rode hard. Imagine: you're going up a hill with 100 guys in the peloton. Gradually 50 get dropped, then 20 more. Then you're down to 15 – it's a race of attrition. To make things harder, you attack – raise the tempo even more. That's the essence of road racing.

But I was supposed to wait for Nate.

At the end of the day I wore the leader's jersey while Nate had lost about 20 minutes. The Subaru-Montgomery team director was furious.

I wanted to talk to my mother. I could barely figure out how to dial the States, but I finally got through and explained the situation.

'To hell with them,' she said. 'Don't let anybody intimidate you.'

I put my head down and I raced. I was the winner, giving the US national team a victory in a European race. Our team was ecstatic. As I came down from the podium, Chris told me something I've never forgotten.

Pushing himself *Armstrong competing as a young man in the Ironman Triathlon, just after he signed a cycling sponsorship deal with Subaru-Montgomery.*

Vying for position *A view of the peloton – the large pack of riders that start out the race – as they cycle through the French countryside during stage 6 of the 1999 Tour de France, between Amiens and Maubeuge, on July 9.*

'You're gonna win the Tour de France one day,' he said.

My reputation was as a single-day racer: I would win on adrenaline and anger, chopping off my competitors one by one. But the Tour was another thing entirely. It required a longer view. It was a matter of continuing to ride and ride when there was no rush of adrenaline left.

In 1995 I finally gained an understanding of the demanding nature of the Tour. I finished it, winning a stage in the closing days. But the knowledge came at too high a price.

Late in the race, our Motorola teammate Fabio Casartelli, the 1992 Olympic champion, was killed on a high-speed descent. He hit a kerb with the back of his head and fractured his skull. I had known Fabio since I first started riding internationally. He was a relaxed fun-loving man, a joker. Some of the top Italians were more serious, but Fabio was all sweetness.

That night we had a team meeting to discuss whether we should keep riding. Personally, I wanted to stop. It was the first time I had encountered death and I didn't know how to handle it. Then Fabio's wife came to see us and she said she wanted us to keep riding because that was what Fabio would have wanted.

The next day the peloton rode in honour of Fabio and gave our team a ceremonial victory. It was virtually a funeral procession. The following morning we began the race again in earnest. That night, Och, the team manager, told us that Fabio had especially wanted to win the next stage, into Limoges. As soon as Och had stopped speaking I knew that I wanted to win it for Fabio.

About halfway through the day I found myself with 25 guys at the front. I did what came naturally to me: I attacked – too early, as usual. You never attack early and on a downhill but I went so fast that I had a 30 second lead in a finger-snap. I went faster than I'd ever ridden. It was a tactical punch in the face – insane, but it worked.

I won by a minute and I didn't feel a moment's pain. I know I rode with a higher purpose that day. Fabio was with me. At the finish line I felt I was winning for Fabio and his family and for the mourning country of Italy.

I had learned what it means to ride the Tour de France. It's not about the bike. It's a metaphor for life: not only the longest race in the world but also the most exalting and heartbreaking and potentially tragic.

I understood now there were no short cuts. I wouldn't be able to win a Tour de France until I had enough iron in my legs and lungs and brain and heart. Until I was a man. Fabio had been a man. I was still trying to get there.

Of *course* I should have known that something was wrong with me.
But athletes, especially cyclists, are in the business of denial. It's a sport
of self-abuse and you do not give in to pain. So I didn't pay any attention
to the fact that I didn't feel well in 1996. When my right testicle became
swollen, I told myself to live with it.

I thought I was just rundown. 'Suck it up,' I said to myself, 'you
can't afford to be tired.' I dropped out of the Tour de France after just
five days. 'I couldn't breathe,' I told the press. Looking back, they were
ominous words.

At the Olympic Games in Atlanta, my body gave out again. I was 6th in
the time trial and 12th in the road race, respectable but disappointing. Back
home in Austin, I told myself it was flu.

Why was this taking so long?

I celebrated my 25th birthday on September 18. A couple of days later
I had a bad coughing attack and I splattered the bathroom sink with
blood. I couldn't believe that mass of blood and clotted matter had come
from my own body.

Frightened, I dialled my neighbour, Dr Rick Parker, a good friend.
While Rick was on his way I eyed the bloody residue in the sink and turned
on the taps. I didn't want Rick to see it. I was embarrassed.

Rick checked my nose and mouth. 'You could be bleeding from your
sinuses. You may have cracked one.'

I was so relieved I jumped at the first suggestion that it wasn't serious
and left it at that.

A few nights later I had dinner with Rick and his wife, but I was so sore
in my right testicle that I couldn't get comfortable at the table. I almost
told Rick, but I was too self-conscious. It hardly seemed like something to
bring up over dinner.

When I woke the next morning, my testicle was swollen almost to the
size of an orange. I dialled Rick again. He insisted he would get me to see a
specialist that afternoon.

Dr Jim Reeves was a prominent Austin urologist with a deep voice and
a way of making everything seem routine – despite the fact that he was
seriously alarmed by what he found.

My testicle was enlarged to three times its normal size, hard and
painful to the touch. Reeves said, 'Just to be safe, I'm going to send you
for an ultrasound.'

The lab was in another building. I figured I'd be out of there in a few minutes. An hour later, I was still on the table. Why was this taking so long?

Without a word, the technician left the room and returned with the chief radiologist. I lay there in silence as he went over me for another 15 minutes.

'We need to take a chest X-ray,' he said.

Why would they look at my chest? Nothing hurt there. I was getting angry now, and scared. A new technician went through the X-ray process.

Down the hallway, I cornered the chief radiologist. 'Hey, what's going on?'

'Well, I don't want to step on Dr Reeves' toes, but perhaps he's checking you for some cancer-related activity. He's waiting for you in his office.'

There was an icy feeling in the pit of my stomach.

As I walked into Dr Reeves' office I noticed that the building was empty. Everyone was gone.

Rick arrived, looking grim. Dr Reeves pulled out my X-rays. An X-ray is like a photo negative: abnormalities come out white.

My chest looked like a snowstorm.

'This is serious,' Dr Reeves said. 'It looks like testicular cancer with large metastasis to the lungs. I've scheduled you for surgery tomorrow morning to remove the testicle.'

I have cancer.

'Shouldn't I get a second opinion?'

Dr Reeves elaborated. Testicular cancer was considered very treatable, thanks to advances in chemotherapy, but early diagnosis was key. The question was, how far had it spread? He recommended I see Dr Dudley Youman, a renowned Austin-based oncologist. Speed was essential; every day would count.

I got up to leave. I had a lot of calls to make and one of them was to my mother. Somehow I'd have to tell her that her only child had cancer.

I drove slowly. I was in shock. Cancer would change everything for me, I realised. Who would I be if I wasn't Lance Armstrong, world-class cyclist?

Inside my house the phone was ringing. My friend Scott.

'Hey, Lance, what's going on?'

'A lot,' I said angrily.

'What do you mean?'

I opened my mouth, closed it and opened it again. 'I have cancer,' I said and started to cry.

In that moment it occurred to me I might lose not just my sport. I could lose my life.

Facing up to 'stage three'

I was in surgery for about 3 hours. The next morning, Dr Youman came by to give me the initial results of the pathology reports. He said it appeared that the cancer was spreading rapidly.

In the 24 hours since I'd been diagnosed, I'd done as much homework as I could. I knew oncologists broke testicular cancer down into three stages: in stage one, the cancer was confined and the patients had excellent prognoses; in stage two, the cancer had moved into the abdominal lymph nodes; and in stage three, it had spread to vital organs such as the lungs.

Rick arrived, looking grim. Dr Reeves pulled out my X-rays. An X-ray is like a photo negative: abnormalities come out white. My chest looked like a snowstorm.

The tests showed that I was in stage three.

The cancer was not just spreading, it was galloping. Youman decided I should begin chemotherapy directly because every day might count.

My mother drew up a calendar to keep track of my treatment and made lists of my medications. She ran my illness as if it were a project. She made an appointment with a nutritionist who gave us a list of food compatible with the drugs. Immediately my mother began steaming huge bowls of broccoli for me.

But beneath all of the manic activity I could tell that she was struggling. She tried not to show me but I knew that at night she would go into her room and cry.

It was time to go public. I held a news conference to announce that I would not be cycling. Everyone was there: Bill, my agent, several sponsors and, on the phone, reporters from Europe. There was an audible murmur when I said the word 'cancer' and I could see the shock on the faces.

My first chemo treatment was strangely undramatic. For one thing, I didn't feel sick. My mother had prepared me to be disturbed by my first

Know your testicles

TESTICULAR CANCER is rare, affecting one in 450 men before the age of 50, but it is the most common cancer in men aged 15-45. It is also more common in white men – in particular, Scandinavians – than in other races. With advances in chemotherapy, the disease is considered very treatable, and 90 per cent of men make a full recovery. The sooner any cancer is detected, the better the prognosis, so it is important to check for abnormalities. Don't do as Lance Armstrong did and tell yourself to 'suck it up'.

Make self-examination a part of your routine, once a month, after a bath or shower, when the warm water has softened the scrotum. Examine the scrotum for lumps on the skin or swellings beneath it. Let the scrotum and testicles rest in your palm and feel for differences between the testicles. Using both hands, gently roll each testicle between thumb and forefinger. It is common for one to be slightly

larger than the other, or to hang lower, but any marked increase in size or weight, any swelling or lump should be further investigated. Cancer rarely develops in both testicles at once, so if in doubt as to what is 'normal', compare them. Don't be alarmed if you feel something bumpy at the top and back of the testicle: this is the epididymis, a sperm-carrying duct. The testicle itself should be round, soft and smooth.

Even if you find a lump, it is probably benign (fewer than four in every 100 testicular lumps are cancerous), but be sure to see your doctor. Never ignore symptoms of pain or discomfort: sudden swelling or tenderness, discharge, uncomfortable heaviness in the scrotum; a dull ache in a testicle or the lower abdomen.

Lance's experience led to suggestions that cycling caused testicular cancer, but this has been largely discounted. High cholesterol, industrial chemicals and long-term cannabis use are all possible factors.

COLOUR-CODED WARNING The yellowy-green area seen in the upper centre of the ultrasound picture indicates the presence of cancer in this testicle.

encounter with other cancer patients. Instead I felt a sense of belonging. I was relieved to be able to talk to other people who shared the illness. By the time my mother got back I was chatting with a guy my grandfather's age. 'Hey, Mom,' I said. 'This is Paul and he's got prostate cancer.'

No health insurance

A couple of days after I started chemo, I opened a letter from the hospital: *Our records show that you have no health insurance.*

It was a lousy piece of timing. I was in the midst of changing employers and my insurance with Motorola had expired. I would have to pay for treatment myself.

I was wiped out financially, I assumed. I had just gone from making $2 million a year to nothing. I would have no income because the companies that sponsored me would surely cut me off since I couldn't race.

The Porsche that I treasured now seemed like pure self-indulgence. Within days it was gone, because I thought I might need every dime. But I think, too, that I was beginning to need to simplify things.

I reported to the hospital for a brain scan. Dr Youman took one look at the image and said, 'You have two spots.'

I couldn't seem to get any good news: *It's in your lungs, it's stage three, you have no insurance, now it's in your brain.*

When something climbs into your mind, that's personal. I tried negotiating with it. 'If the deal is I never cycle again but I live, I'll take it,' I thought.

I began to receive mountains of mail and one evening I opened a letter from a Dr Steven Wolff, who explained that he was an oncologist as well as an ardent cycling fan. He urged me to get a second opinion and offered to arrange consultations for me. From that moment my treatment became a medical collaboration.

On Wolff's recommendation, I flew to Indiana to meet Dr Craig Nichols, who was sober and realistic, but he exuded optimism, too. 'We've cured a lot worse,' he said.

Then he stunned me, saying he would like to tailor my treatment to get me back on the bike. There was a chemo that was much more caustic in the short term but which would not be as debilitating to my lungs. If I could withstand three cycles, I just might get rid of the cancer and recover enough to compete.

Nichols favoured surgery to remove the brain tumours. The standard treatment was radiation, but one potential effect could be a slight loss of balance. Nothing serious to the ordinary person but enough to keep me from riding a bike down an Alp – balance is something you need in that situation.

Accompanying Nichols was Scott Shapiro, a neurosurgeon. His hair curled over his collar and he seemed too casual to be a doctor.

I was in a state of disbelief and it made me blunt. 'Why should you be the person who operates on my head?'

'Because as good as you are at cycling' – he paused – 'I'm a lot better at brain surgery.'

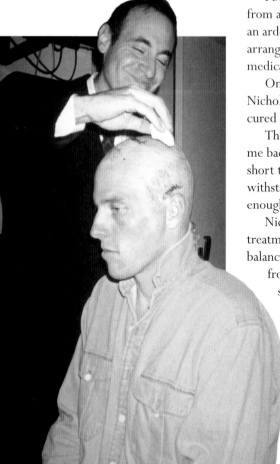

Delicate surgery *Lance Armstrong's neurosurgeon, Scott Shapiro, removes the bandages from his head after performing 6 hours of brain surgery on him at the Indiana University School of Medicine Hospital.*

I laughed and knew that I liked him. 'This is where I want to do my treatment,' I said.

The night before brain surgery I thought about death. I asked myself what I believed. I had never prayed a lot but I knew this much: I believed in belief for its own shining sake. To continue believing in yourself, in the doctors, in the treatment – that was the most important thing. Without belief we would be left with nothing but an overwhelming doom. So, I believed.

All I know about the surgery is what Dr Shapiro related to me. I was on the table for roughly 6 hours as he made the incisions and removed the lesions.

I woke up slowly … '*I'm alive.*'

One day I noticed marks on my skin like brown stains. They were chemo burns. The drugs were scorching my tissues from the inside out. My physique was shot. It was as though my body was being steadily diminished. I looked like a stooped, limping old man.

Shapiro was bending over me. No matter how good the surgeon, once he has put you back together he waits anxiously to see if you are responsive.

'Can you tell me your name?'

'Lance Armstrong,' I said. 'And I can kick your ass on a bike any day.'

I dropped back into bottomless sleep.

He came by the next morning and told me the surgery had been a complete success. 'Now it's a matter of hoping like hell it doesn't come back,' he added.

I began to get good news. None of my sponsors was bailing out on me even though each of them had the right to terminate the deal – and none of them so much as asked when I would ride a bike again. And they got a health provider to cover the costs of my treatment.

The good news continued. After a couple of days of chemo my blood counts improved. But as I approached the end of the week, the euphoria of coming through surgery wore off and the sickness of the chemo took over. All I wanted to do was stare at the wall. And there were two more cycles yet to come.

The question was, which would the chemo kill first: the cancer or me? What a casual bystander associates with cancer – loss of hair, a sickly pallor, wasting away – are actually the side effects of the treatment. Chemo was a burning in my veins, a continuous hacking up of tar-like matter from deep in my chest, a doubling-over need to go to the bathroom.

By the third cycle I was on my hands and knees fighting nausea. By the fourth – the highest number prescribed – I was in the foetal position, retching around the clock.

One day I noticed marks on my skin like brown stains. They were chemo burns. The drugs were scorching my tissues from the inside out. My physique was shot. It was as though my body was being steadily diminished. I looked like a stooped, limping old man.

The irony was, the worse I felt, the better I got. At my sickest, I started to beat the thing. Gradually the tumour markers began to drop. From now on it was just a matter of getting through the last of the treatments. I was almost well. But I sure didn't feel like it.

Dr Nichols said that as my health improved I might feel that I had a larger purpose than just myself. Cancer could be an opportunity. He had seen all kinds of cancer patients become activists against the disease and he hoped I would be one of them. I hoped so, too. I was beginning to see cancer as something I was given for the good of others. I had a new sense of purpose and it had nothing to do with my exploits on a bike. I no longer felt it was my role in life to be a cyclist. Maybe it was to be a cancer survivor.

I called Bill, my agent, and asked him to research what it took to start a charitable foundation. I knew that because my case was a cause célèbre, people would listen, but I didn't want a personal pulpit. I wanted the foundation to manifest all of the issues I had dealt with the past few months, above all the idea that cancer did not have to be a death sentence. It could be a route to a better life.

Against the odds

People think of my comeback as a triumph, but in the beginning it was a disaster.

My first pro race in 18 months was the Ruta del Sol, a five-day jaunt through Spain. I finished 14th and caused a stir, but I was depressed. I was used to leading. Two weeks later, in the arduous eight-day race from Paris to Nice, I quit. I took off my number, abandoned the race and flew home. The decision had nothing to do with how I felt physically. I simply didn't know if cycling was what I wanted to do for the rest of my life.

Peak performance *Riding for the US Postal Service and wearing the coveted yellow jersey, Armstrong races against the Swiss champion, Alexander Zülle, during stage 15 of the 1999 Tour de France, from St Gaudens to Piau-Engaly, on July 20.*

I was a bum. I played golf every day. I drank beer, lay on the sofa and channel-surfed. But it wasn't fun. The truth was, I felt ashamed. *Son, you can't quit.* But I'd quit.

I'd had a job and a life and then I got sick, and when I tried to go back to my life nothing was the same – and I couldn't handle it.

I now know that surviving cancer involved more than just a convalescence of the body. My mind and my soul had to convalesce too.

I was willing to sacrifice the entire 1999 season to prepare for the Tour de France. I picked only a handful of events that would help me peak in July. Cancer had completely reshaped my body. In old pictures I looked like a football player with a thick neck and big upper body. Now I was almost gaunt, leaner in body and more balanced in spirit.

The first stage of the Tour was a time trial over 8km to determine who would ride at the front of the peloton. The riders who wanted to contend in the overall needed to finish among the top three or four. Alexander Zülle of Switzerland broke the course record with a time of 8 minutes and 7 seconds.

It was my turn. I focused on the technique of the ride. I had no idea what my time was. I just pedalled.

I crossed the line and glanced at the clock: 8.02.

I was the leader of the Tour de France. For the first time in my career I would wear the yellow jersey.

We set off across the northern plains of France. All day, every day, my teammates in the US Postal Service rode in front of me, protecting me from wind, crashes and other competitors. Over those first ten days we had just one aim – to stay near the front and out of trouble. I gave up the yellow jersey for the time being, saving myself.

Triumph over adversity *Armstrong speeds past the Arc de Triomphe on the 20th and final stage of the 1999 Tour de France, from Arpajon to Paris, on July 25.*

We arrived in Metz for the 56km time trial, which I won, beating Zülle by 58 seconds. I was so tired I was cross-eyed, but as I pulled the yellow jersey over my head I decided that's where it needed to stay.

We entered the mountains. I held a lead of 2 minutes and 20 seconds, but in the mountains you could fall hopelessly behind in a single day. I was sure to come under heavy attack, but what my adversaries didn't know was how hard I had trained for this part of the race. It was time to show them.

On the final ascent into Sestriere all of us were struggling. We had covered the best part of 240km (150 miles) that day and from here on it would be a question of who cracked and who didn't.

It was time to go. I swung to the inside of the group and accelerated. My bike seemed to jump ahead. I glanced over my shoulder, half expecting to see Zülle on my wheel. No one was there.

Now I could see the finish line. It was uphill the rest of the way. I drove towards the peak.

Was I thinking about cancer as I rode those last few yards? I'd be lying if I said I was. But I think that everything I'd been through, the cancer and the disbelief within the sport that I could come back, made me faster.

Somehow we had controlled the mountains and after three weeks and 3,540km (2,200 miles) I led the race.

I won the final time trial and was now assured of winning the Tour de France. My closest competitor was Zülle, who trailed overall by 7 minutes and 37 seconds — an impossible margin to make up on the final stage into Paris.

I felt a swell of emotion as we rode onto the Champs-Élysées and I was ushered to the podium for the victory ceremony. I said, 'Where's my Mom?' and the crowd opened and I grabbed her. Someone asked her if my victory was against the odds.

'Lance's whole life has been against the odds,' she told him. ■

Where are they now?

LANCE ARMSTRONG'S STORY is truly the stuff of legend. After his triumph over cancer and his victory in the 1999 Tour de France, he went on to win the Tour for the following six consecutive years, establishing a new world record.

He had meanwhile created the Lance Armstrong Foundation and taken up the role of advocate for people living with cancer. Within a decade, his organisation helped to raise $265 million, and his inspirational story won him many awards. He retired from racing on July 24, 2005, but returned to road racing in January 2009, making his very public comeback in the name of cancer awareness.

In 2007, with a group of fellow sports stars, Armstrong founded Athletes for Hope, to encourage professional athletes to involve themselves in charitable causes, and to inspire non-athletes to volunteer for community support work.

His career has been dogged by allegations of the use of performance-enhancing drugs. Such charges were the subject of a book, *L.A. Confidential – Les Secrets de Lance Armstrong*, in 2004, and of articles in French newspapers *L'Équipe* and *Le Monde*, as well as the *LA Times*. Armstrong described the rumours as a 'witch hunt', stating that he must be 'the most tested athlete in history'.

His private life, too, has been grist to the newspaper mill. With his wife Kristin he fathered a son, Luke, in 1999, and twins Isabelle and Grace in 2001, using sperm banked before he began treatment, amid fears that chemotherapy would destroy his fertility. The couple filed for divorce in September 2003, though Armstrong remains a devoted hands-on father. Since then he has dated singer-songwriter Sheryl Crow and actress Kate Hudson.

In December 2008, Armstrong announced that his girlfriend, Anna Hansen, was carrying his child, conceived by natural means.

NEVADA CANCER INSTITUTE CELEBRATES ITS PARTNERSHIP WITH LANCE ARMSTRONG FOUNDATION

THE WINNER Armstrong takes to the podium (left) in 2005 with his children, Luke, Grace and Isabelle, on his 7th Tour de France win. Away from racing (above) he speaks out for cancer sufferers at the Nevada Cancer Institute.

WHILE EXPLORING **THE SOUTH PACIFIC ISLANDS**, American Tami Oldham and her British boyfriend, Richard Sharp, were offered a dream job – to sail a yacht, the *Hazana*, from Tahiti to San Diego. Tami had just agreed to marry Richard, but mother nature was about to turn their lives upside down.

LOST AT SEA

With a grand gesture, Richard waved to me – 'Let's go!'

I shifted the engine into forward. The *Hazana* gathered speed and we headed out of Papeete Harbour on Tahiti. It was September 22, 1983, at 13.30 hours. In a month we'd be back in my home town of San Diego, California.

I took the wheel as Richard hoisted the mainsail. I steered the boat into the wind, and the *Hazana* comfortably heeled over. I reflected on how hard it had been for Richard to say goodbye to his boat; the *Mayaluga* had been his home for many years, and he had sailed her halfway round the world before he met me in San Diego. Richard and I started dating and when he asked me to join him on the boat trip he had planned to the South Pacific, I agreed, knowing I had never felt this way about any man before. Richard was Mr Right, my knight in shining armour, my hero.

The log entry for our first day out read: 'Perfect day. Making 5 knots in calm sea.' But by day three we were pounding into the wind. *Hazana* held up well and there was no way we'd be easing the sheets[1] to make the ride more comfortable – we had committed to deliver *Hazana* for the owners, the Cromptons, and it was San Diego or bust.

On October 9, day 18, the weather channel informed us that there was a tropical storm brewing off the coast of Central America. They were referring to it as Raymond. Richard wrote in the log: 'Watch this one.'

'Storms come and go,' I thought, 'often petering out.' Unfazed, I kept up our daily routine – cooking, cleaning, steering, reading, writing to friends.

The next day the wind veered to the north. At 05.00, we changed our heading to get as far north of Raymond's track as possible. The storm was quickly surpassing the two horrendous storms I'd experienced in the Pacific before I met Richard. We were both seasoned sailors, but this was turning into the worst weather we'd faced together. All through that day, the wind steadily increased. Tropical Storm Raymond was now classed as a hurricane.

The tether breaks

At 09.30 on October 11, the forecast put Hurricane Raymond spinning along a northwest course. Richard screamed at the radio, 'Why the bloody hell are you tacking to the north? Stay the hell away from us!' He had let down his reserve, and more than anger exploded – it was fear. Richard recorded in the logbook: 'We're in the firing line.'

We flew every sail to its maximum capacity. It would be pointless to start the engine, for by now we were sailing way beyond hull speed. Richard's nervousness and fear were obvious. I had never seen him like this. Adrenaline surged through me – fight or flight. There was no way to fly out of this mess, so it was fight. Fight, fight, fight.

The next morning broke cinder-grey with spotty sunlight shedding an overcast hue on brothy seas. By 10.00 hours the seas arched into skyscrapers, looming over our boat. The anenometer, which measures wind speed, read a steady 60 knots (110km/h) and we were forced to take down all sail. By noon the wind was a sustained 100 knots (185km/h).

The happy couple *Richard and Tami prepare for their cruise, unaware of the tragedy that awaited them at the mercy of Hurricane Raymond.*

---

1 Sheets Ropes that control a sail's setting in relation to the wind.

Richard handed me the EPIRB (emergency position-indicating radio device), saying, 'I want you to put this on.'

'What about you?'

'Tami, if we had two I'd put one on. Just make me feel better and put the bloody thing on.'

So I did. Richard fastened his safety harness, and took the wheel. I sat huddled against the cockpit coaming[2]. We were helpless while staring at the raging scene around us. The sound of the screaming wind was unnerving. The ascent of the boat over monstrous waves sent the hull airborne into a freefall that smashed down with a shudder. I shouted to Richard.

'Is this it? Can it get any worse?'

'No. Hang on, be my brave girl. Some day we'll tell our grandchildren how we survived Hurricane Raymond.'

'If we survive,' I hollered back.

'We will. Go below and try to rest.'

'What happens if we roll over? I don't want to leave you alone.'

'The boat would right itself. Look, I'm secure,' he said, giving a sharp tug on his tether. 'I'd come right back up with it.'

I looked at his tether secured to the cleat[3] on the cockpit coaming.

'Go below,' he urged. 'Keep your eye on the barometer. Let me know the moment it starts rising.'

Reluctantly I got up, then squeezed Richard's hand.

'Hold on,' he yelled and cranked the wheel. I tumbled sideways as the hull was knocked down. An avalanche of white water hit us. The boat ominously shuddered from bow to stern.

Richard glanced anxiously at me, fear jumping from his intense blue eyes. Behind him rose sheer cliffs of white water. My eyes questioned his – I couldn't hide my terror. He faltered, then winked at me, thrusting his chin up, a signal for me to go below. His forced grin and lingering eye contact disappeared as I slammed the hatch shut.

I made my way down to the cabin below. I collapsed into the hammock and secured the tether of my safety harness around the table leg. I looked up at the clock: it was 13.00 hours. My eyes dropped to the barometer: it was terrifyingly low. I was flung from side to side in the hammock. No sooner had I closed my eyes than all motion stopped. Something felt very wrong, it became too quiet, this trough too deep.

'Oh my God!' I heard Richard scream.

My eyes popped open.

Whomp! I covered my head as I sailed into oblivion.

Initial calm *The yacht* Hazana, *a Trintella 44, set off with sails billowing, but Hurricane Raymond hit it with such force that the mast was totally sheared off.*

---

2 Coaming A raised section of a ship, which keeps out water.
3 Cleat A secured device, often metal and with two protruding 'horns', onto which rope is attached.

I opened my eyes and saw blue sky and wispy white clouds outside. My head throbbed. I went to touch it, but things – I didn't know what – lay on top of me, smothering me, crushing me. What was going on? I couldn't think. I couldn't remember. Where was I? My hammock hung cock-eyed.

I struggled to free myself from the dead weight that pinned me down. Cans of food, books, pillows, clothes and a door spilled off me as I struggled to sit up.

Where was I? What had happened? I was confused. The clock on the wall showed 4pm. That didn't seem right … I was obviously on a boat – what boat? My weakened hands tried to unclip the tether that was still clipped onto the table leg. Once unclipped, I strained to see around me. My vision was blurry, the pain in my head excruciating. Putting my hand

The greatest storms on earth

A HURRICANE is a formidable force of nature; before it is spent it will expend as much energy as 10,000 nuclear bombs. The first prerequisite for hurricane formation is surface water on the ocean warmed to around 27°C (80°F) – hence talk of a hurricane 'season', lasting from early summer through to autumn. The second and third essential factors are converging low-level winds, and light winds at a high level.

As the sea sends up warm, moist air, which forms clouds, a centre of low pressure is created, around which colliding, spiralling winds may rush, whirling upwards, releasing heat and moisture. Meanwhile, the revolving earth causes the column to twist around the 'eye' – the still and cloudless centre, about 32km (20 miles) across – of the gathering tropical storm. The 'eye wall' surrounding the centre is the scene of the worst havoc.

Shearing winds, above the cloud level, will usually ensure that the impending cataclysm 'blows over', sending streaming clouds for hundreds of miles. But with light winds, the heat builds up and the winds spiral upwards. When the storm's wind speed reaches 120km/h (75mph), it is classified as a hurricane.

Hurricanes can travel at speeds of more than 240km/h (150mph), with gusts above 320km/h (200mph). They are also vast, averaging 320-485km (200-300 miles) in diameter, although size isn't everything: smaller hurricanes can be more damaging than larger, relatively more 'tame' ones.

The naming of hurricanes provides a shorthand means of identifying one from another. Tropical storms and hurricanes were first given female names in 1953; in 1979, male names were added to a rotating, six-yearly approved annual list. Hurricanes are named alphabetically, in chronological order, so the first tropical storm of the year will begin with A. The list runs from A to W, excluding Q and U. When a hurricane has proved particularly devastating, its name is 'retired' and replaced. Thus Katrina joined the disgraced Rita, Dennis, Stan, William and others in retirement, after the appalling damage and loss of life caused in New Orleans.

AN ILL WIND
A satellite image of Hurricane Katrina, the vicious storm that devastated Louisiana, taken on August 29, 2005.

to my brow, I flinched. I looked at my hand and saw crimson. Uncontrollable shivers engulfed me.

Laboriously, I crawled out of the wreckage. I stood up unsteadily. The water was over knee-high. I felt faint. Slowly I waded through the obstacles floating in the water, heading for the forward cabin.

'Hello,' I called out. My voice sounded strange.

Cautiously moving towards the bow, I peeked in a mirror. I saw a frazzled image, its face covered in blood, the forehead cut wide open. Strands of hair, wild and matted with blood, shot out from its skull. I screamed. The ungodly sight was me.

'No!' I shouted, crashing into the bulkhead as I tried to escape.

I stumbled into the V-berth[4]. Everything there was topsy-turvy. The storage hammocks were overturned, spilled clothes lay everywhere. Cans of food and broken dishes lay strewn about. I backed into the main salon.

'Ray,' I apprehensively called. 'Ray? It's not Ray. Ray's the hurricane. Hurricane Raymond. Where's Richard? . . . "Oh my God," that's what he said.'

Fear dropped me to my knees. I retched. Richard had not come below with me. 'Richard?' I screamed. 'RICHAAARRRD!'

I crawled towards the companionway[5] ladder. 'Richard? Richard?' I screamed over and over.

Frantic search

The ladder had broken off its latches and lay sideways against the navigation station seat. I pushed it out of my way and climbed up on the back of the settee, screaming Richard's name. I hoisted myself up into the cockpit. I saw Richard's safety line secured to the cleat on the cockpit coaming. The tether hung over the side of the hull. My God, could he be on the other end?

I lunged for the safety line, grabbed it tight, and yanked hard. It flew into the cockpit, the metal making a sharp craaack against the glass fibre. There lay the bitter end – the D-ring[6] had parted.

Desperately I looked in every direction. Where was the howling wind? Where was the pelting rain? The ocean swell was a slow-rolling 2m (6ft), not monstrous like it had been.

I became a lunatic. Forcing the seat lockers open, I threw cushions, anything that would float, overboard. He's out there somewhere. Maybe he's alive. Oh, God, please . . . 'HOLD ON RICHARD, I'LL FIND YOU.'

He could be alive. It's only been 3 hours. [It was actually 27 hours.]

His last plea, 'Oh my God,' roared in my brain. It must have been a huge wave. We rolled, and Richard . . . 'Oh my love . . . Richard, WHERE ARE YOU?' I surveyed the ocean all around me, to the edge of the horizon. He was nowhere to be seen.

Hazana was ravaged. The mainmast was gone except for a piece just over a metre still attached to the main boom. The mizzen mast, the one

---

4 V-berth Beds at the V-shaped front of a boat, at the bow.

5 Companionway The staircase leading to a cabin.

6 D-ring A metal clip, shaped like a letter D, that fastens onto a strap, usually so that it can be secured to another surface.

I peeked in a mirror. I saw a frazzled image, its face covered in blood, the forehead cut wide open. Strands of hair, wild and matted with blood, shot out from its skull. I screamed. The ungodly sight was me.

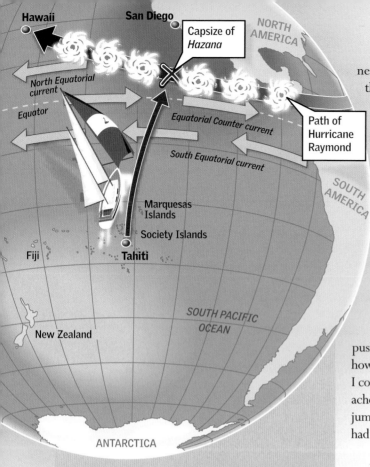

Hit by a storm Despite their attempts to get *Hazana* as far north of the storm as possible, Tami and Richard were intercepted by Hurricane Raymond as they headed from Tahiti, in the southern Pacific Ocean, to San Diego, 2,415km (1,500 miles) away. Once the storm subsided, Tami navigated to Hawaii, using the stars.

next to the mainmast, was in the water, banging against the hull, held on by the starboard – right side – shroud[7]. Stainless-steel rigging hung in the water.

'Richard, Richard,' I howled. He couldn't be gone. In total fear I clung to the boom[8] and lay dazed, my cheek against the cold aluminium.

'GET UP. MOVE.' An inner voice slammed into my thoughts.

Bawling, I crept over the boom, reached into the companionway and groped for the binoculars. Miraculously they were still strapped in their place. I scanned the ocean around me. All I saw was a vast desolate sea, with rolling 2m (6ft) swells. Nothing, not one damned thing, was out there.

'Try the engine!' The inner voice barked.

I pulled out the choke, adjusted the throttle, and pushed the engine's start button. Nothing. I hadn't realised how much hope I was holding that the engine would start. I couldn't think clearly. My head throbbed and my body ached. There was nothing else I could think to do, short of jumping overboard and ending this nightmare. If Richard had beckoned, I would have jumped.

'Don't, he could be alive.'

I fell down into a deep puddle. 'Richard. Richard,' I bellowed, 'Where are you?' I couldn't believe he wasn't there. 'Oh why, why, why, didn't you come below?' In despair I sank to my knees and became submerged in water up to my waist. I gasped and thought, 'My god, the boat's sinking, I've got to get out of here.'

I staggered to the companionway and boosted myself up. I struggled to move the heavy life-raft from the back of the cockpit to the middle of the boat, where I secured it to the cabin-top handrail. Frantically I inflated it and inside found fishing gear, hand flares, a medical kit, half a dozen cans of water and a sponge. Grabbing biscuits, cans of beans, tuna and peaches I threw them into a duffel bag. I also threw the radio receiver in and loaded the bag into the life-raft. As I was grabbing the solar bag[9], a swell hit *Hazana* broadside, causing her to roll. Everything in the raft tumbled overboard.

'Not the radio!' I screamed, as I watched the bag sink.

Wailing in utter frustration, I crawled inside the life-raft, shaking with fear and futility. I cried myself to sleep, not caring if the ship and I sank.

For the next few hours I slept and dozed until finally I forced myself to get up. There was so much I should be doing.

---

7 Shroud A set of ropes that form part of the rigging and support the mast.
8 Boom A spar that attaches to the bottom of a sail, allowing the sail's angle to be altered.
9 Solar bag A bag with solar panels, enabling it to work as a mobile solar-powered generator.

'You need to get the water out of the boat.' The thought drifted into my brain. I obeyed. I went over to the navigation station and turned on the bilge pump. Nothing happened. I resorted to the manual bilge pump, but with all the debris in the water, its screen fouled quickly. I didn't have the strength to deal with it and gave up. But *Hazana* didn't appear to be taking on any more water. 'I could slow down,' I told myself, 'deal with it a little at a time.'

I had tried and failed to get the EPIRB working. Now I staggered to the navigation station. It was littered with broken glass. I wiped glass off the seat and sat down. Grabbing the VHF radio's microphone, I called for help: 'Mayday. Mayday. Does anybody hear me?' Nothing: broken like everything else.

Putting my hand to my forehead, I felt a burn from the gash. There were sutures on board but I couldn't bring myself to sew my head shut. Instead, I rubbed on some alcohol and drew the skin together as tightly as I could tolerate. I put several large butterfly bandages on the long wound. Pus and blood oozed out. I pulled my tangled hair up in a bandanna.

I cranked the handle on the tap and waited through each airy splutter as a cup filled with water. Then I drank greedily. Later I discovered that I had a quarter of a tank of water. This meant that although I would have to be thrifty with the supply I didn't have to ration myself.

I grabbed a sleeping bag, Richard's flowered shirt and his guitar, and pushed it all topside[10]. I made a bed in the cockpit and lashed the wheel to keep the rudder straight. This would help *Hazana* make as much headway as possible with the current. 'Good night, love,' I uttered to the star-filled sky.

I couldn't think clearly My head throbbed and my body ached. There was nothing else I could think to do, short of jumping overboard and ending this nightmare. If Richard had beckoned, I would have jumped.

My face felt on fire. I opened my eyes, blinded by the sun. Not another day.

I found a spoon below and filled it with peanut butter because it was easy. Back in the sun, I sat licking my spoon and trying to figure out how to get moving. The spinnaker[11] pole caught my eye. A length had been sheared off when the mainmast broke and fell over. If I put it on its end, it could act as a mast. I peered down into the anchor chain locker. It was about a metre deep. I would need to fill up the locker to make the pole rise higher in the air.

I crammed blankets, pillows and anything else I could find into the chain locker. I stood the pole upright. It reached a full 2.75m (9ft) into the air. Something was finally being accomplished. I spent a whole day creating the rig to hold the pole and sail in place. I pulled the storm jib out of its bag and hauled the sail up the pole. It was slow to fill, but it did. I had only about 4m² (45 sq ft) of sail, but that was more than I'd had before. I finally felt something different from pain. I felt hope.

Even if the pace was only a knot or two an hour, at least I was making way and had some control over my direction. Besides, I knew that if I didn't get home my mother would never, ever stop looking for me.

---

10 Topside The side of a ship that is above the waterline.
11 Spinnaker A large triangular sail that sits opposite the mainsail.

Heading for Hawaii

The next day broke clear and warm, with *Hazana* moving like a rocking horse in slow motion. If the weather held it would be a perfect day for taking sun sights. The sextant hadn't broken in the capsize, which was a miracle. I recalled the basics of celestial navigation. The sextant helps the mariner to locate a position by using two objects to measure altitudes above sea level. My two objects were the horizon line and the sun. My tentative plan was to reach the northern 19th latitude, turn left and hopefully reach Hawaii, which stretches between latitude 19°N and 20°N.

It's important to have the exact time when taking a sun sight. Using my wristwatch I was able to pinpoint my position. I found myself to be on longitude 134°W by latitude 18°N. This was good news. I was closer to Hawaii than I had thought.

Another long day. I was trying to read a paperback thriller I'd found while I munched on kidney beans from a tin. I couldn't focus on the print. Half asleep, I saw, as if in a dream, a ship, a big ship, smoke curling from its stack.

I grabbed the flare gun out of the waterproof bag I kept in the cockpit.

BAM! The flare shot towards heaven, its brightness competing with the sun. BAM! I fired the second flare.

I stared at the ship. Nothing. It didn't even alter course.

BAM! went the third flare. The ship was getting smaller.

I had tied a red T-shirt to one of the oars and I grabbed it now. I rushed to the bow, frantically waving it. Nothing. The ship did not alter course one degree. It diminished quickly over the horizon. I was later to see another ship and an aeroplane but neither of them spotted me.

I was shocked. How could they not have seen me? I stomped about the deck, kicking whatever got in my way.

Full of rage, I decided to try to remove the 4ft section of the broken mainmast that was still attached to the boom and was always in my way. I found the hammer and the screwdriver and, sitting down on the deck, I took out all my anger on the clevis pin[12]. It didn't budge. Finally, getting under the boom, I used my feet to lift the mast the fraction of an inch needed to relieve the pressure on the pin. As it gave way, the foot of the mainmast toppled from the boom and fell on top of me, trapping me.

Flat on my back near the edge of the deck, I was terrified I'd fall overboard. As I tried to move, the jagged edges of the mainmast cut into my stomach. It weighed a ton. I lay there gasping, staring at the sky, mustering every ounce of strength I could find to shove the massive piece of aluminium off me. 'One, two, three!' Every muscle in my body strained to break free. As the chunk of aluminium rolled off me, I caught myself along the edge just before the momentum could hurl me overboard.

I lay back on the deck panting. How much more could I take?

After the horror of almost falling off the boat, I decided to trail a rope off the stern in case I fell in. Even with *Hazana* travelling at only one or two knots, I knew I might not have the strength to swim fast enough to catch up

---

12 Clevis pin A U-shaped pin often used in sailing-boat rigging, which connects the parts together, but allows some rotation.

with her. If I did fall in I could at least attempt to grab the rope. It terrified me to think that I could possibly drown after all these lonely and miserable days of struggling to survive.

Most days were about the same, sailing along at a snail's pace, but I did see progress each time I noted my position on the chart, plus, if I kept rationing, I should have enough water and food to survive.

I established a routine of waking up some time between three and six in the morning. I'd check the rig, meditate on the bow, open a can and eat whatever was in it. Then I'd scan the horizon with the binoculars and sit and steer for hours and hours.

My daily schedule was focussed around my three daily sun sights. Noon was the most exciting time of day, because I would take my second sun sight and calculate how far I had travelled in the past 24 hours. It was always somewhere between 20 and 60 nautical miles (35-110km). I just prayed I would hit one of the Hawaiian Islands and not sail past them.

Sundown was the loneliest time. How many sunsets had I enjoyed with Richard? Sometimes I'd talk to him – dare him to come to me. Back at the wheel, I adjusted my pillows and steered with my foot. I searched the sky for my constellation friends. When I could no longer keep my eyes open, I lashed the wheel and crawled into the sleeping bag, hugging Richard's shirt.

Celestial navigation

'*And all I ask is a tall ship and a star to steer her by ...*'

JOHN MASEFIELD'S POEM 'SEA FEVER', written in the early 1900s, did not anticipate the wonders of the Global Positioning System (GPS), but it celebrated the ancient art and science of celestial navigation. Fortunately for Tami, she had knowledge of this art.

Since the dawn of history, the human race has been 'wayfinding', using the position of the sun, moon, stars and planets to navigate the oceans. The basic premise of celestial navigation is that an unknown position can be deduced by reference to a known position. It has its roots in the belief, not challenged until the 16th century, that the Earth is the still centre around which the heavenly bodies move.

As long ago as 2000 BC, the Phoenicians used charts and observations of celestial bodies by which to navigate. The Vikings used the sun and the Pole Star (or North Star, Polaris) to guide them on their voyages. It was, though, in those days, a somewhat hit or miss undertaking.

More refined mathematical celestial navigation came later. In 1731, an invaluable piece of navigational equipment, the sextant, was invented independently in England and America. This precise instrument measures the angle of the elevation of a heavenly body above the horizon (called the 'altitude'), in degrees, minutes and seconds. Spot-on timing is essential (just four seconds of error can put calculations off by a nautical mile), as is a *Nautical Almanac*. Without these, if state-of-the-art equipment fails, mariners can but vainly raise their eyes to the heavens.

LIFE-SAVING DEVICE Tami used a sextant – the name means 'one-sixth' because the curved part is a sixth of a circle – to guide her to land.

It was day 35. I estimated I was still 230km (143 miles) from Hawaii. I was starting to see floating objects – signs of humanity like plastic fizzy-drink bottles, a tattered tarp, flip-flops and a Styrofoam float.

Then, on the morning of day 38, as I headed for the bow to check the rig, I stopped short. 'It can't be – can it?' I squinted, trying to focus. 'It's got to be.'

'Land ho!'

On the horizon I saw an isolated cloud-like shape. At first light I thought it was low cumulous clouds. But by noon the mass became a granite-coloured smudge in front of me. Could it be Hawaii?

I went back to the wheel and for an hour I steered towards the increasingly defined land mass, afraid to believe it was land and afraid to believe it wasn't. Finally I believed I was seeing land; it had to be the island. Hawaii was right where I thought it should be. A great relief flooded over me. My spine seemed to melt as I held my head in my hands and cried.

Suddenly excitement rushed through me, and I stood up and shouted, 'LAND! Land ho!' Then I danced about like a warrior, quickly wearing myself out. This calls for a celebration. Scrambling below I sought out the beer and a cigar that I had under one of the seats. Topside I climbed on the boom, lit the cigar and popped open the bottle.

'Oh God, I'm so excited. And grateful. I'm so very, very grateful. Thank you.' But, 'What will I tell Richard's family? How will I tell them? How will I be able to tell anyone about Richard?' Emotion choked me.

On my 41st day alone at sea I sailed to within a few miles of the entrance to Hilo Harbour. At 02.30 the lights in the bay beckoned me, but I dared not go closer because of the huge reef that stretched far offshore. Only a fool or a sailor with local knowledge would attempt the hazardous entrance at night. So in the early morning I tacked back and forth just off the reef-strewn entrance. I was so near and yet so agonisingly far away.

As dawn strolled aimlessly across the sky I went back to the wheel and altered course for the harbour entrance. No sooner had I done this than I noticed a large ship heading out of the harbour. I grabbed the flare gun and started shooting. The ship seemed to pause. I shot off more flares and then grabbed the oar with the faded red T-shirt. At the bow, I waved it back and forth. Suddenly the vessel flashed its running lights and altered course.

'My God, they see me. They actually see me.'

Altogether Tami spent 41 days alone at sea and although reaching Hawaii meant that she was safe, her ordeal wasn't over yet. She first had the heartbreaking job of telling Richard's family that he was lost at sea. She also had to explain to the Hazana's owners, the Cromptons, what had happened to their boat. Then the police needed to interview her because Richard was a British citizen missing at sea, and all the while she had to contend with the media attention that her story had generated. Through it all, she was supported by her family, who helped her in her attempt to come to terms with the devastating events she had endured.

Today Tami lives in Friday Harbor, San Juan Island, Washington, with her husband Ed Ashcraft and their two daughters, Kelli and Brook. She continues to be an enthusiastic sailor. ∎

Homecoming *Tami was overjoyed to return safely, but her happiness was marred by the fact that Richard didn't make it back with her — by sending her below deck while he steered, Richard had sacrificed his own life to keep her safe.*

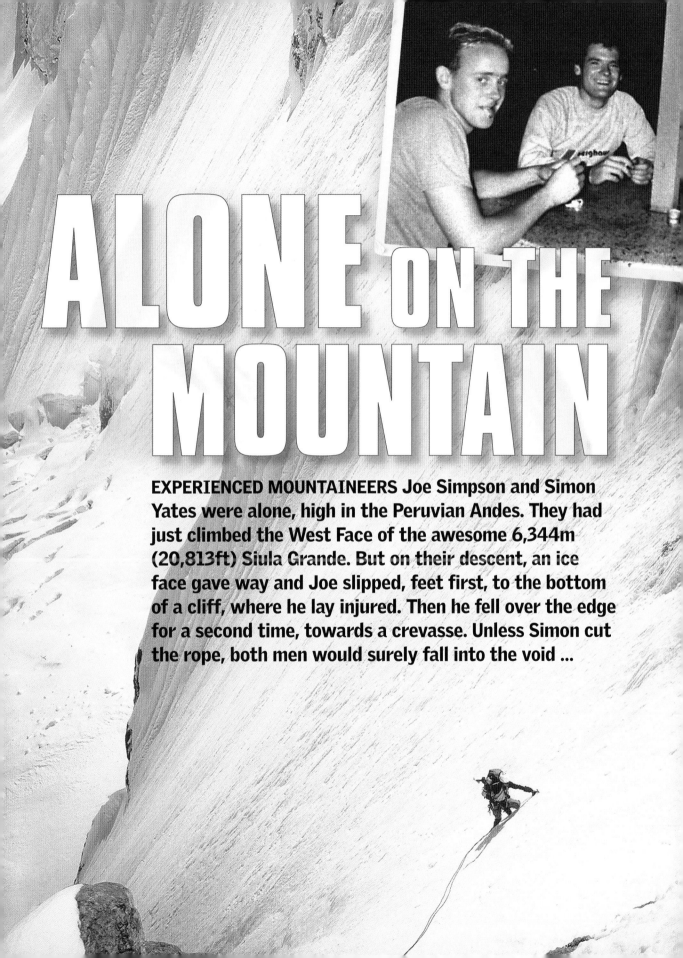

ALONE ON THE MOUNTAIN

EXPERIENCED MOUNTAINEERS Joe Simpson and Simon Yates were alone, high in the Peruvian Andes. They had just climbed the West Face of the awesome 6,344m (20,813ft) Siula Grande. But on their descent, an ice face gave way and Joe slipped, feet first, to the bottom of a cliff, where he lay injured. Then he fell over the edge for a second time, towards a crevasse. Unless Simon cut the rope, both men would surely fall into the void …

Peak after peak *Siula Grande lies in the isolated Cordillera Huayhuash range in the Peruvian section of the Andes, the world's longest mountain range at 7,200km (4,475 miles).*

Men against the mountain *Joe Simpson makes his way up a steep slope of ice on the first day of the climb (previous page, background). Three weeks before the ordeal, he and his climbing partner, Simon Yates, relax in a Peruvian nightclub (previous page, inset).*

The rope slipped. I bounced down a few inches, then again.

I knew what was about to happen: Simon was coming down. I was pulling him off. I hung still and waited for it to happen, scarcely able to hold my head up. An awful weariness washed through me and, with it, a fervent hope that this endless hanging would soon be over.

Everyone said it – if there are just two of you, an injury could turn into a death sentence.

Anger surged through me. It warmed me, shook me, driving the cold off in a tirade of obscenities and frustrated tears. I cried for myself and swore at myself. Everything came down to *me*. It was *my* knee that was smashed, ruptured, twisted, crushed. *I* had fallen and *I* was dying – and Simon with me.

The rope jolted down a few inches. 'How long will you be, Simon?' I thought. 'How long before you join me?' It would be soon. I could feel the rope tremble again, wire-tight. 'So! It ends here. I hope somebody finds us and knows we climbed the West Face of Siula Grande. I don't want to disappear without a trace. They'd never know we did it.'

The wind swung me in a gentle circle. I looked at the waiting crevasse. It was big – 6m (20ft) wide at least. I guessed that I was hanging 15m (50ft) above it. Below me it was covered with snow, but to the right a dark space yawned.

Another jerk. Cold had long since won its battle. There was no feeling in my arms and legs. Everything slowed and softened. Thoughts became idle questions, never answered. I accepted that I was to die. I was so senselessly cold that I craved sleep and cared nothing for the consequences.

My torch beam died. I saw stars above me. They seemed far away – farther than I'd ever seen them before – and brighter. Some moved, little winking moves, on and off, on and off, floating the brightest sparks of light down to me.

Then what I had waited for pounced on me. Like something come alive, the rope lashed violently against my face. The stars went out, and I fell. I fell silently, endlessly into nothingness, as if dreaming of falling. I fell fast, faster than thought, and my stomach protested at the swooping speed of it. I swept down, and from far above I saw myself falling and felt nothing. So this is it!

When I hit the snow roof, a whoomphing impact on my back broke the dream, and the snow engulfed me. I wasn't stopping, and for a blinding moment I was frightened. Now the crevasse! 'Ahhh … No!'

The acceleration took me again, mercifully fast, too fast for the scream that died above me.

The whitest flashes burst in my eyes as a terrible impact whipped me into stillness. They continued – bursting electric flashes in my eyes – as snow followed down onto me. The shock had stunned me, so that for a time I lay numb, hardly conscious of what had happened. I lay still, with open mouth, open eyes staring into blackness.

I couldn't breathe. I retched. Pressure pain in my chest. Retching and gagging, trying hard for air. Nothing. I felt the dull roaring sound of shingles on a beach, and I relaxed. I shut my eyes, and gave in to grey fading shadows. My chest spasmed, then heaved out, and my head suddenly cleared as cold air flowed in.

I was alive.

A burning, searing agony reached up from my leg. It was bent beneath me. Heck! I couldn't be dead and feel that! It kept burning, and I laughed – alive – and laughed again, a real, happy laugh. I laughed through the burning, feeling tears rolling down my face. I couldn't see what was so damned funny, but I laughed anyway. Crying and laughing at high pitch as something tight and twisted uncurled within me.

I stopped laughing abruptly. The tension took hold again.

What had stopped me?

Black space

I could see nothing. I lay on my side, crumpled strangely. I moved an arm cautiously and touched a hard wall. Ice! It was the wall of the crevasse. I continued the search and felt my arm drop into space. There was a drop close by me. I stifled the urge to move away from it. Behind me I felt my legs lying against a slope, and snow sloped steeply beneath me. I was on a ledge, or a bridge. I wasn't slipping, but I didn't know which way to move to make myself safe.

'Just keep still. That's it … *Don't move …* Ah!'

I couldn't stop myself. Pain in my knee jolted through me, demanding movement. I had to get my weight off it. I moved, and slipped. Every muscle gripped down at the snow. '*Don't move.*'

The movement slowed, then stopped. I groped for the ice hammer attached to a cord clipped to my harness. I had to hammer an ice screw into the wall without pushing myself off the ledge I was perched on.

It proved harder than expected. Once I had found the last remaining screw attached to my harness, I had to twist round and face the wall. My eyes had adjusted to the darkness. Starlight and the moon glimmering through my entry hole in the roof above gave enough light for me to see the abysses on either side. I could see grey-shadowed ice walls and the stark blackness of the drops, too deep for the light to penetrate. As I began to hammer the screw into the ice I tried to ignore the black space beyond my shoulder. The hammer blows echoed round the ice walls, and from deep

Setting out *Joe Simpson (left) leads the way towards base camp before the climb, with mules carrying his and his companions' equipment.*

below, from the depths of blackness at my shoulder, I heard second and third echoes drift up. I shuddered. The black space held untold horrors.

I hit the screw and felt my body slide sideways with each blow. When it was driven in to its hilt, I clipped an oblong ring called a carabiner through the eye of the screw and hurriedly searched for the rope at my waist. The black spaces menaced, and my stomach knotted in squeezing clenches.

I hauled myself into a half-sitting position close to the wall, facing the drop on my left. I dared not let go of the ice screw for more than a few seconds, but my frozen fingers needed longer to tie the knot. After six attempts I was at the point of tears when suddenly I found that I had tied a knot of sorts. I clipped it to the ice screw, smiling foolishly. I was safe from the black spaces.

I relaxed against the comforting tightness of the rope and looked up at the hole in the roof, where the cloudless sky was packed with stars, and moonlight was adding its glow to their sparkle. The tension in my stomach flowed away. I began to order my mind into normal thoughts, 'I'm only – what? – 50ft down this crevasse. It's sheltered. I can get out in the morning if I wait for Simon.'

'Simon!?' I spoke his name in a startled voice. It hadn't occurred to me that he might be dead, and the enormity of it struck me. Dead? I couldn't conceive of him dead, *not now ... not after I've survived*. I'd have heard him, seen him come over the cliff.

I began to giggle again. Despite my efforts, I couldn't prevent it, and the echoes bounced back at me from the ice walls, sounding cracked and manic. I sat hunched against the ice wall, laughing convulsively and shivering. A calm rational voice in my head told me it was the cold and the shock. The rest of me went quietly mad, while this calm voice told me what was happening and left me feeling as if I were split in two – one half laughing and the other looking on with unemotional objectivity. After a time I realised it had all stopped, and I was whole again.

I searched in my rucksack for the spare torch battery. When I had inserted it, I switched on the beam and looked into the black space by

Spectacular landscape *Peru's mountain ranges are full of breathtaking scenery. The climbers encountered the coppered green lake below on their approach to the West Face of Siula Grande.*

my side. The ice caught the light, so that it gleamed in blue, silver and green reflections, and I could see small rocks frozen into the surface at regular intervals.

I could see down 30m (100ft). The walls, 6m (20ft) apart, showed no sign of narrowing. In front of me the opposite wall of the crevasse reared up in a tangle of broken ice blocks, and 15m (50ft) above me they arched over to form the roof. The slope to my right fell away steeply for about 9m (30ft). Beyond it lay a drop into darkness.

The roof covered the crevasse to my right and fell away in frozen chaos to my left. I was in a huge cavern of snow and ice. Only the small hole above, winking starlight at me, gave any view of another world, and unless I climbed the blocks, it was as unreachable as the stars.

I turned the torch off. The darkness seemed more oppressive than ever.

Discovering what I had fallen into hadn't cleared my mind. I was alone. Simon was my only chance of escape. But I was convinced that if he was not dead, then he would think that I was. He would see the crevasse and the cliff, and he would know that I was dead. The irony of falling 30m (100ft) and surviving unscathed was unbearable.

I swore bitterly, and the echoes from the darkness made it a futile gesture. I screamed with frustration and anger until my throat dried and I could shout no more. I tried to think of what would happen. 'He won't leave unless he's sure. How do I know he's not dead already? Did he fall with me? Find out. Pull the rope!'

I tugged on the loose rope. It moved easily. When I turned my torch on, I noticed the rope hanging down from the roof. As I pulled, I became excited. This was a chance to escape. I waited for the rope to come tight. When Simon had fallen, he must have hit the slope and stopped. He must be dead, after that fall. 'When the rope comes tight, I can climb up it. His body will anchor it solidly. Yes, that's it …'

This was a chance to escape. I waited for the rope to come tight. When Simon had fallen, he must have hit the slope and stopped. He must be dead, after that fall. When the rope comes tight, I can climb up it.

I saw the rope flick down, and my hopes sank. I drew the slack rope to me and stared at the end. Cut! I couldn't take my eyes from it. White and pink nylon filaments sprayed out from the end.

I suppose I had known all along. It had been madness to have believed in it, but everything was getting that way. I wasn't meant to get out of here. Damn it! I turned off the torch and sobbed quietly in the dark.

It was cold when I woke. Sleep had taken me unawares. I felt calm. It was going to end in the crevasse. I felt pleased to be able to accept it calmly. I thought it might take a few days. I imagined how long it would seem: a long period of twilight and darkness, drifting from exhausted sleep into half-consciousness, ebbing away quietly. It seemed pretty sordid. I hadn't expected a blaze of glory when the end came, but I didn't want it to be like this – a slow, pathetic fade into nothing.

I sat up and turned on the torch. Looking at the wall above the ice screw, I thought it might be possible to climb out using my axes. I fastened a special friction knot, called a Prussik, to the rope. I would climb while still attached to the screw. If I fell, the Prussik might stop me.

An hour later I had made four attempts to climb the vertical ice wall. Only once had I managed to get myself clear of the ice bridge, but then I fell, my injured leg folding agonisingly beneath me again. I screamed, and twisted to free it. Then I lay still, waiting for the pain to ease. I would not try again. I sat on my sack and turned off the torch. I could see my legs in the gloom. There was a delay before I realised the significance of this. I glanced up to the patch of dim light in the roof and checked my watch: it was 5 o'clock. Simon would be coming down the cliff as soon as it was light. I shouted his name loudly. It echoed round me, and I shouted again. I would shout regularly until he heard me or until I was certain he had gone.

A long time later I stopped shouting. The sound could not be heard through the walls of snow and ice. He had gone. I was dead. I picked absently at the end of the rope, trying to come to a decision. I wasn't prepared to spend another night on the ledge. I wasn't going through that madness again, but I cringed from doing the only thing left to me. Without deciding, I took some coils in my hand and threw the rope down to the right. It flew clean out into space and curled over the drop before falling out of sight. It jerked tight. I clipped myself to the rope and lay on my side. I hesitated, looking at the ice screw buried in the wall. The Prussik knot hung below it. I thought that I should take it with me. If there was empty space at the end of the rope, I would be unable to regain the ledge without it.

I let myself slide off the ledge and watched the Prussik get smaller as I abseiled down the slope to the drop. If there was nothing there, I didn't want to come back.

Plunge to the depths

The snow made soft rustling noises as it slithered into the depths. I stared at the ice screw far above me, watching it getting smaller. The ice bridge that had stopped my fall stood out clearly. Beyond it the open cavern of the crevasse faded into shadows. I gripped the rope gently and let it slide through the belay plate, a device for securing the rope, at a constant rate.

The desire to stop abseiling was almost unbearable. I had no idea what lay below, and was certain of only two things: Simon had gone and he would not return. This meant that to stay on the ice ledge would finish me. There was no escape upwards, and the drop on the other side was nothing more than an invitation to end it all quickly. It would be a long time before cold and exhaustion overtook me on the ice bridge, and the idea had forced me to this choice: abseil until I could find a way out, or die in the process. I would meet death rather than wait for it to come to me.

I couldn't bring myself to look down. I dared not risk turning to discover another deep hole. I wasn't that brave. If it was to end here, I wanted it to be sudden and unexpected; so I kept my eyes fixed on the ice screw far above me.

The slope became steeper. When I was about 15m (50ft) below the ice screw, I suddenly felt my legs swing beneath me into open space. My grip stopped the rope involuntarily. This was the drop I had seen from the bridge! I stared up at the bridge trying to make myself release the rope again, but the knowledge that I could abseil until the rope ran out and then fall into space made me clench it even harder. At last I released it and abseiled slowly over the drop until I was hanging vertically on the rope. The wall of the drop was hard, clear water ice. I could no longer see the ice screw, so I stared into the ice as I continued to lower myself. But as the light round me grew fainter, the dread spilled over, and I could contain myself no longer. I stopped.

I wanted to cry, but couldn't. I felt paralysed, incapable of thinking, as waves of panic swept through me. For a helpless, immeasurable time I hung shaking on the rope, with my helmet pressed to the ice wall and my eyes tightly closed. I had to see what was beneath me because, for all my convictions, I didn't have the courage to do it blind. I swung round quickly, catching my smashed knee on the ice wall and howling in pain and fright. Instead of seeing the rope twisting loosely in a void beneath me, I stared blankly at the snow below my feet, not fully believing what I was seeing. A floor! There was a snow-covered floor 4.5m (15ft) below me.

I let out a cry of delight and relief that boomed round the crevasse. I yelled again and again, listening to the echoes, and laughed between the yells.

I was at the bottom of the crevasse.

Into the abyss Joe Simpson and Simon Yates had set out to scale the almost-vertical West Face of Siula Grande. This they managed successfully, setting up camps en route (1st, 2nd, 3rd and 4th bivis – bivouacs – shown right). It was when they began their descent that they encountered difficult terrain. Joe slipped down an ice cliff **A**, badly breaking his leg. Simon lowered him partway down the mountain **B** before Joe plummeted over the edge towards a crevasse **C**. Unable even to see Joe, Simon couldn't pull him back up and, after an hour, cut the rope, leaving Joe to fall into the abyss. Even after Joe had made his miraculous escape from the crevasse, he still faced a three-day crawl **D** back to base camp.

SIULA GRANDE
6,344m (20,813ft)

4th bivi

3rd bivi

A

2nd bivi

B

Ice cliff

C

1st bivi

D

The right decision

When I recovered my wits, I looked more carefully at the carpet of snow above which I was dangling. My jubilation was tempered when I spotted dark holes in the surface. I wasn't at the bottom after all. The crevasse opened up into a pear-shaped dome, its sides curving away to a width of 15m (50ft) before narrowing again. The snow floor cut through the flat end of this cavern, while the walls above me tapered in to form the thin end of the pear, barely 3m (10ft) across and nearly 30m (100ft) high. Small fragments of snow pattered down from the roof.

I looked round the enclosed vault of snow and ice. The walls opposite closed in, but didn't meet. A narrow gap had been filled with snow from above to form a cone that rose all the way to the roof. It was about 4.5m (15ft) wide at the base and as little as a metre or so across at the top. A pillar of gold light beamed diagonally from the hole in the roof. Mesmerised by this beam of sunlight, I forgot about the uncertain floor below and let myself slide down the rope. I was going to reach that sunbeam. How and when were not considered. I just knew I would.

My whole outlook had changed. I could do something positive. I could crawl and climb until I had escaped from this grave. Before, helplessness had been my worst enemy. Now, I had a plan. I felt invigorated, full of energy and optimism. Confidence swept over me as I realised how right I had been to leave the ledge. I had made the right decision against the worst of my fears.

My boots touched the snow, and I sat in my harness hanging above the snow and examined the surface. The floor was suspended across the crevasse, dividing the abyss below from the upper chamber where I sat. The snow slope running up to the sunshine lay 12m (40ft) from me. The inviting floor between me and the slope tempted me to run across it. The idea made me chuckle – I had forgotten that my right leg was useless. OK, crawl. But which way? Straight across or keeping near to the back wall?

It was a difficult decision. The last thing I wanted was to destroy the floor and leave myself stranded on the wrong side of an uncrossable gap. I glanced nervously at the beam of sunlight, trying to draw strength from it, and made my mind up. I would cross in the middle. It was the shortest distance.

I lowered myself until I was sitting on the snow but with most of my weight still on the rope. It was agonising to inch the rope out and let my weight down. I found myself holding my breath, every muscle tensed. I wondered whether I would end up sinking slowly through the snow.

The floor was holding. I breathed deeply and released my aching hand from the rope. I sat very still for 5 minutes. There was no choice but to attempt to cross the gap. I let out 12m (40ft) of rope and tied the remaining 9m (30ft) to my harness. Then, lying spreadeagled on my stomach, I began to wiggle stealthily towards the snow cone, anxiety easing as I got closer. An occasional muffled thumping told me that snow had fallen away beneath the floor. I would freeze rigidly at the slightest sound, holding my breath and feeling my heart hammering, then move off again. The black holes in the floor were all behind me when I passed the halfway point, and I sensed that I was now crawling over thicker and stronger snow.

My whole outlook had changed. I could do something positive. I could crawl and climb until I had escaped from this grave. Before, helplessness had been my worst enemy. Now, I had a plan.

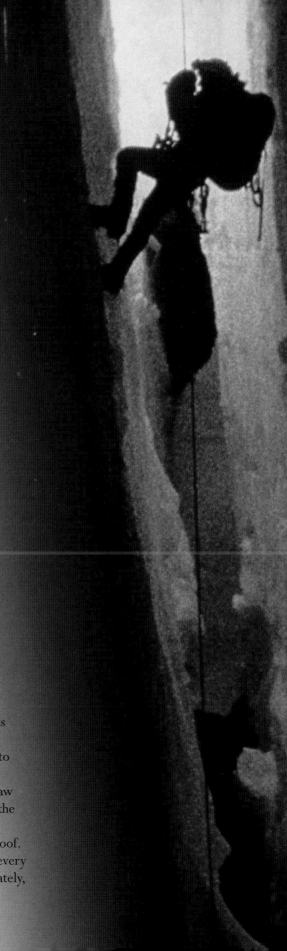

After 10 minutes I lay slumped against the slope rising towards the golden sun in the roof. I felt a slight breeze on my cheek, a chill, deathly brush from deep below. The light in the chamber was a strange mix of blue-grey shadows and dancing reflections from the surrounding ice walls. I rested at the base of the snow cone, absorbing the feel of the crevasse. For all its hushed, cold menace, there was a feeling of sacredness about the chamber, with its magnificent vaulted crystal ceiling. The menace was in my imagination, but I couldn't stop it playing on my mind, as if this thing had waited for a victim with the impersonal patience of the centuries. It had me now, and without the sunbeam I might have sat there numbed and defeated by its implacable stillness. I shivered. The air was uncomfortably cold, well below freezing. It was time to climb.

I stood up gingerly on my left leg, letting my damaged limb hang uselessly. At first I wasn't sure how to set about climbing the slope, which I guessed to be 40m (130ft) high – 10 minutes' work with two legs.

It was the angle of the slope that worried me. To begin with, it rose at only 45 degrees, but as it gained height, the angle increased. The top 6m (20ft) looked almost vertical. I suppressed a growing pessimism by telling myself that I was lucky to have found a slope at all.

The initial steps were clumsy and uncoordinated. I dug my ice axes deep into the snow above me and hauled myself up with my arms. I realised it wouldn't work on the steeper slope above. If an axe ripped free, I would fall. I tried to work out a better method.

I tried lifting the injured leg up and groaned as the knee crunched and refused to bend properly. Pain flared up as I leaned down and dug a step in the snow, then another smaller step below it. When I had finished, I planted both axes in the slope above, gritted my teeth, and heaved my burning leg up to the lower step. Bracing myself on the axes, I made a convulsive hop off my good leg. A searing pain burst from my knee and then faded as the good leg found a foothold on the higher step. I bent down to dig another two steps and repeat the pattern. Bend, hop, rest. Bend, hop, rest … I was sweating profusely despite the cold.

After 2½ hours the slope had steepened considerably, and I had to be especially careful when I hopped. I glanced at the roof above and was delighted to see the sun nearly touching me. Looking down, I saw that I was two-thirds of the way up the snow cone. I was level with the ice bridge.

It took another 2½ hours to reach a point 3m (10ft) below the roof. The angle of the snow had become almost impossibly difficult, and every hop had to be a measured gamble against losing my balance. Fortunately,

Heading for safety *Joe, with his shattered leg heavily bound, sits on a mule as he is led away from Siula Grande at the start of the agonising two-day journey from the base camp to the nearest town, Cajatambo.*

as the cone narrowed, I found that I could get a solid axe placement in the ice wall to my left. I felt exhausted, and sickened by the repeated twisted, crunching spasms in my knee. I bent into the slope again and hopped. The snow roof brushed my helmet. I was directly beneath a head-sized hole in the snow. The glare from the sun was blinding. I hefted my leg into the new step I had dug, and prepared to make another hop.

Escape

If anyone had seen me emerge from the crevasse, they would have laughed. My head popped up through the snow roof, and I stared gopher-like at the scene outside. I stood on one leg, with my head stuck out of the snow, swivelling round to take in the most stupendous view I had ever seen. There wasn't a cloud in the sky, and the sun glared from its azure emptiness with ferocious heat.

I hauled my axe from the crevasse and drove it into the snow outside. When I hopped and rolled out of the yawning drop, I lay against the snow, numb with relief. I didn't want to move and risk disturbing the peace of lying there motionless in the snow. I felt drowsy from the sun and wanted to sleep and forget. I had escaped, and for the moment that was enough.

I flicked my eyes from view to view without moving my head, registering the familiar landscape as if for the first time. The ring of mountains surrounding the glacier was so spectacular that I hardly recognised what I was seeing. I could see ice fields and delicately fluted ridges. The glacier curled away to the north and broke up into a maze of crevasses on the black moraines at its snout. The moraines tumbled chaotically through a wide rocky valley until they reached the bank of a lake in the far distance. Just beyond, another lake flashed sunlight off its surface. The Sarapo mountain blocked my view, but I knew that the second lake ended at another bank of moraines, and beyond that lay the tents.

Joe's incredible journey was not yet over. He was still 60m (200ft) above the glacier and 10km (6 miles) from base camp. With no supplies, a broken leg and frostbite, he knew he had to make it there before Simon struck camp — and that was assuming Simon had survived. Fashioning a rudimentary splint for his leg, he forced himself to hop and crawl over the rough terrain, and not to give in to exhaustion and pain. Joe eventually reached camp after three days. He knew that if Simon had not cut the rope, the likelihood was that they would both have died. But now Simon was able to get him to hospital for urgent medical treatment — after a two-day journey by mule and pick-up truck — and Joe survived to climb again. ■

Where are they now?

WHEN JOE SIMPSON (below) returned from Peru, he was told by his surgeon that he would never walk again. How that surgeon underestimated his patient! With the help of physiotherapists, Joe would not just walk but was able to return to climbing – if anything, he says, at a higher standard.

Joe's extraordinary story of survival, told in his book *Touching the Void*, was made into a film, which saw him and Simon Yates return to Siula Grande and which went on to win a BAFTA – the highest British film award. Joe has written further books on mountains and climbing, establishing himself as a master of the genre. He is also in great demand as a motivational speaker on the international circuit.

His writings are far more than big boys' adventure stories; they are meditative and discursive. In *This Game of Ghosts*, a memoir and sequel to *Touching the Void*, Joe tells of a crippling fall in the Himalayas that nearly broke him. In *Storms of Silence*, which relates how he and four other climbers were forced to abandon an attempt on Cho Oyu in Tibet, he seethes against the suffering of the Tibetan people by the occupying Chinese (see *Persecuted for My Faith*, page 363), and questions the ethics of playing rich men's games in poor men's lands.

His book *The Beckoning Silence* is concerned not only with Joe's own attempts to climb the infamous North Face of the Eiger, but with the deaths of his friends and heroes on that mountain. In *Dark Shadows Falling*, Joe embraces the subjects of recent tragedies, the exploitation of sherpas and the disasters waiting to happen as amateurs and dilettantes set out to scale the peaks. As a departure, he is also working on a novel.

Although injuries threatened to put an end to his climbing career, Joe hopes that ankle surgery will enable him to return to the mountains. He lives in Sheffield, UK, and is renovating a house in Ireland, where he can indulge his passion for fly-fishing and paragliding.

And what of Simon Yates, destined to be remembered forever after as the man who cut the rope? He, too, has continued to climb in some of the most far-flung mountain ranges, runs an expedition company, and has an alternate career as a speaker and award-winning writer. He is married with two children and lives in Penrith, Cumbria.

To find out more information on Joe Simpson visit www.noordinaryjoe.co.uk.

ABOVE THE WORLD

THE SPACE RACE between the USA and the Soviet Union took a decisive turn on March 18, 1965. As Voskhod 2 orbited Earth, cosmonaut Alexei Leonov prepared to take man's first tentative steps in space. Success – and survival – would depend on one man's skill and untried equipment.

After we entered orbit, my commander, Pavel Belyayev, requested permission to extend the airlock chamber in preparation for my space walk. The airlock was a narrow, collapsible set of interconnected rubberised canvas cylinders. Permission granted, Pasha activated the devices that started to pump air into the small rubber tubes which ran the length of the hollow canvas chamber. From a coiled length of 70cm (28in), the airlock quickly extended to its full length of 2m (6½ft). In the meantime, I had strapped the bulky breathing apparatus, containing metal tanks with 90 minutes' worth of oxygen, onto my back. I was ready to clamber inside the airlock and undergo decompression before exiting into space.

Once inside the airlock, I closed the hatch and waited for the nitrogen to be purged from my blood. To avoid suffering from what divers call the bends, I had to maintain the same partial pressure of oxygen in my blood once I emerged into space. With the pressure inside the airlock finally equal to the zero pressure outside the spacecraft, I reported I was ready to exit.

Ground control had to carry out careful checks of all my systems before granting permission to open the outer hatch. When it opened I was lying on my back. There wasn't enough space to turn or move much. But I craned my neck backwards to catch my first, unobstructed, glimpse of the earth.

'Start your mission'

What I saw as the hatch opened took my breath away. Night was turning to day. The small portion of the earth's surface I could see as I leaned back was deep blue. The sky beyond the curving horizon was dark, illuminated with bright stars as I looked due south towards the South Pole. I craned my neck back until it hurt. I wanted to see more. Moving at 30,000km/h (18,000mph), the scene below me rapidly began to change. Very soon the outline of the African continent came into view.

All the time I was waiting for the moment when I would be given permission to ease myself free of the spacecraft. It seemed a long wait. Then my earpiece crackled into life.

'Diamond Two,' Mission Control radioed, 'we can see you very well. It is time for you to start your mission.'

My heart was racing. The moment I had waited for for so long had arrived. It took me just a few seconds to push my upper body out of the airlock. I brought my feet to its rim, holding onto a special rail and took a final look around before I let myself go.

The silence of open space was broken only by the sounds of my beating heart and my breathing, muffled by headphones inside my helmet. Suspended 500km (310 miles) above the surface of the earth, I was attached by just an umbilical cord of cables to our spacecraft, Voskhod 2, as it rapidly orbited the earth. Yet it felt as if I were almost motionless, floating above a vast blue sphere.

'So the world really is round,' I said softly to myself. For a few moments I felt totally alone in this pristine new environment, taking in the beauty of the panorama below me.

All the time I was waiting for the moment when I would be given permission to ease myself free of the spacecraft. It seemed a long wait. Then my earpiece crackled into life.

Read all about it *During the Cold War — a long period of tension between the USA and the USSR that started in the 1940s — readers eagerly awaited news of the latest developments in the hotly contested Space Race. Each side wanted to prove its superiority, and where better than the vast arena of outer space?*

By now we were passing over the Mediterranean. It was as if I was looking at a gigantic, colourful map. I could see the whole of the Black Sea. To my left were Greece and Italy, ahead was the Crimea, and to my right lay the snow-capped Caucasus Mountains and the Volga river. When I raised my head I could see the Baltic Sea.

Then I pulled my thoughts back and responded to Mission Control.

'I'm feeling perfect,' I reported as I pulled the breathing tubes connected to my life-support system out of the airlock. With a small kick, as if pushing away from the side of a swimming pool, I stepped away from the rim of the airlock.

I was walking in space. The first man ever to do so. Nothing will ever compare to the exhilaration I felt in that moment.

I felt insignificant, like an ant, compared to the immensity of the universe. At the same time I felt enormously powerful. High above the surface of the Earth, I felt the power of the human intellect that had placed me there. I felt like a representative of the human race.

Then a voice filled the void: 'Attention. Attention.' It was Pasha, addressing me and, it seemed, the rest of humankind. 'Your attention, please. A human being has made the first-ever walk in open space. He is at this very moment flying free in space.'

Then another voice cut in. 'How do you feel, Lyosha?' That voice sounded familiar, too. But I couldn't place it until it continued and I realised that the speaker was Leonid Brezhnev, the Soviet leader.

Special monitors had been installed in the Kremlin so that the Communist Party's leaders could follow our space flight via a direct link with Mission Control. Brezhnev's address to me was broadcast on state radio and television across the Soviet Union. So was my reply, though at the time I hardly knew how to respond.

'Thank you. I'm feeling perfect. I will do my best to fulfil my mission. I'll see you back on the ground' was all I could think to say. It was a brief exchange because I had work to do and it was proving a great deal tougher than I had thought. While I had been floating free of the spacecraft, I had been facing the sun. The light was intense and the heat incredible. I felt sweat accumulating in drops on my face and running down under my shirt collar.

An unforeseen problem

My pressurised suit was extremely stiff and I had to exert a tremendous pull against the inflated rubber to bend my arms and legs. There was no gravity to give me leverage in the vacuum. Even the slightest movement required extreme effort. It was not planned that I would spend much time outside the spacecraft. So great was the concern about the huge psychological barrier it was feared man might face in the void of open space, that I had a web of sensors attached to my body. Information on my pulse, blood pressure and even the alpha-rhythm waves in my brain was being constantly monitored, by both Pasha and Mission Control.

The tranquillity of space was profound – far greater than diving deep beneath the surface of an ocean. And I felt a huge desire to disturb this motionless environment by moving my body, my arms and my legs

Giant steps *The cosmonaut Alexei Leonov climbs out of the hatch of Voskhod 2 in the first of the sequence of images below. He then floats free of the spacecraft, to which he is still attached by a steel 'umbilical cord', completing the world's first space walk. In the bottom picture he turns the somersault that made world news.*

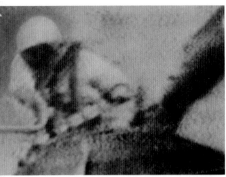

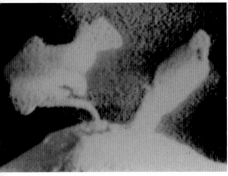

Dressing for space

THE SUIT IN WHICH ALEXEI LEONOV made his historic space walk was a new and untested invention, unlike any piece of space kit worn before. In contrast, the clothes that Yuri Gagarin – the first man in space – had worn were not designed for any specific activity, but were intended only to keep him comfortable during the flight (and warm in the event of a crash).

Leonov's suit, on the other hand, was specially designed for 'extra-vehicle activity'. The basic idea of the suit was that it should function like a Thermos: it had several layers with gaps between them to prevent the movement of heat. There were two separate inner layers, each hermetically sealed, and the outer layer had a shiny surface to reflect the sun's heat. The problem with the layering was that it tended to make the suit stiff – like wearing three overcoats at once – but the Soviet engineers thought they had achieved a reasonable compromise between complete protection and reasonable manoeuvrability. Leonov's experience proved that they had got the balance wrong: in the total vacuum of space, the suit expanded and became as hard and rigid as an inflated leather football.

The suit's saving graces were its unbreakable steel umbilical cord and the pressure valve that allowed Leonov to deflate the suit manually. The fact that he was being supplied with an oxygen-rich mix meant that he could breathe freely even after letting much of the air out. Leonov's suit nearly killed him, but it also saved his life.

A NATIONAL TREASURE Alexei Leonov's pioneering spacesuit is housed at the Russian Space Museum.

as much as I could, given the restrictions of my spacesuit. I felt like a seagull with wings outstretched, soaring above the earth. I gave myself a hefty push away from the side of the spacecraft, and immediately started tumbling uncontrollably, rolling head over heels until my umbilical cord of communication and breathing cables saved me from drifting off into space. After being yanked to a sharp halt, I had to struggle back to the craft, hauling myself fist over fist along the umbilical cord.

As I pulled myself back towards the spacecraft I was struck by how fragile and vulnerable it looked in the vastness of the universe. The brightness of the sunlight reflecting off its rounded hull gave the Voskhod space capsule such a deep golden sheen that it truly earned its name 'Sunrise'. My senses were so heightened that everything I saw in that short time left such deep impressions in my memory that they will last my entire lifetime.

When I pulled level with Voskhod 2, my body temperature had risen even higher and I was extremely tired. I knew it was time to re-enter the spacecraft. I had been in open space for more than 10 minutes. I still had 40 minutes of oxygen left in my autonomous life-support backpack and had a burning desire to stay outside for longer. But not only would it mean disobeying orders, in another 5 minutes our orbit would take us

Public adulation *Alexei Leonov received a hero's welcome from the Soviet Union on his return to Earth.*

away from the sun and into darkness. I still had to negotiate my way back into the spacecraft through the airlock, which would be difficult enough without the handicap of working in the dark.

But as I edged closer to the airlock's entrance I realised I had a very serious problem. My spacesuit had ballooned in the vacuum to such a degree that my feet had pulled away from my boots and my fingers no longer reached the gloves attached to my sleeves. The suit had been tested in a pressure chamber simulating a much lesser altitude and no such deformation had occurred. Now the suit was so misshapen that it would be impossible for me to enter the airlock feet first as I had done in training.

I had to find another way to get back inside the spacecraft, and quickly. The only way I could see of doing this was by pulling myself into the airlock gradually, head first. Even to do so, I would have to reduce the size of my spacesuit by carefully bleeding off some of the high-pressure oxygen in the suit, via a valve in its lining. I knew this might mean risking oxygen starvation, but I had no choice. If I did not re-enter the craft within the next 40 minutes my life-support reserves would be spent.

The only solution was to reduce the pressure in my suit by opening the pressure valve and letting out a little oxygen at a time as I tried to inch inside the airlock. At first I thought of reporting what I planned to do to Mission Control, but I decided against it. I did not want to create nervousness on the ground. And anyway, there was no time for discussion. I was the only one who could solve the problem, and I knew I had to do it fast.

Re-entering the spacecraft this way also meant I would have to perform a somersault once inside the airlock in order to close the outer hatch. It would take far longer than scheduled and I was not sure my life-support system would hold out. The exhilaration I had felt just minutes before as I looked down at the earth evaporated. Bathed in sweat, with my heart racing, I knew I could not afford to panic. I was only too aware of how fear could affect the ability to think and to take whatever action was needed. But time was running out …

I could feel my temperature rising dangerously high, starting with a rush of heat from my feet travelling up my legs and arms, due to the immense exertion all this manoeuvring involved. It was taking far longer than it was supposed to. Even when I at last managed to pull myself entirely into the airlock, I had to perform another almost impossible manoeuvre. I had to curl my body round in order to reach the hatch to close the airlock, so that Pasha could activate the mechanism to equalise the pressure between it and the spacecraft. Once Pasha was sure the hatch was closed and the pressure had equalised, he triggered the inner hatch open and I scrambled back into the spacecraft, drenched with sweat, heart still racing.

My serious problems when re-entering the spacecraft were, thankfully, not televised. My family was spared the worry and anxiety they would have had to endure had they known how close I came to being stranded alone in space.

From the moment our mission looked to be in jeopardy, transmissions from our spacecraft, which had been broadcast on both radio and television, were suddenly suspended without explanation. In their place, Mozart's Requiem was played on state radio. The custom in the Soviet Union at that time was for such solemn music to be played after a senior political figure had died, but before an official announcement of the death was made.

We knew nothing of the news blackout. Nothing could have been further from our minds. As I tried to catch my breath after struggling so hard to re-enter the spacecraft, I knew that if my physical training had not been so intensive I would never have been able to perform the complicated manoeuvres that saved my life.

Pasha also realised how close I had come to being stranded outside the spacecraft, how very nearly it had turned into disaster. But he was calm.

As soon as I opened my helmet to wipe the sweat from my eyes I was drenched again. Exhausted, my adrenalin was pumping so hard there was no immediate chance of my resting. But eventually I drifted into a fitful sleep. My dream was no longer simply a dream. I had actually walked in space. ∎

What happened next?

THE SPACE WALK THAT ALMOST WENT WRONG was not the last hazardous incident that Leonov faced during the Voskhod 2 mission. During the re-entry into the earth's atmosphere, one of the retro-rockets misfired and a service module that was supposed to fall away failed to detach. This resulted in the command module touching down in the snowy uplands of the Ural mountains, far from the designated landing area. Leonov and Belyayev spent an uncomfortable night sitting in the module while wolves pawed at the escape hatch.

Leonov never achieved his greatest professional ambition, which was to be the first man on the moon. He was due to make a 'moonshot' in 1970, but the project was cancelled when the Americans beat the Soviets to it. He did go back into space – and made history again – in 1973, when he was one of the cosmonauts on the Soyuz ship that docked in orbit with an Apollo craft. On July 17, the hatches between the two conjoined spacecraft were opened and Leonov extended a hand to the American mission commander, Tom Stafford. It was the first international handshake in space.

After the Soyuz-Apollo mission, Leonov became head of the cosmonaut corps, and went on to serve as Deputy Director of the Yuri Gagarin Cosmonaut Training Centre in 'Star City', near Moscow. He retired from the post in 1991, the year the USSR collapsed and funding for space exploration dried up. He then took a post as vice-president of one of the many new private banks that sprung up in those years. Throughout it all, Leonov maintained a love of art. He made the first sketches of Earth from a point outside the planet, and his dramatic spacescapes – which he called 'astro-paintings' – are now collectors' items.

FRIENDS IN SPACE Leonov (left) shakes hands with US astronaut Tom Stafford; it was a symbolic gesture during the Cold War.

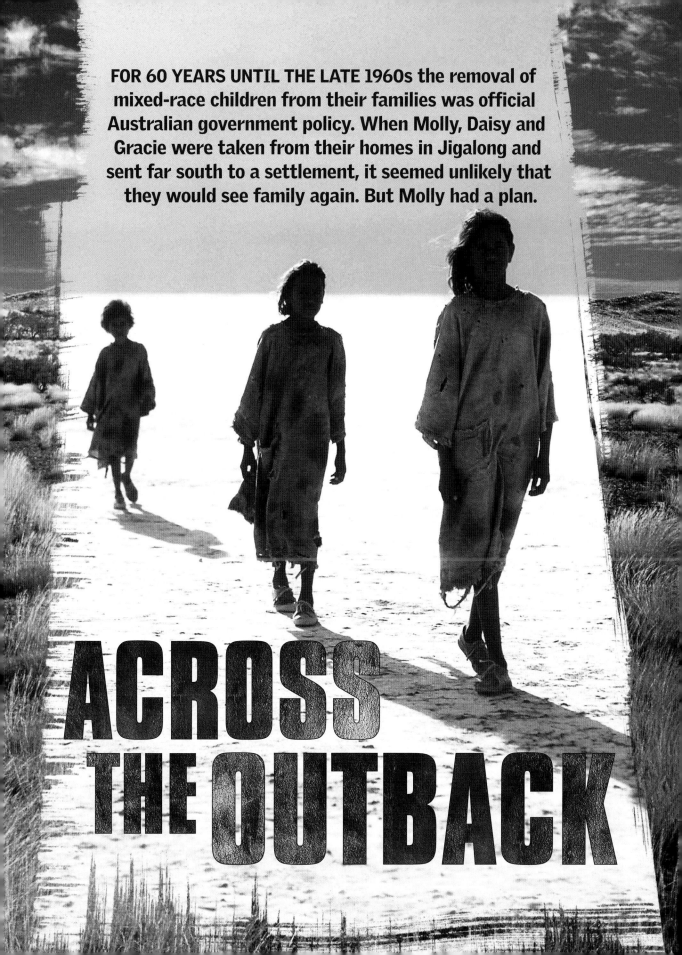

FOR 60 YEARS UNTIL THE LATE 1960s the removal of mixed-race children from their families was official Australian government policy. When Molly, Daisy and Gracie were taken from their homes in Jigalong and sent far south to a settlement, it seemed unlikely that they would see family again. But Molly had a plan.

ACROSS THE OUTBACK

The journey from Jigalong had taken days and days. In July 1931, Constable Riggs, Protector of Aborigines, had arrived at the camp in the Pilbara region of northwest Australia, and taken Molly and Gracie away on the back of his big bay horse. It took him a while to track down Daisy, but soon all three little girls were taken by car and train, always under police escort, to board a ship at Port Hedland. After five days at sea, they reached the port of Fremantle, the busiest seaport in Western Australia, full of men rushing about and yelling, and cargo being unloaded. And then came more car travel for the bewildered children, inland by stages to their destination, the Moore River Native Settlement, north of Perth.

It was still dark, wet and cold at 5.30 on an August morning a few days later. The little ones protested loudly at being forced to rise at that ungodly hour for their first day at school. Molly got up reluctantly and walked out onto the verandah, peeped through the lattice and smiled secretly to herself. Gracie and Daisy joined her, but they didn't care for the grey, dismal day and said so.

The girls waited for the others in the dormitory to join them, then made their way through the slushy mud to the dining room. After a breakfast of weevily porridge, bread and tea, they returned to the dormitory to wait for the school bell. Molly, Daisy and Gracie were going to be taught to read and write. This was to be their first day at school.

But 14-year-old Molly had decided that she and her 'sisters'[1] were not staying at the Moore River Native Settlement. She had no desire to live in this strange place among people she didn't know. It was still too early for classes, so most of the smaller girls slipped back into bed. Molly, Gracie and Daisy did the same but they squashed into the one bed, with the two younger girls at the head and Molly at the end.

Molly finished combing her light brown hair and lay watching the others. At the other end of the bed, Daisy and Gracie were whispering to each other. Thirteen-year-old Daisy had the same coloured hair as her elder 'sister', while 11-year-old Gracie had straight, black hair that hung down to her shoulders. The girls had inherited features from their white fathers. The only obvious Aboriginal characteristics were their dark brown eyes and their ability to control their facial expressions, so that when they reached maturity they would develop the look of the quiet, dignified Aboriginal women from the Pilbara region.

The other girls were now getting ready for school, and the three watched all the activity. Bossing and bullying were everywhere and there were squeals of, 'Don't, you're hurting my head', as tangled knots were combed out.

As soon as the other girls left the overcrowded dormitory, Molly beckoned her two sisters to come closer, then whispered urgently, 'We're not going to school, so grab your bags. We're not staying here.' Daisy and Gracie were stunned and stood staring at her.

But 14-year-old Molly had decided that she and her 'sisters' were not staying at the Moore River Native Settlement. She had no desire to live in this strange place among people she didn't know.

1 Daisy was Molly's half-sister; Gracie was her cousin.

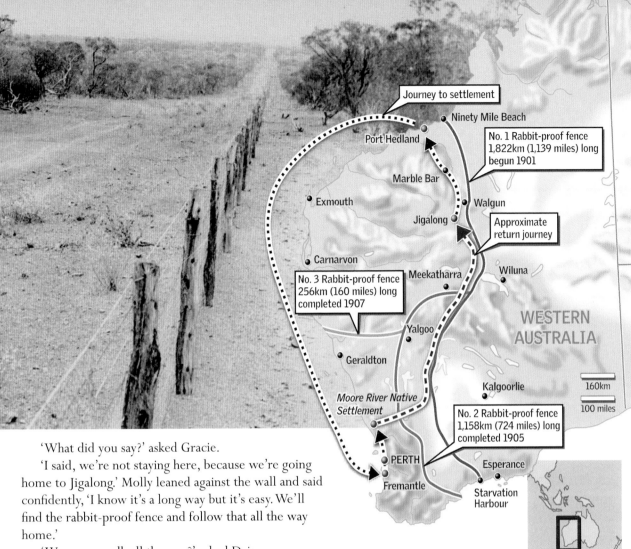

Journey to settlement

Ninety Mile Beach

Port Hedland

**No. 1 Rabbit-proof fence
1,822km (1,139 miles) long
begun 1901**

Marble Bar

Exmouth

Walgun

Jigalong

**Approximate
return journey**

Carnarvon

Meekatharra

Wiluna

**No. 3 Rabbit-proof fence
256km (160 miles) long
completed 1907**

Yalgoo

*WESTERN
AUSTRALIA*

Geraldton

*Moore River Native
Settlement*

Kalgoorlie

160km

100 miles

**No. 2 Rabbit-proof fence
1,158km (724 miles) long
completed 1905**

PERTH

Esperance

Fremantle

Starvation
Harbour

'What did you say?' asked Gracie.

'I said, we're not staying here, because we're going home to Jigalong.' Molly leaned against the wall and said confidently, 'I know it's a long way but it's easy. We'll find the rabbit-proof fence and follow that all the way home.'

'We gunna walk all the way?' asked Daisy.

'Yeah,' replied Molly, getting impatient now. 'So don't waste time.'

Where is the fence?

Finding the rabbit-proof fence seemed like a simple solution for Molly, whose father, Thomas Craig, was an inspector who travelled up and down the fences. Thomas Craig had told her often enough that the fence stretched from coast to coast, south to north. It was just a matter of locating it then following it to Jigalong.

The two youngsters trusted their big sister because she had always been the bossy one who made all the decisions at home. So they did the normal thing and said, 'Alright, Dgudu[2], we'll run away with you.'

They put their meagre possessions into calico bags and pulled the long drawstrings and slung them around their necks. Each put on two dresses and two pairs of calico bloomers. They checked they hadn't missed anything.

'Come on, run, you two,' Molly said sharply as she started to run towards the river, dashing down the sandy slope of the cliffs, dodging small

2 **Dgudu** Older sister.

Landmark to freedom

Three rabbit-proof fences were built by the state government in the early 20th century in a bid to hold back an invasion of rabbits from the east. No. 1 fence, which eventually led the girls back to Jigalong, runs the length of Western Australia, from Starvation Harbour, near Esperance, in the south, to Ninety Mile Beach on the north coast. Fences 2 and 3 had to be erected when rabbits broke west of the line of No. 1 fence.

shrubs on the way. They slowed down only when they reached the bottom. Molly strode on along the muddy banks, pausing to urge her young sisters to try to keep up with her. The girls watched the swirling currents and the white and brown foam that clung to the trunks of the young river gums.

'The river is too deep and fast here, let's try up further,' Molly said, leading the way through the thick young suckers and washed-up logs. Daisy and Gracie were fighting their way through the tea-trees when they heard Molly call out somewhere down the track. 'Yardini![3] Bukala![4] Bukala!'

They ran as fast as they could along the muddy path. Molly stood near a large river gum. As they gasped for breath, she said, 'We gunna cross here.'

A tree leaned over the water creating a bridge for them to cross safely to the other side. They knew that they had found the perfect place to cross the flooded river. The girls climbed onto the trunk and walked cautiously to the end. They tried to shut out the sounds and sights of the gushing water and concentrated on reaching the bank. They made it safely.

They sloshed through the wet, chocolate-coloured banks for another 2 hours, then decided to rest among the thick reeds behind the tall river gums. A few minutes later, Molly stood up and told her young sisters to get up. 'We go kyalie[5] now all the way.' They obeyed without any protests. Ducking under the hanging branches of the paperbark trees they hurried on.

Molly had no fear because the wilderness was her kin. It provided shelter, food and sustenance. She had learned bushcraft skills and survival techniques from an expert, her step-father, a former nomad from the desert. She had memorised the direction in which they had travelled: north then west to the settlement. Also, she had caught a glimpse of the sun behind the clouds during their first day. That enabled her to determine that she was moving in the right direction.

Once they had left the flooded river area the three were able to speed up as they passed through an open landscape and under giant marri gums with thick trunks covered with brownish-grey flaky bark.

---

3 Yardini Come here!
4 Bukala Hurry!
5 Kyalie North.

Remote homeland *Today Jigalong (seen from the air, below) is a tiny community of fewer than 300 people. It is remarkable how Molly was able to find her way home to this pinprick of human habitation in the vastness of the Australian outback.*

The girls trod gingerly over dry, decayed honky nuts that had fallen from the marri gum, trying not to slip. The sand plains were covered with acacia thickets and prickly grevilleas that scratched their bare legs. They tried not to let the discomfort bother them but this was difficult in the cold weather. Stepping around the prickly, dense undergrowth onto patches of white sand, the girls continued at their steady pace, pausing only to climb through boundary fences.

Molly was pleased that the mud and slush were behind them. They were now on the heathlands, which contain some of Australia's most beautiful and unusual wild flowers – the beautiful kangaroo paw flowers.

It started to drizzle again; the girls looked up and saw that there were only scattered clouds, so they trudged on unperturbed through the open forest of banksia, prickly bark and Christmas trees that covered the low sand dunes. Eventually, the showers passed over them heading inland.

Gracie and Daisy longed for a meal of meat, hot damper[6] and sweet tea. They continued north, through the wet countryside, never knowing what was waiting for them over the next rise.

On their second day they came into a section of bushland that had been burned black by fire. In a few weeks' time, this charcoal landscape would be revived by the rain to become a green wilderness again, full of beautiful flowers and animals. The three girls walked in silence over the next hill where they saw an unexpected but welcome sight. Coming towards them were two Mardu men from the Pilbara region on their way home from hunting.

Molly held the girls back and whispered softly, 'Wait.'

So the girls waited for the men to come closer. When they saw the men's catch, they drooled – a cooked kangaroo and two murrandus[7]. They were more interested in the bush tucker than in the two hunters, who introduced themselves and told the girls that they were from Marble Bar in the Pilbara.

'Where are you girls going?' asked one of the men.

'We are running away back home to Jigalong,' replied Molly.

'Well, you girls want to be careful, this country is different from ours, you know,' advised the old man with white hair and a bushy white beard.

'They got a Mardu policeman, a proper cheeky fullah. He flog 'em young runaway gels like you three,' he added, very concerned for them as they were from the Pilbara too. 'He's a good tracker, that Mardu.'

Molly was confident that their footprints would have been washed away by the rain. The men gave them a kangaroo tail and one of the murrandus. The girls thanked them and said goodbye.

Keeping one step ahead

They kept walking until dusk, when they set about preparing a wuungku[8] from branches of trees and shrubs. They decided that it was safe to light a small fire in the centre of the shelter. After a supper of kangaroo tail and murrandu, washed down with rain water, they loaded wood on the fire and slept snugly.

Beauty in the desert *The girls were familiar with the Western Australian desert's colourful array of plantlife, such as the Kangaroo paw flower (top) and the wattle, or acacia (below), useful for providing shelter from man and beast.*

---

6 Damper Unleavened bread.
7 Murrandu A goanna, a type of monitor lizard.
8 Wuungku A shelter.

The next morning the wind was blowing strong and cold. They realised that they must push on farther into the wilderness, covering as much ground as they could during the daylight hours. In this weather and country they had been covering 24-30km (15-18 miles) a day. By midday, the girls were hit with pangs of hunger. Gracie was irritable and began to stamp her feet in protest. Suddenly she got caught in dense, tangled scarlet runner creepers and fell with a thud. She lay there groaning softly to herself.

'We gunna die. We got nothing to eat.'

'Oh shut up and stop whingeing,' ordered Molly. 'We gotta hurry up.'

Gracie withdrew into herself, refusing to talk. She followed Molly and Daisy in a sullen trance, looking neither right nor left. Suddenly Molly shouted excitedly, 'Look over there.'

'What is it, Dgudu?' Daisy wanted to know. Gracie looked up to see rabbit burrows in the sand dunes.

'We gunna catch them to eat,' replied Molly.

The girls hadn't eaten since the morning and it was now late afternoon. A rabbit warren was an exciting find. The three set about blocking the entrances, leaving only one open. Then they sat behind some acacia bushes and waited. After what seemed like ages, out came the rabbits. One, then two, then more.

'Now,' ordered Molly. 'Go.' She leaped up and chased the rabbits. Molly and Gracie were excellent runners. They caught a rabbit each, while their knock-kneed little sister could not catch even the slowest.

It was past dusk when they found a suitable place to make camp. The girls were in good spirits as they made a fire in a hole in the ground and cooked the rabbits in the ashes, after gutting them roughly using a sharp green stick. They ate one for supper with water from a soak they found. The other rabbit was for breakfast.

The morning was pleasant, quiet and peaceful. The girls appeared relaxed as they walked along. Then all of a sudden they stopped and gasped. In a clearing were two of the biggest and blackest kangaroos they had ever seen.

'Look at them, they're standing up and fighting like men,' whispered Molly. 'But they can't see us up here.'

'I'm frightened, Dgudu,' Gracie whispered.

'Me too, Dgudu,' said Daisy moving closer to Molly.

'Come on, let's get away from here. We'll walk around them. They won't see us if we crawl behind these bushes,' Molly whispered.

The two smaller girls didn't want to be attacked by kangaroos, and were relieved when they had climbed the boundary fence. Only then could they feel safe. The girls sat on a fallen log, trying to recover from the sight of the fighting animals. The silence was broken suddenly by an alarmed Molly, who pulled Gracie up roughly by the arms.

'Run under that big tree over there,' she yelled, pointing to a large banksia tree. 'Climb up and hide there. You too, Daisy. Come on.' There they lay, stretched out on the rough branches not daring to move. At last they heard it: a search plane sent to look for them. The girls listened while the plane circled above them, then it gave up and returned home. Several minutes passed before Molly decided it was safe to climb down. On the ground they quickened their pace, keeping close to the trees in case they needed to hide again.

All of a sudden they stopped and gasped.
In a clearing were two of the biggest and blackest kangaroos they had ever seen. 'Look at them, they're standing up and fighting like men,' whispered Molly.

No one took any notice of the change in the weather until they were caught in the showers. They were drenched. Overcome with gloom and despair, they heard the sounds of fowls, squeaky windmills and barking dogs. They reminded them of Jigalong, Walgun and Murra Munda stations, but most of all these sounds brought back memories of their loved ones. As they approached a farmhouse Molly gently urged the two sisters forward.

'Go in there and ask the missus for some food to eat. Hurry up. I'll wait here,' she said as she settled down behind a marri gum.

Daisy and Gracie went willingly because they were very hungry. Approaching the farmhouse, they looked about them. The barking dogs, chained near their kennels, gave the girls a scare as they tried to rush past. Fortunately the chains held. The girls opened the wooden gate and were greeted by a little girl playing with her toys on the verandah.

'Mummy,' she yelled, 'there's two girls outside and they're all wet.'

The child's mother came to the door and asked, 'You the runaways from the settlement?'

'Yes,' they replied shyly.

'Where's the other one?' she asked.

'She's outside near the big tree, on the other side of the fence,' Gracie said.

'Go and tell her to come inside and dry herself while I make something to eat,' the woman said. A Mrs Flanagan, she'd received a phone call from Superintendent Neal asking her to watch out for three absconders. Mrs Flanagan asked the girls a lot of questions, especially about their destination.

'We are going to find the rabbit-proof fence and follow it home to Jigalong,' Molly said.

Mrs Flanagan made thick mutton and tomato chutney sandwiches, which the girls stared at as if mesmerised. The aroma was overpowering;

Parched land *A typical desert scene, north of Kalgoorlie, in Western Australia, shows the kind of unforgiving landscape the three girls had to cross on their journey.*

The Stolen Generations

THE CHIEF ARCHITECT of the plan to remove mixed-race children from their families was one Auber Octavius Neville. He was born in Northumberland, in Victorian Britain, in 1875, when Benjamin Disraeli was Prime Minister. He emigrated with his family to Australia as a child, and in adult life became a public servant, rising via the role of Chief Protector of Aborigines to Commissioner for Native Affairs.

In Neville's mind, to remove part-Aboriginal children from their parents was a means of protecting them, 'whether they like it or not. They cannot remain as they are,' he told the Moseley Royal Commission, which, in 1934, was investigating the administration of Aboriginals.

Continuing to justify his cruel-to-be-kind approach, he stated, 'The children who have been removed as wards of the Chief Protector have been removed because I desired to be satisfied that the conditions surrounding their upbringing were satisfactory, which they certainly were not.'

Before his retirement in 1940, Neville wrote a text, *Australia's Coloured Minority*, detailing his plan for the absorption of part-Aboriginal people into white Australian society, and acknowledging that European colonisation had been detrimental to the Aborigines.

In his zeal to 'uplift the Native race' and to 'protect Aborigines against themselves', Neville was well-intentioned but profoundly ignorant of the beauty, subtlety and integrity of societies such as the Mardu's. At the height of Neville's policy, in the mid 20th century, an estimated 100,000 children were taken from their extended families, often forcibly, by police. They became the 'Stolen Generations'. In many cases, child and parents never saw each other again.

It was for these removals that the Australian Prime Minister Kevin Rudd made a formal Apology to the indigenous peoples of Australia on February 13, 2008.

SEPARATED FROM THEIR PARENTS From left, Silvia, Louise and Marjorie, three of the so-called Stolen Generations, hear the Apology at Parliament House in Canberra.

they could almost taste the mutton and crusty bread. They devoured them greedily, and a feeling of contentment prevailed in the warm, dry kitchen.

Mrs Flanagan filled a couple of paper bags with tea leaves, sugar, flour and salt and half a leg of mutton and fruit cake and bread. 'Come with me and I'll give you some dry clothes and warm coats,' she said. She pulled out some old army uniforms – a greatcoat for Molly and jackets for Gracie and Daisy.

Watching the three girls disappear into the open woodlands, she said to herself, 'Those girls are too young to be wandering around in the bush. They'll perish for sure. It's a wonder they didn't catch pneumonia. I'll have to report this to Mr Neal for their own good,' she said. 'It's my duty.'

A kilometre away, the three sisters agreed that from that point onwards they would follow a routine. Whenever they arrived at a homestead, Daisy and Gracie would enter the yard and ask for food while Molly waited a safe distance away, out of sight. Thankfully, food was never refused. These handouts sustained the girls during their long trek home.

Molly decided to continue in the same direction for a couple of hours at least – just to foil their would-be captors. 'You know, we shouldn't have told her where we were heading,' Molly said. 'They might have someone waiting for us along the rabbit-proof fence. Never mind. We'll go this way for now.'

Finding the fence

News of their escape was spreading across the country. The whole state was told about them when an article appeared in the *West Australian* on August 11, 1931. Within days of the newspaper announcement, responses came in from all around. Reports were exchanged back and forth. But the girls continued trekking on, unaware of the search parties being assembled by the police. They didn't know that they were just a few days ahead of the searchers and their would-be captors.

Within a week, the scratches on their legs had become festering sores. 'My legs are sore, Dgudu,' cried Gracie. 'I can't walk.'

'My legs hurt too,' chimed in Daisy.

'Mine are sore, too,' said Molly. 'But we can't hang around here all day. I'll carry Daisy first, have a rest, then it will be your turn, Gracie.'

Progress was slow and laborious. When Molly's turn came to have a break from carrying them, the younger sisters took turns piggybacking each other.

The three girls had been on the run for over a month. They had left the landscape of mallee gums, acacia trees and green fields and found themselves in a very different countryside; one of red soil, tall, thick mulgas and gidgies[9] and the bright green kurrajong trees that stood out against the other grey-green vegetation. Molly, Daisy and Gracie were at home in this part of the country.

To fool possible informants, they would approach a homestead from one direction and pretend to go off the opposite way. They would double back when all was clear. Their simple meals were just like the ones they ate at home – especially when they managed to find birds, birds' eggs, rabbits and lizards. But their festering sores were still aching and they could find no relief.

One day about midday, when the sun was high in the azure sky, Daisy and Gracie heard an excited shriek from Molly who, as usual, was walking ahead of them. 'I've found it – I've found the rabbit-proof fence. See,' she yelled, pointing to the fence. 'This will take us all the way home to Jigalong.'

'But how do you know that's the rabbit-proof fence, Dgudu?' asked Daisy, puzzled. She didn't notice anything special about this fence.

'This fence is straight, see,' Molly explained. 'And it's clear on each side.'

She should know; after all, her father was the inspector of the fence and he had told her all about it. From when she was young, Molly had learned that the fence was an important landmark for the Mardu people of the Western Desert, who migrated south from the remote regions.

'We're nearly home,' said Molly without realising that they had merely reached the halfway mark, and that they still had almost 800km

---

9 Mulgas and gidgies Acacias.

(500 miles) to go. 'We found the fence now. It gunna be easy,' she said to her younger sisters.

By mid afternoon, they had entered a clearing among the mulga and gidgi trees and found some promising murrandu holes. At that very moment, they heard a man yelling from down the track, 'Hey, you girls. Wait.'

They saw an Aboriginal man riding a bike. The three dashed into the bush forgetting the pain of the sores on their legs.

'Don't run away. I want to talk to you,' he shouted. Peeping out from the bushes they saw that he was holding something in one hand. 'Look, I've got some food to give you. See,' he said. 'Come on, don't be frightened.'

Their need and desire for food overcame fear. The man's name was Don and he explained that he worked on Pindathuna Station near the rabbit-proof fence. He shared his lunch of tinned meat and bread with them.

'Where are you going?' he asked them.

'We gunna follow the railway line to Wiluna,' said Molly to throw him off the scent.

Stockman Don Willocks reported the incident to his boss, who telephoned Constable Robert Larsen at the Yalgoo police station. Larsen had led an earlier search party for the girls and was keen to follow up these sightings. At last he would be able to inform Inspector Simpson at Geraldton that contact had been made with the girls.

A tracker named Ben was brought into the search and he and Larsen travelled to Pindathuna to pick up Willocks. It was impossible to find the tracks because heavy rains had washed them away. Nevertheless, the search party proceeded along the rabbit-proof fence for a few kilometres, searching for tracks. Finally, however, Larsen recorded that the tracking was discontinued, 'owing to the tracker having sore feet, myself having to attend the Police Court on Monday 7/9/31, I decided to return to Yalgoo'.

Party of two

The girls had been on the run for some five weeks and were surviving on bush tucker and water. One day in a clearing close to the fence, the girls spied an emu and six tiny black-and-white striped chicks. Molly and Daisy chased and captured a chick each. They plucked and cooked the emu chicks for supper, accompanied by damper and washed down with tea.

Home was drawing nearer each day. The girls reached the railway siding near Mt Russel Station several days after passing the town of Meekatharra. Here Gracie decided that she had had enough. 'I'm going to the station to see those people working over there,' a determined Gracie told her sisters. Fifteen minutes later she returned. 'That woman, the muda-muda[10] one working here, told me that my mummy left Walgun Station and is living in Wiluna,' she said excitedly. 'I am going with her when the train comes.'

Gracie was plain tired of walking; her bare feet were very sore. The pleadings of her sisters fell on deaf ears. She flatly refused to go any farther.

'I don't want to die,' she said finally as she turned her back to walk away from them. 'I'm going to my mummy in Wiluna.'

10 Muda-muda Mixed-race.

Molly and Daisy continued north on their incredible journey. The day they parted was the hottest since their abscondment. The military coat and jackets were discarded and Molly and Daisy decided to rest beside a creek bed. There was enough water in it to quench their thirst and fill their billycan. The girls were able to take advantage of the longer hours of daylight. They could rise early and cover a good distance before nightfall.

When they climbed through the southern boundary fence of Station 594 – a cattle station along the Canning Stock Route, south of Jigalong – Molly and Daisy were relieved. They had been there before to visit their aunt's camp. When they saw the campsite they almost ran but they didn't have the energy. Their aunt, Molly's step-father's sister, greeted them in the traditional manner by crying with them and for those who had passed away since their last meeting.

'Where did you girls come from? Where have you been?' she asked. Their relations couldn't believe what the girls told them.

The two sisters sank gratefully into the warm bath their aunt prepared. They had grown used to washing at the windmills and pools along the way. The supper of beef stew, bread and tea revived them. Molly and Daisy found that they could only manage small quantities as their stomachs had shrunk.

'You'll soon be fixed when you get back to your mummies,' said their aunt warmly. 'They will fatten you up again.'

After supper they sat around the fire, sharing their experiences late into the night. Then both stretched out on comfortable beds and fell asleep.

The two sisters awoke the next day refreshed after the good night's sleep.

'Not far to go, Dgudu,' said Daisy.

'No, not far now. We'll be home soon,' replied Molly.

When they had almost finished breakfast, their cousin Joey came over and joined them and accepted a mug of tea.

'We're going back to Jigalong this morning as soon as the boss finishes his breakfast,' he said.

Molly and Daisy were ready in a few minutes and didn't have to wait long. Picking up their calico bags, which were now the same colour as the red earth, they walked towards Joey and his boss. They turned and waved goodbye to their aunt and cousin – the others were still asleep – and joined the maintenance workers of the rabbit-proof fence.

'You two girls can take it in turns riding this camel back to Jigalong,' said Ron Clarkson, the contract worker, as he patted the animal. The camel raised its head, looking around everywhere and chewing without pausing.

Daisy enjoyed the ride and welcomed the chance to watch the passing scenery from above ground level. The sun was setting when they entered the main gate to Munda Mindi, a livestock station, and made a camp. Soon they would be reunited with their mothers. That night they slept a dreamless sleep.

For breakfast the following morning they ate bread and jam, salted beef and sweet, black tea. Molly took her turn to ride while Daisy walked beside her. They were passing through country familiar to Daisy, so she took great delight showing her big sister where her family had camped and where bush tucker was plentiful.

The silence one late afternoon in October 1931 was broken occasionally by the cawing of crows and the swishing of the camels' tails as they brushed away pesky bush flies. Now it was Molly's turn to point out special places to Daisy. They passed close to the clay-pan where Molly was born.

As they drew closer, nervous excitement was building up inside them. Both girls took in the familiar landscape of the red earth, the dry spinifex grass and grey-green mulga trees. There was nothing to compare with the beauty of these plains that stretched out in all directions.

They could see the black hills where their families hunted. They were approaching the campsite now; dogs were barking and people were shouting and pointing at them. Some were sitting in the creek bed, wailing quietly. Molly and Daisy were home – after an epic barefoot journey of nine weeks. ■

What happened next?

MOLLY CRAIG MARRIED AN ABORIGINAL STOCKMAN, Toby Kelly, with whom she had two daughters, Doris and Annabelle. In 1940, Molly was once more taken to the Moore River Native Settlement with her two little girls, and in 1941 she again ran away, taking only the infant Annabelle with her.

Doris grew up from the age of four believing that her mother had chosen to abandon her. 'We were always told, "You're in this mission because your mother didn't love you."' It would be 20 years before mother and daughter were reunited and Doris learned the truth. Annabelle, meanwhile, had been taken from Molly and placed in an institution. She became, in adult life, Anna Wyld, and although she sent her daughter Helen with gifts, she herself never saw Molly again.

Doris was married with four children before she made the trip to meet her parents, to discover that she had a big, welcoming family. 'I felt, in a way, I was home.'

Follow the Rabbit-Proof Fence was the second of a trilogy of novels by Doris Pilkington Garimara, documenting the lives of three generations of women. It was made into the film *Rabbit-Proof Fence* in 2002. The first book, *Caprice: A Stockman's Daughter*, won Doris literary acclaim. The third book, *Under the Wintamarra Tree*, recounts Doris's own escape from Moore River.

In 2002, Doris was appointed co-patron of the National Sorry Day Committee's 'Journey of Healing'. In 2006 she published *Home to Mother*, a retelling for children of *Rabbit-Proof Fence*, and in the same year she was awarded an Order of Australia for services to the arts in indigenous literature. This was followed by the 2008 Australia Council Red Ochre Award for her outstanding contribution to Aboriginal art.

Molly Kelly did not live to see her daughter garner such rewards. In January 2004, at the age of 87, at home in Jigalong, she took an afternoon nap from which she failed to wake.

After the original three girls' escape from Moore River, Gracie was taken back and never returned to Jigalong. Daisy was reunited with her family and they subsequently moved away. She married, had four children, and eventually returned with them to live at Jigalong.

LATE FAME Molly (above, in 2004) lived to see her remarkable journey captured in print and on film, thanks to her daughter Doris (left).

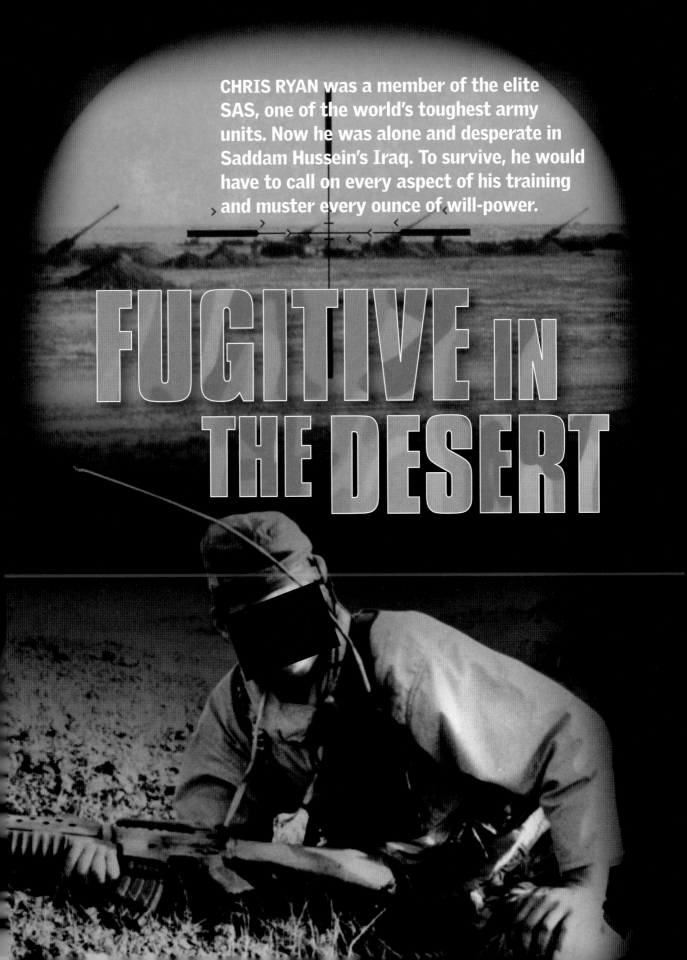

CHRIS RYAN was a member of the elite SAS, one of the world's toughest army units. Now he was alone and desperate in Saddam Hussein's Iraq. To survive, he would have to call on every aspect of his training and muster every ounce of will-power.

FUGITIVE IN THE DESERT

Bid for safety Chris Ryan's route through Iraq (bottom) took him from his first laying-up point, LUP1, over a treacherous 320km (200 miles) of desert terrain. He knew that following the course of the Euphrates river would bring him to the Syrian border – and safety.

Disaster hit us on Thursday night, January 24, 1991. Our SAS patrol, Bravo Two Zero, had been helicoptered from Saudi Arabia 320km (200 miles) into northern Iraq to lie up in an observation post and report on Scud missile-launchers on the move. But on this ninth day of the air-bombardment phase of the Gulf War, we'd stirred up a hornets' nest.

The observation post we chose turned out to be close to an anti-aircraft gun position. Then a boy herding goats spotted us, and, at dusk, we were attacked by Iraqis with automatic rifles. After a firefight, we were forced to run for it. We decided to make for the nearest friendly country, Syria.

There were eight of us, speed-marching for our lives in single file, with the patrol commander, Andy McNab[1], in the normal middle slot and me at the front. At about 11pm I stopped and turned round to confer with Andy. Stan, a muscular Australian, was behind me, then Vince, a tall, slim sergeant from Swindon … but no one else.

'Where's the rest of the patrol?' I demanded.

'I don't know,' Vince replied. 'They split off somewhere.'

I thought, 'Oh, my God!' I couldn't understand how it had happened. The moon came out from behind the clouds and lit up the barren plain. It seemed impossible that the others could have gone far. But the desert had swallowed them up.

We slogged on. Although the Syrian border was only 130km (80 miles) northwest from our observation post, we were aiming due north for the Euphrates, to get water; then we could follow the river to the frontier. By 5am we'd covered about 65km (40 miles). A fundamental SAS rule is that during escape and evasion you don't move in daylight. We holed up for the day in the best shelter we could find: some tank ruts 40cm (15in) deep.

Already thirst was a problem – both of my water bottles were empty – and I had nothing left to eat but ten cracker-type biscuits; I'd abandoned my ten days' rations when we all ditched our heavy haversacks during the fight with the Iraqis. Since the start of the operation none of our radios had worked – we realised much later that we'd been given the wrong frequencies – and we hadn't been able to get through to base. Nor could we contact the rest of the patrol. 'Andy! Andy!' I shouted into my TACBE (tactical rescue beacon, for sending messages to surveillance aircraft or for contacting other TACBEs). The night yielded no reply.

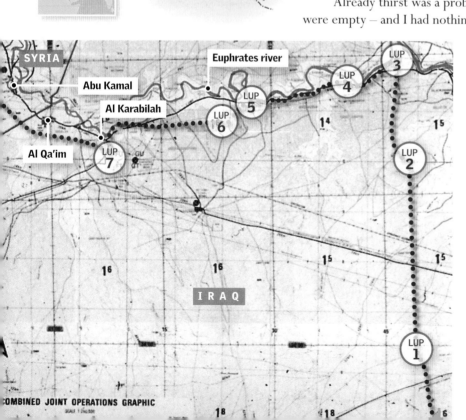

---

1 Some names have been changed.

Things now went from bad to worse. It snowed. We couldn't believe it. In Saudi Arabia the nights had been quite warm; nobody had warned us it would be different up here. The wind knifed through my thin combat fatigues. Never had I endured such agony from cold.

Vince was badly hit by hypothermia and deteriorating fast. When we set off again at nightfall he kept lagging behind, calling through the snow flurries, 'I want to go to sleep. I'm tired.'

I told him. 'If we lie down and sleep, we'll freeze to death.'

When Stan and I stopped for a rest, we realised Vince was no longer with us. We backtracked for 20 minutes, searching, but there was no sign of him. He must have curled up somewhere and dozed off.

'We've got to leave him,' I said, 'or we'll both be killed.' It was a terrible decision to have to take but I saw no alternative. With heavy hearts we cracked on.

At about noon the next day, Saturday, we had left the snow behind and were lying up in a wadi, a dry watercourse, being revived by the sun.

'Don't!' I said fiercely. I knew we'd get no help from the Iraqis. Apart from being enemies in war, we were infidels. Yet Stan was determined. 'I trust the guy. He seems friendly.'

A goatherd, a young man in a big old overcoat, came and sat on a rock near by, chewing stalks of dead grass. Stan whispered, 'He might have a vehicle he'd lend us.'

Stan jumped up and grabbed him. The startled goatherd let out a stream of Arabic and pointed down the wadi. Stan turned to me. 'I'll go with him and see if we can get a tractor.'

'Don't!' I said fiercely. I knew we'd get no help from the Iraqis. Apart from being enemies in war, we were infidels. Yet Stan was determined. 'I trust the guy. He seems friendly.' And away he went with the goatherd.

All alone

I had agreed to wait for Stan until 6.30pm. By 5.30 I was in a state of high anxiety. I kept hoping to see a vehicle heading out – but no. At 6.30, as darkness settled, I started walking north. I was thirsty, hungry and cold, and my last friend had gone.

'Now,' I thought, 'I'm on my own.'

For 15 minutes I walked steadily over level, open ground, with my 203 (a grenade-launcher attached to an automatic rifle) slung over my shoulder. I also had a rocket-launcher (a simple, tube-like device that is thrown away after firing), a night-sight (an image intensifier for seeing in the dark), a torch, knife, compass and escape map.

Then I happened to look back and saw headlights: two Land Rover-type vehicles were advancing towards me at a purposeful crawl. Stan's been captured. This is the enemy. It was going to be them or me. I dropped to the ground, trying to stop myself shaking. If anyone says he's not frightened in a firefight, I don't believe him. SAS guys are subject to the same fear as anyone else. The regiment's strength lies in intensive training to control it.

The vehicles kept coming: 45m (50yd). I aimed the rocket-launcher between the front pair of lights and pulled the trigger. Whoosh! The rocket took the vehicle head-on, stopping it in a cloud of smoke. I grabbed my 203

Real-life action men

ALL OF THE SPECIAL FORCES around the world are modelled on – or at least inspired by – the SAS. Right from the start, the main role of the Special Air Service (SAS) has been, as it was with the Bravo Two Zero patrol, intelligence-gathering behind enemy lines.

The Special Air Service was founded during the Second World War by a young officer, David Stirling, a brilliant maverick in the British Army. Stirling was convinced that a small group of highly trained soldiers could inflict more damage on the enemy than a larger unit of regular troops. He took his idea to Middle East headquarters in Cairo, where he was then based, and managed to persuade the Deputy Commander, General Ritchie, to back the idea. The name Special Air Service was a deliberate obfuscation – designed to make the German enemy think that there was a British parachute brigade on hand in North Africa.

The fact that the SAS tends to operate in 'deep battlespace' means that the regiment's soldiers have to

be experts in survival techniques. SAS methods have been studied by many non-military organisations and individuals, and their impact had been far-reaching.

The SAS approach to survival is summed up in the acronym PLAN, which stands for Protection (finding shelter); Location (signalling your presence so you can be found); Acquisition (of food, or at least of water); and Navigation (making your own way to safety).

Chris Ryan implemented PLAN when lost in northern Iraq – with the exception of Location, because he decidedly did not want to be found by any of the people who were looking for him. What saved him in the end was an ineffable fifth point in the four-point PLAN. It might be termed 'W': the unconquerable will to live.

DESERT FORCE Early SAS recruits return in their Jeep from a desert raiding party in 1943, to be greeted by their commander, Colonel David Stirling, on the right.

and smacked a grenade on the bonnet of the second vehicle. Now I was up and running towards the enemy, spraying the vehicles with automatic rifle fire.

Then I ran off until I had to slow down because my throat was heaving, my chest exploding, my mouth as dry as the desert. I came to some tilled fields. Then, at last, between the trunks of palm trees near a village, I saw water – the Euphrates. Edging out over a platform of bushes that sank into the river under my weight, I filled both my bottles and drank one down. The feeling of relief was incredible. I refilled the empty bottle.

By then it was nearly 5am on Sunday, January 27, my third day on the run and I needed somewhere to lie up for the day. I found a hollow among loose rocks in a wadi. There, a wave of loneliness swept over me. My biscuits were finished. My feet were raw and bleeding. I was cut off from all communications with friends and still far inside a hostile country.

'If things get on top of you,' my mum used to say, 'have a good cry.' So I tried to cry – but couldn't. Instead, my face crumpled up and I laughed. But somehow it did the trick; it let go of the tension.

The civilian population along the river had been alerted to look out for Coalition soldiers on the run, so when I came out of my hiding place on this freezing winter night, amazing numbers of Iraqis were outdoors. Again and again I sensed people ahead of me, brought up the night-sight for a better look, and had to make a detour. It was a frustrating zigzag all the time. I covered 30-40km (20-25 miles) but progressed only 10km (6 miles) towards the frontier.

Despair sets in

Monday, January 28: I reached a road in the early hours of darkness, got out my map and calculated that I was still some 80km (50 miles) from Syria. Then I felt and heard a tremendous rumble. A Scud missile – nearly 12m (40ft) long – passed me on its launcher, a huge articulated truck.

That's what I'm here for – to find Scuds! I whipped out my TACBE, but as usual got no response. The drama of Coalition aircraft coming in to destroy both launcher and missile was not to be.

I came to a tunnel underneath the road, built for pedestrians and animals to walk through, and decided to hide in it. It was a bad decision. At full daylight I heard goatbells approaching. I saw the lead animal of the herd come into view, and just had time to scoot out of the other end of the tunnel and up the sloping embankment of the road.

There I lay on my back, trapped between the tunnel mouth and the road with its traffic. The goats emerged below me, pushing and jostling. Last came the goatherd, an old man. As he walked out, the top of his head was barely a metre below my boots. I lay rigid, praying he wouldn't look back and see me. Little as I wanted to kill an innocent civilian, I was desperate. I held my breath as the party moved slowly away, up into the wadi.

That Tuesday night I crept onwards through an extremely confusing, irregular pattern of buildings. On the ground, insulated landlines ran all over the place. I seemed to have strayed into some kind of communications complex.

I moved with every sense on full alert, my 203 at the ready. Water was again an urgent necessity. I was seriously dehydrated. Then – wonder of wonders – I reached a stream. The water looked crystal-clear. I filled my bottles, thinking, 'I'm in luck!'

But I got a bad fright when I found myself in a transport park and right next to a Russian-made Jeep. I couldn't see through its windows; for all I knew, it could have been full of people. I held my breath, 203 levelled, waiting for it to erupt. When nothing happened I backed off.

Ahead were houses, and I could hear voices. I pushed off to the right, walking on tiptoe or crawling on hands and knees, trying to find my way out of the complex. I had been inside it for 5 hours when at last I worked my way to a road and saw three sentries manning a vehicle control point. Near them stood a line of anti-aircraft gun positions. The ground was almost flat.

I couldn't go forward and couldn't go back. I was trapped. Dawn was approaching. My only possible refuge was a culvert under the road. About the diameter of a 45 gallon drum, it was full of dead bushes, decomposing rubbish and excrement.

I crawled in, desperate for a drink. Then came a horrendous disappointment. I raised one of my bottles to my lips – and the water tasted vicious and metallic. I spat it straight out, but it left a burning sensation in my mouth. The second bottle was also undrinkable.

It was now the morning of Wednesday, January 30, and I felt very frightened. If I didn't reach the border soon, I would be too weak to carry on. I worked out from my map that I still had at least 30km (18 miles) to go.

At the beginning of the year I had been at the peak of physical fitness. Now my whole body was going downhill fast. My tongue was completely dry, like a piece of old leather; my teeth had all come loose, and I had lost so much weight that lying down was agonising. Spine, hips, ribs, knees, elbows, shoulders – everything hurt.

Tortured by thirst, drifting in and out of consciousness, I somehow stuck out the 11 hours of daylight. I didn't see how I was going to avoid the control point and gun positions, but when eventually darkness fell, my morale took a lift again.

When I did drop off to sleep I saw a phantom scene from home: our living room in Hereford, at Christmas, with my wife Janet asking me, 'Chris, will you switch the Christmas tree lights on?' and our two-year-old daughter Sarah, who shares my zest for life, jumping up and saying, 'Daddy, I'll do it!' and flicking the switch. In the filthy culvert I distinctly heard her baby voice.

Tortured by thirst, drifting in and out of consciousness, I somehow stuck out the 11 hours of daylight. I didn't see how I was going to avoid the control point and gun positions, but when eventually darkness fell, my morale took a lift again. The night was black as pitch. I eased myself halfway between the sentries and the guns and started walking at full speed. Behind me, nobody moved. I got clean away.

As I hobbled over the rocks and gravel, my feet so excruciatingly painful I thought they were going to burst, hallucinations began. Suddenly, Sarah

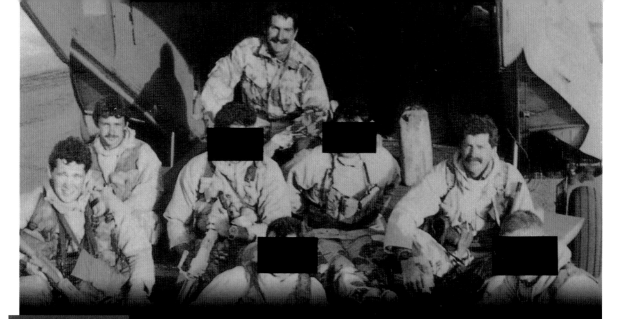

Where are they now?

EIGHT SAS SOLDIERS were sent into Iraq as part of the Bravo Two Zero patrol. Three of the men died on Iraqi soil, and three went on to write accounts of the mission. Chris Ryan's tale of his escape was the first publication in a writing career that now includes a spate of thrillers, children's adventure stories, a fitness manual and a survival guide, as well as a romantic novel published under the unlikely pseudonym of Molly Jackson. He has also made a TV series about elite police units around the world. He presently lives in the USA, where he works as a bodyguard.

Andy McNab, the leader of the Bravo Two Zero patrol, wrote a harrowing book about his experiences as a prisoner of the Iraqis. He too has produced a string of novels based on his military know-how, as well as an autobiography. Unlike Ryan, though, he is not a media figure: in interviews, his features are shrouded in shadows. McNab's account of the disastrous mission was criticised because it blamed Vince Phillips, one of the soldiers who died, for compromising the patrol. Among the critics was one of the Bravo Two Zero survivors, Mike Coburn (called 'Mark the Kiwi' in Ryan's and McNab's accounts). He in turn wrote a book that took issue with McNab's version of events and with the conduct of the army command in Iraq. The British Ministry of Defence mounted a long legal challenge to prevent the book from being published, and when that failed, won the right to confiscate any profits from it.

TO BOLDLY GO Bravo Two Zero members prepare for their Iraqi mission (above), positioned on the tailgate of a Chinook helicopter. Chris Ryan is on the far left. The other soldiers who survived are here seen with their faces blocked out, to preserve their anonymity.

was toddling ahead of me, leading the way through the dark. I thought I could pick her up in my arms. Even when I realised she wasn't there, I knew that it was only the thought of her, and my need to see her again, that were keeping me going.

On I stumbled, and saw the lights of a town, far out on the horizon. I took it to be Al Karabilah, an Iraqi town on the Syrian border. My heart sank: surely the border couldn't still be that far?

Then I came to a barrier of barbed wire: three coils in the bottom row, two on top of them, and one on top of that. Having no pliers to cut with, I decided that the only way to go was over the top. Luckily the builders had made the mistake of bracing the coils by putting in three posts, close to each other, every 23m (25yd). Linked with barbed wire, they formed 'bridges'. I went up and over one of these. The barrier seemed so insignificant I assumed it must mark some inner border, and that I would come to the true frontier farther on.

I set off yet again, on the same compass bearing. Never in my life have I pushed myself so hard. I think I was brain-dead that night, stumbling grimly onwards. Sarah returned to keep me company and lead me.

Thursday, January 31: early morning. I'd been on the run for eight days and seven nights. It was six days since I had finished my biscuits, three since I'd had any water. My body wasn't going to last another day.

A medal for Sarah

Then I saw a white stone farmhouse just over a kilometre away. The people living in that house must have water. I was closing in on the building, my gun in my hands, when a young man with dark curly hair came out. I pointed at the ground, asking, 'Is this Syria?' He nodded, repeating, 'Seeria! Seeria!' then pointed over my shoulder. 'Iraq!'

I looked back the way he was gesturing and realised I must have passed Al Karabilah early in the night without noticing it. The town I had seen was Abu Kamal, inside Syria. That line of barbed wire was the frontier after all. I'd been in Syria for hours.

I discovered that the complex I had walked through was Al Qa'im, a nuclear refinery, and the terrible-tasting water I'd taken from the stream was nuclear effluent.

At the British Embassy in Damascus, I discovered that the complex I had walked through was Al Qa'im, a nuclear refinery, and the terrible-tasting water I'd taken from the stream was nuclear effluent. Later, medical checks showed that I had a blood disorder caused by drinking dirty water from the Euphrates, but no radioactive poisoning.

In ten days I had lost 16kg (36lb). Some of my teeth remained loose, but otherwise I made a full physical recovery. The psychological scars, though, took longer to heal. Lying in bed, I would still see incidents from the patrol, such as abandoning the search for Vince.

When I returned to Al Jawf, the SAS forward-operating base in Saudi Arabia from which Bravo Two Zero had set out, I learned that repeated attempts were made to find us, but we'd been expected to head south for Saudi Arabia rather than for Syria, and our TACBEs were many miles beyond the range of the aircraft listening for messages.

My fellow survivors were returned as prisoners of war: Andy, Dinger, Mark – and Stan, who had been captured and beaten after the goatherd led him to some militiamen. I learned that the patrol had split because Andy heard a jet overhead and stopped to try to contact the pilot on his TACBE. The three of us ahead didn't hear him calling, 'Go to ground!' and carried on walking.

Until I was told at the British Embassy in Damascus, 'You're going to get a medal for this,' it hadn't occurred to me that my escape was anything exceptional. I'd just been for a walk of nearly 320km (200 miles) that proved rather more arduous than expected. Most people, I think, don't know what they're capable of until they're put to the test.

In December 1991, at Buckingham Palace, I received the Military Medal from the Queen. I came home and pinned it on Sarah. ■

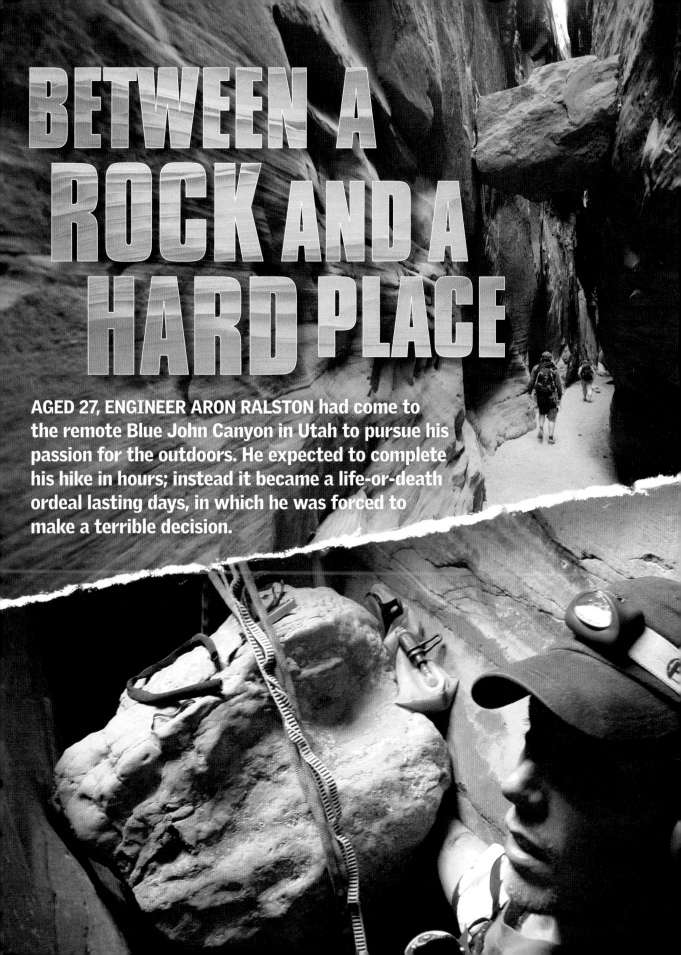

BETWEEN A ROCK AND A HARD PLACE

AGED 27, ENGINEER ARON RALSTON had come to the remote Blue John Canyon in Utah to pursue his passion for the outdoors. He expected to complete his hike in hours; instead it became a life-or-death ordeal lasting days, in which he was forced to make a terrible decision.

In the open section of Blue John Canyon, I pass a wide yellow

arroyo, a dried-up creek bed, coming in from my right. The capstone layer is more resistant to erosion than the ruddy-hued sandstone cliffs of the scenic slot canyons. This creates towers of coloured stone that dot the upper reaches of the canyon's cliffs. All this beauty keeps a smile on my face.

I have half a mile until the narrow slot above the 20m (65ft) high Big Drop rappel. This marks the midpoint of my descent in Blue John and Horseshoe canyons. I've come about 11km (7 miles) from my bike, left by the Robbers' Roost access road, after biking about 13km (8 miles) from my pick-up truck at the Horseshoe Canyon parking area.

I barely notice the canyon closing in. Then I reach the first drop-off, a 'dryfall'. Were there water in the canyon, this would be a waterfall. A dark embedded layer, resistant to erosion, forms the lip.

From where I'm standing to the continuing canyon bottom is about 3m (10ft). I use in-cut handholds to lower myself. My legs dangle maybe a metre off the floor. I let go and drop off the overhang, landing in a sandy concavity.

In my path are two van-sized chockstones – boulders suspended between the canyon walls – one just off the canyon bottom, the next on the floor. I scramble over both blockages. The twisting, deepening canyon narrows to a little over a metre. Colossal flood action has scooped out balls of rock and wedged logs overhead.

In this narrow section, silt from floods coats the walls 3.5m (12ft) above the floor. I stop to take photographs. The camera says it is 2.41pm, on Saturday, April 26, 2003.

Then I see five chockstones wedged at varying heights off the canyon floor. With half a metre of clearance under the first suspended chockstone, I have to crawl under it on my belly. The remaining chockstones are higher.

My arm is stuck

At another drop-off, a little higher than the overhang I descended minutes ago, the slot narrows to a metre and continues at that width down the canyon. It's possible to move up or down fairly easily, feet and back pushing in opposite directions against the walls. This is known as stemming.

Below where I'm standing is a chockstone the size of a bus tyre, stuck a metre out. If I can step onto it, I'll have a 3 metre height to descend. Stemming across the canyon, one foot and one hand on each wall, I traverse out.

I kick at the boulder: it's jammed tightly enough to hold my weight. I lower myself, and the chockstone supports me but teeters slightly. I squat and grip the rear of the lodged boulder, turning to face back up-canyon. Sliding my belly over the front edge, I dangle off the chockstone.

The stone responds with a scraping quake as my weight applies torque. This is trouble. I let go of the rotating boulder to land on rounded rocks below. The falling chockstone consumes the sky. Fear shoots my hands over my head. I can't move backwards or I'll fall over a small ledge. My only hope is to push off the falling rock and get my head out of its way.

The next 3 seconds play out in slow motion. The rock smashes my left hand against the south wall; I yank my left arm back as the rock ricochets, crushes my right hand and ensnares my right wrist; the rock slides another foot down the wall with my arm in tow, tearing skin off my forearm. Then silence.

I stare at the sight of my arm vanishing into an implausibly small gap between the boulder and the canyon wall. My nervous system's pain response overcomes the initial shock. Flaring agony throws me into a panic. I yank my arm in a naive attempt to pull it out. But I'm stuck.

Frantic, I cry out, 'Oh shit, oh shit!' I heave against the boulder, pushing with my left hand, lifting with my knees pressed under the rock. Standing on a 30cm (12in) shelf, I brace my thighs and thrust upwards, grunting, 'Come on … move!' Nothing.

With my left hand, I wipe my forehead. My chest heaves. I need a drink, but when I suck on my hydration-system hose, my reservoir is empty. I have a litre of water in my backpack. Extracting the bottle, I unscrew the top and, before I realise what I'm doing, gulp a third of my water in 5 seconds.

Who will find me?

Gravity and friction have wedged the chockstone just over a metre above the canyon floor. My right thumb is grey; there is no feeling. I can't extend my fingers. I try to wiggle each one. There isn't the slightest twitch.

Judging from the paleness of my trapped hand, and the fact that there's no blood loss, it's probable that I have no circulation to it. It seems to be isolated from my body's circulatory, nervous and motor-control systems. Not good.

No one knows where I am, trapped in the dimly lit bottom of a canyon. Miles from my truck, I am in an infrequently visited place with no means of contacting anyone outside the throw of my voice.

The easy ideas come first, some more wishful than realistic. Maybe other canyoneers will find me. If I'm not out by Monday, my roommates will miss me. I don't have enough water to wait that long – 650ml after my chug a few minutes ago. Survival time in the desert without water is between two and three days. I figure I'll make it to Monday night. Rescue before then will be about as probable as winning the lottery.

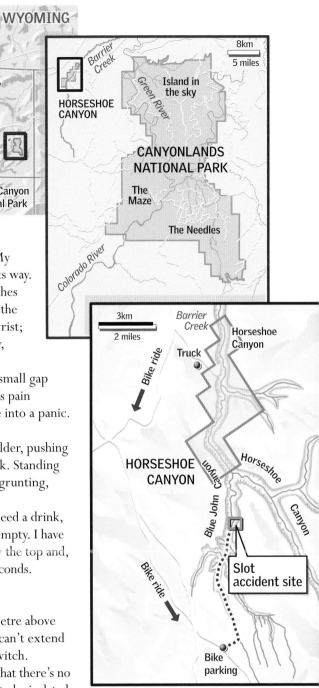

Meeting the challenge *Aron's adventure began at the Horseshoe Canyon offshoot of the Canyonlands National Park in Utah, a forbidding landscape of canyons, mesas — steep, flat-topped hills — and deep river gorges. When trapped, he was very much alone — a long way from his bike and even further from his truck.*

I settle on a sip of water every 90 minutes. It will give me something to look forward to. I organise my options in order of preference: excavate the rock around my hand with my multi-use tool; rig ropes to lift the boulder off my hand; or amputate my arm.

I scratch a 10cm (4in) line across the boulder. If I can remove the stone below this line back about 15cm (6in), I will be able to free my hand.

Tapping, then pounding, my multi-tool's 3in stainless-steel blade against the stone, I try to hit the same spot with each strike. Everything else – the pain, thoughts of rescue, the accident – recedes. I'm taking action. But the going is slow. I unfold the file from the tool, and use it to etch the boulder.

When I stop to clean the file, the grooves are filled with metal flecks. I'm wearing down the edge without any effect on the chockstone. I realise this boulder isn't sandstone. It seems to have come from the darker, erosion-resistant layer that formed the overhanging lip I'd hung from before dropping into the sand about 2 hours ago.

Chipping and lifting have played out unsuccessfully.

I contemplate amputating my arm. My biggest concerns are a cutting tool that can do the job, and a tourniquet that will keep me from bleeding out.

I wonder if it wouldn't be faster to carve out the wall. Switching back to the blade, I strike the wall above my right wrist. My arm is in the way. The knife skitters across the pink sloping canyonside.

There will be daylight until around 9pm. I brush grit from my right forearm and return to hacking. Tick, tick, tick. Pathetically minute, the sound of my knife tapping at the rock resounds through the canyon.

Daylight comes

In the coldest hours before dawn, from 3 until 6, I hack at the chockstone. I take stock of the rock I've managed to eliminate during 15 tiring hours. I would have to chip for 150 hours to free my hand. It's cold in the depths of the fissure, but I can see daylight on the north wall 20m (66ft) above me. I turn off my headlamp. I have made it through the night.

Around 9.30am a dagger of sunlight appears on the canyon floor, a metre behind my shoes. After 5 minutes, I can extend my left leg behind me so the sunshine caresses my ankle. For 10 minutes, I relish the soothing warmth on my calves, alternating between stretching out my left and right leg as sunlight moves across the floor. Climbing up the north wall, the light dagger bends and warps over the sandstone undulations until it ascends above my leg's reach. It is the only direct sun I will get.

It is time to rig a lifting system. If I can rotate the chockstone up maybe a foot, I can pull out my hand. I unclip my fluorescent yellow webbing and string the 8m (25ft) length back and forth across the chockstone.

A triangular horn sticks out in the middle of the shelf 2m (6ft) over my head. I tie my rope to the webbing and try throwing the rope, then drawing the webbing over the horn. Time after time, it pulls free and falls to the sand.

A fissure on the horn catches my eye. The next time I throw and pull the rope, as the knot is about to crest the horn, I twitch the webbing. It responds by slipping back into the slot. Aha! Untying rope and webbing, I slip a rappel ring[1] over the yellow strap and tie knots in the webbing. I tug with my left hand, tightening the loop around the outcropping. The webbing doesn't creep at all as I apply my weight.

Unfortunately, I don't have pulleys with me; I do have carabiners[2], though they'll have greater friction loss. I call upon my training in search and rescue and design a scheme that will replicate the systems we use to evacuate patients from rock-faces. I add loops clipped to carabiners to connect the rope back to itself. With two changes in direction, I've theoretically tripled the force applied at the haul point. The friction is probably halving that advantage.

At the end of the haul line, I tie slip-knots that slide onto stopper knots, creating foot loops. I can now put most of my weight on the line. However, because I'm using a dynamic climbing rope, meant to absorb the energy of a fall, I lose much of the force I'm exerting. I never once budge the rock.

Losing hope

Chipping and lifting have played out unsuccessfully. I contemplate amputating my arm. My biggest concerns are a cutting tool that can do the job, and a tourniquet that will keep me from bleeding out.

Even with my sharper multi-tool blade, I won't be able to saw through my bones. I've seen the hacksaws that Civil War doctors used, and I don't have even a rudimentary saw.

Loops of webbing tied around my forearm are too loose to stop my circulation. I clip the gate of my last unused carabiner through the loops and rotate it twice. The purple webbing presses deeply into my forearm, and the skin nearer my wrist takes on the pallor of a fish belly. I've fashioned an effective tourniquet.

I wonder about my courage and as a test hold the shorter blade of my multi-tool to my skin a few inches from my trapped wrist, indenting my flesh. I feel vaguely ill and I retch. The optimism that has graced me is gone. Lonely and scared, I whimper to myself, 'I am going to die.'

But a regimen of fidgeting and rest has got me through another night. It is a ghost-white sunrise. The day resolves to a cloudless blue.

I haven't given amputation a full chance. The problem is staunching the blood. How can I improve my tourniquet? I need something more elastic than webbing … That's it! Elastic! The neoprene tubing insulation from my water pack is perfect – stretchy but strong.

Using my left hand to wrap the black neoprene twice around my right forearm, I tie an overhand knot and tighten one end in my teeth, then triple the knot. I twist the carabiner six times. What little pink is left in my forearm fades to white, and the flesh between my elbow and the tourniquet flashes to bright red. Oh yeah, this is way better than the webbing.

Ready for the next step, I take my multi-tool and hold the longer knife blade against my upper forearm. I press on the blade and draw the knife

---

1 **Rappel ring** Ring attached to the end of a rope in abseiling.
2 **Carabiner** Metal ring with a spring-loaded gate, used to connect ropes.

across. Nothing happens. I press harder. No cut, nothing. Extracting the sharper short knife, I saw at my forearm, growing frustrated. How the hell am I going to carve through two bones with a knife that won't cut my skin?

Embittered, I set the knife atop the chockstone and loosen the tourniquet. After a minute, the weak blood flow in my arm raises irritated red lines where I was sawing with the knife.

The dagger of sunlight appears, and I stretch out to it. Then, for the first time, I feel pressure in my bladder. I unzip my shorts, and turn to urinate. The sand soaks up the liquid before it can puddle, seemingly absorbing my urine faster than it falls.

Mustering courage

Around 3.35 on Monday afternoon, I have to urinate again. 'How is this possible?' I wonder. That's twice today, despite the fact that I'm dehydrated.

I transfer the contents of my bladder into my empty water reservoir, saving the orangish-brown discharge for the unappetising but inevitable time when it will be the only liquid I have. I should have saved the first batch, I realise. It was clearer and didn't smell as nasty.

Slowly, I become aware of my knife. Suddenly, I know what I am about to do. Mustering my courage, I tie my tourniquet as refined yesterday.

Folding open the shorter of the two knives, I grasp it in my fist. I pick a spot. My fist thrusts the 4cm (1½ in) blade down, burying it to the hilt in the meat of my forearm.

My vision warps with astonishment. I bend my head to my arm, and my surroundings leave behind hallucinogenic trails. Yesterday it didn't seem possible for my knife to get through my skin, but it did. When I wiggle the tool slightly, I feel the blade knocking on my radius – my upper forearm bone.

There is barely any sensation below skin level. The leathery-tough epidermis is twice as thick as I thought. Yellow fatty tissue lies under my skin. When I root around, burgundy-coloured blood seeps into the wound. I tap the bone again. The soft thock-thock tells me I have reached the end of this experiment. I cannot cut through my bones.

Sweating from the adrenaline, I set my multi-tool on the chockstone and pick up my water bottle. It's not time for my next sip, but I've earned this. As the first drops splash my lip, I continue to tilt the bottle up, feeling like I'm doing something naughty, but I don't care; the fact that I shouldn't makes me enjoy it more.

I close my eyes … Oh, God. After an all-too-brief 3 seconds, I swallow the last of my water, and it's gone. My body wails for the water to keep coming, but there's not a drop left. I don't linger on it. I disengage the tourniquet – it's making my whole arm ache. The bleeding is less than I would have expected. I make the connection that since the chockstone has pinched off the arteries in my hand, it has reduced the blood flow in my arm.

Confusion, delirium and cold compete through the night, warping small segments of time into infinities of struggle against the cruel elements.

Mosquitoes and a breeze usher in the morning, and after 2 hours of swatting at the nagging insects, torrents of gold light splash on the walls behind me, flushing the oppression from the canyon.

Improvised surgery *Aron devised a tourniquet (top) from neoprene tubing and a carabiner, knowing that he would have to staunch the blood flow if he successfully amputated his arm. His multi-tool (below) provided the knife and pliers he needed to perform the rudimentary 'operation'.*

I update my tallies in my head: 96 hours of sleep deprivation, 90 hours trapped, 29 hours that I've been sipping my urine, and 25 hours since I finished off my fresh water.

What am I missing here? What have I ignored because it wasn't obvious? Arching my head back, I see several stones lodged in the debris around a chockstone. Slate-black with a reddish tint, an egg-shaped stone stands out; it doesn't seem to be sandstone but a mineralised layer. Reaching up above my head, I pull out the rock.

The black stone in my hand is the weight of a shot-put. I can lift it without straining myself, and smash it into the boulder without letting go of it.

My left hand quickly bruises from the recoil of each blow of my hand-held hammer. After dozens of hits, I have to stop.

It is now Thursday. I should have died days ago. I don't understand how I lived through last night's frigid conditions.

Since the hammer rock tenderised my left hand, all I've had left to do is wait. Nothing gives even a hint that the stillness will break. But I can make it break. I can ignore the pain and resume smashing the chockstone with the hand-held wrecking ball. I reach for the rock.

The bruises on my thumb scream for reprieve from the first blow through to the fifth, when I pause. Adrenaline channels into anger, and I raise the hammer again. Bonk! Again I strike the boulder, the pain in my hand flaring. Screeaatch! Rage blooms in my mind, amid a cloud of pulverised grit.

I force myself to stop. I've created a mess. I take my knife and begin using the blade to brush the dirt away from the open wound. Sweeping grit off my thumb, I accidentally gouge myself. A thin piece of decayed flesh peels back like a skin of boiled milk.

Out of curiosity, I poke my thumb with the knife. On second prodding, the blade releases a tell-tale hiss. Escaping gases are not good. The smell, faint to my desensitised nose, is the stench of a far-off carcass.

Will to live *Free at last, and standing next to a welcome pool of water below the Big Drop, Aron stopped to photograph himself, one of the first shots taken post-amputation.*

Epiphany

Realisation hits me – my hand is poisoning my body. I lash out in fury, trying to yank my forearm out from the sandstone handcuff, wanting to rid myself of any connection to this decomposing appendage.

I thrash myself forward and back, side to side, up and down. I scream as I batter my body to and fro against the canyon walls. I feel my arm bend unnaturally in the grip of the chockstone. An epiphany strikes me with the magnificent glory of a holy intervention. Like bending a 2 x 4in piece of wood in a vice, I can bow my arm until it snaps!

Under the power of this divine interaction, I crouch under the boulder and drop as far down as I can. I put my left hand under the boulder and push hard, to exert maximum downward force on my radius bone. A muted cap-gun shot reverberates up and down the canyon. I feel a gap between the edges of my cleanly broken arm bone.

HOW LOW CAN YOU GO? Narrow Slot Canyon, in Zion National Park, Utah, provides an exhilarating challenge for a canyoneer.

Sculpted by nature

SLOT CANYONS are among the wonders of the natural world, things of beauty and mystery. They exert a powerful fascination for cavers and canyoneers, but are not for the faint-hearted or the claustrophobic. They are formed – usually of sandstone or limestone; sometimes of basalt or granite – by the passage of water over millions of years, and while they may be only a metre or so wide, they can be 100m (330ft) deep.

To reach the bottom of these canyons, it is often necessary to wade through water, to scramble over boulders, and to rappel/abseil down a sheer rock-face, using a rope and friction devices, executing a series of backward leaps. Chockstones – loose boulders, wedged between the canyon walls – are not uncommon.

Nowhere in the world is there a greater density of slot canyons than in the US state of Utah. Sculpted by nature, these canyons mainly comprise sandstone in shades of red and orange, on which the sunshine magically plays.

The more inaccessible a slot canyon, the greater its appeal to aficionados, for whom remote Blue John Canyon offers some of the most exciting challenges in the American west. It is part of the 'Robbers' Roost' area, the one-time stamping ground of outlaws such as Butch Cassidy, the Sundance Kid and Kid Curry. Blue John itself is named after John Griffith, a small-time crook, horse thief, robber and wrangler, who had the physical distinction of having one blue eye and one brown.

Without pause, I hump my body up over the chockstone. I grab the back of the chockstone with my left hand, pulling with every bit of ferocity I can muster, and a second cap-gun shot ends the anticipation of my ulna bone. Sweating and euphoric, I touch my right arm below my wrist, and pull my right shoulder away from the boulder. Both bones have splintered.

Overcome with excitement, I skip the tourniquet, place the shorter and sharper of my multi-tool's blades between two blue veins and push the knife into my wrist to its hilt. In a blaze of pain, I know the job is just starting.

The alternative is a slow demise. My first act is to sever as much skin as I can, without tearing the noodle-like veins. Once I've opened a large enough hole, I stow the knife, holding its handle in my teeth, poke my left forefinger and thumb inside my arm and feel around. Sorting through bizarre and unfamiliar textures, I feel bundles of muscle fibres and two pairs of cleanly fractured but jagged bone ends. Prodding and pinching, I can distinguish between the hard tendons and the soft, rubbery arteries.

Withdrawing my bloody fingers, I isolate a strand of muscle between the knife and my thumb, and using the blade like a paring knife, slice through a filament. I repeat the action a dozen times.

When I find any of the pencil-thick arteries, I tug it a little and remove it from the strand about to be severed. Finally, about a third of the way through the assorted soft tissues, I cut a vein. I haven't put on my tourniquet yet. The desire to keep cutting, to get free, is so powerful that I rationalise I haven't lost much blood yet, only a few drops.

The 'operation'

Another 20 minutes slip past. I am engrossed in making the surgical work go as fast as possible. Stymied by the centimetre wide yellowish tendon in the middle of my forearm, I stop the operation to don my tourniquet. By this time, several ounces of blood have dripped onto the canyon wall. The blood loss has accelerated, and I don't want to lose blood unnecessarily.

Continuing with the surgery, I clear out the muscles surrounding the tendon. Sawing aggressively, I can't put a dent in the amazingly strong tendon. It's like a double-thick strip of fibre-reinforced box-packaging tape, creased over itself in tiny folds. I reconfigure my blood-slippery multi-tool for the pliers. I squeeze and twist, tearing away a fragment.

Little by little, I rip through the tendon, then switch back to the knife, using my teeth. I put the knife's edge under a pale white nerve strand and pluck it, like lifting a guitar string off its frets, until it snaps. A flood of pain recalibrates my personal scale of what hurt feels like – it's as though I had thrust my arm into a cauldron of magma.

Minutes later, I recover enough to continue. The last step is stretching the skin of my outer wrist tight and sawing the blade into the wall, as if slicing gristle on a board. The adrenaline surges through me.

It is 11.32am on Thursday, May 1, 2003. For the second time in my life, I am being born. This time I understand the significance as none of us can the first time. Pulling tight the remaining connective tissues, I rock the knife against the wall, and the final thin strand of flesh tears loose. I fall back against the northern wall of the canyon, my mind surfing on euphoria.

Finally, about a third of the way through the assorted soft tissues, I cut a vein. I haven't put on my tourniquet yet.

I am free!

The exhilarating shock is the most intense feeling of my life. I feel drugged and off balance but buoyed by my freedom. My head bobs and dips to my chest before I right it and steady myself against the wall.

I set my knife on the chockstone and package my stump in a plastic grocery bag and a makeshift sling. I need to get moving. I toss a few loose articles into my pack – the empty water reservoir, the bottle of urine, my pocket knife – and pause as I pick up my camera. I take two photos of my severed hand. White bone ends protrude from the gory muddle. It is an unsentimental goodbye. I grab two dozen coils of climbing rope in my left hand and stumble off down the canyon.

Successfully negotiating the 20m (65ft) Big Drop, Aron hiked on until he met some walkers. A helicopter was looking for him, and soon he was in hospital. Since then, fitted with a new prosthetic arm, he has returned to Blue John Canyon. ■

Where are they now?

THE CHOCKSTONE THAT CRUSHED ARON RALSTON'S ARM did not crush his spirit, nor has his ordeal discouraged him from seeking adventure. Using a prosthetic arm, and snapping on special attachments, he has been able to return to mountaineering, skiing, rock-climbing and rafting. In 2008 he was in South America, climbing 6,000m (20,000ft) peaks. 'And I went to Alaska,' he says, 'and climbed Denali, also known as Mount McKinley, and skied off the summit, which is around 20,300ft.' He also plans to lead a party through the Grand Canyon, in the footsteps of one of his heroes, John Wesley Powell, a fellow amputee who led the first such expedition, in 1869.

Aron is active on the motivational-speaking circuit, addressing corporate groups and schools, as well as speaking out for the wilderness. 'That's an important part of my life. I feel like I'm giving back to the wilderness, which gave me my story and gave me my life again.'

He sounds happy, robust, entirely well-adjusted, but the truth is that it has been tough for him, emotionally and physically. The man named 2003 *GQ* Man of the Year and *Vanity Fair* Person of the Year was for some while in torment. 'I've gone through my struggles,' he confesses. 'When I was laid up after the accident, with all the surgery, and with the pain, I felt really depressed. I was on powerful painkillers. I couldn't relate to my family, I felt disconnected from them, and I couldn't do anything without a lot of help.' He was also battling a bone infection, and with even the strongest antibiotics was given only a 50–50 chance of survival.

With the publication of his book detailing his adventures, he began a gruelling three-month world tour, an endless round of interviews, which pushed him to the edge of distress and left him contemplating suicide. 'I felt I'd lost my life. I didn't get out of the canyon in order to do this.'

Today he lives with his girlfriend, Jessica, in Boulder, Colorado, and is going through adjustments, which are the subject of his second book, a work provisionally titled *Climbing to Consciousness*.

'In my fantasy, I envisage that I can be married, have children, be in a committed relationship and still go on adventures and live the life I've been used to living. For most of the past five years I have been gone from my home about 300 days out of the year, but that's not realistic. It might have to be just one adventure a year. Then, in some ways, to be in a relationship ... there's adventure in that, too.'

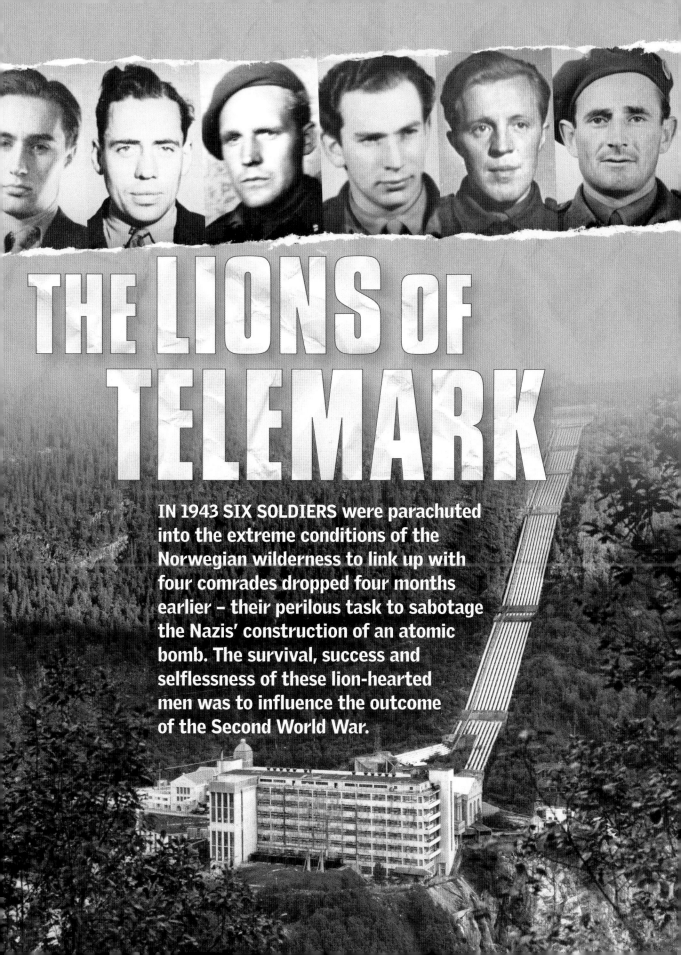

THE LIONS OF TELEMARK

IN 1943 SIX SOLDIERS were parachuted into the extreme conditions of the Norwegian wilderness to link up with four comrades dropped four months earlier – their perilous task to sabotage the Nazis' construction of an atomic bomb. The survival, success and selflessness of these lion-hearted men was to influence the outcome of the Second World War.

On the night of November 19, 1942, two Halifax
bombers, each of them towing a Horsa glider filled with British
commandos, took off from a base in Scotland. The two pairs of aircraft
were headed for the county of Telemark, in southern Norway, where they
were to meet up with four British-trained Norwegian agents who had been
parachuted in a month before. The job of the Norwegian scouts was to guide
in the planes in using a radio beacon, then lead the commandos to their
objective – an industrial plant called Vemork, close to the town of Rjukan.
The aim of the mission was to blow up this factory. The attackers had not
been told why it had to be destroyed; all they knew was that its output
had a secret and deeply sinister significance for the German war effort.

Operation Freshman, as it was codenamed, had been meticulously
planned – and it went horribly wrong. For reasons that have never
been established, one of the Halifaxes began to lose altitude soon after
crossing the Norwegian coastline, and released its glider well short of the
target zone. The glider, with the tow rope still attached to its nose, was
dragged earthward and crash-landed on a mountainside. Three of the 17
commandos on board were killed outright; six were badly injured. The
Halifax, meanwhile, cleared the summit of the mountain, only to plough
into the next peak, 8km (5 miles) on. All four crewmen died. As for the
second Halifax, it reached the area where the four Norwegians were
waiting, and for a short while was locked in on the Eureka radio beacon.
But somehow the Halifax pilot lost his grip on this invisible lifeline, and
could not visually identify the rendezvous amid the confusing jigsaw of
lakes and snowfields. To the dismay of the men on the ground, he gave up
the search when he was directly above them, and turned for home with the
glider still in tow. But as he appoached the Norwegian coast the tow-line
between the aircraft, made brittle by ice and buffeted by high winds,
snapped in two. The glider went down too fast and too steeply, and when it
hit the ground eight of the men on board were killed, five more badly hurt.

All the surviving commandos from both gliders were quickly rounded
up by the Gestapo. The commandos from the first glider were briefly
interrogated, then – against all the rules of war – taken out and shot. As for
the injured men, they were not treated for their wounds, but administered
poison by a German medical officer. The five uninjured men were
interrogated under torture over a matter of weeks, after which they too
were shot. From the wreckage of one of the gliders, the Germans retrieved
a map on which the Vemork plant was ringed in blue ink.

From Freshman to Gunnerside

The bloody outcome of Operation Freshman was a double disaster. Not
only did the attack fail utterly, but the Germans were now aware that the
Allies knew what went on at Vemork, and dearly wanted to stop it. The
significance of Vemork lay in the fact that it was the only plant in Europe
capable of producing 'heavy water', a substance that (given the technology
available in the 1940s) was central to the process of producing weapons-
grade plutonium (see page 162). Vemork's production of heavy water
proved that the Nazi nuclear programme was well under way. By the same

Heroes, every one *Six of the brave
Norwegian soldiers (previous page,
left to right: Joachim Rønneberg, Knut
Haukelid, Kasper Idland, Fredrik
Kayser, Birger Strømsheim and Hans
Storhaug) who attacked Vemork
hydroelectric plant (previous page,
background) in Operation Gunnerside.
In all, nine men took part in the raid,
with a tenth left behind to radio the
outcome back to Britain.*

token, cutting the supply of heavy water was the best way of stopping that programme in its tracks.

So another attempt had to be made to strike at Vemork. This time the task was assigned to the Special Operations Executive (SOE), the organisation set up by Winston Churchill to conduct sabotage behind enemy lines – or, as he put it 'to set Europe ablaze'. The leadership of SOE quickly concluded that the operation would be best carried out by a small band of committed Norwegians rather than a large contingent of British sappers. Many Norwegian soldiers and fighters had escaped their homeland by boat or other means when the Germans invaded. Hundreds of them were now stranded in Britain, waiting and hoping for an opportunity to hit back at the enemy. It was from this pool of talent that SOE had drawn the four operatives who had parachuted into Norway ahead of the ill-fated Freshman operation. Known collectively by the codename 'Grouse', they were Arne Kjelstrup, Jens Poulsson, Knut Haugland and Claus Helberg. All but Kjelstrup were born and raised in Rjukan. They knew the mountain country around the Vemork plant: it was their boyhood playground, the place where they had learned to ski. That was why they were selected for the mission in the first place. The four Grouse men were now ordered to stay put on the bleak Hardanger plateau, though it had never been the plan that they would have to remain there for weeks or months. They had very few supplies, but somehow they were to keep out of sight and stay alive as the fearsome and unforgiving Norwegian winter set in. Meanwhile, SOE would come up with a new plan, and a new team to implement it.

16. The leader will bear in mind that the stocks of fluid in the basement are the main target, and that these must be destroyed regardless of the remaining targets.

17. Any Norwegian guards in the building will be bound and gagged.

18. German guards will be put out of action as circumstances demand.

19. Charge laying will proceed according to instruction given at S.T.S.17.   Priority of targets will be as follows:
    a) Basement H.C. plant
    b) 1st floor Electrolyser No.1. (N.X. Corner)

Acting under orders *The Special Operations Executive (SOE) compiled an exhaustive dossier of material relating to Operation Gunnerside, now stored in the National Archives for England and Wales at Kew, London. Typed instructions were precise and matter of fact, right down to the different treatment to be meted out to Norwegian and German guards – 'bound and gagged' and 'put out of action', respectively.*

The new operation against Vemork was to be called Gunnerside, because this was the name of the Yorkshire estate where Sir Charles Hambro, head of SOE, liked to shoot gamebirds – and the first task of the new group would be to find Grouse. The officer selected to lead the operation was Joachim Rønneberg, a 22-year-old lieutenant in the Royal Norwegian Army. He was swiftly despatched to London to be briefed by Leif Tronstad, head of Section IV of the Norwegian High Command, which dealt with intelligence and sabotage in the home country. Before the war, Tronstad had been a professor at the Norwegian Institute of Technology. It was SOE's immense good fortune that in this capacity Tronstad had been responsible for designing the Vemork plant. He had been on site when it was built, and he knew its every corridor and cranny. This was naturally a huge boon for the planning of the operation.

But the things that Tronstad told Rønneberg about Vemork made the idea of attacking it sound little short of suicidal. For sound industrial reasons, the Vemork hydroelectric plant was built on a narrow ridge half way up an impossibly steep gorge. The mountainside rose almost vertically behind the complex, and at the top there were huge reservoirs of water that provided power to the plant's turbines. In front of the plant, the rockface fell away in a sheer drop of 200m (660ft) to the river at the bottom of the gorge. So the main block, where the heavy water was accumulating, was unreachable – like a cupboard fixed far too high on a kitchen wall. There were only two ways to get into Vemork: a railway that ran along a narrow shelf cut out of the rock, through a gateway and into the plant's main yard; and a suspended road, about 75m (250ft) long, that stretched like a drawbridge across the gorge. The gorge itself was all but unclimbable, especially in winter when it was coated with ice; and the bridge was easy to defend against attack. The reservoirs were closely patrolled, and after the Freshman debacle all approaches from above had been sown with mines. There was a garrison of German soldiers inside the plant, and there were machine-gun posts and floodlights positioned on rooftops.

The plant could not effectively be bombed from the air, and in any case the precious heavy water was collected in a basement room of the main building, which was a faceless seven-storey structure made of steel and concrete. The 'high-concentration room', as it was called, was as solidly constructed as a bank vault. Even a direct hit with a bomb was unlikely to damage it. So Vemork as a whole was an accidental fortress, as loftily inaccessible as a Tibetan monastery and as impregnable as a Norman keep. Nevertheless, Rønneberg's mission was to find a way to get his men inside the complex, to penetrate the high-concentration room undetected by the Germans, and to destroy the canisters containing the heavy water. He and his men were then to get themselves out, or to die fighting inside the plant. That was the essence of Operation Gunnerside.

Rønneburg selected the five men to go to Vemork with him. The man he chose as his second-in-command was Knut Haukelid, seven years Rønneberg's senior, and a rugged outdoorsman even by Norwegian standards. The others were Hans Storhaug (nicknamed 'The Chicken'), Fredrik Kayser, Birger Strømsheim, Fredrik Kayser and Kasper Idland. They were all passionate anti-Nazis, all junior officers or NCOs in the Norwegian Army, and all volunteers for this mission. The Gunnerside men were transferred to a training camp where they learned more about their task, and acquired the special skills necessary to carry it out. A wooden mock-up of the high-concentration room was built for them, complete with realistic models of the heavy-water cells, looking like a row of tall, thin fire extinguishers. The men practised moulding plastic explosive and attaching it to each of the cells, setting the fiddly fuses and detonators, working

Plan of attack *The dossier produced by the SOE in advance of the operation included a map of the Telemark region (opposite, top) and a detailed sketch of the focus of the attack (below).* **(A)** *Plant outbuildings at the end of the railway line.* **(B)** *The main plant building, which the saboteurs had to enter via a cable-duct after the door leading down to the basement was not unlocked as planned.* **(C)** *The crucial basement area housing the heavy water cells.*

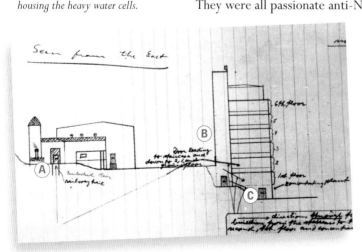

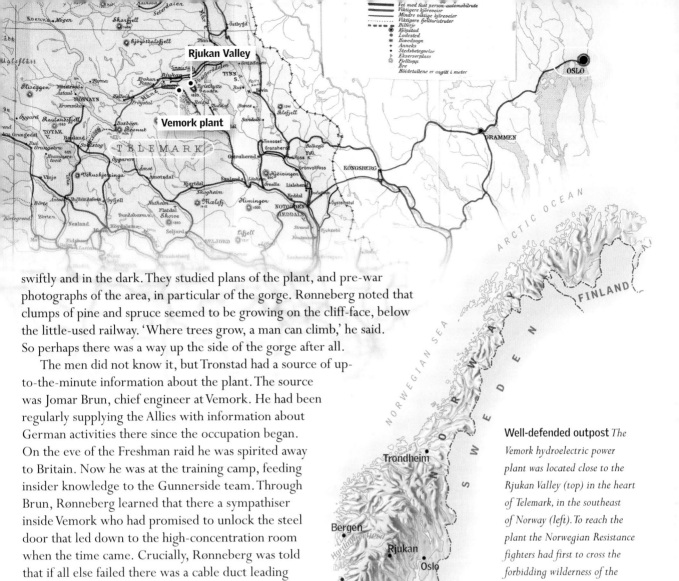

Rjukan Valley

Vemork plant

TELEMARK

OSLO

DRAMMEN

KONOSBERG

ARCTIC OCEAN

FINLAND

NORWEGIAN SEA

N O R W A Y

S W E D E N

Trondheim

Bergen

Rjukan

Oslo

Stavanger

Well-defended outpost *The
Vemork hydroelectric power
plant was located close to the
Rjukan Valley (top) in the heart
of Telemark, in the southeast
of Norway (left). To reach the
plant the Norwegian Resistance
fighters had first to cross the
forbidding wilderness of the
Hardanger plateau from the west.*

swiftly and in the dark. They studied plans of the plant, and pre-war
photographs of the area, in particular of the gorge. Rønneberg noted that
clumps of pine and spruce seemed to be growing on the cliff-face, below
the little-used railway. 'Where trees grow, a man can climb,' he said.
So perhaps there was a way up the side of the gorge after all.

The men did not know it, but Tronstad had a source of up-
to-the-minute information about the plant. The source
was Jomar Brun, chief engineer at Vemork. He had been
regularly supplying the Allies with information about
German activities there since the occupation began.
On the eve of the Freshman raid he was spirited away
to Britain. Now he was at the training camp, feeding
insider knowledge to the Gunnerside team. Through
Brun, Rønneberg learned that there a sympathiser
inside Vemork who had promised to unlock the steel
door that led down to the high-concentration room
when the time came. Crucially, Rønneberg was told
that if all else failed there was a cable duct leading
from outside the plant to a room right next to where
the heavy water was drip-drip-dripping into metal
canisters. Brun had recently crawled down the duct
himself to inspect a leaking pipe, so he knew a man could just about
squeeze through. This, surely, was the Achilles' heel of Fortress Vemork …

Rendezvous in the snow

On February 17, 1943, the six Norwegian patriots leaped from a British
bomber and parachuted down onto the frozen Hardanger plateau.
Somewhere in this vast white wilderness was the cabin where the four
men of the advance party, who had been hiding out on Hardanger since
the middle of October. They knew their fellow-countrymen were coming,
and for them it was not a moment too soon. The Grouse men had been
living on short rations for months, supplemented by soup made from
the brains and offal of reindeer (far more nutritious than the lean cuts of
meat). The Grouse contingent were all physically exhausted, and seriously
malnourished. They sorely needed the fresh supplies of food that the
Gunnerside team were bringing with them.

The Nazi A-bomb

THE NAZI NUCLEAR PROGRAMME got under way on the first day of the war. On September 1, 1939, a group of German physicists formed the *Uranverein* – 'the Uranium Club' – its function to build an atom bomb. The club held its first meeting on September 16. Among those present were Otto Hahn, the so-called 'father of nuclear chemistry' and a future Nobel prize winner, and Hans Geiger, inventor of the Geiger counter. Notable by their absence was a large contingent of German physicists – some of them Jewish – who had fled Germany when Hitler came to power. The loss of their expertise put the German atom-bomb programme at a disadvantage. Moreover, many of the physicists who fled the Nazis later found work on the Manhattan Project that led to the dropping of the first atomb bomb on Hiroshima. So their forced emigration represented a double blow to Hitler's nuclear ambitions.

By the beginning of the 1940s, it was common knowledge in scientific circles that certain forms of uranium and plutonium could be used to make a devastating weapon. The technical problem for both Germany and the Allies was to acquire sufficient quantities of the right type (or 'isotope') of these materials. Germany's method depended on using non-fissile uranium ore to 'breed' weapons-grade plutonium in a reactor. This process is itself a kind of dampened-down nuclear reaction. It depends entirely on the availability of a substance to 'soak up' some of the electrons released during nuclear fission, and so prevent the reaction becoming uncontrollable.

'Heavy water' was this vital substance. It is chemically similar to ordinary water, except that the nucleus of each molecule contains a neutron (standard water molecules have no neutrons). 'Heavy water' exists naturally, but only in tiny quantities. So it needed to be artificially manufactured in industrial amounts. That is what the plant at Vemork was doing.

HEAVY WATER PRODUCTION The SOE dossier contained an image of the inside of Vemork hydroelectric plant.

But no sooner had Rønneberg's men landed on Norwegian soil than a vicious storm blew up. It quickly turned into a blizzard the like of which none of them had ever experienced. Battling against the fierce wind and the biting snow, they found their way to a deserted hut and forced the door. They bedded down, hoping that the next morning they might be able to set out in search of their comrades. But the storm did not let up the next day, or the day after that. In fact it grew stronger. The men were imprisoned by the weather. Two of them fell ill, and the unrelenting cold made all of them weary and stiff. It was not until the fifth morning that the day dawned bright and clear, and at last they could look for the members of Grouse.

Rønneberg's men set out that afternoon towards the cabin where they knew Grouse were holed up. To their astonishment, they soon saw a man heading towards them through the snow. They quickly apprehended the man who, taking them at first to be Germans, immediately began to proclaim that he was a good, loyal Nazi. This protestation almost got him killed, particularly since Gunnerside were under orders to be ruthless, and dispose of anyone they encountered who might jeopardise the mission. But Rønnenberg thought better of shooting him on the spot. He questioned the man, who gave his name as Kristian Kristiansen and admitted that he was a hunter on the trail of reindeer to sell on the black market. Rønneberg decided to use the man's local knowledge, and ordered him at gunpoint to lead them to Grouse's cabin. Kristiansen could barely believe what he had stumbled into: to be press-ganged in the middle of nowhere by a gang of Norwegian-speaking British soldiers …

The next day there was another strange encounter. Kristiansen spotted two men on skis up ahead. The Gunnerside team took cover in the snow, while Knut Haukelid was sent ahead to see who they were. He came up behind them unobserved, and got close enough to see that the men were filthy and ragged, like tramps. Their matted beards obscured their jaundiced features, and their shoulders were hunched like old men. Haukelid coughed loudly and the men span round. Now he knew them, beards or no beards: it was Helberg and Kjelstrup. The two contingents had found each other at last. 'We were delighted at meeting again,' Haukelid said. 'And we expressed our feelings as strongly as young Norwegians can. There was back-slapping and much strong hearty cursing.'

Rønneberg released Kristiansen that evening, having given him a bar of English chocolate and a blood-curdling warning not to breathe a word of what he had seen. That night, over a celebratory dinner of reindeer, dried fruit and coffee, Rønneberg took his men through the details of the plan. They would divide into two groups – a demolition party under the command of Rønneberg himself, and a covering party under Haukelid. Both groups would have a full set of explosives. If anything happened to the demolition party, it was down to the covering party to finish the job, whatever the cost. The covering party were also to guard the escape route, and give the German guards something to think about once the alarm was raised. All of them were to wear their British army uniforms: it had to be clear to the Germans that this was a British military operation, not the work of the Norwegian resistance, because a Norwegian-led act of sabotage would bring reprisals against the local population. They would attack in five days' time.

In the meantime, Claus Helberg was detailed to don civilian clothes, so that he could ski out alone to the gorge and reconnoitre. Rønneberg needed him to identify a negotiable path down to the river, and a climbable route up the other side to the railway line that ran into the plant. Helberg spent a pleasant afternoon exploring the foot of the gorge. He found a small furrow in the rockface a mile or two downriver from the plant. There were cracks big enough for a hand or the toe of a boot, and roots and branches that a man could hold onto. It would be a heck of a climb – especially in the cold and the dark and carrying a heavy kit bag –but it was just about negotiable by a climber who was very good – or very desperate. Helberg reported his find to Rønneberg, along with the good news that the railway appeared to be unpatrolled. So long as the tracks were not mined, they ought to be able to get to the very gates of Vemork without being spotted.

A night on the mountain

At 8pm on February 28th, Operation Gunnerside finally began. The men left the hut that was their forward base. The weather had turned mild, and a thaw was setting in. The snow was turning soft as they made their steep descent, and there were times when they had to take off their skis and wade thigh-deep through the snow. The thick woods that hid them from view also impeded their progress: the men stumbled on hidden roots, or got tangled in inconvenient branches. There came a point when there was both a gap in the forest and a break in the cloud – and in that moonlit moment they caught a glimpse of the target, looming large across the other side of the gorge. For some of the men it was their first sight of Vemork; others already knew that huge, squat rectangle of concrete, having watched it being built when they were boys. All of them could hear it: Vemork emitted a low thrumming sound, rhythmic like a giant heartbeat.

The raiders arrived at the bottom of the gorge, and splashed quickly across the melting surface of the still-frozen river. It occurred to some of them that if the thaw proceeded any quicker, they would be cut off by fast-flowing water on the way back. Helberg led the way to the place where the 200m (660ft) ascent of the gorge was to begin. The weather made the climb more perilous than even Helberg had imagined. The warm wind that had brought the thaw grew strong, and knocked them sideways as they clung with their fingertips to tiny splits and wrinkles in the cliff-face. The covering of ice, which in cold weather adhered to the rock like dry plaster, was now slippery and brittle. Rivulets of ice-cold water ran down, numbing the men's fingers as they scrabbled and fumbled for a sure hold. It was little short of miraculous that all of them made it to the top, where for a minute they lay down beside the railway to recover their breath and their nerve.

It was now gone 11pm. The men moved silently forward to a small transformer shed, next to the track about 400m (¼ mile) from the entrance to Vemork. Some of them went inside the hut to keep warm; Rønneberg stayed outside to watch and wait. He could see the two German soldiers who manned the bridge across the gorge, and he knew that the guard would be relieved at midnight. Half an hour after that, when the new sentries had had a chance to relax into their dull nocturnal routine, the raiders would go in. Sure enough, two soldiers emerged from the barrack yard at 11.57pm, and the two men on the bridge trudged wearily back the other way. The Norwegians crouched silently by the shed, biding their time, while the loud throb of the factory marked out the passing seconds like a great ticking clock.

At 12.30am precisely, Rønneberg gave the signal. Arne Kjelstrup, armed with a long pair of metal-cutters, scurried up to the gate and sheared through the padlocked chain that held it shut. That flimsy chain was all that barred the way into one of Germany's most secret and highly prized military installations, and it was broken in seconds. Kjelstrup swung the gate ajar, and the other men rushed forward through the gap. The men of the covering team immediately fanned out to their preordained posts. Haukelid and Poulsson took up a position behind some storage tanks, where they had a clear view of the guards' barracks. In the event of an alert, they could mow the Germans down as they came out of the door. Storhaug went forward to a position where he could cover the two sentries on the bridge. Helberg stayed close to the open railway gate to guard the escape route.

Rønneberg and the demolition team headed straight for the electrolysis building. They rounded the corner to get to the steel door that they had been promised would be left open for them. To Rønneberg's dismay, it was locked. Strømsheim and Idland went off in search of other doors, while Rønneberg retraced his steps, looking for the cable duct that Tronstad had told him about. On the way he came across a low window. He peered through scratches in the black-out paint and saw that beyond the glass – tantalisingly close – was the high-concentration room he had come to destroy. He could see the rows of canisters, looking just like the mock-ups he had practised on, and he could see a Norwegian civilian sitting at a desk. It would have been easy to smash the glass and climb straight in, but Rønneberg didn't dare: the noise could easily alert the guards in the barracks, only metres away. It would take more time, but he would have to use the cable-duct. There it was: a hole in the wall, like the narrow doorway of an igloo, a short way up the wall at the top of a metal ladder.

Rønneberg finished his preparations and put a match to the shortest fuse. 'Run up the stairs,' he told the nightwatchman as they all left the high concentration area. 'You have 30 seconds.'

Rønneberg climbed the ladder and, pushing his rucksack of plastic explosives ahead of him, wriggled into the hole. Fredrik Kayser crawled in right behind him. They dragged themselves over the mass of cables and pipes, until they came to an open hole in the floor of the tunnel. They dropped through this hole and found themselves – exactly as they had hoped – in a basement area adjacent to the high concentration room. They were standing outside the door, on which hung a notice saying 'No Admittance'. Rønneberg opened the door and stepped in. 'Hands up,' he said to the astounded night watchman. 'We are British soldiers'.

Kayser kept the watchman under guard, and took his key to the steel door leading back out into the yard. Rønneberg set about laying the charges. The explosives were malleable and sticky, like plasticine. He began to wrap a long sausage-shaped charge around the neck of each of the 18 cells, and planted fuses in each one. He was half way through the task when there was crash of glass. It was Idland and Strømsheim, kicking in the window that Rønneberg had peered through earlier. They didn't know he was already in there, and so had decided that to reach the objective they had to take the terrible risk of alerting the Germans to their presence.

But the Germans remained oblivious; they heard nothing above the constant hum of the factory turbines. Rønneberg finished his preparations and put a match to the shortest fuse. 'Run up the stairs,' he told the nightwatchman as they all left the high concentration room. 'You have 30 seconds.' The soldiers then dashed out of the basement, and raced towards the railway gate. They were no more than 20m (65ft) from the building when they heard a muffled, almost anticlimactic thud. Whatever happened now, it was mission accomplished: about 500 litres (110 gallons) of heavy water, the product of many months' output, was gushing down the drains in the floor of the high-concentration room.

The covering party, still in position, heard the explosion and expected all hell to break loose. But the reaction of the Germans was almost comically low-key. One soldier sauntered out of the barracks and peered into the night. He shone his torch up at the high reservoirs, thinking perhaps that the crumbling snow has set off a land mine up on the heights. He swept the torch around the yard, and its beam of his torch nearly fell on Haukelid. If it had, the German would have been cut down in an instant, and a full-scale firefight would have ensued. But the German soldier did not spot the Norwegian commandos crouching in the darkness. He went back indoors – so saving his own life and probably the lives of some of the raiders.

Rønneberg and his men now withdrew, swiftly and quietly. They slid and scrambled back down the gorge as fast as they dared. **The river at the bottom was still passable, but only just: they jumped and skipped from one unstable ice floe to the next, like children playing a deadly game of hopscotch.** As they reached the far side of the river the sirens went off in the plant. The urgent, screeching noise drove them on, like an animal snapping at their heels. But no Nazi posse emerged to pursue them: the Germans were frantically searching for the saboteurs inside the Vemork plant, believing that they could not possibly have made good their escape.

It took Rønneberg's men the rest of the night and most of next day to reach the relative safety of their hut on the Hardanger plateau. They were still only about 11km (7 miles) from the plant, but the mercurial Norwegian weather had changed again, and a ferocious storm was blowing. This time the harsh conditions were a blessing: no search party would be out looking for them yet; they could lay down and sleep.

It was several days before Rønneburg deemed it safe enough for them to move on. In the first days of March, the men of Telemark put on civilian clothes, and went their separate ways: five skied together all the way to neutral Sweden, and from there were flown back to Britain; two decamped to Oslo to await further orders; two remained incognito on the Hardanger plateau. By the time the Germans searched the area, their quarry was long gone, or had receded invisibly into civilian life. The Germans were in any case looking not for a tiny group of Norwegian patriots, but for a small army of British commandos – for surely no lesser force could have pulled off the raid on Vemork. The Wehrmacht in Norway ended up chasing its own ski tracks all over Hardanger.

Unforgotten heroes

It is remarkable that all the Vemork raiders came out of Operation Gunnerside alive, and also that not one shot was fired in anger during the attack. But the war was far from over, and there was still plenty of shooting to be done. In the months and years that followed the heavy-water operation, many of the participants went back to Norway to fight for the liberation of their country. By the time victory came, they had all done enough to be considered national war heroes – even without the vital work they did at Vemork.

> **The river at the bottom was still passable,** but only just: they jumped and skipped from one unstable ice floe to the next, like children playing a deadly game of hopscotch.

But it is for the Telemark raid that Joachim Rønneberg, Knut Haukelid and their comrades-in-arms will be remembered. Leif Tronstad said as much shortly before the men set off to carry out the attack. On a Scottish airfield he had remarked to Rønneberg: 'I cannot tell you why this mission is so important, but if you succeed it will live in Norway's memory for 100 years.' That prophecy is well on the way to coming true – and not just in Norway. The lion-hearted men of Telemark are remembered by all the nations that fought to defeat Nazism. In the years and decades since the war, it has often been claimed that no single military action did more to alter the course of the war than Operation Gunnerside.

But perhaps the most admiring assessment of the Telemark raiders was made by an enemy. General Nikolaus von Falkenhorst, commander of the Wehrmacht in Norway, went to Vemork the day after the attack to survey the damage. Standing in the high-concentration room, looking at the wreckage of the heavy-water cells, and with Nazi Germany's nuclear ambitions lying in puddles all around him, von Falkenhorst declared that this clinically executed strike was 'the finest coup I have seen in this war.' ■

What happened next?

THE RAID ON THE VEMORK PLANT was not the end of Joachim Rønneberg and Knut Haukelid's clandestine fight against the Nazi occupation.

Both men continued to work for the Norwegian Resistance till the end of the war. Rønneberg put his saboteur's expertise to use in the classic fashion: blowing up railway lines and bridges in order to hinder the German forces in Norway. In February 1944, Haukelid led a group of saboteurs who sank a ferry as it carried containers of heavy water across Lake Tinnsjå. It was en route to a secure plant in Germany where work on the atom bomb was to continue. The sinking of the ferry seriously hampered Nazi plans to build an atomic device, and helped to ensure the Allies won the race for the Bomb.

After the war, Rønneberg enjoyed a long career in the Norwegian Broadcasting Corporation. Haukelid continued to serve in the Norwegian military, and rose to the rank of Lieutenant General. Both men were awarded Norway's highest decoration for gallantry, the Krigskorset med Sverd (War Cross with Sword), as well as Britain's Distinguished Service Order (DSO). Haukelid was also a holder of the Military Cross (MC), which he received from the hand of Winston Churchill.

The story of the raid on Telemark was first portrayed on film in 1948, in a Franco-Norwegian production by the name of *Operation Swallow: The Battle for Heavy Water*. In it, Haukelid and many of the others played themselves. Rønneberg declined to do so; his role was taken by an actor. The story was told again in the 1965 blockbuster *The Heroes of Telemark*, starring Kirk Douglas and Richard Harris. The Hollywood version of events, Rønneberg has said, 'had little to do with reality'.

COME FROZEN HELL OR HIGH ADVENTURE...

THEIR MISSION: Stop the Nazis from developing the atom bomb!

COLUMBIA PICTURES presents A Benton Film Production

KIRK DOUGLAS · RICHARD HARRIS

IN ANTHONY MANN'S

THE HEROES OF TELEMARK

THE STUFF OF MOVIES A poster of the 1965 film depicting the role of the Norwegian Resistance.

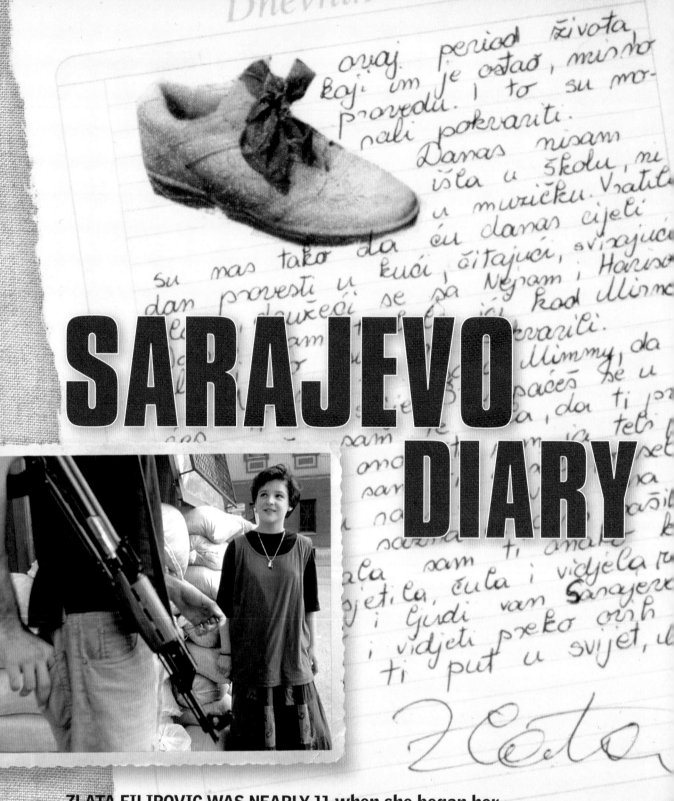

SARAJEVO DIARY

ZLATA FILIPOVIC WAS NEARLY 11 when she began her diary. With war looming, it marked the start of a dark period in her young life, a time when tasks as simple as getting food and water meant risking your life.

Thursday, November 14, 1991. War in Croatia, war in Dubrovnik. Mummy and Daddy keep watching the news on television. Mummy often cries looking at the terrible pictures. They talk mostly politics with their friends. What is politics? I haven't a clue. And I'm not really interested.

December 26 Christmas was wonderful. There was a big Christmas tree, decorations, presents, and lots of wonderful food and drink. A friend phoned from Dubrovnik. I'm keeping my fingers crossed for him and all the people and children in Dubrovnik.

It'll be New Year's Eve soon. Mummy and Daddy and our friends aren't planning a party this year. They don't talk about it much. Is it because of the war in Dubrovnik? I don't understand.

Thursday, March 5, 1992 Things are hotting up here in Sarajevo. On Sunday, a small group of armed civilians killed a Serbian wedding guest and wounded the priest. On Monday the city was full of barricades. At 6 o'clock people got fed up and went out into the streets. The peace procession set out from the cathedral and made its way through the entire city. People sang and cried, 'Bosnia, Bosnia' and 'We'll Live Together'. We joined in.

The next day everything was the same as before. Music lessons, school. Yesterday our teacher told us to go home early. Something was wrong! There was a panic. The girls started screaming and the boys quietly blinked their eyes. Daddy came home from work early that day, too, but everything turned out OK. It's all too much!

Tuesday, March 24 The blue helmets have arrived in Sarajevo. Daddy drove me to the building of the UN Peace Force Command. He told me that now the blue flag is flying in Sarajevo we can hope for something better.

Sunday, April 5 I'm trying to concentrate so I can do my homework. Something is going on in town. You can hear gunfire from the hills. Columns of people are spreading out, trying to stop something, but they don't know what. The radio keeps playing the same song 'Sarajevo, My Love'. My stomach is in knots. I'm afraid of war.

Soon much of Sarajevo was suffering intensive shelling and gunfire from the Serbian Army located in the hills surrounding the city. Schools and offices were closed, and the people – including many of the Filipovics' family and friends – fled the city.

Saturday, May 2 The shooting started around noon. Mummy, Daddy and I ran down to our cellar. The cellar is ugly, dark, smelly. Mummy, who's terrified of mice, had two fears to cope with. We listened to the pounding shells, the shooting, the thundering noise overhead.

When the shooting died down a bit, Daddy ran to our flat and brought us back some sandwiches. He said he could smell burning and that the phones weren't working. He brought our television set down to the cellar. We learned that the main post office was on fire, and that they had kidnapped our president. At around 8pm we went back to the flat. We're worried about Grandma and Grandad. A terrible day, the worst, most awful day in my 11-year-old life.

Fragmented country *A complex mix of ethnic groups live in Bosnia and Herzegovina (see page 171). Underlying tensions between them led to trouble in the capital city of Sarajevo.*

War child *Zlata decorated the neatly written pages of her diary (opposite) with whatever materials she could find. The tools of war became part of everyday life for Zlata (inset).*

Dodging snipers *Bosnian civilians flee gunshots in August 1992. To walk outside in Sarajevo during the siege was to risk being hit by one of the many snipers who lay in wait in the hills.*

Tuesday May 5 Shooting seems to be dying down. I hope they come to some agreement, so that we can live and breathe as human beings again. I want it to stop for ever, PEACE!

We've rearranged things in the flat. Our bedrooms face the hills, which is where they're shooting from, so we turned a safe corner of the sitting room into a bedroom, and sleep on mattresses on the floor. It's safer there, although once the shooting starts no place is safe except for the cellar.

Thursday, May 7 I was almost positive the war would stop, but today … Today a shell fell on the park in front of my house, the park where I used to play with my friends. A lot of people were hurt. NINA IS DEAD. A piece of shrapnel lodged in her brain and she died. We went to kindergarten together, and we used to play in the park. Is it possible I'll never see Nina again? I feel sad. A disgusting war has destroyed a young child's life.

Over the next few weeks government buildings, offices and the Olympic stadium were destroyed. Many more Sarajevans left the city. Zlata's uncle was injured, but he survived.

Wednesday, May 27 SLAUGHTER! MASSACRE! TEARS! HORROR! CRIME! BLOOD! SCREAMS! DESPAIR!

That's what Vase Miskina Street looks like today. Two shells exploded in the street and one in the market. Mummy was nearby at the time. Daddy and I were beside ourselves because she hadn't come home. I saw some of it on television but I still can't believe it.

We kept going to the window hoping to see Mummy. They released a list of the dead and wounded. At 2pm Daddy decided to go and check the hospital. I looked out of the window and I saw Mummy running across the bridge. As she came into the house she started shaking and crying. Through her tears she told us how she had seen dismembered bodies.

Friday, June 5 There's been no electricity for quite some time, and we kept thinking about the food in the freezer. Daddy found an old wood-burning stove, and some wood in the cellar, and we lit the stove out in the yard and cooked everything. We had the neighbours round, and ate veal and chicken, squid, cherry strudel, meat and potato pies. Who knows when we'll be able to cook like this again. Food is becoming a real problem.

Tuesday, June 16 I was in the kitchen laying the table for lunch when I heard a terrible bang and glass breaking. Now all our windows are broken except the ones in my bedroom. We cleared away the glass and put plastic sheeting over the windows. I picked up a piece of shrapnel and the tail-end of a grenade, put them in a box and thanked God I had been in the kitchen, because I could have been hit.

Sunday, July 5 I don't remember when I last left the house. It must be almost two months ago. I really miss Grandma and Grandad. I used to go there every day. I spend my days in the house and in the cellar. That's my wartime childhood. And it's summer. I feel caged up. I can see the park in front of the house. Empty, deserted, no children, no joy. Everything around me smells of war. I wish I could play the piano, but I can't because it's in 'the dangerous room'. How long is this going to go on????

Monday, July 20 I watch the world through the window. Just a piece of the world. There are lots of beautiful pedigree dogs roaming the streets. Their owners probably had to let them go because they couldn't feed them any more. Yesterday I watched a cocker spaniel cross the bridge, not knowing which way to go. He was lost. He wanted to go forward, but then he stopped, turned round and looked back. He was probably looking for his master. Even animals aren't spared by the war.

By the end of August the shooting had died down enough for Zlata to attend a summer school and occasionally visit the few friends who remained in the city. At home they had no electricity or running water. Zlata's father developed a hernia from carrying the heavy water cans, so her mother had to make the trip; it took about 2 hours to get enough for their daily needs.

In October, Mrs Filipovic was issued with papers that would enable her to work in Holland, taking Zlata with her, but they failed to get places on an exit convoy.

The scarred city

THE SIEGE OF SARAJEVO formed part of the wider war that engulfed Yugoslavia in the 1990s. The republic of Bosnia and Herzegovina was in ethnic terms the most diverse of the Yugoslav republics. Slightly less than half the population were Bosniaks (Muslim Bosnians), about a third were Serbs and most of the rest were Croats. In 1992, the Croats and Muslims of Bosnia voted for independence from Yugoslavia – much against the will of the Serbs who lived there. The Serb-dominated Yugoslav army promptly invaded Bosnia, and laid siege to Sarajevo in April 1992. Serb artillery, deployed in the mountains above the city, shelled the civilian population ceaselessly for almost four years. It was the longest siege in modern military history, and it cost the lives of more than 12,000 people. At least 50,000 were wounded or injured.

Serb guns were withdrawn in February 1996, under the terms of the Dayton peace accords, and over the next ten years Sarajevo was slowly repaired and rebuilt. Most of the city centre has been restored, and Sarajevo – now the capital of the sovereign state of Bosnia and Herzegovina – has become a fashionable tourist destination. But reminders of the siege are everywhere. There are, for example, many cemeteries, as well as stalls selling beautifully decorated shell cases, a uniquely Sarajevan souvenir. Most poignant of all are the so-called 'Sarajevo roses'. These are the hundreds of marks in the pavements made by mortar blasts; if an explosion is known to have killed someone, the scar has been filled with red resin. Each looks like a spray of scarlet flowers or a fossilised puddle of congealing blood.

DIRECT HIT Sarajevo's parliament building was hit by an artillery shell, fired from Serb positions in the surrounding hills, on August 20, 1992.

Thursday, November 19 Nothing new on the political front. Resolutions are being adopted, negotiating takes place, and we are dying, freezing, starving, crying. It seems to me that politics invited this war. Among our friends, in our family, there are Serbs, Croats and Muslims. It's a mixed group and I never knew who was what. We know who is good and who isn't. Now politics has put capital letters on them, it wants to separate them. I simply don't understand it.

Sunday, November 29 It's cold. There is wood at the market but, like everything else, only for Deutsche Marks, and that's very expensive. I keep thinking that the lovely trees from our park are probably there – the lime, birch and plane trees that made Sarajevo so pretty – selling for hard currency.

The days are getting shorter. Mummy, Daddy and I play cards by candlelight, or we read something and talk, and, at about 9 o'clock in the evening, friends come to listen to the news on Radio France Internationale.

Thursday, December 3 Today is my first wartime birthday. Twelve years old. As usual there was no electricity. The whole neighbourhood got together in the evening. I got chocolate, vitamins, jewellery, soap. The table was nicely laid, with little rolls, a fish and rice salad, corned beef and a birthday cake. It was nice, but something was missing. Peace was missing!

Monday December 28 My music teacher came to the flat and I had my first piano lesson since March. When there's not shooting it's as if the war were over. But this business with the electricity and water, this darkness, this winter, the shortage of wood and food, brings me back to reality.

As I sit writing, I look over at Mummy and Daddy. They are reading. They look even sadder to me in the light of the oil lamp (we have no more wax candles, so we make oil lamps). Daddy has lost a lot of weight – at least four stone. I think even his glasses are too big for him. Mummy has lost weight too. She's shrunk, somehow, the war has given her wrinkles.

Monday, March 15, 1993 My throat hurts, I'm sneezing and coughing. The second spring of the war. There are no trees to blossom, no birds twittering, because the war has destroyed them as well. There are not even any pigeons – once so common in Sarajevo. How can I feel spring, when spring is something that awakens life, and here everything seems to have died.

Monday, April 5 School has started again. We have all our regular subjects except for physical education. Our form teacher is SUPER.

Monday April 19 I've grown, and I have nothing to wear. Everything's too small, tight and short for me. I arranged to see if I can use some of Martina's things

Reassuring presence *Zlata stands close to a UN soldier, seen wearing the distinctive blue helmet. At first, the UN's involvement brought hopes of an early peace, but it wasn't to be.*

[Zlata's friend Martina had left Sarajevo a year before]. Keka wrote and said, 'Take anything that can brighten up your day, Zlata.' I found myself a black patchwork skirt, white tennis shoes, walking shoes and a more feminine pair.

Saturday, May 8 I went to music school today and saw the marketplace. You should see all the food. Almost anything for hard currency: one egg costs 5 DM, a bar of chocolate 20 DM, biscuits 40 DM. Ordinary people can't afford these prices. We get humanitarian aid packages and help each other out. Now, window sills and balconies have been turned into vegetable gardens. Instead of beautiful geraniums we have lettuce, onions, parsley and carrots.

Friday, July 30 It's hot. I watch people lug water home. You should see the different kinds of carts people invent. Two-wheelers, three-wheelers, shopping trolleys, hospital tables, even a sledge on roller skates. The various sounds and screeching of the wheels is what wakes us up every morning in Sarajevo.

Sunday, September 5 All eyes and ears turn to Geneva. More agreements, negotiations. Today we heard that letters aren't coming into Sarajevo any more. That's worse than not having electricity, water and gas.

A neighbour brought me a real live orange today. Mummy said, 'Let's see whether I remember how to peel it.' It was so nice and juicy. YUMMY!

Thursday, October 7 There's no shooting (thank God). I go to school, read, play the piano. We've lost two years listening to gunfire, battling with electricity, water, food and waiting for peace. I've grown, though I don't know how. I don't eat fruit or vegetables, I don't eat meat. I am a child of rice, peas and spaghetti. I often dream about chicken, pizza …

Sunday, October 17 Yesterday was truly horrible. Five hundred and ninety shells from 4.30am. Six dead, 56 wounded. We were down in the cold, dark cellar. AGAIN! Just as you relax, it starts up again. Why do these people want to destroy us? We haven't done anything. We're innocent. But helpless!

This was the last entry in Zlata's diary. She submitted the journal to a teacher, who had it published in Serbo-Croat with the help of UNICEF. A photographer took it to France where a publishing house liked it and sent back a contract. Zlata and her parents managed to get out of Sarajevo in December 1993. ■

Where are they now?

ZLATA'S ANGUISHED DIARY turned out to be her ticket to a safer life. Her publisher persuaded the French government to help her to escape the siege, and together with her parents she was evacuated from Sarajevo just before Christmas 1993. Zlata arrived in France to a hero's welcome. Newspapers called her the 'Anne Frank of Sarajevo', and she spent her first months away from the war being flown around the world to promote her newly published book and meeting with politicians. She was just 13.

After a couple of years in Paris, the Filipovic family moved to Ireland. In 1996, Zlata and her parents returned to Bosnia. Although the fighting had stopped, the country lay in ruins and after three months they decided that the peace was too uncertain to gamble their future on, so they returned to their new home in Ireland. Zlata left school in 1998 and moved to England to study human sciences at Oxford University, followed by a postgraduate degree in Peace Studies at Trinity College, Dublin.

The little Bosnian girl is now an Irishwoman in her 30s. But Zlata is still a writer, with the horror of war her theme. She has penned short stories, made documentary films and co-edited an anthology of children's war diaries. She has also served on the Executive Committee of Amnesty International for Ireland.

TED EDWARDS, a 40-something ex-steelworker, drama teacher, folk singer, explorer and asthmatic, was unemployed with an overdraft. When he discovered that a section of the Sahara Desert – 560km (350 miles) of sun-scorched terrain between Araouane in Mali and Oualata in Mauritania – was still unexplored, he snatched up the chance to fulfil a childhood dream. But what lay ahead was to become a nightmare.

BEYOND THE LAST OASIS

First, it was the scorpion. The desert night being warm,

I pushed a foot out of my sleeping bag to cool off, and felt a sting. A great acid-like pain began to spread throughout the lower leg and up beyond the knee. It was as if someone had spilled boiling fat on my leg. Then it gripped my heart.

Although painkillers had little effect, I told myself not to worry. Scorpion stings are usually fatal only to the very small or weak – and I, a 14 stone ex-steelworker, was neither.

By dawn it was just my leg that hurt but, as the proverb says, misfortunes never come singly. Several gallons of my precious drinking water had leaked away during the night. One of my four jerrycans, the one with an ill-fitting cap, had fallen over in the soft sand.

I was now down to 10 gallons, and this was the fourth day of my expedition. I estimated it would take 16 days: a solo crossing of the Empty Quarter of the Western Sahara, 560km (350 miles) from Araouane in Mali to Oualata in Mauritania. I still had 480km (300 miles) to go. My camels, Trad and Peggy, carrying my supplies, drank their fill before we set out. Ten gallons should be enough for me. But I had no reserve. (On a previous desert trip I'd discovered that the much-vaunted desert stills – constructed by digging a hole, filling it with a sheet of plastic and hoping that the condensation would fill a bowl with water – were unreliable.)

Next night I camped in a hollow and lay down exhausted. I'd had to drag the camels by their head ropes through ankle-deep dunes. I did not sleep for long. Soon after midnight a thunderstorm broke, and the rain poured down. It rattled on my space blanket, it clattered into my pan, and thudded against my jerrycans. Towards dawn it slackened a little, and I leaped out of my damp bag and packed it. There was not a sign of my camels.

The situation was serious. I was alone in the world's biggest desert, and beyond the point of no return. The chances of walking back and finding Araouane, a speck of a settlement, even on a compass bearing, were remote. Nor could I carry enough water to reach Oualata. I had to find those camels.

Precious water *A well that Ted Edwards encountered on the Araouane Road. The water here had to be retrieved from 36m (120ft) below ground.*

The hollow in which I had camped was about 460m (500yd) across. For half an hour I circled its rim, searching for camel tracks, but a camel's foot is designed not to sink in and it leaves shallow prints even in ideal conditions. The heavy raindrops had turned the sand into a mass of little craters.

I had a brainwave. On each foot a camel has two large toenails about 4cm (1½in) apart. They leave twin holes. Trad and Peggy would have had to dig their toenails in for traction when climbing out of the hollow. The place to look, therefore, was on the steepest part of the slope.

Amid those millions of raindrop holes all over the desert floor I would never have seen the regular pattern I was seeking just by intense staring. The situation called for the 'half-look', a trick I had learned as a child tracking rabbits through early-morning grass in Hindley, Lancashire. Close scrutiny showed the same green grass everywhere, but half-looking, out of the corners of one's eyes, would reveal a distinct line where less dew clung to the blades.

By half-looking I spotted the toenail marks of the girls' passage. I followed them into the next hollow, lost them, then picked them up again. Eventually, after a few kilometres, I came across two rain-soaked camels chewing cud unconcernedly in yet another hidden hollow. I had taken to the habit of talking to Trad and Peggy as if they were human companions, and was convinced that they voiced their views presumably by telepathy. Peggy gazed at me aloofly. 'And now I suppose you expect us to carry something for you in this weather!' I was massively relieved.

Eight thirty saw the girls loaded up with my supplies and the great trek continuing. I hoisted up the skirt of my *bou-bou* (loose Arab robe) into a sort of mini, giving me more the appearance of an ancient Greek than an Arab.

My stung leg was almost back to normal. I had partly made up for the lost drinking water by collecting rain in a plastic sheet. And when I checked with map and compass the accuracy of my navigation, I was amazed to find my estimate of distance to be correct. It put a spring into my previously weary step. I actually skipped down the valley that stretched before me.

After an excellent lunch – sardines, spaghetti, onions and tomato purée – the sun came out and I dried my gear. The world was a wonderful place. Every time I breasted a rise, a new vista of valleys, each half a kilometre (¼ mile) wide and 30m (100ft) deep, thrilled me in the knowledge that mine were possibly the first human eyes to see it

I had left the burdens of civilisation behind. I was now living a completely separate life, and the only problem I had in the world was to reach Oualata. Nothing else mattered. I can't remember ever being so happy.

Chance of a lifetime

My love of deserts was kindled in childhood by a present of Bible stories in comic-strip form. Camels looked incredibly noble beasts. I made up my mind that some day I would own one and travel the wilderness. This seemed to be a marvellous idea, for did I not enjoy building sandcastles at Blackpool?

Then, in 1979, by which time I was a 40-year-old redundant steelworker and a qualified (but unemployed) drama teacher, I read Geoffrey Moorhouse's book *The Fearful Void*. This classic tale of his unsuccessful 1972 attempt to cross the Sahara by camel had a section that really excited me. It mentioned that the country between Araouane and Oualata was unexplored. I sat back dumbfounded. I had assumed that all of Africa was well traversed, but here was a bit left. My old desert ambitions came to the fore. I accepted the challenge. After months of having job applications rejected, and feeling that society considered me useless, I now had a purpose. I was ecstatic!

I sought expert advice. Gerard Morgan-Grenville, author of a Sahara handbook, warned me of the presence of iron ore that could affect my compass. I bought maps of the area. Drawn from aerial photographs, they simply showed the extent of *aklé* (big crescent-shaped dunes) that lies between the two settlements. Elsewhere, the great expanse of nothing was worrying.

I resolved to tackle the journey alone, because most of the desert travellers' problems I read about seemed to stem from relationships with companions. Then, having decided that camels would be more reliable than a motor vehicle, I went to Tunisia to learn to handle them.

I discovered that a camel will mount only the gentlest of hills, and that riding a camel downhill is hair-raising. All of its joints seem to disengage and click and jerk. A camel makes throat noises like a gurgling drain and its smell is phenomenal. Yet, as I was assured by Mehdi, an Arab friend, it knows a tantalising secret.

One evening Mehdi and I were discussing religion and began to list the names by which the universal Spirit is known: God, Allah, Jehovah, Brahma, Elohim and others. Eventually we ran out of names. 'The camel knows more,' said Mehdi. 'A camel looks…' He searched for the word and imitated a camel's expression. 'Haughty?' I prompted. Mehdi agreed. 'A camel looks haughty because he knows the *thousandth* name of Allah!'

Setting off with the 'girls'

I worked out that by getting to Araouane as cheaply as possible I could mount my expedition for £1,000. I did temporary teaching to raise money, sold some possessions and went without food.

My friends in Eccles, Lancashire, where I had a flat, doubted my sanity. They were not alone. The *Sunday Times*, when I asked for sponsorship, replied: 'candidly, as outlined your trek looks suicidal.' However, shortly before Christmas 1982 Alistair Macdonald of BBC North West television told me he wanted to film part of the expedition as a BBC documentary.

On February 6, 1983, we were in Araouane. I had bought two camels and their saddles for about £650. The white one I called Pegasus (quickly shortened to Peggy) since I had first seen her near an airfield. The brown one was nervous about motor vehicles, and because of this fear of progress I named her The Traditionalist, or Trad.

Long trek *Ted approaches Araouane, the starting point for his historic crossing of the Empty Quarter.*

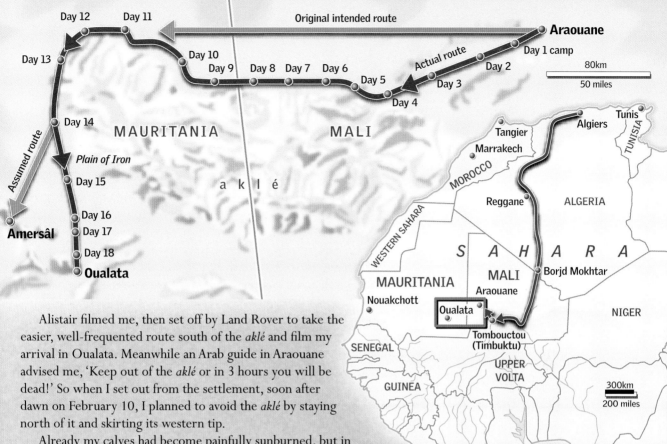

Alistair filmed me, then set off by Land Rover to take the easier, well-frequented route south of the *aklé* and film my arrival in Oualata. Meanwhile an Arab guide in Araouane advised me, 'Keep out of the *aklé* or in 3 hours you will be dead!' So when I set out from the settlement, soon after dawn on February 10, I planned to avoid the *aklé* by staying north of it and skirting its western tip.

Already my calves had become painfully sunburned, but in order to conserve the strength of the camels I decided to walk at this early stage rather than ride. I tied Peggy's head rope to Trad, and tied Trad's rope around my waist. On sand one walks in short, quick steps. My rhythmic tread and the creaking of the camels' loads echoed through the quiet valleys. On the first day we did 15 miles, and on the third day 22 miles. Not until Day 7, shortly after 11am, when the temperature was above 32°C (90°F), did we see our first tree.

Trad's eyes bulged; Peggy drooled. I called a halt and the girls set about the task of pruning. The tree, 3m (10ft) high with spiky leaves and full of sap, was obviously a favourite camel food. I did not know its name, but I called it a 'Manna tree'. I later found out it was a tamarisk. Desert Arabs used the sap in cakes – which they called *manna*.

Paying the price

Day 8. We were on the move at 7.15am, the sun struggling with sparse clouds. I saw green lizards, a desert fox, scarabs and the occasional raven, the desert's dustman. Always there were the flies. They were difficult to ignore. They would buzz inside ears, crawl over lips and around nostrils and eyes.

The *aklé* – hundreds of feet high in places and incredibly beautiful, the type of dunes beloved of Hollywood – lay to my left, but isolated *aklé* began to spring up in my path. I continually sank into its sand up to my calves, which fortunately no longer hurt from sunburn. The camels, reluctant to tackle the inclines, had to be pulled. It dawned on me that

Across the Empty Quarter Ted's 19 day journey (top) took him west from Araouane in Mali to Oualata in Mauritania, though not by the route he originally intended, including a detour he attempted to Amersâl. To get to the start of his solo adventure Ted had already crossed much of the Sahara and northwest Africa, from Algiers to Timbuktu and beyond (above).

exploration is much like genius: 10 per cent inspiration and 90 per cent perspiration. I thought longingly of Eccles's pubs and the local bitter.

At 10.30am, when the sky was a deep flawless blue from horizon to horizon, I felt I had to stop for a while. This was a new development. I, who thought nothing of walking the 400km (250 miles) Pennine Way in 12½ days, needed a rest. But I had been working hard, every day a tough 17 hours, and now the price was becoming evident. I decided that frequent rests would preserve what strength remained.

The refreshing effect of the first rest, though, soon wore off. I became 'dune happy' – my term for the condition whereby if I saw an uphill slope I headed straight for its summit, instead of going round the dune to keep my route as level as possible and conserve energy.

Most of my lunchtime break was spent repairing the sand-filled tape recorder into which I spoke my diary, and filming with the cinecamera Alistair had loaned me. After setting up the camera and starting the clockwork motor I had precisely 18 seconds to run and drag the camels into shot.

At 3pm, in a temperature that exceeded 38°C (100°F), we set out over the scorching sand. Two hours later I had to rest again. The sun was now directly in front of me, burning into my eyeballs. A slight breeze had built up, but was so hot it was like walking past an open furnace door.

Trad, who was about 15 years old, approaching middle age for a camel, folded onto the ground. Peggy, aged about ten, and prone to sulking, simply stood and stared. Camels are as individual as people, in ability as well as personality. Some can go for 15 days or longer without water, others as little as three days. Trad and Peggy looked as if they were beginning to die.

As the sun dipped, the air cooled rapidly. At 5.40pm I found another Manna tree. We stopped for the night. The tree was essential to the well-being of my bonny lassies.

With dead wood from the tree I lit a fire. That evening as I sat drinking tea, the fire's embers glowing, I reflected that the exhilaration of the past few days was ebbing like our strength. The real battle was about to begin.

Obstinate Peggy

We crossed the border into Mauritania at 8.15am on Day 9. The day was, if anything, hotter than the previous one, the perfect canopy of blue framing the golden powerhouse of the sun. I slogged on, forcing each footstep forward. By 11am, my legs would carry me no farther. I couched Peggy and took off my boots (a camel will not accept footwear upon its neck).

'Sorry, m'dear,' I said, as I swung myself on board her saddle.

She turned her head, roaring into my face, 'I WON'T!'

A whack to her rear with my camel stick made her rise, grumbling. Then she lay on her side, pitching me unceremoniously from my perch. The second time I leaped into the saddle she rose and before I was properly settled she threw me into the air. I landed in the sand. A tremendous pain shot through my left side. Three of my ribs were broken. But I remember thinking, 'Thank God the pain is on one side and not in the middle. My back is all right.'

I crawled over to the shade of a Manna tree. I could go no farther that morning. I weighed up my situation. I had about 270km (170 miles) left,

The inhospitable desert

THE WORLD'S LARGEST HOT DESERT, the Sahara sprawls over most of northern Africa, consuming a third of the continent, an area roughly the size of the USA. It is a place of stark contrasts, of shifting seas of sand dunes, of vast gravel plains, dry lake beds and mountains, under featureless skies. In the blazing heat of the day, temperatures can soar to 50°C (122°F) and more; at night they can drop below freezing. Some areas may wait years for even the most ineffectual rainfall. Fierce winds may blow for days, wreaking havoc.

Landlocked Mali is mostly plains, fed by the rivers Senegal and Niger. It is desert in the north, except for a few oases along the ancient camel routes, around which the nomadic Tuareg people still live. Most of the country's population inhabit the savannah to the south.

The village of Araouane is a station on the trans-Saharan caravan routes, a former oasis 270km (168 miles) north of fabled Timbuktu on the road to the salt mines of Taoudenni. It has been inhabited since the 11th century by Bedouin salt traders, and the houses are often buried in sand up to their roofs, the mosque up to its minaret.

Mauritania, too, is mainly desert, dunes, rocky plateaus,

hills and canyons. Here, also, fertile ground has been settled around the few oases and along the coastal plains to the south, crossed by the River Senegal.

Like Araouane, Oualata traces its history back to the days when southeastern Mauritania was a station on the caravan route, for traders carrying salt, ivory, metals, cloths and sacred texts. In the 1970s, many of its people were driven off the land to nearby towns by drought and famine. In recent times, though, something of a miracle has been wrought. Thanks to the combined efforts of the Mauritanian government and a Spanish humanitarian organisation, ruined houses have been restored, water piped in, and a market garden planted with the capacity to feed the 800-strong community.

Despite its air of perpetuity and infinity, the landscape of the Sahara (which means 'desert' in Arabic) was not ever thus. It would have looked quite different 6,000 years ago, according to German scientists, who believe that it was once carpeted with grass and sprigged with shrub. Climate change, they say, has led to its desiccation, forcing human populations to migrate to the fertile river valleys of the Tigris, Euphrates and Nile.

BEAUTY IN THE DESERT Malian nomads cross the Sahara (below). In the oasis town of Oualata, where Ted Edwards ended his journey, some houses have elaborately decorated doorways (above).

but only 6 gallons of water. I would have to average around 34km (21 miles) a day, a daunting task even without injury and fatigue. I dared not risk riding again for a while. The camel's motion would induce too much pain. It would be several days before there was enough light at night to walk safely.

Next day, after plodding through 2 hours of *aklé*, a strong wind whipping sand into our faces, we staggered into firm sand, which in turn petered out to become a vast table top of a plain, dotted by scrub – a welcome change.

My various pains, including a rheumatic shoulder, the legacy of teenage winter camping with inadequate ground insulation, had blended into a general dull ache on my entire left side. I managed to ignore it, however, at 4pm, when the sun dipped redly. It was time for an important celebration. I had achieved the halfway point across the Empty Quarter. I erected the camera tripod, and using my camel stick as a pole, soon had the Union Jack fluttering grandly. It was a proud moment.

Next was a luxury I had been promising myself for days: a bath. The thunderstorm on Day 5 had certainly refreshed me somewhat, but of late the girls had taken to turning away their noses. I agonised over the quantity of water needed for the operation and decided to sacrifice a pint. With my hands I dug a small hole in the sand, lined it with my plastic sheet and poured in the priceless liquid. Then, systematically, I cleaned every part of my body.

The psychological effects were dramatic. I laughed, seemingly for no reason. I even did a little dance, naked on the wind-blown plain. For my festive meal I had freeze-dried spicy beef and mashed potatoes, plus a handful of boiled sweets and four cans of lager, saved for this special occasion. There seemed to be no point in dressing for dinner.

It was time for an important celebration. I had achieved the halfway point across the Empty Quarter. I erected the camera tripod, and using my camel stick as a pole, soon had the Union Jack fluttering grandly.

Day 11. We had passed *Aklé* Corner, as I called it, and were circumventing the area of *aklé* that projected 25 miles to the north. Unfortunately we tried to round the tip too sharply and found ourselves in dense *aklé*. Shifting sand seemed to be in every direction. The only way out was north. So, reluctantly, we turned our backs on Oualata and trudged into the open desert.

At 5pm, having covered 40km (25 miles) that day, I unloaded the camels and heard a *clump*. Peggy had trodden on a jerrycan. Too late, I noticed a dark patch of sand around it. I leaped over and lifted the can in time to see the last drop of water drip from its split bottom seam.

I measured out my remaining water. I now had only 15 pints. A disaster.

Dead man walking

When I had finished my midday rest the following day and tried to lift my rucksack onto Trad's saddle, it slipped from my fingers onto the sand. I simply hadn't the strength in my hands to hold it. Until that moment I had not fully realised how weak I'd become and the revelation shook me. Somehow I lifted my rucksack from the sand and, using knees and hips, tied it in place. I lay down that night thinking that one more mishap would finish me.

An hour after setting off on Day 13, the land became flatter. At last we seemed to have rounded the *aklé* and could turn southwest, on a bearing of 222 degrees by my compass. According to the map, 65km (40 miles) of firm sand lay ahead. But 20km (12 miles) later we struck *aklé* again. We had turned too soon.

I spoke into my tape recorder: 'Half-past twelve. *Aklé* as far as the eye can see. I think I'm a dead man. If I go back north to get out of it I haven't enough water to survive. I've only one chance, to carry on southwest.'

So I ventured into that mountainous sand sea with its burning sun, air and wind. Soon I stopped wandering round the dunes and along the arms of the crescents, seeking level areas. I took a straight line southwest, dragging the unwilling camels up slopes and down almost sheer cliffs of soft sand, causing enormous avalanches of sand and camels. The beauty of those dunes passed unnoticed as we carved a great gash over their pristine surfaces. I don't know if this new tactic gained me any miles but it gave the illusion of greater speed.

For a whole hour we ploughed on, and then for another. I recalled the Arab guide in Araouane: '*Keep out of the aklé or in 3 hours you will be dead!*' But greater than my fear of dying was my anger that this desert should delay me, that it should try to keep me from my appointment in Oualata. I screamed my hatred at those dunes.

And the dunes capitulated. Suddenly there it was before me, a great flat plain just beyond the next dune. I stood on the plain, breathing heavily and grinning. I realised, once more, that I did love this desert. I loved her for what she was and for what she could do to me.

I did not realise that she had not yet finished with me.

The ravens gather

On Day 14 we came across outcrops of iron ore: flat, rusty slabs, the bare bones of the planet thrusting through the flesh. That day we covered almost 37km (23 miles). It wasn't good enough. I was now down to about 3 pints of water. So I made a fundamental change of plan. Instead of heading for Oualata (three days' march at my present pace) I would go to Amersâl, a water-hole west of Oualata. It was only 85km (53 miles) away according to my calculations. Two days' hard walking should get me there.

I set out for Amersâl next morning but felt exhausted and had to rest half-hourly. I was lying on the ground, staring into the desert, when shadows blotted out the sun. A pair of ravens, wings outstretched, were above me, gliding down to inspect what was apparently their lunch. They must have spotted my staggering series of collapses. I yelled at them and they kept their distance. These birds are said to carve out the eyes of victims not yet dead.

The next time I collapsed I thought I heard voices in conversation, but dismissed it as the onset of delirium. When I heard the unmistakable sound of a camel's cough I had to investigate.

Rounding a dune I saw two camels, and a man and a boy, Arabs, squatting on the ground. People! The first I had seen for more than two weeks.

'*Salaam allaikum*,' I said grinning, using one of my few Arab phrases. They were surprised and suspicious. I conveyed by signs that I needed

Desert saviour *One of the nomads that Ted tracked down on Day 17. By this point Ted had run out of water, and the provisions the nomads shared with him undoubtedly saved his life.*

Made for desert life

THE REDOUBTABLE TRAD AND PEGGY were dromedaries, the single-humped *Camelus dromedarius*, able to negotiate great oceans of sand and superbly adapted for survival in the pitiless Sahara.

A hefty beast, it can weigh up to 700kg (110 stone), and stands around 1.85m (6ft) high to the shoulder, 2.15m (7ft) to the top of the hump. With its long, powerfully muscled legs, it can carry heavy loads for long distances. In fact, a camel can bear up to 450kg (over 70 stone), though it is far happier with a burden of around a third of that. Its ambling speed, laden, is around 40km (25 miles) a day.

The dromedary's feet are equipped with broad, leathery pads between two toes, which spread to prevent them from sinking into sand. With its large, coarse mouth and 34 sharp teeth, it can make short work of rough, dry, thorny bushes, gulping the food down and later regurgitating it, chewing it in cud form. It can close its nostrils to exclude dust and sand, and by twitching its nose it cools incoming air, condensing moisture from its breath. Double rows of eyelashes, cartoonishly beguiling, and fur linings to the ears act as dust and sand filters, while bushy eyebrows provide sun shields. Leathery patches on the knees and chest make for comfortable kneeling and rising.

The animal's defining characteristic is its hump – here it can store 36kg (80lb) of fat, to draw on for energy when food is scarce. The dromedary can get by for a week with very little sustenance, and can function well having lost a quarter of its body weight.

PATIENT AND ABIDING
A single-humped dromedary camel; domesticated animals can live up to 40 or 50 years.

Because it doesn't pant, and perspires only in extreme heat, it conserves precious body fluids. When given a chance to fill up with water, it can take on board 136 litres (30 gallons) in under 15 minutes.

Camels have been a good friend and servant to man for perhaps 4,000 years. Dromedaries are used not only as pack animals, but for racing, drawing ploughs and turning waterwheels. They are raised for meat and highly nutritious milk, and for wool.

The dromedary's shaggy, two-humped relative, found in Asia, is the Bactrian camel. To remember which is which, picture a D and a B lying on their backs.

water. They understood but had none with them. They were out hunting bish, a local species of gazelle. Where had I come from? I told them. They obviously didn't believe me.

Suddenly they got to their feet, jumped expertly on board their camels and trotted off north. Returning to my camels, I lay on the sand, not one iota of strength left. It was time for a major decision: whether I was to live or die.

The pain in my body was phenomenal, and death seemed a very viable alternative. I could dispatch myself with my sheath knife; we of the North are of Viking blood and die with sword in hand. Against this I weighed the arguments for survival. Amersâl was 64km (40 miles) away, a punishing walk in daytime. I had about a pint of water left.

My mind wandered to England. I had with me a few photographs from home. I took them out, looked at them, and remembered. The sun sank and was gone. As the air cooled, my strength began to return, and with it came hope. And while there was hope, there must be life. I put away the photographs and stood, unsteadily. I decided to live.

Tempers flare

There was an acacia tree not far away. Slowly I walked the girls over to it and left them to prune it as I collected wood and lit a fire. I used half a pint of water, my last tea bag and my last sugar to brew hot, sweet tea, sipping it at first, then taking a huge gulp, feeling it run down my throat and seemingly permeate every crevice of my being. I strapped my water bottle containing the last half-pint to Peggy's saddle, in case by carrying it myself I was tempted to drink it.

We set off that evening to walk in the cool of the night, Peggy tied to Trad, and Trad's head rope knotted firmly around my waist. Ignoring my body's pleas for clemency, I marched on my compass bearing for Amersâl.

There was a roar from Peggy at the back. Her saddle had slipped forward onto her neck. Repair was routine. However, owing to my fatigue, I forgot the first move; I forgot to untie myself from Trad. She came, too. Peggy, annoyed at the saddle's weight, reared up. Trad took this as a personal attack and went for Peggy.

With teeth, heads and legs they joined battle, more than a ton of confused, angry flesh whirling about in the sand. I was still tied to Trad and being flung about like a rag doll. I tried pulling Trad away, but the strength of a man is nothing compared with that of an angry camel. The knot in Trad's head rope was impossibly tight and behind me. I had to get loose before serious injury resulted. In desperation I drew my sheath knife and cut myself free.

For some seconds more the camels milled and roared, then they stood, shivering with fright, their eyes rolling white. I spoke to them soothingly, and led them to separate clumps of grass to calm them. The battle site was a mass of equipment, saddles and churned sand. I searched for, and found, my water bottle. Miraculously the cap was still on and my half-pint was still inside.

Fateful error

Day 16. 2am. According to my calculations the distance to Amersâl had become a mere 35km (22 miles). I slept, my legs having given their all. For much of the rest of that blistering, interminable day we tried to shelter beneath some acacias. The wind rose and became a sandstorm, partially burying me. I learned later that the temperature reached more than 49°C (120°F). As the sun sank I drank my last drop of water and loaded the camels – 25 minutes, and flop; 25 minutes and flop. We staggered on until after midnight.

Day 17. This would be my last day. I had to find water, or the prospect of water. I had already passed the point where Amersâl should have been. The sun was gaining height, but there was no stopping until I found water.

I found fresh camel tracks. For an hour I followed them, then looked up to see three ragged tents. People were there, looking at me. I was safe. They brought me a large bowl of camel's milk, then glasses of sweet tea. Later, when they had fetched water, I drank 2 gallons of what was virtually thin mud. Life surged back as if by some miracle.

I climbed 100ft to the top of a ridge, hoping to find the route to Oualata, but all I saw was mile after mile of valleys. Panic welled up inside me. I had drunk the last of the water for breakfast. Was I going to fail at this late stage?

The nomads told me I was 30km (19 miles) from Oualata. For at least two days I had been almost 40 degrees off course. My compass was influenced by the iron ore of which I had been warned. I owed my life to aiming for Amersâl. The compass error meant that I headed in fact for Oualata. But if I had aimed for Oualata, I would have missed it completely, striding on into the open desert and almost-certain death.

I stayed the night with the nomads, and we feasted on my remaining spaghetti and onions. In the morning they presented me with 1½ gallons of water, and I set off again, rested and refreshed.

The day heated up and there, suddenly, was the escarpment on which Oualata stands. The rocky apron of land just dropped away for 300m (1,000ft) into a great valley. All I had to do was find a way down into that valley and turn left. Within the hour I could be in Oualata.

Even at that last stage the desert had cards up her sleeve. I found a side alley leading down the escarpment. The camels followed me slowly. It took us 2 hours to reach the valley floor. We went along it for about an hour and came to a dead end. It was the wrong valley.

We tried to climb out of it, but within 4.5m (15ft) of the top the rocks became just a little steeper. The girls rebelled. They stopped. I pulled and pushed, stroked and cajoled, but they would not go that last distance. I had to lead the poor, tired animals back down to the valley floor. By now it was dusk. We spent the night there.

On Day 19 I managed to escape from the valley by returning to the spot where we entered it. I climbed 30m (100ft) to the top of a ridge, hoping to find the route to Oualata, but all I saw was mile after mile of valleys. Panic welled up inside me. I had drunk the last of the water for breakfast. Was I going to fail at this late stage? After enduring so much, must I fall at the last fence?

Dragging the camels after me I eventually got to the rim of an enormous valley, several miles across, which surely had to be Oualata's. There was no strength left in any of us. Trad and Peggy were collapsing at every opportunity. It was 1.30pm, with the appalling sun close to its zenith. I sat in the shade of Peggy and waited, for coolness, rescue, death.

At 3.30pm, somehow, I stood up for one last effort. A side valley led to the main valley. It was a tough scramble down to the sandy bottom, especially for the camels, but we found camel tracks there. My legs gave up and I asked the impossible of Peggy. Moaning all the while, she complied. We went down the valley at a crawl. It was all I could do to clutch the sides of Peggy's saddle to keep myself on board.

Then the main valley opened out around us. There was a mob of camels and people, and a well. One figure detached itself from the crowd, smiling.

'*Salaam allaikum*,' he beamed.

'Oualata?' I croaked.

He pointed. The town gleamed white in the late afternoon sun. We had arrived.

The waterman drew water and poured it into a huge metal bucket. The camels, whose last drink had been 20 days previously, made it vanish faster than he could draw it. When they had drunk their fill I drank, too.

Alistair Macdonald, who had given me up for dead, greeted me like a prodigal. We killed the fatted champagne bottle, knocking it back in plastic cups. Days later I arrived at Manchester Airport.

At first my friends did not recognise me. My weight had fallen from a rotund 14 stone to little more than a skeletal 10. Gradually I returned to my former self. My broken ribs healed.

Memories of the worst aspects of my adventure receded, though they would never vanish and, like old men with their wars, I would always speak of them when the adrenalin flowed. But of the real things I could not speak; of the bond between man and beast, and land. There would be moments in the churn of daily life when I would drift away and look inwardly outward to the sand, to the silent stars, and to the roar of the stinging storm.

I often wondered what became of my bonny lassies. I was obliged to sell Peggy for a fraction of what I paid for her, and Trad I gave to the local administrative head of Oualata, at his suggestion. I hope they found the easier life they had so richly earned when they set a 20-day record for camels' waterlessness and ensured their place in camel annals for evermore. ∎

Where are they now?

UNDETERRED BY HIS GRUELLING TRIP across the Sahara, in August 1984, Ted Edwards set off, in the teeth of a howling gale, to be the first person to walk solo across Iceland, 820km (510 miles) from the east coast to the west, with 33kg (72lb) of equipment on his back – an experience recalled in his book *Fight The Wild Island*. 'It was,' he says with masterly understatement, 'no picnic'.

On his return from Reykjavik he found a letter waiting for him from an expert on Iceland, advising him that his trip was impossible.

In August 1985, Ted was in Tanzania, on another solo expedition, to retrace the steps of Henry Morton Stanley, on his famous 1,600km (1,000 mile) expedition from Zanzibar to the village of Ujiji on the shores of Lake Tanganyika, where Stanley found the missing explorer Dr David Livingstone. 'There,' Ted Edwards relates, 'near Morogoro, I discovered the site of the lost city of Sima-Mwenni.'

Not content with confining his adventures to some of the earth's most inhospitable regions, Ted Edwards meanwhile had his eyes on the heavens. In 1984 he wrote to Sir Keith Joseph, who was then Secretary of State for Education and Science in the UK, enquiring about the possibility of sending a British man into space with NASA, and volunteering his services. The response was in the negative.

Discouraged, but never a quitter, Ted then wrote to the State Committee for Science and Technology at the Kremlin, again offering his services, but he received no reply.

If he had had his way, he would have been the first writer in space, and one of two Britons aboard the doomed Space Shuttle *Challenger*, which disintegrated over the Atlantic 73 seconds into its flight, with the loss of all seven of its crew members.

Although he was moved profoundly by the tragedy, Ted's enthusiasm for space flight remained undimmed. In 1990 and 1992 he was tipped to go into space with the Soviet Union, but was excluded by the Soviets' age criteria.

PLEASE DON'T LEAVE ME!

SURROUNDED BY A WALL OF FLAMES, the 12-year-old girl had no option but to put all her hope and trust in a courageous firefighter.

'Let's go, Mum!' Shirley Young begged her mother. It was a Thursday in August 1990 – late-shopping night at Manukau City Shopping Centre in South Auckland. One of the highlights of the week for the 12-year-old Maori girl was to spend a few hours at what was then New Zealand's biggest mall with her aunt and cousin. Her mother, Gaylene, a single parent struggling to improve her job prospects, appreciated having a few hours by herself to catch up on her studies.

Gaylene pulled on a woollen cardigan and drove the trio to the mall in her sister's white Cortina, stopping at the kerb on busy Wiri Station Road to drop them off. As Shirley headed across the car park to join the throng of shoppers she suddenly realised she didn't have her purse. 'Wait, Mum!' she yelled, running back. 'I forgot my money.' Shirley opened the passenger door and leaned in to talk to her mother.

Farther back along the busy road, Buddy Marsh shifted gears on his huge Scania tanker as he headed up the rise. The 40 tonne truck and trailer held more than 30,000 litres (nearly 8,000 gallons) of petrol destined for a service station in central Auckland. A cautious driver, Marsh kept well to the left of the two-lane road but, as he neared the mall, a taxi, which had pulled out of the car park, blocked his lane. Marsh swung his rig away. A glance in his mirrors showed the trailer just clearing the front of the taxi. Then, as he looked ahead, Marsh gasped in horror. Not 20m (65ft) away, directly in his path, was a stationary white car.

Petrol sprayed both vehicles and ignited instantly. Carried on by its momentum, the trailer jackknifed, reared over the kerb and toppled on top of the wrecked car.

Marsh yanked on the steering wheel and hit the air brakes, locking up several of the 14 sets of wheels. The truck slammed into the rear of the car, spinning it round like a child's toy and rupturing its fuel tank. Petrol sprayed both vehicles and ignited instantly. Carried on by its momentum, the trailer jackknifed, reared over the kerb and toppled on top of the wrecked car.

Into the inferno

One second Gaylene Young was talking to her daughter, the next she was whirling round in a vortex of crumpling metal. Gaylene sat stunned as flames poured into the car and a single, terrible thought rose up in her mind. 'Shirley! Where is she?' Gaylene groped frantically round in the darkness but the passenger seat was empty. Thank God. She's made it out of here. An excruciating pain shot up her legs: her trainers and tracksuit trousers were on fire. Gaylene struggled to open the buckled doors, but they wouldn't budge.

'No!' she screamed, 'I won't die like this.'

'Brian!' Marsh called on his two-way radio to his shiftmate Brian Dixon in another truck, 'I've had an accident! I'm on fire! Call the emergency services!'

Marsh jumped down and ran round the front of the tanker to the burning car. Flames were licking the trailer's tanks. Worse, fuel was leaking from relief valves on the overturned trailer and spewing from a hole in its front compartment. The whole rig could blow. Marsh reached the car just as bystander David Petera hauled Gaylene out, smothering her flaming clothes with his own body. Petera and others then carried her a safe distance away.

Above the hiss of escaping compressed air and the roaring fire, Marsh heard a voice calling, 'Mum! Mum!' At first he could see nothing. Then, as he searched underneath the toppled trailer, he saw a young, dark-haired girl trapped in a tiny space between a rear wheel and the chassis. 'Mum!' she cried. 'Mum!'

Marsh grabbed her beneath the arms. 'You'll be all right. You're coming with me,' he said. But he couldn't budge her: her lower body was pinned to the ground by the wheel assembly. 'I want my mum!' she wailed.

Petera crawled in alongside him and together they tried to find a way of freeing the girl. Through a gap in the chassis, Marsh could see a stream of fuel spilling from the tanker into the gutter. 'We've got to get her out now!' he told Petera.

'Try inching the truck forward,' Petera suggested. Marsh ran back to the cab and jumped up into the burning seat; the interior was ablaze. He reached through the flames to the melting dashboard and twisted the ignition key. To his amazement, the engine roared into life. In low gear, he coaxed the rig gently forward. Shirley shrieked in pain. 'It's no good,' called Petera. 'She's still trapped.'

A wall of fire ran the length of the tanker, threatening to sweep round under the trailer where Shirley lay. Marsh grabbed a small fire extinguisher from the cab and ran back, spraying it around the girl in the hope of buying a few precious seconds. Then, from above the men, came a thunderous roar. An explosion tore a hole in one of the trailer's four fuel compartments. An immense fireball ballooned into the sky. Shoppers in the car park ran for their lives. Marsh and Petera, shielded by the tanker itself from the full force of the blast, crawled out.

With a blare of sirens, a pump and rescue tender from Manukau Station arrived. Immediately the vehicles stopped, senior firefighter Royd Kennedy had an armful of hose out of the locker and his partner, Mike Keys, was lugging foam containers down behind him. Driver Tod Penberthy was springing to connect the pump to the nearest hydrant. Waiting for the water, Kennedy saw his boots, fireproof overtrousers and the rubber on his breathing apparatus begin to scorch. When they turned the hose on the fire, the heat was so intense that the water steamed away before it reached the flames.

The tanker was burning end to end, shooting flames 100m (330ft) into the air. Petrol poured from holes and relief valves into a widening lake, and a river of fire raced down the road into storm-water drains.

More fire crews arrived. 'Concentrate on pushing the flames away from that tanker!' ordered Divisional Officer Ray Warby, who had arrived to take control. As if to underline his words, the fuel in another compartment exploded in a monstrous fireball, forcing Kennedy and his crewmates back 20m (65ft). The vehicles in the car park around them had begun to melt, their plastic bumpers and mirrors sagging and paint bubbling.

As the firefighters readied themselves for another assault on the fire, a long, high-pitched wail cut through the night. When the eerie sound came again it raised the hair on the back of Kennedy's neck. 'I'll be damned,' he thought, 'it's coming from the tanker.' Shielding his eyes, Kennedy peered into the glare, but saw only a flaming wall 50m (165ft) high. Then, for a

The tanker was burning end to end, shooting flames 100m (330ft) into the air. Petrol poured from holes and relief valves into a widening lake, and a river of fire raced down the road into storm-water drains.

split second, the flames parted. From beneath the trailer he saw something waving. It was the hand of a child.

'Cover me!' Kennedy shouted to colleagues. He dropped his hose and ran into the inferno.

Promise to Shirley

For 10 minutes little Shirley Young had been slowly roasting in a sea of fire. 'It's hopeless,' she told herself, 'no one can hear me in here.' Giddy with pain and petrol fumes, she felt her mind begin to drift and suddenly saw a vivid image of her grandfather and her great-uncle, both of whom had died years before. 'They're guardian angels now,' she thought. 'They'll be watching over me.' The idea gave her new strength. Straining to see through the wall of fire, Shirley glimpsed moving figures. Mustering every ounce of strength, she screamed louder than she had ever done in her life.

As Kennedy neared the flames, the heat hit him like a physical blow, stinging his face through his visor. Shielding his head with his gloved hands and fireproof jacket, he crawled under the trailer. Shirley was trying to hold herself up by clutching a cable over her head, but her hips and thighs were under the wheel assembly and her legs were twisted up, like a grasshopper's, next to her chest.

'I'm scared. Please don't leave me,' she wailed.

Kennedy tucked his air cylinder under her shoulders to support her upper body. 'Don't worry,' he told her. 'I'll stay, I promise you.'

'Is my mum all right?' Shirley asked.

'She's a bit burned, but she got away. My mates will soon get us out, too,' Kennedy replied.

The air was so thick with fumes that the two of them could barely breathe. Kennedy knew it would be only seconds before the vapour ignited. Whoosh! The firefighter braced himself as the air exploded around them. 'This is it,' he thought. 'Now we're goners.'

Shirley whimpered. Kennedy felt sick with helplessness as the flames washed over her. Then, for a moment, the fire drew back. 'This is pretty rough eh, Shirley?' he said, unstrapping his helmet. 'Put this on.' At least it may help save her face, he thought. He pulled the strap tight and flipped down the visor.

More explosions rocked the trailer, and Kennedy's heart sank. 'We don't have a chance now,' he thought. He looked down at the girl's tortured body.

Reliving the ordeal

IT IS LITTLE WONDER, after his harrowing experience, that Royd Kennedy suffered post-traumatic stress disorder (PTSD). The condition is particularly common in the emergency services and the armed forces, although it can afflict anyone who is exposed to a severe traumatic event. According to some estimates, one in five firefighters will experience PTSD at some time, as will one in ten of the general population.

PTSD was first recognised after the Vietnam War. It is, by any other name, the 'shell shock', 'battle fatigue' or 'combat stress' suffered by soldiers in two world wars, but we now know that what has been dubbed the 'invisible injury' is not confined to the military.

Symptoms usually develop within three months of the trauma, although in some cases they do not surface until years later. The sufferer typically relives the event through recurring memories, dreams and flashbacks, and recoils from anything that brings the horrors to mind.

There may be a feeling of emotional numbness, detachment, a deep pessimism and a distancing from loved ones. Irascibility, poor concentration, extreme wariness and agitation may all feature, and there may be continuing depression, phobia, anxiety, panic attacks and dependence on drugs or alcohol.

While some sufferers may be prescribed medication such as antidepressants, many gentle therapies can alleviate PTSD without the risk of adverse side effects. Cognitive behavioural therapy (CBT), anxiety management, counselling and group therapy all have their place, as do practices such as meditation and tai chi.

Royd Kennedy is living proof that it is possible to transcend PTSD and return to good psychological health.

SAFE AT LAST Royd is comforted by a colleague immediately after the terrible events.

'I won't leave you. That I promise.' Then he wrapped his arms tightly round her and waited for the final surge of flame that would immolate them both.

But instead of fire, they were hit by an ice-cold waterfall. 'My mates are here!' yelled Kennedy. Warby appeared through the curtain of water. 'Don't worry, we'll get things moving,' he told Kennedy, then he took stock quickly. The two were shielded from the full force of the main fire above and beside them, but the burning wreckage of the car was in the way, hampering the firefighters' efforts to protect and rescue the pair.

Warby crawled out and ran to Peter Glass, an officer in charge of a rescue tender. 'Get that girl out. I don't care how you do it as long as you do it fast!'

As firefighters sprayed the life-giving water that kept the fire away from Kennedy and Shirley, they were exposed to the full radiated heat of the main tanker blaze. It gnawed through their multilayered bunker coats as if they were tissue paper, and blistered their arms and hands. But they didn't dare back off. If the spray wavered, the fire would instantly sweep back again. Even changing crews was too risky. Ironically, now Shirley and Kennedy began to shiver violently: 80 litres (20 gallons) of freezing water cascaded over them each second. Soon they were in the first stages of hypothermia.

'I'll get someone to relieve you,' Warby yelled to Kennedy.

'No,' Kennedy retorted. 'I must stay with her. I made a promise.'

Peter Glass brought his rescue tender in as close as he dared while a crewman sprinted to the car and hooked a winch cable to the windscreen pillar. The winch was not powerful enough to drag the car out so they rigged it to the rescue tender's crane and, using it like a giant fishing rod, hauled the burning wreck away.

The firefighters were facing yet another potential catastrophe, though. Fed by tonnes of fuel, a torrent of fire was pouring into storm-water drains in the car park and on Wiri Station Road. But what route did the drains take?

The answer came with a deafening explosion. A manhole cover blasted out of the ground at the main entrance of the mall, narrowly missing a woman and flinging her shopping trolley into the air. Rumbling underground explosions began lifting and blowing out manhole covers all over the complex. The entire shopping centre was now permeated with petrol fumes. 'Evacuate the centre,' came the order.

Back at the burning rig, Warby approached Grant Pennycook, a paramedic from a waiting ambulance crew. 'There must be something we can do to ease the girl's pain – could you make it under there?' he asked.

Biting back his fear, Pennycook donned a bunker coat and helmet and headed into the inferno. As he crawled into the tiny space where Shirley and Kennedy lay, he realised he wouldn't have room to get an IV drip going. He considered administering a painkiller, but decided against it: Shirley seemed to be coping and side effects such as the suppression of her breathing might hamper the rescue operation.

Trauma victims need to get to hospital within an hour of injury – dubbed the 'golden hour' by emergency services – to have a decent chance of survival. Crawling out, Pennycook was conscious that timing was vital. Shirley had been under the tanker for more than 30 minutes. She could easily slip into shock and die.

Kennedy had been trying to take her mind off her predicament. 'What do you watch on TV?' he asked, and they talked for a while about her favourite shows. 'If you could go anywhere in the world where would you go?'

'Disneyland,' she said emphatically, 'I love Mickey Mouse.'

Whenever she was startled by a sudden noise Kennedy would explain what the firefighters were doing. 'How bad am I hurt, Royd?' she asked.

Kennedy tried to reassure her, 'You'd got a few broken bones and burns, but it's marvellous what the doctors can do.' Occasionally she would let out stifled moans. 'It's OK, yell all you want,' he encouraged. 'Bite me if it helps.' The pain from the injuries to Shirley's lower body was becoming unbearable. She cried out, burying her hands in Kennedy's thick hair, pulling hard to ease her agony.

The steady flow of water wavered for an instant. 'God no,' thought Kennedy, 'the fire can't take us now.' Shirley barely managed to move her arms as the flames rolled in. Then the water came pouring back and Kennedy was horrified to see that several layers of skin on her arms had slid down and bunched up round her wrists. 'I'm still with you, Shirley,' he said. 'Do you like horses?' he asked, desperate to get her talking again.

'I've never been on a horse.'

Eruption *A giant fireball exploded high into the air at Manukau City Shopping Centre, forcing shoppers to flee for their lives.*

'We're losing her, Warby,' Kennedy shouted. 'Throw me an Air Viva!' Kennedy put the mask of the portable resuscitator over Shirley's face and forced air into her lungs. She stirred a little and opened her eyes.

'When we're out of here, I promise you a ride on my daughter's horse, Gilly.'

As Kennedy talked, he kept a finger on Shirley's wrist to check her pulse. Now it was growing noticeably fainter and more erratic. She'd been trapped for nearly 40 minutes.

With the wreck out of the way, Glass was trying to lift the trailer off the girl. He faced a knife-edge decision. A hydraulic jack would be quicker, but it risked tilting the trailer, tipping out more fuel and incinerating the pair. 'We'll use the air bags. They'll give a straight lift,' Glass told his crew. Made of rubber reinforced with steel, the air bags were capable of lifting a railway wagon into the air. They slid one under each set of rear wheels and began feeding in compressed air. As the trailer moved, they slipped in wooden blocks to keep it on an even keel.

Kennedy felt Shirley's pulse flutter and she closed her eyes. 'Shirley, talk to me!' he pleaded. She rallied for a couple of moments but her pulse was so faint now he could barely feel it. She lifted her head and looked into his eyes. 'If I don't make it, tell Mum I love her,' she whispered.

'We're losing her, Warby,' Kennedy shouted. 'Throw me an Air Viva!' Kennedy put the mask of the portable resuscitator over Shirley's face and forced air into her lungs. She stirred a little and opened her eyes. 'You tell your mum yourself,' he scolded. 'I promised I wouldn't leave you. Now, don't you leave me!'

'I'll hang on,' she murmured.

Guardian angels

Peter Glass's rescue team had run into trouble. Part of the trailer was on soft ground that was sodden from all the water, and the air bag under the wheel trapping Shirley was sinking into the mud instead of lifting up. They blocked one more time and inflated the bag to its maximum, but the wheels had risen only 10cm (4in). 'We must have her out now,' Warby told Glass.

Praying that it would give them that extra few centimetres of lift without tipping the trailer, Glass shoved a small hydraulic ram under the chassis. He flicked the valve open and held his breath. The trailer lifted some more. Now he had a 15cm (6in) gap between ground and wheels; it would have to be enough.

'Go for it!' he yelled. Kennedy gently untangled Shirley's legs from under the wheel; they were crushed so badly they were like jelly in his hands. Warby helped him free her crumpled body from its prison. Then they carried her to the stretcher. Just before Shirley was lifted into the waiting ambulance, she smiled at him and he bent down to give her a kiss on the cheek.

At Middlemore Hospital, a team of surgeons worked through the night on Shirley. For two weeks she lay in intensive care. With tubes in her throat, she couldn't talk for the first few days. But as she drifted in and out of a sedated sleep, she scrawled a note: 'I love you, Mummy.'

Five days after the accident they wheeled Gaylene from her ward, where she was recovering from 20-degree burns on her body, into Shirley's ward. Mother and daughter held hands across their beds and wept with happiness.

As Shirley slowly recovered, she underwent a series of painful skin grafts to her legs. Orthopaedic surgeons found the right calf muscle too badly damaged to repair and decided to amputate her leg below the knee.

Firefighters have an unwritten rule never to visit victims in hospital in case they get too involved and lose judgement on the job. But Kennedy visited Shirley often, eating her chocolates and writing on her chart, 'This kid is far too noisy.'

'She's a miracle child,' says Kennedy. 'No one knows how she survived.'

Shirley knows: 'I had guardian angels watching over me,' she explains. ∎

Where are they now?

'LIFE IS GREAT,' declares Royd Kennedy, now in his fifties. 'I feel alive and 25. My kids are great, I've a fantastic wife, a great job and am living in the best part of the world. What more could you want?' A happy ending, then, but he has come through some very rough times since that night at Manukau.

While still suffering from undiagnosed post-traumatic stress disorder (see page 192), he endured the break-up of his 26 year marriage and estrangement from the three eldest of his four children.

Work in Kuwait and Croatia followed, as well as numerous awards for heroism. An initially successful foray into publishing – Emergency RESCUE Trade Magazines – foundered, causing Royd substantial financial loss. By the time he joined the Queensland Fire and Rescue Service in Australia in June 2000, he was 46 and penniless. Then in 2003 Royd transferred to his present role in Cairns as Far North Regions Strategic Planning Manager.

He is now happily married to Vanessa, a New Zealander 17 years his junior, and they have two children, Ivan and Kasey. 'We live at the beach north of Cairns, and through careful investment and going without, we now have several properties and a 40ft boat. We dive and fish the Great Barrier Reef and generally enjoy life.'

As well as composing technical procedures for mining companies in Queensland along with Vanessa, Royd has also written an autobiography, *Firefighter*, and has embarked on penning a motivational roller-coaster read, *How to Overcome Adversity*. He knows of what he writes.

Following what he modestly calls 'the incident' in Manukau, Royd Kennedy saw Shirley several times and followed her progress. In October 2007, the two were reunited on a New Zealand TV series, *Whatever Happened To ...?* Shirley was by then a beautiful but still sad-eyed young mother, who confessed she suffered from depression. 'I think,' said Royd on camera, 'the biggest miracle is that Shirley survived to create further life'. At these kind words, Shirley visibly brightened. Asked by presenter Paul Holmes, 'Would you do it again?' Royd responded, 'I'd do it in a heartbeat, and I'd expect any firefighter to do the same for my children.'

Royd and Vanessa are today proud Australian citizens, and he recently received the Australia Day Medallion for services to the people of Queensland.

REUNITED Royd (left) in 2007 with Shirley and her husband Damon, and their children Brenhan and Tasmyn.

GROWING UP IN AUSCHWITZ

IN MAY 1944, the Geiringer family, four Jewish refugees from Vienna, were in hiding from the Nazis in Amsterdam. The youngest was Eva, and on the morning of her 15th birthday, the soldiers came to take them away ...

The prison van jolted us towards the gaol. Prison officers bundled us out and separated the men from the women. I clung to Mutti, my mother. She had her eyes on Heinz, my brother, and Pappy, who mouthed, 'Chin up!' to us as we were marched away.

Mutti and I were ordered into a large dormitory. About 40 other women were already confined in there with only the most primitive toilet facilities. I lay on a bunk bed next to Mutti. I couldn't sleep at all.

Throughout the night, new captives were being brought in. There were women with babies who screamed with fear and a chronic asthmatic who suffered attacks throughout the night. Eventually I managed to shut out all the noises and slip into unconsciousness.

The following morning we were given food, the first since my birthday breakfast the day before. Mutti handed me some of her bread while we all tried to guess what our fate was likely to be. We were all afraid we would be sent to a concentration camp. On the third day we were marched to the station and boarded a train for Westerbork, a holding camp for detainees in the country. Our hope was that the war would finish soon and we could remain in Westerbork till then. The accommodation there was reasonable, with clean beds and good toilet facilities. Even better, we were allowed to mix with the men, and Pappy and Heinz soon found us.

Grim destination *Prisoners from Hungary arrive by train at Auschwitz concentration camp in Poland.*

Most of the running of the camp was performed by Jews, some of whom Pappy knew, and a friend of his promised to put us on a work schedule. To our dismay, we heard that a large group of people was about to be transported to Auschwitz. Since we were among the newest arrivals, Pappy's friend had not had a chance to secure work for us. We felt we were bound to be among the unlucky ones.

Our hearts sank as we heard our names called out. We walked to the cattle trucks, carrying our cases. The wagon was so tightly packed we could not sit down and we huddled against each other in a corner. The only comfort was that we were still together.

I could see two tiny barred windows near the ceiling and two pails in the far corner – the only provision for our needs. The wagons shuddered and the cattle train began to move. As the journey went on, we did what we could to help each other, but there wasn't much. People took it in turns to stand so that others could have space to stretch out on the boards.

During the day the doors were opened once, the buckets changed and some bread thrown in – it was like feeding animals in cages. We tried to

Childhood nightmare *Eva Geiringer, shown in a school photograph of 1940 opposite, would have become all too familiar with the railway tracks that led to the gas chambers of Auschwitz (opposite, main picture).*

communicate with the guards, pleading for help, but were ignored by the stony-faced SS. At one halt, machine-guns were trained on us and we were ordered to hand over all the valuables we possessed.

There was so little light in the truck that day and night merged. Sometimes the train stopped for hours. Without movement, the trucks became unbearably hot and airless. The stench from the buckets overpowered us.

Selection begins

After about three days the train jolted to a halt and the doors opened. The SS shouted, 'If anyone is too tired to walk they can go on a lorry to the camp.'

With relief many walked to the waiting lorries, shouting to their relatives, 'We'll see you there!' We learned later that these people had been driven directly to the gas chambers.

Just as I was about to climb down, Mutti handed me a long coat and a grown-up-looking felt hat. 'Put this on.'

'I don't need it,' I protested. It was a boiling hot day but she insisted.

The women were ordered to walk towards the front of the platform while the men were marched towards the back. Pappy grabbed me and said, 'God will protect you, Evertje.' Then my parents embraced for the last time.

We moved along until we came to a group of SS. They were dividing the line – all the old and the children had to go to the right. The process was relentless. At this stage, though, we did not realise what 'selection' really meant.

Then it was my turn. The SS officer looked me up and down and indicated left. I was the youngest person by far in our line. Many mothers lost daughters of my age. Ridiculous though it looked on me, that hat and the long coat had saved my life.

Row upon row of wooden barracks stretched into the distance enclosed by electrified barbed wire. Sentries in watchtowers overlooked the camp surrounds. Even in the heat I shivered.

We were marshalled into a barrack for our 'reception'. And there we waited. We had been without food or drink for more than 24 hours. Eventually eight women dressed in striped blue and grey uniforms appeared – the Kappos, Polish prisoners of war used by the SS to administer the camp.

A heavily built Kappo stood in front of us. 'Can you smell the crematorium?' she shouted. 'That's where your dear relatives have been gassed in what they thought were shower rooms.'

We did not believe her – it was too terrible to contemplate.

One of the Kappos who seemed a bit kinder said, 'Don't drink the tap water. It carries typhus and dysentery.'

We were herded into a building where we had to leave any last belongings, including everything we wore. I did not want to undress, but I knew I had no choice so I walked with the rest, all of us completely naked, into a large shower room.

As we huddled together, the doors were closed and I thought of what the Kappos had told us. Were these showers water or gas? I began to shake with fear and Mutti gripped my hand tightly. Suddenly cold water poured down onto our heads.

As we huddled together, the doors were closed and I thought of what the Kappos had told us. Were these showers water or gas? I began to shake with fear and Mutti gripped my hand tightly. Suddenly cold water poured down onto our heads.

Eventually the flow of water ceased. I looked around for a towel but there were none, nor any clothes. We were ordered to walk towards a couple of prisoners who were shaving everyone's hair. SS men came in to leer at our bodies. Then we were lined up to be tattooed with the numbers on our admission papers. All this had taken hours. I was so thirsty I promised myself I would drink the first water I saw.

At last we were given some clothing – a pair of knickers of indiscriminate size, an overgarment and two odd shoes. We spent some time trying to swap garments and shoes to fit.

The ordeal was finally over. We stepped out into the evening to be marshalled to our quarters. As we began to move, I spied a tap on the wall. I could not resist. Darting over, I turned on the tap and drank. It was so wonderful. Several others copied me before we were pushed back into line.

Roll-call

Birkenau was the largest of the Auschwitz camps, a vast complex of barracks divided by barbed wire and electrified fencing. The compound we were taken to contained about 20 buildings, each housing approximately 500 to 800 women. We had no facilities. We had to sleep ten to a tier of a three-level wooden bunk. That first night I was utterly exhausted. Oblivious to everything, I lay in Mutti's arms and slept.

In the early hours of the following morning we were ordered outside for *Appel* (roll-call). The count lasted 2 hours and we had to stand without

Marked men *A German officer makes his selection from a line of men, all bearing the yellow stars on their chests that identified them as Jews.*

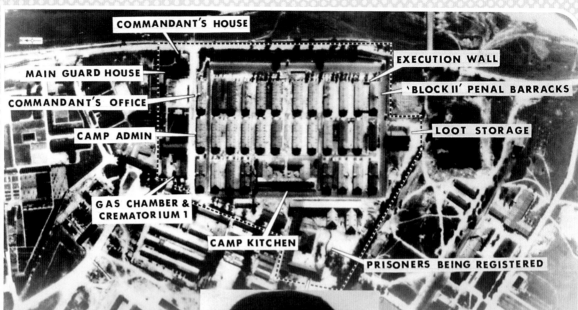

COMMANDANT'S HOUSE

MAIN GUARD HOUSE

COMMANDANT'S OFFICE

CAMP ADMIN

GAS CHAMBER & CREMATORIUM 1

CAMP KITCHEN

EXECUTION WALL

'BLOCK 11' PENAL BARRACKS

LOOT STORAGE

PRISONERS BEING REGISTERED

Auschwitz and the 'Angel of Death'

THE BARE FACTS of the Holocaust are beyond dispute. In 1942, at a conference in the Berlin suburb of Wannsee, the Nazi leadership took the decision to enact a 'final solution to the Jewish question'.

This bureaucratic phrase, a typical Nazi euphemism, denoted a chilling and ambitious plan to annihilate the entire Jewish population of Europe. In every country that came under Nazi control, Jews were registered, then rounded up and deported to concentration camps.

The plan was carried out more effectively in some countries than in others. Almost all of Poland's 3 million Jews, for example, were swallowed up, whereas all but a handful of Denmark's 8,000 Jews managed to escape to neutral Sweden. In total, Hitler's regime succeeded in murdering about

DEATH CAMP SCIENCE Dr Josef Mengele (above) struck terror into the inmates of Auschwitz, who feared his cruel experiments. In the background is the only known photo of Birkenau extermination unit, taken in August 1944. The image was produced from an aerial reconnaissance film.

6 million Jewish men, women and children – slightly less than two-thirds of all Europe's Jews.

There were many concentration camps, but the main site of the final solution was the Birkenau unit of Auschwitz. It was a factory of death, a production line where human beings were efficiently and systematically killed.

But Auschwitz was not just a facility for genocide; it was also a monstrous laboratory that functioned according to 'the lights of perverted science' (as Churchill had put it). Doctor Josef Mengele, whom Eva had briefly encountered at Auschwitz and whom inmates referred to as the 'Angel of Death' and 'Dr Death', conducted unspeakably cruel experiments on inmates of the camp. He had a particular interest in twins, who were always spared immediate consignment to the gas chambers so that he could make use of them. To be an object of fascination to Dr Mengele was a horrible fate; his research nearly always resulted in the death of its subjects.

moving for as long as it took. It was a test of endurance we would have to face twice every day. If just one digit of the count was wrong, the whole process would begin again. Inevitably, as time wore on into the bitter Polish winter, deaths would throw the count out and the ordeal would inflict more deaths the following night.

The first *Appel* was a special torment because we had been given neither food nor water. We were not dismissed until the sun was up and only then were we given a piece of black bread and cold substitute coffee, handed out in tin mugs to one in every five. We quickly learned that possession of one's own mug was necessary to get one's share. Mutti and I eventually had to sacrifice several rations of bread to obtain one.

We were marched to a courtyard surrounded by barbed wire and left there to spend the day. The sun beat down on our newly shaved heads. There was no shade, nowhere to sit and nothing to do. The routine was to be the same for the next three weeks. We were left outside all day. When the skies opened we were drenched and the dust turned into a quagmire. Every refinement of ordinary human living, even shelter, was denied us.

Meeting Dr Death

Early on the second day I began to suffer violent stomach cramps. I awoke shaking with fever and burning with such a high temperature that I could hardly stand. But I knew I had to go out on *Appel* because otherwise the count would not be correct. 'Help me, Mutti,' I moaned. We managed to position ourselves in the last row so I could lean against the wall. By then I was only semi-conscious and by the next day I was no better.

By now the others were beginning to complain. Any inmate with a high fever was a dangerous bunkfellow. 'Take her to the hospital block,' they nagged, but I refused to go. There were rumours going round that patients were being experimented on in the most painful and disgusting ways. But in the end I gave in. We all suspected I had typhus.

Although this 'hospital' was simply another barrack, it had an air of professional efficiency about it. Nurses in aprons bustled around and there

Poignant reminders *Sorting out the piles of executed prisoners' battered shoes and other possessions was Eva's first job at Auschwitz.*

were Jewish doctors in white coats. The atmosphere was reassuring.

A nurse appeared, tall and sturdy with a full head of hair. She cut an unlikely figure among the emaciated forms around her. She moved with purpose and was obviously in charge. When Mutti saw her, she let out a scream, 'Minni!' It was our beloved cousin from Prague – it was wonderful luck for us that she was there.

Minni took me in to see the doctor and made sure I got the correct drugs. Though I was extremely ill she did not want to see me go into the hospital.

That evening as we stood for *Appel* there were thunderstorms. I was burning with fever and delirium. Later Mutti confessed she had been convinced I would not survive the night. But, amazingly, when I awoke at dawn my fever had gone. I still felt very weak but I knew I was going to pull through.

My recovery gave me a new view of life. I told myself it was now up to me. I was determined to survive the war, no matter what they did to me.

At the end of our quarantine, Mutti and I were allocated to a work unit in 'Canada' – a huge compound erected to house the spoils brought from the trains that shunted prisoners to their deaths. Each morning, lorries dumped their personal possessions to be sorted by work parties like ours. We could see piles of clothing, mounds of shoes and one heap, taller than my head, made up of thousands of pairs of spectacles. It still did not dawn on me why they were no longer needed.

We recognised him as Dr Mengele – Dr Death.
The stories of his appalling experiments circulated among the prisoners. We realised that a selection was to be held.

Mutti and I were each given a pair of scissors to undo the linings of coats and look for valuables. We found so many things that it was like opening a pile of presents until I thought of the people who kept their precious things in their coats – particularly when I came across photos. As I gazed at a picture of a bar mitzvah boy surrounded by his smiling family I was hit by the enormity of what I was doing.

Suddenly I knew that none of these people would ever see each other again. I was paralysed by horror and angry that I had allowed myself to enjoy something so ghastly.

After only a few weeks, Mutti and I were transferred to a group who had to carry huge blocks of stone from one side of the camp to the other. Then we had to break them down into tiny pieces with hammers, supervised by brutal Germans. If we dared to rest they would beat us with the butt of a gun. Mutti became very thin, partly from lack of food but also from worry.

At the beginning of October, during the weekly shower session, we noticed a change in the atmosphere. The Kappos were shouting more than usual and fear hung in the air. We were very frightened as we heard the doors close behind us. When water streamed down on our heads, we prayed with relief.

But to our dismay, when the doors opened, there stood several SS men with a slim, immaculately uniformed officer in front. We recognised him as Dr Mengele – Dr Death. The stories of his appalling experiments

Herded together *The women's barracks at Auschwitz, where female prisoners slept, were crammed tightly with tiered rows of bunk beds.*

circulated among the prisoners. We realised that a selection was to be held.

Each of us had to turn slowly in front of him while he scrutinised us with clinical precision. At his indication, the first few women were sent to the right, then one to the left where she stood trembling with fright. When I walked forward he waved me to the right, but I was horrified to see Mutti pushed to the selected side.

I screamed and began to shake uncontrollably as I watched my mother being marched away. It was the blackest moment in my life. I thought it was the last time I would ever see her.

Losing hope

That night I made my way to Minni's barrack, where I blurted out the terrible news.

'I will speak with Herr Dr Mengele tomorrow,' Minni reassured me.

That night, for the first time since our capture, I was without Mutti.

The following day we were moved to Camp C, about 2km (1¼ miles) away, to another work unit. I cried all the way there. I felt that the last ties with my family had been broken.

Feeling totally deserted, I was now losing the courage and hope that had kept me alive. I was too young to be left on my own. Full of self-pity, I could not envisage any future for myself. I didn't see how I could cope in a world without my family.

I began to resign myself to death.

I sat at a bench for 14 hours a day, plaiting strips of rag into rope. One

'Evertje, I'm convinced the war cannot last much longer. Have hope – it will soon be all over.' We exchanged looks of such yearning and love that I still see his face like this in my dreams.

morning a Kappo entered, looking for somebody. When she stood behind me I froze with fear, expecting a blow, but to my astonishment she said in a friendly voice, 'There's someone to see you.'

When I shuffled outside I could hardly believe my eyes.

'Pappy!' I cried. He looked very thin and older than I remembered, but his eyes were full of love. I threw myself into his arms and felt his strength flow into me and pull me back to life.

Then I had to tell him that Mutti had been selected and gassed. He reeled backwards as if I had hit him. He managed to pull himself together for my sake and told me not to give up.

'Evertje, I'm convinced the war cannot last much longer. Have hope – it will soon be all over.'

We exchanged looks of such yearning and love that I still see his face like this in my dreams.

Finding Mutti

As the winter winds blew across the plains, the Kappos wrapped themselves in extra layers of clothing, but we were given nothing more. We shivered to stay alive and each day the cold became more unbearable.

I developed frostbite in my toes so that I could hardly walk. But I was too frightened to go to the hospital. Once people went there most were never seen again.

One day a new group of women arrived. Some were Dutch, from our transport train from Westerbork. They rushed over to me and all began speaking at once. I was confused, but I understood one thing. Mutti was alive! She was lying in the hospital – Minni had saved her.

For the next week I waited outside whenever I could, hoping to see Pappy and tell him the news. He had promised to come back, but he never came. It dawned on me then that I had found my mother but lost my father.

Every day the sound of gunfire came a little closer. The Russians were advancing and the Germans had started to evacuate the camp. Now I knew that Mutti was alive, the last thing I wanted was to be moved on. One day in December several women were ordered to stand on one side. The last number called was mine.

To my joy, we were marched to the hospital block where I plucked up the courage to ask an orderly for Minni.

'What a wonderful woman,' she exclaimed. 'I'll fetch her.'

Minni was delighted to see me and led me to the back of the barrack. She pointed to a top bunk. Suddenly a pitiful figure with a shaved head jerked upright and stared at me.

'Mutti!' I called.

She was almost starved to death. Her arms were paper-thin and she could barely stand – but she was alive.

We lay cuddling each other for days, talking in whispers about everything that had happened to us as the Russian guns sounded in the distance.

At last we were together again.

In August 1945, after Mutti and I had managed to return to Amsterdam, we received a letter from the Red Cross informing us that Heinz had died of exhaustion after a forced march from Auschwitz to Mauthausen. Pappy, who could not have known that Mutti and I had survived, probably gave up hope and died three days before the end of the war.

At this time we were visited at our apartment by Otto Frank who, like us, had lost his family in the camps. Otto and Mutti became close and they married in 1953. ■

Where are they now?

AFTER THE LIBERATION of Auschwitz, Eva and her mother made their way back to Amsterdam. There they received that fateful letter from the Red Cross informing them of Heinz and Pappy's deaths. Pappy died not knowing that his wife and daughter were still alive.

A former neighbour of the Geiringers, Otto Frank, also found his way back to Amsterdam from the Nazi camps in Poland, having lost his wife and two daughters there. Eva had known Otto's youngest daughter Anne before the occupation. Here, in post-war Amsterdam, Eva's bereaved mother and the widower Otto Frank fell in love, and they married in 1953. So it happened that Eva became a posthumous step-sister to the renowned diarist Anne Frank, who had died at Bergen-Belsen concentration camp.

By this time, Eva had also married. She and her new husband, an Israeli economist named Zvi Schloss, settled in Britain, where Eva worked as a photographer and antiques dealer. More than half a century later, Zvi and Eva still live in London. They have three daughters and five grandchildren.

Eva is a founding trustee of the Anne Frank Trust UK and has travelled the world to speak in schools and universities about her experience of the Holocaust. She contributed to a highly successful documentary play entitled *And They Came For Me*, which tells the story of her year in the concentration camps. Eva generally took to the stage at the end of each performance to answer questions from the audience. 'Every day that terrible year, full of suffering, hunger, extreme heat and bitter cold, was a good day,' she has said, 'because we were still alive.'

TRIUMPH OVER ADVERSITY Mutti enjoys her wedding day with Otto Frank, Anne Frank's father (above). In 2001 her daugher, Eva, received an Honorary Doctorate in Civil Law from Northumbria University (left).

KIDNAPPED IN THE JUNGLE

COMING TO THE END OF HIS GAP YEAR, British student Matthew Scott trekked into dangerous territory to see the Lost City of Colombia. He was entering a hostile jungle where guerrillas were known to operate.

'Sorry, señor,' said the guy at the tourist agency in Santa Marta, Colombia, 'the tour left half an hour ago.' Oh no – I'd done it again! I was famous for failing to make my connections. I'd even managed to miss the plane taking me to South America at the start of my gap-year travels. Now, after seven months away, I was looking forward to returning to my family in London and taking up my engineering place at university. But before I left I had one more adventure planned: a six-day trek into the jungle to visit the remains of the Lost City. It was going to be the perfect end to my trip – except that I'd now missed it.

But I wasn't going to give up just yet. I tore through the streets back to my £3-a-night hostel, determined to catch up with the tour by nightfall. Hastily stuffing a pair of black wellingtons, a water bottle and a smelly old T-shirt into a dilapidated rucksack, I raced for a bus that would take me towards base camp.

In my mind, the Lost City, dating from 500 BC but discovered only in 1976, was a must-see. Even though there were several terrorist groups operating in the area, I didn't think I was doing anything risky. I had talked to many other travellers who had been there.

The bus stopped in a small village and a local guide agreed to take me up to the camp. As we climbed the steep path I was struck by the beauty of the mountains. Their sharp slopes were clad in thick jungles and criss-crossed with rivers and streams. My guide told me that the largest river, the Buritaca, was the main route up to the Lost City.

At the camp I was relieved to meet up with the others in our group. I was the youngest; the rest were all in their mid twenties or older: Mathijs, a good chess player from Holland; Reinhilt, a German girl keen on mountaineering; and half a dozen Israelis. They told me there was another group of trekkers at a nearby camp that we might join up with.

Trouble ahead

'Get up.' The words were in Spanish. Then came a prod in the ribs with the butt of a rifle, not hard but insistent. The voice spoke louder. 'Get up! Get up!' What was going on?

I could see two men in uniform, with camouflage caps, black flak jackets and holsters with pistols. Each had a larger gun across his chest and they were searching our bags. I glanced at my watch, a cheap digital: 5.09am.

Suddenly I was on my feet and alert. I had my clothes on in 2 seconds flat. My first thought was, 'This is a robbery.' Then I saw them tying up the guide and the porter, who weren't protesting.

Despite this, everyone stayed calm. It was surreal. We'd all got to know each other over the past two days, hiking along the river, falling asleep to the sound of crickets and frogs and rushing water – 'God's symphony,' someone had called it. We'd bonded. And now we were being kidnapped.

We were herded into the middle of the room and the intruders demanded to know our nationalities. I snatched a word with the guide, as I'd acquired passable Spanish. I figured he ought to know the local paramilitary groups.

'Is this a problem?'

'*Ningún problema.*' No problem.

I could see two men in uniform, with camouflage caps, black flak jackets and holsters with pistols. Each had a larger gun across his chest and they were searching our bags.

Into the unknown *Matthew Scott's journey to the Lost City began in the north of Columbia at the coastal town of Santa Marta, gateway to the Sierra Nevada de Santa Marta. This area of mountains and dense jungle provided the perfect cover for armed guerrillas.*

He was lying, of course, but it made me feel better. I picked up my bag and the two armed men marched us all down the hill to the other tourist camp. I wondered if I could keep going, straight out of the Lost City, and find my way back the way we had come. But when we reached the second camp there were 16 or 17 more men standing around with machine-guns. At this point I realised we might be in trouble.

Now or never

Among the second group was another Briton, Mark Henderson, a 31-year-old TV producer I'd met the night before. We had a lot in common since we both came from the same area of south London. Now, as the guerrillas split us into two groups, I made sure I was with Mark.

There were eight of us in all. We were told to fill our water bottles, then, accompanied by eight armed guards, we were given the order to march. It was now 5.30am.

Our direction led deep into the jungle, away from the Lost City. A guerrilla led the way, with another bringing up the rear; the rest mingled with the column, which soon dissolved into a straggle.

The jungle was thick and lush and we had to grab onto vines to avoid slipping on the muddy paths. I caught up with the lead guerrilla to try to make conversation. At first he said the guerrillas were Colombian army taking us away from bandits, but, finally, he admitted that we were on a two-day march to a camp where the bosses would decide what to do with us.

By the time we had walked for 4 hours everyone was tired. The sun was beating down on the jungle canopy, generating the heat and vapour that would soon turn into the rain that fell like clockwork every afternoon.

At last, the guerrillas called a halt and we were each given a slice of processed cheese and some panella – a honey derivative that comes compacted into a thick disc, with bees entombed inside. It's pretty inedible, but I tried to take as much as possible as it was passed around, breaking up little bits to put in my water bottle. At least it might give me energy.

After we had eaten, the march began again. Soon, we breached the treeline, moving through a scrubby landscape with rocks jutting out of the side of the mountain. Some of the weaker members were starting to feel the pace. I heard a couple of the people behind me complaining to the guards.

'We don't want to go any farther. Where are you taking us anyway?'

I couldn't hear what the guards said in reply, but when I turned back, one of them pointed his gun at me. The message was clear: get walking.

We'd spent the past two days trekking through the mountains with guides and this wasn't much different. Except now the guides had guns.

Shortly after midday we stopped for a second time as it began to rain. Each of us was issued with a sheet of plastic to keep out the wet. There were also meagre rations – a mini chocolate bar and bits of dried guava. The guards were scrupulous in picking up the chocolate wrappings, and people commented on it.

'How nice they don't want to litter the mountainside.'

But Mark and I realised it wasn't that at all – it was because they didn't want our group to be tracked. As we trudged higher and higher into the mountains, we discussed our predicament. We didn't talk about 'escaping' because the Spanish word – *escapar* – is too similar. Instead, we said we were thinking of 'getting away'.

There were two possibilities. First, to hide in the jungle until the column had passed by, then retrace the route to the Lost City and Santa Marta. There was the risk, however, of meeting more guerrillas on the way. The second option was to follow a stream down the mountain until it connected with the Río Buritaca, which would lead us back to Santa Marta.

'Let's go now,' I said.

'I think it's a bad idea,' Mark replied.

'Come on, we can do it. We're in better shape than the others.'

Mark shook his head. 'Too risky.'

Clearly there were risks – getting lost, or being caught and shot. But I was pretty confident we wouldn't be shot. Hostages are more valuable alive than dead and the guerrillas seemed pretty demoralised.

It was now 1pm and soon the rain would be so strong that we would have to stop. The window of opportunity was closing.

As we strode on I was boiling with fury. I couldn't stand the thought of months in the jungle while my life was put on hold. My flight to England was in five days' time. I had planned on going home to my family and then on to university. I didn't want these people to ruin all that.

I made up my mind – I'd follow the river system back to Santa Marta. After alerting Mark and the others, I found a spot in the line where I could not be seen by our captors. I could hear the water on my right-hand side.

I couldn't wait any longer.

Troops hit the ground *Backed by helicopters, soldiers conduct a search of the mountains of the Sierra Nevada de Santa Marta in northern Colombia, in the hope of rescuing the abducted tourists.*

Going it alone

I launched myself feet first off the right-hand side of the narrow ridge, the thick layer of cloud and driving rain helping to conceal my departure. I thought it might be half an hour before I was missed.

Despite this, as I slid on my backside down the steep slope, I was scared I might have been spotted and followed. I scrambled urgently down the scree of rocks and loose tree roots, razor-sharp twigs lacerating my bare arms and my feet skidding in my wellington boots. Eventually I came to a halt. It was time to take stock.

I took off my rucksack and calculated which of the things inside I needed. The sack had holes in it – I'd spent ages trying to sew them up – and even though it left my arms free, it inhibited my full range of movement. I decided to leave it behind. I also threw away my water bottle; my plan was to follow the river, so I reckoned I'd have a regular supply of drinking water.

I decided to keep a torch, a spare sock, which contained my cash card, and the plastic sheet, which was essential – my only shelter against the rain and cold. I rolled it up and stuffed it into one of my wellingtons. I put the sock in the other boot and the torch into my trouser pocket. That left just the clothes I was wearing: a T-shirt, trousers, swimming trunks and socks.

I moved on quickly, still thinking I might be being pursued. Suddenly, one foot gave way and I found myself falling, tumbling over and over, grabbing wildly at vines and roots. I must have dropped more than 12m (40ft).

Hard terrain *The commander of Colombia's army, General Carlos Ospina, oversees his troops as they search for the kidnapped tourists high in the Sierra Nevada de Santa Marta.*

'There's no way they're following me down that,' I said out loud, sure that I was now safe from the guerrillas. Thankful I hadn't broken any bones, I carried on. The descent was now dangerously steep. I turned to face the rock and began to climb down, looking for handholds and footholds. It wasn't easy in wellingtons, but the vines on the trees were generally good. Then one of them broke and I fell, hitting my jaw on a ledge of rock. It bled a lot.

I carried on for 2 hours and, when it got dark, I lay down on the slope, curled up in the plastic sheet. But I couldn't sleep. It was too wet and cold and my mind was racing. How was I going to survive out here in the jungle? How long would it take to find my way back along the river to Santa Marta?

In the morning I located the stream that I had heard from up on the ridge. Here my wellington boots came into their own. The fastest way through the jungle was to walk along the bed of the stream, but even that was overgrown with plants. Sometimes I ended up on all fours, crawling along the water to get under fallen trees that blocked the way. I regularly ran into steep waterfalls and was forced to decide the best way to go. Should I head into the jungle to find an easier descent? Or clamber down the wet rocks?

The cold and the wet were my main enemies, in a valley so deep that the sun's warmth couldn't penetrate. My theory was that the stream would soon bend to the right to join up with the Río Buritaca, which would lead me back to the coast.

Bruising rains

That first day I established a routine that I followed for four days. Rising at 5.30am – my watch kept me sane – I walked hard until 8am, then climbed up the valley slope to find some sun. I allowed myself an hour's rest to warm up, then plunged back down into the gloom of the valley.

As I scrambled along the stream I sang songs, mostly desolate ones about being lost, forcing myself to keep pace with the rhythm of the tune. Though I hadn't eaten anything, I didn't feel hungry. You get hungry when there's food available and here there was no food at all. There were no berries, no fruit, no wildlife but for birds, which I couldn't catch.

The only creatures available were bugs. The masses of mosquitoes drove me crazy, though fortunately this part of Colombia was not malarial. After a while, I learned to cope with them by playing a game – seeing how long I could resist swatting them. Another bigger insect bit even harder. Whenever one of these bloodsuckers landed on me, I would catch it and squeeze its juices onto my tongue – it had a sweet taste I shall never forget.

Later, I pulled the scab off the cut on my chin and ate it. I reasoned it must have some nutritional value.

At 2pm every day the rains came – bruising, torrential, unforgiving. It was impossible to walk any more, so I went to bed, curled under my plastic sheet. I lay in a foetal position, trying to make a cocoon of warmth, but it was as wet inside as out. By the time the rain stopped, if it did, it was pitch-dark.

My jungle nights lasted for some 15 hours. I'd just lie there, trying to sleep, listening to the whining of the mosquitoes, croaking of the frogs and incessant rush of water. Sometimes I thought those nights would never end.

Ingenious uses *Matthew put his limited gear – his trousers, with a torch in the pocket, wellington boots and a single sock containing his cash card – to good use. The sock and the wellingtons provided an unexpected source of moisture when he needed it most, while his plastic sheet, on which his gear is lying, he used as a blanket and shelter.*

Where is the river?

On the fifth day, I couldn't fool myself any longer. I knew I should be heading north, yet had worked out from the sun's position that the stream was taking me southwest – deeper into the jungle. It was clear I wasn't going to find the Río Buritaca that day or any other. I was in the wrong river system and hopelessly lost.

The next day was my lowest point. At this stage I really regretted escaping and would have gone back to my captors with open arms. I hadn't seen any sign of life at all for nearly a week – I was probably in a place where no human beings had ever been before. Another week like this and I would certainly be dead. I put my chances of survival now at 50-50.

Though there didn't seem much hope, I just kept pressing on. I thought of my family and friends back in London and all the plans I had made, like going to university. I really didn't want to miss the start of term, but all of that seemed to exist in a different world.

Kidnap and contraband

IN 2003, when Matthew Scott was taken hostage, Colombia was notorious for being the 'kidnap capital of the world'. At its worst, in 2000, more than 3,500 people were seized. In 2007, 'just' 400 were taken. A hard-line security policy introduced by President Alvaro Uribe alongside peace overtures was proving a partial success.

Colombia is a beautiful country exhausted by decades of civil war, poverty and violent crime. A number of leftist guerrilla groups formed in the 1960s, most notably the ELN (National Liberation Army) and the FARC (Revolutionary Armed Forces of Colombia). The FARC grew to be the biggest and best equipped

of the rebel factions and by 2001 was reckoned to have some 16,000 members, falling to 9,000 in 2008. In violent opposition to the ELN and the FARC, there appeared right-wing paramilitary groups such as the United Self-Defence Forces of Colombia (AUC).

All of these armed groups have been involved with drug trafficking. In 2006 an indictment from the US Department of Justice charged that the FARC supplied 50 per cent of the world's cocaine. This group has also been responsible for most of the kidnappings, including the kidnap in February 2002 of presidential candidate Ingrid Betancourt, who was freed in July 2008.

Although the ELN, which snatched Matthew and his companions, is more rooted in ideology than the FARC, it, too, has profited from the illegal drugs industry, kidnapping and extortion. But hostages have also been seized by criminals with no political affiliations.

Some 3 million Colombians have been displaced by fighting in the country; they often subsist in shanty towns, deprived of basic health services and education, as initiatives continue to try to bring peace to this strife-torn land.

STANDING GUARD A soldier watches over a huge haul of marijuana in Cali, Colombia; in all, the packages contain more than 6.7 tonnes of the drug, seized from FARC rebels.

To keep me going I also made resolutions. If I ever got out of this, I promised to appreciate every second of my life. I swore I'd remember that each meal is a luxury that many can ill afford. And I promised myself that I would be more open and honest with everyone, especially my family.

I was finding it impossible to sleep for more than an hour a night. And now the cold and lack of food was starting to make me hallucinate. Once, I imagined I could go to the shop on the corner and rent a horse to get out of the jungle. Why on earth hadn't I thought of it before?

Boredom led me to fantasise, and I craved food and warmth. I imagined walking into a restaurant and ordering soup, perhaps tomato. And I wanted a baked potato, cut into quarters, with a little butter and a lot of salt, and then a huge amount of cheese. And, on top of that, chutney. Not pickle, chutney.

I fantasised about food. 'When I get home,' I said to myself, 'I'll learn how to cook.'

I tried not to look at my watch as that made the time go even more slowly.

Signs of humanity

I decided to abandon the stream and make for the ridge. On day seven, I started at 5.30am, as usual, but I felt light-headed and weak – the climbing was taking its toll. Then, miraculously, I stumbled across a path cutting across the valley; there was a camp, or some kind of construction, at the bottom. It was an absolute miracle. Though I'm an atheist, I sank to my knees and gave thanks to God. I didn't know what else to do.

The camp consisted of a little platform with four poles for a mosquito net and, on a fifth pole, an empty plastic packet of peas and carrots. I felt so happy. It was the first trace I had seen of humanity.

But as the path led upwards again, I could manage just ten paces or so before I had to sit down and rest. I made it only about halfway up the hill before the 2 o'clock deluge.

That 'night' was the worst so far. As well as being on a steep slope, which gave me bad pressure sores, there was a tropical storm with lightning and thunder that just rolled on and on. The rain was bruising. Every time I changed position, the plastic and I slithered down the slope.

As I was no longer close to the river, I had no drinking water. I had been using the front section of my torch as a cup. Though it leaked around the lens, I could get a decent mouthful from the river if I used it quickly enough.

But the torch end wasn't much use now. I had to come up with a plan to catch some of the water cascading down all around me. I took off my boots and set them down with sticks in the top to hold them open. But when I next slithered down the slope, I knocked the boots over. After that, I placed them above my position and, to my relief, they did trap some rain.

Now I was higher up, there was a view. The next day, I heard a wonderful, man-made sound. The throb of distant helicopters. Suddenly one was coming towards me. It was overhead, about 50m (160ft) away. Surely they were looking for me? I waved and jumped up and down and threw my plastic sheet in the air. They didn't see me. The sound died away.

By the tenth day, I was feeling sick, dizzy and nauseous, collapsing frequently as I pressed uphill. My feet were painful and clearly infected. I was worried I had trench foot, which is caused by water, and I was still using my wellingtons to catch the rain at night. But I had to drink and, during the day, regularly sucked moisture from the spare sock in my boot.

I arrived on a ridge above a wide flat valley. I could see irregular green shapes carved out of the jungle below that looked like signs of human activity. My heart leaped. If the land was cultivated, that meant permanent residents, almost certainly Indians.

I found an abandoned hut, containing pots, a water bottle and a gourd. There were also some rotten potatoes – the first food I'd seen. I was tempted to eat them, though in the end I decided not to. I knew that if left too long, potatoes turn green and create a toxin – they wouldn't do me any good.

'I'll find people tomorrow,' I told myself.

I had to.

Then, miraculously, I stumbled across a path cutting across the valley; there was a camp, or some kind of construction, at the bottom. It was an absolute miracle. Though I'm an atheist, I sank to my knees and gave thanks to God.

Help at last

The next morning I rounded a corner and stopped in amazement. Ahead of me on the path were two donkeys, which quickly shied off when I approached. Then I saw five cows beside a path leading to two large houses surrounded by a fence of thick vegetation.

'*Hola!*' I shouted, but there was no reply. The houses were abandoned. I was keeping a tight rein on my emotions, yet I really had hoped there would be somebody there.

I thought back on my life, on what an easy 19 years it had been. To think that I could just walk down the street and buy Coca-Cola. That I had spent every night of my life in a bed. That I used to eat good food, cuts of meat with rice and vegetables. Yet here I was, face to face with the effort it took for simple people to get food off the land.

These were my thoughts when, suddenly, I saw three figures walking towards me. They were Indians: a man, a woman and a girl. I was so happy.

They were absolutely astonished to see me. Fortunately they spoke a little Spanish.

'Hello. I haven't had food in 11 days. I have been lost.' I tried to explain I'd been captured and had escaped.

I offered them money to guide me to Santa Marta. They said it would take three days. They gave me panella, which I ate eagerly, and I drank a lot of their water. Then they told me to wait while they collected their donkeys.

After they'd gone, as I lay in the sun, I had terrible misgivings. I should never have let these people out of my sight. These were the first human beings I had seen in 11 days and I had just let them walk away. Now I had no idea if I would ever see them again.

'I'm a fool,' I said. 'An absolute fool.' Letting them go might be the worst decision I had ever made in my life.

To my relief, they came back.

We set off at once for their village, walking hard, and I struggled to keep up. I kept asking, 'Are we nearly there yet?' over and over like a child. Unlike the paramilitaries, who always said the next stop was 'one hour' off, these people were cruelly honest. The village was still miles away.

As the rain began to fall, it became obvious that I wasn't going to make it that far.

When we reached two huts occupied by an Indian woman called Oonca and her children, they finally agreed to call a halt.

Oonca took me into a hut with a fire. It was glorious. For the first time in 12 days, I began to dry out. I collapsed onto a hammock and they gave me two oranges, my first solid food. Then, as the others stoked the fire, I fell into a dreamless sleep.

The ordeal is over

'Go! Go! Go!' The command was barely audible above the clatter of the rotor blades. The Colombian army helicopter touched down and I was lifted aboard by two soldiers. The door was still open as the helicopter wheeled away over the jungle towards Santa Marta.

Welcome back *Matthew Scott arrives home to a press conference at Heathrow Airport on September 26, 2003 – to the obvious relief of his parents, James and Kate.*

FREE AT LAST Four Israeli hostages stand next to British backpacker Mark Henderson (right). They were released after more than 100 days in captivity, on December 22, 2003.

What happened next?

ON THE NIGHT of Monday, December 22, 2003, a single bell tolled from the tower of St Cuthbert's Church in Pateley Bridge, in the North Yorkshire Dales. Here a candle had been burning every day for local man Mark Henderson since he was taken hostage. The church bell was ringing out the good news: after 102 gruelling days, Mark and all the other captives had been freed.

The party had been held by members of the ELN (see page 212), who were demanding an investigation into abuses of the human rights of peasants in the Sierra Nevada region by right-wing paramilitary forces. Two captives had been released a month earlier. Now Mark and his remaining companions – Israelis Benny Daniel, Ido Guy, Erez Altawi and Orpaz Ohayon – were granted their liberty.

They had been walking under armed guard to a meeting point since the Friday; there they waited with masked rebels to be collected by a humanitarian commission in two helicopters. After 3 months and 10 days, they were gaunt and dishevelled. As Mark confessed, at times they had been close to despair. 'We felt we may just be forgotten by our governments.'

Their hopes had been raised, then dashed, when it seemed that the rebels had decided to renege on a promise to release them by Christmas. The gunmen's attitude seemed to have softened with the intervention of the UN Secretary General, Kofi Annan, and the release of a UN report into the mistreatment of the peasants.

With the escape of Matthew Scott, Mark had feared there might be reprisals against the rest of the group. But, after venting his fury, screaming and cocking his gun, the rebel leader took a philosophical view. 'There is no need to get him. The tigers will.'

That morning, after three more hours of relentless walking behind my rescuers, I'd stumbled into the village of Don Diego. And now, after 12 days in the Sierra Nevada, my ordeal was over.

In the hospital at Santa Marta, I was handed a mobile phone.

My dad picked up the phone at home in Clapham and I said, 'Hello, big man, how's it going?'

'It's Matt!' he shouted. I could hear Mum crying in the background.

When she came on the line, she asked what I wanted when I got home.

'A baked potato,' I said, 'with lots of cheese and chutney.' ∎

LEOPARD ATTACK

AN ENRAGED LEOPARD was on the loose in Victoria Falls, Zimbabwe. For Paul Connolly, a supremely fit expedition leader, it would become a fight to the death.

Rosemarie Honman woke at four in the morning to the loud noise of her five big dogs yapping and fighting. At the back door of her house in Victoria Falls, Zimbabwe, she yelled at them to shut up, then went to the kennel and threw their water bowl over them.

Three ran from the kennel and she dragged a fourth into the open. The last dog, Scruff, seemed to be making a strange throaty noise and wouldn't budge, so she left him. At dawn Scruff emerged, his ears and paws bleeding. Yet the strange, rumbling growl continued inside the kennel.

Honman called her gardener, who shone a flashlight into the dark enclosure. Two blazing eyes, bright as fireworks, glowed in the beam. 'It's a bloody leopard!' Honman shouted.

Retreating to the house, she telephoned her neighbour, Fanie Pretorius, a retired big-game hunter and safari guide. He grabbed a shotgun and called Steven Zvinongoza, chief warden of the area's national park; the two men then hurried to the Honman home.

Pretorius knew leopards almost never attacked humans, but if this animal had been cornered and taunted by dogs it would be frightened – and dangerous.

From the safety of the kitchen doorway they lobbed stones at the kennel, 3m (10ft) away. Spitting and snarling, the leopard slunk out into the daylight and charged. The two men jumped inside the house and slammed the door in the leopard's face. It thudded into the door, then dropped to the ground and crept away through the trees.

'We should shoot it because it will attack people,' Pretorius said.

'Let it be,' Zvinongoza replied. 'It will go back to the wild if we leave it alone.'

Direct approach

Honman quickly telephoned her neighbours to warn them of the danger. But she didn't call Paul and Marie Connolly, whose big garden was just over the wall. The family, she thought, was not at home.

In fact, that Friday morning, July 30, 1998, Paul Connolly had just returned from a solo kayak expedition on the Congo River. The oldest of his four daughters was away at boarding school, and Marie had taken the youngest to visit her parents in Belgium. Their two other girls had left for school. Every door of the family's big thatched house was flung wide to catch the cool morning air.

Though trained as a lawyer, Connolly, 45, had pioneered white-water rafting trips for tourists on the Zambezi River in Zimbabwe. Now he ran canoe safaris and expeditions to remote parts of Africa. Dressed as usual in denim bush shirt and shorts, a green baseball cap pulled low over his dark brows and suntanned face, he was vigorous, agile and – at about 1.8m (6ft) tall and weighing 75kg (165lb) – superbly fit.

Shortly after 9am, he was sitting in his office, detached from the main house, having a cup of coffee with Marilyn Ndlovu. A neighbour, she had stopped by with her daughter Violet, aged 3. Suddenly they heard the

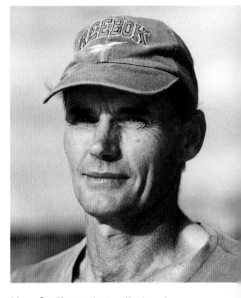

Man of action *Paul Connolly showed no fear as he approached the leopard, which turned on him at his home in the Victoria Falls area of Zimbabwe, a landlocked country in southern Africa (below).*

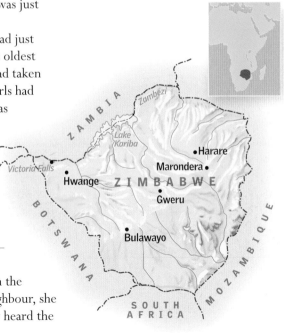

Breaking and entering *Even the inside of the house wasn't safe from the angry leopard, as it threw itself through a kitchen window.*

housekeeper screaming in the backyard. Connolly jumped up and raced out of the door.

'Boss, get the gun!' yelled Tanyara Ngwenya, the gardener. 'Leopard! Leopard!'

'Where?' Connolly demanded. Ngwenya pointed towards the back of the house. In the shadows, Connolly saw a handsome young female leopard, at least 0.75m (2½ft) high at the shoulder and well over 2m (6ft) long from its nose to the end of its twitching tail.

On tough, daily training runs along bush roads, Connolly had often met dangerous wild animals face to face. His first instinct was to run straight at them, yelling loudly and waving; once he had even stopped a charging lioness in her tracks. At other times, nimble footwork had saved him from charging buffalo, elephants and even warthogs.

Crouching low, the leopard was 18m (20yd) away and slinking past the bedroom windows, pausing to peer curiously into each one. Connolly marched boldly towards it. 'Push off!' he yelled. 'Go away!'

For an instant, man and cat stared at each other in the bright sunlight. Then, a yellowy blur of lightning, the leopard shot across the yard straight at Connolly. Even as he braced himself for the hit, Connolly had a quick-flash thought: 'How incredibly beautiful this animal is!'

In one last mighty spring, the leopard flew at his throat. With no time to duck or dodge, Connolly threw up his left arm to protect his face. Sharp teeth punctured his hand and wrist and a massive weight crashed into his chest.

Twisting to absorb the impact, Connolly shot his arm straight out from the shoulder. Fangs clamped on his wrist, and the leopard stretched upwards, its back legs on the ground and its front claws thrashing the air. Tanyara Ngwenya bravely darted in from behind, grabbed the leopard's tail and pulled with all his strength.

Bitter fight

Connolly glimpsed little Violet Ndlovu standing nearby. 'Get the child!' he yelled. 'Run!' With a scream, Violet's mother grabbed her daughter and raced indoors.

Connolly felt a surge of confidence. The leopard's weight was about 45kg (100lb), and holding it up was no problem. 'I can sort this out,' he thought. Then his foot slipped on the courtyard tiles. Man and leopard fell sideways and came down on the ground facing each other, Connolly's left hand still in its jaws. The leopard's ears were pinned flat, its yellow eyes blazing. From deep down in its belly came loud grunts. Tanyara Ngwenya sprang away and fled inside.

Connolly grabbed the soft folds of the animal's throat with his right hand and squeezed with his full strength, trying to crush its windpipe. But the leopard was all muscle, with anger seething at its core. One hand alone wasn't enough.

So, with a huge effort, Connolly slithered up onto his knees and, half-crouching over the leopard, finally dragged his hand from its jaws. Now he could lock both hands round the leopard's throat.

In a fury, the animal drew in its back legs and struck upwards at Connolly's arching body, kicking repeatedly and fast, its extended claws shredding Connolly's shirt. Knowing he was close to being disembowelled, Connolly let go and sprang to his feet.

The door was just a couple of paces away. Connolly crept slowly towards it, his gaze locked on the leopard's eyes.

Suddenly the animal attacked him again. Connolly barely had time to lift his right arm in defence before the leopard's teeth sank into his wrist.

Leaning back to keep his face and throat out of range, Connolly found the strength to rain desperate one-handed punches on the leopard's nose. The animal half-closed its eyes and shook its head. Clearly, the punches hurt.

The silent hunter

ALTHOUGH FEARED AS A 'MAN-EATER', the leopard is far more threatened by people than the other way around. Indeed, leopards today are fighting for their very existence in the wild. They are killed by trophy hunters and shot or poisoned by poachers for their beautiful coats and by farmers protecting their livestock. Their habitats are also increasingly being destroyed. Thanks to its extraordinary adaptability, the leopard is among nature's great survivors, though, and it is a strong man who takes on one of these big cats.

In terms of proportion, a leopard is identical to a domestic cat, although it is many times larger and stronger. It has a powerful neck and low-slung body on short, strong limbs, and can exhibit an astonishing turn of speed – up to 60km/h (37mph). A male leopard can weigh 65-90kg (140-200lb), with females somewhat lighter at 35-65kg (80-140lb).

There have been tales of leopards attacking people throughout recorded history, but these opportunistic hunters will often take more helpless prey, which they patiently stalk before pouncing on them. Leopards benefit from night vision and can strike under cover of darkness. Antelopes and impalas, gazelles, monkeys and wildebeest, even young giraffes are all fair game, but they will also feed off rodents, birds, reptiles, domestic dogs, lambs and poultry, and indeed, if they are starving, on human beings. Solitary hunters, leopards cannot afford to be wounded, and will fight back with intense ferocity. They are defensive of their territories, and will kill small competitors on their patch, such as jackals, wild cats and lion cubs.

It is a measure of the strength of a leopard's jaw that it can kill and carry prey two or three times its weight for miles before hauling it high up into a tree, to devour it in safety.

The struggle over *This leopard-skin rug, now hanging in Paul Connolly's home, is a vivid reminder of his boxing match with a big cat.*

Face to face, man and cat slugged it out.

With both fists, Connolly threw blows at its face as if hammering a punchbag. Blood flew from his wound and the leopard's vivid face-markings blurred in his eyes.

Abruptly the leopard let go. Connolly jumped across the threshold into the kitchen and slammed the door. With all the kitchen windows and doors shut he figured he was safe. His arms were bleeding and the pain was agonising. Wild-animal wounds, he knew, were invariably infected and must be quickly cleansed. As he moved to the kitchen sink, he glanced out of the big window.

The leopard was in a half-crouch, looking up. As soon as it spotted him, the big cat hurled itself at the window.

The leopard's left paw hit the window first, followed by its head. As the glass exploded, the animal landed in the kitchen's stainless-steel sink. It slashed out at Connolly's face with both front paws.

Clenching his right fist and drawing back his arm, Connolly delivered a haymaker punch to the leopard's nose. The animal reeled back but quickly rebounded, lashing out again.

Face to face, man and cat slugged it out. With both fists, Connolly threw blows at its face as if hammering a punchbag. Blood flew from his wound and the leopard's vivid face-markings blurred in his eyes.

The leopard tried to block his furious assault, blood spraying from a cut in its right paw. Dazed, confused and off-balance, it struggled desperately to fight out of its corner.

For 20 long seconds the deadly boxing match continued. Connolly felt his energy flag, but saw the leopard begin to cringe. Connolly punched harder and faster.

The big cat now retreated until it was balancing on the window sill. Connolly leaned over the sink and gave it one last, hard punch that became a kind of push. The animal dropped to the ground outside.

Connolly shouted to the women to stay in the TV room where they were hiding and ran to the bathroom where he bathed his arms in hot water. Suddenly he heard the double blast of a shotgun. Drawn by the screams from Connolly's yard, Fanie Pretorius and park warden Steven Zvinongoza had rushed to the scene.

Paul Connolly's lacerated arms required 37 stitches, but he is philosophical about the encounter. 'Things like this are bound to happen,' he says. 'It's the price we pay for being able to enjoy the enchantment of Africa.'

The leopard's skin is now a handsome rug in his hallway. ∎

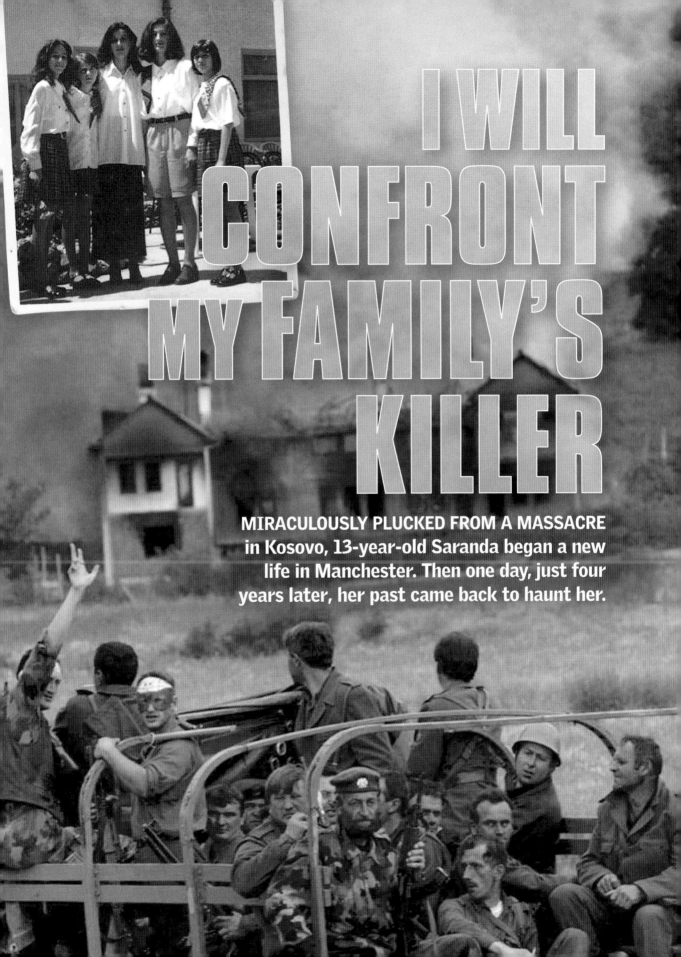

I WILL CONFRONT MY FAMILY'S KILLER

MIRACULOUSLY PLUCKED FROM A MASSACRE in Kosovo, 13-year-old Saranda began a new life in Manchester. Then one day, just four years later, her past came back to haunt her.

Family life shattered *A shot from the family album (previous page, inset) shows Saranda on the right in happier times. Little did she know the horrors she would face when the Serbian army (previous page, below, driving past a burning house near Podujevo, Kosovo) moved in.*

The normally bustling streets of Podujevo in the wooded hills of Kosovo near the Serbian border are disconcertingly quiet. For days there have been rumours that the Serbian paramilitary forces camped on the outskirts of town have come to 'cleanse' the area of ethnic Albanians.

In a house on Ivana Kosancica Street, Sala Bogujevci and her sister-in-law Shefkate sit, tense and scared. The day before they had begged their husbands, 'Go into the hills and hide or the Serbs will kill you.' Knowing that Serbs generally left women and children alone, the men had fled reluctantly. Now, their children are playing quietly indoors. Thirteen-year-old dark-haired Saranda is old enough to understand the danger. Her stomach knots as she hears shattering glass down the street and the sound of shouting and swearing. From the window she sees about 20 men approaching. They are long-haired, unshaven and dressed in the green camouflage of the Scorpions, a feared Serbian paramilitary unit. Saranda freezes. 'They're coming to our house!'

She runs to help to round up the children. They gather around their mothers, clutching at them, as heavily armed men storm the house. The soldiers herd them and another family into a neighbour's walled garden.

'Take off your headscarves!' one of the men shouts. They begin to search the women and children. In the trouser pocket of Saranda's 9-year-old brother, Shpetim, a Scorpion finds some marbles and tosses them to the ground. 'Now collect,' he bellows at the boy. Sala – a former medical student who gave up her career to bring up her three children – bends down to rescue her son's marbles. Shefkate begs, 'Please! They are only children.' In reply, a soldier hits her, pushes her down, steps back, raises his rifle.

'No!' The group screams as he opens fire. Saranda tightly hugs her cousin, 12-year-old Fatos. Then the other soldiers start shooting. Scores of bullets rip into the women and children. Saranda loses her footing and slides down the wall, bodies collapsing on top of her. As she falls she is riveted by the face of one of the killers – a tall, square-jawed man with ice-cold eyes, barking out orders.

At last the shooting stops and there is silence. Saranda hears only the gurgle of someone trying to breathe. Her brother Shpetim is draped across her thighs. His head has been blown away. She hears the sound of a new ammunition clip being slid into a gun. Saranda instinctively shields her head with her left arm as more bullets tear into the bodies around her.

Razed to the ground *An aerial shot of buildings in Pristina, the capital of Kosovo. Such scenes of utter devastation were common during periods of tension between Albanians and Serbs.*

Escape to England

As the plane comes in to land in Manchester, Saranda sees lights stretching into the darkness. It's been four months since the massacre. Saranda was pulled from the heap of bodies alive. So were cousin Fatos and his sister Jehona, ten, and brother Genc, six. But Saranda's mother, brothers and grandmother died.

The children were rescued from a Pristina hospital, looted of equipment, by British army surgeon Lieutenant Colonel David Vassallo after NATO troops liberated Kosovo on June 12, 1999. Vassallo emailed details of the children's injuries to doctors in Britain. When Manchester specialists Stuart Watson and Jim Bruce offered to carry out surgery, their medical evacuation was arranged. Saranda's father Safet and uncle Selatin were also on the plane, reunited with the children after Saranda smuggled a note from her hospital bed.

From the airport, Saranda and her cousins were taken to Manchester's Withington Hospital. Watson and Bruce realised the children needed urgent treatment for 31 gunshot wounds in total. Saranda's left arm received 13 bullets and she was shot in her leg and back. But Watson told her gently, 'There's a lot we can do to help you.'

In a 13 hour operation, Watson began mending her damaged bones and nerves and took skin grafts from her back to rebuild ruptured tissue. He also carried out surgery on Jehona, shot in the shoulders, arm and leg. Genc and Fatos were treated for gunshot wounds in both legs. Their sister Lirie, eight, found in Belgrade by Red Cross workers, had a neck injury and had to be fed through her stomach until she too was operated on in Manchester.

They each began recovering, though the process was slow and they had many operations. They moved into a refugee reception unit and, still weak, were taken by taxi to school, where they were taught in a small, separate unit of Kosovan children.

One of their earliest visitors was Pam Dawes, a volunteer with the charity Manchester Aid to Kosovo (MaK), formed by local people. Saranda found living in a sprawling city strange, but nonetheless she told Pam, 'I'm glad we're in Manchester. We feel safe here.' Another new friend, Methodist minister Bruce Thompson, helped the family deal with their grief.

Saranda learned English quicker than the others and through her they began to connect with a new world. Helped by Thompson and MaK, they moved into two houses – Saranda and Safet in one, Selatin and his four children in the other. Saranda became mother and big sister to her cousins.

Small acts of kindness played a big part in helping the Bogujevcis to settle into their new lives. At Christmas, Pam took each of the children a big box of chocolates, presents from MaK. After Saranda's third operation, her English tutor Bernard Brown cheered her up with a get-well card written in careful Albanian, learned from fellow refugees.

On her first day at mainstream school, Saranda was trying to make sense of her timetable when a girl with curly reddish hair sat beside her. 'Give us a look.' Moments later she was showing Saranda to her classroom. In time, the cousins learned bus routes, ran errands to nearby shops and picked up local accents. Their new routine was comforting after all they had been through.

In 2001 Pam took the Bogujevcis with her own family on holiday to Scotland. 'For the first time you could see them relax, be happy and carefree, and just be children.'

Securing justice

Still, nothing prepared Saranda, now a striking and calmly spoken young woman, for the news they later received from Serbian human rights lawyer Natasa Kandic. Sasa Cvjetan, a paramilitary and prominent member of Belgrade's criminal underworld, was to go on trial for his part in the

Ancient conflict zone *Kosovo lies to the south of Serbia and Montenegro. At the time of the conflict with Serbia at the end of the 1990s, around 90 per cent of the population was Albanian, 5 per cent Serb, and yet Kosovo was seen by Serbs as central to their national identity. When the Albanian majority called for an independent Kosovan state, a passionate Serbian response was inevitable. Kosovo finally declared its independence in February 2008.*

Shefkate begs, 'Please! They are only children.' In reply, a soldier hits her, pushes her down, steps back, raises his rifle. 'No!' The group screams as he opens fire.

An oasis of joy

ON MARCH 28, 2009, on the 10th anniversary of the massacre in Podujevo, a ceremony of dedication was held at the town to mark the establishment of the 'Manchester Peace Park', a true labour of love and a work in progress.

It was cousins Saranda, Fatos and Jehona who requested that a park be created, so that the people of Podujevo might enjoy the kind of generous, social, open spaces afforded by the parks of Manchester. It would be a symbol of healing and renewal, a celebration of the close bonds between Britain and Kosovo.

Manchester Aid to Kosovo (MaK) set about fundraising for the park. In 2004, landscape architect Jane Knight of the Eden Project in Cornwall began to draw up designs for a disused 22 acre site on the edge of town, working with others, not least the townspeople themselves, such as the teenage volunteers of the Peace Boys of Podujevo. Links have been forged with Kosovan ecologists, with local schools, and with Women in Action, which includes young widows and women whose lives have been blighted by war. In a town where unemployment stands at around 80 per cent, trainee gardeners have been recruited.

When the park is complete, it will have facilities for basketball, volleyball and football, and much more besides, including woodland walks, a picnic area and a playground. A central meeting place is equipped for performances.

The public dedication was attended by the survivors, bereaved families and representatives of MaK and the Eden Project. The weekend of the ceremony was focused on remembrance, and in the town centre a banner, bearing the word 'peace' in hundreds of languages, was unfurled.

The Travelling Band from Manchester were central in helping to lead the event. 'Much of our celebration of life and recovery comes through working with musicians,' says Pam. Dennis Wrigley, an initiator and early leader of Manchester Aid to Kosovo, sent a dedication, expressing the hope that the park be 'an oasis of joy'.

To learn more about MaK and the Peace Park, visit www.makonline.org.

PLACE OF COMFORT Saranda at the dedication ceremony for the Peace Park, surrounded by friends and family from Kosovo and the UK.

massacre that day in Podujevo, and as the five Bogujevci children were the only survivors, Kandic was desperate for them to go to Belgrade to testify.

Safet and Selatin agreed it was important for their children to secure justice for the murder of their relatives. Yet the prospect of facing one of the Scorpions in court was terrifying.

The trial was about to begin when, in Belgrade, the Serbian prime minister was assassinated. The trial was postponed. 'If the Serbs can't protect their own prime minister,' Safet argued, 'then they won't be able to protect us either, so I'm afraid of the children going there.' Their fathers asked if they could testify via a video link from Manchester, but were turned down. They requested UN protection in Belgrade, but it wasn't possible for foreign armed forces to enter Serbia.

While the family grappled with a monumental decision, they visited Podujevo to unveil a plaque in the garden marking the fourth anniversary of the massacre. It was the first time Saranda had been back. She saw the bullet marks on the wall. 'It's like the day it happened. I feel like I'm here with them – my mum, my grandmother, my brothers, my auntie, my cousin, everyone. I can see the whole thing …'

Once more she heard Genc shouting, 'Look what they have done,' and gazed down at her brother Shpetim resting on her legs, his head blown off.

Out of her nightmare, Saranda Bogujevci plucked a new determination. She would go back to Belgrade to stop such horror happening to others.

Giving evidence

The door of their plane swung open at Belgrade Airport on a July day. The cousins flinched when they saw armed men on the Tarmac. The entire terminal had been sealed off. A convoy of Jeeps and cars with darkened windows was waiting outside with 30 armed officers from Serbia's special unit for witness protection, who would guard them round the clock.

At their hotel, they took over a whole floor under heavy guard and the dining room was sealed off for their exclusive use. But when Natasa Kandic briefed the children about what would happen in court, it was too much for Genc. Just ten, and with a bullet still lodged in his groin, he pleaded, 'I don't want to see their faces, I don't want to stay.' A relative took him away to Kosovo for the duration of the trial.

For the others, the five days in Belgrade were an ordeal. First, each of the children had to identify Cvjetan separately. At Belgrade state prison they peered in turn through a one-way glass at five prisoners lined up behind it.

Tattooed and muscular through long hours of body-building behind bars, the men tried to confuse the children. Four of them snarled and looked menacing, while Cvjetan, his hair now cropped, smiled. But Lirie, who was still waiting for her neck wounds to heal sufficiently to allow cosmetic surgery, blurted out, 'That's him! The one in the red sweater!' All the cousins identified Cvjetan as the killer.

Finally it was Saranda's turn to give evidence in court. Dressed in a black T-shirt and jeans, she entered Chamber Three of Belgrade's District Court and took her seat opposite the Serbian woman judge. She felt hot – the court was stifling – then scared of the questioning she would face. She turned her eyes to Cvjetan. He was sitting just feet from her, about the same distance as when he'd been slaughtering her family.

As a former Scorpion told the court how he saw Cvjetan hurriedly reloading his weapon, Saranda remembered her father telling her he counted 97 empty shell casings in the garden.

She gave her evidence in English with a UN translator at her side. Still looking frail – after skin grafts and five operations – she spoke with authority and determination. 'I was 13, almost 14 years of age. We lived in a house …' For 2 hours she talked through the massacre unflinchingly. At one point her translator had to break off and turn away before he could continue.

Guilty *Sasa Cvjetan makes his way to the Court of Justice in the Serbian town of Prokuplje, accused of killing ethnic Albanian civilians, including members of Saranda's family. Thanks in large part to Saranda's testimony, he was found guilty.*

'He threw away his [empty] gun and took someone else's weapon ... when I slid to the ground he was still firing and he hit me twice ...'

Saranda looked at Cvjetan often as she spoke. Not once did he look at her, but she began to feel a power over him. Finally he was having to face up to what he had done to her family. 'I remember him,' Saranda said. 'I recognise the expression in his eyes.'

Jailed

Eight months after their gruelling ordeal, the Bogujevcis were back home in Manchester when they received the news they had craved – Cvjetan had been found guilty and sentenced to a maximum of 20 years in jail.

The children and their fathers hugged each other in relief; their bravery had won justice for their loved ones. They were the first children ever to give evidence at a war crimes trial. In recognition of this, the Anne Frank Trust UK presented them with an international award for moral courage.

Saranda will never forget the tragedy, but the nightmare was over. 'I wanted to tell these people they can never destroy this family.' ∎

Where are they now?

FOLLOWING HER RETURN TO BELGRADE to testify against Sasa Cvjetan, Saranda and her family – her cousins Fatos, Jehona, Lirie and Genc along with their fathers – pursued her personal campaign for justice for her murdered relatives. Another Scorpion, Dejan Demirovic, accused with Cvjetan, had fled to Canada in 2001, before he could be arrested, and was tried *in absentia*.

A hearing before the Canadian Refugee Board was set for January 2004 and Saranda travelled to Canada to testify about her ordeal. In October 2005,

Demirovic was deported from Toronto via Milan, and immediately detained in Belgrade's central prison. He has since been released due to lack of evidence, but Saranda and her cousins have continued in their quest to bring the guilty to justice, and have given evidence in other trials since.

Saranda has recently graduated and works in the interactive arts, concentrating on photography. 'A lot of my work is to do with my experience during the war, and in Kosovo, so I've concentrated a lot on landscape, trying to tell a story through objects rather than people – the journeys I used to take as a kid in Kosovo, the power station where my dad worked, the buildings around Manchester.'

She has an extraordinarily positive outlook. 'Manchester is my second home. We've met so many great people and had so much support. The anniversary, the dedication, make you want to celebrate the lives of those who died, instead of always thinking of the worst that has happened. As a kid, that's what I remember, with my family always being happy, always together. You can't change what happened in the past, but you can change what happens in the future.'

THROUGH THE LOOKING GLASS Back in Kosovo, Saranda takes a self-portrait photograph. In the background is a painting of her two brothers, killed in the massacre.

Edwards's lungs were aching, and he was running desperately short of air. He had to make a split-second decision: 'Do I go back up to the surface, or do I rescue him now?'

Even though Tony must have been under the water for about 8 minutes, Edwards realised it wasn't the moment to take a risk.

He shot back to the surface, gulped for air and dived one last time. Seconds later he grabbed an arm and dragged a limp Tony Wicks to the surface. 'I've found him!' Edwards yelled. 'He's not breathing!' Chris Davidson ran back to his office, cancelled the divers and called instead for specialist paramedics.

Treading water, with Tony's head cradled in the crook of his left arm, Edwards felt halfway up the boy's neck for his carotid pulse and pressed gently for 5 seconds. Nothing.

The boy's eyes were open. Steely-grey, they bulged out of his face. Edwards blew on them in the hope the eyelids would flicker. No reaction.

He's got to be dead, thought Edwards. Tony's skin was clammy and paper-white. The only colour in him was his ginger crew-cut hair.

Fighting for life

Tilting Tony's head back with his right hand to ensure a clear airway to his lungs, Edwards began mouth-to-mouth resuscitation, all the while manoeuvring himself and the boy nearer the pontoon. He managed to hook his left arm round one of the supporting posts, but was still treading water.

Then his toes felt something metallic. Edwards put his feet down flat and found he was standing on a submerged supermarket trolley.

Now that he had something to take his weight, he held Tony's shoulders out of the water, tilted his head back and placed his mouth over the boy's to continue resuscitation.

Slowly, colour returned to Tony's skin. Three minutes after being plucked from the canal bed, a noise came from the boy's mouth. But his body remained limp, his eyes blind. Still Edwards refused to give up.

'How is he?' bellowed a voice. Looking up, Edwards saw a fireman kneeling on the pontoon. He felt the boy's neck again. This time there was no mistaking the tell-tale sensation under his fingers: a pulse! He called out, 'He's alive! I'm sure he's alive!' The fireman reached down for Tony.

'Have you got oxygen?' Edwards asked. The fireman nodded. 'Get that first,' Edwards told him. 'I'll carry on with the resuscitation. We've got to keep this going – I don't want to lose him now!'

As the oxygen arrived, Edwards passed the still-unconscious Tony up onto the pontoon. The fireman placed the boy in the recovery position. Thick black water and vomit trickled from Tony's mouth. But when the oxygen

Happy together *Tony Wicks (right) and his friend Joshua Soper (left) fully appreciate the dangers of playing near canals now, after Tony's dramatic rescue.*

Take a deep breath In common with other mammals, human beings have an innate 'dive reflex', which, some scientists believe, may be a legacy of an aquatic phase in our evolution. The instant our faces are immersed in water, the dive reflex (bradycardia) is triggered. As receptors send out emergency signals, the heartbeat slows automatically, reducing the body's need for oxygen. Blood flow to the abdominal organs and muscles decreases, and blood is redistributed to vital organs such as the brain and heart.

Some 20,000 exponents of the internationally competitive sport of 'freediving' develop and exploit the body's natural responses, enabling them to dive, with no additional oxygen, to depths where the lungs contract to the size of a fist, for minutes at a time. Like whales and dolphins, freedivers say, we have the ability to swim deep beneath the waves – but unlike whales and dolphins, we have to train our minds and bodies for 'apnoea', a temporary inability to breathe, as pearl divers, seen above, have done for centuries.

The record for 'static apnoea' (holding the breath under water) stands at 10 minutes. Tony Wicks's survival was nothing short of miraculous. After 8 minutes under water, most people will have drowned.

mask was put on him he coughed and spluttered, obviously breathing, albeit erratically.

Moments later an ambulance crew arrived. Paramedics wrapped Tony in blankets and strapped him to a stretcher for the 4 minute dash to Doncaster Royal Infirmary. Just 10 minutes had passed since Joshua had knocked on the door.

As he picked up his clothes, Edwards had a new fear. Tony must have been under that water for at least 8 minutes. If he lives, what sort of state is he going to be in? In his police days, he had pulled a suicide from a gas oven. He had saved her life but she was left with permanent brain damage.

Meanwhile, back in her flat, Nadine Wicks had decided she would go and look for Tony. But where?

'Mrs Wicks?' Two police officers were standing at her door with Joshua, who was sobbing. 'Will you come with us? Tony's been fished out of the canal. He's in the infirmary.'

Coming back to life

In the resuscitation room, Tony lay wrapped in a blanket as doctors desperately tried to warm him up. He was still unconscious and his veins collapsed at the first prick of a rehydration needle.

Thanks to Edwards, he was still breathing. The shock of his hot body hitting cold water had thrown him into a sort of suspended animation, or 'dive reflex', where the pulse falls dramatically and blood is redirected from the skin and intestines to heart muscle and brain. Babies can survive this way under water for up to an hour, but the infirmary's medical team had never heard of it happening in a child of Tony's age.

So many doctors and nurses were swarming around Tony that Nadine could not get near her son. He looked so small, submerged under tubes and dials.

'Has he been baptised?' a nurse asked her. 'Would you like a priest?'

Next morning, Bob Edwards was driving to his office in Leeds when his mobile phone rang. It was a local radio station. Tony Wicks had just regained consciousness, they told him. 'Do you know how he is?' asked Edwards, dreading the reply.

'Oh, he's fine; he's sitting up in bed, asking for breakfast.'

When Edwards walked into the ward later that day, he discovered that Tony had suffered no ill effects beyond a sore throat from a tube the doctors had inserted.

Nadine rushed over and grabbed his hand. 'I just can't believe you risked your life to save my Tony,' she sobbed. 'I don't know how to thank you.'

'There's one way *you* can thank me, young man,' smiled Edwards, perching by Tony's bed. 'Promise me you'll take some swimming lessons!' ∎

IT'S STILL ME INSIDE

HORRIBLY BURNED WHEN AN ARGENTINE jet fighter bombed his troop ship during the Falklands War, Simon Weston, a soldier of 3 Company Welsh Guards, wasn't expected to make it. But he won through, and has been an inspiration to thousands.

At 2.10pm on June 8, 1982, I was down below on the tank deck of the troop-landing ship *Sir Galahad*, waiting to land with my mortar platoon at Fitzroy to open a new advance on Port Stanley. What I could not see were the Argentine Skyhawk attack jets that had suddenly appeared and were now streaking across the water towards my ship.

'If anything goes wrong now, at least they'll have some blood to slap into us,' I joked to Byron Cordey as I sat down with my back against some boxes of plasma.

I'd played rugby with Byron. He was one of the big lads in Prince of Wales Company who were disembarking just ahead of us. There was a definite buzz in the air as we got ready to go ashore and do some fighting.

I spotted Yorkie Walker stretched out on top of a stack of packing cases, his hands behind his head, his beret tilted over his face in a way that was peculiarly his. I wondered what would be a good way of waking him up. 'I know,' I thought, 'I'll shout "air raid!" down his ear.'

But someone else did it for me. At that precise moment, a voice echoed, loud and urgent, down the whole length of the tank deck. 'Air-raid warning red! Get down! Get down!' All around me people sprang into action. Facing the stern, I managed to get myself into a sort of semi-crouch, then decided to look up through the open deck above me in the hope of catching a glimpse of an enemy plane.

The bomb came through the port side of the ship and across in front of me, a great grey streak flying from right to left. It had sliced through the port engine room and flew across the roadway towards the starboard engine room against whose bulkheads I had dumped my kit. I heard jet engines screaming from above as the planes went over, then there was a brilliant flash from the engine room, and the beginning of my personal Hiroshima.

The flash was yellow and orange, like an oil-rig flare. A moment later there was the warmth of summer in the air, only there was no breeze, nothing moving at all.

Nobody did anything. Nobody said anything. A cloud bellied outwards and upwards and we just watched it engulf us. It was all so quiet. The lad next to me was standing as still as a statue.

Suddenly everybody sprang back to life, but now men were shadows, silhouettes with brilliant, whole-body haloes of the most beautiful colours I had ever seen. I felt the air sucked from my lungs and then a surge of hot air washed over me. No sensation yet of the cruel, excruciating, unrelenting heat: in that first blinding flash all my exposed nerve endings had been scorched away.

I can't have been more than 6m (20ft) away when the bomb, a 2,000-pounder, exploded. I thought that they had napalmed the ship. Pain drew my eyes to the backs of my hands and I watched, transfixed by the horror, as they fried and melted, the skin bubbling and flaking away from the bone like the leaves of a book burning on a bonfire before being carried away by the wind.

I looked around me for help. Other people were in desperate trouble. I saw a mate from my depot days and tried to help him to his feet. His uniform was blazing and the flames ate into my palms as I lifted against the weight. It was useless. My hands were strangely slippery, as if they had wet soap on them and I was trying to grip a pole. My mate slid time and again from my grasp and I finally staggered back defeated. It was then that I saw, on the front of his burning combat jacket, the layers and layers of skin that had flaked off my palms. My hands were raw.

Men were mutilated and burning, and fought to rip off their clothing or douse the flames and beat at their faces, arms, legs, hair. A human fireball crumpled less than a metre from me like a disintegrating Guy Fawkes. I remembered Yorkie and tried to get near him, but I couldn't. Everything was on fire, even the blood in the first-aid boxes was ablaze. I knew he'd had it.

I didn't know what to do next. All I wanted was to get out, but I didn't know which way to run. Another friend careered past me, a human torch, his hands and face melting as he collapsed onto the red-hot deck. I blundered away blindly and saw others standing stock-still, mesmerised, their heads swollen like dark, smouldering footballs, their eyes piercing through their charred faces like the eyes of coal miners, their blackened hands held in the air as if in surrender. Then they, too, started to run.

Undisguised horror

It got worse. The large consignment of petrol for the Land Rovers began to spurt out of the jerrycans and ignite in great sheets of flame. Our 81mm mortar bombs started to cook. Bullets and grenades on men's belts began to explode. Shrapnel whizzed past my head as I stumbled around in the dark, dark smoke.

I was suffocating; I was on fire and nobody could help me. I was in a hundred separate agonies as I ran towards where I'd left my sub-machine gun. My thought was that I wanted to shoot myself. I stumbled over men on the floor. I could not be sure who they all were; their faces were too blackened or disfigured, but some I recognised by their voices, by the pleas and the screams of comrades I had laughed and joked with for so many years. Even more grotesque, I knew others by the shape of their teeth as the flames peeled back their lips into hideous grins.

I couldn't find my gun; but if somebody had handed me one at that point I would surely have released my friends from their torment and then I would have turned it on myself.

A movement. A barely felt ripple in the smoke on my face. Instinct made me turn and face the direction it was flowing from. The fresh air had

The air was cool and clean and sweet as I charged up the stairs. I felt as if I was running all the way to heaven.

to be forward, through the wall of flames where the roadway widened out into the tank deck proper. I would have to run through the flames. There was nowhere else to go.

I charged along the roadway, fighting with every ounce of strength and determination I had left. I emerged into a passageway to find bodies lying all over the floor – live bodies, unburned but in shock; they still hadn't reacted. I ran on thanking God that many of my comrades were still alive. I surged along a passage towards the front of a ship. I came to a door but I couldn't open it. My hands were so badly burned. Someone swung it open. A big Marine on the other side yelled, 'Keep on up the stairs until you can't go any further. There you'll be safe.' He looked at me with undisguised horror.

The air was cool and clean and sweet as I charged up the stairs. I felt as if I was running all the way to heaven.

A huge pall of black smoke hung over the *Sir Galahad* in the clear still air. It was a shock to remember what a beautiful day it was. There appeared to be no panic on that upper deck, just men giving what comfort they could to their injured mates.

'Sit down here and let's sort you out,' said a Guardsman who steered me gently towards an empty bit of floor space.

Rescue operation

The Guardsman found a medic, and the two of them cut my trousers and boots off and threw them over the side. They jettisoned all the money in my pockets, too, and the set of poker dice that had helped me win it. Then I was parted from the gold St Christopher medal that Mam had given me for my 18th birthday, and that she'd been anxious to know I'd got with me when I'd left England on the *QE2* for the Falklands. And – every bit as precious – the photograph of my little niece Rebecca in the bath that my sister Helen had given me the last time I left my home town of Nelson in mid-Glamorgan. Then they ripped my syrette of morphine from my jacket and jabbed it into my arm, painted a big 'M' and the time of application onto my favourite, non-army-issue green T-shirt and sat me with my back against a pillar.

Sea King and Wessex helicopters had launched a rescue operation within seconds of the bomb raid. The pilots were amazing, shuttling ceaselessly back and forth to bring casualties off to the battalion's aid post ashore. I was dressed in just my underpants and T-shirt as I rose up into the Sea King. The cold bit into the open wounds on my legs. I started to shiver.

We flew straight to Ajax Bay, a trip of just 5 minutes. All that afternoon and evening, helicopters continued to bring load after load of casualties. At one point there was a shout that all the treatment areas were completely full. Medics rushed around trying to distribute even shares of their expertise and loving care. I was told there were 143 casualties, including 46 who had died.

They came to cut the rings off my fingers. By now my eyelids had swollen and I couldn't see a thing. My hands and fingers were enclosed in sterile plastic bags and I was swimming in and out of consciousness. My body was 46 per cent burned.

'I'm thirsty,' I cried out. 'I need water.'

All I got, though, was saline solution.

Fight over the far islands

TO THE BRITISH they are the Falklands, named after the naval treasurer Viscount Falkland when English sailors landed there in 1690. To the Argentines they are Las Islas Malvinas. This archipelago in the South Atlantic, 650km (400 miles) southeast of South America – comprising East and West Falkland, along with a constellation of hundreds of mostly unpopulated smaller islands – was declared a British colony in 1833. Argentina has always disputed British ownership.

In April 1982, Argentina's ruling military junta, under General Leopoldo Galtieri, ordered an invasion. Forces overran the British garrison, and within 3 hours the 80 Marines surrendered.

In London, Prime Minister Margaret Thatcher was advised by naval chiefs that a task force could be despatched to reclaim the territories – an objective achieved within 74 days, though at vast expense and with

TO STANLEY The *Sir Galahad* was waiting to land at Fitzroy, near Bluff Cove, on the east of East Falkland – in preparation for an advance on Stanley – when it was blown apart by Skyhawk attack bombers.

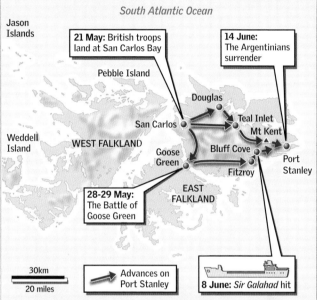

South Atlantic Ocean

Jason Islands

21 May: British troops land at San Carlos Bay

14 June: The Argentinians surrender

Pebble Island

Douglas

San Carlos

Teal Inlet

Mt Kent

Weddell Island

WEST FALKLAND

Goose Green

Bluff Cove

Port Stanley

Fitzroy

28-29 May: The Battle of Goose Green

EAST FALKLAND

30km / 20 miles

Advances on Port Stanley

8 June: *Sir Galahad* hit

FLYING THE FLAG A column of 45 Royal Marine Commandos march towards Port Stanley.

tragic loss of life. Indeed, the retaking of the islands involved more than 100 British ships and 28,000 men and women, of whom 255 were killed on land and at sea, and 777 were wounded.

By the time of the attack on the *Sir Galahad* and her sister ship *Sir Tristram*, Britain had already lost HMS *Sheffield, Ardent, Antelope, Coventry* and the container ship *Atlantic Conveyor*.

The loss of life among the Argentine conscripted forces was three times that of the British. The sinking of the *General Belgrano* by HMS *Conqueror* on May 2, at a cost of 323 Argentine lives, was a source of fierce controversy when it was revealed that the cruiser, a survivor of Pearl Harbor, had been outside a 200 mile (320km) exclusion zone imposed by the British, and was sailing away from the conflict.

On June 13, Argentine commander General Mario Menéndez surrendered, under pressure from his demoralised troops. In all, there was more than one death for every two of the 1,800 islanders.

I passed out again, and woke up to a sound that made my blood run cold. 'Air-raid warning green!'

Please God, no. Was it for real or was I just reliving the nightmare of the voice that had echoed down on the tank deck? The medics began shifting stretchers. When they got to me there was another shout.

'Air-raid warning red! Get down! Get down! Get down!'

Another blur. I came round in a helicopter. I felt us land on the deck of a ship and I was being lifted by kind hands.

'All right, lad, we've got you now.' I didn't have a clue where I was, but somehow I knew I was going to be safe.

As we made our approach to RAF Brize Norton, several weeks after the attack on *Galahad,* the captain made an announcement: 'Ladies and gentlemen, you have just entered the *Guinness Book of Records.* The flight from Montevideo has taken us just 16 hours, a new record.'

It was only later that I discovered part of the reason for the rush was that I was on board. Apparently my injuries were so bad that I could have croaked at any moment.

Full honours *The Duke of Edinburgh pins the South Atlantic Medal, awarded for service during the Falklands War, on Guardsman Simon Weston at Buckingham Palace.*

Touching down was a great relief. I had come home. I didn't know quite what faced me now but at least I had returned, which was more than many of my friends had done.

My first thoughts were of my family, and particularly my mother. I knew that she would be there to greet me if she possibly could, but I had no idea what she had been told. I was very apprehensive. How would she react when she saw me?

I was driven by ambulance from the landing strip to the RAF hospital at Wroughton. One of the RAF boys waiting to carry me inside said, 'Welcome home, lad, we'll look after you now.' Those were the first words anyone had really said to me since we'd arrived, but they didn't sink in properly. I was still looking for my family.

'Look at that poor boy,' my mother said to Gran, her voice full of emotion.

I didn't realise that she hadn't recognised her own son. Then when I called out, 'Hello, Mam,' she turned and our eyes met.

She was completely stunned; it was as if she suddenly couldn't breathe. She didn't say anything to me. She couldn't.

The RAF boys whisked me away so that she could compose herself. When I saw her a few minutes later she was still in tears.

'Don't cry, Mam,' I said. 'I'm alright. I'm alive.'

There wasn't time to say more. The doctors were eager to helicopter the injured men to the Queen Elizabeth Military Hospital in Woolwich. I said a brief goodbye to Mam and my stretcher was lifted through the doors of a big Chinook helicopter. It was the worst helicopter ride of my life. Chinooks vibrate violently in the middle, and that was just where I was sited. I felt totally helpless. The sheets I was lying on had wrinkled and stuck to my back. It was agony.

The first specialist I saw was Colonel McDermott, a plastic surgeon who specialised in treating burns victims. He decided I should be lowered into a bath to soak the dressings on my back and legs. I can still hear my screams as they lifted me in. Every single individual nerve ending was on fire.

Colonel McDermott decided to concentrate initially on my hands and my eyes. The incessant pain in my hands was the only thing reminding me that these strange mutilated objects belonged to me.

'As long as you can sort out my eyes and my hands I don't care what you do,' I said.

'Those are first on the list.'

Agonising operations

They were due to operate on my eyelids for the first time on July 5. In the pre-op room I took a deep breath and told Colonel McDermott about the nightmare I'd had ever since I was choppered to Ajax Bay.

'The thing is, I'm petrified of going blind, absolutely petrified …'

The Colonel smiled through his mask. 'Well that's not too unreasonable, but you won't go blind if we can get the eyelids working properly.'

The idea was to remove thin layers of living skin from my thighs, shoulders and rump, with a machine like a cheese parer, then to lay it out on cotton wool before stitching some of it onto the backs of my hands and using some to rebuild my scorched melted lids. The thinner the graft the higher the 'percentage take'.

The blink reflex is a remarkable thing, the Colonel told me, and it can usually outpace any foreign body flying towards the eye, or any flash, so it is very rare that the front surface of the eye is directly burned. In my case the blink reflex had closed the lids firmly.

The trouble was that in having closed so efficiently and therefore taken the brunt of the thermal injury, the lids themselves were at risk of scarring up and contracting, which would cause secondary exposure of the cornea. The colonel wanted to prevent this at all costs, because sooner or later it would lead to ulceration and to perforation of the eye itself. That is one way in which eyes can be lost.

The colonel chose a relatively hairless part of my shoulder from which to take this graft. With luck this would mean that there would be little growth of hair on my lower eyelids.

These first few operations at Woolwich also brought home to me another aspect of my recovery that I had not been aware of. My body was 46 per cent burned, and all the affected areas needed to be resurfaced with fresh skin. What I had thought of as my unscarred areas rapidly became donor sites for the areas that were badly burned. And let me tell you, having just one split-skin graft off part of me that I'd thought had escaped the inferno was bad enough. Having that area and others harvested again and again for yet more skin was absolutely excruciating, and meant that

'Look at that poor boy,' my mother said to Gran, her voice full of emotion. I didn't realise that she hadn't recognised her own son.

those parts too became scarred. I kept on believing that it would be all right. But the agony of the operations had only just begun.

Of all those injured on the *Sir Galahad*, I was the last to leave hospital in 1983. My body looked like a pink-and-white chessboard where patches of skin had been lifted from one part to be grafted to another. After 35 operations, the worst of my physical battle against the burns I'd suffered may have been over, but my battle to come to terms with them had scarcely started. Being filmed for the TV documentary *Simon's War*, first shown that year, had provided some light relief and the public response was overwhelming with more than 1,000 letters from people I had never met. Physically I was beginning to feel better, but once the attention died down and I was home again I began to be tormented again by nightmares and flashbacks. I was off drugs and my mind was back together, and I was having

Facing their demons

IN NOVEMBER 1991, as part of his emotional recovery, Simon Weston returned to the Falklands, an experience recalled in his book *Going Back*. 'I wanted to go to San Carlos, to the freezer plant used as a hospital where I almost died, and to the shore where they put the boys to rest.' He adds, 'A strange idea had resurfaced, that one day I would meet the pilot who dropped the bomb on *Sir Galahad*.'

That meeting took place in an apartment in Buenos Aires, arousing conflicting emotions – rage, forgiveness, tolerance. The pilot responsible for the deaths of 46 men and the injury of 97 others was named Carlos Cachon. Although he knew nothing of the tally of the killed and wounded, he had known, of course, that the bomb had wrought terrible destruction, and on his return from the war, records Weston, he had begun to suffer cramps in his back, a pain that woke him in the early hours – a pain that shifted to his mind. 'He had wanted to meet someone from the other side, if possible someone from *Sir Galahad*, to express his sympathy, make human contact, find the human face behind the smoke and flames.'

When Cachon was approached it was like an answer to his prayer: 'Like touching heaven with my hands.' For both, it was a way to lay down some ghosts.

In the years since the Falklands War, Simon has brought hope and inspiration to many. He works tirelessly for charity – although his own charity, Weston Spirit, closed in 2008, after bringing opportunities to 85,000 vulnerable young people in the UK. Simon's story has been the subject of five BBC documentaries, including the TV tie-in to *Going Back*. He has also turned his hand to fiction, and even a children's book, *A Nod from Nelson*. In 1992 he was awarded the OBE. Simon and his wife Lucy have three children, James, Stuart and Caitlin.

TOGETHER IN PEACE At long last, Simon meets the pilot who dropped the bomb, Carlos Cachon. Left to right: Carlos's wife, Graciela, Caitlin, Simon, James, Carlos, with Stuart on his shoulders, and Lucy.

to face the future and the fact that there were things I could never do again. The dream of playing rugby had long since been shattered.

I was desperately trying to live like a normal human being, but I had to look at life in a different way because people looked at me differently. Inside I was normal, but outside I was scarred. I wanted to go places and do things, but everywhere people stopped and stared. Most people felt revulsion when they saw me. They seemed to think that I was scarred on the brain too. Somebody at a darts trip to Hereford said, 'Oi, when you gonna take your mask off then?'

From despair to hope

In October 1984 I reported back to Woolwich for yet another operation on my hands. Not long after I was summoned to London to the medical discharge board. After a day of tests, I found myself seated in front of a doctor. It took a time for what he was saying to sink in. I suppose I was clutching at straws, hoping to catch some stray word of hope or encouragement in among all the medical mumbo-jumbo. But ultimately what it boiled down to was that I was unfit for further military service.

I was 23, and I wanted to enjoy my life to the full. I still looked like a panda with those white eyes in the middle of a red face and my Miss Piggy nose. You try to put up a front but it drags the stuffing right out of you. The scars would settle in time, but I didn't quite feel ready to go job-hunting. I guess I was afraid of employers' reactions. Inside I was still the same old Simon Weston; it was just that everyone else looked at my face first – and I knew only too well what they saw. In the outside world, people still said to me, 'You're wonderful, you're a hero,' and then they'd pat the old boy on the back and buy him a drink. And I'd wake up in the morning feeling awful and I'd look in the mirror and I'd think, 'what's the point?' I got more and more lazy and lethargic. I was drinking myself into oblivion. I stopped caring about myself and about everything, I didn't wash, I didn't brush my teeth, I just wanted to sit in my room alone all day.

Over and over I blamed myself for being alive while my mates had died. Out of the 30 of us in mortar platoon, only eight had survived.

At the end of her tether, my Mam decided to get in touch with my other 'family' to see if they could help.

The Welsh Guards couldn't have responded more quickly. An officer called at our house a few days later on what I thought was just a passing visit. We swapped a few pleasantries, and then I was asked if I'd like to go to Germany to watch the team play rugby.

'Yes, sir,' I said. No hesitation.

Depression is a circle and you're a pea in the centre, rattling around. You're stuck. But there is a door in that circle, and everyone has the key to open it. My regiment was my key. When I got to Germany and discovered that they hadn't forgotten me and they were still my mates and treated me quite normally – they were used to seeing injured soldiers all the time and were not going to bend over backwards for me. I was cured.

Then in the summer of 1986 I was invited by the Guards Association of Australasia to make the first of my goodwill tours down under. While

Tying the knot *Simon married Lucy Tetherington on May 12, 1990, at the Guards Chapel in London.*

Helping others *Simon trains for the New York Marathon in Central Park on October 31, 1998, with other team members. They ran on behalf of his charity, Weston Spirit.*

at Woolwich it had also been arranged that when I was better I should join Operation Raleigh as a signaller. Sitting on a plane with Raleigh founder John Blashford-Snell, I said, 'I never did find out who nominated me.'

'I shouldn't really tell you this,' he said, 'but I'll give you a clue. It is someone very closely associated with your part of the world, who has followed your progress with a lot of interest and concern.'

'My mam?' I ventured.

'No. As a matter of fact, it was the Prince of Wales.'

Love conquers all

If I hadn't got injured, I would have never met Lucy, my wife. One of my greatest fears was that I would never find another girlfriend, never find a girl to settle down with and enjoy the life most people take for granted – marriage, home, kids, work, just the ordinary things people do.

We met through Weston Spirit, the charity I had co-founded in Liverpool in 1988 to remotivate unemployed young people, where Lucy was working as a volunteer. She also worked part-time, giving keep-fit classes and was studying leisure management at college.

We married in Guards Chapel at Wellington Barracks, in London's Birdcage Walk, on May 12, 1990, exactly eight years after I had sailed for the Falklands on the *QE2*.

Ours is a very balanced partnership and there's no doubt that meeting Lucy started to punch pegs into holes for me. It's like sitting in front of a great big jigsaw puzzle and you have to put this piece there and that piece there.

How I look has never been an issue between us. In fact, Lucy says she loves my bald head because she can spot me easily in the supermarket. It only seems to bother other people but that's their problem really, not ours.

About the time we got married, we were invited out to dinner, in Swansea, and as we came down the stairs Lucy got taken away by the women. The first thing they said to her was, 'We didn't expect you to be quite so pretty.'

'What did they mean by that?' she asked me later. 'Just because you're scarred, does that mean they thought you wouldn't find anyone attractive to marry?' We sometimes get jibes like that, but on the whole people are lovely.

It's a wonderful feeling to be with Lucy. She never makes me feel bad, no matter what is going on, and she's so funny we laugh constantly. Apart from occasional fallings out, she completed an awful lot for me.

Love will do that for you every time. Between two people it is probably the most powerful emotion there is, but in people themselves, the greatest power in the world is hope. Without hope you have nothing. Hope is what keeps you going: hope that things will work out right; that you'll meet the right person; that things will resolve themselves; hope that war doesn't happen. Hope is truly the most wonderful emotion you can imagine. ∎

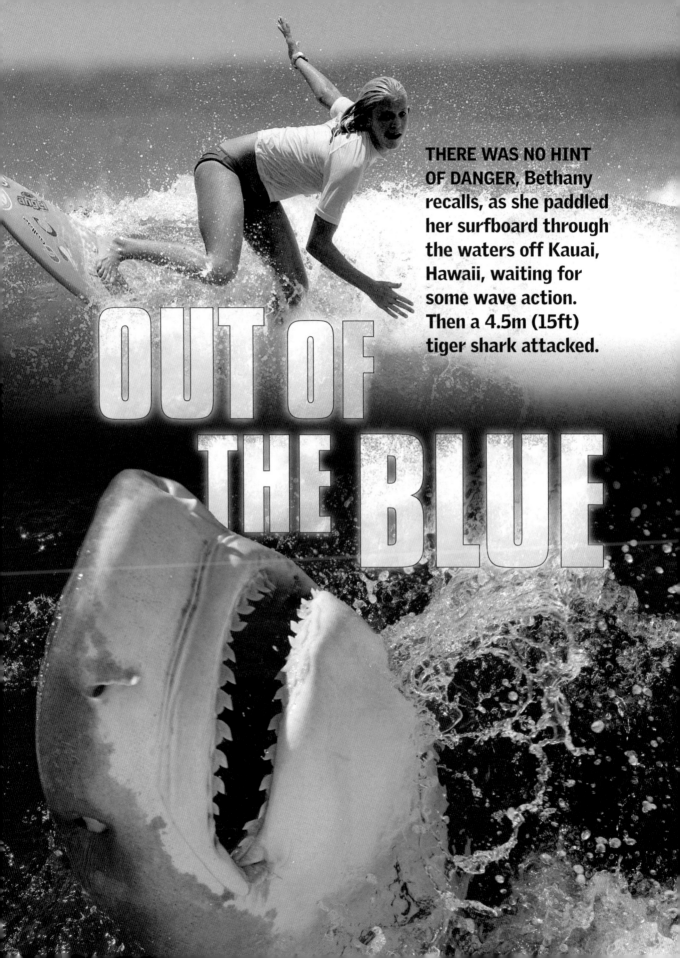

OUT OF THE BLUE

THERE WAS NO HINT OF DANGER, Bethany recalls, as she paddled her surfboard through the waters off Kauai, Hawaii, waiting for some wave action. Then a 4.5m (15ft) tiger shark attacked.

Mighty predator *The tiger shark that attacked Bethany was eventually captured. Its bite mark identified it as the culprit.*

I had no warning at all, not even the slightest hint of danger on the horizon. The water was crystal-clear and calm — it was more like swimming in a pool, rather than the deep ocean waters in Kauai, Hawaii. The waves were small and inconsistent and I was just kind of rolling along with them, relaxing on my surfboard with my left arm dangling in the cool water. I remember thinking, 'I hope the surf picks up soon,' when suddenly there was a flash of grey.

That's all it took: a split second. I felt a lot of pressure and a couple of fast tugs. I saw the jaws of a 4.5m (15ft) tiger shark cover the top of my board and my left arm. Then I watched in shock as the water around me turned bright red. My left arm was gone almost to the armpit, along with a huge, crescent-shaped chunk of my red, white and blue surfboard.

It had been a morning like any other. My mum Cheri and I set off before dawn looking for a good surf spot. When we arrived at our destination, a place called Cannons, the sun wasn't up yet. I got out of the car to take a look, but it was too dark to see the water. I couldn't hear much either. If the surf is really big, you can actually hear it cracking on the reef from a long way away. 'It doesn't seem like much is happening,' I said.

'I guess we should head back,' Mum said with a sigh. She was equally disappointed. 'Maybe the surf will come up tomorrow.' I knew that if I didn't surf, I would be home doing social studies, English or maths. Because I was working to be a professional surfer, I was educated at home so I'd have the time to practise, but my parents piled on the homework.

I had started entering competitions while I was still at junior school. Travelling round the state of Hawaii isn't easy or cheap and my parents aren't rich; Dad is a waiter and Mum is a cleaner. We had to come up with the money for entry fees, airline tickets, car rentals, food and hotel costs.

And unlike with golf or some other sports, if you win, there is little or no money, especially in the child and girl divisions. But my parents were willing to make sacrifices for me. With their support, I entered my first major competition at the age of eight, the Rell Sunn contest at Makaha Beach on the island of Oahu. The waves were big and I could feel the adrenalin rush. A lot of youngsters get intimidated when the surf starts getting huge. Me? I live for it — the bigger the better! I ended up winning all my heats and the division championships.

After that, I entered more contests and did pretty well in most. It seemed possible that I could become a professional surfer like a couple of other girls from my island have done. At least my parents and my two older brothers thought so. It was what I wanted more than anything in the world.

As Mum and I were driving away from Cannons, I made one last effort, 'Let's just try Tunnels Beach.' Tunnels is a short walk from Cannons; surfers like it because far out on the edge of the reef is a lightning-fast wave almost all year.

'Of course, we can go and take a look,' Mum replied. A black pick-up truck turned into the car park, with Alana Blanchard, my best friend, her

15-year-old brother Byron and her dad Holt. Even though the waves were lousy, it was sunny, the water was warm and my friends were here to hang out with.

'Can I stay, Mum?' I asked.

'Just make sure Holt brings you home,' she called and, with that, I raced down the trail with my friends to Tunnels Beach. I was happy that I was going surfing; I was happy to be with my friends. I felt the warm water slosh against my ankles and, just before I jumped in, I looked at my watch. It was 6.40am on that beautiful Halloween morning in 2003.

Praying for help

Lying on my surfboard, watching my blood spread in the water around me, I said to my friends, in a loud, yet not panicked voice, 'I just got attacked by a shark.' Byron and Holt got to me in a flash. Holt's face was white and his eyes were wide. 'Oh, my God!' he said, but he didn't freak out. Instead, he took control of the situation: he pushed me by the tail of my board and I caught a small wave that washed me over the reef. It's a miracle that it was high tide. If it had been low tide, we would have had to go all the way round the reef to get to shore. As it was, the beach was still 400m (¼ mile) away.

My arm was bleeding badly, but not spewing blood like it should have with a major artery open. I know now that wounds like mine often cause the arteries to roll back and tighten. I was praying like mad: 'Please, God, help me, let me get to the beach,' over and over again.

Holt took off his grey long-sleeved surfing top. The reef was shallow now, only a couple of feet deep, so he stood up and tied the top around the stub of my arm to act as a tourniquet. Then he had me grab onto the bottom of his swimming trunks and hold on tight as he paddled both of us towards the shore. Byron was already ahead of us, stroking like mad to the beach to call emergency services. Holt kept making me answer questions like, 'Bethany, are you still with me? How are you doing?' I think he wanted to make sure that I didn't pass out in the middle of the ocean. So I was talking, just answering his questions and praying out loud and watching the beach get closer and closer.

Once we reached the shore, Holt lifted me off the surfboard and laid me on the sand. He then tied a surfboard lead round my arm to stop the bleeding. At that point, everything went black and I'm not sure how long I was out of it. I kept coming in and out of consciousness. What happened after that is confusing: a mix of sights, sounds and feelings. I remember being cold. I heard this happens when you lose a lot of blood. People brought beach towels and wrapped me up in them.

I remember starting to feel pain in my stump and thinking, 'This hurts a lot.' And I know I said, 'I want my mum!' I remember being very thirsty and asking Alana for water.

She ran up to a visitor, Fred Murray, who had heard cries for help and dashed to the beach while the rest of his group, here on Kauai for a family reunion, relaxed at a rented home on the seafront.

'Come with me!' he yelled, and they both raced back to get one of his relatives, Paul Wheeler, who was a captain and a paramedic at a fire station.

I saw the jaws of a 15ft tiger shark cover the top of my board and my left arm. Then I watched in shock as the water around me turned bright red. My left arm was gone almost to the armpit.

Giant bite *The force of the shark's bite is clear from the damage done to Bethany's surfboard. It was almost cut in two by the massive jaws.*

F.Y.I.

Napali Coast

A'Haena Beach Park

↙ Bethany's Location at Tunnels

Park Co... →

Paddle to Beach...

Kauai
• Lihue
Niihau
Oahu
Honolulu
Molokai
Maui

HAWAII

PACIFIC OCEAN

Hawaii
• Hilo

Scene of the attack *The Napali Coast (above, on a postcard marked up after the event) was regarded as one of the safest places to surf before Bethany's ordeal at Tunnels Beach. It was the first-ever recorded shark attack on the north shore of Kauai, the oldest of the Hawaiian islands, which sit in the middle of the Pacific Ocean (above, right).*

Alana explained to him, as best she could in her state of shock, what had happened and that I needed water.

Paul didn't hesitate. He bolted out of the door to help me. I remember his face and the compassion in his voice. Everyone was relieved there was a professional on the scene. Paul examined the wound. Alana came with water, but Paul advised against it. 'I know you're thirsty,' he said, 'but you're going to need surgery and you need an empty stomach.'

A neighbour brought a small first-aid kit and Paul slipped on gloves so he could wrap my wound in gauze to keep it clean. I remember wincing as he covered it up, but I knew he had to do it. Paul felt my pulse. He shook his head. 'She's lost a lot of blood,' he said quietly.

I remember thinking, 'Why is the ambulance taking so long? Please, please hurry!' Again, I kept passing out, only catching glimpses of what was going on and bits of frantic conversation.

Favourable odds

Emergency vehicles arrived. I remember their sirens, high-pitched and shrill. I remember being stuck with needles and being slid onto a stretcher and into the back of the ambulance. I remember most clearly what the Kauai paramedic said to me. He spoke softly and held my hand as we were pulling out of the Tunnels' car park. He whispered in my ear, 'God will never leave you or forsake you.'

My dad had been scheduled for knee surgery that morning and was already at the hospital on the operating table, anaesthetised from the waist down. Dr David Rovinsky, his orthopaedic surgeon, was preparing to start the operation when an emergency-room nurse burst into the room. 'Just to warn you, Dr Rovinsky,' she announced. 'There's a 13-year-old girl coming, a shark attack victim. We're going to need this room right away.'

My dad heard her and knew that the 13-year-old girl had to be either me or Alana.

The doctor tried to calm him. 'I'll go and try to find out what's happening.' Within 5 minutes Dr Rovinsky returned. His face was pale and there were tears in his eyes. 'Tom, it's Bethany,' he said softly. 'She's in a stable condition. That's all I know. I'm going to have to wheel you out. Bethany's coming in here.'

My dad later told me that his hour in the recovery room was torture. 'I tried to will the feeling back into my legs so I could run in there and see you,' he admitted.

Mum had been informed only that I'd been attacked but given no details of my injury. As she rushed to the hospital, her long-standing friend Evelyn Cook reached her on her mobile phone. 'Cheri, she's lost an arm.' Mum dropped the phone, pulled the car over to the edge of the road, stared at her two hands on the steering wheel and started weeping.

Dr Rovinsky assured my parents that the odds were in my favour: I was young, in great physical shape, the cut had been direct rather than a ragged tear and my calmness had kept my heartbeat slow enough to keep

Killer of the warm ocean

SHARKS HAVE a long evolutionary history, reaching back more than 200 million years and pre-dating even the earliest dinosaurs. Little wonder, then, that they have highly refined instincts, assuring them of first place among the oceans' most dangerous killers.

Of more than 350 species of shark, only 20 pose a serious threat to human beings, and of these, just four species account for the 60-70 attacks registered each year around the world. Legend has the great white as the most dangerous shark of all, but while it prowls in colder seas, the tiger shark (below) is the serial killer of warm tropical waters, often inhabiting the shallows and lurking around the reefs.

The tiger shark is a big beast. The largest recorded was 7.4m (almost 25ft) long, but the more usual length is 3.25-4.25m (10-14ft), at a weight of around 385-635kg (850-1,400lb). Despite its size, it is a fleet swimmer, capable of sustained

speeds of 32km/h (20mph), and of travelling around 80km (50 miles) in a day.

The tiger shark is solitary except when breeding, and can live 50 years in the wild. Its sharply serrated teeth, which are continually replaced, can crunch through flesh, bone and even the carapace of sea turtles. As well as good eyesight even in murky waters, it has an acute sense of smell that can pick up minute traces of blood; it is further equipped with sensors that can detect even small movements in potential prey.

The tiger shark's indiscriminate eating habits have earned it the reputation of the dustbin of the sea. It will devour fish, seals, turtles, sea birds and other sharks, including small members of its own species. It also eats foreign objects of no nutritional value. There are stories of tiger sharks being found with tin cans, baseballs and car registration plates in their digestive tracts.

the severed artery from quickly draining my blood supply. Everyone's fast reactions had also been a big help. 'She's got everything going for her.'

First, Dr Rovinsky had to clean the wound thoroughly, since shark bites tend to have a high risk of infection. Then he isolated the nerves and cut them, causing them to retract and reducing the potential for 'phantom pain' – the feeling of an ache in a portion of a limb that no longer exists in reality, but still sends signals to the brain. Most of the wound was then left open, but packed with gauze for several days to ensure that no infection took place.

Three days later, Dr Rovinsky performed a second operation that included closing the wound by using a flap of my skin.

At one point in the days that followed, I said to Dad, 'I want to be the best surf photographer in the world.' That was my way of saying, 'I know my surfing days are over.' He tried to smile. He knew what I meant.

But a few days later I started thinking about going surfing again. However, the doctor had said I had to stay out of the water for three to four weeks after the second operation. In the meantime, there was plenty to occupy my time and thoughts. The main thing was getting used to the reality of my injury. When a nurse came to change the dressing on my arm a couple of days after I was released from the hospital, it was the first time that any of us had seen just how much of my arm was missing. My grandmother went out on the porch and cried. It upset my brother Timmy so much that he went to his room and stayed in bed all afternoon.

It's hard for me to describe the joy I felt as I rode the wave in for the first time after the attack. Even though I was all wet, I felt tears trickling down my face. Everyone was cheering.

My parents had a difficult time too. As for me, when I looked at that little stump of an arm held together with long black stitches, I almost fainted. It was a lot worse than I'd imagined. I knew then that I was going to need help from someone much bigger than me if I was ever to get back in the water.

In my first weeks at home, my family and I experienced an outpouring of *aloha*. For those in Hawaii, *aloha* means much more than hello and goodbye. It goes back to the old Hawaiian traditions and it means a mutual regard and affection of one person for another without any expectation of something in return. It means you do something from the pureness of your heart.

I was really moved by the number of people who wanted to help to raise money for my family. People didn't ask us; they just looked at the situation we were in and said, 'I want to help this family. They're going to need it.'

On Saturday, November 15, only a few weeks after the attack, hundreds and hundreds of people descended on the main ballroom of a hotel in Lihue for a silent auction that included more than 500 donated items. Because I was still trying to build up my strength, I couldn't attend, which was upsetting. On a huge stage, some of the island's most sought-after names performed. Even rock icon Graham Nash, formerly of the legendary Crosby, Stills, Nash and Young, came to sing on my behalf. The bidding was fast and furious, and when it was over, donations totalled about $75,000. It made us feel humble and loved.

That *aloha* spirit wasn't limited to Hawaii. My parents were astounded to get thousands of letters from all over the world, many with gifts of money. We really don't know why so many people wrote, prayed or gave, but we are very, very grateful for each one.

One organisation, Save Our Seas, learned what had happened to me and heard me say in an interview that if I couldn't surf again, maybe I would take surf pictures. So they offered to train me. But first there was something I had to do.

One day a small group of family and friends went with me to a beach off the beaten track. We arrived late in the afternoon, and when we came down the path, we saw that the place was about as good as it ever gets. The surfing area was packed with local talent.

Alana and I walked into the surf together just like we did on that early Halloween morning. It felt good to step into the liquid warmth and taste the salty water. It was like coming back home after a long, long trip. To think I had come so close to losing for ever all these things that I loved so much: the ocean, my family and my friends.

Alana paddled through the rolling white water (surfers call this soup) and headed farther out to the blue unbroken waves. I decided to make it easy on myself and ride some soup to begin with. In some ways, it was like learning to surf all over again. I had to learn how to paddle evenly with one arm and when I felt the wave pick me up, I had to put my hand flat on the centre of the deck to get to my feet rather than grab the surfboard rail the way you would if you had two hands.

A close bond *Bethany (left) and Alana (right) still surf together and remain best friends.*

My first couple of tries didn't work: I couldn't get up. I thought it was going to be easier than it was. My dad kept shouting, 'Bethany, try one more time. This one will be it!'

Then it happened. A wave rolled through, I caught it, put my hand on the deck to push up and I was standing. It's hard for me to describe the joy I felt as I rode the wave in for the first time after the attack. Even though I was all wet, I felt tears trickling down my face. Everyone was cheering.

Sometimes people ask me if I am ever scared of sharks now that I am surfing again. The answer is yes; sometimes my heart pounds when I see a shadow under the water. Sometimes I have nightmares. And I'm not ready to go out and surf Tunnels again.

Helping others

The other day I got an email telling me about someone who lost his arm. He's a teenager and very athletic like me, except his sport is wakeboarding. I grabbed the phone, called his house and said, 'Hey, Logan, this is Bethany Hamilton from Kauai, Hawaii. You probably heard I lost my arm to a shark.'

'Yeah,' he said softly.

'I just want you to know that I'm surfing in the national finals with one arm.'

'Yeah? Cool,' he said.

'Look, I know you may not feel great at the moment. But I know that you can do loads of stuff too. You can and you will. OK?'

We chatted a while and I could feel his mood brightening. 'Keep in touch and let me know what you're up to,' I added.

Moments like this make me think I may be able to do more good having one arm than when I had two. I think this was God's plan for me. I'm not saying God made the shark bite me. I think he knew it would happen and he made a way for my life to be happy and meaningful in spite of it happening. ∎

Where are they now?

BETHANY NOT ONLY RETURNED to the sport she loved but has continued to surf competitively. Just three months after the shark attack, she came fifth in a local competition. In July 2004 she won the ESPY (Excellence in Sports Performance Yearly) Award for Best Comeback Athlete of the Year, and was presented with a special award for courage at the Teen Choice Awards. In 2005 Bethany took first place in the NSSA (National Scholastic Surfing Association) top youth surf championship. And in 2008 she began competing full-time on the ASP (Association of Surfing Professionals) World Qualifying Series, taking third place in her first attempt, against many of the world's best female surfers.

Bethany has featured in *People* and *Time* magazines, and has appeared on the Oprah Winfrey and Ellen DeGeneres shows, on *Tonight* and on a programme titled *Fearless*. Celebrity status, though, has never gone to her head. When it was suggested that she tell her story, in what became *Soul Surfer: A True Story of Faith, Family and Fighting to Get Back on the Board*, Bethany at first resisted. 'It actually took a lot of convincing by my family and friends, because I'm not someone who likes to talk a lot about myself, or thinks I'm any big deal.'

Her rigorous training regime might see her out of bed and on the beach at 5.30am, to catch the waves before the crowds arrive. She has had to work to strengthen her right arm and to build her leg muscles, takes short sprints between surf sessions, and rides a bike. At home she stretches to improve her body alignment and even does press-ups by leaning her left shoulder against the bed.

In 2005, Bethany launched two fragrance ranges, 'Stoked' for women and 'Wired' for men – both named after surfing terms – pledging a percentage of profits to the Christian humanitarian organisation World Vision.

Of her incredible courage and tenacity Bethany has said, simply, 'I just love surfing. It's my love of surfing and life that make me want to help people, and to show people that anything is possible.'

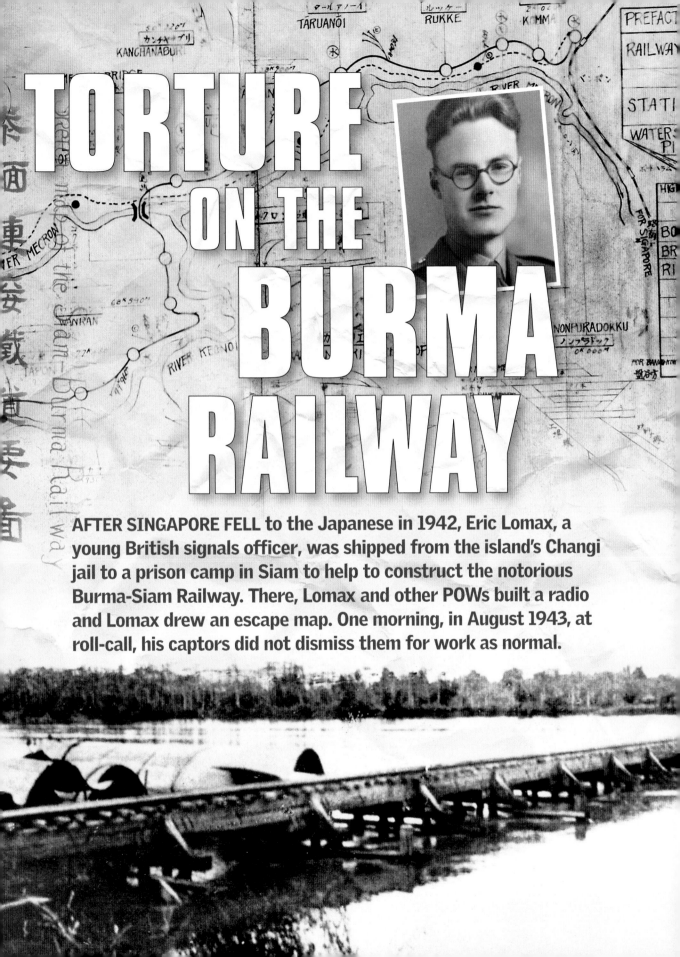

TORTURE ON THE BURMA RAILWAY

AFTER SINGAPORE FELL to the Japanese in 1942, Eric Lomax, a young British signals officer, was shipped from the island's Changi jail to a prison camp in Siam to help to construct the notorious Burma-Siam Railway. There, Lomax and other POWs built a radio and Lomax drew an escape map. One morning, in August 1943, at roll-call, his captors did not dismiss them for work as normal.

The Japanese guards kept every POW standing to attention in the assembly area while a group of them walked back into the huts; the rest surrounded us with fixed bayonets. We could hear them moving around inside the huts. A crescendo of pulling, clattering and dragging began.

An hour passed. The sun was now high and hot, but we were forbidden to move. The search went on and on, piling up behind us as they threw out motor-car batteries, dynamos, boxes and an incredible array of tools – all of them stolen from the Japanese. A lot of activity seemed to be centred around Lance Thew's corner of our long hut. Sergeant Major Thew of the Royal Army Ordnance Corps was our radio maker. After about 3 hours, Thew was called and he went into the hut. The guards had found the radio.

Thew was taken away from the camp with all his kit. Two days after his removal, a messenger from the Airfield Camp at Kanburi, about a mile away, told us that as soon as Thew had got there a long interrogation was followed by a terrible beating. He was then made to come to attention, barely able to stand, and forced to hold this position all day and all night for two days. On September 10, Fred Smith, a sergeant in the Royal Artillery, followed Thew to the Airfield Camp.

On September 21 we found out what they intended for the rest of us who had shared the hut. Early in the morning, four unshaven Japanese soldiers filed in. One said they were here to remove five officers to 'another camp': Major Bill Smith, Major Slater, Major Knight, Lieutenant Mackay and Lieutenant Lomax. As he spoke, a truck drew up outside.

I had to do some quick thinking. I knew there was a good chance of a firing squad or hanging party at the end of the road they would bring us down. I considered that if we were going to make a break for it and head up-country on the 1,600km (1,000 mile) walk to the Burma Road we would be better off with the map. I asked permission to use the latrine, where I reached into the hollow bamboo in the back wall where I kept the map. It came out with difficulty, and I tucked it into my shirt. Back in the hut, I slipped it into a Royal Signals instrument mechanic's leather bag in which I kept the smaller items of my kit.

The five of us boarded the truck, and were taken to Kanburi. The guards conducted us to the main guardroom, where we were brusquely ordered to stand to attention outside, well away from any protection from the sun. There we stood beside a long ditch, neatly spaced like five telegraph poles along a road. The intense heat of the sun, the irritation of flies and mosquitoes feeding on sweaty, itching skin, the painful contraction of eyes against the light and even the fear of violent death had been superseded, towards evening, by the even more powerful sensation of a burning thirst. They gave us nothing to drink.

No mercy

As dusk fell the five of us were moved into a closer and more compact group in front of the guardroom. A noisy party of Japanese and Koreans approached us through the dark. They looked like NCOs, their uniforms dishevelled, one or two of them unsteady on their feet. All of them carried pick-handles. Major Bill Smith was called out in front of our line and told to raise his arms right up over his head. He was 50 years old and his tall, gaunt figure, his thin arms held out like a scarecrow's, looked terribly weak. A hefty Japanese sergeant lifted his pick and delivered a blow across Smith's back that knocked him down. He was trodden on and kicked back into an upright position. All the thugs now set to in earnest as blows went home on the squirming body. Bill Smith cried out repeatedly, appealing for mercy, but to no avail. I could not tell how long it all took. How does one measure such time? Blows had replaced the normal empty seconds of time passing, but I think it took about 40 minutes until he lay still.

My friend, Morton 'Mac' Mackay, an artillery officer in his early 40s, was called forward. The flailing pick-handles rose and fell ceaselessly until in due course his body was dragged along and dumped beside Smith's, who was still alive, in the ditch. The moments while I was waiting my turn were the worst of my life. To have to witness the torture of others and to see the preparations for the attack on one's own body is a punishment in itself. This experience is the beginning of a form of insanity.

Then me. It must have been about midnight. I took off my spectacles and my watch carefully, turned and laid them down on the table behind me in the guardroom, as if I was preparing to go into a swimming pool.

I was called forward. I stood to attention. They stood facing me, breathing heavily. There was a pause. It seemed to drag on for minutes. Then I went down with a blow that shook every bone, and which released a sensation of scorching liquid pain searing through my entire body. Sudden blows struck me all over, tremendous flashes of solid light that burned and agonised. I could identify the periodic stamping of boots on the back of my head, crunching my face into the gravel; the crack of bones snapping; my teeth breaking.

At one point I realised that my hips were being damaged and I remember looking up and seeing the picks coming down towards them, and putting my arms up to deflect the blows. It went on and on. I thought I was dying. I have never forgotten crying out, 'Jesus,' crying out for help in the utter despair of hopelessness. I rolled into a deep ditch of foul stagnant water, which, in the second or two before consciousness was finally extinguished, flowed over me with the freshness of a pure and sweet spring.

Later the following morning, after we had been left out all night, we saw a small procession approaching: a POW with a red cross on his sleeve, two teams of stretcher-bearers and a Japanese guard. The stretcher parties lifted up the two bodies that looked the worst, while the rest of us were told to follow on foot. The POW with the red cross introduced himself as a Dutch doctor for the Netherlands forces in Java. He took us to the camp hospital and told us that his instructions were to repair us.

Quiet medical orderlies laid us out like sardines. The remains of our clothing were stripped off and they washed us gently from head to toe. They gave us freshly made lime juice to drink. Nothing ever tasted so refreshing.

When most of the dirt and blood had been removed, it was possible to assess the damage. For my part, both my forearms were broken and several of my ribs were cracked. One hip was clearly damaged. There did not seem to be any skin on my back. I was in such pain that I could not begin to locate its source. The four others were in as bad state; everyone had broken ribs, but by some chance I was the only one with fractured limbs.

The doctor set the broken bones in my arms and put them in splints. There was no anaesthetic, but the additional pain hardly seemed noticeable. We tried to sleep for the remainder of the day, sipping lime juice, the only medicine that the doctor had in his little hospital.

For two or three days we lay in our refuge, too sore to move. Our food was very good, the best the camp could supply. Many little delicacies were smuggled to us by other POWs, and we drank gallon after gallon of lime juice. With each passing day we felt better. Our skin was losing the intense black of the bruising; pale patches began to show up as our bodies mended themselves.

Meanwhile, somebody must have gathered up our kit from the guardroom and brought it to us. My spectacles and watch were still intact. I found only one thing missing: my map of Siam and Burma showing the route of the railway.

Meeting the Kempeitai

At 4 o'clock in the morning of October 7, 1943, we were roused from our sleep. Three or four figures were standing in the shadows at the door of the hospital hut. I caught glimpses of them as they paced about. The insignia on their collars was unmistakable; these were the Kempeitai, the Japanese secret police, whose reputation was like the Gestapo's. They represented something cold and calculating, an organisation that lurked on the edges of the worst imaginings of all the prisoners on the railway.

A lorry was waiting outside. I was the last out, the long splints on both my arms making every task painful. As dawn was breaking we were driven swiftly through the main gates of Kanburi POW camp. We thought that this could easily be our last journey.

We found ourselves being driven into the town of Kanburi itself along a narrow street of merchant houses. We stopped at a tall building that had a special protective wall built out into the street. We had not been aware that the Kempeitai had a local headquarters.

The insignia on their collars was unmistakable; these were the Kempeitai, the Japanese secret police, whose reputation was like the Gestapo's. They represented something cold and calculating.

The Death Railway

IN JUNE 1942, Japanese shipping in the Andaman Sea came under attack from Allied submarines, making it difficult for the Imperial Army to supply its forces in Burma. To counter this threat, the Japanese High Command decided to build an overland supply line, a railway that would join with other lines to link Bangkok in Siam (now Thailand) to Rangoon (now Yangon) in Burma (now also called Myanmar). The new section would pass through some 400km (250 miles) of dense jungle, across high mountains and over deep ravines. Japanese engineers estimated it would take five years to build; the order came back to complete it in 18 months or less.

Construction started in October 1942. The workforce consisted of Allied prisoners of war – British, Australian, Dutch and a few Americans – alongside forced labourers from Burma, China, Java, Malaya and India. The men toiled from before dawn till after dark, in baking heat or else in the thick mud of the monsoon. They cleared forests, dug cuttings, hauled logs and rocks, laid tracks and constructed bridges. The conditions were so punishing that they amounted to a form of daily torture – even without the brutal treatment meted out by their Japanese guards. Anyone deemed not to be working hard enough was beaten, or forced to stand for hours holding a heavy rock above his head.

Rations were extremely meagre – just rice and a few vegetables, often maggoty or rotten. All the men quickly grew weak or sick with malnutrition. Diseases such as malaria, dysentery and cholera became rife, and took a daily toll. As many as 50,000 POWs had died on the railway by the time it was completed late in 1943. The death count among the forced labourers is not known for certain, but may have been as high as 250,000. One Australian veteran later said that the building of the railway by such methods 'can only be regarded as a cold-blooded, merciless crime against mankind, obviously premeditated.'

HARD LABOUR In a drawing made by a POW in 1943, four prisoners haul a log across the River Kwai to be used in the building of a bridge. It formed part of the Burma-Siam Railway (left), linking into existing lines at Nong Pladuk in the south and Thanbyuzayat to the north. Working parties were based at each end and eventually met at Neiki.

To Rangoon
Martaban
Moulmein
River Kwai Noi
Thanbyuzayat
(northern junction)
Tanbaya (Hospital)
SIAM
(THAILAND)
Ye
Three
Pagodas
Pass
Neiki
(meeting point of
railway workers)
Tamajao
Rin Tin
Hintok
Hellfire Pass
Kunyu
River Mea Kahung
Andaman
Sea
Tavoy River
BURMA
(MYANMAR)
Kwai Bridge
Kanchanaburi (Japanese HQ)
Wanran
Nong Pladuk
(start of railway)
Chungkai
(Hospital)
Bampong
Tavoy
30km
20 miles
To Singapore
Bangkok
Gulf of
Thailand
CHINA
INDIA

We were quickly hustled out of the truck and through a gloomy passage into the yard at the back of the building. The yard was long and narrow, its left side bounded by a wall; and along part of its length were blocks of little hutch-like cages. We were each ushered into one of these cells through a small, low door. The front of each was made of bamboo latticework; each was about 1.5m (5ft) long, a little more than 0.75m (2½ft) wide, and less than 1.5m (5ft) high. The top was solid, a flat surface presenting itself to the sunlight like a hot plate.

We were allowed to take into our box one blanket each, a drinking cup or mug and the shirts that we were wearing. The rest of our kit and our footwear were removed. They caged us like animals.

I lay down on the floor, diagonally across the cell; I am over 1.8m (6ft) tall and I had to lie cramped, my arms held up to prevent my own weight crushing the unset bones. The heat was suffocating when the sun came up.

In the afternoon they gave us a small bowl of heavily salted rice formed into leaden balls. There was another helping of this dehydrating mush in the evening. It was all we got for the rest of our stay in that place. I felt more and more hungry, and I was thirsty all the time.

At least I was supping with the very long wooden spoon made for me by one of the medical officers in Kanburi. It was the only way I could feed myself, since I couldn't raise my arms high enough to use a normal spoon, and the Japanese wanted me alive enough to let me keep my special utensil.

They caged us like animals.

I lay down on the floor, diagonally across the cell; I am over 6ft tall and I had to lie cramped, my arms held up to prevent my own weight crushing the unset bones.

The cell became an oven in the afternoon. Ants, vicious large red ones, crawled all over it and over me, my splints preventing me from sweeping them away from my legs and back.

It is impossible to account precisely for the next few days; my mind was confused, sometimes even to the point of oblivion. I think that one full day and night elapsed before the interrogation started.

Some time early in the morning I was taken by two guards into the main building, where I was pushed into a room constructed entirely of a dark tropical hardwood that gave the chamber a permanent twilit atmosphere. Across a plain narrow table, also made of dark timber, two Japanese were seated. One of them was a large, broad, muscular, shaven-headed man wearing the uniform of a Japanese NCO, his face and thickset neck full of latent violence. The other figure, in private's uniform, was far smaller. He had a good head of very black hair, a wide mouth and defined cheekbones, and looked very unmilitary beside his thuggish colleague. There was no ease between them; it was obvious who was in charge.

The smaller man opened up, speaking a heavily accented but quite fluent English. He introduced himself as an interpreter whose job was to assist the NCO of 'the special police', as he put it, in his investigation into the 'widespread anti-Japanese activities' that had been occurring in POW camps in the neighbourhood.

The NCO then shouted in a series of short barks, and the small man began his task of translation, speaking like a mechanical voice with almost no inflection of interest. 'Lomax, we have already examined Thew and Smith and they have made full confessions to making and using a wireless. They have already told us about the part you have played. We are satisfied that you are guilty. Lomax, you will be killed shortly whatever happens. But it will be to your advantage in the time remaining to tell the whole truth. You know how we can deal with people when we wish to be unpleasant.'

Waiting for death

They wanted to know about my family history, about my schooling, my war record, my spare-time activities. Here I was trying to explain the migrations of my Lancastrian and Scottish ancestors to uncomprehending Japanese men in a Siamese village. The pointlessness of what we were doing began to overwhelm me.

Their real interest was anti-Japanese activities in the camp and they tried to cross-check whatever they had already got from Smith and Thew, which was not much. I tried to be vague. Once, the interpreter let slip that Fred and Lance were still being kept in the building. It gave me a brief surge of hope to know that they were still alive.

They were obsessed with radios, of course, but waited a long time before introducing the subject of transmitters. Then they went at me. In these questions they revealed their extreme ignorance, wanting to know how a simple receiver could be converted into a transmitter, for example – which can't be done. I tried to tell them that the technical problems of making a transmitter were too great for a group of prisoners with the pathetic materials available to them.

At some point they brought in a different NCO, the first one having failed to get the answers they were looking for. So far they had not laid a finger on me, but the endless barrage of ludicrous questions and the deprivation of sleep were bad enough. I sat hour after hour balancing my broken arms on my thighs, longing for rest. Once or twice they woke me at night and brought me to the room. There was little inflection in the interpreter's voice; it filled my dreams with its flat repetitive questions. I hated him more and more. He was the one asking the questions, driving me on. I was sick of the sight of him; I would have killed him for his endless insistence.

It is a strange feeling, being sentenced to death in your early 20s. It made me feel relaxed, in a strange way, to know that I was living on borrowed time. Yet day after day the psychological torment continued. I expected death, but had no clear image of an ending that would make sense to me. It occurred to me that my family would never find my grave.

Casualties of hard labour

A haunting image, produced by one of the POWs, shows medical workers, identified by their cross-bearing armbands, helping to stretcher dead, sick and injured prisoners to the train in the background.

One morning I was taken into that room and there on the table, spread out carefully, was my map. It looked so fine, so neatly done. The NCO and the interpreter stood at the window with their backs to me. The room was silent. They left me standing there for a long time.

Then they turned and from both of them came a storm of fake anger. They had obviously known about it all along, but were now trying to shock me. 'This is a very good map … why did you make it? From where did you steal the paper, where did you get your information? Were you planning to escape on your own? With others? Who are they?'

The interpreter was now getting deeper into his role as interrogator, as though he was enjoying it. They were really worked up; I could feel their frustration at being sent round in circles by my stubborn refusals. There was a violent electricity in the air.

Suddenly the NCO grabbed my shoulder and pulled me out, half-stumbling, his fingers pinching my flesh where he grabbed my shirt. Out in the yard he tied me to a bench with a rope. The questioning recommenced. The interpreter's voice: 'Lomax, you will tell us why you made the map.' The NCO picked up a rough tree branch. Each question from the small man by my side was followed by a terrible blow with the branch to my chest and stomach. 'Lomax, you will tell. Then it will stop.'

I think I felt the interpreter's hand on my hand; a strange gesture, the obscene contrast between this gesture of comfort and the pitiless violence. Suddenly the NCO stopped hitting me. He went off to the side and

Captive patients *Prisoners mend their broken bodies on a hospital ward at Changi Prison in Singapore. It was to this hospital that POWs on the point of death were often sent.*

I saw him coming back holding a hosepipe. He directed the full flow of the gushing pipe into my nostrils and mouth. Water poured down my windpipe and throat and filled my lungs and stomach. The torrent was unimaginably choking. This is the sensation of drowning, on dry land, on a hot dry afternoon. Your humanity bursts from within you as you gag and choke. I tried very hard to will unconsciousness, but no relief came. He was too skilful to risk losing me altogether. When I was choking uncontrollably, the NCO took the hose away. The flat, urgent voice of the interpreter resumed; the other man hit me with the branch a few more times. I had nothing to say; I was beyond invention. So they turned on the tap again, and again there was that nausea of rising water from inside my bodily cavity, a flood welling up from within and choking me.

They alternated beatings and half-drownings. I have no idea whether it finished that day, or if there was more the following day. I eventually found myself back in my cage. I must have been dragged there.

Then the interrogations stopped. One morning our cages – Thew and Smith were with us now – were opened and the small interpreter took charge of us. Incredibly, the seven of us were all still alive. Our kit was brought out into the yard. We asked a lot of questions, but there were no replies from the young translator-interrogator. A truck drove up, with a number of guards on board. As I was climbing aboard, with Mac's help, the interpreter walked up to me and said gravely, 'Keep your chin up.' He stood there in the yard, a tiny figure standing among the larger regular soldiers.

During the journey we were able to speak quietly beneath the noise of the engine as the guards talked among themselves. We spoke about our interrogations. My companions' warmth, and the solidarity of their anger, was worth so much. There was an extraordinary urgency about this whispered conversation: we were sure that this time we were about to die.

But instead we were taken to a station 50km (30 miles) away, back at the beginning of the railway. A train arrived quite soon, an ordinary local passenger train full of civilians. It moved off eastwards towards Bangkok. On the south side were extensive new railway yards, with rows of wagons, flatcars and shunting engines and a large number of Japanese C56 steam locomotives. The presence of all this machinery could only mean that the Burma to Siam railway had been completed in record time.

Court martial

At the main railway station in Bangkok, the Kempeitai agents handed us over to a squad of soldiers and we were driven away to a large nondescript building with guards standing to attention outside it. Next day we moved again, this time to the grounds of a grand house. One of the outbuildings had been turned into a large cell. We occupied that cell for 36 days, sitting with our knees spread and ankles locked from 7 in the morning until 10 at night, with the exception of a bare hour of daily exercise. We suffered the cramps and rigors of unsupple muscles forced into this unfamiliar position. On the morning of November 22, 1943, we were abruptly told to smarten ourselves up and were taken into the main building and into a large room with long windows. Several Japanese officers sat along a table with their backs to the light. They clearly formed a court martial. The president of the court appeared to be a lieutenant general.

He asked us if we had anything to say. Jim Slater spoke up with considerable courage, saying that we had been punished enough. He described the beatings at Kanburi, pointing to my broken arms, and my torture by the Kempeitai. If the judge had not been aware of our treatment before, he certainly betrayed no interest now and pronounced sentence. Thew and Fred Smith, ten years' imprisonment each; Bill Smith, Slater, Knight, Mackay and Lomax, five years each. For the first time since the discovery of the radio under Thew's bed, the threat of imminent death had been lifted.

A few days after our trial we were put into uniform again and moved 1,930km (1,200 miles) south to Singapore. Our new home was to be Outram Road, a punitive military prison where we were kept in our cells almost all the time. The worst new enemy we faced, even compared to the dirt and hunger, was perhaps the most formidable of all: silence. It seemed particularly sadistic to make Fred Smith and I share a cell and forbid us to speak to each other and at the same time deprive us of books and distractions of any kind.

As always, there were some people who were humane enough to take risks to help us. One of the Japanese prison staff removed my splints when the bones seemed to be set, and took away my long spoon, but only after I had assured him that I could manage without it.

Piecing together information was like rubbing at a dirty window with a rag, making blurred peepholes that allowed us to catch a glimpse of the situation at Outram Road. We discovered that in the past some men in our block had become so ill they had quietly died in their cells, from a combination of disease, brutality and starvation. For this was a place in which the living were turned into ghosts — starved, diseased creatures wasted down to their skeletal outlines. The most tantalising rumour was that occasionally prisoners on the point of death were sent away to a hospital at Changi jail. For many prisoners, Changi was a dreadful place; only Outram Road made it homely to us. I was determined to get there.

By the end of April 1944 my fellow officers were all very ill. We couldn't take much more. Then the Japanese gave me my chance when they took the unprecedented step of placing extremely sick men in a group of cells on the ground floor. I had found that I could drive up my pulse rate by deep and accelerated breathing, so procuring a state that frightened my cell mate and even me. One day, when there was a warder in earshot, I worked my pulse up, cried out and twisted and clutched myself. My performance had an effect: the warder had me carried down to one of the 'sick' cells. After two months I made another attempt to frighten the warders and this time the symptoms hardly needed to be simulated. It's not too difficult to feign imminent death when you already look like a corpse. I was bundled onto a stretcher, my kit was loaded on top of me and I was put into an open truck, which drove off through what smelt like countryside. I kept my eyes shut; I was beyond fear, but I hoped that I was not being taken to some lonely execution ground.

After about half an hour there was a right-hand turn, a near stop, another right-hand turn, which interrupted the sunlight — and then, an English voice. The stretcher was lifted off the truck and I was carried away. I saw around me the functional and naked walls of a modern jail. I was still a prisoner. But this was what I had been trying to achieve for months; I was inside Changi at last, and I began to cry, an uncontrollable cascade; tears of relief and joy.

In April 1945, Bron Rogers, the Australian Army doctor from Hobart who ran one of the hospital wards at Changi, told us that the Nazi armies were nearly destroyed and Berlin was under attack. But around the overcrowded blocks and yards of Changi there were rumours of trenches being dug nearby, of preparations for mass murder. When we heard that Rangoon had been captured on May 3, our exhilaration was poisoned by fear.

One evening, early in August, Bron gathered us round and told us that a new type of bomb had been used over Japan, destroying the city of Hiroshima. On August 9, reports from a secret radio spoke of another bomb of almost cosmic power and another Japanese city destroyed. Six days later Japan surrendered. Four days after that, the gates of hell were opened. We exulted, but we were aware that the real victory for us was to have survived.

The privacy of the torture victim is more impregnable than any island fortress. My experiences had put a huge distance between me and my previous life, yet I behaved – was expected to behave – as though I were the same person.

Prisoners of war don't find it easy to settle. Back in Edinburgh in November 1945 I was already living in a world of my own. The privacy of the torture victim is more impregnable than any island fortress. My experiences had put a huge distance between me and my previous life, yet I behaved – was expected to behave – as though I were the same person. The nightmares began soon after my return: I was back in Outram Road, never to be released.

In the cold light of day, my anger turned to the Japanese who had beaten, interrogated or tortured me. I wanted to do violence to them, specifically to revenge myself on the hateful little interrogator at Kanburi with his dreadful English pronunciation, his mechanical questions and his way of being in the room yet seeming to be detached from it. I wished to drown him, cage him and beat him. I still thought of his voice: *Lomax, you will be killed shortly*; *Lomax, you will tell us.* ■

What happened next?

FLASHBACKS CONTINUED to haunt Eric Lomax for years, wrecking his first marriage. He was determined to punish his inquisitor. But who was he? In October 1989 a friend gave Lomax a newspaper clipping about a book called *Crosses and Tigers* by Takashi Nagase. Ever since the war, Nagase had worked to atone for the atrocities he had witnessed in Kanburi camp. He had led pilgrimages to Kanburi War Cemetery and spoken at many rallies in Japan to promote friendship and understanding among Pacific War veterans. Lomax found the book extraordinarily difficult to read, the horrors described terrifyingly familiar. He now realised that the author was the man he was looking for.

His second wife Patti suggested that he write to Nagase. He refused. So in October 1991 she wrote to him instead, asking Nagase to correspond with Lomax, 'for he has lived with unanswered questions ... all these years ... and I hope that contact between you could be a healing experience for both of you.' Nagase replied. He promised to answer any questions, but most of all he wanted to meet Lomax in person and apologise. 'Please tell him to live long until I can see him.'

Eric Lomax and Takashi Nagase, now both in their 70s, finally met at the little museum by the River Kwai Bridge on March 26, 1993 (below left, with Patti on left). 'A tiny man in an elegant straw hat, loose kimono-like jacket and trousers, he came onto the terrace, walking past a carefully preserved locomotive, a veteran of the Royal Siamese Railway, built in Glasgow,' Lomax recalls.

'He began with a formal bow, his face working and agitated. I stepped forward, took his hand and said, *"Ohayo gozaimasu, Nagase san, ogenki desu ha?"'* (Good morning, Mr Nagase, how are you?)

'He looked up at me; he was trembling, in tears, saying over and over, "I am very, very, sorry ... I never forgot you." Now we were face to face, his grief seemed far more acute than mine.' As the two men sat holding hands they began to forge a friendship of forgiveness that has lasted ever since. Lomax adds, 'The day we met again I told him I could remember his very last words to me. He asked what they were and laughed when I said, "Keep your chin up."'

NEW YORK. 9/11. In the panic and horror of the attack on the Twin Towers, a banker working on a floor where the second plane struck manages to find a way out, helping a stranger to escape the carnage all around them.

THE LONG WAY DOWN

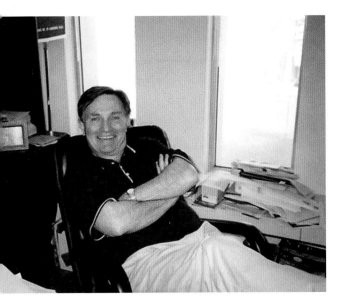

Before the attack *Brian Clark, an executive vice president at Euro Brokers, in his office on the 84th floor of the South Tower, about a year before the attack.*

Like any normal day I arrived at about 7.15 in the morning. That particular day was more or less flawless weather – a beautiful day, blue sky. I got my morning coffee and went about my normal chores. Sitting at my desk on the 84th floor of the South Tower of the World Trade Center, Tower Two, facing the door with the window behind me, at about 8.46 I heard an enormous *thump*. I didn't feel any vibration, but there was a noticeable sound like a *boom* or *thump,* and the lights buzzed for a second.

There was suddenly this glare, and my attention was immediately caught. I spun my head around, and the entire airspace behind me was filled with flame. My immediate thought was there had been an explosion one or two floors above our office. Being one of the fire marshals, I was equipped with a whistle and flashlight in my office. I jumped up, grabbed them and yelled, 'Get out! Everybody get out!' This all took me 5 seconds. When I looked behind me out of the window, the flames were all gone, and thousands of papers were just fluttering in the air, the edges of which were all on fire. It was like flaming confetti. Very strange.

I didn't realise at the time that the area in which all this was happening was so huge. In my mind it was two floors up. So I ran out of my office, into an open-plan area, and I said, 'Come on, let's go, there has been an explosion,' and I started to get people off the floor.

We were a trading operation. Our customers were not individuals, but large financial trading institutions around the world. So we had in our trading floor many television sets tuned to financial news information. Well, all of these stations cut away to their news departments, and there were these breaking news stories that a plane had hit the World Trade Center. The story developed literally within minutes, and we understood fairly soon, I would say within 3 or 4 minutes, that an airliner had hit One World Trade Center.

Second strike

We knew now that the damage had been done to Tower One, not our tower, so we relaxed a little bit about evacuation. Nonetheless, many people in the first minute had bolted for the stairs and were on their way down. Now there were photographs of One World Trade Center and the smoke coming out of the upper floors. The fire marshals like myself were content to let people go or stay.

I called my wife and told her, 'You know, you won't believe this but Tower One has been hit. We are fine where we are. Relax, turn on the TV, find out what's happening.'

At about 8.55 there was an announcement. First the strobe lights flashed, as they did during the normal fire drills. The alarm system gave a little bit of a *whoop whoop*, to alert you to an announcement about to be made. Then the very familiar voice, the one we heard all the time, came

Terror strikes *The moment before an airliner hit the South Tower of the World Trade Center (previous page, left), causing a massive explosion (centre). Within an hour, the tower had collapsed (right).*

over the system and said, 'Building Two is secure. There is no need to evacuate Building Two. Repeat, Building Two is secure ...'

And they went through the whole story again. So this was reinforcement that there was no need to evacuate. I am strictly guessing but I would think we were perhaps down to about 25 people left on our floor at the time of the announcement. (I had gone for a walk through our office.) So, the pressure seemed to be off, and there wasn't a panic, although we were greatly concerned about what was going on in Tower One.

If you went to the north wall windows, you could look up and see the flames and the smoke and people now starting to jump. I could not take myself to the window to view that. I just didn't want that image burned in my brain. One girl in particular – Susan her name was – turned from the window when she saw a person jump. She hadn't noticed it before, and she spun around in tears, almost frantically, ran to me and said 'Oh, Brian, it's terrible. People are dying.'

I said, 'Susan, it's a terrible tragedy,' and I put my arms around her, and I said 'Come on, let's get you more composed,' and we walked out of the trading floor down the hall. In the building the centre core was crossed by hallways. There was a north-south hallway and an east-west hallway. I walked with her from the east side through the centre core to the west side, where the ladies room was, and she went into the ladies room.

I continued on to the west side near my office. I was fairly near the windows talking with two or three people, including especially Bobby Coll. At apparently 9.03 – I didn't check my watch – the second plane hit the south side of our building at approximately the 78th, 79th and 80th floors. Our room fell apart at that moment, complete destruction without an explosion. The lights went out, but we were near the window so there was daylight. Again, this sort of *thump*, this explosion without fire and flame, a very strange sensation.

There was a kind of twist to the building when it got hit. The ceiling tiles and some of the brackets fell; some air-conditioning ducts, speakers, cables and things like that that were in the ceiling also fell. I seem to have a sense that floor tiles even buckled a bit or were moved. Some of the walls were actually torn in a jagged direction rather than up and down. Again perhaps explained by the torque, some of the door frames popped out of the wall and partially or fully fell.

If you went to the north wall windows, you could look up and see the flames and the smoke and people now starting to jump. I could not take myself to the window to view that.

Terrible decision *People can be seen hanging out of broken windows of the North Tower of the World Trade Center after the terrorist attack, deciding whether to jump to their deaths or not.*

Running for their lives *Pedestrians flee the area surrounding the World Trade Center as the South Tower collapses, engulfing the whole area in a giant cloud of dust and debris.*

Rescue mission

For 7-10 seconds there was this enormous sway in the building. It was one way, and I just felt in my heart, 'Oh my gosh, we are going over.' That's what it felt like. Now, on windy days prior to that there was a little bit of a sway to the building. You got used to it; you didn't notice it. The window blinds would go *clack clack* as they swung. But, for those agonising seconds I thought it was over – a horrible feeling – but then the building righted itself. It didn't sway back and forth; it just went one way, it seemed, and then back, and we were stable again.

I was looking at Bobby Coll square in the eyes, and we knew in an instant that it was terrorism. I mean, there wasn't for sure terrorism on people's minds when the first building had been hit. Was it pilot error? Was it instrument error? Or just a one-off suicide? Horrible as it was, you didn't know for certain that it was terrorism. But when the second building got hit you instantly calculated the two of them: terrorism.

So we knew we were in a difficult situation. I switched on the flashlight, and we started out of the room. Our room was not black with smoke but sort of white with chalky construction dust. It was incredibly dusty and dirty as we made our way out of the room and over some debris, and we went to the crossroads in the middle of the building.

At that point, had we gone 3 or 4 metres straight ahead to the east, we would have come to Stairway B. We didn't know where this plane had hit, we didn't know if it was a plane, we didn't know anything other than suddenly we were in chaos and our building had been hit. I could have turned right 3yd to Stairway C, closer to the impact point. I had no idea what condition that stairway was in. Miraculously, at random I turned left to Stairway A, which was the farthest from the impact.

So we started down that stairway. We only went three floors. There was a group of seven of us, myself and six others. I remember some of the names. I know everybody at Euro Brokers, but in my mind somehow I blanked out who those other grey shapes were; they were a little farther up the stairs, not in the light of the flashlight. I do remember Bobby Coll, Kevin York, David Vera and Ron DiFrancesco.

We met two people who had come up from the 80th floor, a heavy-set woman and by comparison a rather frail male companion of hers, a workmate. She was saying from the landing below, 'Stop, stop you've got to go up. You can't go down. There is too much smoke and flames below.' I had my flashlight, and I was shining it in each face as people made comments; an argument ensued as to what we should do.

At the same moment as this argument was going on I heard *bang, bang, bang, thump, thump, thump*, 'Help! Help! I'm buried. I can't breathe. Is anybody there? Can you help me?' A strange voice coming from within the

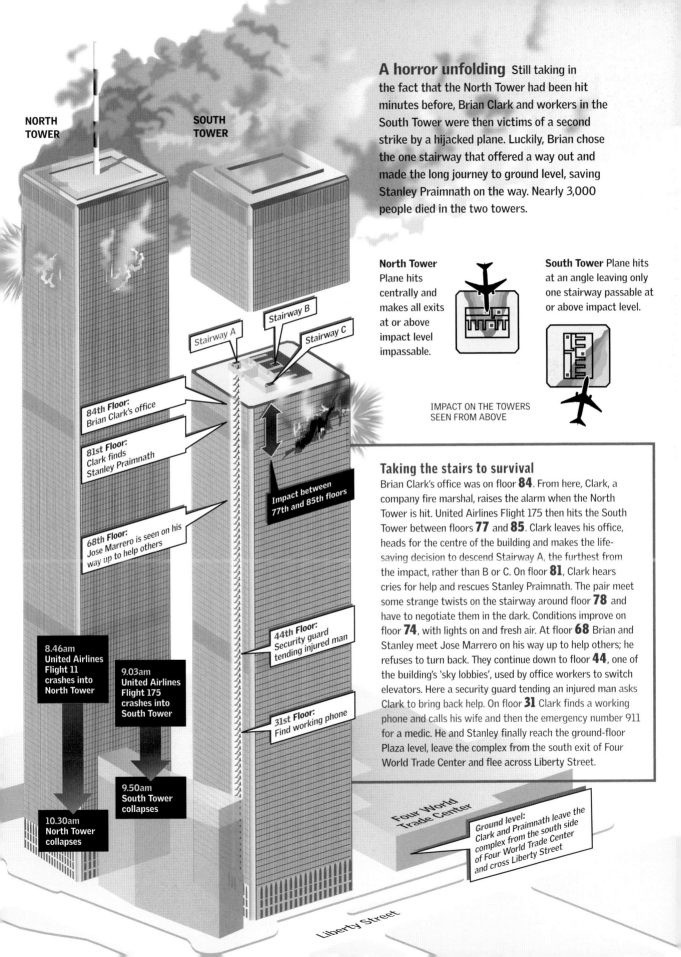

NORTH TOWER

SOUTH TOWER

A horror unfolding Still taking in the fact that the North Tower had been hit minutes before, Brian Clark and workers in the South Tower were then victims of a second strike by a hijacked plane. Luckily, Brian chose the one stairway that offered a way out and made the long journey to ground level, saving Stanley Praimnath on the way. Nearly 3,000 people died in the two towers.

North Tower Plane hits centrally and makes all exits at or above impact level impassable.

South Tower Plane hits at an angle leaving only one stairway passable at or above impact level.

IMPACT ON THE TOWERS
SEEN FROM ABOVE

Stairway A

Stairway B

Stairway C

84th Floor:
Brian Clark's office

81st Floor:
Clark finds
Stanley Praimnath

Impact between
77th and 85th floors

68th Floor:
Jose Marrero is seen on his
way up to help others

44th Floor:
Security guard
tending injured man

31st Floor:
Find working phone

8.46am
United Airlines
Flight 11
crashes into
North Tower

9.03am
United Airlines
Flight 175
crashes into
South Tower

9.50am
South Tower
collapses

10.30am
North Tower
collapses

Taking the stairs to survival

Brian Clark's office was on floor **84**. From here, Clark, a company fire marshal, raises the alarm when the North Tower is hit. United Airlines Flight 175 then hits the South Tower between floors **77** and **85**. Clark leaves his office, heads for the centre of the building and makes the life-saving decision to descend Stairway A, the furthest from the impact, rather than B or C. On floor **81**, Clark hears cries for help and rescues Stanley Praimnath. The pair meet some strange twists on the stairway around floor **78** and have to negotiate them in the dark. Conditions improve on floor **74**, with lights on and fresh air. At floor **68** Brian and Stanley meet Jose Marrero on his way up to help others; he refuses to turn back. They continue down to floor **44**, one of the building's 'sky lobbies', used by office workers to switch elevators. Here a security guard tending an injured man asks Clark to bring back help. On floor **31** Clark finds a working phone and calls his wife and then the emergency number 911 for a medic. He and Stanley finally reach the ground-floor Plaza level, leave the complex from the south exit of Four World Trade Center and flee across Liberty Street.

Four World Trade Center

Ground level:
Clark and Praimnath leave the
complex from the south side
of Four World Trade Center
and cross Liberty Street

Liberty Street

81st floor. I heard this voice, and it caused me to lose concentration in this argument that was going on about whether to head up or down.

I grabbed Ron by the sleeve and I said, 'Come on, Ron. Let's get this fellow.' The fire-escape door had blown away from the wall a bit, but we were able to squeeze onto the 81st floor. It was in darkness, but again I had my flashlight. I scanned the room, and I said, 'Who's there? Where are you?'

He said, 'Oh, I can see your light.'

What my light beam revealed was similar to what you might meet on a very foggy road at night, because there was white dust everywhere. He said, 'No, to the right … to the left …' In about a minute, Ron and I located his voice. He said, 'Can you see my hand?' His hand was sticking out of some debris, waving frantically, and my light picked it up. I said, 'OK, I see you now.'

And at that moment my associate Ron who came down with me was overcome with smoke. He had a gym bag or a briefcase with him, and he was putting it in front of his face in an attempt to filter the air. It clearly wasn't working, and Ron, with eyes shut, backed off the floor. He was almost completely overcome by the smoke.

Miraculously, I was in a kind of bubble. I was breathing fine. I was squinting a bit, but I could work, and I struggled to get debris away from Stanley – I found out later his name was Stanley Praimnath; he worked at Fuji Bank.

We got to the point I couldn't do any more work from my side, and I said, 'You've got to jump. You've got to get over this last barrier.' Well, he jumped once and fell back down. I said, 'Come on, you've got to do this. It's the only way out.' I reached in again, and Stanley jumped, and I got him by the collar or the shoulder or somewhere there. I pulled him out and onto me, and we fell in a heap and embraced.

Ron had gone. He was not there when we got back to the stairs. The other people had gone up as I left with Ron to go in on the 81st floor. I had this vision of Bobby Coll and Kevin York each with a hand under one elbow of this heavy-set woman, saying things like, 'Come on. We are in this together. We will help you.' And up they went. And Dave Vera, who had a walkie-talkie, started back up the stairs as well. That's the last I saw of those people.

So Stanley and I went back to the stairs on the 81st floor, and we began down. The first five floors were difficult, because plasterboard had been blown off the wall and was lying propped up against the railing. We had to move it, shove it to the side. The sprinkler system had turned on so there was water sloshing down the stairways. It was dark.

The stairways didn't go straight down. There was one particular area, around the 78th floor I think, where you actually came to some strange twists. So we had to figure that out in the darkness, but we made some fortunate decisions. Around the 74th floor, I would say, we broke into what I call fresh air. The lights were on. It was normal conditions. There was not a problem breathing, and there was nobody there, not a soul, just Stanley and me. We were starting to have normal conversation. He was cut and bruised a bit, but he was fine conversing.

A hard rain *The air was so thick with dust and debris after the collapse of the World Trade Center that it looked like a snowstorm. People struggled to breathe as they escaped the scene.*

A moonscape outside

We continued on down. On the 68th floor, we met one man walking up. The man's name was Jose Marrero. He worked for Euro Brokers for many years, in our security department, and he was also one of our fire marshals. Jose had been with many people of ours all the way down into the 30s and 40s on the stairway and figured, I guess, that he had done his job. Then he heard Dave Vera, who had started down with me, on his walkie-talkie saying that he needed help; he was helping people, could he get help?

So Jose, hero that he was, was walking back up. I said, 'Jose, Dave's a big boy, he can get out. We've just come through hell to get here. Come on down with us.'

'No, no, no,' he said. 'I'll be fine. I can help.' Then Jose kept marching up. Jose was about 35 years old and quite fit, but when I passed him he was understandably labouring to climb the stairs. But he kept going.

Stanley and I continued down until we got to the 44th floor, seeing nobody. On the 44th floor we went off, because I knew that was one of the sky lobbies – the intermediate floors where people change elevators – in the Trade Center. Conditions were normal other than there was nobody there, except for a security guard who was tending to a man moaning in pain, with massive head wounds. The security guard was saying, 'I need help. My phones don't work, but I need medical attention for this man. I'll stay with him, I'll tend him, but you must promise to get help as soon as you can telephone somebody.' Stanley and I said 'OK' and went back to the stairs.

We went down again. Easy travel, just the two of us. Lights on, fresh air all the way down to the 31st floor, where we went in at random and got into somebody's conference room, and each grabbed a phone.

I called my wife – I hadn't talked to her since about 8.55, I suppose, and this was about 9.40. My wife had turned on the TV, and the first thing she had seen was the second plane slam into our building. So she had no idea where I was for that 45 minute stretch. I told her I was fine. Stanley talked to his wife, told her similar news.

I then called 911 – coincidence 9/11 – and was put on hold. After telling my story to two different operators and getting passed up the line, I was asked for a third time to tell somebody else my story. I said, 'I'm gonna tell you this once, and then I'm hanging up.' I went through the details about the 44th floor, man on the ground, need a medic, need a stretcher, goodbye.' We were probably in that conference room for 4 minutes I would think, and then it was back to the stairs.

Transformed skyline *The outline of Lower Manhattan is changed forever after the Twin Towers collapse, sending smoke billowing wildly across the city.*

Remembering the dead

IN THE AFTERMATH of the events of 9/11, the need was felt to create a sacred space, a memorial to the thousands of innocent victims and rescuers who had lost their lives in the terrorist attacks, and to acknowledge the courage and endurance of the many survivors who took great risks to save others.

In 2003, the Lower Manhattan Development Corporation launched a competition to design a fitting memorial, attracting 5,200 entries from 63 nations. The 13 member 'jury' who reviewed proposals included Maya Lin, designer of the Vietnam Veterans Memorial at Washington D.C., and deputy mayor Patricia Harris.

The design chosen from a shortlist of eight was by Israeli architect Michael Arad of Handel Architects, who collaborated with landscape architects Peter Walker and Partners on the design. It features two square pools with cascading waterfalls where the towers stood, surrounded by a 'forest' of almost 400 swamp white oak and sweetgum trees, to provide 'a green rebirth in spring, welcome shade through the heat of summer, and seasonal colour in the fall'. On the parapets surrounding the pools will be inscribed the names of victims. Numerous benches will be provided for those who wish to sit in contemplation.

PHOENIX FROM THE ASHES The new Memorial Plaza (right) will cover New York's 'Ground Zero', where the shattered remains of the World Trade Center (below) stood after the Twin Towers collapsed.

The Memorial Plaza, dubbed 'Reflecting Absence', is to be one of the most sustainable, green plazas ever built. It is scheduled for completion in 2011.

Although the memorial proposals were at first well received, the project has not been without its critics, who point to lack of progress and complain of the expense. Few would argue, though, with the mission statement of the National September 11 Memorial & Museum at the World Trade Center, which includes the sentiment: 'May the lives remembered, the deeds recognised, and the spirit reawakened by eternal beacons, which reaffirm respect for life, strengthen our resolve to preserve freedom, and inspire an end to hatred, ignorance and intolerance.'

Of course, we had no idea that the building was about to fall. We were taking our time. In fact, I said to Stanley at one point, 'Hey, let's not go too fast here. I'd hate to break an ankle.' We went all the way down to the Plaza level. We came out and stared, awestruck. What we looked at was normally a flowing fountain, vendors with their wagons, business people coming to and from the building, tourists everywhere. It was a beautiful people place, yet this area, several acres I'm sure, was dead; it was a moonscape. It looked like it had been deserted for 100 years, and we had just discovered it.

The towers collapse

It was surreal. We stared at it for 20 or 30 seconds with our jaws dropped, saying, 'What is happening here?' We went down an escalator that wasn't working – all electricity was off, other than the emergency electricity in the stairway – and through some revolving doors. We were passing firemen and policemen who were going about their business, walking at normal speeds. I didn't sense any panic. There were other evacuees like Stanley and me, but there was no running or crowds. It was more or less deserted.

We got out to the south exit of Four World Trade Center on the southeast corner of the complex. Firemen and policemen stood at the door. One said, 'Whoa, wait a minute fellows, if you are gonna cross Liberty Street, you had better go for it. There is debris falling from above.'

I crept out from under the eaves. I said, 'All right, Stanley, I don't see anything coming. Are you ready?' He said, 'Yup,' and after one more check, I said, 'All right, let's go,' and we ran across Liberty Street, which is quite wide at that point, several lanes. There was nobody there.

We ran across the street and up another block and caught our breath. There was a deli owner there. I said, 'Have you got any water?' He went in and just handed us this water in bottles and said, 'Here you go.' I said, 'Thank you.' He said, 'In fact, here is a breakfast platter. I don't think anybody is going to be picking that up.' And he gave me this great tray with some fresh fruit on it and some rolls.

I carried this with me another block to the west side of Trinity Church, where we met a couple of ministers. That's when Stanley broke down. He cried to these ministers, 'This man saved my life.' He said I just pulled him up like Superman. I don't remember having this extraordinary strength, but he says it really did happen that way. He completely broke down.

I was overcome with emotion as well, and I said, 'You know, Stanley, you may think I saved your life but I think you saved my life, too. You got me out of that argument as to whether I should go up or go down. I'm here, and I'm fine, and it's because of your voice in the darkness that I made it.' We embraced, and the ministers had a quick prayer, and one of them said, 'You know, the church is open if you would like to go in there.'

Stanley and I looked at each other, nodded and said, 'All right, let's do that.' So we walked to the south side of Trinity Church, which is a street that slopes up. As we walked up, we got higher and higher, and we could now turn round and see the World Trade Center. Stanley said to me, 'You know, I think those buildings could go down.' I said, 'There is no way. Those are steel structures.' But I didn't finish the sentence before Tower Two started to slide down.

He cried to these ministers, 'This man saved my life.' He said I just pulled him up like Superman. I don't remember having this extraordinary strength, but he says it really did happen that way.

Heading home

I would say that we'd been out of the building maybe 5 minutes when it collapsed. It disappeared into its own dust. We stared, watching, with nobody running or anything initially. But then this great tsunami of dust came over the church. Everybody looked up, and, as in a disaster movie, everybody started running in fear of the debris and dust that might be in there. You didn't want to breathe that junk, so we ran down Broadway and went into a building as the dust and smoke was catching up to our backsides. We got into that lobby with many other people doing the same thing. The air was clean in there, and people were milling around.

I realised then that I was still carrying the silly fruit platter, so I plumped that down on the reception desk there, and people started digging into it. It was an odd thing that I didn't just chuck it aside when I was running. I wasn't even aware that I was carrying it.

We stayed for at least half an hour, I suppose. The ash settled. We went out the east side of that building, which was onto New Street. It was like a winter's day, grey sky. I suppose it was a ¼in of dust and ash everywhere, but it looked like freshly fallen fine snow. We walked in amazement down the street. We wandered over to the east side of Manhattan, the East River. Stanley gave me his business card, and thank goodness he did, because in the crowd that was walking, he and I suddenly got parted. He just disappeared into the crowd. I yelled and looked and walked back and forth but he was gone.

I was very grateful I had his business card at that point, because I knew that he was real. My initial thought was, 'Whoa, this was an angel; this didn't happen.' It was a strange feeling that slipped over me. But, hey, I had his business card, so I knew he was real.

I wandered up FDR Drive on the east side of the island, thinking I was going to have to walk to mid-town to get home somehow to northern New Jersey where I live. But in this fog, in this white, wintry day, I heard someone on a bullhorn, 'Next ferry for Jersey City.' 'That's strange,' I thought. I didn't even know there were ferries over here. Well, what the ferry company had done was reroute their ferries to the east side of the island; there's a pier over there, Pier 11. I thought, 'This is wonderful.'

I jumped on that ferry. They certainly weren't charging. We sailed around the southern tip of Manhattan, up the Hudson River, and as we got parallel to the World Trade Center – the wind was blowing from north to south that day – it was then that I and many other people realised for the first time that both towers were completely down.

It was just a surreal feeling. Disbelief. How could this happen? Of course, at the time we knew nothing about the planes being hijacked, nothing about the Pentagon, nothing about the plane going down in Pennsylvania, or the FAA getting all planes out of the air. We were completely in the dark. But we could look off to the Trade Center on our right and see that this building I had worked in for 27 years was gone. It was a staggering thought. There was silence. People just couldn't believe it.

We sailed in silence to Harborside in Jersey City and got off the ferry. Well, I ran to the ticket booth. I think I was the first person there. I asked the lady if I could use the phone, and she said, 'Absolutely.' I called my

Then this great tsunami of dust came over the church. Everybody looked up, and, as in a disaster movie, everybody started running in fear of the debris and dust that might be in there. You didn't want to breathe that junk.

wife, and I could hear the cheers back at home. They wanted to come and get me. I said, 'Well, look, I know the traffic in the area will be horrible.'

So I ended up walking about a mile to Hoboken train terminal, and caught a train to my station. Then I got in my car and drove 15 minutes to my home. When I hit the driveway, I honked the horn awfully loudly many times. There was then a front lawn full of tears and a reunion.

That's my story. It was a long, horrific day, but for me it turned out all right. Ron, I learned later, had gone up to the 91st floor. He lay on the floor there for 10 minutes until he panicked. He told me, 'I had to see my wife. I had to see my kids at all costs. I was gonna make it out.' And he went to the stairway and went all the way down, following me, I guess, by 5-7 minutes.

For many others, I'm deeply saddened that they aren't here. We lost 61 people in total, including Susan whom I had tried to comfort, 61 friends that we worked with and laughed with for years. ∎

Where are they now?

A WEEK AFTER 9/11, Brian Clark had a strange and vivid dream in which he saw, at the foot of his bed, the heroic Jose, whom he had passed on his way downstairs, as the young man made his way up in a vain bid to help Dave Vera. In the dream, Jose was wearing a bright and blousy white shirt and a glorious smile. 'Jose, you're alive!' said Brian. 'How did you do that? You fooled everybody.' Only by his smile did Jose respond, as if to say 'You'll figure it out.' The dream left Brian with the firm conviction that not only was Jose fine, but so were all 61 of his co-workers who had perished. It was deeply consoling. He has never, he says, had nightmares about 9/11.

Just ten days after 9/11, Euro Brokers was back in business, in borrowed offices overlooking Manhattan's Staten Island Ferry Terminal, and Brian was asked to administer the Euro Brokers Relief Fund, responsible for collecting and distributing money to bereaved relatives in financial need. It was an ideal role for him, and therapeutic.

He had known personally the colleagues who died and had been there on 9/11. 'I had helped manage Euro Brokers for 27 years so people trusted me. I had these great, long conversations with relatives,' he says, 're-creating what it was like.'

He and Stanley Praimnath became firm friends. The two men's story was told in a Sky One documentary, *United by 9/11*, in September 2005. A book by Stanley, written with William Hennessey and titled *Plucked From the Fire*, was published by Rosedog. Brian credits his upbringing – the values instilled in him by his parents and his grandmother – for the fact that he went unhesitatingly to Stanley's aid. 'I was quickly able to switch positions, to think, "If I was in that stranger's place, what would I want to happen? I'd want someone to come and get me."'

The return to work was actually healing for most of Euro Brokers' surviving staff. They had had a shared trauma and could help and support each other. 'The temporary quarters were makeshift, but it worked. Because we were all together, we didn't care. We were just happy to be there.' They were also given counselling with their peer groups as part of their rehabilitation.

The company has since relocated to permanent offices within a mile of Ground Zero. Five years after 9/11, Brian retired and is now enjoying life at the house he and his wife Dianne have shared for 35 years. They have three grandchildren close by, and four more in Toronto.

SURVIVORS Brian Clark (right) with Stanley Praimnath, the man he selflessly rescued from the burning tower.

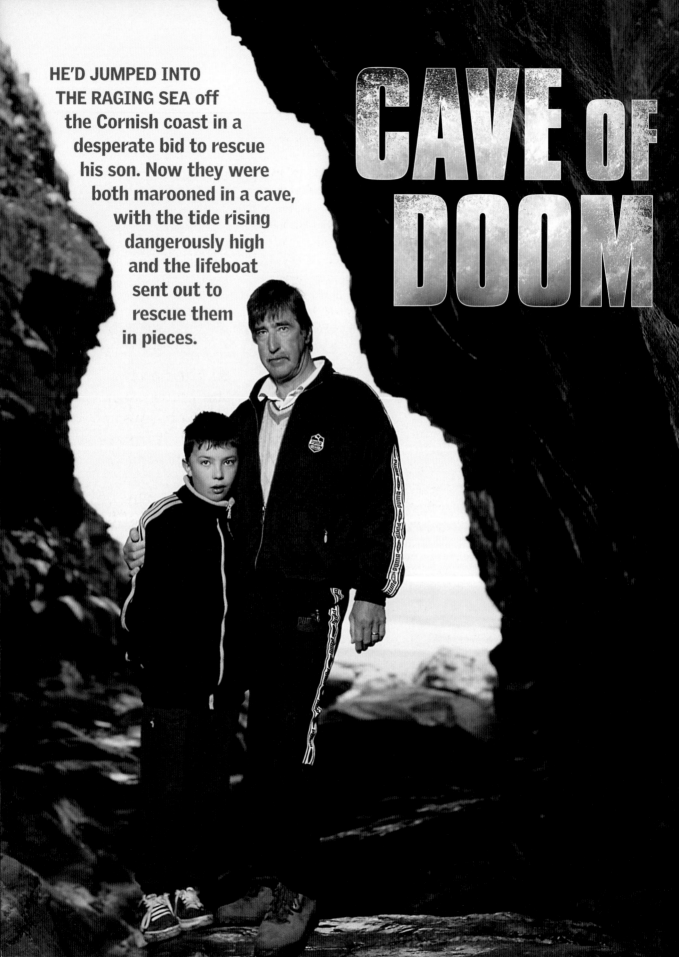

HE'D JUMPED INTO THE RAGING SEA off the Cornish coast in a desperate bid to rescue his son. Now they were both marooned in a cave, with the tide rising dangerously high and the lifeboat sent out to rescue them in pieces.

CAVE OF DOOM

'I'm off to the beach,' announced 11-year-old James Leeds, coming into the dining room of the family's Cornish hotel, Willapark Manor. Nick Leeds looked up from serving wine to the 38 guests tucking into Sunday lunch and smiled at the small bright-eyed, black-haired boy.

'Have a good time,' he replied. He had no qualms. James was mature for his age and always told his parents where he was going.

Nick glanced beyond the dining-room windows at the Atlantic rollers slicking up the popular surfing beach of Bossiney Cove, 180m (200yd) away. He never tired of this evocative smugglers' coast of gentle coves cradled in high black slate cliffs. A mile north was Tintagel Castle, legendary birthplace of King Arthur, whose golden round table was said to lie deep under the mound of Bossiney Castle, just across the fields from the hotel.

A quietly spoken yet sociable man, Nick had bought the neglected turn-of-the-century cliff-top villa in 1982 and had worked hard to transform it into a 14-bedroom hotel, with the help of his wife Liz.

Today, September 6, 1998, she was busy in the kitchen while Nick and their 23-year-old daughter Kate worked in the restaurant. Nick, a tennis nut, was looking forward to a quiet afternoon watching Tim Henman on television.

It was 4.45pm when Nick heard his wife screaming. He rushed into the hall. In front of Liz stood James's friend Christopher Hill in wet trunks, sobbing, 'James has been swept out. I think he's hurt.'

At the beach, the waves had started coming in much bigger and faster than usual. The two boys had climbed onto a 6m (20ft) high rock, but one wave that dwarfed all the others had engulfed them. James's legs had been swiped from under him and the retreating wave had sucked him into the Atlantic.

'James! James!' echoed round Nick's head as he raced out of the hotel, still in the white shirt, bow tie and waistcoat he wore for waiting at tables.

Time for action

He loved all their seven children equally, but Nick had a special bond with his youngest son. They shared a love of the sea and often played guitar together.

Nick cursed his leather soles as he careered clumsily in Christopher's tracks across 90m (100yd) of damp grass to the cliff edge. The sea was pounding into the cove 55m (180ft) below. A swarming sickness tugged at his stomach. He sprinted down the twisting cliff path, in places no more than a slippery gully, and in 5 minutes he was on the rock from which James had been swept.

It was next to a cave, 12m (40ft) high and 8m (25ft) wide, which disappeared 25m (80ft) into the cliff like a damp black railway tunnel.

Nick stripped to his underpants, desperately scanning the huge waves and the gaps between for a glimpse of his son's dark head bobbing above the frothing blue water. Nothing.

As a father he could not wait for help. He had to do something.

'Throw me that float,' he yelled to Christopher, gesturing at a buoyancy aid attached by a rope to a steel post.

Although Nick was only of average build, his passion for playing tennis had kept him fitter than most 52-year-olds. Even in these terrifying conditions, he might stand a chance. Clutching the buoyancy aid, Nick jumped.

At the beach, the waves had started coming in much bigger and faster than usual. The two boys had climbed onto a 6m (20ft) high rock, but one wave that dwarfed all the others had engulfed them.

Like his son, he was a good swimmer, but he found himself being hurled around. Suddenly he could not move his legs. The buoyancy-aid rope was tangled round his ankles. Kicking and struggling, he managed to free himself.

Wave after wave dumped down on his head. His strength began to fail, but he could not give up on his son. James might have been washed into the cave.

If only he could get in there too, he could at least comfort the boy. 'I just can't bear the idea of him alone and frightened,' he thought.

Three times the sea swept Nick towards the cave. Three times he lunged at the rocks, but it was worse than gripping wet soap. Swept out again, choking and gasping, he surfaced long enough to yell, 'Please God! Help me!'

Enormous waves

After calling the emergency services at Port Isaac, Liz scrambled down to the beach. She saw James's clothes and changing bag thrashing around in the angry water. On the rock she spotted her husband's watch and a single shoe.

She was a strong and optimistic woman, but at that moment her spirit deserted her.

Then she felt two arms go round her. It was Kate. The two women hugged each other and cried.

Suddenly a wave hurled Nick into the depths of the cave. On the right, a great shoulder of smooth rock extended its entire length. He threw out his arms, grabbing anything that would stop him being sucked back out.

At last! A handhold. He was more than halfway inside, where the rock narrowed to a twisted floor-to-ceiling slash, dividing the front of the cave from another chamber behind it.

Up to his shoulders in water, Nick gulped air. 'What next?' he wondered. Then he heard a voice high above, 'Dad? I love you, Dad.'

Nick peered into the darkness. 'Round this way!' James yelled down from the roof of the cave.

He had climbed into a narrow crevice 6m (20ft) above his father, where he was clinging on by his fingertips.

Clambering up a 60-degree face of ice-smooth slate was not easy, but eventually Nick manoeuvred himself into the small space behind James.

He reached out and put his arm across the boy's back to reassure and protect him.

It was the most wonderful moment of Nick's life. 'I love you too,' he said. 'I really thought I'd lost you.'

At 5.16pm, more than half an hour after James Leeds had been washed into the sea, local coastguard Ken Richards joined Liz on the rock. 'They must be in the cave,' Liz told him, praying for it to be true.

'We'll do everything to get them out,' Richards reassured her.

Two helicopters and two lifeboats were already on their way. On top

Reaching the unreachable *The day after the dramatic rescue of Nick and James Leeds, the damaged lifeboat was retrieved from the cave where father, son and the two lifeboatmen were trapped. Even in calm weather, the almost sheer cliffs make access to the cave a hazardous task.*

of the cliff, three coastguard teams were setting up ropes and lights, and getting ready to be lowered down the cliff.

The Atlantic had the same kind of heavy groundswell that had claimed the lives of two surfers just along the coast three years before. Even worse, 275m (300yd) out was a series of sandbars. Every time the 4-4.5m (12-15ft) waves hit one of these, they gained an extra 4.5m (15ft) in height. The biggest were coming in every 6 minutes. And those waves were going to get a whole load bigger before high water at 6.20pm.

Rescuers overboard

'James, it's a helicopter!' Nick's spirits soared. 'They've come to get us.'

Squeezed into the narrow gap behind his son, Nick kept his darkest fear from James: if the cave fills completely, we'll drown before anybody can save us. The water was only 2.5m (8ft) below — and rising fast.

Nick realised that the throb of engines was coming from directly above their heads. He looked up and saw a sliver of daylight coming down a shaft the size of a tiny chimney. If he could just push James into it, at least his son might be safe, however high the tide rose.

But the shaft was blocked by a yellow buoy. Nick stretched up and pushed at it. It would not move. He punched at it, hoping to work it loose, but the sea had jammed it there with such force that it was stuck fast.

Then his ears popped. The air pressure in the cave had changed. He heard a rumbling to his right. Turning his head, he saw a big wave rushing down the cave. It was going to swamp them. 'Breathe in,' he shouted to James, flexing his muscles so his body filled the crevice to shield his son.

The water thudded into him, a solid, unforgiving mass. The noise was deafening.

Suddenly he was tumbling in the backwash. Winded and weightless in a helter-skelter of white water, Nick's helpless body cannoned into the rocks.

Clambering back up to his son, he saw the Port Isaac inshore lifeboat just outside the mouth of the cave.

'We're here, we're here!' Nick shouted, waving frantically. Then he saw huge waves powering in behind it. One swept two of the crew overboard,

September 6, 1998

16.30 James swept away
A huge wave sweeps James Leeds into the Atlantic Ocean. His friend runs for help.

16.45 Nick Leeds alerted
James's father races down to the sea and, seeing no sign of his son, leaps into the water, aiming for the cave where James is trapped.

17.16 Coastguard arrives
The coastguard reassures Liz that two lifeboats and two helicopters are on their way.

17.30 Roped down
Coastguards prepare to lower themselves down, but are unable to get to the cave.

18.20 High tide The waves get higher. A lifeboat is wrecked and two lifeboatmen are also stranded in the cave.

19.00 Battered by waves
Nick injures his arm and James fractures his skull.

20.50 Rescue at last Nick, James and the lifeboatmen emerge from the cave.

Willapark Manor Hotel

Bossiney

Bossiney Cove

dashing any hope of rescue for father and son. The backwash flushed the battered lifeboat out of the cave as the remaining crewman tried frantically to restart the engine

Nick was desperate. It was getting dark and the two lifeboatmen were stranded somewhere in the cave, out of sight.

From outside, a beam of light played crazy patterns on the rock. Another rescue boat? But Nick knew that the waves were now too high for anybody to get into the cave. 'If we can hang on until the tide turns,' he told James, 'we'll get out.' But when would that be?

Still on the cliff path, Liz Leeds saw one of the coastguard team dangling on his ropes just beneath the cave's upper lip. Seeing him gesturing at the coastguard, pointing his thumb down and shaking his head, she shuddered.

'Ma'am! Ma'am!' Ken Richards shouted at her. 'You must go up top for your own safety.'

Unaware that the thumb-down gesture meant simply that getting into the cave was impossible, she turned and walked away – certain she would never see her husband and son again.

Nick smelled fumes. The surging tide had smashed the wrecked lifeboat back into the cave, and leaking fuel was vaporising in the incessant spray, making it hard to breathe.

For those in peril on the seas

FOR 365 DAYS A YEAR, 24 hours a day, some 4,800 volunteers in the UK and the Republic of Ireland stand by to crew lifeboats at the summons of their pagers. Only one in ten of these men and women is professionally employed on our seas or waterways. Yet they are all the backbone of the Royal National Lifeboat Institution (RNLI), which receives no government funding, relying entirely on charitable donations.

There are 231 lifeboat stations around Great Britain and Ireland, including four on the River Thames. In 2008 alone, RNLI lifeboats rescued 8,000 people – an average of 22 a day.

It was Sir William Hillary, a Yorkshire-born Quaker, soldier and adventurer (motto: 'With courage nothing is impossible'), who first argued for a lifeboat service, having himself prompted and coordinated dramatic sea rescues off his adopted home, the Isle of Man. He printed and distributed pamphlets, lobbied the Admiralty (the British government department with responsibility for naval affairs) and approached all sovereigns and governments with naval power in Europe and the Americas. His appeals led, in 1824,

to the foundation of the National Institution for the Preservation of Life from Shipwreck.

The lifeboat crews of Port Isaac in Cornwall have a long, distinguished history of awards and commendations for bravery, dating from 1859. For their efforts to rescue Nick and James Leeds, helmsman Kevin Dingle and crew member Mike Edkins received the thanks of the Institution, inscribed on vellum. Crew member Paul Pollington and auxiliary coastguard Kenneth C. Richards received framed letters of thanks.

Some rescues off Port Isaac have certainly been unusual. In 1975, the station was awarded a Certificate of Merit by the RSPCA, after the lifeboats joined a rescue when 30 bullocks plunged over a cliff at Port Quin.

Huge waves knocked him off his perch and tossed him into a frantic whirlpool of rocks and driftwood, which crashed into his head. A layer of skin was grated from his back, buttocks and shoulders, but he was so cold he felt no pain. Each time he managed to scrabble back up to James.

'We're not going to get out of here are we, Dad?'

'Yes, we are,' Nick gasped. 'Just hang in there and don't let go.'

Again Nick was thrown down. When he tried to climb out, his left arm no longer worked. His shoulder joint had been crushed like a ping-pong ball and his strength was spent.

'James!' he shouted up. 'You'll have to make it on your own.'

Terrified, James yelled for all his worth into the blackness, 'My dad's dying! My dad's dying!'

Don't give up!

Suddenly, above the noise of the surf, he heard a shout, 'Don't give up! Help's coming.' It was lifeboatman Mike Edkins who, along with fellow crew member Kevin Dingle, was squeezed in a tiny hole nearer the cave mouth.

Nick had barely clawed his way, one-handed, back up to his son when another huge wave flushed them both right into the rear chamber of the cave.

James fractured his skull in the fall. But although his head was badly bruised and swelling, he was still in better shape than his father, who was shaking and exhausted, his useless left arm dangling limply at his side.

All at once James realised that survival depended on him. He heard the voice shouting again. 'Keep him warm. Don't let him go to sleep.'

For the next hour James stayed as close as he possibly could to his gallant father. To stave off hypothermia and keep Nick awake, James kept on talking, saying anything that came into his head. If Nick lost consciousness, he would die.

'We're going to make it, Dad,' he urged through chattering teeth, searching all the time with salt-stung eyes for any sign that the tide was losing its terrible rage.

Again he saw light bobbing into the cave from outside. James could not let his father slip away now. His innate good sense overcoming his small boy's fear, he cajoled, bullied, coaxed, 'Wake up, Dad. C'mon. Don't go to sleep!'

It was 8.50pm. Although the tide had turned more than 2 hours before, the surf in the cave had been too lethal for a search attempt.

Now, out of the gloomy depths of the cave, emerged the trapped lifeboatmen Mike Edkins and Kevin Dingle, helped by two coastguards.

Moments later two figures, one much smaller than the other, crawled out into the eerie glare of the searchlights. After nearly 5 hours in the water, Nick and James Leeds clung tightly to each other for warmth and strength. Both knew there could be no greater thing that a father could do for his son or a son for his father than to save the other's life.

Nick and James were transported to the North Devon Hospital, Barnstaple, by an RAF helicopter that had earlier plucked the third Port Isaac lifeboatman safely from the sea.

The following year, both father and son received British Gold Hero awards from the Association of Retired and Persons Over Fifty. ■

To stave off hypothermia and keep Nick awake, James kept on talking, saying anything that came into his head. If Nick lost consciousness, he would die.

HIGH-FLYING EXECUTIVE Mary Quin got more than she bargained for on a Christmas trip to Yemen. Instead of the peace she sought, she was kidnapped, along with 18 other tourists, four of whom died in a dramatic rescue attempt. The event changed Mary's life for ever, as she attempted to understand the circumstances that turn men into captors.

CAUGHT IN THE CROSSFIRE

It had been a stressful year. Assigned to manage three small businesses by Rank Xerox, I found them an awkward mix, with major political and ego battles getting in the way of real accomplishment. My relatives were far away in New Zealand and since I had little interest in spending Christmas alone at my house north of New York, it was a good time for me to travel – preferably to somewhere warm, with limited email or voicemail access. Yemen fitted the bill perfectly.

When I applied for my visa, I considered that the only unusual risk about Yemen – beyond the normal difficulties of travel in any developing country – was the incidence of kidnapping. Yemen's tribes had a reputation for kidnapping foreigners and demanding some benefit from the government for the hostages' release. However, no hostages had ever been harmed.

I had already started packing for my trip when I heard, on December 17, 1998, that the USA and Britain had launched a four-day air offence against Iraq after Saddam Hussein had yet again failed to cooperate with the UN weapons inspection. Obviously, anti-American violence by Islamic terrorists was a threat. But Iraq was a long way from Yemen – and what kind of wimp lets a remote chance of something bad happening dissuade her from an adventure? Not me. Nevertheless, I packed both my New Zealand and American passports.

Killing ground *In this field (background), Mary Quin and the other hostages were forced by their kidnappers to stand on top of a dividing wall as human shields. Mary was drawn to Yemen partly by its ancient sites, such as the desert city of Marib (opposite, below left).*

Relaxed and happy *At the start of their Yemen adventure holiday, members of the tour group smiled for the camera at a roadside restaurant in the Hadramawt region, unaware of the drama about to unfold. In a kidnapping that lasted just 24 hours, four of the group would lose their lives.*

Ambushed

Yemen was everything I'd hoped: palaces perched on top of rocky outcrops; camels moving silently across the vast desert of the Empty Quarter; skyscrapers built of mud in the walled oasis towns. With 18 other adventure travellers, mostly British, with three Americans and two Australians, our tour leader and local drivers, we travelled round the country in a convoy of five Toyota Land Cruisers.

It was now December 28 and we left the town of Habban for a 320km (200 miles) trip to the port city of Aden. Crossing the barren beauty of the deserts of Shabwah and Abyan provinces, we stopped a couple of times to photograph stunning views of mountain plateaus and canyons.

This main route was used by a steady flow of trucks and battered cars. We thought nothing of it when a white pick-up truck, its bed crammed full of men, pulled onto the road between our first and second vehicles. After a while it swerved sideways, blocking the path of the second Land Cruiser. Several rifle shots cracked across the emptiness of the desert. I was in the fourth vehicle, sitting in the back with three women, including softly spoken Ruth, a classically Celtic-looking Scot with freckles and short red hair – we could almost have passed for sisters.

Three armed men had surrounded the Land Cruiser in front. Our driver was tense; his left hand grasped the door handle and his right closed round the stock of the rifle on the seat beside him as he muttered in Arabic. I knew at once that this was an ambush and we were about to be kidnapped. My first instinct was to escape. But the passenger door to my left opened onto the middle of the road where there was no shelter. I couldn't get to the other door.

I turned to check the road behind us. The last of our convoy had also stopped. More armed men came running from all directions, shouting and firing shots into the air.

I counted about 18 men, most of them wearing the red-and-white checked khafiya, or headscarf, wrapped across their faces. Suddenly, I remembered something my detective father had told me many years before: if you ever witness a crime, pay attention to the time that it happens. It was 3 minutes before 11am. Against the desert background, the scene reminded me of a B-grade cowboy film. My reaction was fascination rather than fear.

Only the front vehicle in our convoy had escaped. In it was our tour leader with the only driver who spoke English and the only traveller who spoke Arabic. At least they could get help.

'Who Americans?' We were sitting on two blankets spread out under some trees. Beyond the trees was an open area with four low earth walls, three parallel to each other and the other closing them off at one end; each was about half a metre or so high and broad enough to stand on, which identified this space as fields, used for crops in the rainy season. There was no sign of any human habitation.

The leader, perhaps in his early 30s, with intense eyes and thick wavy hair, bent down on one knee in front of us. 'Who Americans?' he demanded. I later learned that this man was Abu Hassan. His interest in Americans was not a good sign.

I handed over my New Zealand passport. Hassan and two others mulled over our passports and compared them with what was obviously a list of

Desert splendour *The ruined ciiy of Marib is believed by some to have been the home of the legendary Queen of Sheba. Yemen's ancient sites and spectacular landscapes attract adventurous visitors despite the threats of kidnapping and terrorism.*

the travellers. 'Any more Americans?' It seemed less and less likely that this was about a tribal grievance. These kidnappers had a different agenda.

With no introductions offered and little else to distinguish the gang members, we gave them names based mostly on differences in clothing – Purple Skirt (the traditional wraparound futa), Yellow Pants (a fetching pair of canary-coloured trousers) and Grey Shirt. The manager in me was instinctively assessing the performance of the kidnappers. Most of them were milling about in a nervous, disorganised way and seemed unsure what they should be doing. 'I could run a kidnapping better than this,' I thought.

Another gang member squatted to the left of Hassan, nervously tossing a hand grenade from one hand to the other, his eyes glittering with excitement. Unlike the rest of the kidnappers, Hassan did not bother to cover his face as he spoke. 'We are mujahideen.'

Yellow Pants spoke reasonably good English and acted as the official interpreter. We were ordered to collect our water bottles and rucksacks. I took the opportunity to switch from sandals to sturdier walking shoes and to stuff a fleece in my rucksack. One of the youngest kidnappers, a bright-eyed boy, pointed towards my sandals. Never one to argue with anyone holding a gun, I handed them over. 'Be my guest,' I smiled at him.

Led by half a dozen armed guards we headed out in single file across a broad valley, over a hill and down into a dry river bed, a wadi, a walk of about 50 minutes, where we halted under the shade of overhanging rocks. I noticed that Peter Rowe, a mathematics professor at Durham University, wore only flip-flops and was having difficulty navigating the uneven terrain strewn with sharp volcanic stones and rocks.

Abu Hassan came to address us, Yellow Pants at his side. Another gang member squatted to the left of Hassan, nervously tossing a hand grenade from one hand to the other, his eyes glittering with excitement. Unlike the rest of the kidnappers, Hassan did not bother to cover his face as he spoke. 'We are mujahideen. You are not responsible for the bombings in Iraq but your countries are. Our friends are in prison. When the government releases them, you can go. Don't be afraid.'

'How can I not be afraid with that guy playing with his hand grenade right next to me?' Catherine, a young Australian woman, said angrily. Hassan spoke abruptly to Grenade, who stood up and moved away. The terse explanation for our capture was over.

'Who is Mary?'

We spoke little to each other during the afternoon, sharing only a few whispered exchanges. The sun still burned its harsh light into the narrow valley, reflecting off the bleached walls of the wadi and the dust-covered leaves of parched, stunted trees. The kidnappers took turns to kneel and pray.

The men of our party were taken away, one by one. Were they going to be interrogated? Executed? We eight women were left under the overhanging rocks. 'At least in an Arab country women are less likely to be raped,' whispered Catherine. She had spoken the word in all our minds.

Just then several kidnappers reappeared and ordered us to hand over our rucksacks and all our jewellery. After 5 minutes, Hassan returned.

'Who is Mary?'

I stood to face Hassan, noticing my American passport in his hand.

'I was born in New Zealand. All my family live in New Zealand.' I paused to allow Yellow Pants to translate. 'But I work in America. I have an American passport so I can work there.'

The two men exchanged a few words in Arabic. Then Hassan handed me my American passport and walked away. I was only a woman, after all, and not even a 'real' American. Hardly worth his time and trouble.

All the men in our group returned unharmed. The kidnappers, blinded by the limited roles of women in their own culture, did not bother to assess the bargaining value of their female hostages. There was another employee of a large American corporation on the trip and we were potentially more valuable than some of the male hostages who did not have employers with such deep pockets or influence. I found out later that Xerox had put the corporate jet on standby to evacuate me.

We all crammed onto the two blankets. As the sun set, the air chilled. I had a spot near one edge, but after an hour of trying to sleep, uncomfortable about my exposure to scorpions or spiders, I sat up and watched the night sky. The beams of torches suddenly spilled onto the blankets and the kidnappers called to us to get up. My watch showed it was close to 9pm. We retraced our steps through the darkness of the wadi. The kidnappers seemed light-hearted and one of them bantered a few English words. 'Don't worry. Tomorrow, Britannia,' he said.

The prospect that this would soon be over, that the day's events would be little more than an inconvenience and an exciting travel story, was reassuring. Back near the vehicles we found a long row of blankets and our sleeping bags in a heap. Spending the night in the warmth of my own sleeping bag, with plenty of room, seemed like staying in a four-star hotel.

Armed rescue

Before retiring for the night, I casually walked across the field towards some bushes, seeking a private toilet spot. The kidnappers, huddled round a fire, showed no sign of stopping me. Squatting out of sight, I considered the possibility of escaping right then, simply disappearing into the surrounding darkness. But this was southern Yemen and many minefields had not yet been cleared since the 1994 civil war. I decided it was wiser to wait until our situation became clearer.

At midnight we were woken again. Dinner time. A big plastic bag of stew – goat? camel? mutton? It was tough but I chewed through two rubbery chunks and took a handful of the dates offered for dessert. A smaller plastic bag contained what Yellow Pants called sauce. As I crawled back inside my sleeping bag, I heard Brian, a genial 52-year-old postal worker from Peterborough, helpfully explaining the difference in meaning between 'sauce' and 'gravy'. Our captor was delighted at this chance to refine his English.

The next morning the atmosphere in the camp was much more relaxed. We didn't speak much, just exchanged looks of disbelief as we

I considered the possibility of escaping right then, simply disappearing into the surrounding darkness. But this was southern Yemen, and many minefields had not yet been cleared since the 1994 civil war.

each realised it hadn't been a dream. We really were hostages. Opening my suitcase, I noticed how much was missing: binoculars, torch, leather belt, warm jacket. My small photo album was still there, so I removed a picture of my five brothers and sisters. I wondered if the kidnapping was on TV yet, or if my family was still unaware of what had happened?

Under my skirt I stepped into a change of underwear, then drew on some dark brown trousers. I thought about changing my long-sleeved T-shirt but that would involve a greater degree of exposure. A swish of deodorant would have to do. I pulled out my wide-brimmed straw hat for protection from the sun.

Several of our group discovered their boots were missing. Catherine complained. To my surprise, 5 minutes later Purple Skirt came over to us and dropped half a dozen pairs of boots, plus my sandals, on the ground. 'I am sorry,' he said, 'Some of our people are criminals.'

'No joking,' I laughed to myself.

About 7am we were rounded up and led to a different spot in the wadi. I settled down with my book, *War and Peace*, a hasty last-minute airport purchase. The morning dragged on.

Someone arrived with cartons of juice and biscuits and, as the delivery man turned to go, one of the kidnappers asked, 'Go market. You want something?' Incredible! We asked for bottled water, oranges and bananas, bread – and rolls of toilet paper.

I climbed up the hillside and discovered there was a view of our previous night's campsite. 'There have been vehicles coming and going all morning,' said one of the other hostages already at the viewpoint.

After about 10 minutes, we heard the sound of gunfire. I looked at my watch. It was 3 minutes before 11am – exactly 24 hours since the ambush. I felt worried.

'Oh shit,' I said to the others, 'I think someone is trying to rescue us.' I did not know it then, but my fear was well founded. Of all the hostages killed in a kidnapping, most die during an armed rescue attempt.

The kidnappers were just as surprised. They made us all sit together in the wadi, then hustled us back over the hill and across the open valley to the campsite, where we were herded behind one of the low walls. Suddenly a shell exploded right overhead and we threw ourselves down on the ground. We were right in the line of fire.

Human shields

At gunpoint, we were made to get up and stand on the top of a wall, our hands in the air. They were using us as human shields. The incoming gunfire did not stop. We stood on the wall for about 10 minutes, hearts pounding. The bullets made distinctive zinging sounds. 'Just like in films,' I thought.

Except that I could be killed at any second.

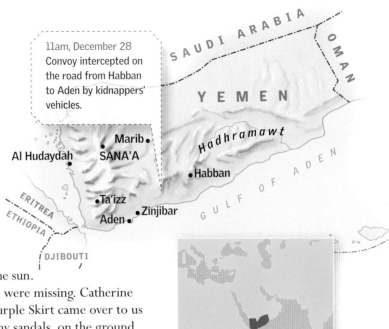

11am, December 28 Convoy intercepted on the road from Habban to Aden by kidnappers' vehicles.

Ambushed en route *The convoy of five Land Cruisers was intercepted as it made its way through the Yemeni desert. The kidnappers' first mistake was to allow the lead vehicle to escape.*

Terror in the land of Sheba

LEGENDARY HOME OF THE QUEEN OF SHEBA, burial place of Job, Yemen was once known as *Arabia Felix*, fortunate Arabia. It does not seem so fortunate today.

The Republic of Yemen is the poorest country in the Middle East, and one of the poorest in the world, with its oil reserves depleted, severe water shortages and widespread malnutrition. Rebel groups pose a continuing threat to law and order.

While famine is a real and present danger, the country is fertile territory, at least for those who would recruit terrorists from a generation of disaffected young men with bleak or non-existent prospects.

On October 12, 2000, two suicide bombers attacked the guided-missile destroyer USS *Cole* as it was refuelling in Aden harbour. Seventeen naval personnel were killed and 39 injured in the ensuing explosions. And in September 2008 suicide bombers struck again, at the US Embassy in the heart of the Yemeni capital, Sana'a, killing 16 people, mainly Yemeni troops. No Americans were hurt. A group called 'Islamic Jihad in Yemen' claimed responsibility and threatened further attacks.

Yemen's President, Ali Abdullah Saleh, in power since 1978, had allied his country with the US in its 'war on terror' since the attack on the USS *Cole*, but his government had been accused of laxness, or complicity with terrorists, after 23 prisoners tunnelled out of a Sana'a prison in 2006.

Saleh had also pursued a programme under which jihadis, those pursuing the Islamic holy war, were allowed to go free if they promised to reform. Yemeni courts commuted a death sentence for Jamal al-Badawi, convicted of masterminding the USS *Cole* strike, giving him instead 15 years in prison.

Mary Quin's kidnapper, Abu Hassan, also leader of the Al Jihad gang, was shown no such clemency, though, and was executed for his role in the attack on the *Cole*, and for hostage-taking and murder.

Fruits of terror Abu Hassan, shown in his prison cell in Zinjibar (left), was executed for his part in the kidnapping in 1999. A year later the destroyer USS *Cole* became the target of bombers in the port of Aden (above).

The kidnapper we called Grey Shirt shouted to us to go forwards across the field and then to stop but keep our arms up. The bullets kept flying and shells and grenades were exploding in the sky, creating small grey clouds against the perfect blue.

If you are going to be shot at, it helps to do it with people who have a sense of humour. Catherine commented, 'If this is what it's like to be rescued, I'd just as soon stay a hostage.'

Peter suggested that we should write a new section for the Yemeni guidebooks. I asked Ruth if her Arab language phrase book had any helpful suggestions. 'Ach, the book doesna' seem to address this particular situation.' Her canny humour was immensely reassuring.

We sensed the attackers were gradually encircling the campsite, although they were still too far away for us to see them. I didn't see how we could survive this two-way gunfight, but yet I felt certain I would survive. I could even imagine myself back at work, telling colleagues about what had happened. After 45 minutes, we were all still alive and no one was screaming or panicking.

Run for it

The nearest of the attacking forces was now in shouting distance. The kidnappers were lying against the earth wall where we stood, firing between our legs. I turned to look at Catherine next to me. Tears were streaming down her face. I held her hand. At that moment, I knew that the one choice I was free to make, that human beings are always free to make in any circumstance, was about my own behaviour. I would not let these terrorists see that I was afraid.

'You can do this,' I told myself. 'You are still alive. Just one more minute. You can do this. You can stay alive for just one more minute.' Time and again I felt air move against my face as a bullet shot past me.

I could not believe this was the day, the place, where my life would end. Besides, I thought, 'If I die now, I won't get to see how it all ends.'

Purple Skirt grabbed the back of my shirt, just below my neck, and I felt the hard barrel of his Kalashnikov jammed against my spine. He continued shouting, the tension in his voice escalating as he prodded me forwards across the open field, towards the rescue force. I had an image of a bullet shattering my spine into a thousand pieces. The universe now consisted of only Purple Skirt and me.

We came to the central wall. I went up and over. 'Just one more minute. You can do this.' Suddenly I could no longer feel the gun. I turned. To my surprise, Purple Skirt was lying on his side on the ground, groaning.

He was struggling to get up. I could see no blood and his rifle lay on the ground in front of him. I decided to make a run for it. After a couple of steps, fearful that Purple Skirt might have enough life left in him to fire off another round, I turned and made a grab for the gun. With a shock I found he had grabbed the other end. I pulled as hard as I could on the barrel, trying to keep it pointed off to the side of me, Purple Skirt screaming, 'No! No! No!'

He was stronger than I expected. I brought my right foot down hard on his head, gaining enough extra leverage to rip the gun from his hands. For a moment I suddenly knew I was capable of killing another human being. It shocked me. One problem – I didn't know how to use a rifle.

I turned and began to run across the next open field. As I ran across the desert carrying the Kalashnikov, I felt like a cross between Lawrence of Arabia and Rambo. Crazy thoughts flew through my brain. It seemed to me that time had slowed down, that I ran in slow motion. The desert was shrouded in a pale blue-white veil that seemed always to part just a little in front of me. I was not afraid. Now I could die on my own terms, not as a victim.

As I came closer to the third wall, I snapped out of the adrenalin-induced high and wondered what lay on the other side. I had assumed it was the Yemeni army, but what if it were a competing terrorist organisation?

I tossed the rifle off to my right, ran up over the wall in a few strides and threw myself flat on the ground.

As I ran across the desert carrying the Kalashnikov, I felt like a cross between Lawrence of Arabia and Rambo ... Now I could die on my own terms, not as a victim.

My heart was thumping and my breath coming in gasps. Slowly, barely raising my head, I turned and looked round. Within about 5 metres of me, three soldiers in desert-coloured camouflage crouched among the bushes. One gave me a thumbs-up signal and another motioned with his hand for me to lie low. I didn't need any encouragement.

I did survive. But Ruth, Peter and two others did not. At the end of the 2 hour gun battle, four tourists, two kidnappers and possibly one soldier were dead and two of the tourists were injured. Three kidnappers were captured alive, but a dozen more, including the murderous Grey Shirt, escaped into the open desert.

Understanding the captors

The first weeks after the kidnapping were a strange time in which nothing seemed real. People asked if the experience left me feeling anxious. On the contrary, I felt invincible: driving recklessly, not bothering to lock my front door. I did my best to imitate life as usual during the day, but business issues seemed so trivial. I spent my evenings searching the internet, seeking the latest news and researching, to try to understand my captors and their motives. Before I could leave the past behind, I had to understand it.

I quickly became aware that several British men had been arrested in Yemen, accused of a bombing conspiracy, just prior to the kidnapping. These were the 'soldiers' whose release Abu Hassan demanded in exchange for us hostages. Hassan had recruited them into the Aden-Abyan Islamic Army (AAIA) in his fight against the broadly pro-Western government of President Saleh. From reports of the Yemeni trial of the five British-born 'terrorists', I learned the prosecution asserted that the conspiracy had links to Finsbury Park mosque in London.

One of the accused was Mohsin Ghailan, stepson of the notorious hook-handed, one-eyed Abu Hamza. Just after the trial started, Yemen security forces apprehended four more foreigners, among them

17-year-old Mohammed Mustafa Kamel, the son of Abu Hamza. After sending emails requesting an appointment with the radical cleric I flew to London and went to the Finsbury Park mosque.

I draped a black shawl over my head and shoulders and was escorted to an office door hidden behind a heavy curtain under a stairwell. Abu Hamza was sitting behind a desk. To my surprise, four young children were playing on the floor round his feet.

'Salaam alaikum,' I said in greeting. 'I have come to talk about Yemen. I am one of the tourists taken hostage.'

Abu Hamza was momentarily speechless. He looked closely at me with his good eye, then leaned back in his chair.

'Do you object to people like me visiting Muslim countries?' I asked.

'No, I don't object if people visit respectfully. Like you,' he nodded towards my head-covering. 'I object to tourists who abuse Muslim hospitality and I object to the use made of tourist dollars. You do not know this, but tourism is the reason the government gives for allowing gambling, alcohol and usury banks.'

'What is your ultimate goal?' I asked. 'Do you realistically think every country will eventually become Muslim, even England?'

'I don't intend everyone should be converted to Islam,' the cleric replied, 'but the image of Islam has been distorted. Western countries want Muslim countries to be poor and weak. I want peace for those who want peace, war for those who love war.'

Hamza asked me about my own impressions of Islam and whether I would go back to a Muslim country after what had happened. I told him there were good and bad aspects to all religions and I hoped one day to return to Yemen.

Rest in peace *Although it initially caused her some anxiety to return to the scene of her kidnapping, Mary Quin quickly overcame it to pay her respects to Ruth and Peter and her fellow tourists who died in the rescue attempt. She placed a wreath at the foot of the wall where they were killed.*

The return

I did go back to Yemen. I talked to the police and I was allowed into prison to talk to the convicted terrorists, including Abu Hamza's son and stepson. Whether for money or religious zeal, they had chosen to associate with the AAIA, to participate in terrorist training and, I believe, intended to bomb civilian targets in Aden.

At no time did any of them express any regret. I did not want even to mention my murdered fellow travellers, feeling that their memories would be dishonoured by speaking of them in this despicable company.

British-born Mohammed Mustafa Kamel and Mohsin Ghailan both served their prison sentences in Yemen for their involvement in a terrorist bombing campaign and have since returned to the UK.

For me now, though, it was a relief to return to the fresh air and blue skies outside of the prison. I had an even more important goal to accomplish. I asked to be taken back to the place where we had faced 2 hours of gunfire.

As we travelled the rutted road across the desert, I noticed that my heartbeat was increasing: adrenalin was surging through me in readiness for danger.

But when we reached the two fields with their low earth walls, I felt only a sense of relief, like a child who sees there is nothing to fear when the light is turned on in a darkened room.

'It's just a field,' I said to myself, 'just a field.'

At the foot of the wall where Ruth and Peter had died, I laid a wreath. 'Rest in peace. Wherever your spirits might be,' I told them. ■

Where are they now?

FAR FROM BEING DETERRED by her experiences in Yemen, Mary Quin was determined to 'fight back through feminism', to pursue the cause of global women's rights and to see more of the Middle East. In 2000, having quit her high-powered corporate job, she travelled to Egypt as part of an initiative to promote hygiene and health and to discourage female circumcision. In the same year, she attended a conference in Tajikistan, concerned with the plight of women under the Taliban. With eight other delegates, she crossed the border into a part of Afghanistan controlled by the Northern Alliance, where she visited villages, schools, refugee camps, even a jail where she spoke with captured Taliban fighters.

Despite her ordeal, she has never felt the need for counselling. She is just so sad for the four tourists who died, thankful for her escape, and abidingly grateful for the full life she is living.

Following the publicity surrounding her story, Mary received an email from Ray Kaufman, a finance executive,

expressing his admiration. The two met, were instantly attracted, and now live as a couple in Anchorage, Alaska. There Mary founded an organic retailing company, Tuliqi LLC, and a year later, 'out of the blue', was asked to run NANA Management Services, one of Alaska's ten largest companies. NANA is a native-owned corporation with a dedication to preserving the culture and values of the Iñupiat, descendants of the first people to live in northwest Alaska.

Somehow, Mary still finds time for Tuliqi, and for numerous hobbies. She and Ray hunt, fish and take their boat out on Prince William Sound, loving life in one of the world's last great wilderness. They have travelled to Zimbabwe, Namibia and Tanzania, where she put into practice what she had learned on a course in digital photography.

'What happened in Yemen has not in any way put me off travelling to interesting places or to developing countries,' says Mary. 'You figure, "What are the odds of you being in that sort of situation twice in your life?"'

She and Ray did, though, have one hair-raising encounter in Africa – with a deadly black mamba in the rafters of their hut.

KATE ADIE RECOUNTS THE STORY of the terrifying events in Beijing's Tiananmen Square – when getting the story meant putting herself right in the firing line.

DODGING TANKS AND BULLETS

Pulling together *The world watched as students demonstrated in Beijing, China, in 1989. They were calling for greater freedom and democracy.*

Facing danger *A lone man standing before a line of tanks at Tiananmen Square (previous page, top) came to symbolise the stand against the Chinese authorities. Kate Adie (previous page, bottom) had to show similar courage to get news of the demonstrations to the outside world.*

As a foreign correspondent for the BBC, I go where I am sent, experience having taught me to travel light, with not much more than the essentials: toothbrush (and a spare), a medicinal bottle of Scotch (also possible for teeth cleaning if there is no water) and a torch. I have learned to take tough, workaday clothes and a small hand mirror and very tiny hairbrush that can be stuffed into the pocket of my jeans.

At the beginning of June 1989, the student demonstrations in Beijing had been worldwide news for weeks. Day after day, pictures appeared of the students camping in Tiananmen Square, arguing, writing posters and parading banners. Many news organisations were starting to scale down their presence and it wasn't clear if there would be any significant developments.

The colourful mayhem in the square (highly conservative by comparison with student behaviour in Europe) was anathema to the ruling old men of China. Tiananmen, a stretch of concrete of hideous proportions, was where they liked to see the grandeur and unity of China displayed: serried ranks and orderly extravaganzas near the mausoleum containing the body of Chairman Mao. But so far there had been no overt government action.

Because one of our correspondents had lost his voice and another had to return home, I was sent to Beijing and headed straight for Tiananmen.

The square was a huge, messy, sprawling sort of carnival; but instead of fun and jollity there was passion and debate. Food was a preoccupation:

pennants fluttered from small tents plastered with bits of paper – testimonials from the hunger strikers inside. Next to them, bespectacled lads picked their way through bedrolls, crumpled newspapers and wooden stools, delivering bamboo boxes of noodles and sacks of buns.

Television crews from many countries roamed around, finding the students who spoke English. That in itself was a novelty. Trying to report in China has always been difficult and to find oneself free to ask questions, with young people eager and unafraid to talk, was extraordinary. 'Democracy' was a word used loosely by everyone, but the students used the words 'reform' and 'anti-corruption' much more frequently.

I make no claim at all to being a 'China watcher'. As on so many other stories, I brought only curiosity and a layman's knowledge to this vast country, so different from the West. Chinese society has traditionally been divided into households, rather than individuals, for taxation and other governmental purposes, so the concept of the group, the mass, has an emotional tug that a Western crowd does not parallel.

Warning signs

In the early hours of June 3, columns of soldiers had made their way towards the city centre, but were stopped by local people. The troops were unarmed and appeared rather unsure of themselves. What was significant was the number of ordinary Beijing residents who demanded that the soldiers leave the students in peace, a gesture of support not lost on the authorities. Students were one thing – but the workers? The old men grew alarmed.

The day passed, warm and muggy, and as usual we could gain no information whatsoever about official reactions. Towards evening, another column of soldiers had a much noisier confrontation with civilians at a flyover a mile from the square. All over Beijing – but unknown to most of us at the centre – similar scenes were played out for several hours and any move the soldiers tried to make was blocked by a swarm of angry citizens.

We were conscious that the appearance of uniforms marked another step up the ladder of tension. However, the students in the square merely went deeper into discussion and there were still sightseers and Chinese families wandering over the concrete expanse, revelling in the strangeness of it all.

Just before midnight, I sat at the edge of the square, nattering to a couple of students who spoke excellent English. They gigglingly admitted to being boyfriend and girlfriend, asking shyly if it was rude to hold hands in public in Britain. They weren't sure where the demonstrations were leading, but were certain that the country's new-found economic wealth had been grabbed by the inner circle of privileged party members.

They dreaded the end of their studies, because the system still deployed graduates at the state's behest to work anywhere in the country, so they couldn't guarantee staying in Beijing, or together.

Outnumbered *Chinese policemen are surrounded by students near Tiananmen Square on May 4, 1989. Hundreds of thousands of students and workers joined in the demonstrations.*

'Are students in Britain ordered to different cities to work?' they asked. I wondered where to begin.

They perched on the railings, holding hands and dreaming, both smartly dressed and bathed in the strange tangerine-orange lights of the square. At that moment I got an odd feeling. I'm not overtly superstitious, but occasionally there is the unmistakable frisson of something – something that passes broodingly overhead, unseen but emanating darkness.

The front line

At a quarter to midnight, I headed with the crew – cameraman Bob Poole and sound recordist Alan Smith – back to the Palace Hotel, where we had our editing machines and extra phone lines. We'd also bagged a few rooms in the gloomy old Beijing Hotel on Chang An, one of the main roads leading to Tiananmen, with a view of the square from its balconies.

At 7 minutes past midnight, I overheard a radio crackle: 'There's shooting, there's shooting at Fuxingmen.' We hurtled out, finding one of the drivers who spoke a little English, and headed for the location just west of Tiananmen, avoiding the main roads. There was clearly something very odd going on – hundreds of people were creeping out of their houses, pointing and shouting.

We got our first sight of army trucks heading across the end of a small street, and abandoned the car to walk down and join the little crowd watching a fire 100m (330ft) in the distance. Puzzled, we saw two people fall to the ground. I couldn't figure out what was going on, as I was standing in the middle of the lane transfixed; an armoured personnel carrier had roared by and a truck on the main road was on fire. There was thunderous noise, petrol fumes and smoke. And the chatter of continuous gunfire.

As we scuttled to the edge of the main road, a truck went by with soldiers standing apparently ramrod-stiff. It took several seconds to realise that they were holding their automatic weapons absolutely straight and hammering bullets along the pavements and down all the side streets. We filmed a few shots and looked into the distance to see scores of trucks and armoured personnel carriers heading towards us.

People power *Demonstrators, who attacked the Chinese military during the uprisings, watch as a tank goes up in flames.*

'This is what an invading army looks like,' I thought, shaking with helplessness. We raced away down the lane, past the small cottages that make up the traditional maze of housing, looking for our car. We spotted the driver, who was surrounded by a shouting crowd; seeing our camera, a man detached himself and pulled us into his cottage doorway. We found ourselves in a tiny room, with every household article stacked neatly, a bare floor well swept and a blue-screened TV on a lace mat. On a low chair was a woman, a huge blossoming peony of blood in her stomach – the bullet exit wound. The man crouched in the other chair, evidently trying to explain that they'd been watching together when …

A commotion at the door. Could we take a wounded woman to hospital? There was an air of panic as we tried to cram ourselves into the car, with several relatives refusing to be left behind. The woman's skull was a mangle of brains and hair, though she was still alive. We careered down dark streets to the children's hospital; we found ourselves heading into hell.

Scores of people were jamming the entrance, distraught, screaming, demented. In the 20 minutes we were there, 40 casualties were brought in by bicycle, rickshaw, carried on a park bench. All the injuries were bullet wounds. There were elderly women, teenagers, children – not one seemed to be a college student.

We pushed our way into the operating theatre. It was a scene of mayhem: the living and the dead alike fetching up on the tables, with the staff slinging corpses onto the ground. The whole floor was red with running blood. Doctors and nurses clutched at us, pointing to the camera and begging us to take pictures – but quickly. After a few minutes, two men erupted from another door and shrieked at us. We legged it, for the camera was precious.

The big picture

I have no grand ideas about reporting. You make your way to the centre of the action, look and listen, ask questions and verify, then shift the story as fast as possible. You can never report everything and what you see may be unrepresentative of the whole. On the other hand, you may underestimate the scale of what you see. Trying to gauge the significance of any event while it is in progress is a dangerous game.

On that night of June 3, I took a minute or so just to listen. Normally Beijing, still then a city of bicycles, was as silent as a country village at night. But I could hear the rumble of military vehicles 500m (550yd) to the south and the sound of gunfire echoing from all sides. The guns spoke of city-wide trouble, continuous and violent. An hour later I listened again and the volleys were nonstop, chattering across Beijing – some very far away. To be unable to show the full extent of what happened is not only frustrating, but a measure of the arbitrary and piecemeal nature of any reporting. That night, I felt it more strongly than ever before – or since.

We tried time and again to get near the square, eventually abandoning the car, but it began to dawn on us that the killing was taking place well away from Tiananmen. Ordinary citizens were being killed in their homes, the bullets ripping through the soft bricks. Onlookers, the curious, the disbelieving and the frightened who ventured out into the narrow lanes were being mown down. At one point I found myself between two men about 300m (330yd) from the endless passage of army vehicles. The man on my right was crying and gripping my arm; on my left, the other man spoke a few words of English. As I turned to him, I felt the grip on my right arm slip – and at my feet was a silent heap, absolutely still.

Seat of power *Beijing, formerly known as Peking in English, sits in the northeast corner of the People's Republic of China. Although now outstripped in terms of size and wealth by Shanghai, it remains the centre of government and the ruling Communist Party.*

At that point I wondered if we were going to survive. 'Should we stay out?' I shouted to Bob.

'Course we should.'

'I agree.'

We both knew we had gone beyond the boundary of risk where we would normally call it a day. The Chinese army was killing indiscriminately with powerful weapons, and the secret police and other officials were said to be hunting for foreign journalists. A major worry was that after more than 2½ hours on the streets, we had seen just one other member of the media – a Canadian TV cameraman. The majority of press, I later learned, were still in the square – or had stayed in the Beijing Hotel to watch from the balcony.

Escape and evade

Along Chang An, we could see signs of resistance – stones littered the road and the number of vehicles on fire was growing. As we made our way towards Tiananmen, we were having problems with students who tried to drag us this way and that, to show us another body or a wrecked vehicle. This only made us more vulnerable, drawing attention to the camera.

A ponytailed man who said he was called Li attached himself to us. Too old to be a student, he had a dark characterful face and spoke a little English. He instantly understood the problem, shushing the students and guiding us nimbly through back alleys and courtyards. I put my faith in him – and prayed that he wasn't a secret policeman.

A line of troops blocked our access to the square, which by about 3am was partially under the control of the army. There were still thousands of students standing defiantly, confronting the soldiers, and when we walked nearer I realised they were singing the Internationale.

As they sang, there was a tremendous roar of gunfire; this started a stampede, with bicycles and rickshaws intermingled. Li pointed to the far side of the boulevard and we dashed across a couple of hundred yards while people fell around us. In the shadow of a government building, we lay on the ground and considered our options.

We were breathless, bewildered and outraged. I knew I had to get on a phone to London for the main evening news bulletin; there was only an hour or so before the deadline. I felt it imperative to deliver an eyewitness report.

The crowd soon re-formed in front of the soldiers and we risked a 'stand-up' – just a few seconds of me talking to camera – but it was interrupted four times by immense volleys and rushing students. More than an hour later, we got a take, having witnessed ambulance drivers being injured and white-coated medical staff being shot. I decided to head back to the hotel on my own with the one precious cassette.

'Run for it!'

The route lay across a long expanse of open ground, running parallel to the soldiers' line. I set off at a hard run and had gone only about 50m (55yd) when the firing began again. There was chaos, hundreds of people blundering in all directions. My arm flipped upwards, I lost the cassette and simultaneously a young man cannoned into me. I went full length over him

The China crisis

ON JUNE 4, 2007, watched by plain-clothes policemen, 70-year-old Ding Zilin, a former lecturer in Marxist philosophy at the People's University in Beijing, laid flowers on the pavement in memory of her 17-year-old son, one of those killed by soldiers. It was the first time she had been allowed to do so. Ding was organiser of a group of bereaved relatives, under the banner of the 'Tiananmen Mothers', who keep alive the memories of the 1989 massacre.

China has been in many ways transformed since that dark day, achieving an 'economic miracle'. Living standards have improved for the majority; exports and financial reserves have rocketed. Such is the standing of the People's Republic in the eyes of the world, that it had the honour of hosting the spectacular 2008 Olympic Games. Critics point to a continuing poor human rights record, inequality and rampant corruption. Not everyone regards the new consumerism as a good thing. And still in China people are punished for raising the spectre of Tiananmen Square. In March 2009, a former soldier, Zhang Shijun, was detained after posting on the internet an open letter to president Hu Jintao, urging the government to reconsider its condemnation of the demonstrations that led to the slaughter. 'I feel like my spirit is stuck there on the night of June 3,' confessed Zhang.

A major catalyst for the demonstrations was the death of Hu Yaobang, who two years earlier had been humiliated and forced to resign as Secretary General of the Communist Party, after he called for rapid reform and expressed contempt for 'Maoist excesses'. Deng Xiaoping (below) and his Communist colleagues now faced a political crisis in which the legitimacy of the party's power monopoly was questioned, at a time when communist regimes around the world were crumbling.

After ordering that the demonstrations be crushed, Deng steered the country onto a path of change, announcing in the spring of 1992 that 'to get rich is glorious'. Hoardings proclaimed the message: 'Development is the Irrefutable Argument.'

Deng Xiaoping died on February 19, 1997. The exact toll of the dead of June 1989 has never been disclosed.

and lay with my face on the Tarmac, watching little scarlet ticks flashing on the ground just a yard away. I had no notion that they were bullets. I crawled after the tape and turned to apologise to the young man. He had a huge seeping hole in his back – and I had blood running down my arm. The bullet that took a nick out of my elbow had killed him.

I set off again, possessed with fear and rage, running towards the Beijing Hotel just beyond the edge of the square, hoping the BBC was somewhere in the rooms we'd rented. 'A safe haven,' I was squeaking to myself, and then found the gates fastened shut with wire.

'Bugger that,' I thought, and like an animal went for the wall.

I got up in one go, clawing at the stone, and only when I got to the top did I realise it was at least 2.5m (8ft) high. Too chicken to jump, I half-slid down the other side and trotted across the compound, which was eerily

A policeman went for the tape in my hand. I kicked him in the groin, punched the second with my left hand and body-charged the third. I'm no fighter, but surprise and a sense of outrage are enough.

silent. The lobby was dimly lit. Too late, I spotted three policemen inside. Also coming across the lobby were two non-Chinese, shouting as the glass door was pushed open, 'Run for it – they'll arrest you!'

By then I was halfway through, and mad.

A policeman went for the tape in my hand. I kicked him in the groin, punched the second with my left hand and body-charged the third. I'm no fighter, but surprise and a sense of outrage are enough.

I hurtled to the stairs as the two strangers obstructed the cops. I had no idea on which floor we had our office, so I hammered on doors until I struck lucky. I looked a complete fright, blood and grit everywhere, and with my fingers locked so rigidly round the cassette it had to be prised free.

I mustered everything I could to find the right words, which would both paint a picture accurately and convey a sense of the scale and atmosphere. We could not send TV pictures directly – all we had was a telephone line.

After such a night there should have been some respite, but neither the Chinese army nor the protestors had given up. Even though the streets had quietened and the students had been marshalled from the square under army guard, a short time after I'd left, with Bob and Alan making it safely back, the city was in defiant mood. There were frequent bursts of gunfire – so much so that it became the norm, like Beirut in wartime.

Our stories were 'pigeoned' out – taken to the airport by a roundabout route and smuggled abroad. Drivers risked their lives to help us, and friends of people who worked in our local bureau bamboozled officials and fought off plain-clothes police to protect our tapes.

The city was prey to rumour and fear: patients were being hauled out of hospital, the crematoria were working overtime – was it true they threw the injured in, still alive, along with the dead? We were refused permission to visit the Beijing Union Hospital, but I thought it necessary to have a go, and we sneaked in.

Nervous young doctors shepherded us to a small room in which there were several patients with gunshot wounds. The doctors were frantic that we should see what they were having to deal with, but also terrified – patients and bodies had been removed, without the permission of families, to who knows where.

Suddenly, we heard raised voices and saw uniformed men heading our way. A nurse screamed, 'They kill you!' and a young woman doctor shouted, 'With me, with me!' and set off at breakneck speed.

We galloped after her, hearing men shouting orders behind us. She dived down a narrow set of steps and pelted through a basement. We knocked into stores of old equipment as we fled, ending up in the coke cellar, where this young woman, tears streaming down her face and shouting 'Run, run!', pointed to a window of light at the top of a heap of coke.

We scrabbled out, finding ourselves in a side street we knew, and made for the hotel.

And so it went on. The old men had held on to the antimacassared armchairs of power through simple brutality; now they had scores to settle.

Aftermath

On the afternoon of June 4, having spent the morning broadcasting over the phone to London and cutting the story to send to the airport, I went to my hotel room and cried uncontrollably for a long time. I kept thinking not only of those who had wanted to change their country and been blown away, but also of those who had risked everything for us – the strangers, mere journalists.

Nobody has ever been able to put a number on those killed in Beijing in June 1989. Perhaps 2-3,000 died, with many more injured. The regime has probably destroyed any detailed evidence and cannot bring itself to admit that it might have made a mistake.

Instead, it produces glossy publications such as *The Truth About the Beijing Turmoil*, and writes: 'The measures adopted by the Chinese government to put down the rebellion have not only won the acclaim and support of the Chinese people, but have also won the understanding and support of the governments and people of many other countries.'

Liars. That's why it's worth being a reporter. ■

What happened next?

KATE ADIE BECAME THE BBC's new chief correspondent in 1989, and one of her first assignments was to cover the demonstrations in Beijing. Over the next 14 years, she became one of the UK's most highly respected and best-known reporters, a familiar face in some of the world's most war-ravaged regions. It became a joke within the British army that when Kate Adie showed up in flak jacket and camouflage, they knew they were in a hot spot. 'I never desired to go into war zones,' she has said. 'I never had any thought about it. It sort of just happened as part of the job.'

She covered the Gulf War. She was there as the former Yugoslavia tore itself apart. She has reported on the genocide in Rwanda and the brutal civil war in Sierra Leone. (See *Sarajevo Diary*, page 168, and *The Fight to Save Tenneh*, page 64.)

Adie has been shot, she had a knife held to her throat in Bosnia, and has had a gun held to her face. In 1991, in Georgia, she contracted hepatitis. She returned from Kurdistan with tick-borne Congo-Crimea haemorrhagic fever. A Land Rover in which

she was travelling in Sarajevo in 1992 was shot at, leaving her with a fragment of bullet in her foot. She has endured bedbugs and primitive or non-existent toilet facilities; she has eaten food of dubious provenance.

In recognition of her courageous work, Adie has received numerous accolades in the UK, including three Royal Television Society Awards and BAFTA's Richard Dimbleby Award. In 1993 she stood down from front-line reporting, although she continues to present *From Our Own Correspondent* on BBC Radio 4. In the same year she received an OBE.

In 2002, Adie's book *The Kindness of Strangers* was published. Billed as an 'autobiography', it is largely a compelling, often witty account of her working career. In 2004 she followed up with *Corsets to Camouflage: Women and War*. In 2005 came *Nobody's Child*, an intriguing exploration of foundling children, written with the empathy and insight of one who was herself adopted – although not abandoned. *Into Danger: Risking Your Life for Work*, published in 2008, is an illuminating study of people whose professions – legal and illegal – place them in peril.

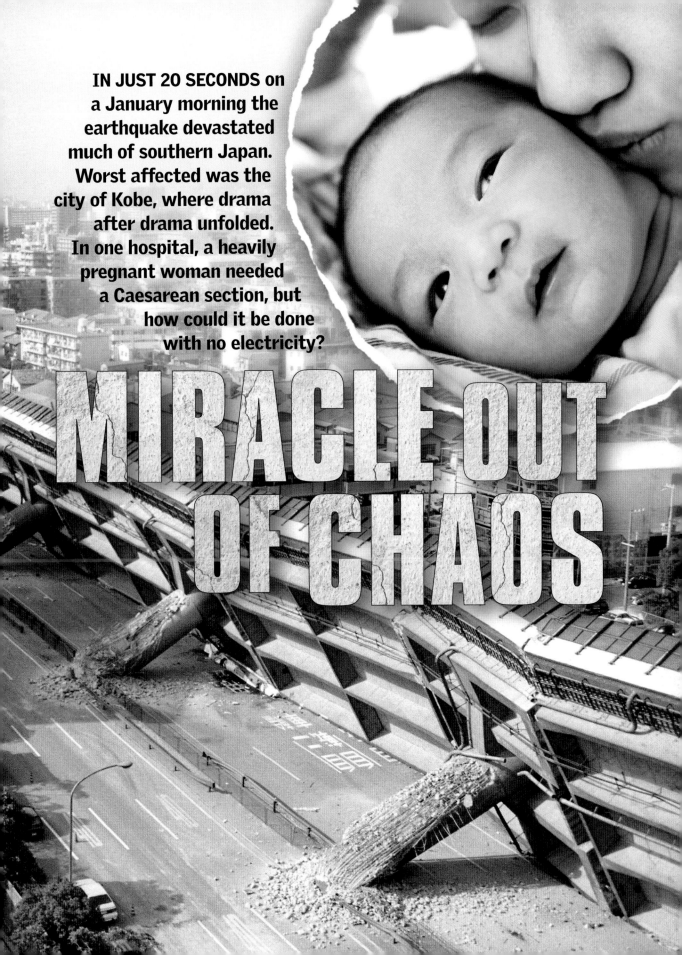

IN JUST 20 SECONDS on a January morning the earthquake devastated much of southern Japan. Worst affected was the city of Kobe, where drama after drama unfolded. In one hospital, a heavily pregnant woman needed a Caesarean section, but how could it be done with no electricity?

MIRACLE OUT OF CHAOS

Frozen in time *On January 17, 1995, just before 5.47am, this clock stopped, never to run again. It marked the precise moment when the Great Hanshin, or Kobe, Earthquake began.*

In the earthquake-prone nation of Japan, Kobe was

an oasis of peace. For four centuries the elegant city on Osaka Bay managed to avoid disaster. One morning in January 1995, those four centuries of good luck were erased, and in 20 devastating seconds a once-beautiful metropolis became a landscape of death.

The night before, Fukuko Kanehara had been resting badly. In the final month of her pregnancy and unable to find a comfortable position in which to sleep, she rose from her futon more than once, careful not to disturb her little son who lay beside her.

Earlier that day the pretty 34-year-old telephoned her obstetrician, Dr Tetsuo Otani. She was beginning to experience early labour. This was disquieting because her baby was to be delivered by Caesarean section on Friday, four days away. She said her pains were not severe, and Dr Otani assured her there was no cause for worry.

Finally, at around 3am on Tuesday, January 17, 1995, Fukuko fell into a sound sleep. It did not last long. At first she thought someone was trying to shake her awake, but in the next heart-stopping instant she knew what it was: an earthquake. The floor was bucking under her, and the house resounded with the din of glass and crockery shattering and furniture crashing.

Instinctively she threw herself across her son, Masayoshi, who had been jarred into terrified consciousness. She cradled him in one arm and with the other kept trying to hold onto something solid. The whole house seemed to be moving. Her husband called out to her, and she called back to reassure him. But she was certain the house was about to crash down on them.

And then, like a passing train, the ominous rumble faded. The floor of the room bounced a few times more in the slackening grip of aftershocks, then lay still.

The earthquake was over.

Hironori Kanehara pushed through the clutter on the floor and felt his way towards his wife and son in the pitch blackness. Husband and wife held onto each other, exchanging assurances that they were all right. The couple tried to turn on a light, but there was no electricity. They turned on a tap. Water trickled out for a minute, then gurgled dry.

Stretched to the limit

Numb, they sat in silence for a while. Their little boy fell asleep. Before long, the first streaks of grey light had appeared in the window, and Fukuko whispered, 'I think I have to go to the hospital now.'

Her husband flinched, imagining the chaos in the city streets outside. 'You're sure?' he asked her.

'The pains are coming very hard,' she answered.

Fukuko's doctor, who lived on Rokko Island, a man-made spit of land in Osaka Bay, was already on his way to work. By great good luck his family was safe. The hospital, a 20-bed maternity clinic, of which he and his obstetrician father were codirectors, was 13km (8 miles) away on the mainland. He didn't know whether the mainland bridge was even standing.

He had ten patients at his clinic who would need his help – if there was still a clinic. Peering through the milky morning light, he was relieved to see that the mainland bridge was largely intact. But once across, he realised that worse was to come.

Streets had buckled or been torn open by the ferocity of the quake, and railway overpasses had crashed to the tracks. He looped left and veered right, following open streets, always trying to stay on a course towards the clinic.

Part of the elevated Hanshin Expressway, Kobe's main east-west artery, was tipped over on its side. The concrete pylons that bore its weight had snapped at the base, tipping nearly 1 kilometre (half a mile) of four-lane highway into the street below. The cars and trucks that had been riding on it lay smashed and crumpled, their dead drivers and passengers still pinned inside.

But Dr Otani's three-storey clinic was intact. And both his parents, who lived next door, and the patients were safe. When Dr Otani dashed inside, he saw that his father had already taken charge, and all hands were at work repairing the damage and restoring order. None of the mothers or new babies was harmed. When the power failed, the emergency electrical system had cut in as it was supposed to.

Many of the staff were busy filling baths, buckets and whatever else might hold water in any quantity. The clinic could no more function without water than it could without electricity. The staff worried that the supply would last only until the city's holding tanks ran dry.

The quake was having other unforeseen consequences. Within the hour, four women who had gone into stress-induced labour appeared. One was in only the 23rd week of her pregnancy, dangerously premature. Two were near full term. The fourth was Fukuko Kanehara, accompanied by her husband and their little boy.

The staff felt overwhelmed. They delivered about 350 babies a year in the small clinic. Four in one day, even under the best circumstances, would stretch them to the limit.

Then their emergency power system failed. All of the sophisticated, electrically powered equipment on which they had come to rely was rendered useless.

Utter devastation *Two survivors try to salvage what they can from their home after it was destroyed in the earthquake.*

Life and death decision

Shortly after Fukuko Kanehara arrived, Dr Tetsuo Otani had given her an injection to slow her labour, and her husband, assured that all was well and that the birth of the baby was still hours, maybe days away, had gone back home with his sleepy son.

He had made it to the clinic, driving through still-empty streets, in 30 minutes; getting back took 3 hours. Thousands of terrified people, fleeing the city in cars, on bicycles and on foot, were choking roads already constricted by the quake's devastation. Meanwhile, Dr Otani and his father were working out a plan. Both full-term pregnancies could be safely delivered by whatever light was available. But the other two patients were not so easily dealt with.

The premature baby, whose survival chances were only one in four, would require the controlled environment of an incubator. For that they would need electricity if the infant was to have any chance at all. As for

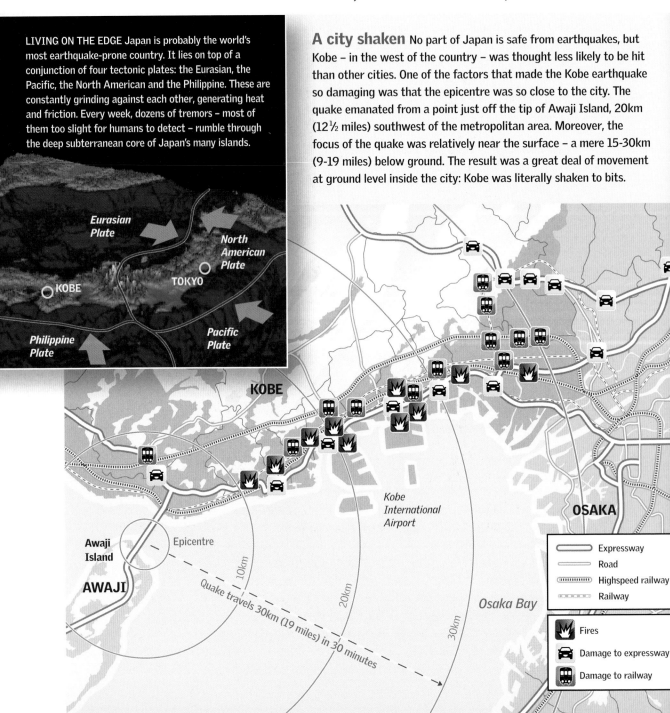

LIVING ON THE EDGE Japan is probably the world's most earthquake-prone country. It lies on top of a conjunction of four tectonic plates: the Eurasian, the Pacific, the North American and the Philippine. These are constantly grinding against each other, generating heat and friction. Every week, dozens of tremors – most of them too slight for humans to detect – rumble through the deep subterranean core of Japan's many islands.

Eurasian Plate

North American Plate

KOBE

TOKYO

Philippine Plate

Pacific Plate

A city shaken No part of Japan is safe from earthquakes, but Kobe – in the west of the country – was thought less likely to be hit than other cities. One of the factors that made the Kobe earthquake so damaging was that the epicentre was so close to the city. The quake emanated from a point just off the tip of Awaji Island, 20km (12½ miles) southwest of the metropolitan area. Moreover, the focus of the quake was relatively near the surface – a mere 15-30km (9-19 miles) below ground. The result was a great deal of movement at ground level inside the city: Kobe was literally shaken to bits.

KOBE

Kobe International Airport

OSAKA

Awaji Island

Epicentre

AWAJI

10km

20km

30km

Quake travels 30km (19 miles) in 30 minutes

Osaka Bay

Expressway

Road

Highspeed railway

Railway

Fires

Damage to expressway

Damage to railway

Fukuko Kanehara, neither doctor liked to think about doing a Caesarean section without other essential, electrically powered equipment.

Obviously it would be better to transfer these two women to a hospital that still had electricity. But there were not enough ambulances for the lengthening list of earthquake victims. And from what they heard on the radio, electric power had been lost throughout greater Kobe.

At 4pm the doctors could wait no longer. They would have to deliver the premature baby. With no functioning incubator the staff did all they could, but the baby girl, born 17 weeks too soon, lived only 2 hours.

Shaken but determined, Dr Otani turned his attention to Fukuko. Although he was just 39, he had already studied and practised obstetrics in Japan, the United States and Australia. He specialised in difficult pregnancies and had done many Caesarean sections. In addition, his father had performed more than 1,000. But neither had ever performed one without the advanced instrumentation they were used to.

By late afternoon they had begun to realise that they might have to do one now. A nurse came to report that the baby's heartbeat was decelerating. If this continued, the baby would be in jeopardy. Without electronic monitoring devices, they simply could not tell. The baby could slip away while they were still debating whether to intervene.

The two doctors explained to Fukuko why they had to go ahead with the operation even though the electricity was still out. Silently she nodded her assent. At 5.18pm Dr Otani administered a general anaesthetic, nitrous oxide, with a hand pump. Eight nurses were in attendance in the third-floor operating room. Three of them held torches trained directly on Fukuko's extended abdomen as the elder Dr Otani made the incision.

Dark side of the city

Kobe was the San Francisco of Japan – everyone loved it. Sheltered by the Rokko Mountains to the north and sloping sharply down to Osaka Bay and the Inland Sea, it was an urbane, fun-loving city of spectacular views and stylish shops. It became a major port after shipping was diverted there from Yokohama – all but destroyed in the earthquake of 1923 – and eventually developed into the world's sixth-busiest port, and a metropolis that served more than 18 million people.

Geologically it was a disaster waiting to happen. Some sections of the downtown area, lying in old river beds, were dangerously vulnerable to earth tremors, and so were its water mains. And in a city without water, every wooden house is a potential fire trap. Yet national earthquake fears were focused on high-risk Tokyo, 440km (275 miles) away. By comparison Kobe was considered safe. It had not suffered a major earthquake in 400 years.

That all changed with the first shocks, a series of horizontal lurches. At the epicentre of the quake was the fishing village of Hokudan-cho on Awaji Island, 10km (6 miles) offshore from Kobe. Walls buckled in the first 3 seconds, roofs caved in, gas and water pipes snapped and power lines were torn apart. Nearly every building collapsed. Of the thousands to die in what would officially be designated the Great Hanshin Earthquake, the first 38 probably died in Hokudan-cho.

Perilous journey *Like a scene from a Hollywood disaster movie, a bus teeters on the edge of an expressway, which has been torn apart by the earthquake.*

After the tremors *Further damage and fatalities resulted from the many fires that started in Kobe after the initial quake had done its damage.*

Hurtling outwards with cataclysmic force, the shock waves slammed into unstable landfills and squeezed them dry, forcing underground water to the surface, where spouts of sand and water shot 3m (10ft) into the air.

Seemingly firm terrain was transformed into quicksand. Buildings on the reclaimed harbour islands keeled over or slid down into ground suddenly turned to the consistency of pudding. Roads, car parks and railway tracks sank out of sight. Part of Rokko Island shifted 5m (16ft) out to sea. And work on a 4km (2½ mile) suspension bridge under construction between Awaji Island and Kobe would have to go back to the drawing board – the earthquake had lengthened the distance to be spanned by 1.2m (4ft).

Now in full fury, the killer quake surged on through the earth's crust, tearing great gashes in softer rock near the surface. It smashed into the mainland and laid waste to towns and villages all the way to Kyoto, 90km (56 miles) from the epicentre, damaging 62 centuries-old temples and revered shrines in the ancient imperial capital. It killed 25 people in Osaka, Japan's second-largest city.

But it was Kobe that felt the full brunt of the earthquake. Many wooden houses tumbled like matchwood; others were buried under avalanching cliffs. In the commercial centre, multi-storey buildings of steel and stone shivered, twisted and toppled. Train tracks, including those for the famous high-speed bullet trains, lay snarled and twisted like strands of discarded silver ribbon. Railway carriages were flipped over, and the three-storey Itami Station was rolled on its side, crushing a dozen parked cars.

What made the earthquake all the more devastating was that there had been no warning.

'You can go'

People were crushed in their beds as they slept, or were buried under mountains of rubble or trapped by fire. Short-circuited electrical wires or overturned ovens sparked fires fuelled by propane heating gas spewing from fractured pipes, and the fires were whipped along by the stiff winter wind.

The Kobe fire department found itself all but helpless in the face of obstructed streets and ruptured water mains. Unchecked, the flames devoured everything in their path, leaping from house to house.

The fires burned into the night until there was nothing left to destroy. By then acres of central Kobe had become a smouldering wasteland of ash and charred, misshapen metal. There were already more than 2,000 known dead, and some 230,000 people were without adequate food, shelter or sanitation. Scores of injured citizens stumbled through the glass-littered streets, not knowing where to turn.

Hiyoshi-cho was a typical working-class neighbourhood, crowded with traditional wooden dwellings of two storeys and criss-crossed by streets barely 2m (6ft) wide. Most people who lived in it were the city's day labourers, binmen and street cleaners. Tomiya Kuwano, 47, lived there with his wife and three children. He sold clothing in a shop around the corner from his house. His elderly parents lived in a second-floor bedroom above the shop, where they also helped out.

When the quake hit, registering about 6.4 on the Richter scale, it set all of Hiyoshi-cho quavering. Since the houses were unsupported by any inner beams – the walls were merely room partitions – they either buckled and caved in, or sent their upper floors tumbling out into the street.

Tomiya Kuwano's house fell in on itself. The second floor dropped straight down onto the first. Fortunately the whole family slept upstairs, and no one was hurt. They all came scurrying out of the debris in the dark.

Their neighbours were also streaming into the street in a state of shock. Tomiya knew about the danger of aftershocks. 'Stay out of your houses!' he warned. After organising teams to search for people who might still be trapped, he ran to see whether his own mother and father were all right.

As he ran through the ruins of his neighbourhood in the cold dawn, a stark reality hit him: not a single building remained intact. He could see some houses burning in the distance, and a gusty wind was blowing from that direction. Fear began welling up in his stomach. By now the sun was higher in the sky, shining on the corner where his parents' house was in plain view – but there was no house. What was left was a pile of splintered wood.

He ran around the wreckage, searching for a way in, calling out to his parents. Through a window of what had been the second-floor bedroom, now on the ground, he could see his father on his hands and knees. 'I'm coming, Father!' Tomiya cried out.

'I'm all right,' his father called back. 'Find your mother. She was downstairs in the kitchen.'

Tomiya ran to the kitchen door, jammed tight in its upended wall. And as he struggled with the door, his father came limping around the corner with a torch. They shone it through a narrow opening. Tomiya's father shouted to his wife, 'Sumiko, do you hear me? Do you see the light?'

'I can see the light, yes,' his wife answered. 'I hear you.'

'Crawl towards the light.'

'I can't move. Something heavy has fallen across my legs.'

Her husband frantically tried to hammer or squeeze his way in. Tomiya felt heat at his back and was suddenly sick with horror. The fire, which only minutes before had been 275m (300yd) away, was now just across the narrow street and lunging towards them.

'We have to go,' shouted the son, his heart breaking.

The fire was nearly over their heads now, reaching for the fresh kindling of smashed houses on their side of the street. The heat was blistering.

As he ran through the ruins of his neighbourhood in the cold dawn, a stark reality hit him: not a single building remained intact.

Lessons of the Kobe quake

BEFORE 1995, Japanese people assumed that their country was well prepared to deal with earthquakes. They believed that most buildings had been constructed to withstand a seismic shock, and that the authorities had a plan in place to deal with the consequences of a major incident. The Kobe quake shattered that faith as surely as it destroyed the city.

Many countrywide procedural changes were made in the wake of the disaster. The armed forces, for example, were given a mandate for 'autonomous dispatch': they no longer have to wait for a formal request for help from a regional governor before mobilising. In Kobe, the collapse of the freeway had hindered efforts to get food and medication to survivors, so the government undertook to construct a national network of quakeproof roads – aid can now be moved quickly to a disaster site. And many more highly sophisticated seismic detection sites have been constructed across Japan, allowing emergency planners to make judgments about the nature and scale of a disaster before first-hand reports come in.

At Kobe, there were places where the shaking had turned solid ground to sandy mush – a phenomenon called liquefaction. Buildings on such ground tended to topple sideways into the neighbouring structure, causing entire streets to 'domino'. When the time came to reconstruct them, they were placed farther apart to prevent this. Other architectural measures included the installation of rubber shock absorbers in the foundations of buildings and the piers supporting roadways: when a tremor hits, they should bounce rather than tumble. And throughout Kobe there are now predesignated evacuation sites. Immense water tanks have also been installed beneath four of the city's parks – sunken reservoirs strong enough not to crack however violent the quake – as well as stockpiles of emergency rations.

None of these things can stop an earthquake happening. But next time the worst happens everyone will be better equipped to respond.

'We have to go now, Mother!' Tomiya called out, sobbing.

The old woman must have felt the fire closing in. 'Go. You can go,' they heard her say.

But the father remained on his knees, his palms pressed together in front of his face in the Buddhist attitude of prayer. 'I'm sorry, Sumiko,' he kept saying. Firelight glinted on the tears in his eyes.

A far corner of the house caught fire. 'Please, Father!' Tomiya begged. But his father remained kneeling, weeping, telling his wife again and again how sorry he was. A neighbour ran under the canopy of flame and helped Tomiya lift him up to his feet.

Even as they dragged him away, the old man was calling out to his wife of 50 years. 'Forgive me, Sumiko,' he said. 'I'm sorry.'

'Go,' she replied. 'I forgive you.'

Loss of faith

Decades of assumptions were shattered by those 20 seconds of the Great Hanshin Earthquake. The people of post-war Japan had put their trust in an elaborate 'earthquake-proofing' plan that they were convinced would avert disaster. Twenty seconds was all it took to leave that faith in tatters.

Japanese officials seemed no more able to deal with the quake than the average citizen. Authorities at every level appeared overwhelmed by the enormity of the task. The most fundamental principles of disaster control were neglected. Cordoning off the main roads for emergency vehicles should have been a top priority, but no one gave such an order. Traffic in Kobe degenerated into citywide gridlock, and fire engines and ambulances sat stranded in a sea of cars while houses burned down and the injured bled to death on the street.

The first rescue teams had little more than some shovels and crowbars – no chainsaws, no heat-sensing equipment, no search dogs, no radios, no system of coordinated communications – to help to locate survivors in the rubble. It was four crucial hours before the mandatory written request for help was sent to the armed forces. Blankets, emergency rations and first-aid kits had to be tracked down in far-flung warehouses.

While those officials charged with helping people floundered, the people themselves shone. The crisis brought out all that is best in the civil, disciplined, close-knit Japanese. '*Shoganai*,' they said – 'It can't be helped' – and patiently they set about extricating themselves from the wreckage of their lives.

Some 250 students of the Kobe University of Mercantile Marine designated themselves a rescue battalion. Armed with saws, axes and crowbars, small teams ventured out into the community looking for people in trouble. Before darkness forced them to quit, these students had pulled more than 100 trapped and injured victims of the quake from the ruins.

To the chagrin of the authorities, the Yamaguchi-gumi syndicate, the largest of the Japanese crime families, was winning praise and headlines for its efficiency at providing earthquake relief. Headquartered in Kobe and 30,000-strong, the syndicate opened its enclave in Kobe's Nada ward and, even before the aftershocks ended, began giving away water from its own well and food from its own kitchen. The word soon spread, and by mid afternoon there were 200 people at the gate.

It was only the beginning. Within days, truckloads of rice, noodles, baby food, overcoats, nappies, sleeping bags, oil heaters, portable ovens and torches were being unloaded by young syndicate men.

The gang's walled citadel was transformed. The car park became a supply depot, with everything labelled and neatly stacked in tents. Soon the young men were handing out 8,000 meals a day to all comers, and a fleet of 15 rented vans was snaking through the city delivering boxes of relief supplies to hospitals, refugee centres and churches.

One parishioner felt obliged to remind her priest that this charity came from tainted hands. 'God works in mysterious ways,' the good father replied. 'Will you take some bananas?'

She would.

Terror in the hospital

There were 160 patients at the 200-bed Miyaji Hospital on the day of the earthquake, and all but one were asleep when it struck. The one, an elderly woman on the fourth floor, was walking back to her room and was slammed to her knees by the powerful first shock. Somehow she got back up on her feet and staggered out to an enclosed passageway that connected the two hospital wings. Seconds later the spasms racked the building and tore one end of the passageway out of its moorings, dropping it and the woman straight down to the third floor.

Hurt, dazed, in danger of being flung all the way to the ground, she clung on for her life. Finally a nurse spotted the trembling woman and crawled out to drag her inside.

A doctor on the night watch, along with day-shift nurses who had been asleep in hospital dormitory rooms when the quake hit, rushed into a chaos of overturned files and runaway trolleys. They knew that the first floor had collapsed almost to ground level. Word spread that two staff members were trapped in a dormitory room.

The 20 doctors and nurses began shepherding bedraggled men and women down the stairs – only to face a new problem. With the cave-in of the first floor, all of the hospital entrances had been obliterated. The only way out was through what had once been a window on the second floor. But the building was air-conditioned, and all of its windows were hermetically sealed. People congregated at what was a wall of glass, now only a few feet above the pavement.

Then someone solved the problem: he took a metal chair and threw it through the window. Others laid a futon over the edges of glass, and mattresses on the pavement outside. The exodus began. Nurses led patients across the street to a Nissan car showroom whose big display windows had been blown out.

Bedding down *A lack of housing after the earthquake forced some 1,100 people to cram together into an unheated municipal gymnasium.*

Meanwhile, nurse Chihiro Fujiwara was cut off from the world. Asleep in a dormitory room, she had been jerked into terrified wakefulness by chunks of plaster falling on her head. The tall metal lockers alongside her bed bounced in time to the quake's thrusts. She had pulled the blankets over her head and rolled onto her side, curled in a tight ball just before the lockers fell on her. Then she heard the walls cracking, and something even heavier fell across the lockers. All she knew was the room went pitch dark, and she couldn't move.

Her dormitory room was at the far end of the collapsed first floor. She was sharing it with a colleague, nurse Mihoko Morioka, who was in a bed only 2m (6½ft) away. Apparently Mihoko was badly hurt. Chihiro could hear her weeping and calling out through the wall of debris between them, 'Help me!'

They were friends as well as colleagues, and often talked excitedly about Mihoko's coming wedding.

Chihiro could not help her.

'Be brave, Mihoko,' she pleaded. 'They will find us soon.'

Rescue

The Miyaji Hospital was a family affair. Dr Tomoo Miyaji started it as a clinic in 1965 and kept on expanding and modernising it over the years. Dr Miyaji was president, and his wife and two of their three children, also doctors, were on the medical staff.

He had rushed to the hospital prepared to lead the rescue effort. But when he arrived, he saw that the staff had already safely evacuated the patients. At that moment he had only one other concern: saving the two nurses still imprisoned in the first-floor dormitory room.

A rescue team had arrived, and a crane and other equipment were called in. But the team had barely begun lifting the heavy wreckage and digging through the rubble when everything was called to a halt. Engineers had concluded that a few key beams had fallen in such a way that they were all that was keeping the ceiling and the rest of the building off the first floor. What was left of the nurse's dormitory room was in the narrow space under the beams. Disturbing the wreckage was likely to bring the ceiling and the building above it slamming down. If the trapped nurses were alive now, they would not be then.

The only alternative was the slow, laborious job of tunnelling up from under to reach the two women.

Among the squads of firefighters and soldiers starting to burrow through the concrete foundation of the building was a young man named Hideo Abe, Mihoko Morioka's fiancé. He and Mihoko were planning to be married in October. The evening before the quake, they'd had dinner at his apartment, and his last sight of her was when he waved goodbye from his balcony as she set off to walk the few short blocks to the hospital.

Although his apartment building collapsed, Hideo escaped unharmed. It was inconceivable to him that harm could come to Mihoko, protected by the stone and steel shell of Miyaji Hospital. But as soon as it was light, he ran over there and learned the bad news first-hand.

Now he followed behind the crews with drills and jackhammers, helping to clear away the rubble as the rescuers broke through the foundation and drilled into the basement. After hours of effort, they started drilling up into the basement ceiling, up into the collapsed first floor.

Overhead, Chihiro Fujiwara felt the vibrations. Then she heard sounds of grinding, hammering and eventually voices shouting their names. She called back, but without much hope of being heard. Light-headed and weak, she had lain there with her knees nearly up to her chin for almost half a day without food or water. She again called to her friend Mihoko. But there was no sound from the other side of the darkness. Chihiro realised she had not heard Mihoko's voice for hours.

Finally she felt the rescuers cutting away the steel springs under her bed. The next thing she knew, they were lifting her down into a dim light and pulling her through a tunnel, then out into the street. It was dark. She had been buried alive for 11 hours.

'What about Mihoko-san – the other nurse?' were her first words to the nearest rescue worker. He tried to answer, then looked away. As they carried her across the street, she saw Hideo Abe, his head in his hands and his eyes red-rimmed. At that moment she knew the answer.

A 'simple' operation

With modern surgical techniques, a Caesarean section is usually a simple operation. But it's far from safe when the lights are out and you have no electricity, noted Dr Tetsuo Otani grimly as he monitored the anaesthetic while his father made the initial incision. They stood in the pool of light made by the torches held by three nurses. Beyond the medical team, the operating room lay in deep shadow.

From time to time one or another of the doctors would summon the torches closer or point to a particular area for them to illuminate. Only the harsh alternative for Fukuko Kanehara's unborn baby made major surgery in such conditions an acceptable risk.

Luckily they had anaesthesia and sterile containers filled with cotton swabs and gauze. The anaesthetic machine had been pushed off to one side: without electricity it was useless. Normally it would regulate the flow of gases for the patient continuously and automatically. Instead, the younger Dr Otani had to make adjustments manually, constantly watching to check that Fukuko was breathing enough nitrous oxide to keep her asleep and taking in enough oxygen to counteract the possibility of asphyxia in her baby.

They knew this would be difficult because a surgeon performing a Caesarean section works amid considerable blood, plus all the amniotic fluid in which the foetus has lain. These fluids had to be sponged away constantly with gauze pads and big cotton swabs. It was a tedious job that electric suction devices would have swiftly disposed of.

But what weighed most heavily on the doctors and nurses as they laboured on was that the only vital signs they could monitor were the mother's blood pressure and heart rate. They knew nothing about the foetus except that the heart was beating. When the uterus was finally opened, though, they could all see that the foetus was an apparently healthy baby girl. Eyes met, and hidden smiles were exchanged behind their surgical masks.

Every person in that operating room had assisted or been witness to the births of thousands of babies, but this was one they would never forget. And when the younger Dr Otani lifted the infant then sucked the amniotic fluid from her airway, and the baby let out her first cry, a surge of elation swept through the group.

The little girl, who would be named Yuki, weighed 3.47kg (7.65lb) and was presented to Fukuko Kanehara in a candlelit room as soon as the happy mother came out of the anaesthetic at around 7pm.

During that time, her husband had made several futile attempts to reach the clinic by car. He finally got there at 2pm the next day. When he came into her room, he saw his wife with intravenous tubes going into her. Unaware that the baby had been born, he assumed she was being prepared for the delivery. 'It's going to be just fine,' he said. 'Don't worry.'

She replied, smiling, 'I won't.' And in a happy ending to at least one earthquake story, she sent him to the nursery to see his new daughter. ■

What happened next?

IN DECEMBER 1995, 11 months after the Kobe earthquake, a strange and beautiful memorial was erected. In the town centre the municipal authorities constructed a series of pavilions made entirely from hand-painted lights. They formed an amazing and spectacular sight in this place where so many buildings had fallen down.

The idea and the lights themselves came from Italy, where such displays are called *luminarie*. The Italian government staged the event as a gift, something to lift the spirits of the stricken people of Kobe. Those first *luminarie* were such a success that they have been repeated every year since. On each occasion the twinkling edifices are new and different, and so is the theme of the festival. In 1997 it was entitled 'The Stars of the Earth'; in 2006, 'The Magic of the Sky'; in 2008, 'The Light of the Infinite'. The festival lasts for two weeks, but the illuminations are turned on for only an hour or two each evening, which somehow makes them seem all the more special and spellbinding.

The Kobe Luminarie draw about 5 million visitors each year. The roads nearby are closed, and vast crowds shuffle through the empty streets towards the illuminations. Inside the final building there is usually a large commemorative wreath festooned with brass bells; the idea is that people throw coins at the bells to hear them ring, and in that moment they think of those who died. It all adds up to a new Japanese tradition, a celebration of life and hope in the darkest days of winter.

SHINING LIGHTS Participants gather round the 2009 Kobe Luminarie to pay their respects to earthquake victims.

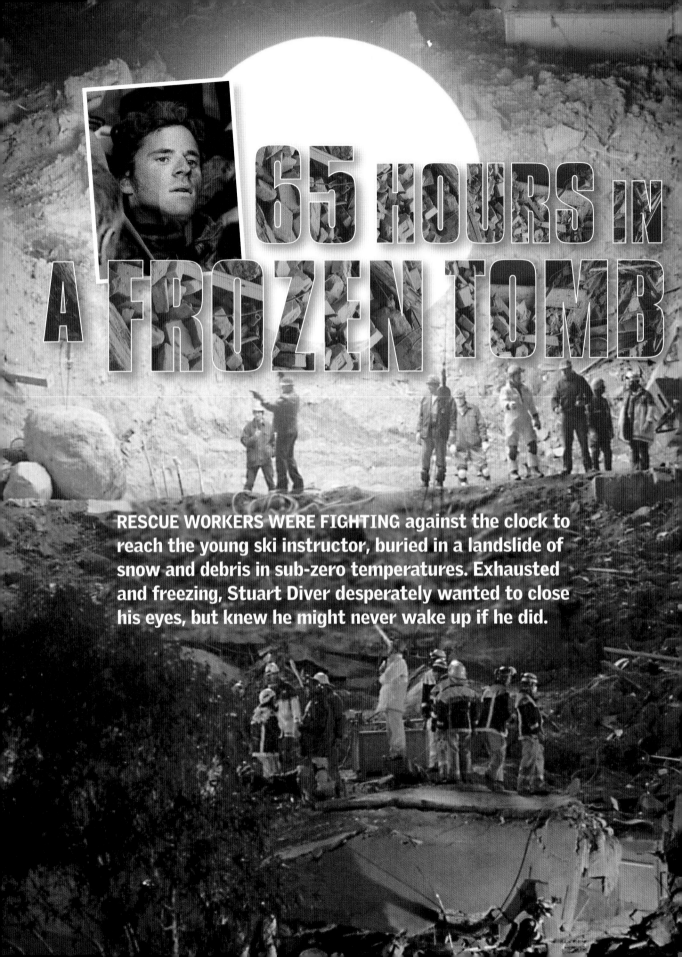

65 HOURS IN A FROZEN TOMB

RESCUE WORKERS WERE FIGHTING against the clock to reach the young ski instructor, buried in a landslide of snow and debris in sub-zero temperatures. Exhausted and freezing, Stuart Diver desperately wanted to close his eyes, but knew he might never wake up if he did.

'Goodnight, Sal.' Stuart Diver kissed his wife, switched off his bedside lamp and lay back with a feeling of pleasure. It was Wednesday, July 30, 1997, and the end of a long, tiring day for the couple, both 27. It was peak season in Thredbo, a bustling Alpine town of some 4,000 people in Australia's Snowy Mountains. Stuart had worked 8 hours as a ski instructor, and his wife Sally had put in a long shift at a local hotel, where she organised conferences.

Stuart had met Sally – bright and energetic – at the Royal Melbourne Institute of Technology eight years earlier, and with their shared passion for the outdoors, they were soon inseparable. One rare time when they were apart, Stuart drove 6 hours from Thredbo to Sydney to propose to her. 'What about getting engaged today, Sal?' he asked. She laughed her bubbly laugh and replied, 'Oh, yes!' Following their marriage in 1995, their dream was to start their own outdoor adventure business. They now lived in the Bimbadeen staff lodge, a four-storey concrete-block structure set on a slope opposite Thredbo's main ski slope.

A steady snow was now covering the roof of their lodge, and as Stuart slept, the first warning sign came: a sudden thundering roar. His eyes flicked open. His bedside clock read 11.37pm. Within moments, the bed trembled, and the roar grew louder. Stuart and Sally screamed as the windows, walls and ceiling crashed around them.

Seconds later when the tumult subsided, Stuart tried to sit up, but bashed his head against something hard. It felt like concrete. With mounting horror, he realised the building must have collapsed, and that he and Sally were trapped in a space no bigger than a coffin. Neither could move.

Too late

'Help me, Stuart!' Sally cried. Stuart ran his hand along her body and discovered a big concrete beam across her waist, pinning her to the bed. Their wrought-iron bedhead had fallen forward, trapping her head. Miraculously both had missed him.

'Stuart!' Sally screamed, as water poured over her face. Desperately, Stuart heaved at the bedhead to no avail. He placed his hand on Sally's mouth, trying to keep her from drowning, but their cavity continued to fill.

Now they heard a rumbling, rushing sound. Water! If a water main had ruptured above them, it could flood their tomb and drown them. A split-second later, an icy, reeking mixture of water and heating fuel rushed through the gaps above Stuart's head, filling the small space.

'Stuart!' Sally screamed, as water poured over her face. Desperately, Stuart heaved at the bedhead to no avail. He placed his hand on Sally's mouth, trying to keep her from drowning, but their cavity continued to fill. Beneath his hand, Stuart felt Sally's submerged face contort in horror.

Stuart pushed himself onto his elbows. The water had just started lapping his lips when suddenly it drained away. He reached down to his wife. She was quiet now. She was gone. He wished he would die too – if only to be with Sally. 'Just do it,' he pleaded, 'and make it quick.'

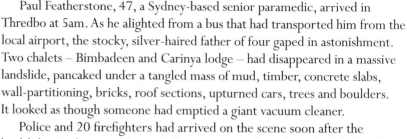

Paul Featherstone, 47, a Sydney-based senior paramedic, arrived in Thredbo at 5am. As he alighted from a bus that had transported him from the local airport, the stocky, silver-haired father of four gaped in astonishment. Two chalets – Bimbadeen and Carinya lodge – had disappeared in a massive landslide, pancaked under a tangled mass of mud, timber, concrete slabs, wall-partitioning, bricks, roof sections, upturned cars, trees and boulders. It looked as though someone had emptied a giant vacuum cleaner.

Police and 20 firefighters had arrived on the scene soon after the landslide, Featherstone learned. But a senior police officer had declared the site too unstable to try rescuing anyone. Now, more than 5 hours later, it was still off-limits.

As a member of the New South Wales Ambulance Service's Special Casualty Access Team (SCAT) – an elite group specialised in treating patients in rugged terrain – Featherstone was used to emergencies. But he had never seen anything like this. It's hard to imagine anyone surviving, he thought.

Stuart Diver lay stunned in the icy mud all around him. 'You've taken my wife!' he shouted upwards, choking with grief. Within minutes, however, his despair gave way to a fierce determination. He sensed Sally's spirit with him. If he gave up without a fight, he felt he'd be letting her down. He vowed to survive as long as he could.

Now another torrent of water swamped him. This time he jammed his left hand against the wall and the other on the muddy bed. Then he pushed upwards, straining to keep his nose and mouth above the freezing water.

Stuart had completed two wilderness-survival courses that taught the urgency of preserving core-body temperature in sub-zero conditions. Already his hands and feet were numb. When the water subsided, he put his hands under his armpits to conserve heat. He wiggled his toes vigorously. He must do everything he could, he decided, to keep warm.

By the time a wintry sun rose over Thredbo, more than 200 firefighters, police, ambulance and other rescuers had arrived. In a makeshift headquarters, police area commander Charlie Sanderson explained that at least 11 men and seven women were under the rubble. 'Screams were heard soon after the tragedy,' he said, 'but there's been no sound since then. We have the gravest fears for them all.'

A team of geophysicists finally declared the site stable at 10am and Sanderson briefed workers on rescue procedure. Three siren blasts, he warned, would mean the rubble was slipping. 'Then get the hell out!'

At 10.30am, 11 hours after the accident, Featherstone joined emergency-service workers and volunteers on the landslip. Hand-to-hand in a human chain, they passed pieces of shattered concrete, furniture, bedding, bricks and timber to waiting trucks. Firefighters crawled over the landslip and peered into gaps, yelling, 'Rescue team above – can you hear me?' But the only sounds were from birds overhead and the gurgle of water below.

Stuart had been inundated five times by sudden bursts of water. Thirst and hunger gnawed at him. He pondered drinking the next gush. But with

July 30, 1997

23.37 Landslide With little warning, Sally and Stuart's lodge collapses, trapping them under rubble and concrete. When water floods in, Sally cannot escape and drowns.

July 31

05.00 Paramedic Paul Featherstone arrives He joins other rescue workers, but the risk of further landslides means the site is still off-limits.

10.00 Rescue begins The site is declared stable and a team of 200 rescue workers starts work, forming a human chain to clear the debris.

Aug 1

06.00 One body recovered Hopes are fading that any survivors will be found.

Aug 2

5.30 Firefighter makes contact with Stuart Rescuers now focus on the spot where Stuart is trapped, desperately trying to remove the rubble around him. Featherstone provides crucial support.

17.17 Pulled free 65 hours later, Stuart is free at last.

fuel and possibly sewage in it, he knew it could be toxic. Even worse than his thirst was the cold. It clawed at his body. He tried to keep his feet moving, but soon lost all energy. Then he felt a cotton cover at the end of the bed. Stretching down, he ripped a piece of the material free. It just covered his stomach and thighs, helping conserve body heat. Next he found a polar fleece jacket he had left on the bed after dinner and struggled into it.

Now, as Stuart sunk into a deep, sluggish state, he heard a faint noise. Somewhere, a man was shouting. People are looking for me! he realised. He felt a surge of excitement.

'Hello!' he shouted over and over. No response. His spirits sank. He'd been trapped for 29 hours.

By dawn on Friday, August 1, one body had been recovered. The chances of finding a survivor now, Featherstone believed, were growing slimmer and slimmer. When someone is exposed to extended sub-zero conditions, the body temperature drops, blood flow to vital organs slows, organs shut down, and the victim dies of hypothermia, usually within 24 hours.

Clearing continued throughout the morning. Suddenly an alarm blasted three times. Featherstone moved with the others to the edge of the slip. As he waited for the all-clear, music drifted from Thredbo's chapel, 'Amazing Grace, how sweet the sound, that saved a wretch like me … '.

Work finally resumed, and later, as the sun set, the temperature dropped to around -8°C (18°F).

At 5.30 the next morning, more than two days after the disaster, firefighter Steve Hirst was moving debris when he heard a sound somewhere below him. Lying on his stomach, Hirst yelled, 'Rescue party working overhead. Can you hear me?'

'I hear you!'

'What's your name?'

'Stuart Diver.'

'What's your condition?' Hirst shouted.

'I'm OK.'

'Is there anyone with you?'

'My wife, Sally, but she's dead.'

News of the survivor spread quickly, and the recovery team tore at the rubble where the voice had been heard. After an hour, workers exposed a huge slab of concrete. Through a jagged, half-metre-wide opening, they heard Stuart's voice, stronger now. 'He must be just underneath,' Hirst said.

Village destroyed *A dramatic aerial view shows the extent of the damage caused by the landslide at Thredbo, which claimed the lives of 18 people. The threat of further landslides in this unstable terrain hampered rescue workers in their desperate attempts to find survivors.*

How Stuart was saved Although rescue workers now knew where Stuart Diver was located, reaching him and freeing him from his frozen tomb would prove to be a dangerous race against time.

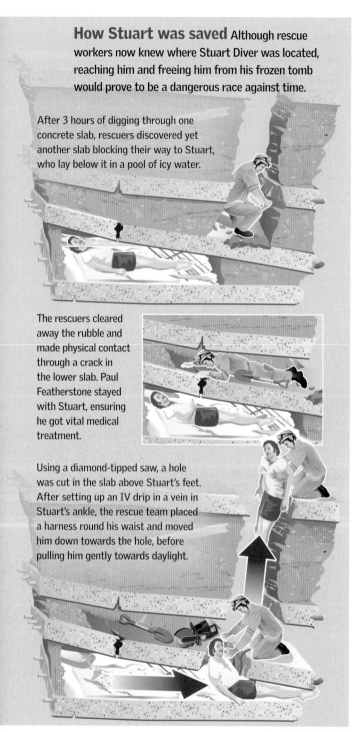

After 3 hours of digging through one concrete slab, rescuers discovered yet another slab blocking their way to Stuart, who lay below it in a pool of icy water.

The rescuers cleared away the rubble and made physical contact through a crack in the lower slab. Paul Featherstone stayed with Stuart, ensuring he got vital medical treatment.

Using a diamond-tipped saw, a hole was cut in the slab above Stuart's feet. After setting up an IV drip in a vein in Stuart's ankle, the rescue team placed a harness round his waist and moved him down towards the hole, before pulling him gently towards daylight.

He and six other rescuers wriggled through the gap into a small chamber, and began clearing more rubble. Soon they discovered another concrete slab 2m (6½ft) lower. After more than 3 hours of digging, a rescuer's light illuminated a crack in the lower slab.

'I can see your light!' Stuart called. 'It's above me.' Silence shrouded the chamber as the men were struck by a sickening realisation: Stuart was underneath yet another slab.

Extreme caution

A fireman saw Stuart poke four fingertips through the crack. Squeezing them gently the fireman said, 'Mate, I've never felt hands so cold.'

Featherstone crawled into the tunnel, pressing close to the crack. 'G'day, Stuart. My name's Paul Featherstone. I'm a paramedic. How are you feeling?'

Suddenly the warning siren blasted three times and a colleague pulled Featherstone from the tunnel. Immediately, he ran to the site controller. 'That guy could die unless I'm down there to settle him,' Featherstone said. 'I'm going back.' This was a risk, he added, that he had to take. 'Give me a skeleton crew of spotters,' he suggested. 'They can watch for movement while I'm in the hole.'

The controller reluctantly agreed, and Featherstone scrambled back down the tunnel.

He handed Stuart a mask, which he clamped over his nose and mouth, and connected it to an oxygen cylinder. Next Featherstone passed Stuart a warm-air hose, attached to a generator on the surface, to place inside his fleece. Featherstone then gave Stuart a pulse oximeter, which he attached to his thumb. This would allow the paramedic to monitor Stuart's pulse.

Featherstone knew his patient's kidneys and liver could malfunction, increasing lactic acid and potassium in his blood to toxic levels, a condition known as acidosis. If Stuart moved suddenly or his heart rate rose, toxins might flood his system, triggering a heart attack. When the pulse oximeter's beep quickened, the paramedic would need to calm him.

Suddenly Stuart began weeping. 'I've got to tell you how Sal died,' he said. 'It's tearing me apart.'

Deeply moved, the paramedic replied quietly, 'Fire away.' As Stuart described how he had tried to save Sally, Featherstone struggled for the right words to say. 'You did all you could possibly do,' he said eventually.

Finally, he grabbed a bottle of electrolyte-and-nutrient solution and, through the crack, inserted a tube from its stopper into Stuart's mouth. Featherstone restricted him to two half-mouthfuls every 20 minutes because he knew Stuart's stomach would have shrunk and any more might cause him to vomit and choke.

After clearing the rubble, and when they were sure of Stuart's exact location, the rescuers started cutting a manhole in the slab above Stuart's feet, using a diamond-tipped circular saw. Dust billowed, and the tunnel filled with a deafening squeal. The pulse monitor began emitting rapid beeps. Stuart's pulse, already more than 100, went up to a worrying 150.

'Stop work!' Featherstone ordered. When the drilling stopped, he reassured Stuart. 'Everything is safe. We're making the noise to get you out as quickly as possible.' His words helped. Stuart's pulse immediately dropped and his respiration slowed.

Finally, after cutting through the slab immediately above Stuart and clearing other debris, the hole over his feet was large enough for a tunneller to enter. After three more hours of digging, Featherstone slid into the cavity to prepare his patient for moving. 'But before we can get him out, we must set up an IV,' Featherstone said. The better Stuart was hydrated, the less likely he'd be to suffer heart failure when moved.

A doctor now reached into the cavity, inserting an intravenous line into a vein in Stuart's ankle. Featherstone took his temperature. It was 34.7°C (94°F), three below normal. His patient was hypothermic, but his pulse was strong, and he didn't appear physically distressed. 'So far, so good, but we're not there yet,' he thought.

The paramedic manoeuvred a harness round Stuart's waist, then gently pulled him feet-first until his head was beneath the manhole. Through the gap, Stuart glimpsed a patch of open sky. He smiled. 'I thought I'd never see daylight again.'

Featherstone realised the following moments would be critical. If acidosis was imminent, it could strike when Stuart was hauled from the hole.

'Before we bring him out,' the paramedic told colleagues, 'we need to make a phone call.' With his mobile phone, he called Stuart's parents, who had driven from Melbourne the day after the landslide. Featherstone knew this might be their last chance to speak to their son.

'How're you doing, Tiger?' Steve Diver asked.

'Happy to be out of here, Dad,' Stuart replied. Then the phone connection broke.

The pulse oximeter now beeped rapidly. Featherstone placed a steadying hand on his patient. 'No, mate,' he said. 'We have to take this slowly.' Stuart's pulse returned to normal.

'OK, Stu, here we go,' the paramedic said. 'Let us do the grunt. You just relax.'

Moment of release *After nearly three days trapped in his frozen tomb, Stuart Diver is finally pulled from the rubble of the ski lodge.*

As two firemen pulled from above, Featherstone and another paramedic held Stuart under his arms. Soon his head was partly out of the manhole. On the surface, rescuers slid a rescue board through both holes in the concrete slabs, and Featherstone positioned it behind Stuart's back. 'Let's do it,' the paramedic said. With a concerted heave, rescuers hoisted Stuart to the surface. It was 5.17pm on Saturday, August 2 – 65 hours after the landslide.

Stuart looked all around him. 'That sky's fantastic!' he exclaimed. 'Well done, guys.'

The only survivor of the landslide, Stuart was airlifted to Canberra Hospital. There, doctors were astonished to discover that he had suffered only frostbite, dehydration, superficial cuts and hypothermia.

Stuart returned to his parents' home in Melbourne to continue his recovery. A few days later, Paul Featherstone came by to see him.

Featherstone insists he's no hero. 'It's what I do,' he says of his work. 'You can only do your best. And often, that's enough.'

Before Sally Diver's funeral service in Melbourne, Stuart looked into her coffin in the chapel. 'She looks so beautiful,' he thought, 'so at peace.'

Stuart kissed her gently. 'See you later, Sal,' he said. On one finger, along with his own wedding ring, he was now wearing Sally's wedding and engagement rings. 'Part of her will always be with me,' he says. 'Always!' ■

Where are they now?

STUART DIVER still lives in Thredbo, the Snowy Mountains ski resort where he so nearly met his death. He remarried in 2002, five years after the catastrophe that took the life of his first wife. Today, he owns a small boutique hotel on the mountain above the site of the avalanche.

A coroner's inquest held in 1998 found that the landslide was, in the end, man-made, caused by a long-standing leak in an underground water pipe that fatally weakened the geological structure of the mountainside. The New South Wales government admitted liability, and settled out of court with the families of all the victims. Diver settled separately in 2004. His case was dealt with on its own due to an odd circumstance: his brother Euan was Thredbo's assistant engineer at the time of the landslide. Euan had conducted a routine inspection of the village on the very day it occurred; he saw nothing to make him suspect a calamity was about to occur.

Inevitably perhaps, Stuart Diver became a kind of national hero in the months and years after his ordeal. His fortitude and courage were held up as an example to his fellow Australians, and he became the subject of many a newspaper article and school essay.

He published a book of his own about his dreadful experience, and his story was turned into a made-for-TV movie called *Heroes' Mountain*. In this dramatisation, the part of Diver was played by Craig McLachlan, best known as Henry Mitchell in *Neighbours*.

Diver made good use of his strange celebrity to publicise the work of the Salvation Army, which had provided comfort to him during his 65 hours underground. 'I believe in hope,' said Diver, speaking at a charity event in 2006. 'No matter what happens to you, no matter how bad it all gets, there is always hope. There must be. I am living proof of that.'

AS THE RIVER ROSE HIGHER in the Cornish village of Boscastle, a giant wave threatened to engulf all in its path. How would the villagers survive the onslaught?

THE DAY THE SKY FELL IN

Rumbles of thunder and splatting rain hit Boscastle in the middle of the afternoon of August 16, 2004. Holidaymakers exploring the quaint village and harbour on Cornwall's north coast scuttled for cover. In The Spinning Wheel café, owner and chef John Smart, 55, put a tray of scones to bake in the oven so that the homely smell would bring people in. His wife Francilla, 41, served afternoon teas as the café filled up.

Partners for 25 years, with one son each, the couple had married in March. Giving up teaching jobs in London, they'd slaved for six years to make a success of the continental-style café. John prayed business wouldn't be interrupted because August brought a third of their income.

In ruins *Francilla and John Smart stand in what remained of their café, The Spinning Wheel, after it was destroyed by the flash floods.*

Next door but one, Boscastle Bakery was doing a brisk trade in wet-day comfort food. Nev Chamberlain and his wife Susan had been up since 4am baking the pasties and cakes now in demand. Two doors down in the Rock Shop, another in the line of shops on Bridge Walk, backing onto the river, Yvonne Gaskell was relieved that 40 containers of organic ice cream had come that morning. 'But we're running low on clotted cream,' she warned her husband Russell.

That wet August Monday afternoon at least 1,000 people crammed into the gift shops, pubs and tea shops in the village of Boscastle, none of whom had the least suspicion of the disaster brewing.

The thunderstorm that had developed over the north Cornish coast had stalled. Instead of drifting away with the wind, the unstable black cloud boiled high into the heavens, triggering excessive rain. Falling like buckets of bricks, it landed in the 20km^2 (8 sq miles) of waterlogged moorland that funnelled water into a steep-sided valley. Boscastle was at the bottom of that valley.

The first sign of something strange was the angry note of the river. Instead of babbling past the village's car park and shops then rippling between meadowy banks to the sea, the usually shallow current frothed and swirled. John Smart noticed a tang of damp woodland mingling with the aroma of his scones and looked out of his back door. Worry touched his thin, lined face. Filled with debris, the river already licked along the top of the walkway behind the shop. He'd never seen it so high. Just as he reached out to save his flowerpots they were swept away.

The roar of the river became so loud that Yvonne Gaskell ran up the stairs to the flat above the Rock Shop and peered over the balcony. 'Oh my God!' she cried. Huge and smooth, an avalanche of soil-coloured water 2m (6ft) high surged down the river towards her. She flew inside and yelled at Russell that a wave was coming.

Outside, people jumped clear as the wave swept around the bridge, filling the roads on both sides so that nobody could cross.

Water poured over the window ledge, 1m (3ft) above the floor, into The Spinning Wheel. 'I'm afraid we have to close,' John Smart told his customers, trying not to scare them.

One woman was adamant. 'I've paid for this tea so I'm going to drink it,' she said, but finished it quickly as tables and chairs started to drift around. In the Riverside Hotel at the bottom end of Bridge Walk, owner Peter Templar, a sturdy 58-year-old, watched the Test Match cricket on TV. He heard a tremendous crack. A 2m (6ft) wave roared past the back windows.

In the 11 years since he and his wife Margaret, 56, had taken on the hotel, they'd seen flooding like this only once before. Templar ran to fetch sandbags and laid them across the door. 'The water won't come any higher,' he told Margaret.

Deluge begins

But within a few minutes water was pouring through the back wall. Customers began leaving the crowded tea room and Templar checked the upper rooms to warn guests to leave. When he came down the water was knee-high. 'Everyone out now!' he shouted. 'We'll head for the car park.'

They'd be safer up there. Holding hands and bracing their legs against the surging current, Templar and his wife, daughter, son-in-law, two grandchildren, staff members and dog inched along the line of shops to Cornish Stores, a grocery shop facing the car park at the top end. Owner Guy Lane-de-Courtin, a rangy 35-year-old, grabbed Templar's hand and pulled the family to safety on the steps leading to his flat over the shop.

The steps were already crowded with others trying to reach their cars, which now bobbed like pedalos on a boating lake, the huge volume of water penned up by a 2m (6ft) stone wall at the foot of the steps. 'We'll

Driven to destruction *Such was the force of the flooding in Boscastle that many cars were swept away and thrown around as if they were no more than toys.*

wait here until it goes down,' Templar told his family. He couldn't have known that the hills above would soon be awash with more than 18cm (7in) of rain – two months' normal rainfall. The deluge had hardly started.

Eleven kilometres (7 miles) away in the village of Delabole, fire-station officer Mark Saltern heard rain drumming on the roof of his joinery workshop and was not surprised when his pager went off. A burly man of 41 who still played football for the village, he'd been a part-time fireman for 19 years and was no stranger to floods. In minutes, he and six men were surging through flooded lanes in their fire engine. From the bend above Boscastle they saw brown water battering the bridge and rising into the slate-and-stone buildings. Aghast, a fireman asked, 'What are we going to do?'

Saltern had spent many an afternoon exploring the gift shops and buying ice creams with his wife and two kids. 'This is serious but manageable,' he thought. And he couldn't imagine it getting worse. 'Life jackets on, lads,' he said.

The fire crew warned people on the bridge to move away. Forked lightning jabbed out of the black sky; thunder cracked. Holding a rope stretched between them and gasping from the force of the rain, they rounded the corner to Bridge Walk.

Outside Cornish Stores, they saw people huddled on the wall damming the water in the car park; others were crowded on the stairs to two flats above the shops. 'Get inside!' Saltern ordered them. 'The wall will collapse at any minute.'

Terrifying torrent

In the bakery he spotted Susan Chamberlain kneeling on the floor. She was blotting up water with rags and wringing them into a bucket, not realising that racing water had risen halfway up the back window behind her. Saltern saw a tree whirl past. 'Get upstairs, quick!' he shouted. 'If the window goes you'll be dead.'

Neither his radio nor mobile could get a signal so he grabbed the bakery phone and called Fire Control in Truro. 'This is a major incident, send all the help you can.'

A shout came from outside, 'The wall's going!'

'I've got to go,' Saltern said. He hung up just as the car-park wall burst outwards.

A torrent of terrifying power surged down the street, cars surfing at more than 60km/h (40mph) on a huge black wave. Guy Lane-de-Courtin watched his white van bounce off the gents' lavatory and hit an electric pole. Cables came down, firing sparks. Dipping and spinning, the van shot down the street. Other cars followed, some with yellow lights flashing and alarms going.

Saltern spotted his crew on the stairs to the Smarts' flat and waded towards them. Rising a metre in seconds, the water was halfway up his thighs when his men reached out and grabbed him. They raced up to the flat. 'Wipe your feet!' Francilla joked as they staggered in, drenched and mud-caked.

But then the whole place shook as if a bomb had exploded in the basement. Horrified, Templar realised their haven was in terrible danger.

Now ten people plus six firemen were crowded into the Smarts' flat, with 24 others above Cornish Stores next door. Cataracts of water as high as the first floor sluiced along both sides of the building. Cars and trees whirled past at eye level. And still the water rose. Watching recycling bins pirouette like synchronised swimmers as they floated past, Peter Templar breathed a sigh of relief. It's a strong stone building, we'll be safe here, he thought.

But then the whole place shook as if a bomb had exploded in the basement. Horrified, Templar realised their haven was in terrible danger. The outside wall took the whole brunt of the torrent. Trees and vehicles rammed into it. Any moment the wall would crack then collapse, taking the house and all the people with it. He said to Lane-de-Courtin, 'Guy, we need to get out of here!'

The immense cataract now hurled vehicles over the bridge and formed standing waves 3m (10ft) high. One car travelling like a torpedo smashed into the Harbour Light, a 500-year-old barn and one of Cornwall's most photographed buildings. In a blink it was gone.

Everywhere people fought for their lives. Washed out of her cottage, Emily Maugham grabbed a drainpipe that pulled away from the wall. A neighbour stretching out of his door grabbed her an instant before she was swept away.

In a rented holiday cottage with his two Staffordshire bull terriers, a few doors along, security officer Andy Trethewey saw the front of the bakery opposite explode. A bomb-burst of dark-brown water thundered into his front door and chased him into the kitchen. Springing up on the worktop, he thrust one dog on top of a cupboard and put the other on the fridge as it floated past. His head bent under the ceiling, he felt cold water rising higher and higher right up to his chin.

Above The Spinning Wheel, firemen who went onto the balcony to empty water from their boots came back with worried faces. The building vibrated from the pressure of water, its level rising still higher. One of the firemen, Ken Goodman, a builder, knew that the unimaginable power of the racing flood would undermine the foundations. If one building collapsed the rest would go down like dominoes. But he pinned a confident smile on his face.

He closed the flat door and watched the water rise up the glass. How long would it hold? 'Come on,' he said cheerfully. 'Let's go higher.'

In the attic bedroom, Mark Saltern found a big skylight and climbed out into the roof valley. Muffled thuds came from the small window opposite. It was Peter Templar, wielding a power tool like a hammer as he stood on a lavatory cistern and tried to smash a way out.

Safe, at last *Help arrives for one villager, who is hoisted above the rising flood waters by rescue workers into a helicopter above.*

Pulling together *The day after the flooding, Boscastle's residents combined forces, digging a channel to help them to clear any remaining water.*

Saltern's firemen opened the window. Even up here, they felt the building tremble as it was hit by debris. 'We have to get out before it goes,' Templar shouted. Below him, Guy Lane-de-Courtin stood with one foot on the lavatory-seat lid and the other on the cistern.

One by one, 24 men, women and children – and Izzy the German shepherd – stood on the lavatory then climbed onto his leg and reached upwards. Firemen grabbed their hands. Once outside they dived head-first though the attic skylight of the Smarts' flat.

With a crowd of drenched, cold and frightened people in their bedroom, Francilla handed out all the T-shirts and towels she had and tried not to think about what the torrent was doing to their café. Would they lose everything?

Still on the roof, Mark Saltern tried his radio and was amazed to get through. 'I've got 40 here including the crew, all safe and well,' he reported to Control. Below, he saw weeping children gazing up at him. 'Don't worry, you're safe now,' he said with a smile. But he was fibbing. In all his years as a fireman he'd never felt so unsafe or more scared. Then he heard the sound he'd been praying for – a helicopter.

Deadly peril

Approaching in blinding rain at 4.19pm and expecting to rescue people on top of a car, the crew of the first Royal Navy helicopter came upon a scene of devastation. Desperate people hung out of windows while others struggled to smash a way out through roof tiles. Marine captain Pete McLelland radioed the Aeronautical Rescue Coordination Centre: 'Get all available rescue teams and standby aircraft. We're in danger of losing people in their houses.'

From the ridge of the roof Mark Saltern spotted adults and children huddled on top of the visitor centre in the car park. Their lives were in deadly peril for the roof was only just above the water and half of it had already collapsed. As the helicopter descended towards him, Saltern waved it forward.

Moments later the yellow RAF helicopter that followed was hovering 6m (20ft) over Bridge Walk and Sergeant 'Shuie' Thompson, lowered on a wire, landed on the roof next to Saltern. 'How many have you got?' he asked.

'Forty people and a dog.'

'You're joking!'

Two at a time, the refugees were winched straight out of the attic window. 'Brush your hair, love, there'll be TV cameras out there,' fireman Ken Goodman told a nervous woman who was on her way up before she knew it.

In the Rock Shop next door, Russell and Yvonne Gaskell built a ladder of beer cases up to their attic window so they could get out. They joined the line as the big Sea King helicopter made three trips, shuttling people to a playing field at the top of the hill. In all, about 120 people were airlifted by seven different helicopters.

It was getting dark when Andy Trethewey, still with water up to his chin, felt the level begin to fall. Soon he could wade out into the street and a fireman helped to rescue the dogs. Sue Chamberlain – with scores of others trapped in shops and houses – was piggybacked to safety through the knee-deep quagmire of mud and debris left by the water.

Of the bakery, nothing was left. Other shops and cafés, like the hotel, were filled knee-deep with oozing mud. But even in the face of destruction and ruin, the people of Boscastle celebrated a miracle. Not one person died and only three – one blister, one heart problem, one broken thumb – were taken to hospital. 'Everyone behaved calmly and sensibly and we got away with it,' says Mark Saltern. 'That's the miracle of Boscastle.'

Two nights later, John and Francilla Smart joined 40 villagers outside the devastated Wellington Hotel. Undaunted, they'd come to sing folk songs. 'We sing here every Wednesday night,' said John. 'There's no reason to stop – and we'll be open again in spring.' Boscastle was already fighting back. ■

What happened next?

THE REGENERATION OF BOSCASTLE was to prove almost as much a spiritual as a material undertaking. As a four-year programme of rebuilding and improvement was in train, the residents of the historic village were looking to their own resources to ensure that Boscastle would bounce back.

Fears that tourists would stay away proved unfounded. In the summer of 2005, with the approach of the first anniversary of the flood, and with all but five businesses reopened, the village was said to be 'bursting at the seams' with visitors: if anything, the flood had put Boscastle on the map.

In October 2005, the first annual Boscastle Festival of Food, Arts and Crafts was staged and proved a huge success. Then in 2007 came the first annual Boscastle Walking Festival, in which local people act as guides.

After the devastating floods there was a shift in local thinking, a heightened concern for environmental issues. By 2008, many of the village businesses had signed up to the Green Tourism Business Scheme (GTBS). After independent inspections, Boscastle gained five GTBS Gold Awards, with more to follow – the highest concentration of gold achievers in any small community in the UK. 'Boscastle is a fantastic example of how a society can get along,' said GTBS director Andrea Nicholas. 'They have become a stronger community through adversity.'

'The flood has had an impact on people's thinking,' said Adrian Prescott, B&B owner and secretary of Boscastle's Chamber of Commerce. 'Everybody took stock of the fact that we are custodians of the environment. Despite the fact that we've all got individual businesses, we work as a unit rather than compete with each other ... We'd like to see other areas taking on our ethos of cooperation. If that happened you'd see some real change.'

Is there a danger, though, that the Valency and Jordan rivers could again swamp the resort? At the tourist information centre they are completely sanguine. 'The new flood defences are holding up well,' they say.

CELEBRATION The 2005 Mayday procession in Boscastle showed how far the villagers had moved on since the disaster.

AN EVENING WALK ALONG LONELY Morecambe Bay turned into a nightmare for Terry Howlett, trapped overnight in quicksand. It was morning before help arrived and the race against the tide began.

THE SAND'S EATING ME ALIVE!

The air was tangy with mud and brine as the train rattled into the Lancashire town of Carnforth. Terry Howlett took a deep, invigorating breath as he stepped onto the platform, glad to be back.

It was a breezy Saturday evening in August 1996, and Howlett had travelled here from his home in Darlington, County Durham, with a lot on his mind. After buying a meal, he headed off to his favourite spot – the eerie wilderness of shifting sandbanks, muddy channels and racing tides of Morecambe Bay.

He'd first discovered this lonely place while on leave from the Navy in 1988 and had returned often. Its haunting magic never failed to lift his spirits.

A long causeway jutted out for more than a mile into the bay's flat and desolate shore. Howlett walked towards the sea, feeling the tranquillity of the marshes gathering him in, as he wrestled with his thoughts.

A painful football injury had brought his naval career as a weapons technician to an end. After three knee operations, he could no longer go to sea and had to resign. No quitter, Howlett had willingly taken on a string of casual jobs, but none had led to anything.

Now his knee was healed and, as he approached his 30th birthday, he was anxious to get on with his life. Above all, he told himself, he needed to get more qualifications – 'If I keep going, I could get through to college.'

Coming to the end of the causeway, Terry wandered onto the beach. In the moonlight, he could make out the channel of a river some 180m (200yd) broad. The tide was well out, leaving an expanse of rippled sand dotted with pools. Thinking that he'd be able to walk for hours on the salt grasses beyond, he continued on.

But after a dozen steps he felt himself sinking into the soft sand. Windmilling his arms to keep his balance, he tried to leap free, but he only sank deeper. In seconds he was up to his knees in a man-hungry pudding of cold, oozing jelly. Quicksand.

Howlett was stunned. There had been nothing on the surface to suggest it was soft or dangerous. As local people well knew, the swirling of river or tidal currents sometimes digs out isolated hollows that fill with a porridge-like sediment. Only an expert eye can detect these melgraves, as they are called, and they have a voracious appetite. Shrimp-fishermen's horses, motorbikes, even dump trucks have been swallowed up.

Howlett had read that farmers who got stuck in quicksand while rounding up sheep would spreadeagle themselves to distribute their weight. But it was too late for that. The sand was already climbing up his thighs. 'My God, it's eating me alive!'

Fear gripped Howlett, and he yelled for help. Nobody heard. He had an awful vision of himself choking to death as his nose and throat filled with sand. 'I'll disappear and nobody will ever know what happened to me.'

The clammy sand nuzzled up to his crotch, seeped inside his trousers and crawled over his belly. One more inch … another inch …

Admire it from afar *A sign at Morecambe Bay warns of the dangers awaiting anyone who ventures onto the vast expanse of treacherous sand.*

Saviours of the sand *After his terrifying ordeal, a grateful Terry Howlett (opposite, front row, centre) poses with some of his rescuers.*

Hardly daring to breathe, he sank to his waist – then stopped. He tried wriggling his toes, but his feet seemed cast in concrete. Although Howlett's body was immobile, his brain was spinning. And, suddenly, he was electrified by a frightening thought: 'When will the tide come in again?'

Thinking back, he remembered that the tide had been going out when he reached the beach, which meant it wouldn't be back for another 9 or 10 hours. 'I've got a chance after all,' he thought.

Cupping his fingers, he began to scoop away the sand around his waist that was holding him prisoner. But as fast as he dug, the muck oozed back into place. After an hour his fingers were numb and sore, his legs raging with cramps.

Then he heard a roar like a waterfall. Moments later a vicious rain-squall struck. Drenched in seconds, Terry buried his face in his hands and bowed his head. Gripped in jaws of sand, he had nowhere to run.

Calling for help

The storm rattled through the night. At the crack of dawn, Tony Gardner, 54, got up to check his sheep and stepped out to a glorious morning.

A grey-bearded stonemason from Yorkshire, Gardner spent weekends on the small hill farm that had been in his family for generations.

The sky was clear and sunny, the air cool and still. His boots were swishing through the grass when suddenly he heard something and paused to listen. Was somebody shouting?

Far below, Gardner saw a herd of cows being taken in for milking. 'The farmer's calling his stock,' he thought.

An hour later, returning home, Gardner heard the same sound. Puzzled, he called his wife Frances to come and listen. 'It's got a rhythm to it, sounds like "help me, help me",' she said. Driving along the road, the Gardners saw no climber trapped on the rocks, no road accident. 'It must be coming from the shore,' Gardner told his wife. He dialled 999.

Minutes later, police constable Ian Nickson met the Gardners at the beach and the three of them set off towards the cries at a run. After a mile, Gardner paused. 'Where are you?' he yelled.

'Over here!' a hoarse voice replied.

Gardner blinked and stared. Incredibly, somebody was out there, buried to the waist in sand.

'Right, I've got you!' Gardner called, running along the beach.

'You're OK, lad, we've found you now,' he said, when he reached Terry. 'How on earth did you get here?'

For 9 hours Howlett had scratched vainly at the sand, pausing only to hug himself to preserve body heat. Since dawn he'd been shouting for help, his energy flagging as he grew more and more desperate. Incredibly, his cries had been heard 2.5km (1½ miles) away.

Nickson arrived on the scene moments later. 'Don't worry, son, we'll have you out in a jiffy,' he said cheerfully. Howlett slumped with a feeling of relief as Nickson radioed police headquarters.

Gripping Howlett beneath the armpits, the policeman and farmer pulled firmly upwards. But Howlett's body wouldn't budge.

'We're stretching him in two,' Nickson said finally. He radioed headquarters again. 'We can't get the trapped man out. Request coastguard, the fire brigade and an ambulance.'

Their biggest enemy now, Gardner realised, was not the quicksand but the sea. Tides in the bay were fierce; some days the sea level rose by more than 6m (20ft) in a very short time. He glanced at the policeman. 'You'd best check the tide.'

On his radio, Nickson was advised to expect high tide at 7.38. It was already 7.30. 'We're all right, the tide's nearly full,' he said.

But Gardner was suspicious. He gazed out towards the bay. 'If the tide's full,' he wondered, 'where's the water?'

Perilous beauty of Morecambe Bay

FED BY FIVE RIVERS – the Leven, Kent, Keer, Lune and Wyre – Morecambe Bay is the largest continuous area of intertidal sand and mudflats in the UK. At high tide it is a 'great inner sea'. At low tide, 310km² (120 sq miles) of sand are revealed. This is a birdwatchers' paradise, a site of international importance for waders. It is wild, expansive and beautiful, but, with its quicksands, and with tides that are said to advance faster than a galloping horse, it is utterly treacherous. Waters flood in, surging between the sand ridges, cutting off the unwary. The gullies and rivers running into the bay change daily, and what is firm sand one day may be quicksand the next.

The bay's reputation as a death trap was compounded in February 2004 when 23 young Chinese cockle-pickers drowned. 'They didn't stand a chance,' one despairing local expert commented. 'They were out in the middle,' says Paul Calland of Bay Search and Rescue (see page 332). 'You can walk out, or drive out, and it *looks* safe ... but you can be 10 miles out, then the tide comes in all around you.'

Before the advent of the railway and speedy road travel, people would take short cuts across the bay, though many lost their lives. At one point, guides were provided by the priories of Conishead and Cartmel. Then, in 1538, the Duchy of Lancaster appointed an official Royal Guide – a tradition upheld today. Cedric Robinson, Queen's Guide to the Sands of Morecambe Bay, and the 25th person to hold the post, has guided hundreds of thousands of visitors across the bay, in what has become an internationally famous walk, frequently undertaken for charities, including Bay Search and Rescue. In his book, *Between the Tides: The Perilous Beauty of Morecambe Bay*, Robinson explains how the Kent estuary has become more dangerous than ever, as a result of its frequent changes of course – and how, with global warming, dolphin and salmon have become frequent visitors.

water droplets

rising water source

sand particles

underground spring rises as tide comes in

water liquefies surrounding loose sand

1m

0.5

0

HIDDEN DANGER Quicksand is formed when rising water oversaturates the sand so that friction between the particles is reduced, producing a mushy 'soup', usually no more than a metre or so deep, which cannot bear weight. If you are caught, don't struggle or panic, or you will become stuck. Try to float on the sand, on your back.

Leading Frances by the elbow until they were out of Howlett's earshot, he whispered, 'My bet is there's still a tide to come up the channel.'

Hauntingly deserted through the night, the area was now bustling with rescuers. Firemen ferried air-bottles, ropes, ladders and rescue gear from their trucks. Local fire chief Bob Gleeson, called in to supervise the rescue, stood back on high ground with the Gardners.

Paramedics in green overalls arrived. Sue Williamson, 38, had two red blankets tucked under one arm and carried a bag filled with emergency equipment. John Dockray, the fire station commander, introduced her. 'This is Terry Howlett and we'll have him out in a few minutes,' he said.

To the rescue!

THE HOURS OF FRUSTRATING LABOUR to free Terry Howlett were traumatic not just for Terry but for his 32 rescuers. He had so nearly drowned before their eyes. Surely, reasoned coastguards Gary Parsons and Adrian Swenson, there had to be a better way.

Watching hovercraft racing at 100km/h (60mph) over sands at Carnforth, Gary had his first bright idea. He bought an old ex-racer, which would cover in 12 minutes a distance that would take 3 hours on foot, and in 2001 launched Bay Hovercraft Rescue. He named the craft after Ada Hillard, who lived on the bay and who, having once nearly lost a family member to its clutches, became a major benefactor.

The hovercraft had its limitations. It would not carry enough equipment or rescuers, was not well equipped to carry injured casualties and would not go through the long, coarse grass around the bay. Always learning from experience, and thinking laterally, Gary and the team acquired an ex-military, all-terrain, amphibious personnel carrier (see below) and Bay Hovercraft Rescue became Bay Search and

Rescue. Originally designed for use in snow, the vehicle has seating for 18 and makes short work of sand, mud and even quicksand.

The next acquisition was a second-hand airboat of the sort that negotiates the swamplands of Florida's Everglades, and which proved their worth in flooded New Orleans in the wake of Hurricane Katrina. Another stroke of genius has been the use of a tool known as a concrete poker to free anyone trapped. Using the 'Bay Search and Rescue Technique', the team can free someone from quicksand in 4-5 minutes, and they regularly practise by extracting one another.

This 12-man operation is called out to the bay on average eight to ten times a year, and can help in other emergency situations such as deep snow, ice and blizzards. Says Paul Calland, an operational team leader, 'We're a bit like the military in that we train constantly – and hope that it never happens.'

To find out more about Bay Search and Rescue, including how to make a donation, visit www.baysearchandrescue. org.uk.

Pulling together *With the waters rising fast, a whole team of rescuers battled to free Terry from the quicksand, but he was stuck fast.*

'It's Sunday morning,' Sue teased smilingly. 'You should be in church, not stuck down a hole!'

Terry's wan smile triggered in Williamson a childhood memory of finding a seabird covered with oil. The stricken gull had looked at her with the same bright and trusting eyes as she'd carried it tenderly to a refuge. Her heart went out to him.

As the firemen tried to lift Howlett up, he grimaced, then yelled with pain. 'My legs!' he gasped.

Dockray looked on with concern. Mud and sand rescues cropped up several times a year on Morecambe Bay, but the victims were seldom more than shin-deep. The usual technique was to sit them down on a board to take the weight off their legs, then work on lifting their feet. This one was different. 'The lad's in deep,' he worried.

Something else troubled Dockray. He had the same thought as Gardner. If it was high tide, where was the water? He radioed fireman Barry Maguire to double-check tide times. 'High water's 8.38, John,' Maguire answered, knowing it was summer and an extra hour had to be added.

Dockray checked his watch. It was 7.50 and the water would come licking up the river channel any minute. He told his men and the mood of relaxed cheerfulness abruptly changed.

On their minds was the memory of a similar incident. In 1980 a teenage boy was trapped on his trail bike in soft mud. Frantic efforts to dig him out failed. As the water rose, the mask of a breathing set was fitted over his face, but he tore it off and drowned before the firemen's eyes.

With grim determination, the rescue team redoubled their efforts. Using a sand lance, a 1.2m (4ft) steel tube attached by rubber hose to an air cylinder, firemen blasted air through the tube in an attempt to loosen the quicksand's grip. But the jets of air only drove the suspended water out of the sand, making it even harder.

Up the beach, Bob Gleeson weighed up the options: a mechanical digger would sink; getting firehoses to jet the sand from the hole would take too long.

It might already be too late. A tongue of frothy water was now sweeping into the river channel at the speed of a wave running up a beach. When Howlett saw Sue Williamson glance over her shoulder and in a frenzy

Froth and muddy water bubbled around Terry's face, making him cough. His bad knee was agony. To blot out the pain and fear he thought of his mother and his gran. He loved them both dearly and dreaded to think of their anguish as they were told of his death.

renew her attack on the muck, he understood. He felt sorry for the rescuers. These were good people trying so hard to get him out. 'If they have to watch me drown, it'll be really tough on them,' he thought.

In moments the in-rushing water bubbled round his waist and poured over his rescuers' legs. Its speed was frightening.

Watching the desperate scene, Gleeson calculated that the water was rising at about 5cm (2in) a minute. Fireman Steve Darby approached. 'We're not getting him out – we've got to get a breathing set on him.'

Gleeson hadn't broached this earlier in case Howlett was spooked. Like the boy who'd died in the mud, he might panic at the idea of going underwater. Steve Darby was already starting to take off his uniform. His plan was to don a breathing set and sit beside Howlett under the water.

'He's out!'

Lugging a coiled hose over his shoulder, auxiliary coastguard Tom Hayhurst, 56, and his team of seven carried pipes and hoses along the beach to what looked like a football scrum of wet and half-dressed people out in the water.

They began setting up a high-pressure water jet that would blast away the mud trapping Howlett. Again and again, the team had to stop to extricate each other as they sank down into the wet sand.

Water was now swirling around Howlett's chest. He steeled himself to remain calm. 'I'm so scared – but I won't think about it.' Even as he made himself smile, he could feel the cold wetness licking around his ribs.

While Hayhurst's men tried to help the firemen, on shore Gleeson told Dockray. 'John, it's getting dangerous for the men. You've got 5 minutes, then I'm ordering them out.'

Howlett bent his head back and upwards as the water swirled beneath his chin. Working knee-deep in water next to him, one of the paramedics pushed the nozzle down the side of the trapped man's leg and the power jet began pushing the sand aside.

Froth and muddy water bubbled around Terry's face, making him cough. His bad knee was agony. To blot out the pain and fear he thought of his mother and his gran. He loved them both dearly and dreaded to think of their anguish as they were told of his death.

But suddenly the sand round his feet shifted. 'I can move my toes!' Howlett cried, spitting water. As the firemen strained to heave him upwards, his right leg pulled clear. A cheer went up.

'Don't you dare put that foot down!' Dockray yelled, then, 'Keep pulling lads,' as the rescuers grabbed Howlett by the arms and shoulders for one mighty last-ditch effort.

Howlett screamed with pain. Then a great shout went up. 'He's out!' A cradle of helping hands carried the exhausted man up the beach and he was laid in a nest of coats and blankets. Down on the shore, the tide, 1-1.2m (3-4ft) deep now, swept over the spot where he'd been trapped.

Flown by helicopter to hospital suffering severe hypothermia, Terry was released the next day. His ordeal, he says, was a reminder of how precious life is. 'You think you're totally alone, without hope, then someone reaches out to help you. It's made me believe in myself again, and in my future.' ■

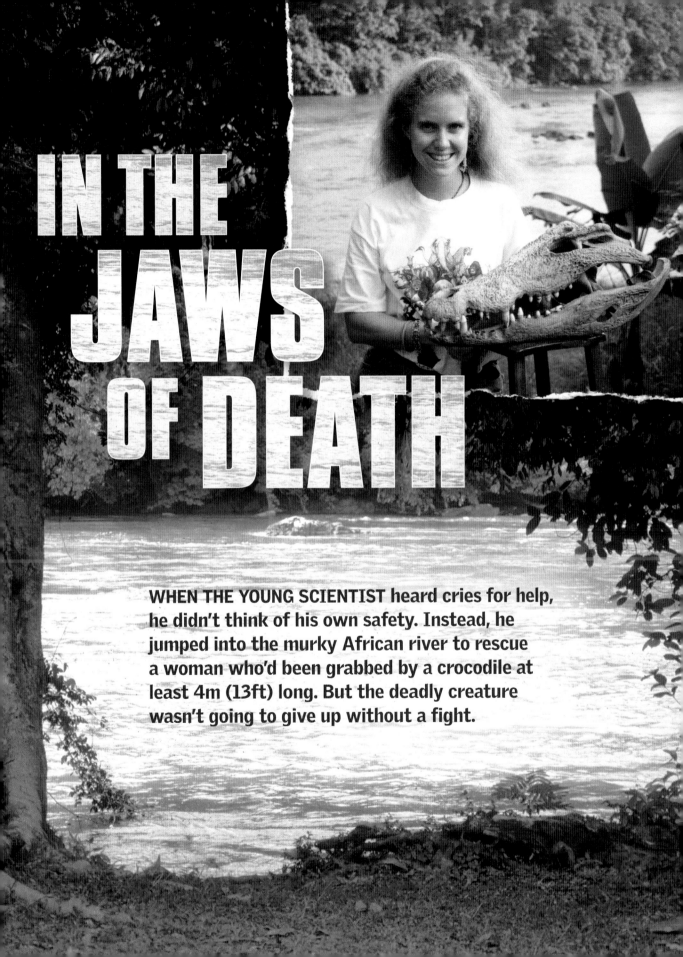

IN THE JAWS OF DEATH

WHEN THE YOUNG SCIENTIST heard cries for help, he didn't think of his own safety. Instead, he jumped into the murky African river to rescue a woman who'd been grabbed by a crocodile at least 4m (13ft) long. But the deadly creature wasn't going to give up without a fight.

The day had been hot and humid,
and Sandy Rossi looked forward to her customary pre-dinner swim. With no running water at the remote African jungle camp, everyone bathed in the Epulu river.

Rossi, 27, had arrived three months before to be tutor and nanny to the two children of John and Terese Hart, naturalists from New York studying the vast Ituri forest of central Zaire [now the Democratic Republic of Congo]. Sandy, a former Peace Corps volunteer, told her parents back home in Missouri that the job was perfect for her.

Now, on March 14, 1993, she took Bekah, 10, and JoJo, 3, into the water. Ken Cochrane, a 28-year-old research assistant from California, joined them.

Sandy looked at her watch: 6.10pm. 'Time to get out. It's going to be dark soon,' she called. Ken herded the reluctant children ashore while Sandy waded out waist-deep, lathering up her thick, shoulder-length hair. Bending forward, she rinsed it with both hands.

A snout and two yellow reptilian eyes broke the surface of the river. The beast sensed prey moving in the water. Off in the twilight, it sighted splashing. Submerging without a ripple, the more than 4m (13ft) long reptile tucked its clawed and webbed feet against its 136kg (300lb) body. Its powerful tail drove it swiftly through the murky water.

Whoomph! Knocked off her feet, Sandy tumbled underwater. A crushing pain in her left forearm took her breath away. She sensed a malevolent, primal presence beside her. She'd been grabbed by a crocodile.

Instinctively, she thought first of the children. 'I've got to warn Ken.' Pushing her feet against the sandy river bottom, she thrust her head to the surface. Ken stood 3m (10ft) away, knee-deep in the water, his back to her.

Behind him, Sandy saw the children on the river bank reaching for their towels. 'Crocodile!' she gasped. Ken shot her a disapproving look. 'Don't even joke about that,' he admonished.

Ambushed

The crocodile jerked her under again, savaging her like a rag doll. Its great jaws were studded with around 70 wicked teeth designed to penetrate flesh and hold its victim underwater until it drowned. She felt the bones in her forearm grind sickeningly. 'I'm going to be dragged off and eaten by this thing and Ken doesn't believe me!' Reaching over the snout with her free arm, she clasped the fingers of her left hand protruding out of the far side of its jaws, and locked her arms together. Again she pushed with her legs, staggering upright. Breaking the surface, she screamed, 'Crocodile!'

Ken froze. Sandy stood in waist-deep water, straining to hold up the great, ugly green head, its frightful jaws clamped around her left arm. In a heartbeat she was gone.

Ken dived into the churning water, reaching her as she emerged spluttering, 'It's got my arm!' Getting behind her, he grabbed her shoulders. Then he began pulling her backwards towards the bank, reassuring her, 'Hang on, Sandy.'

Suddenly, the water stilled. Ken knew crocodiles rarely give up their prey. The reptiles kill more than 400 people a year in such watery ambushes.

Ken's hand grazed something underwater. A chill ran up his spine as he realised it was the crocodile's snout. He fingered rows of frightful teeth clamping Sandy's wrist. 'Oh my God, it's still got her.'

Desperately, he tried to prise the jaws apart, but it was as if they were welded shut. Without warning, the crocodile exploded into a frenzied roll, jerking Sandy away. Ken lunged for her waist and held on tight.

'If I don't let go, it will rip her arm off.' Reluctantly he released her and watched her corkscrew underwater, a blur of honey-blonde hair and pale face entwined around the thrashing animal. He hovered over her spinning body, feeling helpless against the overwhelming strength of this monster. How do you fight a crocodile with your bare hands?

'I can't die like this'

The sudden, wrenching torque snapped the bones in Sandy's upper arm like twigs. Anger at the brute ripping her body apart welled up through her fear and pain, and with it came a fierce determination to survive. 'It can have my arm,' she resolved, 'but not my life. I can't die like this!' Quick thinking and a cool head had got Sandy out of tough situations before. Once, in Mali with the Peace Corps, she was attacked by killer bees, and narrowly escaped injury by jumping into a ditch and pulling her jacket over her head. Now she struggled to remain calm. 'What do I know about crocodiles?' A scene from the movie *Crocodile Dundee* flashed before her.

River scene *The rock-strewn waters of the Epulu river, in the Ituri Forest region of northern Congo, look peaceful enough, but dangers can lurk beneath the surface.*

The perfect predator

IT WAS A NILE CROCODILE (*Crocodylus niloticus*) that so nearly took Sandy Rossi's life. Along with the salt-water crocodile, it is the most dangerous of the species. It has between 60 and 72 teeth, and if one is lost another will grow. The teeth have a highly sensitive nervous system, which, triggered by an object entering the mouth, signals to the jaws to snap shut – its jaw strength is up to 30 times that of the most tenacious large dog. Curiously, though, the opposing muscles are so weak that it would take only the pressure of two fingers to prevent it from opening its mouth. With its long snout, yawning gape, powerful claws, and the ability to lie with its eyes above water, combined with a fast turn of speed over short distances, the Nile crocodile is perfectly adapted for ambush predation.

It is capable of taking almost any animal within attacking range, although it will tend to avoid other large predators such as big cats. Its sights are usually set on prey such as wildebeest, zebras, warthogs, antelopes, goats, sheep and cattle.

As Sandy knew, a crocodile's gambit is to grab a mammal from the water's edge, and to drag it down to drown it. Because it cannot chew, the crocodile clamps its jaws and spins its body to rip off large chunks of flesh. When sharing prey, crocodiles may use each other as they bite and twist in what is known as the 'death roll'. In a similar way, they may use branches or stones to secure their quarry.

The oldest animals on earth, pre-dating the dinosaurs, crocodiles have changed little over 65 million years, yet they are the most advanced of all reptiles, having a four-chambered heart, a diaphragm and a cerebral cortex. They can live for 100 years, although life expectancy is generally closer to 70.

An ability to slow their metabolism means crocodiles can go long periods without food. They survive well even with a missing limb, and their immunity to infection has led to hopes that crocodile blood might be used to fight infections in people.

The Nile crocodile is today an endangered species, due to the destruction of its habitats and the value of its skin for leather.

Crocs drown their prey in a death roll, Mick Dundee had said. It's not just trying to drag me off, Sandy now realised. It's trying to drown me.

Abruptly, the spinning ceased. The reptile lay motionless, holding her underwater. Planting her feet on the bottom, she pushed to the surface.

'Hang on,' Ken encouraged, as her head surfaced and she filled her lungs. 'We'll get you away from this thing.'

The vicious spinning left her disoriented and sickened. She recalled hearing that punching predators on the nose made them let go. She rained blows on the beast's snout with her free arm.

Ken, probing beneath the water, located the crocodile's bony eye sockets. He gouged hard with his thumbs, but they just bent back against a triple layer of impenetrable, leathery eyelids. Cursing, he tore at the great reptile's throat with both hands. The beast never flinched.

By now, the crocodile had drawn them around 8m (25ft) from the river bank into the strong current. Already on tiptoe, Sandy could barely get her face above water.

Ken was afraid of ripping Sandy's arm off if he pulled on her, so he seized the reptile's head and hauled for dear life, towing the crocodile towards the bank. Sandy helped as best she could, trying to ignore the crushing pain in her arm. Pure defiance burned in her blue eyes. 'We're going to beat this thing!' she yelled.

Ken pounded the beast with short jabbing rights, but it was like punching the front of a tank. Sandy's face was pale, contorted in pain, but Ken saw her jaw set in grim determination. 'She's counting on me. I can't let her down,' he thought.

Panting with exertion, inch by inch, together they gained a foot, then a few more. When they reached waist-deep water, the bank was tantalisingly near. Ken looked over his shoulder. Just a bit further.

Whoosh! The crocodile snapped into another death roll, batting Ken aside.

Sandy gritted her teeth as she went under. 'I'll tuck and roll with it, then, when it stops, I won't be dead.' She feared drowning more than she feared the crocodile. With her good arm she tried to protect her head from the big rocks littering the river bottom. 'One, two … ' she counted the rolls … 'three, four … ride it out then get air … five, six, seven … stopped!'

Ken hauled her up. He glanced over his shoulder at the river bank, his heart sinking; they were chest-deep again. It would be easy for the crocodile to sweep them out into midstream.

Frantically, he and Sandy heaved for shore. They worked in a metre or two. Then the crocodile spun wildly again.

This time Sandy managed to fill her lungs before being dragged under. She focused on counting rolls. 'Two … five … eight … Sweet Jesus, help me, it isn't going to stop,' she prayed. At ten rolls the crocodile finally ceased and lay still.

Lungs bursting, she fumbled for the river bottom with her feet. Nothing. She flailed out in every direction in the murky water. Nauseated and disoriented, she couldn't tell up from down. A stream of air bubbles trickled past her face. Follow them up. She moved towards a pale glimmer.

A watery image of Ken's face appeared above her; she reached for it, but the crocodile held her in deep water now. She never knew it was possible to hold her breath so long. Scissor-kicking, she lunged for Ken with her right hand, catching his wrist. She clawed her way up his bicep, then his shoulder, heaving with all her remaining strength as he pulled her to him.

Her face broke the surface, mouth wide, sucking great, sobbing breaths. With his own 6ft 2in frame neck-deep, Ken knew Sandy could no longer touch the bottom.

Not once had the great reptile surfaced. There was no need; it could stay submerged for up to an hour while its victim drowned. The brute's walnut-sized brain knew nothing of giving in. Greater resistance prompted

Sandy's saviour *Sandy (left) with the man who battled the crocodile to save her life, Ken Cochrane.*

ever more violent and aggressive attack. When a crocodile, the closest living reptilian relative of the dinosaur, has prey in its jaws, no creature on Earth can make it release its death grip.

The beast snapped into another series of rolls. In deeper water now there was no resisting the current as they spiralled downstream around a bend.

After the bend the water became shallower. Ken now stood thigh-deep, braced against a flood-gauge pole, wrestling the crocodile's head.

Growing even more frenzied, the creature twirled Sandy with such fury she smashed into the flood gauge, snapping it in half. The broken point speared through her left shoulder, driving deep into her ribcage and narrowly missing her lungs. Stabbing pain shot through her. 'If you black out, you'll die,' she thought, fighting for consciousness.

The creature rose out of the water, swinging its huge head back and forth. It opened its jaws wide and gulped down Sandy's forearm. Then, with its cold reptilian eyes locked on Sandy, it slithered backwards into the river.

Ken grabbed her waist, heaving backwards for shore like a man possessed. With no thought now of saving her arm, he was locked in a macabre tug of war with the crocodile for Sandy's life. Heels dug into the mud, he strained against the monster as it lashed its great tail, its flailing razor-sharp claws slashing his legs, neither man nor beast giving an inch.

Sandy steeled herself and pulled as hard as she could, her legs kicking for the beach. Backs to the shore, legs hammering into the mud, they suddenly rocketed out of the water and sprawled onto land. Dazed, they lay with chests heaving. In the dim light, Ken looked down and saw a bloody, chewed stump of bone and muscle where Sandy's left forearm had been; what was left of her hand dangled by a few strands of sinew and skin. The ferocity of the attack had rammed her elbow and broken upper-arm bones into her shoulder, swelling her upper arm to three times its normal size.

The creature rose out of the water, swinging its huge head back and forth. It opened its jaws wide and gulped down Sandy's forearm. Then, with its cold reptilian eyes locked on Sandy, it slithered backwards into the river.

They were only a foot from the water's edge, but before Ken could move Sandy he had to apply a tourniquet. Otherwise she'd bleed to death. Using a T-shirt, he tied the tourniquet tight around Sandy's arm, tucking what remained of her left hand against the pressure point.

Together, they ran up the embankment. At the crest, relief flooded over Sandy. 'It can't get me now.'

Road to recovery

Sandy's recovery was not assured. She had lost a lot of blood. At 6.50 that evening, Ken drove her to the village clinic, where a proper tourniquet was attached, and she was given antibiotics. It was 8pm before Sandy was placed on a mattress in a four-wheel drive, and Ken set off across the rough jungle roads.

They arrived at the field hospital 3 hours later, where a Dutch doctor amputated the remains of Sandy's hand. The next day she was flown to

Nairobi for more expert care, but the doctors there advised only rest, large doses of antibiotics and a transfusion to boost her strength before she returned to the United States for specialist surgery. Ken had the same blood type, so he donated some blood for Sandy.

'Ken risked his life to save mine,' Sandy said. 'He's like a big brother to me.'

But Ken had the last words: 'Sandy's alive because she refused to give up.'

Sandy returned to the United States, where surgeons took muscle from her back and skin grafts from her leg to fashion tissue around the raw bone to support a prosthesis. ■

Where are they now?

'IT COULD HAVE BEEN a lot worse,' says Sandy, reflecting on her life-or-death struggle with the crocodile. 'He got my arm. I got my life. It was an OK trade.' Emotionally as well as physically, she has made an extraordinary recovery, taking a view that to mope around would be 'sort of stupid'.

Her upper arm had sustained multiple fractures. It took 18 months to heal, in the course of which she developed all kinds of coping strategies, ways of doing things one-handed, so she has not felt great need of a prosthesis, and in no way has her perceived disability held her back. She has been married since 1997 to Jeffrey (seen below holding a pumpkin), and she works from their home in South Dakota, making elevation maps for the US Geological Survey.

The couple have two children, Dominic, 10, bottom right, and Josie, 8, on the left. 'They're just as smart as whips,' she says, 'they keep me going. Every so often, it's "How come *we* have to help with the laundry, and our friends don't?" I'm always very blunt. I say, "Look, I'm sorry you're stuck with a mom with one hand. Now get over it!"' In more ways than one she is an object of curiosity. 'Their friends know me as "the crazy crocodile lady".'

After her story was first told in *Reader's Digest*, she had a couple of amusing encounters. In New York, on a bus in the Bronx, a man looked up from his magazine, blinked at her and told her, 'I know you. I just read about you!' More amazingly, she relates, 'I was on the beach at Mombasa, Kenya, a couple of years after the attack, and this guy was reading something. He happened to look up as I walked by. Looked down. Looked up. Looked down. Looked up. And not only was he reading about me in *Reader's Digest*, but it was the Swedish edition. It was really hilarious.'

Sandy has stayed in contact with Ken, and feels abiding gratitude to him. 'He was amazing. I absolutely wouldn't be here without him. I don't think he's ever got the right kind of kudos for what he did.'

If there is one thing she has lost, she says, it is spontaneity. 'You can't just dash out the door, you have to stop and think, "Do I need anything? Am I going to have to do things differently?"' Still, she refuses to let it get her down. 'The way I always look at it, there is no point in getting out of the water, just to be depressed about your life. You can either be a victim or a survivor, and surviving is about living.'

IN 1914, ERNEST SHACKLETON set out to traverse Antarctica. But his ship, *Endurance*, became trapped in thickening pack ice, the crew marooned on an ice floe. When the floe broke up, the men had no choice but to take to the lifeboats. After five harrowing days at sea, they reached remote Elephant Island. How would they ever be found?

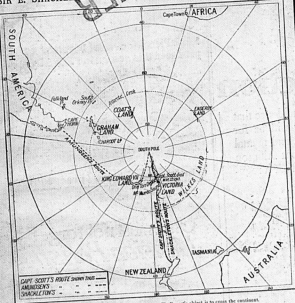

THE DAILY MIRROR, Tuesday, December 30, 1913.

Boxing as a Moral Training for Boys.

The Daily Mirror
THE MORNING JOURNAL WITH THE SECOND LARGEST NET SALE.

No. 3,177.   Registered at the G.P.O. as a Newspaper.   TUESDAY, DECEMBER 30, 1913.   One Halfpenny.

SIR E. SHACKLETON TO LEAD A BRITISH ANTARCTIC EXPEDITION FROM SEA TO SEA

Sir Ernest Shackleton.—(Swaine.)

Map showing routes of previous expeditions. Sir Ernest's object is to cross the continent.

CAPT. SCOTT'S ROUTE SHOWN THUS
AMUNDSEN'S
SHACKLETON'S

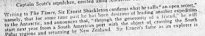

Captain Scott's sepulchre, erected amid Antarctic wastes. It marks the spot where the bodies were found.

Captain R. F. Scott.—(Thomson.)

Writing to *The Times*, Sir Ernest Shackleton confirms what he calls "an open secret," namely, that for some time past he has been desirous of leading another expedition to the Antarctic, and announces that, "through the generosity of a friend," he will start next year from a South American port with the object of crossing the South Polar regions and returning by New Zealand. Sir Ernest's fame as an explorer is world-wide. Twice he has served on South Polar expeditions, once in 19— the late Captain Scott, and once when he commanded the expedition which the Nimrod in 1907 and returned in 1909, after he had himself penetrated ninety-seven miles of the Pole. Sir Ernest was born at Kilkee in 187— created a knight in 1909.

HEROES OF THE
ANTARCTIC

An examination of our stores showed that we had rations to last five weeks. I decided that the party must be limited to one hot meal a day.

There was no chance of any search being made for us on Elephant Island. The nearest port was Stanley, in the Falklands, 870km (540 miles) away, but we could scarcely hope to beat up against the prevailing northwesterly wind in a frail boat with a small sail area. South Georgia was 1,290km (800 miles) away, but lay in the area of the west winds, and I could count on finding whalers at the whaling stations on the east coast. A boat party might make the voyage and be back with relief within a month, provided that the boat survive the great seas.

The ocean south of Cape Horn in mid May is known to be the most storm-swept area of water in the world. The weather then is unsettled, the gales almost unceasing. We had to face these conditions in a small and weather-beaten boat. I told Frank Wild, the Second in Command, that he would have to stay behind to hold the party together. Skipper Frank Worsley I would take with me, for I had a very high opinion of his navigation. Four others would be required. Second Officer Tom Crean begged to come. I promised to take him. I called the men together, explained my plan, and asked for volunteers. I finally selected Harry McNeish, the carpenter, and able seamen Timothy McCarthy and John Vincent.

The decision made, I walked through the blizzard with Worsley to examine the *James Caird*, the 6m (20ft) ship's whaler. She appeared to have shrunk when I viewed her in the light of our new undertaking. I called McCarthy and asked him to make her more seaworthy. But the gale was more severe than ever. We could not proceed with our preparations that day. The tents were suffering in the wind but at dark, about 5pm, we all turned in, after a supper consisting of a pannikin[1] of hot milk, one of our precious biscuits, and a cold penguin leg each.

The gale was stronger than ever the following morning (April 20). No work could be done. Blizzard and snow, snow and blizzard, sudden lulls and fierce returns. During the lulls we could see on the horizon bergs of all shapes and sizes driving along before the gale, and the sinister appearance of the swift moving masses made us thankful that, instead of battling with the storm amid the ice, we were required only to face the drift from the glaciers and inland heights. The gusts might knock us off our feet, but at least we fell on solid ground.

There was a lull in the bad weather on April 21, and the carpenter started to collect material for the decking of the *James Caird*. He fitted the mast of one of the other ship's boats, the *Stancomb-Wills*, inside the *James Caird*, with the object of preventing our boat buckling in the heavy seas. He had not sufficient wood to provide a deck, but by using the sledge runners

Battling the ice *The crew of* Endurance *attempted to cut away the ice that formed round the ship in the Weddell Sea, but it was to no avail, and she was eventually crushed. The men were then forced to take to the seas in the ship's three on-board vessels: the* James Caird, *the* Stancomb-Wills *and the* Dudley Docker.

---

1 Pannikin A small metal cup.

and box lids he made a framework extending from the forecastle[2] aft to a well. It provided a base for a canvas covering.

We set aside stores for the boat journey and chose essential equipment from the scanty stock at our disposal. Two 10 gallon casks had to be filled with water melted from ice collected at the foot of the glacier.

On April 23, we could see a line of pack ice, 8km (5 miles) out. Winter was advancing, and soon the pack might close round the island and stay our departure. I climbed to the summit of the seaward rocks and examined the ice. The belt of pack appeared sufficiently broken for our purposes, and I decided that, unless conditions forbade it, we would start out next morning.

We turned out at dawn, launched the *Stancomb-Wills* and loaded her with stores, gear and ballast, which would be transferred to the *James Caird* when the heavier boat had been launched. The ballast consisted of bags made from blankets filled with sand. In addition, we had a number of boulders and about 115kg (250lb) of ice, which would supplement our casks of water.

The swell made things difficult. Many of us got wet to the waist dragging the boat out. The *James Caird* was soon clear of the breakers. The *Stancomb-Wills* came alongside, transferred her load, and went back to the shore for more. The water casks were towed behind the *Stancomb-Wills* on this journey, and the swell drove the boat onto the rocks. One of the casks was slightly stove in. Sea water entered it and the contents were now brackish.

By midday the *James Caird* was ready. I said goodbye to the men. Then, setting our jib, we cut the painter[3] and moved away. The men staying behind waved to us and gave three cheers.

I had all sails set, and the wind took us rapidly to the line of the pack. As we entered it I stood with arms round the mast, directing the steering, to avoid the great lumps of ice that were flung about in the heave of the sea. The pack thickened and we were forced to turn east, towards a gap I had seen in the morning from the high ground. At four in the afternoon we found the channel. Dropping sail, we rowed through, and by 5.30pm we were clear of the pack with open water before us. We passed one more piece of ice in the darkness an hour later, but the pack lay behind, and with a fair wind swelling our sails we steered our little craft through the night.

The swell was very heavy, and when the time came for our evening meal we found great difficulty in keeping the Primus lamp alight and preventing the hoosh[4] splashing out of the pot. The pot had

Crushed *The ship's dogs look on as the ice becomes ever more tightly packed around* Endurance.

---

2 **Forecastle** The forward part of a ship, where the crew have their quarters.
3 **Painter** A rope attached to the bow of a ship, so it can be tied or towed.
4 **Hoosh** A thick stew made from pemmican (dried meat/fat).

to be lifted whenever the movement of the boat threatened to cause a disaster. The lamp had to be protected from water, for sprays were coming over the bows and our flimsy decking was by no means watertight. All these operations were conducted in the confined space under the decking, where the men lay or knelt and adjusted themselves as best they could to the angles of our cases and ballast. It was uncomfortable, but without the decking we could not have used the cooker at all.

I decided to run north for two days while the wind held before turning east for South Georgia. We took 2 hourly spells at the tiller. The men not on watch crawled into the sodden sleeping bags but there was no comfort. The bags and cases seemed to be alive in the unfailing knack of presenting their most uncomfortable angles to our rest-seeking bodies. Cramped in our narrow quarters and continually wet by the spray, we suffered severely from cold.

Freezing breath

We made progress, but there were times when we lay hove to[5], drifting across the storm-whitened seas watching the uprearing masses of water, flung to and fro. Deep seemed the valleys when we lay between the reeling seas. High were the hills when we perched momentarily on the top of giant combers[6]. So small was our boat and so great were the seas that often our sail flapped idly in the calm between the crests of two waves. Then we would climb the next slope and catch the full fury of the gale where the whiteness of the breaking water surged around us.

The wind worked into a gale on the third day out. The increasing seas discovered the weaknesses of our decking. The continuous blows shifted the box lids and sledge runners so that the canvas sagged and accumulated water. Then icy trickles poured into the boat. The nails that the carpenter had extracted from cases at Elephant Island and used to fasten the battens were too short to make firm the decking. Water entered the boat at a dozen points. Much baling was necessary, and nothing could prevent our gear from becoming sodden. There were no dry places, and at last we simply covered our heads with our Burberrys[7] and endured the all-pervading water. There was one fairly dry spot under the solid original decking at the bows, and we managed to protect some of our biscuit from salt water; but I do not think any of us got the taste of salt out of our mouths during the voyage.

The order of the watch was 4 hours on and 4 off, three men to the watch. One man had the tiller ropes, the second attended to the sail, and the third baled. While a new watch was shivering in the wind and spray, the men who had been relieved groped among the soaked sleeping bags and tried to steal a little of the warmth created by the last occupants. But the boulders that we had taken aboard for ballast had to be shifted continually in order to trim the boat. The moving of the boulders was weary and painful work. Another of our troubles was the chafing of our legs by wet clothes, which had not been changed for seven months. The

5 **Hove to** Term used to describe a boat that has turned into the wind and stopped.
6 **Comber** A long, curling wave.
7 **Burberrys** Raincoats.

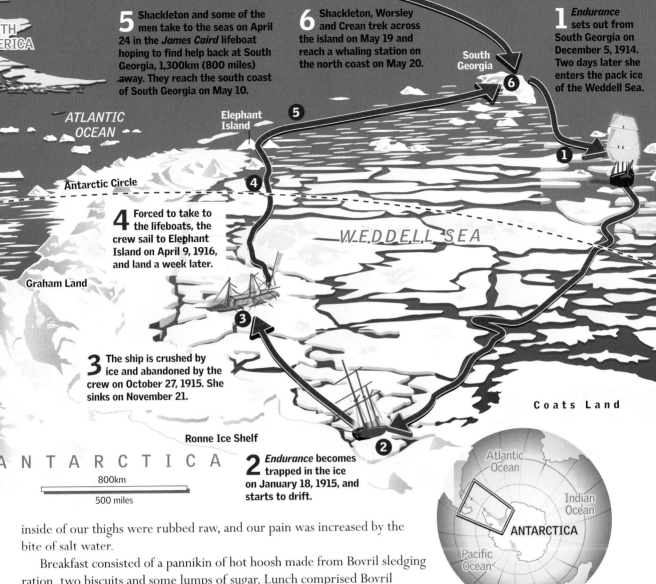

5 Shackleton and some of the men take to the seas on April 24 in the *James Caird* lifeboat hoping to find help back at South Georgia, 1,300km (800 miles) away. They reach the south coast of South Georgia on May 10.

6 Shackleton, Worsley and Crean trek across the island on May 19 and reach a whaling station on the north coast on May 20.

1 *Endurance* sets out from South Georgia on December 5, 1914. Two days later she enters the pack ice of the Weddell Sea.

South Georgia

ATLANTIC OCEAN

Elephant Island

Antarctic Circle

4 Forced to take to the lifeboats, the crew sail to Elephant Island on April 9, 1916, and land a week later.

WEDDELL SEA

Graham Land

3 The ship is crushed by ice and abandoned by the crew on October 27, 1915. She sinks on November 21.

Coats Land

Ronne Ice Shelf

A N T A R C T I C A

2 *Endurance* becomes trapped in the ice on January 18, 1915, and starts to drift.

800km

500 miles

Atlantic Ocean

Indian Ocean

ANTARCTICA

Pacific Ocean

inside of our thighs were rubbed raw, and our pain was increased by the bite of salt water.

Breakfast consisted of a pannikin of hot hoosh made from Bovril sledging ration, two biscuits and some lumps of sugar. Lunch comprised Bovril sledging ration, eaten raw, and a pannikin of hot milk. Tea was the same.

A severe southwesterly gale on the fourth day out forced us to heave to. On the fifth day the gale was so fierce we were compelled to put out a sea anchor to keep the *James Caird*'s head up to the sea. Even then the crests of the waves often would curl right over us and we shipped a great deal of water, which necessitated unceasing baling. Looking out abeam[8], we would see a hollow like a tunnel as the crest of a big wave toppled. A thousand times it appeared as though the *James Caird* must be engulfed. The southwesterly gale had its birthplace above the Antarctic continent, and its freezing breath lowered the temperature towards zero. The sprays froze upon the boat and gave bows, sides and decking a coat of mail. We could not allow the load of ice to grow, and we crawled about, chipping at it with the available tools.

When daylight came on the sixth day we saw that the *James Caird* was not rising to the oncoming seas. The weight of the ice that had formed upon

Amazing journey

Ernest Shackleton may have failed completely in his mission to cross the Antarctic, but as the First World War raged on other continents he and his men achieved heroic status by surviving in the coldest of conditions with but three lifeboats and limited supplies between them. The only casualty was their ship, the Norwegian-built *Endurance*, smashed by the unforgiving ice.

---

8 Abeam At right angles from the centre of a ship.

her during the night was having its effect, and she was becoming more like a log than a boat. We broke away the spare oars and threw them overboard. Two of the sleeping bags went over the side. We now had four bags. The reduction of weight relieved the boat, and vigorous scraping did more.

We suffered severely from the cold, for, though the temperature was rising, our vitality was declining owing to shortage of food, exposure and the necessity of maintaining our cramped positions day and night. I found it was necessary to prepare hot milk for all hands during the night, in order to sustain life till dawn. One of the memories from those days is of Crean singing at the tiller. He always sang while steering, and nobody ever discovered what the song was. It was devoid of tune and as monotonous as the chanting of a Buddhist monk; yet somehow it was cheerful.

On the tenth night Worsley could not straighten his body after his spell at the tiller. He was thoroughly cramped, and we had to drag him beneath the decking and massage him before he could unbend himself and get into a sleeping bag. A hard gale came up on the eleventh day (May 5). Snow squalls added to the discomfort produced by a tremendous cross-sea[9]. At midnight I was at the tiller and noticed a line of clear sky. I called to the others that the sky was clearing, then realised that what I had seen was not a rift in the clouds but the white crest of an enormous wave.

Tough guys *Skipper Frank Worsley (left), a New Zealander, and the Irish Second Officer Tom Crean (right) were two of the men Shackleton selected to strike out with him from Elephant Island on the* James Caird. *They were then the two he chose to make the final trek across South Georgia.*

During 26 years' experience of the ocean I had not encountered a wave so gigantic. It was a mighty upheaval of the ocean, a thing apart from the big white-capped seas that had been our enemies for many days.

I shouted, 'For God's sake, hold on! It's got us!' White surged the foam of the breaking sea around us. We felt our boat lifted and flung like a cork in breaking surf. We were in a seething chaos of tortured water; but somehow the boat lived through it, half full of water, sagging to the dead weight and shuddering under the blow. We baled with the energy of men fighting for life, and after 10 minutes felt the boat renew her life beneath us. She floated again and ceased to lurch drunkenly.

All our gear was thoroughly wet again. Not until 3am, when we were chilled to the limit of endurance, did we manage to get the stove alight and make ourselves hot drinks. Vincent had for the past week ceased to be an active member of the crew. I could not account for his collapse. Physically, he was one of the strongest men in the boat. Our supply of water was running low. The hot drink at night was essential, but the daily allowance of water had to be cut to half a pint a man. Our thirst was increased by the fact we were now using the brackish water in the cask that had been slightly stove in when the boat was being loaded.

9 Cross-sea A sea with two wave systems, with the waves running in contrary directions.

Craving water

Thirst possessed us. Lack of water is the most severe privation that men can be condemned to, and we found the salt water in our clothing and the salt spray that lashed our faces made our thirst grow to a burning pain.

May 6 and the following day passed in a sort of nightmare. Our mouths were dry and our tongues swollen. The wind was strong and the heavy sea forced us to navigate carefully, but any thought of our peril from the waves was buried beneath the consciousness of our raging thirst. On the morning of May 8 we saw two shags on a mass of kelp, and at 12.30pm, through a rift in the clouds, McCarthy caught a glimpse of the black cliffs of South Georgia, 14 days after our departure from Elephant Island.

Rollers showed the presence of reefs along the coast. The rocks were close to the surface, and over them the great waves broke, swirling viciously and spouting 12m (40ft) into the air. The rocky coast descended sheer to the sea. To have attempted landing would have been suicidal. There was nothing for it but to haul off till the following morning.

At 5am the wind increased to one of the worst hurricanes any of us had experienced. A great cross-sea was running, and the wind shrieked as it tore the tops off the waves and converted the whole seascape into a haze of driving spray. The *James Caird* was bumping heavily, and the water was pouring in everywhere. Our thirst was forgotten in the realisation of our imminent danger, as we baled unceasingly. The afternoon wore away as we edged down the coast, with the thunder of breakers in our ears.

Just after 6pm, in the dark, things changed for the best. The wind shifted. As soon as the gale eased, the pin that locked the mast to the thwart[10] fell out. It must have been on the point of doing this throughout the hurricane; and if it had gone, nothing could have saved us; the mast would have snapped like a carrot.

We stood offshore, tired to the point of apathy. Our water had long been finished. The pangs of thirst attacked us with redoubled intensity, and I felt that we must land the following day at almost any hazard. When May 10 dawned there was practically no wind, but a high cross-sea. We sighted an indentation, which I thought must be King Haakon Bay, and about noon we sighted a line of jagged reef that seemed to bar the entrance to the bay. A gap in the reef appeared, and we made for it, but the wind shifted and we could not approach it directly. That afternoon we bore up, tacking five times in the strong wind. The last tack enabled us to get through, and at last we were in the bay. Dusk was approaching. A small cove,

---

10 Thwart Bench seat that runs the width of a boat.

Precise instructions *Shackleton gave the order to abandon ship on October 27, 1915. The men had to made camp on dangerous ice, prompting Shackleton to issue detailed instructions (below) on what each was to do in the event of the ice breaking. A set of instructions was pinned to each tent at the camp, which they called Ocean Camp.*

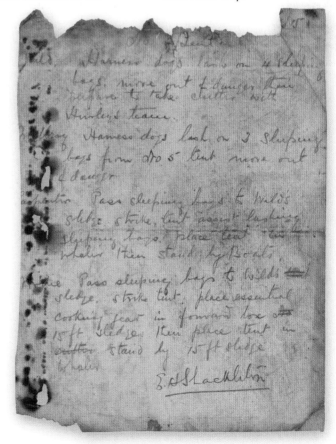

with a boulder-strewn beach guarded by a reef, made a break in the cliffs on the south side of the bay, and we turned in that direction. I stood in the bows directing the steering as we ran through the kelp and made the passage of the reef. The entrance was so narrow that we had to take in the oars, and the swell was piling itself right over the reef into the cove; but in a minute we were inside and the *James Caird* touched the beach.

Vital kit for the Antarctic

SHACKLETON'S CREW WAS KITTED OUT for its Antarctic expedition by the firm of Burberry in London. The same outfitters provided Scott and Amundsen with their cold-weather gear. Standard Antarctic kit at that time consisted mostly of woollen garments: Jaeger woollen long johns and vest, a sweater, double-thickness woollen trousers, wool socks, wool muffler, wool balaclava.

On top, every man wore Burberry's patented cotton-gabardine coat – a voluminous hooded garment designed to keep out the freezing wind. This apparel would have done the main job of insulating the explorers and protecting them from the driving snow, but a problem arose when their clothes soaked up sweat as the men worked, quickly becoming damp. Wool, once wet, is scratchy,

loses its insulating properties and is hard to dry. In a half-open boat, soaked to the skin with freezing sea water, Shackleton and his men would have suffered agonies of discomfort.

On their feet, the men of the *Endurance* wore either military-style leather hobnail boots or 'finnesko' ('Finnish shoes'). These were soft high boots made of reindeer fur that, for extra insulation, could be stuffed with the local dry straw-like grass. Modern Antarctic explorers tend to favour US Army 'bunny boots'. These look like snow-white Dr Martens, and are said to insulate the feet when it is as cold as -40 or even -60°C (-40 to -76°F).

BEST FOOT FORWARD A boot (left) most likely worn by James Mann Wordie, the ship's geologist. Boots were just part of the extreme weather kit issued to the crew (below).

I sprang ashore and climbed some rocks with a line. A slip on the wet rocks 6m (20ft) up nearly closed my part of the story just when we were achieving safety. A jagged piece of rock held me and at the same time bruised me sorely. However, I made fast the line, and in a few minutes we were all safe on the beach. We heard a gurgling sound and, peering around, found a stream of fresh water. A moment later we were down on our knees drinking the pure ice-cold water in long draughts that put new life into us.

We carried the stores and gear above the high water mark and threw the ballast out of the boat. We attempted to pull the boat up the beach, and discovered how weak we had become. It would be necessary to have food and rest before we beached the boat. We set a watch to fend the *James Caird* off the rocks of the beach. To the left of the cove, I had noticed a little cave as we were running in. We carried the sleeping bags round and found a hollow in the rock-face. There we prepared a hot meal, and when the food was finished I ordered the men to turn in. I took the first watch beside the *James Caird*.

I found a flat rock for my feet, which were in a bad way owing to cold, wetness and lack of exercise in the boat, and laboured to keep the *James Caird* clear of the beach. Occasionally I had to rush into the seething water. After several hours I found my desire for sleep irresistible and called Crean. I could hear him groaning as he stumbled over the sharp rocks on his way down the beach. I arranged for 1 hour watches during the remainder of the night and then took Crean's place among the sleeping men.

Sustenance at last

After sunrise we set about getting the boat ashore, first bracing ourselves for the task with another meal. Inch by inch we dragged the *James Caird* above the high water mark. King Haakon Bay is a 13km (8 mile) sound with sides formed by steep mountains furrowed by glaciers. These barred our way inland from the cove. We must sail to the head of the sound where snow slopes gave us hope that an overland journey could begin.

Crean and I climbed the tussock slope behind the beach. We found the nests of albatrosses, and, to our delight, the nests contained young birds. Our most pressing anxiety was a shortage of fuel for the cooker. We had rations for ten more days and we knew now that we could get birds for food. During the morning we started a fire in the cave with wood from the topsides of the boat. We estimated that the young albatrosses weighed at least 3kg (6lb) each when cleaned and dressed for the pot. Four birds went into the pot for six men, with a Bovril ration for thickening. The flesh was white and succulent, and the bones, not fully formed, melted in our mouths. When we had eaten, we dried our tobacco in the embers and smoked contentedly. We made an attempt to dry our clothes, which were soaked with salt water, but did not meet with much success.

The condition of the party generally, and particularly of McNeish and Vincent, would prevent us putting to sea again except under dire necessity. We were still 240km (150 miles) away from Stromness Whaling Station by sea. The alternative was to attempt the crossing of the island. Several days must elapse before our strength would be sufficiently recovered to allow us to row or sail to the head of the bay.

A slip on the wet rocks 20ft up nearly closed my part of the story just when we were achieving safety. A jagged piece of rock held me and at the same time bruised me sorely.

To the whaling station

On May 15 we loaded the boat and sailed up the bay, and ran the boat ashore on a beach. There were hundreds of sea elephants[11] lying about. A cold, drizzling rain was falling. We hauled the *James Caird* above high water mark and turned her over for shelter. Soon we had converted her into a cabin, turfing it round with tussocks. A sea elephant provided us with fuel and meat, and that evening found a fairly contented party.

Our path towards the whaling stations led up a snow slope that appeared to lead to a pass in the great Allardyce Range. An ice sheet covered most of the interior, filling the valleys and disguising the configuration of the land, which, indeed, showed only in rocky ridges and peaks. I planned to climb to the pass and then be guided by the configuration of the country in the selection of a route to where the whaling stations were in the bays Leith, Husvik and Stromness. Worsley reckoned from the chart that the distance from our camp to Husvik was 27km (17 miles), but we could not expect to follow a direct line.

Worsley and Crean were coming with me, and we decided to leave the sleeping bags behind and make the journey in light marching order. We would take three days' provisions, the Primus lamp, the small cooker, the carpenter's adze (for use as an ice axe), the 15m (50ft) rope and a box of matches. I was unfortunate as regards footwear, as I had given away my heavy boots on the floe, and had now a comparatively light pair in poor condition. The carpenter put several screws from the *James Caird* in the soles to provide a grip on the ice.

We turned out at 2am on May 19. The full moon was shining in a practically cloudless sky. We said goodbye and soon were ascending a snow

---

11 Sea elephants Elephant seals.

Rescue mission *The 22 men left behind wave off the* James Caird *and her six-man crew as she leaves Elephant Island. Shackleton's aim was to bring back help for the men before their rations ran out.*

slope. We sank over our ankles and progress was slow. After 2 hours' climbing we were 760m (2,500ft) above sea level. As the ridges drew nearer, moonlight showed us that the interior was broken tremendously. High peaks, impassable cliffs, steep snow slopes and sharply descending glaciers were prominent in all directions. I had hoped to get a view of the country ahead from the top of the slope, but as the surface became more level, thick fog drifted down. We roped ourselves together as a precaution against holes, crevasses and precipices and tramped through the fog for 2 hours.

As daylight came, the fog thinned, and from about 900m (3,000ft) we looked down on what seemed to be a frozen lake with its farther shores obscured by fog. I decided to go down, since the lake lay on our course. When the fog lifted, we saw that our lake stretched to the horizon, and realised we were looking upon the open sea on the east coast of the island. Our chart was inaccurate. There was no way round the shoreline owing to steep cliffs and glaciers. There was nothing for it but to start up again.

We regained the ridge, struck southeast and plodded on towards another sharp ridge between two peaks. The slope became precipitous and it was necessary to cut steps. The adze proved excellent. I cut the last few steps and stood upon the razorback. I looked down a sheer precipice to a chaos of crumpled ice 460m (1,500ft) below. There was no way down.

To the northeast there appeared to be a snow slope that might give a path to the lower country, so we retraced our steps down the slope that had taken us 3 hours to climb. We were now feeling the strain of the unaccustomed marching. We had done little walking since January and our muscles were out of tune.

At the bottom we skirted the base of the mountain above us and once more started for the crest. After another weary climb we reached the top. The same precipice lay below. Looking back, we could see that a fog was rolling up behind us. The creeping grey clouds were a warning that we must get down to lower levels before becoming enveloped.

It was important for us to get down into the next valley before dark. We were now up 1,370m (4,500ft) and the night temperature at that elevation would be very low. We had no tent and no sleeping bags, and our clothes had endured much rough usage during the last ten months. Back we went, and after a detour we reached the top of another ridge in the fading light. After a glance over the top I turned to the two behind me and said, 'Come on, boys.'

Within a minute they stood beside me on the ice ridge. The surface fell away at a sharp incline in front of us, but it merged into a snow slope. We could not see the bottom owing to mist and bad light, and the possibility of the slope ending in a sheer fall occurred to us; but the fog that was creeping up behind allowed no time for hesitation. We descended slowly at first, cutting steps; then the surface became softer, indicating that the gradient was less severe, so we unroped and slid. When we stopped at the foot we found we had descended around 275m (900ft) in 2 minutes.

Improvised shelter *The men who stayed on Elephant Island lashed together the two remaining ship's boats, the* Stancomb-Wills *and the* Dudley Docker, *to form a shelter, which they called the 'Snuggery'.*

Journey's end *The former Stromness Whaling Station, in South Georgia, where Shackleton and his men landed after their arduous journey from Elephant Island.*

We had seen from the top that our course lay between two huge masses of crevasses, and we thought that the road ahead lay clear. This belief and the increasing cold made us abandon the idea of camping. We started up the long ascent. Night was upon us, and for an hour we plodded along in almost complete darkness, watching for crevasses. Then the moon rose and made a silver pathway for our feet. By midnight we were again at an elevation of 1,220m (4,000ft).

After we had descended about 90m (300ft) a thin wind attacked us. We had been on the march for more than 20 hours. Wisps of cloud warned us that wind and snow were likely. After 1am we cut a pit in the snow and started the Primus. Hot food gave us energy. Worsley and Crean sang their old songs. Laughter was in our hearts, though not on our parched and cracked lips.

We were up and away within half an hour, still downward to the coast. Our high hopes were soon shattered. Crevasses warned us that we were on another glacier. I knew there was no glacier in Stromness. Back we turned and tramped up the glacier again.

At 5am we were at the foot of the rocky spurs of the range. We were very tired, and the wind was chilling. We decided to get under the lee of a rock for a rest. The wind was bringing a little drift and the white dust lay on our clothes. Within a minute my companions were fast asleep. I realised it would be disastrous if we all slumbered together, for sleep under such conditions merges into death. After 5 minutes I shook them into consciousness, told them they had slept for half an hour, and gave the word for a fresh start. We

> **Hot food gave us energy.** Worsley and Crean sang their old songs. Laughter was in our hearts, though not on our parched and cracked lips.

were so stiff that for the first 275m (300yd) we marched with our knees bent. A jagged line of peaks with a gap like a broken tooth confronted us. Our course to Stromness lay across it. A very steep slope led up to the ridge and an icy wind burst through it.

We went through the gap at 6am. Husvik Harbour appeared ahead. Down we went. At 6.30 I thought I heard the sound of a steam whistle. I knew that the men at the whaling station would be called from their beds about then. I told the others, and we watched the chronometer for 7 o'clock, when the whalers would be summoned to work. To the minute the whistle came, borne clearly on the wind. It was the first sound created by outside human agency that had come to our ears since we left Stromness Bay in December 1914.

At 1.30pm we climbed round a final ridge and saw a whaling boat entering the bay, 760m (2,500ft) below. A few moments later, the masts of a sailing ship lying at the wharf came in sight. Minute figures moving to and fro caught our gaze, and then we saw the sheds and factory of Stromness Whaling Station. We paused and shook hands.

The sole pathway down was a channel cut by water running from the upland. Through icy water we followed this stream, wet to the waist, shivering, cold and tired. Presently we reached the top of a waterfall and discovered a drop of 9m (30ft) with impassable cliffs on both sides. We fastened our rope to a boulder. Then Worsley and I lowered Crean. I went next, sliding down the rope, and Worsley came last.

We set off towards the whaling station, now not more than 2.5km (1½ miles) distant. We tried to straighten ourselves up a bit. Our beards were long and our hair was matted. We were unwashed and the garments we had worn for a year without change were tattered and stained. When we came to the wharf, I asked a man if Mr Sorlle (the manager) was in the house.

Mr Sorlle came to the door and said, 'Well?'

'My name is Shackleton,' I said. ■

What happened next?

SHACKLETON AND HIS TWO COMPANIONS returned to civilisation, but civilisation at that moment was in tumult. The First World War was raging, and all three men swapped their explorer's kit for soldier's uniform. Shackleton, though in his 40s, volunteered for front-line duty in France. He was eventually commissioned to take part in the anti-Bolshevik intervention against Soviet Russia, and sailed to the Arctic city of Murmansk. Worsley saw service on 'Q-boats', decoy vessels designed to lure German U-boats to the surface, where they could be attacked. Crean was posted to the naval base at Chatham, in Kent, and had a quiet war.

Shackleton published his account of the *Endurance* expedition soon after the armistice in 1918, and earned a living as a public speaker. But he still had the lust to explore, and in 1921 he sailed south once again, intending to explore the fringes of the Antarctic landmass. But his constitution was weakened by years of privation. He died of a heart attack in South Georgia (before reaching Antarctica) and was buried there.

Shackleton had asked Tom Crean to come with him on that last expedition, but Crean declined. He had married

HERO'S MEMORIAL Shackleton (bottom left) died on reaching South Georgia during his last expedition in 1922. He was buried at Grytviken (above) on his wife's instructions.

in 1917, and gone back with his wife to Annascaul, in County Kerry, where he was born. He opened a pub called the South Pole Inn. There he lived out his days, pulling pints and saying nothing about his grand seaborne adventure. Crean died of appendicitis in 1938.

As for Worsley, he accepted Shackleton's invitation to Antarctica, and was with him when he died. At the age of 68, in 1940, Worsley saw action again while serving with the Red Cross in France and Norway. In 1941 he put his naval experience to good use clearing wrecks from the English Channel. He died in 1943.

Shackleton has had a strange posthumous career as a management guru. In 2001 a book called *Shackleton's Way: Leadership Lessons from the Great Antarctic Explorer* made a corporate parable of his exploits. But a truer assessment of his achievement was published in the *Buenos Aires Herald*, soon after the crew of the *Endurance* had been rescued: 'Had Shackleton lived in the days of the Vikings, the bards would have composed a saga to his praise, and would sing it by the side of roaring fires in the great halls of the mighty.'

EDWARD SAWYER WAS
a prisoner of war working
in Hiroshima's dockyards
on August 6, 1945. He lived
to give his own account of
that terrible day – the day
the first atomic bomb was
dropped on a city.

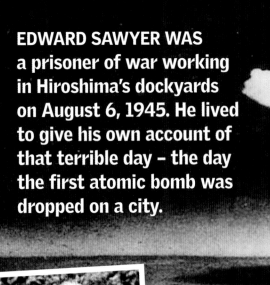

I SURVIVED HIROSHIMA

The door is kicked open and the guard shouts, '*Speedo! Tenko!*'
Then he runs the length of the wooden hut, hitting his stick against the 80
bunk beds. It is 6am and I am jarred back into the misery of another day
as a prisoner of war of the Japanese – 3½ years after my capture on the
Pacific island of Timor, where I was sergeant with an anti-aircraft battery.

Wearily, I lever myself onto an elbow, unroll the green drill trousers I have
used for a pillow and drag them over the long dingy underpants, then tuck in
the khaki shirt I have slept in to keep off the fleas. I roll up the strip of woven
straw matting that separates emaciated hips from the wooden planked bed.

Every day begins in the same way, and there is an apathetic acceptance
of the rude awakenings, the gnawing hunger, the disease and ill health,
even the beatings.

The morning air is fresh, the sky clear as the sun comes up behind
the hills that surround the camp. The Commandant comes out of the
administration building, salutes the Rising Sun flag hanging limp on the
pole above, then paces the assembled company's POWs – Americans,
Australians, British, Chinese, Dutch, Indians and Malays. With eyes front,
we are ordered to bow from the waist. He salutes, then walks up and down
the lines with his retinue and returns to the building.

Working party

We are issued with our midday meal – wooden boxes packed with brown
rice, a few soya beans and radishes and two slivers of sun-dried fish the
size of small sardines. Thus equipped, we set out – 20 men and two armed
guards to each open lorry – for a day's hard labour: in a coal mine, an iron
foundry, digging vegetables or unloading cargo on the docks.

For nearly 20 miles we bounce along potholed roads through the hills,
stopping to offload working parties, until we reach Hiroshima docks at the
delta of the Ota river.

I jump down and a Japanese *hancho* (foreman) points me to 5,000
tonnes of rusting freighter tied up at the wharf. I know it well. For the past
two days I have been unloading its sickly smelling cargo of brown sugar.
There are eight in our working party, four down below, four above storing
the bags in the adjacent warehouse. We toss to see who goes below to work
the first two loads. I lose and go on-board with Keith,
Bluey and Curly, all Australians.
I'm the only English POW
on the ship.

We climb down the long
metal ladder into the stifling
hold. The only light comes from a
dangling electric bulb and a patch
of blue sky visible through the
hatch 9m (30ft) above. We strip
to the waist and start dragging the
2cwt sacks onto the loading board
lowered by the crane, and all the
flies that have been crawling over

Grim headlines *The world wakes
up to the sombre news that the USA
had dropped an atomic bomb on
the Japanese city of Hiroshima
on August 6, 1945.*

the sticky hessian transfer their attentions to our sticky bodies. When four bags have been stacked, we signal to the POW on the deck and step back as the swaying load is hauled out of the hold.

After a brief respite, another four sacks are hauled up and it is time to change shifts. As we start to climb the ladder, the *hancho* orders us back to work another load. We yell up to him that we have done our stint, but he threatens us, so we back down.

Suddenly, a brilliant white light fills every corner of the hold. Blinded by the dazzle, we stagger backwards then sprawl on the floor as the ship is sucked downwards. It rocks and shakes and shudders in the grip of some mighty force, then rises again to lurch violently to starboard with a loud grinding as the side scrapes against the concrete wharf. Large flakes of metal begin to shower down on us from the rusty bulkheads. A thunderous rumbling outside gets louder and louder.

Unearthly noise

The sea is pounding the ship and we hear the rigging being wrenched from the deck by a cyclonic wind. The light has gone out and we lie in the dark, petrified, clinging to the bags while the ship is tossed around and our ears are bombarded by an unearthly noise that thunders on and on.

Slowly, the horrendous turbulence begins to abate and the ship steadies into a listing position. I look up at the patch and the blue sky has turned a leaden grey. Through ringing ears I hear Australian voices.

'Bloody hell! What is it?'

'Could've been a bomb on the dock.'

'I didn't hear an explosion. Did you?'

No one had heard an explosion, so it couldn't have been a bomb.

'What is it, then?'

Death zone The devastation unleashed on Hiroshima by the atomic bomb – exploded 580m (1,900ft) above the city – spread in waves from the Ota river delta (below). Around 90 per cent of the people who lived within 800m (½ mile) of the hypocentre, or 'ground zero', would have died – most of them instantly. It is estimated that at least 70,000 people were killed by the initial blast, intense heat and radiation from the bomb.

SEA OF OKHOTSK

Sapporo

JAPAN

Sendai

TOKYO

SOUTH KOREA

Kyoto · Nagoya

Hiroshima

Kobe Osaka

Kumamoto

Nagasaki

Kagoshima

2,500m

2,000m

1,500m

1,000m

Hypocentre of blast

Ruins of Hiroshima Castle

500m

Docks

Chamber of Commerce and Industry building

Ota river

Complete fire and blast damage

Complete blast damage

We shout up with cupped hands to anyone who can hear us. There is no answer. The temperature in the hold has risen dramatically and the heat is almost unbearable. We decide to climb out. Bluey grasps the ladder and lets go with a yell. The metal is too hot to handle; even the bulkheads below the waterline are warm to touch. We stay in our oven-like hold.

Soon we hear the patter of rain and see large black drops falling through the hatch. There is something sinister about them; we move away as the drops become a steady downpour, soaking and staining the bag on the loading board. With a morbid fascination, we sit looking at this weird black rain until it stops, almost as quickly as it started.

There is now a strange silence outside. It is occasionally shattered by the crack and thud of falling masonry. We shout up again but there is only the echo of our own voices in the sweltering gloom.

A long time passes, then we hear footsteps on the deck. We jump up and call again. A face covered with a surgical mask looks down. He calls in Japanese, 'Wait! Wait! Stay where you are.'

'What has happened?'

'Terrible danger! Fire! Many dead. Wait!' He disappears.

We wait, none the wiser. He returns in about an hour, this dock official, and lowers a wicker basket on a rope. Inside are a bottle of water and boxes of rice rolls wrapped in seaweed. We eat, listening to the sounds of shovelling and shouting in the distance, then to footsteps and voices on the deck.

Terrible suffering

Three masked faces peer down at us. An American voice tells us he is a doctor and he has two Japanese medics with him. He throws down four oilskin coats and tells us to put them on. The ladder has cooled and we climb into a scorched and devastated world. Above our heads the bent crane tilts dangerously, the driver dead in his cabin. The ship's funnel lies on its side; the listing deck is strewn with rigging, the bridge is shattered. Through the port rails we can see the river, carrying dozens of burnt bodies out to sea, some still clinging together in pathetic groups.

Looking up the river, we see what had been the city of Hiroshima. For about 2 sq miles nearly every building has been pulverised into rubble and over all this devastation hangs a leaden pall of smoke.

When the doctor (a US Marine major captured in the Philippines) tells us it was all done by one bomb, it is beyond our comprehension. The stench is real enough and we waste no time putting on the masks, which dull the nauseating smells of burnt flesh, acrid smoke and hot metal.

The charred body of the *hancho* is lying near the bow, and among some fallen rigging is the body of the POW who passed our signals to the crane driver. We look at him sombrely, remembering how we had been kept below, then climb onto the wharf to look for the other three men.

The roof of the warehouse has been blown off. The clock in the wall is still intact with the hands on the blackened face pointing to 8.15. Civil-defence workers are trying to move the dead scattered over the wharf. When they attempt to pick one up, the burnt skin slides off like a jumper peeling off a body.

Suddenly, a brilliant white light fills every corner of the hold. Blinded by the dazzle, we stagger backwards then sprawl on the floor as the ship is sucked downwards.

Sickened, we walk towards the warehouse, where we find the bodies of the other POWs. Two have fallen forward, but the third is still sitting upright, staring grotesquely with eyes slowly melting in waxen rivulets down his red, swollen face. We stare back in stricken silence.

'Come on,' says the major. Having confirmed that we are the only survivors, he becomes anxious. 'There's nothing we can do, so let's get going.' He implies he has seen enough for today to fear reprisals from the Japanese survivors, so we follow him down the quay. Sweating under the oilskin coats, which help to conceal our identity, we hurry past a group of Japanese soldiers digging for survivors, past a blackened wall with a grey, ghostly outline of a human figure who was standing beside it when the flash occurred.

As we go, the major, whose face is cut and bloodied, tells us of his miraculous escape when the hospital he was working in collapsed. He was buried under rubble but clawed his way out to join the rescue operations. He tells us about two women who were entering the hospital together when the bomb went off: one was killed by the flash; the other had her clothes blown off, leaving her alive but naked, her body unmarked.

On the outskirts of the city, we pass a square that has been turned into a medical clearing station. It is crowded with people, many of them burned and bleeding, with long strips of skin hanging from their swollen naked bodies. There is no hysteria or panic, only the quiet desperation of the first-aid teams and the shocked, dazed stares of the onlookers.

For the first time, I feel pity and sorrow for the Japanese. 'Just look at all that terrible suffering,' says the major. 'Why was it necessary? They were almost beaten anyway. Why did they do it? Why? Why?' It is a question soldiers often ask.

The major takes us to an assembly point where some army lorries are lined up, and speaks to the officer in charge. Then a teenage soldier, toting a rifle, escorts us to a lorry. We climb in, take off our coats and give them back to the major. We cannot thank him enough for rescuing us.

First-aid station *Workers treat patients who have been exposed to radiation as best they can at the Fukuromachi Relief Station.*

Four men short

The Japanese soldier climbs in with us and the lorry moves off, twisting and turning to find a clear route from the flattened city. The soldier tugs the laced rear canvas flaps apart to peer out and through the chinks we see the façade of a Christian church still standing, its Gothic arched doorway leading only to smouldering debris. As we climb the hills beyond, there are stark, burnt trees, many uprooted, devoid of any foliage.

When we reach the camp the perimeter fence is flattened and

Why Hiroshima?

LATE IN 1944 the US leadership began to consider how and where their secret bomb might be deployed. A list of possible Japanese targets was drawn up. These included the capital, Tokyo, and the ancient city of Kyoto. The list was submitted to Henry Stimson, secretary of war, who was in charge of all bomb-related matters. He removed Kyoto from the list, partly because he had fond memories of it, having honeymooned there. In April 1945, President Roosevelt died, and was succeeded by Harry S. Truman. In the first days of the new presidency, Stimson told Truman that 'within four months we shall in all probability have completed the most terrible weapon ever known in human history'. Meanwhile, a report of the so-called 'Target Committee' announced that: 'Hiroshima is the largest untouched target. Consideration should be given to this city.' Orders were conveyed that in the meantime Hiroshima and other potential targets should not be attacked with conventional bombs. In July, Japan rejected an American call to surrender or else face 'prompt and utter destruction'. Truman decided to use the bomb. It would administer, wrote Stimson, 'a tremendous shock ... such an effective shock would save many times the number of lives, both American and Japanese, than it would cost.' In other words, it would render a long and bloody invasion unnecessary. On July 25, the order was issued to drop the 'first special bomb as soon as weather will permit visual bombing after about August 3, 1945, on one of the targets: Hiroshima, Kokura, Niigata and Nagasaki.' To Hiroshima's great misfortune, clear blue skies were forecast above the city for the morning of August 6.

DISBELIEF A man, his back badly burned in the bombing, surveys his devastated city.

one roof has been blown off a storehouse. We are told that a freak wind had done the damage. No one believes us when we tell them it was a bomb.

We head for the water tank to splash our bodies over and over, trying to wash away the sights and smells of the day, then we flop exhausted on our bunks. The senior American POW colonel comes in, and sends us off to see the POW doctor, who checks us over. Although physically unscathed, we are feeling emotionally shattered.

Evening roll-call is four men short; only Keith, Bluey, Curly and I know the horror of their instantaneous deaths. Then the guards call us to assemble on the parade ground. The Commandant appears and we bow from the waist as usual. He salutes, orders us to stand at ease, and starts to speak in English.

'Today, America drop big bomb on Hiroshima . . .' His voice rises in anger as he tells of the damage and loss of life, then comes a note of defiance. 'America would not drop big bomb if Japan had big bomb because if Japan had big bomb, Japan would bomb San Francisco . . . '

He repeats it again and again, naming every American city he can think of and we listen with rising anxiety, eyeing the manned machine-gun. Then, to our intense relief, he announces that the camp is to be evacuated and we will be taken by train to Niigata on the northwest coast of Honshu.

When it is time to board the lorries that will transport us to the railway station, I remove one of the planks on my bunk and feel around for the small notebook that has been my pencilled diary for the past 3½ years, and tuck it into my shirt with a dog-eared photograph of my fiancee, Mary. Then I join the others lining up at the lorries.

Darkness is falling as we begin the long ride north. Listening to the rhythm of the wheels on the track, I begin to feel a glimmer of hope that this may be the first leg of my journey back to freedom, the beginning of the end of years of brutal slavery.

Edward Sawyer, like most Far-East POWs, had a long haul back to health. When he was freed in 1945, he weighed 48kg (7st 7lb) and suffered from dysentery, malaria and nervous disorders. Two years of recuperation followed before he was well enough to resume work as a printer. In July 1947, he and Mary married, but they were told they would probably not be able to have a family. Fourteen years later, their only child, a healthy son, was born. ■

What happened next?

IN THE IMMEDIATE AFTERMATH of the explosion, most survivors left the ruins of Hiroshima. But within a month, people were drifting back, building makeshift shacks in the rubble. 'Blue-sky classrooms' were set up in roofless buildings.

These first returnees fell victim to a new misfortune when, in September, the city was hit by a massive typhoon that killed 3,000 people in the Hiroshima prefecture.

In 1946, the governor of Hiroshima convened a conference to discuss ways and means of reconstructing the city, although some of the delegates felt the ruins should be left alone. In 1949 the mayor of Hiroshima asked General MacArthur, supreme commander of the Allied powers, to sanction the idea of Hiroshima as a 'peace memorial city', and he gave the idea his blessing.

In the early 1950s Japan functioned as a logistical base for American and UN troops fighting in Korea. Many Japanese cities experienced an economic boom founded on dollar investment. In Hiroshima, industry took root once more. Machine-tooling factories and food canneries sprung up; the Mazda car firm established itself in the city. By 1958 the population had reached its pre-war figure of 410,000; it is now three times that.

Hiroshima has become a bustling Japanese city like any other, but every year, at 8.15 on the morning of August 6, the city falls silent, a Peace Bell is rung for 1 minute, and prayers are offered for the dead.

A CITY REMEMBERS Doves fly above Peace Memorial Park (left) in 2008 on the 63rd anniversary of the dropping of the A-bomb. Above is what remained of the Chamber of Commerce and Industry, now known as the Atomic Bomb Dome.

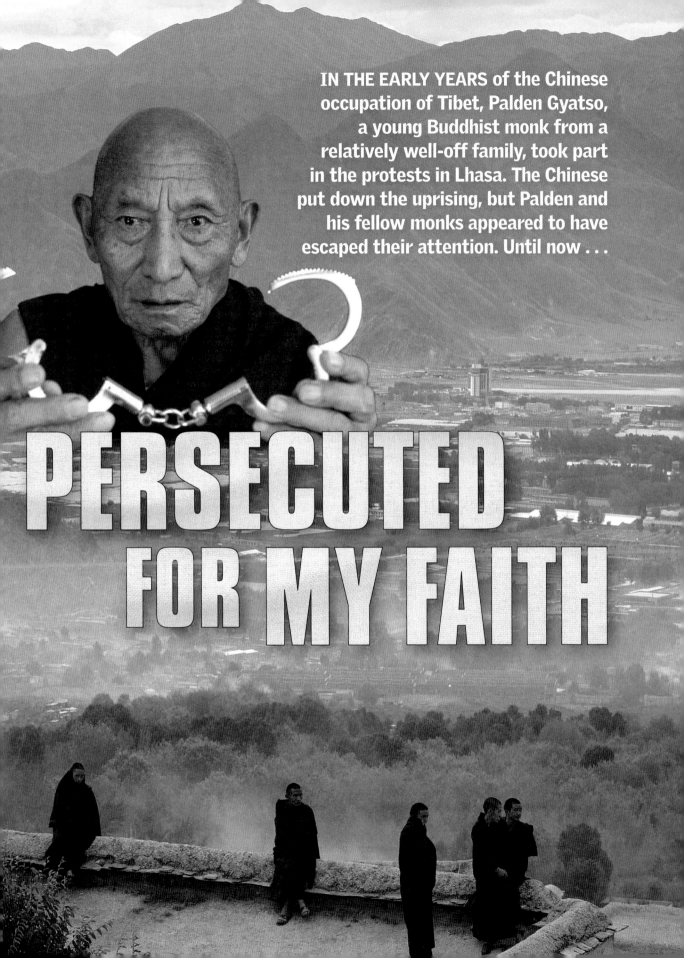

IN THE EARLY YEARS of the Chinese occupation of Tibet, Palden Gyatso, a young Buddhist monk from a relatively well-off family, took part in the protests in Lhasa. The Chinese put down the uprising, but Palden and his fellow monks appeared to have escaped their attention. Until now . . .

PERSECUTED FOR MY FAITH

In June 1959 a novice came to my room in the monastery and told me that all the monks had to gather in the courtyard. Outside, Chinese soldiers were standing along the outer walls, their guns fitted with bayonets. The monks sat on the dusty floor of the yard and beside me was my mentor, Gyen Rigzin Tenpa, one of the most learned monks from Lhasa.

The senior Chinese official announced that 'reactionary bandits' had kidnapped the Dalai Lama. He said the Gadong monastery had to declare where its loyalties lay. Monks who held office in the monastery were told to step forward and their hands were shackled behind their backs.

We were gripped by fear. I looked at Gyen Rigzin Tenpa. His eyes brimmed with tears, but the shackled monks gave no indication that they were afraid. Theirs were the faces of innocent men. They were led away at gunpoint.

We had to attend a 'study session', which involved subjecting us to a barrage of accusation. We were confined to the monastery for a whole month and forced to attend study sessions every day. From my window I could see that the villagers had been forced into the fields for study sessions, penned there like cattle. No one was getting ready for the impending harvest. The Chinese had decreed that there were more important things to do than harvest crops.

A Chinese officer explained the nature of class struggle. He told us there were four classes: landlords, rich farmers, middling farmers and poor farmers. He asked us which class we belonged to and I replied that I was a monk. The officer did not approve of this reply. He said there were class distinctions even in a monastery. Later, because of my family background, I was categorised a rich monk. This meant I had no future in the new proletarian society.

A new investigation team came from Lhasa and searched our quarters. They became very excited by a photo in Gyen's belongings that showed a group of Tibetans with the leaders of the Indian Independence movement in 1946, including Ghandi and Nehru.

Gyen was told to pack some belongings into a small bag and I rushed over to say goodbye as he was ordered into a waiting jeep. Two guards aimed their guns at him and commanded, 'Move.' I was never to see him again.

A soldier took me into an interrogation room and a Chinese officer

Defeated *Tibetan monks lay down their arms in April 1959, surrounded by soldiers of the People's Liberation Army of China, after an unsuccessful armed uprising against Chinese rule.*

introduced himself as Liao. 'This is very serious,' he said and pointed at the photograph. 'You have to acknowledge your teacher was a spy.'

But I refused to make the false allegation. Liao said, 'Do you know the party policy?' The policy was leniency. The Party would forget my crimes if I confessed to them. But if I resisted, the Party would 'fight back'. I said once more that Gyen was not a spy.

Escape plan

Liao's open palm caught me on the side of the face, knocking me backwards. The two guards tied my arms behind my back with a rope and threw the end over a beam. They hoisted me up, wrenching my arms from their sockets. I screamed as their fists thudded into my body. When they untied the rope, Liao began to question me again. All he wanted was for me to implicate Gyen as a spy, but how could I do that? In Tibetan Buddhism the bond between teacher and student is based on devotion and trust. How could I betray him and have a clear conscience?

Some time in summer 1960, the interrogations ended and I was taken to Norbukhungtse monastery. And so my imprisonment in 'the new society' began.

By the end of 1962, I began to think about escaping. I could identify six other prisoners who would come with me, including a young nomad, Dhargye, whose knowledge of the mountains would be invaluable. Our cell had previously been used as a kitchen and when I first came to Norbukhungtse I was set to work blocking up the back door. I knew it would be easy to remove some of the bricks so, one morning, I pretended to be sick and stayed behind. I began to dig into the soft mud with a stick and soon I could feel the bricks moving. I made enough space to get my fingers round them. We would have to go that night, before my excavations were discovered.

At midnight I removed the bricks and saw a single star shining through the hole. Guards paced above, but the wall was too high for them to notice us as we climbed through. We walked all night, heading for the mountains, and by sunrise had reached the top of a ridge. We stopped to rest in a cave.

Dhargye woke me and pointed to a group of Chinese soldiers converging on the village below. They were after us. It was the middle of winter and we left a trail of footprints in the snow, which I knew would give us away. We walked across the mountains for five days. On the fifth day, Dhargye told us that all we had to do was cross a small pass and then

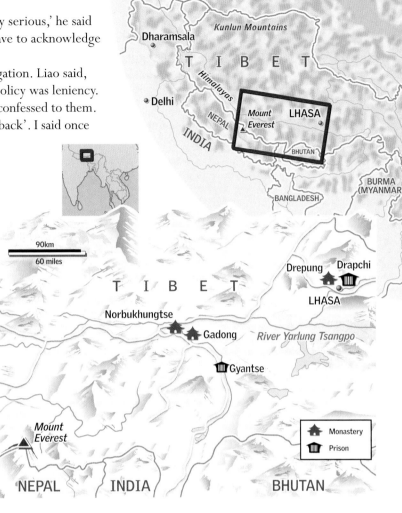

Captive land Remote, mountainous Tibet is now part of the People's Republic of China, which it borders to the north and east. Palden Gyatso was a monk at Gadong monastery when the Chinese occupation began, then held captive at Norbukhungtse monastery. Recaptured after trying to escape to Bhutan, he was thrown into Gyantse prison, where he stayed for 20 years before being moved to Drepung monastery. Palden ended his days of captivity at Drapchi prison before making a long final escape to Nepal.

we would be over the border and safe in Bhutan. Then we saw a group of soldiers riding towards us and gunshots rang out. My companions began to run and I jumped behind a low wall. A bullet hit a stone near me and the next thing I knew the butt of a rifle was landing on my head.

We were shackled and taken to Gyantse Prison, where I was interrogated for a month. I was not given any work, not that there was much I could have done with my wrists and ankles in their shackles. The Chinese used several kinds of cuffs. Some were made from heavy chunks of iron, others were lighter, but the bracelets had serrated edges. My leg-irons were linked by a chain just two rings long. I could move only by shuffling.

I relied on my cell mates for everything. They took it in turns to feed me, wash me and help me over to the sanitary bucket. I still think of them and of how much I would like to repay them.

Sentenced

One day our cell leader told me it had been announced that everyone involved in the escape would be subjected to a *thamzing* – a 'struggle session'. The Party claimed that these sessions allowed the people to vent their anger at representatives of the exploiting class. The *thamzing* always started with a verbal condemnation and usually developed into beatings. Chinese officials watched from a distance and hardly ever intervened. This absolved the Party of all responsibility – if anyone was hurt it was the consequence of the people's anger, not the Party's.

My turn came on a Monday morning. Officials were seated at a table in the yard and the compound was surrounded by soldiers. My heart pounded. Six months had passed since our escape and I still had not been sentenced. I thought I might be sentenced to death, since prisoners bound for execution were often shackled to stop them committing suicide.

One prisoner – a former civil servant determined to prove himself useful to the Chinese – denounced me. 'Why should you want to escape?' he asked.

Here was my opportunity to discredit the Chinese and show my independence. 'I escaped because I feared I would die of starvation,' I replied.

The prisoner hit me hard and I fell to the ground. He put his hand on my neck and pushed me into the dirt. He said, 'The earth is the Party and the sky is the people, and between the earth and the sky there is no escape for you.'

An officer read out my sentence – eight years with a further three years deprivation of political rights. I was glad I was not going to be executed but, together with an earlier sentence, I would have to serve a total of 15 years.

In 1966 we were informed that the Cultural Revolution had been initiated by Chairman Mao and told to reform our thoughts. We were warned that if anyone strayed from the path of progress they would be exterminated like vermin. I couldn't understand what this had to do with Tibet.

In 1975 my sentence should have come to an end but I was sent to work in a factory as a 'reform through labour prisoner'. It wasn't until the spring of 1983 that I was allowed to leave the camp for the monastery of Drepung. There a police search of my room revealed a Tibetan flag and writings by the Dalai Lama. I was sentenced to a further eight years in prison. I was 51 and had spent most of my adult life in Chinese prisons, in my own country.

The 'liberation' of Tibet

WHEN BRITISH EXPLORER Frank Kingdon-Ward visited Tibet in the 1920s, he marvelled that it was 'one great zoological garden'. It is home to the snow leopard, the blue sheep, the red panda and golden monkey. This conjurs up an image of an earthly Eden, and yet, at the time of the invasion of east Tibet by the People's Liberation Army of China in 1950, the country was not quite paradise on Earth. It was, rather, a feudal society, in which serfs laboured on vast manorial estates. The so-called 'liberation' of those serfs would prove to be a brutal process.

In 1951, a Tibetan delegation travelled to Beijing to meet with the Chinese government, and was ordered, under threat of military action, to sign a 'Seventeen-Point Agreement on Measures for the Peaceful Liberation of Tibet'.

Tibet was from then effectively a colony of China, subsumed by the People's Republic. Chinese troops marched upon the Tibetan capital, Lhasa, and there began the suppression of religion, which Mao Zedong reviled as 'poison'. Along with the three other 'olds' – culture, customs, habits – it was to be obliterated.

On March 17, 1959, as the Chinese exacted bloody reprisals against the Tibetan resistance, the nation's leader, the 14th Dalai Lama, fled to India, seeking political asylum and establishing a government in exile. Meanwhile, in his homeland, resistance continued against Mao's 'Great Leap Forward', which saw the killing, torture and imprisonment of many thousands of Buddhist nuns and monks, and the attempted stamping out of Tibetan beliefs and rituals. In the absence of the Dalai Lama, the Chinese installed the Panchen Lama – the other of Tibet's two great Lamas – as a powerless government figurehead.

Thirty years later, in 1989, the Dalai Lama was awarded the Nobel Peace Prize for his non-violent approach to the issue of Tibet. He has warned, 'There is every danger that the entire Tibetan nation, with its own unique cultural heritage, will completely disappear. The present situation is so serious that it is really a question of life and death. If death occurs, nothing is left.'

In 2005, Chinese premier Wen Jiabao offered to hold talks with the Dalai Lama, on the condition that he dropped his demand for independence. The Dalai Lama told the *South China Morning Post*: 'We are willing to be part of the People's Republic of China, to have it govern and guarantee to preserve our Tibetan culture, spirituality and our environment.'

The environment is not the least of these concerns. In the 'great zoological garden', rivers run with toxic waste, great swaths of forest have been cleared, and rare and endangered species are hunted for sport. Historically, Tibetans lived in harmony with nature: the interdependence of all plants and animals is central to Buddhism. Today we understand that we disrupt fragile ecosystems at our peril. Throughout their struggles, many Tibetans have felt ignored by the rest of the world. For this, we may all pay an unforeseen price.

PEACEFUL PROTEST Buddhist monks and other pro-Tibet supporters take to the streets of London on March 7, 2009, to mark the 50th anniversary of the Tibet uprising. Palden Gyatso is at the front, second from the right.

Manifestation of the Buddha

His Holiness the 14th Dalai Lama, Tenzin Gyatso, was born Lhamo Dhondup in 1935, into a farming family in a small village in northeastern Tibet. At barely three years old, he was recognised as the 14th reincarnation of the Buddha of Compassion. He was enthroned in Lhasa on February 22, 1940, as 'Holy Lord, Gentle Glory, Compassionate, Defender of the Faith, Ocean of Wisdom' or, more simply, 'The Wish-fulfilling Gem' or 'The Presence'.

On the death of the 13th Dalai Lama in 1935, the Regent of Tibet had stood on the shores of the sacred 'Oracle Lake' of Lhamo Lhatso, 140km (90 miles) from Lhasa, in whose waters it is said visions of the future may be seen. There the Regent saw three Tibetan characters, Ah, Ka and Ma, along with images of a monastery with roofs the colours of jade and gold, and a house with turquoise tiles. Emissaries were then sent out to scour Tibet.

Heading east, a party led by Lama Kewstang Rinpoche of Sera Monastery, found a place conforming to the Regent's vision. There they found a small boy, Lhamo Dhondup. A series of tests assured them they had found 'The Presence'.

In 1959, when he was 25, the Dalai Lama was forced to flee Tibet, followed by some 80,000 refugees. He had been head of state since November 1950.

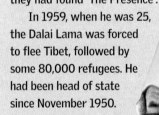

FIFTY YEARS OF EXILE On March 11, 2009, the Dalai Lama attended 50th anniversary proceedings in the seat of the exiled government, in McLeod Ganj, Dharamsala, India.

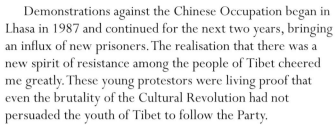

Demonstrations against the Chinese Occupation began in Lhasa in 1987 and continued for the next two years, bringing an influx of new prisoners. The realisation that there was a new spirit of resistance among the people of Tibet cheered me greatly. These young protestors were living proof that even the brutality of the Cultural Revolution had not persuaded the youth of Tibet to follow the Party.

I had openly congratulated the young political prisoners, so it was hardly surprising the authorities should think I was a bad influence. I was moved to Drapchi, the number one prison in Tibet, and interrogated by Paljor, a guard I held responsible for the death of a friend.

'Still you have failed to reform,' he said and pushed a baton into an electric socket. 'Why are you here?'

'Because I put up posters calling for Tibetan independence.'

Paljor pulled the baton from its socket and began to poke me with it. Then, shouting obscenities, he thrust the baton into my mouth. I felt as though my body were being torn apart. I can remember the way the shocks made my body vibrate, holding me in its grip. I passed out and when I woke I found I was lying in a pool of vomit and urine. I spat something out. It was three of my teeth. It would be weeks before I could eat solid food again.

I found myself sharing a dormitory with kindred spirits. All had taken part in demonstrations or written posters demanding independence. The authorities decided that brutality was the only way to react to our rebelliousness, but we said openly we would rather die than submit to the Chinese. Wounds can heal. But once your spirit is broken, everything falls apart. We drew strength from our belief that we were fighting for justice and the freedom of our country.

On the morning of August 25, 1992, my term came to an end. I had convinced the authorities that I intended to go back to the monastery and devote my remaining years to the religious life. In reality I hatched a plan to escape to India with contacts outside the prison. In September, dressed for the first time in a suit, I crossed the border into Nepal. I wasted no time in getting on a bus for Delhi.

Several days later I arrived in the hill station of Dharamsala, where the Dalai Lama had made his home in exile. I had first seen his Holiness in 1951 in the old Tibet. Now I prostrated myself before him.

'Gyen Rigzin Tenpa's pupil,' he said. 'You have faced much hardship.'

I was weeping when I left the room. That meeting had been my life's ambition. I made my way to the temple and, in new monk's robes, offered a prayer that all should be released from suffering. ■

AS THE PILOT TURNED THE TWO-SEATER PLANE back towards Cardiff, he collapsed. His passenger stared uncomprehendingly at the controls of the tiny plane. He was on his own.

MAYDAY! I DON'T KNOW HOW TO FLY

22 MINUTES OF TERROR

It was 6.39pm on Monday, March 30, 1992. Just a few hours earlier, Alan Anderson, a 26-year-old mechanic from Llandow, South Wales, had accepted an invitation from his girlfriend Alison's father, Les Rhoades, to 'come on up for a bumble', a short 'aimless' flight.

Alan, who has a fear of heights, had been so terrified when Les took him up in a four-seater plane the year before that he had sworn he would never fly again. But it was difficult to say no to Les.

In the two years since they had met, Alan and the 63-year-old former mechanical engineer had become like father and son, both delighting in 'taking the mickey', teasing and making fun of one another. So Alan knew he'd never hear the end of it if he refused a ride in the 22-year-old single-engine Rallye Minerva – known as 'Gaydog' after its call sign 'G-AYDG' – which Les owned with five friends.

Sitting beside Les, dual controls in front of him, Alan felt his fears begin to melt away as they flew west from Cardiff along the coast towards Swansea. There was hardly a cloud in the windless sky, and the evening sun bathed the Welsh countryside in a warm glow. 'This is brilliant,' thought Alan. 'It's like flying with my guardian angel.'

After 30 minutes or so, they turned back towards Cardiff and Les reset the plane's radio to Cardiff Airport's approach frequency. Then he pointed to a lone cloud ahead, some 60m (200ft) above them. 'Let's chase it,' he said.

'Do we have to, Les?' joked Alan. 'It's bad enough being up here.'

Suddenly Les's head fell forward and he let go of the control stick. 'Good joke, Les,' thought Alan. Then the plane began to lose altitude and go round in smaller and smaller circles. 'Come on, Les, stop messing around,' said Alan. 'I'm getting scared.' Les still didn't move.

Gaydog slipped into a dive, dropping to 500m (1,700ft) … 450m (1,500ft) … 300m (1,000ft). Terrified, Alan put his hand inside Les's jacket and felt for a heartbeat. There was none.

Through the windscreen Alan could see they were heading straight for the three chimneys of the vast Port Talbot steelworks. Now less than 180m (600ft) from the ground, he pulled on the dual control stick in front of him as he had seen Les do. Gaydog began a steep climb. They missed crashing into the steelworks by seconds.

'Oh God, please help me,' Alan prayed. A jumble of thoughts filled his mind: 'How am I going to tell Alison about her father? … I wonder if she knows how much I love her? … What am I going to do now?'

He shouted into the radio headset he'd been wearing since take-off: 'Help! Help! Mayday!' When no one answered, it dawned on him that his headset was merely for communication between pilot and passenger; it could not transmit. Shakily he removed Les's headset and put it on.

What now? Better pull Les's feet off those two pedals. (Though Alan didn't know it, they were the rudder controls.) Reaching across, he bumped into a black knob protruding from the centre of the control panel. Without realising it he had hit the throttle. Gaydog was now flying at more than 190km/h (120mph).

Pilot out cold

Again Alan shouted 'Mayday!' into his headset, this time pressing the button on the top of the pilot's control stick as Les did when he radioed the tower.

Now his headphones crackled into life. 'Thank God,' thought Alan as he heard John Hibberd, 41-year-old air traffic controller, say, 'Mayday go ahead.'

The instant Hibberd received Alan's mayday call, he checked the control console's directional finder. It told him Alan was to the west of the airport, but he still had to establish Gaydog's exact position; it could be any one of the five aircraft on his radar screen. 'Can you look at the dials ahead of you and see what heading you are on?' he asked Alan.

The compass was unmistakable, hanging at eye level. 'Number 12 next to the east,' Alan read.

'That's fine,' Hibberd told him. 'You're heading directly back to the airport. And how is the pilot now?'

'He's cold,' said Alan shakily.

Hibberd asked Alan if he knew what his altitude was. He was taken aback at Alan's reply, 'Whereabouts on the dial is that one?'

'See if you can see something that says A-L-T.'

'Yeah, I can see that. The little hand is just about on the two, the other one is just below the seven.'

Hibberd was reassured that Alan was flying at around 800m (2,600ft), high enough to avoid television masts, high chimneys or other obstructions. In fact, Alan had misread the altimeter; he was at less than 500m (1,600ft).

Again Alan shouted, 'Mayday!' into his headset, this time pressing the button on the top of the pilot's control stick as Les did when he radioed the tower. Now his headphones crackled into life. 'Thank God,' thought Alan.

Briefing all incoming planes to keep clear, Hibberd urgently paged his fellow air traffic controller Colin Eaton to come and help him.

To Alan, it seemed ages since Hibberd had last spoken. 'Why doesn't he tell me how he's going to help me?', he thought. As long as he clung to the control stick the plane flew steadily and level, because Les had fully 'trimmed' the elevators and rudder. 'But I'll never manage to land,' he thought in a panic. He decided he would circle over the Bristol Channel until the plane ran out of fuel. Then, just before it hit the water, he would unstrap himself and Les, and jump.

Still heading east along the coast, he spotted Cardiff Airport; from 500m (1,600ft) up it looked like a small table top. He pressed the radio button and blurted out, 'Cardiff Airport, I'm just coming over the runway now.'

Meanwhile, John Hibberd had just been contacted by the pilot of a light aircraft – 'Charlie Echo' in radio shorthand – flying some 8km (5 miles) north of the airport, offering his assistance. Miraculously, the pilot was an experienced flying instructor, 26-year-old Robert Legg, who with his student Martin Leighton had been listening to the drama unfold since Alan's first audible mayday call. Hibberd now acknowledged Alan's message and immediately told Legg to head south towards the airport, where he should be able to spot Alan heading towards the Bristol Channel.

Adrenalin surging, Legg turned his single-engine Piper Warrior II to the southwest and began scanning the skies for Gaydog. At last he and Martin spotted Alan's tiny plane some 300m (1,000ft) below them. Robert put Charlie Echo into a shallow full-power dive to catch up with him.

Running back from his tea break, Colin Eaton, a stocky RAF Royal Air Force veteran of 38, slipped into the left-hand seat at the radar-room console. Hibberd, busy instructing incoming planes to switch to the airport's spare frequency and leave the normal one free for Alan and Robert, passed the emergency over to him.

A cool head *Flying instructor Robert Legg displayed great calm as he talked Alan down from the skies.*

'This guy's good'

Eaton radioed Alan, speaking slowly and carefully: 'This is the air traffic controller … There is an aircraft about 7km (4 miles) to the west of you. He is rapidly approaching you to draw alongside, and then he will be speaking to you on this frequency.'

'OK,' replied Alan. 'I've never done this before, mind.'

Robert Legg radioed Alan to tell him he was coming up behind, and asked how much fuel he had left. 'Half a tank on both sides, I think,' said Alan, reading the plane's twin gauges. 'How much longer are we gonna be?'

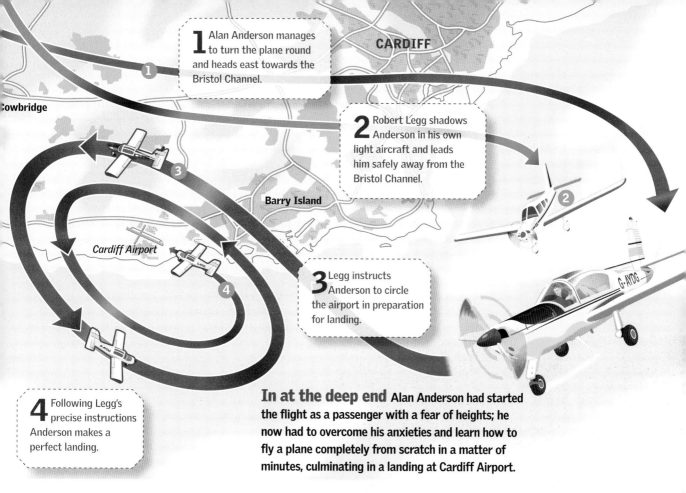

1 Alan Anderson manages to turn the plane round and heads east towards the Bristol Channel.

2 Robert Legg shadows Anderson in his own light aircraft and leads him safely away from the Bristol Channel.

3 Legg instructs Anderson to circle the airport in preparation for landing.

4 Following Legg's precise instructions Anderson makes a perfect landing.

CARDIFF

Cowbridge

Barry Island

Cardiff Airport

In at the deep end Alan Anderson had started the flight as a passenger with a fear of heights; he now had to overcome his anxieties and learn how to fly a plane completely from scratch in a matter of minutes, culminating in a landing at Cardiff Airport.

In the calm, reassuring tone he used with all his students, Legg replied, 'I'll get you down as quickly as possible.'

He didn't know how he was going to get Alan down, but he did know it made no sense for him to keep heading over the Bristol Channel; contrary to Alan's belief, he would have little chance of survival if he crashed into the water.

'Hold the control column in front of you,' Legg told Alan. 'Rotate it gently to the right and put the aircraft into a bank turn to the right.'

He was closing in on Gaydog, now heading north towards the coast. 'If you look to your right, just behind your wing, you may see my aircraft,' he radioed Alan. 'We're going to circle over the airfield in a nice wide circuit and then we're going to bring you down onto the runway.'

Listening to Robert Legg's precise instructions, John Hibberd marvelled at how quickly he had taken control of the situation. 'This guy's good,' he said to Colin Eaton.

By now, Colin Eaton had ordered the 'Local Standby' alert earlier instigated to be upgraded to a 'Full Emergency'. Airport fire crews were in position along the runway. Local police headquarters at Bridgend and county fire brigade headquarters at Cardiff were alerted. A light aircraft and an RAF TriStar tanker were kept out of the airspace; an incoming passenger aircraft was put into a holding pattern. To all intents and purposes, Cardiff Airport was now closed.

Robert Legg was aware that, at 190km/h (120mph), he and Alan were going much too fast for a landing approach. To get Alan to slow down without losing height, he asked him to pull out the throttle slightly.

'Which one is the throttle?' asked Alan.

Below in the radar room, Colin Eaton could hardly believe his ears. 'Good grief,' he said to John Hibberd, 'if he gets down it will be a miracle.'

Robert Legg was shaken, too, but he calmly told Alan how to locate and reduce the throttle. 'Ease gently back on the control column now to maintain your altitude,' he instructed.

Gaydog slowed to about 150km/h (100mph) and Legg breathed a sigh of relief.

Robert brought his plane level with Gaydog, a few hundred feet to Alan's left.

'I can see you,' said Alan. 'Thank Christ you're there!'

Recalling a scene from the film *Airport 1975*, he expected Robert to position Charlie Echo close to Gaydog, jump on board and scramble into the cockpit. 'He'll land it for me,' he thought.

With both planes at 300m (1,000ft) and heading directly for Cardiff's main runway, Legg wondered whether to tell Alan to attempt a landing. 'Hang on,' he told himself. 'He knows the basics now, using the throttle and control stick, but all he's done is make a right turn. Let's not be too hasty.' As a complete novice on his first flight, Alan's chances of landing safely were next to nil. His life hung in the balance.

'We're going to fly over the runway first,' Robert told Alan.

Suddenly Alan asked Robert if there was anyone who could contact Alison and tell her about Les. More than anything, he wanted to put his arms round his girlfriend.

Aware that Alan was on the brink of panic, Robert soothed, 'Yes, we'll get that sorted out for you. Just concentrate on my instructions.'

Carefully he went on, 'We're going to do a left-hand circuit … a nice gentle turn to the left about the same sort of rate as we did before … and we're going to come all the way around again and bring it down on the runway. Do you understand?'

'Yeah, I understand,' said Alan. 'But how do you stop it?'

By now, he realised he had to land Gaydog by himself. Irrationally, he thought, 'Les will be so furious with me if I scratch Gaydog. He loves this plane.'

Robert continued to guide him carefully through the turn, 'Hold the aircraft in a gentle bank … That's fine. Add a little more power. Pull slightly back on the control column to maintain your height.'

'I tell you,' said Alan, 'I've never been so scared in all my life!'

Against all odds *Gaydog is wheeled to safety by firefighters, after a perfect landing.*

After another small turn to the right at about 120m (400ft), Gaydog was positioned to make its final turn to the left and approach the runway. 'This time I'm going to attempt to get you down,' said Robert. 'Just aim for the runway … just a gentle bank turn … as you've done before.'

Perfect landing

The runway still seemed very small to Alan – and very hard. He fully expected to crash. 'Maybe I can make it if I land on the grass,' he thought.

Robert positioned Charlie Echo behind and 30m (100ft) above Gaydog. He hoped he could bring Alan down low enough, and slow enough, to prevent him being badly hurt if he crashed – as he surely must. Three things were in Alan's favour: the Rallye Minerva is a plane that handles very well at low speeds, there was hardly any wind, and the runway was the biggest in South Wales, capable of taking giant 747s.

When Gaydog was under 2km (a mile or so) from the runway, Robert told Alan, 'I'd like you to reduce the throttle slightly … Come over to the right a little … we're aiming for the big tarmac strip to the right of the white and red lights.'

'This is it,' thought Alan as Gaydog floated gradually down to 30m (100ft). 'Either I do this or I die!'

Once Alan was flying over the beginning of the runway, Robert told him, 'Pull the throttle all the way towards you now and pull gently back on the control column … Hold it there … Hold it …'

As Alan concentrated on Robert's every word, the runway seemed to rise up and fill the windscreen. Gaydog touched down on the tarmac in a perfect landing.

In the radar room, Colin Eaton shouted excitedly, 'He's made it!'

When Alan felt the wheels touch the runway he closed his eyes, expecting to crash into parked planes. With no brake on the copilot's side, he had no way of stopping Gaydog. But the plane coasted down the runway, veered into the grass and rolled to a halt – virtually unscathed. To the last, as air traffic controller John Hibberd put it, 'Someone up there was clearly looking out for Alan Anderson.'

Les Rhoades was pronounced dead on arrival at the hospital; an autopsy revealed that he had suffered a massive heart attack.

Alan was treated for shock at the hospital and released. He and Alison were married the following year.

Even though Alan swore he would never fly again, in July 1992 he went up in Gaydog – with a pilot – as a final tribute to Les. A few months later, in November, he received a Royal Association for Disability and Rehabilitation award as one of 1992's 'People of the Year'.

Robert Legg, who shrugged off his actions as 'all in a day's work', received the Royal Aero Club's silver medal for achievement in aviation. ■

A happy ending *In 1993 Alan married his girlfriend Alison, the daughter of stricken pilot Les Rhoades.*

FROM A GOATHERD'S HUT in Somalia to modelling for *Vogue*, Waris Dirie's story is one of survival and triumph. A child of the desert, she lived through drought and deprivation, but it was a brutal rite of passage that would prove her most horrific test and shape her life to come.

FLOWER FROM A CRUEL DESERT

My family was a tribe of herdsmen in the Somalian desert. And as a child, the freedom I had to experience nature's sights, sounds and smells was pure joy. We watched lions baking in the sun. We ran with giraffes, zebras and foxes. We chased hyraxes – rabbit-sized animals – through the sand. I was so happy.

Like the rest of my family, I have no idea exactly how old I am; I can only guess. We lived by the seasons and the sun, planning our moves around our need for rain, planning our day around the span of daylight available.

Our home was a tent-like domed hut woven from grass and built on a framework of sticks; it was a couple of metres in diameter. When it came time to move, we dismantled the hut and tied it to the backs of our camels. Then, when we found a spot with water and foliage, we'd set up again. At night we children slept outside under the stars, cuddled together on a mat. My father slept off to one side, our guardian.

Papa was very handsome, about 1.8m (6ft) tall, slim and lighter-skinned than Mama. My mother was beautiful. Her face was like a Modigliani sculpture and her skin was dark and smooth, as if perfectly chiselled from black marble. My mother named me Waris, the word we used for the desert flower. In my country sometimes it doesn't rain for months. Few living things can survive. But finally the water pours down and the brilliant yellow-orange blooms of the desert flower appear, a miracle of nature.

Becoming a woman

Gradually the happy times disappeared. Life became harder. By five I knew what it was to be an African woman, to live with terrible suffering in a passive, helpless manner.

Women are the backbone of Africa; they do most of the work. Yet women are powerless to make decisions. They have no say, sometimes not even in whom they will marry.

Subsistence living *Waris grew up in a simple Somalian village of thatched huts like the one below. Although it was far removed from the life she now enjoys in Europe, she has never forgotten her roots, and she continues to campaign to improve the lot of women in developing countries.*

In a nomadic culture like the one I was raised in, there is no place for an unmarried woman, so mothers feel it is their duty to ensure their daughters have the best possible opportunity to get a husband. And since the prevailing wisdom in Somalia is that there are bad things between a girl's legs, a woman is considered dirty, oversexed and unmarriageable unless those parts – the clitoris, the labia minora and most of the labia majora – are removed. Then the wound is stitched shut, leaving only a small opening and a scar where the genitals had been – a practice called infibulation.

The actual details of the ritual cutting are never explained to the girls – it's a mystery. You just know that something special is going to happen when your time comes. As a result, all young girls in Somalia anxiously await the ceremony that will mark their becoming a woman. Originally the process occurred when the girls reached puberty, but through time it has been performed on younger and younger girls.

One evening when I was about five, my mother said to me, 'Your father ran into the gypsy woman. She should be here any day now.'

The night before my circumcision, the family made a special fuss over me and I got extra food at dinner. Mama told me not to drink too much water or milk. I lay awake with excitement, until suddenly she was standing over me, motioning. The sky was still dark. I grabbed my little blanket and sleepily stumbled along after her.

We walked out into the brush. 'We'll wait here,' Mama said, and we sat on the cold ground. The day was growing lighter; soon I heard the click-click of the gypsy woman's sandals. Then, without my seeing her approach, she was right beside me.

'Sit over there.' She motioned towards a flat rock.

Mama positioned me on the rock. She sat behind me and pulled my head against her chest, her legs straddling my body. I circled my arms around her thighs. She placed a piece of root from an old tree between my teeth.

'Bite on this.'

I was frozen with fear.

I peered between my legs and saw the gypsy. The old woman foraged through an old carpet-bag and fished out a broken razor blade. I saw dried blood on the jagged edge. She spat on it and wiped it on her dress. My world went dark as Mama tied a blindfold over my eyes.

The next thing I felt was my flesh being cut away. I heard the blade sawing back and forth through my skin. The feeling was indescribable. I didn't move, telling myself the more I did, the longer the torture would take. Unfortunately, my legs began to quiver and shake uncontrollably of their own accord, and I prayed, 'Please, God, let it be over quickly.' Soon it was, because I passed out.

When I woke up, my blindfold was off and I saw the gypsy woman had piled a stack of thorns from an acacia tree next to her. She used these to puncture holes in my skin, then poked a strong white thread through the holes to sew me up. My legs were completely numb, but the pain between them was so intense that I wished I would die.

Africa's most easterly point
Somalia juts out of Africa's east coast like an upturned elbow or a horn, hence the term the 'Horn of Africa'.

My memory ends at that instant, until I opened my eyes and the woman was gone. My legs had been tied together with strips of cloth binding me from my ankles to my hips so I couldn't move. I turned my head towards the rock; it was drenched with blood as if an animal had been slaughtered there. Pieces of my flesh lay on top, drying in the sun.

Waves of heat beat down on my face, until my mother and older sister, Aman, dragged me into the shade of a bush while they finished making a shelter for me. This was the tradition; a little hut was prepared under a tree, where I would rest and recuperate alone for the next few weeks.

After hours of waiting, I was dying to relieve myself. I called my sister, who rolled me over on my side and scooped out a little hole in the sand. 'Go ahead,' she said.

The first drop stung as if my skin were being eaten by acid. After the gypsy sewed me up, the only opening left for urine – and later for menstrual blood – was a minuscule hole the diameter of a matchstick.

As the days dragged on and I lay in my hut, I became infected and ran a high fever. I faded in and out of consciousness. Mama brought me food and water for the next two weeks. Lying there alone with my legs still tied, I could do nothing but wonder, 'Why? What was it all for?' At that age I didn't understand anything about sex. All I knew was that I had been butchered with my mother's permission.

I suffered as a result of my circumcision, but I was lucky. Many girls bleed to death or die from shock, infection or tetanus. Considering the conditions in which the procedure is performed, it's surprising that any of us survive.

Impending marriage

I was around 13 when my father came home one evening and called, 'Come here,' in a soft voice. Normally he was very stern, so I began to feel suspicious.

He sat me on his knee. 'You know,' he began, 'you've been really good.' Now I knew something serious was up. 'You've been working hard as any man, taking good care of the animals. And I want you to know I'm going to miss you very much.'

When he said this, I thought he was afraid I was going to run away like my sister Aman had when he had tried to arrange her marriage.

I hugged him. 'Oh, Papa, I'm not going anywhere.'

He stared at me and said, 'Yes, you are, my darling. I found you a husband.'

'No, Papa, no!' I shook my head. 'I'm not going to marry.'

The next day I met my prospective husband – he was an old man, at least 60, who had a long white beard and walked with a stick. He had agreed to give my father five camels for me.

That evening, after everyone went to sleep, I went to my mother, who was still sitting next to the fire, and whispered, 'I'm going to run away.'

'Shhh, quiet! Where are you going to go?'

'Mogadishu.' My sister Aman was there.

'Go to bed.' Her stern look seemed to say the subject was closed.

While I was sleeping, Mama knelt on the ground beside me and lightly tapped my arm. 'Go – go before he wakes up,' she said softly. So, barefoot and with only a scarf draped around me, I ran off into the black desert night.

I didn't know which direction led to Mogadishu; I just ran. Slowly at first, because I couldn't see. But as the sky lightened, I was off like a gazelle. I ran for hours.

By midday I'd travelled deep into the red sand. The landscape stretched on to eternity. Hungry, thirsty and tired, I slowed and walked.

As I pondered what was going to happen next, I heard, 'Waris … Waris …' My father's voice echoed all around me! I was frightened. If he caught me, I knew that he would make me marry.

Even though I had gotten a head start, Papa had tracked me down by following my footprints through the sand. He was close.

I started to run. I looked back and saw him coming over the hill. He spotted me too. Terrified, I ran faster. It was as if we were surfing waves of sand; I flew up one hill, and he glided down the one behind me. On and on we continued for hours, until I realised I hadn't seen him for some time. He no longer called to me.

I kept running until the sun set, and the night was so black I couldn't see. By then I was starving and my feet were bleeding. I sat down to rest, and fell asleep under a tree.

In the morning I opened my eyes to the burning sun. I got up and continued to run. And so it went for days – days marked by hunger, thirst, fear and pain. When it grew too dark to see, I would stop. At midday I'd sit under a tree and take a siesta.

Blinded by sand *Life in the inhospitable Somalian desert is harsh, with sandstorms further hampering the people's efforts to forge a basic living.*

It was during one of these naps that a slight sound woke me. I opened my eyes and was staring into the face of a lion. I tried to stand, but I hadn't eaten for days, so my weak legs wobbled and folded beneath me.

'Come and get me,' I said to the lion. 'I'm ready.'

The big cat stared at me, and my eyes locked on his. He licked his lips and paced back and forth in front of me, elegantly, sensuously. Finally he turned and walked away, no doubt deciding that I had so little flesh, I wasn't worth eating.

When I realised the lion was not going to kill me, I knew that God had something else planned, some reason to keep me alive. 'What is it?' I asked as I struggled to my feet. 'Direct me.'

Traditions in a traditional nation

SOMALIS USE A RANGE OF SWEEPING, eloquent hand and arm gestures to illustrate their speech, such as a thumb under the chin to denote fullness or a twist of the open hand to suggest 'nothing' or 'no'. It is considered impolite to beckon someone with the index finger – a gesture reserved for dogs – and a thumbs-up is regarded as obscene. Somali men greet one another by three shakes of the hand, then a hand laid upon the heart. Rarely do Somalis of the opposite sex touch when meeting, unless they are related. The customary salutation is 'Assalam Alaikum': 'Peace be upon you.'

There has been little peace for the Somalis since the state was created in 1960 when a British protectorate merged with an Italian colony. But the Horn of Africa nation is starting to recover from recent wars.

In a country steeped in tradition, arranged marriages are common, and, as was to be the case with Waris, young girls are often married off to men much older than themselves. While children take their father's surname and learn about their paternal clan lineage, wives retain their maiden names and position within their own clans.

It is the responsibility of the wealthier elements in a family to help less fortunate members, with gifts of food, money or shelter. Those living in the city might take in child relatives from rural areas and put them through school – although, as Waris's experience shows, children may be exploited.

At mealtimes, men are served first; women and children eat later.

Breakfast for much of the populace might be a millet pancake. For nomads, the staple diet is milk and yoghurt from goats and camels, and grain bought from the sale of livestock. The evening meal could be yoghurt, beans, fresh fruit in season, such as papaya and mango; fish is plentiful in coastal regions. Hands are washed both before and after a meal, and the right hand is used for eating, the left being reserved for prayer and purification.

Women visit one another in their homes, to drink tea or milk together. In towns, men gather in tea shops to set the world to rights. The position of women in this patriarchal society is expressed by an old Somali proverb: 'God created woman from a crooked rib, and anyone who tries to straighten it, breaks it.'

Providing sustenance
A Somalian woman squats down to prepare food in a traditional clay pot.

Back-breaking work

A port city on the Indian Ocean, Mogadishu was beautiful then. Walking along, I craned my neck to look at the stunning white buildings surrounded by palm trees and brightly coloured flowers. Much of the architecture was built by the Italians when the city was the capital of Italian Somaliland, giving the city a Mediterranean feel.

I arrived there several weeks after fleeing home. Along the way, cousins sheltered me, told me news of Aman, and gave me money to complete the journey. Once in the city, I got directions to my sister's neighbourhood and asked some women at a market if they knew Aman.

'I thought you looked familiar!' one cried. Then she told her son to take me to Aman's house. We walked along the quiet streets until we came to a tiny shack. I went inside, found my sister asleep and woke her.

'What are you doing here?' she asked groggily, looking at me as if I were a dream. I sat down and told her my story. At last I had someone to talk to who would understand. She had found a husband, a good man who worked hard. They were expecting their first child.

It was a cramped two-room place, but she grudgingly agreed I could stay as long as I needed. I cleaned the house, scrubbed the clothes and did the shopping in the market. And after Aman gave birth to a beautiful little girl, I helped take care of the baby. It became clear, though, that my sister and I were not alike. She was bossy and treated me like the same little sister she'd left behind five or so years before.

We had other relatives I'd met in Mogadishu, so I went and knocked on the door of Aunt Sahru, my mother's sister, and asked if I could stay with her family for a while.

'You have a friend here,' she said. 'If you want to stay with us, you can.'

Things were off to a better start than I'd imagined. Once again, I began helping around the house.

I had been worried about leaving Mama without anyone to help her with her work, and one day I decided that a partial remedy was to send her money. So I set out to find a job. I stopped at a construction site and convinced the man in charge that I could carry sand and mix as well as the men.

The next morning my career as a construction worker began. It was horrible. I carried back-breaking loads of sand all day and developed enormous blisters on my hands. Everyone thought I would quit, but I stuck it out for a month. By then I had saved $60, which I sent to Mama through an acquaintance, but she never saw a penny of it.

I had started cleaning the house for my aunt again when one day Mohammed Chama Farah, the Somalian ambassador in London, arrived. He was married to yet another aunt, my mother's sister Maruim.

As I dusted my way around the next room, I overheard him say he needed to find a servant before beginning his four-year diplomatic appointment in London. This was my opportunity.

I called Aunt Sahru aside. 'Please ask him if I can be his maid.'

She walked back into the other room, sat beside her brother-in-law and said quietly, 'Why don't you take her? She really is a good cleaner.'

I opened my eyes and was staring into the face of a lion. I tried to stand, but I hadn't eaten for days, so my weak legs wobbled and folded beneath me. 'Come and get me,' I said to the lion. 'I'm ready.'

Uncle Mohammed sat still for a moment, then summoned me. He looked me up and down with disgust. 'OK. Be here tomorrow afternoon. We'll go to London.'

London! I didn't know where it was, but I knew it was very far away, and far away was where I wanted to be. I was on fire with excitement.

The next day Uncle Mohammed picked me up and gave me my passport. I looked at it in wonder, the first paper with my name on it. I hugged Auntie Sahru and waved farewell.

Cool reception

As the driver eased the car out of the airport and into the London morning traffic, I was overcome by such a sad, lonely feeling, in this completely foreign place, with nothing but white, sickly faces around me.

When we stopped in front of my uncle's home, I stared in astonishment. The ambassador's residence was a four-storey mansion. We walked to the front door and entered. Auntie Maruim greeted me in the foyer.

'Come in,' she said coolly. 'Close the door.'

I had planned to rush to her and hug her, but something about the way she stood there in her stylish Western clothes, her hands pressed together, made me freeze in the doorway. 'First I'd like to show you around and explain your duties.'

'Oh,' I said quietly, feeling the last spark of energy leave my body after the long flight. 'Auntie, I'm very tired. I want to lie down. Can I please go to sleep?'

Aunt Maruim took me into her room. The four-poster was the size of my family's entire hut. I climbed under the covers. I had never felt anything so soft and heavenly in my life, and I fell asleep as if I were falling down a long black tunnel.

The following morning I was wandering through the house when she found me. 'Good. You're up. Let's go to the kitchen, and I can show you what you'll be doing.'

I had planned to rush to her and hug her, but something about the way she stood there in her stylish Western clothes, her hands pressed together, made me freeze in the doorway.

I followed in a daze. The room gleamed with blue ceramic tiles and creamy-white cabinets. A six-ring oven dominated the centre. Auntie opened and slammed drawers, calling out, 'And here are the utensils, the cutlery, the linens.' I had no idea what she was talking about.

'At 6.30 each morning you'll serve your uncle's breakfast: herbal tea and two poached eggs. I'd like my coffee in my room at 7. Then you'll make pancakes for the children; they eat at 8 sharp. After breakfast –'

'Auntie, who's going to teach me these things? What's pancakes?'

She stared at me with a sort of panicky look. Exhaling slowly, she said, 'I'll do these things for the first time, Waris. Watch closely. Listen and learn.' I nodded.

I had the routine after the first week and followed it every day for the next four years. For a girl who had never been aware of time, I learned to watch the clock closely – and live by it.

After breakfast I cleaned the kitchen, my aunt's room and her bathroom. Then I worked through each room of the house, dusting, mopping, scrubbing and polishing my way up all four floors. I kept working until I fell into bed around midnight. I never had a day off.

Throughout Africa it's common for more affluent family members to take in the children of their poor relations, and those children work in return for their upkeep. Sometimes the relatives educate the children and treat them like one of their own. Sometimes they don't. Obviously, my aunt and uncle had more important issues on their minds.

During the summer of 1983, when I was about 16, Uncle Mohammed's sister died and her little daughter, Sophie, came to live with us. My uncle enrolled her in All Souls Church of England Primary School, and my morning routine then included walking Sophie to school.

On one of the first mornings, as we strolled, I saw a strange man staring at me. He was white, around 40 and had a ponytail. He had brought his daughter to the school. He didn't hide the fact that he was staring.

After I left Sophie at the door, he walked towards me and started speaking. Since I didn't speak English, I had no idea what he was saying. Frightened, I ran home.

From then on, each time I saw him at the school, he simply smiled politely and went about his business. Then one day he walked up and handed me a card. I tucked it in my pocket and watched as he turned to walk away.

When I got home, I showed the card to one of Auntie Maruim's daughters. 'What does it say?'

'It says he's a photographer.'

I saw that my cousin wanted to get back to the book she was reading, so I hid the card in my room. Some little voice told me to hang onto it.

When Uncle Mohammed's term was coming to an end, he announced the family would be going home. I wasn't excited about returning to Somalia. I wanted to go home wealthy and successful, but I had saved only a pittance from my maid's wages. My dream was to make enough money to buy my mother a house, and to accomplish this, I felt I should stay in England. How I would manage this, I didn't know. But I had faith.

Uncle Mohammed advised us all of the date we were leaving, and of the need to make sure our passports were in order. I did. I promptly sealed mine in a plastic bag, buried it in the garden and announced I couldn't find it. My plan was simple enough: if I didn't have a passport, they couldn't take me back. Uncle was suspicious, but I said, 'Just leave me here. I'll be fine.'

Until the morning of departure, I hadn't really believed that they would leave me all alone. But they did. I stood on the pavement, waved goodbye and watched the car until it was out of sight. I was scared and had to fight an overwhelming feeling of panic.

I picked up my little duffel bag, slung it over my shoulder, unearthed my passport and headed down the street, smiling.

Shining brightly *As part of her glittering modelling career, Waris took to the catwalk for the designer Kenzo in October 1995.*

In front of the camera

I entered a shop that same day and saw a tall, attractive African woman examining some sweaters. We began talking in Somali, and she was quite friendly. Her name was Halwu.

'Where do you live, Waris? What do you do?'

'Oh, you'll think I'm crazy, but I don't have any place to live because my family went back to Somalia today. My uncle was the ambassador, but now the new man is coming. So right this minute, I have no idea where I'm headed.'

She waved to silence me, as if the movement of her hand could sweep away all my problems. 'I have a room at the YMCA. You can come and stay for the night.'

Halwu and I became close friends. After a few days I took a room at the YWCA right across the way. Then I set out to find a job.

'Why don't you start by looking right here?' Halwu said, pointing to McDonald's.

'There's no way. I can't speak English or read. Besides, I don't have a work permit.'

But she knew the ropes, and I began working there, in the kitchen. I washed dishes, wiped counters, scrubbed grills and mopped floors. I went home at night smelling of grease. But I didn't complain, because at least now I could support myself. I was grateful to have a job.

I began going to the free language school, learning English and how to read and write. For the first time in years my days weren't only about work.

Sometimes Halwu took me to nightclubs, where the whole crowd seemed to know her. Overcoming my strict African upbringing, I chatted away, forcing myself to talk with everyone – black, white, male, female. I had to learn survival skills for this new world. My life was moving smoothly. It was about to change dramatically.

One afternoon when I got back home from McDonald's, I pulled out the photographer's card, which I'd stuck in my passport, and marched to Halwu's room. I showed her the card, explained the history and said, 'I never really understood what he wanted.'

'Well,' she said, 'why don't you call and ask him?'

'You talk to him. My English is still not very good.'

She did, and the next day I went to inspect Mike Goss's studio. I had no idea what to expect, but when I opened the door, I stumbled into another world. Hanging everywhere in the lobby were enormous posters featuring beautiful women. 'Oh!' I said, spinning. I just knew – this is it. This is my opportunity.

Mike came out and explained that as soon as he saw me, he had wanted to take my picture. I stared at him with my mouth hanging open. 'That's it? A picture like this?' I waved at the posters.

'Yes,' he said, nodding emphatically. 'You have the most beautiful profile.'

Two days later I returned to the studio. The make-up woman sat me down and started to work, coming at me with cotton wool, brushes, sponges, creams, paints and powders, poking me with her fingers and pulling my skin.

'Now' – the woman stepped back and looked at me with satisfaction – 'look in the mirror.'

I stared in the glass. My face was transformed, all golden, silky and light with make-up. 'Wow! Look at me!'

The woman led me out to Mike, who positioned me on a stool. I studied objects I'd never seen before: the camera, lights, battery packs, cords hanging like snakes.

'OK, Waris,' he said. 'Put your lips together and stare straight ahead. Chin up. That's it – beautiful!'

I heard a click, followed by a loud pop, which made me jump. The flashes went off, the lights blazing for a split second. Somehow the lights made me feel like a different person.

Mike took a piece of paper from the camera and motioned for me to walk over. He pulled off the top layer of paper. As I watched, a woman gradually emerged from the sheet as if by magic. When he handed me the Polaroid, I barely recognised myself. There was a glamorous creature like the ones posing in the lobby. They had transformed me. Instead of Waris the maid, I was Waris the model.

Welcome surgery

My career as a model took off. I worked in Paris, Milan, then New York; I appeared in a Revlon commercial with Cindy Crawford, Claudia Schiffer and Lauren Hutton. These projects kept snowballing, and soon I was in the big fashion magazines: *Elle*, *Glamour*, Italian *Vogue*, and British and American *Vogue*.

But for all the excitement and success of my new life, I carried wounds from the old. The tiny hole the circumciser had left me permitted urine to escape only one drop at a time. It took me about 10 minutes to urinate. My periods were always a nightmare. I couldn't function for several days each month; I simply went to bed and wanted to die so the suffering would stop.

I finally plucked up enough courage to find a specialist doctor. When I went to Dr Michael Macrae's office, I said to him, 'There's something I haven't told you. I'm from Somalia and I ... I ...'

He didn't even let me finish the sentence. 'Go get changed. I want to examine you.' He saw the look of terror on my face. 'It's OK.'

He called in his nurse to show me where to change, how to put the gown on, and asked her if there was someone in the hospital who could speak Somali. But when she came back, she brought a Somali man. I thought, 'Oh, here's the rotten luck, to discuss this using a Somali man to translate!' How much worse could it get?

Dr Macrae said, 'Explain to her that she's closed up way too much – I don't even know how she's made it this far. We need to operate on her as soon as possible.'

I could see the Somali man wasn't happy. He glared at the doctor and then said to me, 'Well, if you really want it, they can open you up. But do you know this is against your culture? Does your family know you're doing this?'

I stared in the glass. My face was transformed, all golden, silky and light with make-up. 'Wow! Look at me!'

A mother's love *With the birth of her son, Aleeke, Waris felt a new respect for her own mother and for all the women of Somalia, spurring her on to campaign on their behalf.*

'No.'

'The first thing I'd do is discuss it with them.'

I nodded. His was the response of a typical African man.

Over a year went by before I was able to have the surgery. I had to overcome some practical problems and my own last-minute doubts, but Dr Macrae did a fine job, and I've always been grateful. He told me, 'You're not alone. Women come in with this problem all the time. A lot of women from the Sudan, Egypt, Somalia. Some of them are pregnant and terrified. So, without the permission of their husbands, they come to me, and I do my best.'

Within three weeks I could sit on the toilet and – whoosh! There's no way to explain what a freedom that was.

My mission

By now I was appearing in commercials and music videos, and working with the biggest photographers in the fashion business. My life was heavenly.

I was even reunited with my family when the BBC made a documentary about me. I asked my mother if she would like to come back and live with me in England or America.

'But what would I do?'

'That's precisely it. You've done enough work. It's time to rest.'

'No. Your father's getting old and he needs me. This is my home. This is all I've ever known.'

One thing she did want was grandchildren, but I had never met a man I wanted to be with. Then one night in New York in 1995 I met a shy musician with a 70s Afro and a funky style. His name was Dana Murray, and I knew from that moment he was my man.

At dinner the next night I laughed and told him that some day I was going to have his baby. My crazy prediction came true with the birth of our son on June 13, 1997. He was beautiful, with silky black hair and long feet and fingers. I named him Aleeke.

After going through the cycle of womanhood that began prematurely with my circumcision at age five and came full circle with my baby's birth when I was about 30, I had even more respect for my own mother. I understood what incredible strength the women in Somalia possess.

Llaura Ziv, a writer for the fashion magazine *Marie Claire*, made an appointment to interview me. When we met, I liked her right away. I said, 'I don't know what kind of story you wanted from me, but all of that fashion-model stuff's been done a million times. If you promise to publish it, I'll give you a real story.'

She said, 'Oh? Well, I'll do my best,' and switched on her tape recorder. I began telling her the story of my circumcision when I was a child. Halfway through the interview, she started crying and turned off the tape.

'I mean, it's horrible, it's disgusting. I never dreamed such things still happen today.'

'That's the point,' I said. 'People in the West don't know.'

The day after the interview, I felt stunned and embarrassed. Everybody would know my most personal secret. My closest friends didn't know what had happened to me as a little girl, and now I was telling millions of strangers.

But after much thought, I realised I needed to talk about my circumcision. First of all, it bothers me deeply. Besides the health problems that I still struggle with, I will never know the pleasures of sex. I feel incomplete, crippled, and knowing that there's nothing I can do to change that is the most hopeless feeling of all.

The second reason was my hope of making people aware that this practice still occurs today. I had to speak not only for me but for the millions of girls living with it and those dying from it.

When the interview came out, the response was dramatic. I began giving more interviews and speaking at schools, community organisations and anywhere I could to publicise the issue. In 1997 the United Nations Population Fund invited me to join its fight to stop female circumcision, or female genital mutilation (FGM), as it is more aptly called today.

That's what I'm working towards.

From the moment God saved me from a lion, I felt He had a plan for me, some reason to keep me alive. My faith tells me God has work for me to do and this is my mission. I pray that one day no woman will have to experience this pain and that it becomes a thing of the past. ∎

Where are they now?

NOW IN HER FORTIES and as radiantly beautiful as ever, Waris Dirie lives in Vienna and continues her tireless fight against female genital mutilation (FGM), through the Waris Dirie Foundation. She served for a time as the United Nations Population Fund's special ambassador for the elimination of FGM, but stood down to devote herself to the Foundation.

Her autobiography, *Desert Flower*, published in 1998, was a huge international best-seller. The book so impressed singer-songwriter Elton John that he bought the film rights, describing it as 'the most beautiful inspiration to anyone'.

Such success and acclaim have inspired Waris to devote her life to the struggle, and she went on to write *Desert Dawn*, in which she told how, 20 years after her escape, she visited her family in a Somalia that was torn apart by war and plagued with famine.

There followed *Desert Children*, the result of research with a team of journalists which revealed that FGM, far from being just an African issue, had ramifications in Europe, where as many as half a million girls and women are affected. According to estimates by UNICEF, 3 million girls in Africa, Asia, the USA, Australia and Europe are still subjected to FGM.

In 2007, the World Demographic Association awarded Waris Dirie the annual *Prix des Générations* in recognition of her fight for the well-being of rising generations of girls. In the same year, the French President Nicolas Sarkozy acknowledged Waris's humanitarian work with the award of the medal of *Chevalier de la Légion d'honneur*.

Also in 2007, she published a fourth book, *Letter to My Mother*, which Waris describes as 'a long, detailed epistle ... about the wounds of my soul that won't heal, about the downside of my career, and about the demon that has long since haunted me'.

WINNING SMILE Waris received the Two Wings Award in 2003 for her work to improve the living conditions of women in developing countries.

BEHIND ENEMY LINES

BY JUNE 1944, GEORGE MILLAR had fought in North Africa, escaped from a POW camp and won a Military Cross. Five days before D-Day, the dashing Scotsman, codenamed Émile, parachuted into occupied France to organise and lead Maquis resistance groups and cripple the rail network in enemy territory.

We were lying under a shower of huge raindrops. The shelter of small criss-crossing pine branches, which we had erected, served to keep heavy rain off for about 10 minutes. Then it was wetter underneath than it was outside. Lying in my feather-lined sleeping bag, I managed to keep in a steamily warm condition. But poor Boulaya was cold as well as wet. Boulaya, whose name was Joseph Barthelet, was on the tall side for a Frenchman. A thin man in his late 30s or early 40s, and a native of Besançon, he spoke English with a London accent and gave the impression he had been fatter before the war. His clothes were appalling, yet he wore them with a rakish air, as though they were a flag – as indeed they were. They were the badge of his dangerous life. The uniform of a captain in the Resistance.

'I think I shall bring big Berger back with me from the other Maquis at Champoux,' Boulaya said. 'And we will look for a location for our new command post. Something a little distant from this Maquis at Vieilley. And we must try to build a rainproof hut if we can get no tents. Of course you will postpone your trip to Besançon today.'

'Why? I might as well be there in the rain as sitting here dripping in the woods.'

'I do wish you wouldn't go, but if you plan an operation on the depot or the station I shall come along as second-in-command.'

The previous evening, two of the Vieilley Maquis had blown up two turntables in Besançon that were used for shifting rolling stock from one line to another. Sixty-three locomotives were now trapped, but the charges had not been strong enough and German engineers thought they could have one turntable moving in a few days.

I told Boulaya of my new plan to destroy the railway. In the very centre of Besançon, the railway lines running to Belfort and Vesoul, to the east and north, as well as the lines to Dijon, to the west, and Dole, to the south, fanned out. I wanted to attack all points of this fan.

Opposite the fan was the restroom for the German railway workers, whom the Maquis always referred to as the 'Bahnhofs'; they had been injected into the French railway system to make it more 'honest and efficient' from the German point of view. Each of them was armed with a pistol, and we had to be prepared for trouble from them. After the previous raid they would be on full alert. On the other side of the lines was Control Post No. 3, where the local pointsman would presumably be sympathetic, but he was dangerous in that he was in constant communication with the depot, and if he was excited or frightened the people at the other end of the line would know that something was wrong.

'We shall need you to go and reason with the man in Control Post No. 3,' I told Boulaya. 'To reason with him by means of a Sten, of course, but at the same time it requires somebody who can keep absolutely calm himself, and talk so smoothly and so fast that the pointsman can continue to give the right answers on the telephone with the minimum of hold up.'

They dressed me up in workman's blue overalls to make my fair hair and British baby face less noticeable, and we set off that morning on our

Dashing saboteur *Behind the smile of the young George Millar (opposite, top) lay a man with nerves of steel. Millar successfully organised sabotage operations on behalf of the French Resistance, including a train derailment in July 1944 (opposite, below).*

His clothes were appalling, yet he wore them with a rakish air, as though they were a flag – as indeed they were. They were the badge of his dangerous life. The uniform of a captain in the Resistance.

bicycles, the Frisé, Maurice and I, to do a recce. The Frisé, so-called because of his huge head with an enormous thickness of dust-coloured curls (I suppose in our army he would have been called 'Curly'), had been a sailor. He was an old 22 year old, tough and cheeky but intelligent. The Frisé learned easily and his personal weapons, a Sten and a Colt, were in perfect condition. Maurice, in his middle or late 20s, had a family in Besançon.

The attractive old town of Besançon, lying on a loop of the wide river Doubs, is entirely surrounded by hills. Twisting and turning through the narrow lanes of the suburbs, the Frisé led me down to the hollow of Besançon itself until, turning sharply under a bridge, we halted beside the railway lines.

Carrying my bicycle across the tracks, I counted the *cœurs d'aiguilles* – sets of points – that would need charges. There were 12 of them. And that did not include the main through line to Belfort I could see forking away nearer the actual station 180m (200yd) farther on. That would take four more charges, making 16 in all.

'I'd forgotten about them,' the Frisé agreed. 'I'll look after them.'

In a hairdresser's shop by the station I bought a large pipe and a tobacco pouch, presents for Boulaya. A member of the feared *Milice* – a paramilitary force created in January 1943 by the Vichy Regime, with German aid, to fight the French Resistance – and a German were having their hair cut. They were agreeing that the Americans would have to give up trying to take the Cherbourg Peninsula and that all the Allied bridge-head would soon be non-existent.

Maurice arrived with information that there were two patrols which patrolled the line at irregular intervals during the night. One was Cossack, the other German. The Cossacks, in the pay of the Nazis, were reported to shoot at everything they saw. They were quartered not far from our route in and out of town.

That afternoon in a wood just outside Besançon, 16 standard 1½lb charges took a good deal of making with only novices to help. And the only type of explosive remaining in our stock was called '808'; excellent stuff, but it had two drawbacks. It had a powerful and sticky smell, and when you handled any quantity of it you got a bad headache. I said nothing, but got them to heat a sufficient quantity of the stuff in boiling water until it was soft enough to handle. With many complaints about the smell, they got down to making the charges. To save material, I put only one primer in each charge and 16 fuses for the 16 charges. When they were made we sewed them into little linen bags.

By 10 o'clock that night five of us were at the rendezvous, an electric pylon where our

Reporting back *The SOE files at the National Archives in Kew, London, include George Millar's full description, headed 'Emile's report', on his landing in France on June 1, 1944.*

George.Reid MILLAR – CHANCELLOR – TREASURER Circuit.

E M I L E ' S   R E P O R T
_____

I dropped in at CHAGNY, some 15 kms. due North of June 1st at 2 a.m.

The reception was organised by the MAQUIS of JACQUES, THEODULE's men, and it was well organised from the air view. I plainly saw the lights and the letter through before I dropped, and I also plainly saw that the aircraft overshot. My lines twisted in the slipstream, but I [made a com]fortable landing about one km. beyond the reception in [a fores]t.

[W]hen I had folded my parachute some armed peasants [found] me, told me that I was a Boche, and led me back roughly [and] who asked me for the password. I gave the word [given] previously to contact THEODULE at the safe house indicated [in] LONDON. JACQUES then had me searched, saying that the [word] for the dropping was "Cambronne". Finally reassured by [my] accent and the name "THEODULE" he said that he was [glad] to see me, and sent me off with a boy guide to a farm.

The following day, having burned my parachute, I moved down to the MAQUIS, which was near the farm. I met the smell of ordure, remembered from maquis I had seen while [f]rom GERMANY. Otherwise JACQUES was well installed. [Buil]t tent-shaped wattle huts covered with railway [sleepers.] There were some twenty maquisards, dirty, dressed in [al]most agreeable.

The second aeroplane that had left with me had failed but the contents of my own aeroplane were interesting. [I] explained the working of the Bazooka and the A/T mine [to the maq]uis and inspected the material they had received on path from the forest ran into the suburbs of Besançon, but there was no sign of the Frisé. We waited for an hour and a half. Spirits, which had been reasonably good up to now, sank completely.

'Obviously, we can't go on now,' said Buhl, a man about my age with a thin, weak face and large dark eyes. Boulaya told me that he was a noted 'killer'. 'If the Frisé isn't here it means he's been picked up by the Boche. With all that stuff on him they'll know he's one of a gang. The whole town will be watched.'

'There is nothing to suggest that Frisé has been taken,' I said, although secretly I thought it might be so.

We set off, gingerly at first, and then gathering pace. After 30 minutes we were in the town proper. As we were coming down the last slippery hill between the high walls before the station – I could already see the blue lights of Control Post No. 3 – the beam of a headlight swung around the corner. We flung ourselves face downwards in the gutter and heard a motorcycle sputtering past. It stopped about 180m (200yd) farther up the hill. The rider appeared to adjust his coat, then he continued on his way. This reassured me. If the man had seen us he would not have dared to stop. On the other hand, he was almost certainly a German. No Frenchman would use a motorcycle at that place and hour. For a second or two I actually thought of turning, I am ashamed to say. But I urged the men on.

The station seemed a million times busier and noisier than in the morning, due to one engine shunting carriages and trucks. We saw the door of the Bahnhofs' hut opening and closing. I had no intention of keeping either myself or the men waiting too long. It was bad for the nerves. My watch said 12.30.

We slouched into the lights, walked down the railway line, and with a brief glance around, I got to work. I felt for the first charge or two as though I were working on the stage of the Palladium. Then I got used to the lights, the noise and the bustle. I had all six charges wedged against the rails and initiated in less than 3 minutes.

Maurice was crouched over the points and working slowly towards me with his charges. Buhl, his Sten gun held along his leg so it did not show, was facing the big control post, and another of the group was lurking in the shadows by the Bahnhofs' hut. There were people moving about everywhere, but the bustle gave me confidence. Maurice had now finished his work. I gave the whistle that was the agreed sign for withdrawal.

I told one of the men to go and tell the rail workers in the shunting yards to clear off, that the station would go up in 20 minutes. As we made for the gate there was an announcement from the control tower: 'All personnel leave this area at once and return to the depot. This is urgent.' And then, very faintly, the metallic voice added, '*Vive La France.*'

The Frisé met us at the gate.

'Where have you been?' I asked, and followed the question with some vile French.

'At the rendezvous,' he lied. 'A Cossack patrol has just passed the railway bridge. When are we going to do the job?'

'The job is done, or at least our part of it. The charges will begin to go off in 15 minutes.'

Risking all *René Parietti ('Maurice'), Joseph Barthelet ('Boulaya') and André Roulier ('Le Frisé') put their lives on the line for the sake of 'La France'.*

The soldiers of the night

IN JUNE 1940, General de Gaulle broadcast a speech from his base in London to his fellow countrymen in France. 'Believe me when I tell you that nothing is lost for France,' he said. 'Whatever happens, the flame of French Resistance must not die and will not die.' Thousands of French men and women took this as a call to arms, and began to organise resistance against the German occupation. In the occupied north of France, numerous separate groups sprang up, many of them ideologically based: communists banded together with other communists, Catholics with Catholics. There were groups such as the *Cheminots*, who specialised in disabling railway lines and engines, as well as a group of Zionist *Résistants* dedicated to smuggling Jews out of France into neutral Spain. The *Maquis* were slightly different: they were made up in the first instance of men and women who had chosen to evade forced conscription into labour battalions to work in German factories. They, the *Maquisards*, fled into the uplands of Haute-Savoie and other impenetrable regions. Thousands hid together in caves and forests, gradually organising themselves into an effective army.

The Special Operations Executive (SOE) in London did its best to support and coordinate the efforts of the various Resistance organisations. It trained agents for secret operations inside France, and set up a network of radio operatives throughout the country. It parachuted caches of arms and other equipment to the *Maquisards*, so that they could take the fight to the Germans. Most crucially, SOE sent in born leaders and experts in sabotage – some of them French, others, like George Millar, British. These highly trained soldiers became the commanders in the open guerrilla war that the Resistance waged against Germany from D-Day on. Once they were fighting in the open, the Resistance successfully harassed and delayed crack German units moving up towards the beachheads in Normandy. And they were more than a match for the unhappy foreign conscripts in the *Wehrmacht*, such as the renegade Russians and Ukrainians that Millar describes as 'Cossacks'.

By that time there was a secret army of 150,000 men and women inside occupied France – every one a 'soldier of the night', as the writer André Malraux later described them. The total number of Resistance fighters cannot be known for sure: perhaps as many as 400,000 brave individuals. What is known is that 220,000 French civilians were later honoured by their government for their part in the war against the Nazis.

READY TO AMBUSH Members of the French Maquis Resistance in 1944 on the island of Corsica, their rifles levelled.

'I must be off.'

'Where are you going?'

'To place my charges, of course.'

I knew it was useless trying to stop him. 'We'll wait at the rendezvous.'

The rest of us had done nearly a quarter of an hour's hard walking and were not far from the Cossacks' barracks when the first charge went off. The whole town was in a hollow, so the noise sounded particularly impressive. There was a vivid flash too. From then on, at irregular intervals spaced over nearly 40 minutes, the explosions came. As I counted 13, 14, 15, 16, I knew that the Frisé also had succeeded. Not one charge had failed.

The sound of machine-gun firing came from the Cossacks' place. We later learned that they thought this was an air raid and were proving to their German masters that they were awake by firing into the air. I was glad they did: the noise sobered my men. They were inclined to get too jubilant and noisy despite my injunctions that withdrawal was the most dangerous part of the whole operation and must be performed in silence.

We hobbled into camp at 5 in the morning. Boulaya and Georges [Molle] were waiting with coffee and a huge omelette. They were jubilant. In his report to Colonel Morin, or 'le patron' as he preferred to be called, Boulaya wrote: 'The Maquis of Vieilley, led by the British officer, Émile, saved the city of Besançon from Allied bombing [making it] useless to the enemy and [saving it] for posterity and for France.'

We decided to blow up all the points from Besançon to Vesoul. I made the rounds of the stations, locating the targets, then planning the attack, and sometimes carrying it out myself with one or two helpers. I was careful never to make too many attacks close to Vieilley. This obliged me to take to cycling again. One of the targets was the station at Montbozon.

Near miss

Although I carried an astonishing number of excellently forged 'personal papers', some of them German, to back up my cover story that I was Georges Henri Maillard, born in Paris, being smelled out in the dark and quietly surrounded by Germans became nearly a mania with me after a night in Montbozon. Berger and I were cycling through the small town and since we were both tired and the curfew approached we decided to stop for the night. The safe house Berger chose to shelter us was opposite the hotel. Berger – who had now come across from the Champoux Maquis – had just turned out the light and moved across the room to the window to pull up the blind in deference to my mania for early morning light.

'Pssst,' he hissed and beckoned me across.

There were Germans in the street below us. One truck already stood under our window, and, while I watched, another rolled silently in, with its motor cut and no headlights. From the hooded back leaped a string of steel-helmeted soldiers. They cast grotesque moon shadows. They were the first Germans I had seen that made no noise with their feet. They had taken off their boots. Berger and I stood there not daring to move.

Like grey ghosts the Germans ran to their posts, surrounding the hotel. Two machine-guns covered the street. Every corner round the hotel was

There were Germans in the street below us. One truck already stood under our window, and, while I watched, another rolled silently in, with its motor cut and no headlights. From the hooded back leaped a string of steel-helmeted soldiers. They cast grotesque moon shadows.

Stretegic target *Besançon, where George Millar and his Maquis colleagues blew up the railway, is the main town in the Franche-Comté region of eastern France. Although a long way from the Normandy beaches of the D-Day landings, it was a key transport hub for the Germans trying to supply their forces further west.*

covered by a grey figure tensely crouched on one knee, and holding a short automatic weapon.

A car came ghosting into the street and slid to a stop beside the trucks. Two officers in steel helmets got out, and stood stiffly to attention in the middle of the road. One of the kneeling grey figures detached itself from a shadow and came across to them. When they spoke, the hearer put the side of his big helmet up against the speaker's mouth. There was something incredibly sinister about the silent conversation.

The two officers tiptoed across the road. Unlike their men, they wore boots. They stood on the steps of the hotel for a moment. Now three men in stocking soles had joined them. One beat on the door with the butt of an automatic rifle. The door opened quickly, too quickly perhaps. The electric light from the open doorway shone out upon the Germans. I saw that they belonged to the *Feldgendarmerie*. They wore great metal plaques hanging on chains from their necks.

They stalked into the hotel. The lights went on one by one in the bedrooms. One pair of shutters was not closed. When the light went on we got a flash picture of an elderly man in a fawn-coloured nightshirt sitting up in bed. Two Germans stood in the doorway looking at him. One of them, an officer, read a paper in his hand, probably the police list of hotel clients. The other German crossed the room and pulled down the blind.

'Can we get out of here by the back?' I whispered to Berger.

'No. And who knows? The whole place may be surrounded. If we move at all we are mincemeat.'

The search continued for 2 hours, then the two officers walked noisily back to their car. The car started, the engine raced. The two trucks followed suit. All three vehicles roared away, the noise from their exhausts gradually dwindling to silence.

Berger nudged me. His finger was on his lips, but there was no need to warn me to keep quiet. I knew already that the silent guards still kneeled around the hotel. Sleep was impossible. At 5 o'clock I got up to see the Germans silently forming up in the roadway. There were 18 of them. Each man got out a cigarette. I watched them through the vertical slit between the shutter and the wall. Their 18 glowing cigarettes were pointing at us. I feared they might see into our window. When all the cigarettes were finished, they turned and marched away looking like a grotesque rectangular animal sliding away into the bluish moonlight.

Next morning I was thankful to get clear of Montbozon. The *Feldgendarmerie* had not found the person they were looking for. And we never knew who that was.

Home for heroes

We had to choose our new headquarters, and one that could not be stealthily surrounded. And for this Georges had selected a resting place for heroes. Half an hour's climb behind our Maquis – more than halfway up the hill to 'La Dame Blanche', the massive, square, empty fortress on the skyline – a band of pine trees separated the edge of the main forest of Chailluz from the topmost steeply sloping hayfields of Vieilley. Armed with saw and billhook, Berger and Georges — both countrymen and experts at such things — had made a very reasonable dwelling for two people in one day. The cabin was rectangular, about 6m (20ft) long by 2.5m (8ft) wide. One of the long sides was open, and faced, through a screen of pine trees, a magnificent view of the Ognon Valley and the hill-lands of the Haute-Saône beyond. The roof — made of stout pine branches covered with small branches and then with straw — was about 3m (10ft) high on the open side and then sloped down to 1.2m (4ft) at the back. Boulaya — who had been promoted to the rank of major by the 'patron' — and I each had a bed made by cutting an indent into the clean soil and filling it with dry hay. At the other side of our beds was a table running the length of the short wall and made with old boards salvaged by me from the fortress up above.

Facing the table were two stout chairs made by driving forked branches into the ground, with a seat and back woven by Berger from creepers. You stepped from the open side of the shack to a 1m (3ft) wide terraced path, which led to two exits and to a lookout post from which we could see the roads and railway far beneath us. Georges made the entry without cutting a single branch. You left a path through the wood, cutting through some bushes on a surface of broken branches that did not show tracks, then down a steep bank, and then winding between small trees, and into the pines. The other exit was only for emergencies. We made a zigzagging path through the pines nearly 90m (100yd) in length. Near its end were the latrine and the refuse dump, and beyond them the concealed exit. If surprised in the shack, the long pathway would give us extra mobility.

When the other Maquisards saw that we were shifting, they too left their old beds in the forest alcoves and moved off to other nests farther from the main camp. We did not tell them where we slept, and they did not disclose their new sleeping places to us. In this way the Maquis became decentralised at nights. For we were nervous.

A vital force *Members of the Maquis Resistance of Vieilley on September 9, 1944.*

Hunted

The attack on the fuel-tanker train at Roches looked like a job for two men. It should be possible to crawl along the embankment from the level crossing, keeping between the railway and the wood, and stalk one, possibly two, German sentries, to find a gap in the guard. Then one of them could climb onto a group of tankers and fix on say three charges (magnetic 'clams' would be best) linked to an incendiary. The other man would have a Sten and lie under the tankers and give protection until the job was done. All the Maquisards were sitting around the fireplace in the new living space, eager to come. It must be someone young, agile, able to crawl and to run if need be.

'I'll take you, Nono,' I said. Not yet 20 he had been in the Vieilley Maquis for about a week. 'We shall go on bicycles and you'll want a rucksack with soft shoes, a Sten and something to blacken our faces and hands. Wear dark clothes. And look me out three "clams" and an incendiary with a small roll of detonating fuse, some ordinary fuse, one of the small boxes with two detonators and a roll of adhesive tape. We leave at 5 o'clock.'

He laid out everything we needed for the operation neatly on the table and checked all the articles off on his list. This was his great day.

As we cycled, Nono was in great spirits. 'What did you do in peacetime?' he asked. 'I suppose you were a soldier, an officer.'

'No. I was a newspaperman.'

'Which paper, Émile?'

'The *Daily* …'

The words died on my lips. There was a German soldier in the wood on the left. He did not seem to notice us and we cycled on for about 3m (3yd), breasting the slope. Then both of us saw what lay ahead – several German lorries were pulled into the side of the road, and the soldiers were examining another cyclist.

'We must turn back.'

As we turned, one of the Germans bellowed down the road, obviously to men concealed behind us, 'Terrorists …'

And before we got any speed up, the man we had seen in the bushes had come out in front of us. **Short and square, I shall remember his face as long as I live.** It was a strong, shiny, very-much-washed-looking face. There was no fear in it. Only satisfaction. I struggled to get my pistol out but it would not move from my pocket. There was only one thing to do – ride for it.

The German had already raised his rifle to the aim position. I would pass him at a range of 2m (2yd). I was between him and Nono. I assumed that I was as good as dead. We were side-by-side picking up speed, when the bang came close to my right eardrum. I could not believe I was still careering down the hill, swerving my bicycle from side to side. Then I realised that they had killed Nono instead of me.

The Germans had some kind of machine-gun going now. The steel was zipping off the road surface all around me. There was only one piece of available cover. I dived into the wood on my right and threw the bicycle down. There were Germans in that wood, but probably higher up.

I hoped that I was in a tongue of the southern part of the forest of Chailluz. On my left was an open glade running up to a small farm. I dared not run up it because it was observed by the Germans. To my right I could hear them smashing through the small trees and bushes. My only hope was to get to the top of the tongue and into the forest proper before they cut me off.

Although I was pouring with sweat, I kept my leather jacket on to protect my body from scratches. My face, hands and bare toes and ankles were soon running with blood and I had to slash my way through the bramble with my parachutist's knife. I could hear the Germans edging ever closer. To make the going harder the wood ran up a steep hill. I had never felt such physical exhaustion.

When I reached the edge of the forest proper I paused a moment. The Germans were struggling through a thicket perhaps 45m (50yd) behind me. I drew my Colt and sent two .45 shells thudding into this thicket. There was an instant answering salvo with a sub-machine gun and rifles, but when I had fired I had dropped down a bank and now, fairly silently on my rubber-soled sandals, I was running through more open woodland.

The bushes and trees through which I had torn my way were hanging with moisture, soaking my corduroy trousers; they were so heavy it was difficult to run. I stopped to roll them up over my knees. Then I heard another party of Germans arrive at the farm in what sounded like two trucks. I must try to make a circle around this second party. The first party was on the move again. I got out the excellent compass given to me in London and checked my direction. Until I found a path I knew I would have to go through the forest using my memory of the map.

After half an hour I struck a path that I recognised. It was just what I needed to take me around the large German party that was now cutting deep into the wood from the farm. I continued running down the path for perhaps 3km (2 miles). All sounds of pursuit had now died, and I was nervous, for an unheard enemy is sinister. It was possible they had set guards along the Marchaux road.

At the edge of the clear space that bordered the road I pulled out a small flask and after drinking nearly half the calvados it contained felt equal to the crossing and climb that now confronted me. I tried to clean the blood off my face with a handkerchief damped in spittle and took off my tell-tale jacket, rolling it into a shape that was easily carried. I changed the magazine in my Colt and thrust it loosely into my trouser pocket.

I strolled across the road, as though I was a cultivator returning from his work. No Germans were in sight. But the road was busy with peasants. As I mounted the hill on the western end of the plateau between Marchaux and Champoux, I heard the church bell of Marchaux begin slowly to toll. I was sure that it was tolling for Nono.

Pushing myself to my fastest pace, I climbed the long hill to the path that I knew so well running along the summit. There was no sign of

Brothers in arms *George Millar (right) stands alongside his Resistance colleague Georges Molle (left). The photo, taken after the liberation, shows the entrance to the sewer in which, on August 15, 1944, the two men were able to escape from the Gestapo.*

Germans on the top, and I made good time back to the Maquis hideout. They were amazed to see me for the rumour was already going around that I was dead. It was only the next day that we knew for certain it was Nono.

The first rain came at midnight. The following morning the Maquis decided that as the rain had set in for several days to move into a barn on the outskirts of Vieilley.

'Isn't that a little risky?' I asked Boulaya.

'No. Of course, I had forgotten. We've been saved by a miracle.'

'After yesterday I am prepared to believe in it. What is your miracle?'

'The Junkers tried to murder Hitler. The army is fighting the SS in several places. There have been shots in the barracks at Besançon. The Gestapo have their hands full for the moment.'

'The Champoux Maquis moved last night,' he said. 'Just as well, too. An hour or two later the Boche were at Champoux. Six hundred men, all searching for you.' ∎

What happened next?

DURING THE THREE MONTHS George Millar spent in France in 1944, he and his French comrades carried out dozens of raids. They destroyed trains and track, blocked roads to stop German troop movements, and ambushed the enemy wherever they could find them. Many times Millar came close to being caught – once he narrowly avoided detection by the Gestapo by hiding in a sewer. Among the tools of his dangerous trade was a doctor's certificate saying that he had incurable throat problems: it accounted for the husky whisper he used to disguise the Scottish lilt to his spoken French.

At the end of the war, Millar left the Army, divorced his first wife, who had been living with someone else, and married a friend of hers, Isabel Paske-Smith. Immediately after the war, he wrote a book entitled simply *Maquis*, which was the first to inform the British public that British officers had worked in France with the French Resistance. Millar went on to have a successful career as a memoirist and travel writer before settling down to a life of farming and shooting on his Dorset estate.

In recognition of his wartime achievements, George Millar was awarded the DSO and the Military Cross. The French recognised his contribution to the liberation of their country with the *Légion d'Honneur* and the *Croix de Guerre*. He was long remembered in the highlands where he fought alongside the Maquis – and not just for his military prowess. So good-looking was he that, 60 years on, women of the Resistance would still sigh 'Ah! Émile!' when his name was mentioned, and lay a hand on their heart. Millar died in 2005.

LA RÉUNION French Resistance fighters meet again in the woods above the village of Vieilley. They are, from left, Claude Dody, Georges Molle, Marcel Boichard and George Millar.

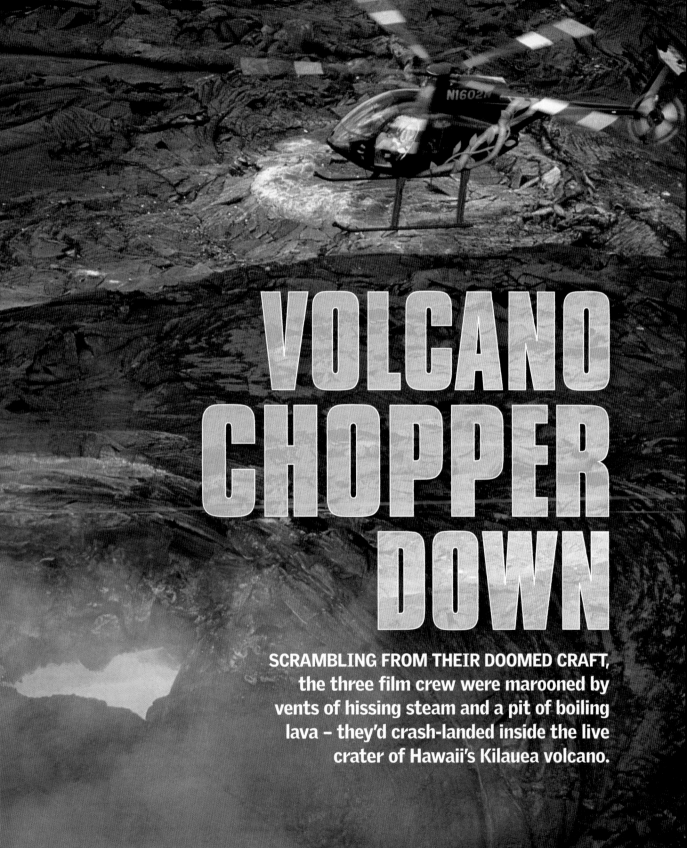

VOLCANO CHOPPER DOWN

SCRAMBLING FROM THEIR DOOMED CRAFT, the three film crew were marooned by vents of hissing steam and a pit of boiling lava – they'd crash-landed inside the live crater of Hawaii's Kilauea volcano.

It had been raining for a week in Hawaii's Volcanoes National Park, and the Hollywood film crew had seen little of the volcano they had come to shoot. On Saturday morning, they couldn't wait any longer. 'Let's go,' Michael Benson announced.

Benson, 49, was in Hawaii to film background footage for the thriller *Sliver*. He was accompanied by camera technician Chris Duddy, 31, and helicopter pilot Craig Hosking, 34. They planned to fly low over the volcano and zoom in on the crater floor with a special camera.

The site chosen was the smoking Pu'u 'O'o vent of Kilauea, the world's most active volcano. Since 1983, its oozing lava had been devouring villages and had added hundreds of acres to the island as it hissed into the sea and solidified. Now, during a quieter period, the crater floor, larger than three football fields, was covered with a thin layer of hardened lava.

As they prepared to film on November 21, 1992, Benson decided to buy a little insurance. He knew some islanders believed in the powers of a volcano goddess called Madame Pele. They pictured her with fiery eyes, lava-black hair and a fondness for gin. So Benson — with a flair for the dramatic — decided to drop a bottle of gin into the crater. 'We need only a few minutes of good weather,' he explained. 'Maybe with a little persuasion, Madame Pele will cooperate.'

As Hosking circled the chopper above the steaming cone, Duddy tossed out the offering. He missed the opening, however, and the bottle exploded on the volcano's rim. 'Close enough,' Benson said. 'She'll get the idea.'

Hosking now hovered over the smoking caldera while Benson filmed the crater floor. 'We got some good footage,' Benson said. 'But to be sure, let's do one more take.'

This 'shoot' was the kind of cinematic challenge that Benson, a veteran of such hits as *Terminator 2* and *Patriot Games*, thrived on. Tall, lean, with brown hair and blue eyes, Benson knew he had a tough, winning team.

With a craggy face and prematurely white hair, Duddy already had more than 40 films to his credit. The gangling Hosking was known as one of the film industry's best helicopter pilots.

At 11.25am, they passed 90m (300ft) above the crater's rim — right over the spot where Duddy had tossed in the bottle. Suddenly, a warning light appeared on the instrument panel. 'We've lost power,' Hosking said. 'We're going down.'

They were descending to the left of a red-hot lava pond at 97km/h (60mph). Clearly they were going down inside the volcano. There was no chance of clearing the rim and returning to the outside for an emergency landing.

Frantically, Hosking peered through breaks in the clouds, looking for a flat

Into the furnace *A helicopter hovers over the rim of Pu'u 'O'o crater at Kilauea, one of the five main volcanoes on the island of Hawaii (see page 404).*

place to set the chopper down. Fortunately, he was steering away from the 1,370°C (2,500°F) lava pool.

As he flared the nose slightly upwards for a controlled landing, the main rotor hit a large boulder, causing the craft to drop the last few feet like a stone. The chopper's tail section broke off, and its batteries were smashed. The radio was dead.

Scrambling from the cabin, the three men fought for air in the sulphurous fumes. 'We've got to get out of here before we suffocate,' Benson said, gasping.

Steam hissed angrily from the ground. Nearby, the lava pond boiled ominously, and the heat beneath the thin rock warmed their feet. 'If there's a hell,' Duddy thought, 'it's definitely like this.'

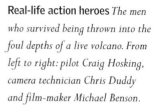

Real-life action heroes *The men who survived being thrown into the foul depths of a live volcano. From left to right: pilot Craig Hosking, camera technician Chris Duddy and film-maker Michael Benson.*

With visibility less than 6m (20ft), they knew no one could spot them from the air. Indeed, no one would even be looking for them for another hour, when they were due back. 'We'll have to hike out,' Hosking said.

With Duddy in the lead, they picked their way towards a rock-strewn slope that angled sharply to the rim 90m (300ft) above. In 15 minutes, they hiked about halfway up the crater wall.

Scrambling through layers of ash and crumbling rock, they sank to their knees, slipping backwards with nearly every step. As the slope increased to 45 degrees they had to crawl. 'Keep three points of contact with the rock,' Hosking said, recalling his climbing experience in the Rocky Mountains. 'Two legs and one arm, or two arms and one leg.'

Finally Duddy clambered onto a ledge. Above him, an overhanging rock-face blocked his route. 'I can't go any farther!' he yelled to the others, 15m (50ft) below. 'Don't come this way!'

Benson and Hosking crouched on another narrow ledge. 'Hang on tight,' Hosking told Benson. 'I'll work my way back. Maybe I can get the chopper radio working.'

'You'll suffocate down there,' Benson argued.

'If we stay here, we'll either fall or choke to death,' Hosking replied. 'My going down is our only hope.' And he disappeared into swirling steam below.

Reaching the crater floor, Hosking was engulfed by foul-smelling hydrogen sulphide and sulphur dioxide. He tore off his shirt and wrapped it around his nose and mouth to filter out the fumes.

Hosking removed the battery from the movie camera. 'If I could rig a connection,' he thought, 'maybe that would power the radio, too.' But he had to fight against blacking out. Again and again, he would crawl 15m (50ft) up the slope where the air was less noxious, take a few deep breaths, then return to splicing the stripped wires to the camera battery.

Finally, after an hour, a spark signalled that the circuit was working. 'This is Hilo Bay Three,' Hosking announced. 'Any aircraft in the vicinity of the vent? We're in the crater.'

'You're in the crater?' responded the pilot of their back-up helicopter.

'Roger. Aircraft not flyable, no injuries, but we can't climb out.'

'We've notified Search and Rescue,' the pilot replied. 'A chopper's on the way.'

The island of fire

KILAUEA, WHERE Craig Hosking's helicopter went down, is the most active volcano in the world. It has been issuing a stream of lava continuously since 1983. This molten rock flows like a slow, burning river to the sea, where it cools and solidifies. As a result, the area of Hawaii has been extended by 2km² (0.8 sq miles) at the southerly foot of the volcano. Kilauea is one of five volcanoes on the island – one is extinct, two are dormant and two are active. The Hawaiian landmass is entirely made up of volcanic material that has gushed from their vents over the course of many millennia.

Most of this volcanic activity proceeds in a rather stately fashion, and – though it is spectacular to observe – it is not unpredictably violent. This is why you can visit the lava fields as a tourist, and hover above the crater in a helicopter. But occasionally Kilauea clears its throat and makes its presence felt more dramatically. In March 2008 a new steam vent inside the main crater exploded with a force equal to an earthquake measuring 3.7 on the Richter scale. A couple of weeks later, small gobbets of fresh lava

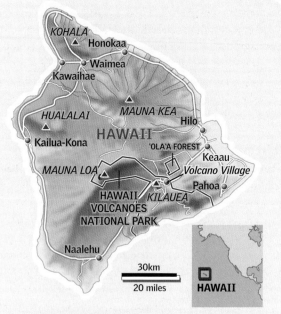

were thrown out of the crater (rather than trickling out) for the first time since 1982. When lava is ejected in this way, it often solidifies in the shape of droplets. Such specimens are known as Pele's tears, after the angry Hawaiian goddess whom the American film-makers tried – and failed – to appease.

Hosking shouted up to his friends, 'I got through! They're sending help!' But Benson and Duddy could not hear him over the lava's grumbling, nor could they see him through the thick smoke.

At 1.30pm, Don Shearer, a contract helicopter pilot on the neighbouring island of Maui, received an urgent call from a dispatcher. 'A helicopter's crashed in the Pu'u 'O'o crater. There are survivors.'

Shearer had worked with park rangers on plane crashes, lost hikers, downed sightseeing helicopters – but never anything in an active volcano. He quickly fuelled up and headed for the island.

As his Hughes 500 chopper approached the crater an hour after receiving the call, the radio picked up one of Hosking's appeals: 'We need help … air.'

'This guy's on his last legs,' Shearer realised. 'If I don't get him out soon, it'll be too late.'

'You'll have to direct me by sound.'

Hosking answered that he understood. 'But what about Mike and Chris?' he wondered. Reluctantly, he realised his best bet was to get out, then help rescuers to pinpoint the whereabouts of Benson and Duddy.

Shearer moved cautiously in the blinding fog, unable to see either floor or walls of the crater. 'To your right,' Hosking said.

Edging sideways, Shearer spotted the wrecked chopper just 9m (30ft) ahead. 'I'm real close,' he radioed Hosking. 'Run towards the noise of the helicopter.'

Hosking sprang forward, crawled onto the left skid of the hovering craft, and hauled himself into the rear seat. Barely able to breathe, Shearer manoeuvred along the crater floor until he thought he was clear of any overhang. Pulling maximum power, he took the chopper straight up, high above the volcano. From the back seat, Hosking threw both arms around Shearer, tears of joy streaming down his cheeks.

Fishing blindly

When Hosking had first climbed down to the wreckage, Benson and Duddy could see him through breaks in the clouds. But then the fumes worsened, and an acidic, blinding fog surrounded each man. They took off their shirts and wrapped them around their faces to filter the poisonous air.

Later, Benson and Duddy heard a helicopter, but couldn't tell where it was. Benson yelled down to where Hosking had been. Maybe he knew what was going on. No reply. 'Is he dead?' Duddy called.

'I don't think anyone could survive down there this long,' Benson replied.

A feeling of doom overcame Duddy. Divorced, with two young children, he thought, 'I don't want to die this way. I want to see my kids grow up.' One by one, he pictured every person in his family. Out loud, he said he loved them.

Park rangers Jeffrey Judd and Neil Akana worked their way to the rim above Benson and Duddy. Extremely unstable, the area could slough off at any moment. Visibility was no more than an arm's length. Fumes at the rim were so pungent they corroded the stainless-steel clips on their climbing ropes. The rangers had to wear gas masks.

Akana snapped himself to a rope and crept to the volcano's crumbling edge. Judd and several firefighters held the rope's other end. 'We're going to throw ropes over the side!' Akana called. 'If you see one, grab it; we'll haul you out!'

Duddy's heart leaped. 'We're down here!' he shouted.

Again and again, Akana threw an orange rope over the side, fishing blindly for the men. Duddy's voice echoed off the crater wall, making it difficult to pinpoint his location. Benson couldn't hear Akana's voice over the lava pit's roar.

The rangers were soon joined by Hosking, who insisted on helping. As darkness fell, however, they returned to their base camp, hoping to come up with another strategy.

Huddling on the cliff, Benson and Duddy shivered as a rainstorm drenched them and temperatures fell to the 50s fahrenheit. Duddy, consumed by fear, called to Benson, 'Maybe it's smarter and quicker just to jump into the crater!'

'Don't do it!' Benson shouted back. 'Be patient.'

Benson's confidence made Duddy think, 'If Mike can take it, so can I.'

'I'm climbing'

On Sunday morning, Shearer learned that corrosive fumes had damaged his chopper's turbine the day before, grounding him. And poor visibility stymied the rangers' efforts to help the trapped men.

Duddy couldn't stand the prospect of another night on the ledge. He looked at his watch: 3pm. 'I can't take it any more,' he called to Benson. 'I'm climbing.'

Signalling danger *Smoke and ash pour dramatically from the crater of Kilauea volcano on April 23, 2006. Hawaii's Volcanoes National Park had to be closed on that day because of high levels of sulphur dioxide in the atmosphere.*

Benson heard his determination. 'OK,' he said. 'Good luck.'

Duddy stood up, reeling from vertigo. He wriggled his fingers into a crack in the cliff. His feet found a toehold. The rock was wet and slick. His arms and legs shook with fear – but he hung on. He could see the top of the rim now. Only 12m (40ft) to go.

About a couple of metres from the top, he was stopped cold by a wall of compacted gravel and stone. Rocks crumbled in his hands as he groped for a hold. 'It's over,' he thought. 'I can't go up or down.' He looked above him. The top was so close. 'I have to try.'

Carefully, he sank both hands into the gravel up to his elbows. In one final, mighty pull, he heaved himself up and landed on his stomach on top of the rim. He lay a moment, gasping in disbelief, then yelled to Benson, 'I made it! I'll make sure they know exactly where you are.' Benson heard nothing above the whistling wind and lava.

Following a rope that rangers had left as a marker, Duddy stumbled down the outside of the cone to the overjoyed rescuers. 'Mike is 150ft below the rim, just to the right of where the ropes are,' he told them. 'You've got to get him out!'

As a stopgap measure, rangers decided to drop packages of food, water, clothing and portable radios over the rim. They hoped that Benson might be able to reach one of them. It would help him through the night.

In the fading twilight, Benson saw something hurtling through the mist. It looked big and striped. 'Oh my God!' he thought. Duddy had been wearing a striped shirt. 'It's Chris!' Then he heard a sickening thud on the crater floor. 'Chris!' he screamed. 'Why didn't I try to stop him?' Suddenly Benson felt responsible for the whole disaster. 'Why did I insist on that final shot?'

Waiting for sunrise on the third day, Benson strained to breathe. His throat was so sore he could no longer call for help. He caught rainwater in the 1.25cm (½in) depression on his light meter's face and sipped every drop. He thought of his wife of 25 years and their two children. They were telling him to be strong. 'We love you,' they seemed to say. 'You're going to be rescued. Stay put.'

The gases he breathed caused strange thoughts to race through his head. As the swirling mist parted briefly, Benson saw a human profile on a distant rock. 'Madame Pele! You're not going to win. I'm getting out of here!'

Then he prayed for a miracle. 'Please, God,' he pleaded, 'make the day clear so they can see me from the air.'

Members of the film crew had managed to track down Tom Hauptman, a daring rescue pilot. Early on Monday, Hauptman flew to the crater rim with ranger Judd in the copilot's seat.

Hearing a loud noise overhead, Benson peered upwards. Suddenly the air cleared, and above he made out the tail rotor of a helicopter. Frantically, he waved – and the pilot waved back. Benson couldn't believe his eyes.

The craft vanished again, but a voice boomed over the chopper's public-address system. 'We're lowering a rescue net!' Benson thanked God for the miracle.

Hauptman programmed his satellite navigation system to home in on the exact spot where he had seen Benson. Now the pilot eased down to rim

Rocks crumbled in his hands as he groped for a hold. 'It's over,' he thought. 'I can't go up or down.' He looked above him. The top was so close. 'I have to try.'

level and hovered delicately, lowering the net into the swirling clouds below. Hauptman waited 10 seconds, then climbed to where he could check his 'catch'. The net was empty. Benson had seen it, but it was just out of reach.

Hauptman waited for another opening in the clouds. He lowered the basket and hovered above the side of the cliff.

This time the rope dangled within Benson's reach. When he pulled it towards him, however, the net snagged on a rock. Hands trembling, Benson struggled to free it. But before he could climb into the net, it began to rise. 'There goes my last chance,' he thought glumly.

But the net came back, this time dangling 3m (10ft) in front of Benson. Without a moment's hesitation, he dived into it. When Hauptman broke into clear air, he let out a whoop. 'We've got a live one!' he screamed to Judd.

Benson, Duddy and Hosking all suffered dehydration, minor abrasions and pulmonary problems. Duddy and Hosking made a full recovery before Benson, who continued having treatment for some time. Rangers believe that his 48 hour survival ordeal inside the active volcano was a world record.

The experience had a profound effect on each of the three men. As Benson summed up at the time, 'They say a cat has nine lives. If I were a cat, I would've used at least five of mine in that volcano. I'm not about to squander what's left.' ■

Where are they now?

IF YOU ARE GOING to be in a helicopter crash, then Craig Hosking is the man you would want to be at the controls. He is one of the most experienced stunt pilots in the world. He gained his helicopter pilot's licence on his 16th birthday (making him the youngest qualified pilot ever) and he has clocked up more than 16,000 hours of flying time – not just in 'copters, but also in planes, gliders and jets. Hosking was not put off show business by his terrifying experience in Hawaii. He has continued to choreograph and direct flight scenes for films such as *The Matrix Reloaded, Mission: Impossible II, Batman Begins, The Hulk* and *Indiana Jones and the Kingdom of the Crystal Skull*. He occasionally appears in front of the camera, too. In *Speed 2*, for example, he can be seen trying to push Sandra Bullock out of a seaplane (right).

Chris Duddy and Michael Benson have also continued to work at the heart of Hollywood's dream factory. Duddy has written, produced and directed many films; he was responsible for the visual effects in movies such as *Titanic, Waterworld* and *Demolition Man*. Four years after the helicopter crash, he married Joely Fisher, half-sister of *Star Wars* actress Carrie Fisher. In 1997 Michael Benson shot a film called *Volcano*. It was not the story of his own brush with death, but a thriller about an underground volcano erupting beneath the streets of Los Angeles.

The men's own story was made into a film, though: as an episode of the American true-life documentary series *I Shouldn't Be Alive* ... As for the volcano footage from Kilauea, it was cut from the final edit of *Sliver*.

NO STRANGER TO DANGER Craig Hosking at the controls of a seaplane in *Speed 2* with actress Sandra Bullock.

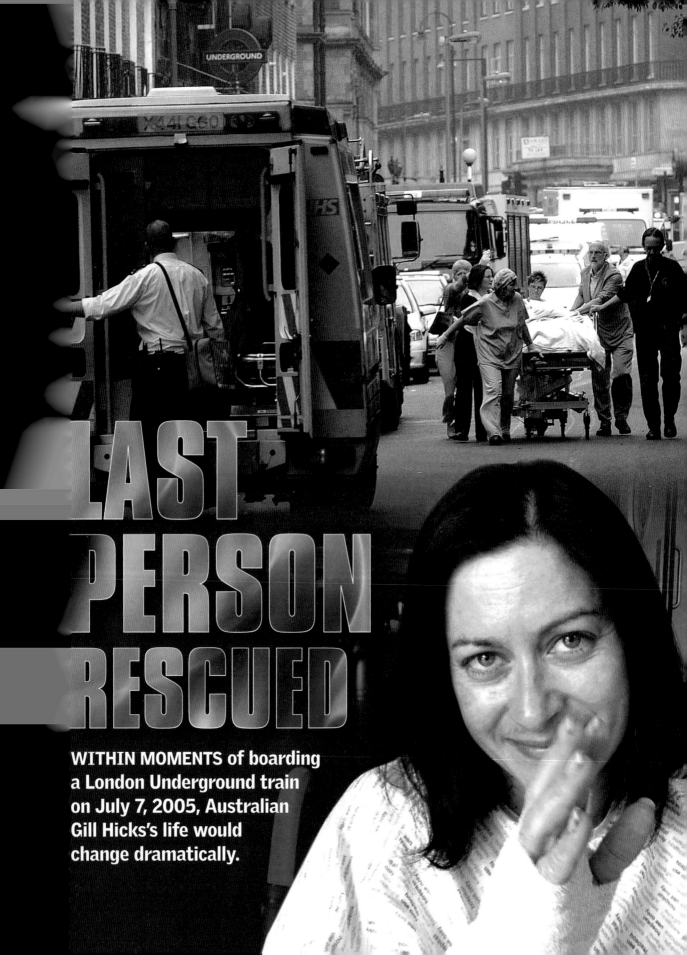

LAST PERSON RESCUED

WITHIN MOMENTS of boarding a London Underground train on July 7, 2005, Australian Gill Hicks's life would change dramatically.

'Hey, watch it!' I say to an aggressive commuter as he pushes past me to squeeze onto the packed tube carriage at King's Cross underground. Phew! It's a tight jam but I'm in, my five-foot-nothing frame sandwiched between tall people breathing down on me. The doors shut and we're moving. I must remember to talk to my colleagues about what we're going to do about the Olympic win.

It could only have been seconds before the whole world changed.

I was falling, descending into an abyss, blackness engulfing me. Then the falling stopped and I lay motionless. Whimpers for help filled the air. What had happened? Where did the train go? Where were we now?

I tried to get up and failed. I raised my arms, dazed, barely able to breathe.

'Help … help me.' I didn't know if I was whispering, shouting or just mouthing the words. I didn't know if I could be heard through all the other calls for help. I just kept saying the words.

'Please, God. Help me, I'm dying,' a voice close to me kept saying. It was a woman I couldn't see. Another voice spoke, suggesting help was on its way. There were more cries for help, occasionally followed by reassurance and comfort, then one by one the voices fell silent. Nothing.

The atmosphere was thick with acrid-smelling smoke. A light was shining almost directly through the train carriage over at me and I could clearly see my legs. They resembled an anatomical drawing. I could see the insides: muscle, tendons and bones. Attached to these were my feet – still perfect, still looking like my feet, but just dangling, as though they had been severed at the ankles. My feet were just hanging by a thread. This couldn't be real, it couldn't be happening. 'My legs are gone,' I thought. 'Dear God, my legs are gone.'

'Priority One'

Somehow I knew that to stay alive, I had to remain calm. If I screamed or cried out, my heart would pump more blood. The more blood my heart pumped, the more I would lose – it was streaming from my wounds, flowing from what resembled my legs.

I still had my scarf on and some clothes. They were in shreds but they were there. I had to stop the bleeding. I raised my arm – it hurt – and managed to slip my scarf from around my neck. Desperately, I ripped at it with my teeth, trying not to pass out. My only thoughts as I fashioned a tourniquet were to hold on, hold on.

I opened my eyes and reached down to tie the left leg first, up around my thigh. Then I reached for my right leg, trying to lift it a little. As I moved my hand up to my thigh, my hand sank, disappearing deep into my leg. My inner thigh was missing. It was gone. How did this happen? What happened?

As I battled drowsiness, I could hear two loud and powerful voices in my head. One was willing me to hold on, to remember those who loved me and needed me; the other was encouraging me to let go, to drift away into a peaceful and permanent sleep.

Was that a light? Someone was here – help had come. I lifted my hand to wave and spoke, 'My name is Gill, my name is Gill.'

A city under attack *Injured commuters are evacuated from the area surrounding Russell Square tube station (opposite, top). Bomb victim Gill Hicks (opposite, bottom), the last person to be rescued alive from the train, takes a welcome break from intensive care during her recovery.*

And then I heard two of the best words I've ever heard – 'Priority One' – and felt someone put a tag of some sort on me. I was a 'Priority One'. That had to be good, very good, very … I started to drift.

A man was holding my hand. He didn't let go. I was so cold, but I could feel his warmth. He was telling me to stay with him. He knew my name and held my hand, tight. He said over and over, 'Stay with us, Gill. Come on, love, come on, Gill, you have got to stay with us.' I needed to know he wouldn't let go – his hand kept me connected, kept me alive.

'My God, please'

'Hello? Hello? You're in St Thomas' Hospital. You've been involved in a major incident. We need to find out who you are.' It was a woman's voice – but it was muffled, like the carriage voices had been. It was as though I was listening to the world from the inside of a fishbowl. My eyes must have opened long enough to see bright lights and people around me. I knew I was safe, but I didn't know where I was, or how I had got there.

'Can you blink for me? Blink once for yes if you can understand me, OK?' I blinked, closing my eyes as tightly as I could, then opening them again, staring back into the light. 'I am going to go through the alphabet, OK my love? When we get to the first letter of your name, blink once. Everything will be all right, my love; we will find out who you are.'

Who I was, before that day, was Gill Hicks, an Australian abroad, living the life of a Londoner after some 15 years working in the UK's capital. Following a decade in publishing and running my own business, I now headed an enormous project for the Design Council, the UK's strategic body for design; was a Fellow of the Royal Society of Arts; and sat on various arts panels, including the board of the Women's Playhouse Trust. These accolades were everything to me, but as I worked harder, it became more difficult to remain the happy-go-lucky Adelaide girl I'd once been. A lovely relationship notwithstanding, I was driven and defined by my job.

A man was holding my hand. He didn't let go. I was so cold, but I could feel his warmth. He was telling me to stay with him. He knew my name and held my hand, tight. He said over and over, 'Stay with us, Gill. Come on, love, come on, Gill, you have got to stay with us.'

I'd been tired when I awoke that day, having slept only fitfully. My partner Joe and I had argued the night before and the dispute had been serious enough, at the time, to make me question whether or not we should go ahead with our plans to marry in December.

But everything had now changed. Less than 13 hours after slamming the door shut on my way to work, Joe and I were reunited in a hospital ICU ward. As I lapsed in and out of consciousness, a team of doctors explained to Joe that my life was hanging by a very fragile thread. Joe told me afterwards how scared he was of seeing me. He had often contemplated what it would be like to lose a limb, and now, with absolute dread, he had to face his fear.

What he saw was a shapeless face with angry dark bruises covering my usually pale, flawless skin. I had no eyelashes or eyebrows – they'd been singed off in the blast – and my hair was filthy, a bloody, matted frizz. It looked as though I had been electrocuted. I was pumped with so much fluid that both my face and my body had swollen, giving the impression that I was much larger than I actually was. Joe's eyes scanned me, slowly, yet quickly, flickering, tracing down my body, trying to find my hand among the tubes and dressings. Then he saw.

The sheet that was covering me came to an abrupt end, simply falling flat onto the bed, highlighting the inescapable facts of the medical briefing. There it was – the end of me.

Every synapse in Joe's body was screaming with anguish and despair. 'My God, please.' Joe was asking for strength, not only for himself, but also for me.

The essence of terror

London had never had an attack of this kind, even during a 30 year history of being under constant terrorist threat from the IRA. However, this was a new order of terror – suicide bombs that deliberately targeted civilians en masse, aimed at London's overcrowded and extremely vulnerable public transport system – in my case, deep underground. This was the essence of terror: there was no prior warning. No one could have stopped this. We – the entire population of London – were all bracketed together as 'enemies'. No discrimination, no pity, no compassion. Just cold-blooded murder.

Outside, as ambulances swarmed to the various hospitals, the city was in organised chaos: streets were cordoned off, emergency-service workers were down in tunnels and police filled the streets, combing for evidence.

Back in Australia, like so many people around the world that day, my brother Graham and his family were watching the news on television, a flash report every 15 minutes or so. Naturally, they felt a connection because I lived in London, but they weren't overly concerned. Why would they be? What were the odds that I would be involved?

It's just never going to be someone you know, especially not someone close.

Graham's wife Jo called, expecting me to answer the

Life-giving hands *Gill Hicks is reunited with two heroic members of British Transport Police – Steve Bryan (left) and Aaron Debnam (right). Aaron had held Gill's hand and encouraged her not to give up.*

Terror at rush hour

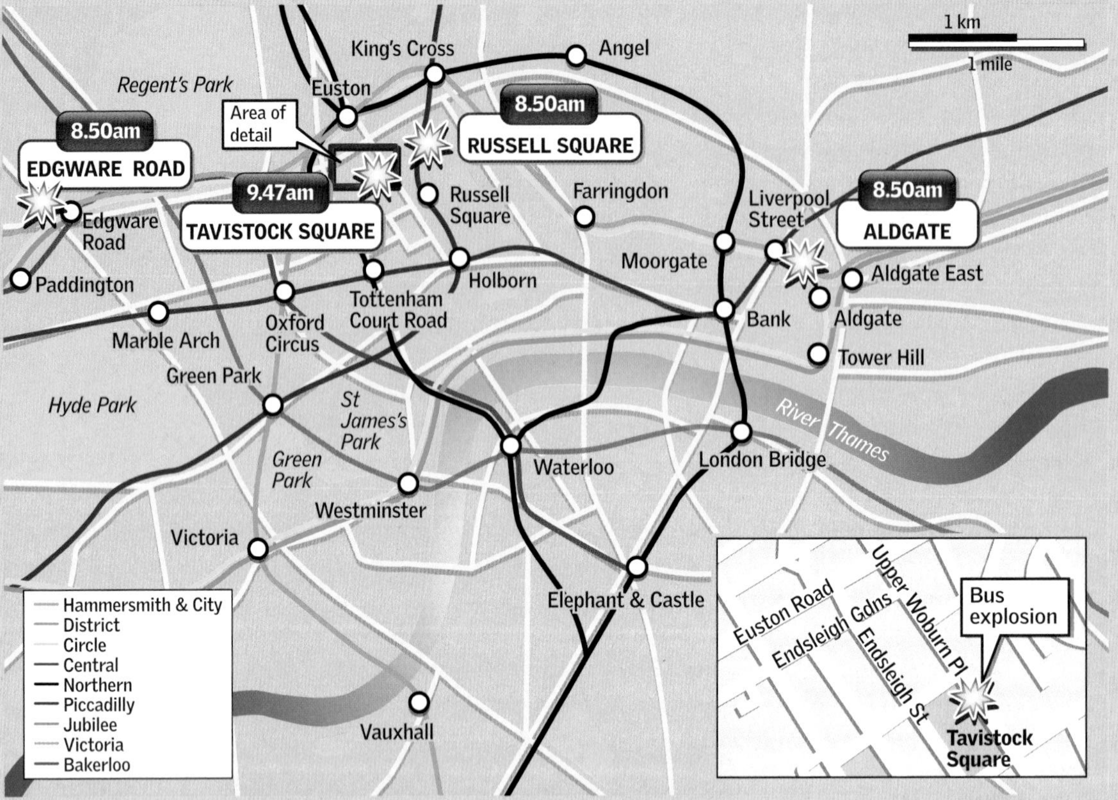
1 km
1 mile
King's Cross
Angel
Regent's Park
Euston
Area of detail
8.50am
EDGWARE ROAD
8.50am
RUSSELL SQUARE
9.47am
TAVISTOCK SQUARE
Russell Square
Farringdon
Liverpool Street
8.50am
ALDGATE
Edgware Road
Paddington
Moorgate
Aldgate East
Holborn
Tottenham Court Road
Oxford Circus
Marble Arch
Bank
Aldgate
Tower Hill
Green Park
Hyde Park
St James's Park
River Thames
Green Park
Waterloo
London Bridge
Westminster
Victoria
Elephant & Castle
Hammersmith & City
District
Circle
Central
Northern
Piccadilly
Jubilee
Victoria
Bakerloo
Vauxhall
Euston Road
Endsleigh Gdns
Upper Woburn Pl
Endsleigh St
Bus explosion
Tavistock Square

COORDINATED ATTACK Within the space of an hour, four bombs had gone off across London, bringing chaos to the city.

AT 8.50AM ON THURSDAY JULY 7, 2007, three bombs exploded simultaneously on the London underground. Three of the suicide bombers had travelled from Yorkshire to meet up with the fourth, Germaine Lindsay, at Luton, where they boarded a train to London's King's Cross. Once in London, Lindsay, 19, boarded a Piccadilly Line train travelling south from King's Cross, 24-year-old Shehzad Tanweer caught a Circle Line train heading east from Liverpool Street, and Mohammad Sidique Khan, 30, took a westbound Circle Line train for Paddington.

Lindsay was in the front carriage of the King's Cross train, and detonated his bomb at Russell Square, killing 26 people as well as himself; he also injured 340 people, including Gill Hicks. The bomb on the eastbound train, on the floor of the second carriage, exploded at Aldgate, killing seven people plus the bomber, and injuring 171, at least ten seriously. On the Paddington train, too, the bomb was in the second carriage. It went off as the train left Edgware Road station, killing six people, plus the bomber, and injuring 163.

Not quite an hour later, with emergency services stretched to breaking point, Hasib Hussain, 18, detonated a bomb on a number 30 bus at the junction of Tavistock Square and Upper Woburn Place. It had been diverted from its usual route from Marble Arch to Hackney because of road closures caused by the tube bombings. Thirteen people, plus the bomber, were killed; 110 were injured. The events, and the appalling toll, defy imagination.

The four bombers, all British citizens, all of whom grew up in Yorkshire, had led apparently unremarkable lives. Jamaican-born Lindsay, a convert to Islam who later moved to Aylesbury in Buckinghamshire, was father to one daughter. His wife gave birth to a son after his death.

phone. She left messages on my mobile and at work. She wasn't worried; I'd call soon enough to say I was all right. If not, she would try again in the morning. They went to bed. Just a few hours later their phone rang – they had those few precious hours of rest before learning that their lives, too, had changed forever.

With experience of the bombings in Bali in 2002, where so many Australian nationals had either lost their lives or been terribly injured, the Australian Government rallied with support that was all-embracing: I was one of theirs and Australian officials reacted like parents. There was no time for red tape – my brother's journey and arrival in London were fully orchestrated within a matter of hours.

With Joe and Graham at my bedside, I held on, but it was a fragile time. Five days after the bombings, I was still in ICU – the birthplace of what I was to call forever afterwards 'Life Two' – and I still had no idea what had happened. Joe worried that I had brain damage because, from what he could tell, I appeared to have no short-term memory. He would tell me something, continuing from an earlier visit, and I would offer a surprised expression, as if I was hearing it for the first time.

Joe was also constantly looking for new ways to communicate with me other than squeezing my one free hand, or through my blinking eyes. As he considered getting me to write down my thoughts, I motioned to him, pointing to where my legs used to be and made a shrugging gesture. Joe understood that I was asking him what had happened. I knew I had lost my legs, and I knew that I was near death, but what I didn't know was how.

'Darling, my darling Gill, you were in a terrorist attack. It was a suicide bomber, darling. That's what happened.'

I was completely shocked. A bomb! Me? I felt like I was choking. I found it difficult to breathe. My heart and mind were trying to understand and remember, but all I could do, automaton-like, was cry. Tears rolled from the corners of my eyes. Joe squeezed my hand. 'It's all right. You're safe now; you're alive. I'm here and I love you so much. I love you, my Boo Boo. I'm so happy to have you back.'

A bomb! Me? I felt like I was choking. I found it difficult to breathe. My heart and mind were trying to understand and remember, but all I could do, automaton-like, was cry.

But I was overwhelmed. I wanted to scream, pull out my tubes and run away. And at the same time, I also wanted to digest the news and give myself time to mourn and reflect. My throat was raw. I had a rasping cough and was still bringing up fragments of whatever it was I had ingested and inhaled in the tunnel. I wanted desperately for the tube wedged into my throat to come out. I hated being so restricted, unable to talk or to drink. I wanted something to soothe my throat … I could have drunk an ocean dry.

'Here… is that better?' The nurse would drop some water from the tip of a giant cotton bud into the side of my mouth. The drops would glide past the tubing to my throat. Those tiny drops of water were my greatest pleasure. 'More, more, more,' my eyes would say and Joe would laugh, learning to drip the water into my mouth.

I would close my eyes and think about a time when I would be able to drink a whole cup of water. It seemed unimaginable, but it kept me going.

It was one of the things that helped me to stay positive: having that personal goal to drink a cup of water again.

I just didn't know what to expect in the future. What can you expect when you are lying in bed, unable to get in or out unless someone comes to help you, unable to turn from side to side, unable to wash? I didn't want people to cry for me. But I also struggled to come to terms with being 'disabled'. I couldn't explain to anyone how distressed I felt at not being able to do anything. I clung to the words of my rehabilitation consultant, Dr Luff, who held my hand one morning, looked me straight in the eye and said, 'You will walk out of here, Gill. I guarantee you that.'

It was on hearing this extraordinary news that an idea was planted in Joe's mind: perhaps we wouldn't have to postpone our wedding date, now little more than five months away. As for me, I would veer between moments of complete delight and sheer terror. One morning nurses would find me spinning round and round, shrieking like a child at a funfair, when I was ensconced in a wheelchair for the first time. At other times, I would wake at night, panicked, to the smell – that acrid mixture of chemicals, dust, skin and hair burning – that lingered no matter how many weeks had passed since that day.

But there was something I had to do. Gruesome as it sounds, I wanted to say goodbye to my old legs, which had been kept as forensic evidence and were in the mortuary. Joe thought it was a bad idea, but he agreed to take me.

With no skin holding them together, they didn't look like legs. But there were my feet, perfect, each toe lovingly painted with my nail polish. I leaned over and touched them, remembering enjoying a foot spa, reflexology, Joe tickling the soles until I begged him to stop. I remembered wearing socks and the feeling of being barefoot on wooden floorboards. I memorised every last detail and said goodbye, signing the papers for them to be cremated.

What I couldn't have foreseen is the degree of unity that Joe and I would build together through these dark times. We'd lived together for seven years, but this was different. I relied on Joe. I needed him. And he rose to the position. He wanted to share the entire experience with me and never to let me feel that I was facing it alone. We created our own impenetrable bubble, a cocoon that we would retreat into whenever the outside world got too much for us. I never had to doubt Joe's commitment or his love.

It was one less piece of the future to worry about.

Making life count

Then, as rehabilitation began in earnest, one immediate question reared its head: what did I want to call my legs? Were they still legs? I didn't need to think for too long though; I blurted out my response as if this had been something I had been considering for some time. 'Let's call them "Stumpingtons",' I said. 'That can be their English name.'

And then, to my astonishment, I went still further: 'I also think they're twins. Boys, definitely boys, but not identical. It's hard to tell them apart,

Silent tribute *On the first anniversary of the London bombings, Gill (front row, 2nd right) gathered with other survivors, relatives and emergency-service workers to take part in a 2 minute silence outside Russell Square tube station.*

On her own two feet

WHEN YOU CONSIDER how much work Gill has done for the cause of peace in a few short years, the word 'tireless' suggests itself, but the truth is that life for anyone with two prosthetic legs is physically exhausting. 'I use about 200 per cent more energy than an able-bodied person,' she says. 'I have to eat lots of bananas and slow-burn foods.'

She had been struggling to come to terms with the prospect of life in a wheelchair when her specialist told her that she would walk out of the hospital. First, though, while her body was still healing, and before she could be fitted with prosthetics, she had to go through intensive physiotherapy to build up her core strength and develop stability. She was going to have to learn to walk all over again.

Little more than a month after the bombings, casts were made of her stumps, so that the artificial legs would be a perfect fit. She learned that she was to have so-called 'Elite Feet', or 'sports feet', designed to offer 'a better sports–life balance'. It was suggested that the legs would be a little shorter than the ones she'd lost, to give a greater sense of gravity, but Gill was having none of that!

Prostheses like Gill's that replace the leg below the knee are known as 'transtibial'. Transtibial amputees, retaining the knee, more readily regain normal movement than 'transfemoral' (above-the-knee) amputees. Gill's legs are held in place with a ratchet attached to a rubber liner that rolls on over the stump and slots into the leg socket.

Gill had had the idea that she would simply be issued with one pair of legs and be ready to go. 'What I didn't appreciate was the ongoing nature of it. You don't get one set of legs and that's it. I'm a lifelong patient. For the first five years there is a lot of change. Every three or four months I get new sockets made for my legs.' Lifestyle is also a consideration. She is hoping for an adaptation to allow her to use an exercise bike. Then there is wear and tear. She laughs. 'The prosthetist hadn't seen a double amputee who'd walked over 200 miles.' (See page 417.)

STEPS TO FREEDOM Gill expertly fits her prosthetic limbs, first rolling a rubber liner over the stumps of her legs.

but to the trained eye, like surgeon Professor Burnand's, or to mine, well … we can tell the difference.'

This set the tone, not only for that session, but also for the rest of my rehabilitation.

My physiotherapists Matt and Nichola dubbed me 'Gillington' from then on and most names were translated into our new language. It may have been a touch juvenile, but it worked for us. It was a difficult time for all of us, so our games lifted the sessions.

Over the months, I did media interviews and met people who are now a part of my life forever. Many of the new numbers in my mobile phone are those of the medical teams and my fellow survivors. Each has their own horrific story and their own perspective, but I have yet to meet a survivor who harbours hatred for the bombers. What we all seem to have in common is a deep desire to 'make life count'.

The happiest day *Gill poses outside medieval St Etheldreda's Church, Holborn, London, on her wedding day with husband Joe, stepdaughter Lily (left) and niece and bridesmaid Maddy (right).*

The Australian Prime Minister John Howard and his wife Janette came to visit me at St Thomas' and stayed for over half an hour. Months later, I stubbornly stood in prosthetics for an entire 2 hours at a private reception hosted by the Queen, even though Her Majesty personally suggested I sit and rest. I was also invited by Prince Charles to Highgrove and appeared on various TV shows.

Lovely as all these moments were, none was as moving as meeting PC Aaron Debnam from the British Transport Police, the man who had kept me alive in the tunnel on the day the bombs exploded.

The wedding

Joe and I got married as planned on December 10, 2005. My dream was to get through the day without a stumble, and I did. Bridesmaids Maddy and Lily, my niece and stepdaughter respectively, helped me get my legs ready the night before – I had special gold tights to cover the prosthetic casings and my limited-edition Adidas chrome trainers to complete the look. I never expected to be married in trainers, but they were the best fit and had a good grip for balancing. My sister-in-law Jo took a picture of them standing on their own: two gold and silver legs.

The breakthroughs and the triumphs have never failed to excite me. I am in constant wonder at what my body has achieved, how this amazing machine has healed itself and adapted to having its limbs missing. I am in awe.

The tasks that may seem ordinary to some are monumental to me, and the achievement of conquering these – well, that's my version of climbing Mount Everest. It's exhilarating and often extremely emotional to carry a hot drink up the stairs for the first time, or to go out alone and cross a road.

With my new mindset, continuing my work at the Design Council no longer seemed as important as it once was. I returned to my office, eager to complete unfinished business, and threw an entire 'URGENT' file in the bin. Nothing had happened with that file for eight months, yet the world hadn't stopped turning. It didn't mean anything now.

Since that day I've asked myself many times if it's good enough just to be alive, or is life about what we do? Not a day passes when I don't wish that the bombings on July 7 hadn't happened. If I could turn the clock back, I would, without hesitation. But, as I see it, I had no choice on that morning. Germaine Lindsay didn't ask me before he detonated his bomb if I was his enemy. He took away my choice by assuming that we all were.

Lovely as all these moments were, none was as moving as meeting PC Aaron Debnam from the British Transport Police, the man who had kept me alive in the tunnel on the day the bombs exploded.

While I didn't have a choice then, I feel I've been presented with many choices since. I could have chosen to let hatred for this act, and for the person who committed it, consume me. I could have chosen to curl up in a ball and cry, asking, 'Why me, why me?' I could have done many things, all of which I was entitled to, but I didn't.

From the moment I was given the option of choosing life, I made a vow: that if I did survive, I would live a full and rich life. I vowed I would never take anything – all that I have – for granted again. I would never forget how precious every single day is. ■

Where are they now?

IT WAS NO IDLE VOW that Gill made to live her new life to the full. In 2006 she was appointed Ambassador for the charity Peace Direct. In 2007 she became an advocate for Leonard Cheshire Disability. Now, drawing on her background in art and design, she has founded M.A.D for Peace, a creative, not-for-profit venture to promote peace, starting within local communities, and rippling out to the wider world, in the belief that 'everyone can make a difference'.

Gill has been justly feted for her courage and has been the subject of articles and TV documentaries. As well as carrying the 2008 Olympic torch in Canberra, she has been awarded an MBE and was named Australian of the Year by Britain's Australia Day Foundation.

In the summer of 2008, she and husband Joe conceived the idea of WALKTALK, a walk of more than 320km (200 miles) from Leeds to London, as M.A.D. for Peace's first major initiative. Designed to promote mutual understanding and respect, it offered an opportunity for a diverse range of people to walk and converse with each other about matters of belief and conscience. Gill, of course, joined the walk, every step of the way. 'It wasn't a march,' she says, 'it wasn't a demonstration; we were actively doing peace by encouraging people to come together.'

On the day of the bombing, when she was rushed to hospital, the last casualty on the train to be rescued, Gill was tagged 'One Unknown'. Now she draws 'a powerful message from all the people who did so much for that little One Unknown. That's what keeps me going to this day and shapes my thoughts and all my projects. Everything stems from that experience of humanity in all its brilliance. We all have the capacity to do so much more than we imagine.'

WALKING FOR PEACE Gill joined with supporters and her husband Joe Kerr to complete the month-long WALKTALK.

RETURNING HOME FROM school to a remote farm in New Brunswick, the young girl found her father collapsed by his tractor in a pool of blood, his head trapped. His life depended on what she and her sister did next.

'WE WON'T LET YOU DIE, DAD'

Glen Hillock watched from the warm comfort of his living room as winds from Chaleur Bay blew snow across his lane. Hillock's farm was the last stop for local school buses, and as a courtesy he tried to keep the lane cleared so they could use it to turn around.

It was almost 3pm. His two youngest daughters, Angie, 11, and Daisy, 8, had come home on an early bus and were watching TV. The bus carrying his eldest daughter, 13-year-old Amber, would arrive in about an hour, and a bit later his wife, Sharon, would return from her clerical job at the Chaleur Regional Hospital in Bathurst, New Brunswick, 40km (25 miles) away. Hillock decided he'd better clear the lane before they arrived.

Monday, January 30, 1995, was a cold day in the shore-front farming community of New Bandon in northern New Brunswick. Before going out, Hillock pulled on his insulated blue mechanic's suit, skidoo boots, thick sheepskin mittens and a wool tuque, a warm Canadian hat.

At nearly 1.9m (6ft 2in) and weighing 77kg (170lb), the 55-year-old farmer was lean and fit. For 23 years now, he had worked the same 20 hectares (50 acres) his father had before him, growing potatoes and grain, keeping a few beef cattle, and in the summer driving a gravel truck for extra income.

With the wind and flurries blowing around him, Hillock walked across to the garage where he stored his ageing 3 tonne Massey Ferguson tractor. The ignition wiring had burned out, so he routinely had to lift the bonnet and jump-start it with a screwdriver. The engine roared to life, but Hillock had been clearing snow for only a few minutes when the tractor ran out of petrol.

He filled the tank, then went to restart the engine, bending under one of the two hydraulic arms that held the metal plough blade more than a metre above the ground.

As Hillock reached towards the ignition, the valve locking the metal arms in place gave way. The 450kg (1,000lb) plough crashed down, one of the arms crushing Hillock's head into a 7cm (3in) space between the arm and the tractor.

Trapped and alone

Agony and terror forced a scream from Hillock, but it came out as a soft moan. His smashed head was locked in place, his eyes fixed open so that he stared helplessly at the engine. His neck was twisted to the left and a metal bar pressing against his throat partially closed his airway. He grabbed the bar and pushed his body up to ease his breathing, then tried to take a step backwards, but his head was trapped.

A deeply religious man, he prayed to God to take care of his family and to free him from this pain. Blood oozed from his eyes, ears, nose and mouth, and a gaping wound in the back of his scalp spilled more blood down the side of the tractor. Though he was clearly visible from the highway just 6m (20ft) away, passing motorists took no notice; he simply looked like a farmer repairing his tractor, not a man whose life was draining away.

At 4pm Amber's school bus pulled into the lane. As it stopped, Amber spotted her father bent over the tractor. 'He's always fixing that thing,' she thought affectionately.

A proud man *Glen Hillock (opposite) knows he wouldn't have survived his horrific ordeal were it not for his cool-headed daughters, Angie (left) and Amber (right), who sprang into action immediately.*

Angie looked at her father. His body seemed to be relaxing, his arms and legs bending; if he slumped any further he'd be strangled. 'Dad!' she screamed. 'Get up! Come on, you're strong!'

The auburn-haired eighth grader said a quick goodbye to the driver and sauntered over towards her father. 'Hi, Dad!' she called but got no response. She noticed a pool of red fluid on the snow beneath the tractor. 'Is that antifreeze?' she wondered.

As she drew nearer, she became alarmed by her father's awkward posture. 'Dad, are you OK?'

She finally looked under the hydraulic arm and was confronted by her father's ghost-white face, bulging eyes and shattered, protruding facial bones. Amber screamed.

'Call 911!' she cried, running into the house. 'Dad's stuck in the tractor!' Her sisters looked back at her, unbelieving. Willing her voice to be calm, Amber dialled 911 herself. 'Go be with him, Angie!' she ordered. Then she spotted 8-year-old Daisy watching her from the kitchen. 'She's too young to see Dad this way,' she thought. 'Go to your room, Daisy,' she said. The younger child stomped off obediently.

Help arrives

Outside, Angie ran barefoot through the snow to her father. The quiet blonde child gasped when she first saw her father's deformed face and head, but quickly leaned down and touched his arm. 'Dad, answer me. Let me know you're alive, OK?'

Hillock moaned and Angie could hear blood gurgling in his throat. 'We won't let you die, Dad!' she cried.

'On TV they're always saying to cover a victim with blankets and keep him conscious,' she thought, and ran back into the house.

Amber was still on the phone, waiting for the police to connect her with the Bathurst Ambulance Service. 'Put your boots on!' she yelled as Angie struggled through the front door with a pile of blankets.

Angie hurriedly stepped into her boots and ran back to her father. She wrapped one blanket around his neck and the rest over the side of the tractor. 'You're going to be OK, Dad.'

But she feared that if he weakened or passed out, he would be strangled by the bar. She clambered onto the tractor and studied the control levers, but decided against testing them, afraid she might injure her father more.

Back alongside the tractor, she struggled in vain to lift the metal arm that held his head in a vice-like grip. Defeated, Angie leaned against the tractor's front wheel and looked into her father's eyes. 'I love you, Dad,' was all she could say.

A yellow and red liquid now dripped from Hillock's nose – blood mixed with the brain fluid from the crack in his skull.

At the sound of a car pulling into the lane, Angie looked up. It was a French-speaking man from a nearby community who wanted to buy potatoes. Amber ran out of the house to speak to him.

'Go next door and get help,' she pleaded. The man sped off in his car, and Amber hurried back to her 911 call.

Angie looked at her father. His body seemed to be relaxing, his arms and legs bending; if he slumped any further he'd be strangled. 'Dad!' she screamed. 'Get up! Come on, you're strong!'

Through a haze of pain and shock, Hillock understood. Groaning, he straightened his legs.

About 2km (1¼ miles) up the road the phone rang at the home of Harry Smith, a retired papermaker. It was his wife's elderly aunt who told him a French-speaking stranger had just come to her door talking excitedly about needing help for the potato man. She meant Glen Hillock.

Harry and his brother Hales, a lobster fisherman, had known Hillock since childhood. 'I'll check on him,' he promised and promptly called his brother.

At 4.15pm, when the brothers arrived on the scene, Hillock had been trapped for almost an hour. Harry Smith took one look at Hillock's face and stepped back in horror.

'Angie,' he said, steadying himself, 'we need a bar to lift up the arm.' With the girl in tow, he ran to the garage to search for something that would do the job. In among Hillock's tools, they found a metal pipe.

The Smiths pushed the pipe underneath the tractor's arm and positioned a concrete block on the ground for leverage. The pipe merely bent when they applied pressure. Hales ran to the garage and soon reappeared with an old driveshaft from a car.

Using the 2m (6½ft) shaft, the two men tried again to lift the arm, pitting all their strength against almost half a tonne. It wouldn't move.

Responding quickly to the many calls for help that Amber had made, neighbours began to arrive. A line of parked cars formed in front of the farm.

Returning from work, Sharon Hillock neared her home and wondered what was happening when she spotted the line of cars in front. As she stepped from the car, Amber appeared. 'Mom!' she cried, grabbing Sharon's arm. 'Dad's had an accident!'

Sharon raced to the tractor, looked into her husband's bloodied face and fixed eyes and thought at once he must be dead. Then he moaned.

While Hales and Harry Smith continued their fight to free him, Sharon put her arms around her husband's waist and hugged him from behind. 'Hang in there, Glen,' she said. 'I'm not ready to lose you.'

A farmer's forgiveness *His red Massey Ferguson 165 tractor had caused Glen Hillock terrible injuries, but it was the first thing he asked about when he woke from his coma.*

Home for the hardy

FAR OUT ON THE EAST COAST OF CANADA, New Brunswick is an ethnic mosaic. As well as its indigenous population of more than 12,000 Mi'kmaq and Maliseets Native Americans, it is also home to a mix of peoples of French, English, Irish and Scots descent, as well as Basque and Jersey fishermen, and later influxes of, among others, Germans, Scandinavians and Asians – making for a rich multicultural heritage. Of a population of 787,100, a third are French-speaking, and just over half are rural dwellers.

Average winter temperatures in the province range from around -7.5°C (18.5°F) to as low as -30 to -35°C (-22 to -31°F) in the extreme northwest. Little wonder, then, that children here should be hardy and resourceful.

New Brunswick is bounded by Quebec's Gaspé Peninsula and Chaleur Bay to the north, by Nova Scotia to the east and, to the south, by the Bay of Fundy, which has some of the world's highest tides. Around 87 per cent of the province is clad with forest, and there are more than 3,000 farms on the land. The rich fishing grounds yield catches such as lobster, herring and mackerel.

It was a Frenchman, Jacques Cartier, who, visiting in 1534, gave Chaleur Bay (Bay of Warmth) its name. Cartier arrived in July. Had he come in February to find sea ice, blizzards and keening winds off the Atlantic, it might have been otherwise named.

Not that the indomitable, hospitable inhabitants of New Brunswick are troubled by winter, which they treat in many ways as a festival of fun. For the local leisure industry, snow is 'white gold', offering opportunities to promote sleigh rides, skating, skiing and snowshoeing.

French deportees, Brits loyal to the Crown and exiled in the American Revolution, Scots and Irish refugees from political pressures and potato famine, fur traders, travellers, adventurers, embattled aboriginals ... It's not too fanciful to say that survival is in the genes of those from New Brunswick.

BIG HORIZONS Although most of New Brunswick comprises forest land, it is also home to a large number of farms. Many sit in isolation on wide expanses of open land.

'He's caught bad'

Percy Scott, a Bathurst District school-bus driver for 24 years, slowed down when he saw the parked cars in front of the Hillocks' lane. As he passed, Harry Smith waved at him to stop.

'He's caught bad,' Smith said, running up to the bus and gesturing back towards Hillock. 'We need help.'

Scott looked back at the 25 children on board. 'We need some of you older boys,' he said. 'Looks like we have a job to do.'

Five Grade 10, 11 and 12 boys from Bathurst High School followed Scott off the bus. 'We should be able to lift this,' Scott told them, gesturing towards the plough blade.

The five youths, used to helping out with farm chores, confidently moved in on either side of Scott. 'Ready?' he said, and the six braced themselves, their knees bent, their fingers jammed into a gap under the loader bucket.

The team heaved upwards and, in an instant, the dreadful blade rose smoothly into the air. As the metal arm released its hold on Hillock, he fell backwards into Sharon's arms. After the sudden release of pressure, blood poured from his mouth and nose.

'Get Angie away!' Laura McNulty, a neighbour and nurse tending to him, urged those gathered round. She didn't want the child to see so much blood.

At the hospital in Bathurst, Dr Mark Fletcher was shocked by the sight of Hillock's grossly disfigured face. He sutured the scalp and stabilised Hillock as best he could. But a CT scan revealed multiple facial fractures and swelling of the brain.

That night, Hillock was transferred by ambulance to the intensive-care unit of the better-equipped hospital at Moncton, 200km (125 miles) away. For the next two days, he was kept in a drug-induced coma and hooked up to a ventilator. Cerebrospinal fluid continued to leak from the frontal crack in his skull.

Day and night, Sharon remained at his side. The hospital where she worked raised money for her travel and lodgings, and a collection in the community provided more than $4,000 to help the family.

When Glen finally awoke, Sharon was holding his hand. He wanted to say something, so the nurses provided a pen and paper. With a weak hand he scribbled, 'What happened to my tractor?'

Sharon smiled through tears of joy. She had her husband back.

A week after the accident, plastic surgeons reconstructed Hillock's face in a 10 hour operation. They inserted six metal plates with 36 screws across the crushed bones and removed bone from his skull to rebuild his right eye socket. Two months later Hillock was well enough to plant his fields and resume farming.

After the accident, Amber and Angie joined the local St John Ambulance Association, volunteering their time to assist injured people at sporting and other community events.

'I don't think you could find better kids than these,' says Hillock. 'I don't think you could find a better community, either.' ∎

The team heaved upwards

and, in an instant, the dreadful blade rose smoothly into the air. As the metal arm released its hold on Hillock, he fell backwards into Sharon's arms. After the sudden release of pressure, blood poured from his mouth and nose.

MAD WHITE GIANT

FROM AN EARLY AGE, Benedict Allen had dreamed of exploring the Amazon Basin, journeying through uncharted territory between the mouths of the Orinoco and Amazon rivers. In 1983, aged 23, he set off alone for South America. For four months he travelled and lived with different tribes, making friends, learning their ways, improving his jungle skills. But nothing could prepare him for what lay ahead.

The 'River Sea'

The Amazon is 6,400km (4,000 miles) long and has the world's largest drainage basin (area of land drained) at 7 million km² (2.7 million sq miles) – covering 40 per cent of South America. Benedict Allen's four-month journey took him 1,130km (700 miles) from the Orinoco to the mouth of the Amazon.

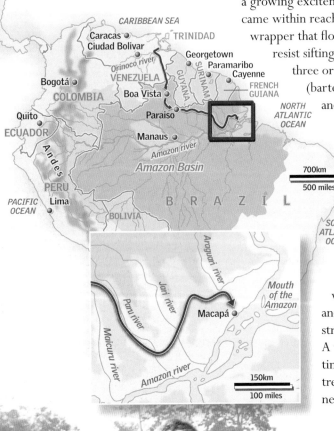

My two guides,

My two guides, Yepe and Pim, were from different tribes. Pim was a Tirio, about 16, bouncy and mischievous. He had agreed to come with me because he wanted to see the sun rise up out of the sea. Yepe was older, a Wayana, with long hair. He was a bachelor in a family group whom we'd met.

After a night of partying, we bid farewell to the group and started our descent of the Paru river. Almost immediately there were signs that we were coming out of the interior. The first was a non-Indian's hut. Pim and Yepe saw it was square, not round, and sat bolt upright in their seats.

The Brazilians were a curiosity at first: real white men, gold miners in their slum shacks. We gaped at them as much as they gaped at us. We had a growing excitement, a trembling in our stomachs, as the outside world came within reach. The Indians marvelled at each Coke bottle and sweet wrapper that floated by. Whenever we stopped, Yepe and Pim could not resist sifting through junk heaps and pilfering what they could. After three or four halts, both had hacked off their hair with scissors (bartered for an arrow), given away their bangles, necklaces and armbands and dressed up in T-shirts and shorts. 'Is wonderful,' said Pim dancing with glee, having just swapped his earrings for a deck of playing cards.

Alcohol flowed. The gold miners paid the Indians to take off their clothes and dance naked on the tables. They jigged to the miners' whistles and handclaps and kept on until they keeled over.

Pim, Cashoe (a dog I had found and nursed back to health), Yepe and I abandoned the canoe to walk east through the forest to the Jari, where we bought a new dugout. Here, the miners were all yellow with malaria. The sight of the decaying men changed Pim and Yepe. They had been led to believe that white men were strong. Was this the future I had brought them to, they asked? A white man's graveyard? As we paddled south, for the first time we saw that a few of the men gaping at us from the trees, leaning on their spades, wore revolvers. I'd sworn never to set foot where there was gold fever.

A new guide

I forced Pim and Yepe on down the river. They didn't know why they were coming, or where they were going. They paddled hopelessly as if stirring soup. I hoped they were mourning the life that they'd left behind in the interior. I feared there was nothing for them ahead but slavery to gold miners and a mind-numbing haze of cheap alcohol.

I persuaded them to tie up the canoe and come hunting in the forest. While Pim was chasing butterflies, Yepe was talking about the jungle spirits, how he could hardly feel any here at all, and how it was better in the forest we had come from.

'Yepe, I want you to take my canoe and leave me. Go upriver again.'

'You not want Yepe any more?'

'I can manage. Gold men are bad people. Yepe must go a long way away and take Pim with you. Go when this sun falls low.'

We took a different route back to the river, and bumped into a settlement of miners. 'Let's go another way,' I said, but Pim had dashed forward and was already mingling with a bunch of silent Indians. The stench of the village, two palm huts with tumbledown roofs, made me queasy. Pim ran to me and grabbed my hand. 'Come, look what I find!' He pulled me over to a square, tin-roofed shack, then jerked me inside.

There was a bench, and on top of the bench was the thing that Pim wanted me to play with. It was made of fine metal. A pair of scales for weighing gold.

Suddenly, a big man was blocking the doorway. 'And what have we got here?'

The voice came from a frog-faced man with pale, white skin and greased-back black hair. He was smiling, but I didn't like his eyes, green and jelly-like. I told him my name, the names of the others, and that we were just passing through to the mouth of the Amazon.

The miner said his name was Mendez. 'You know where you are going on to from here?'

'Continuing south, then up the Iratapuru tributary, then walking east through the forest to the road to Macapá, on the Amazon mouth.'

'I know the track through that forest. I could be your guide for a small consideration.' Mendez also revealed that he knew the river, listing a dozen rapids all of which tallied with those I'd heard about. He would be my guide if I agreed to leave Yepe and Pim with him when we parted. Despite my protestations, he gave them a bottle of cachaca, and took them into his hut to tempt them with gold.

All the way down the Jari, Mendez kept flashing his gold at Yepe and Pim, promising them a share of what they found. We turned up the Iratapuru and journeyed well into the interior again, a week upstream of other human habitation. Mendez had Pim and Yepe eating out of his hand.

'We going be rich, Benedito,' said Yepe, as we glided up to Edwardio's shack. Edwardio, Mendez's friend, would be the fourth miner in the partnership. He was lean, with black eyes, cold and hooded. He was happy that Mendez had got hold of two strong Indians to work for them, but what was the other stranger doing here?

Taking to the water *Benedict Allen navigated part of his route along the Amazon in a dugout canoe (opposite). The rest of his journey he made on foot, often through dense tropical rainforest.*

Gold fever *A gold miner with his next meal slung round his neck and a rifle over his shoulder. Allen tried to stay away from the miners, fearing trouble.*

That evening, I tried to talk to Pim and Yepe, but Mendez ensured they had bottles to their lips for most of the time. Then their heads crashed down on the table.

'You'd better go to bed, Benedito,' said Mendez. 'You've got a lot of paddling to do tomorrow.' He had decided that I should abandon my expedition and go back downriver by myself.

Sensing danger

I woke abruptly in the darkness with the feeling that something was wrong. The sensation was strong enough to make me lift my head from the hammock to listen to the night. It was not that I knew what had disturbed me; it was just that the jungle had taught me to use my senses to the full and I trusted them. Now they had woken me out of my sleep.

I lifted up the mosquito net and reached for my boots. The two Indians were asleep, but the miners were still up. I tiptoed through the dark to the doorway of their hut. They were speaking in Portuguese; I heard them say they were going to cut my throat. Was the Englishman armed? Yes, but no problem. Did his Indian friends mind? No, they couldn't care less.

The words rattled about in my brain. Then I ran. I dashed back for my hammock and mosquito net, and then I was away, and into the black forest. At the river I heard a soft, sighing noise in the trees and knew it was approaching rain. The river water was warm against my legs. I coiled the mooring rope and heaved the canoe clear of the bank. I leaped aboard, colliding with Cashoe, who had been left to guard our stores, and fumbled for the paddle. No one would think of going upstream to find me, I thought, and that was the direction I took.

I looked over my shoulder and saw, fading into the distance, a pale crocodile. It was Edwardio's canoe. I watched until it was lost in the darkness. I was alone.

Rocks and branches were snared in the water, but I steered clear of them by listening to the ripples of the water flow ahead. It was a trick Yepe had taught me. The rain came, tearing at the leaves and dancing on the water.

By day I paddled, living on fish baited with palm berries, and nuts scavenged from the forest floor. At dusk I assembled a camp – just a hammock, mosquito net and canvas-sheeting roof – tucked in the trees a few dozen paces from the river. Each morning I woke in the cool mist, when it was so quiet you could hear the dew dripping, and wondered if this was a dream. But the clammy earth smell was real and so were the canopies of leaves, matted yellow orchids and moss-smothered branches. The red leaves of creepers were heaped like fishing nets over everything else.

Dog-tired, I was looking for the track from the river to the east; the one Mendez had told me led out of the forest. It was my hope; and as long as I knew I had some, that was just fine. With my stores, I could make the jungle a comfortable-enough home for a week or so. I kept a vision of the Amazon mouth – a sunset view of water-like, rippleless glass – in the forefront of my mind.

On the third day, the water ruffled and whitened. I had to pull the canoe by rope up a series of cataracts and then around some rapids. Just

I heard them say they were going to cut my throat. Was the Englishman armed? Yes, but no problem. Did his Indian friends mind? No, they couldn't care less.

People of the rainforest

THE AMAZON RAINFOREST is believed to be the oldest tropical forest in the world, dating back perhaps 100 million years. As well as abounding in countless species of flora and fauna, it has been continuously inhabited by humankind for more than 12,000 years. Today it is home to some 390 ethnic groups – a population approaching 2.8 million – whose history since the 16th century has been one of exploitation at the hands of outsiders.

When Captain Vicente Yáñez Pinzón came to the Amazon in 1500, he was greeted with great friendliness, yet he skirmished with the native people and took 30 of them back to Spain as slaves. In around 1540, Gonzalo Pizarro led a party of *conquistadores* from Quito, Ecuador, in search of the fabled El Dorado, supposed source of unlimited gold. Pizarro's expedition was followed by a group led by Francisco de Orellana, who found many villages of indigenous people along the length of the Amazon. He returned with tales of a land densely and productively populated – and spoke of a tribe of war-like women, the 'Amazons'.

By the time French naturalist and mathematician Charles Marie de la Condamine travelled down the river in 1743, he found no settlements on its banks, and reported, 'All have submitted or retreated far away.' Many of the native people had been enslaved, pressed into service to harvest and spin cotton, or simply hunted down. Slavery continued into the 20th century, fuelled by the rubber trade.

Even well-intentioned visitors to this 'naturalist's paradise', attracted by the sheer diversity of life there, brought with them disease to which the inhabitants had no immunity. According to one estimate, 90 per cent of the indigenous people died within the first century of contact with Europeans, as infections spread from village to village.

Today, this fragile ecosystem is under siege from such depredations as encroaching agriculture, the burning of forest and grasslands, contamination of soil and rivers, illegal timber traffic, mining, and petroleum and hydrocarbon exploitation. In recent times, too, there have been two new menaces to the rainforest peoples – extreme tourism and the fashion for reality TV shows, which put previously uncontacted tribes at risk, not just culturally but epidemiologically, since they have no resistance to such ills as influenza and tuberculosis. In one instance in 2008, it was alleged that a British production company spread flu among a Peruvian tribe, killing four of its members.

FOREST PROVIDER A young boy picks urucum (achiote) high up in a tree (above). The seeds are ground down to a powder and added to food – for a spicy taste – as well as to make-up. It is also valued as an antidote to poisoning that can occur from eating the roots of the manioc, or cassava, plant.

out of the jaws of the rapids, beyond the spray but before we were safe, I jumped into the canoe and took up the paddle again.

'You can start bailing out the water if you want to feel useful, Cashoe!' He was not a dog in my mind, but a member of the expedition team – the one that guarded the stores at night. Cashoe chose this moment to bite into a rice sack and tussle with it playfully.

'Not now, Cashoe! Lie down!' It was already too late. As the rice sacks shifted, giving the canoe a left-hand list, I stuck my paddle out to the right to balance it. Even then I had a feeling of inevitable disaster. There was the sight of the receding calmness of dark russet water; my panicky wild strokes; gravel whisking up from the riverbed and clattering on the canoe underside. The twisting white foam streaked past as we were carried downstream; Cashoe yelping, the bucking worse and worse until at last –

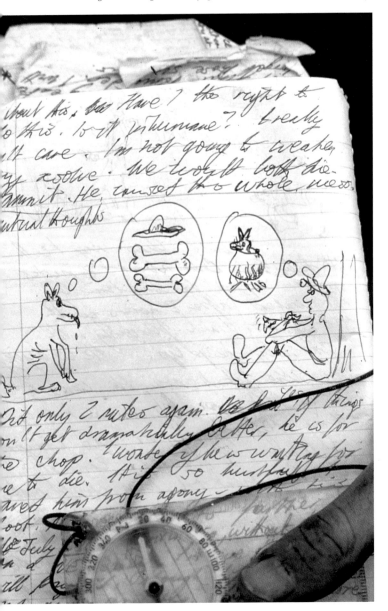

Will to survive Benedict Allen faced a terrible dilemma about his faithful dog, Cashoe, brought on by extreme hunger. It is summed up in the cartoon (below), drawn on one of Allen's few surviving notebook pages.

a relief now – we hit a tree trunk. The dugout crumpled as easily as a matchbox. Cashoe was flung out and I saw him choking in the surf as he was swept downstream.

I fought my way to the riverbank and hauled myself out. I had bashed my head on a rock as I was being flushed downstream, and one of my fingernails had been split as I clawed at the shingle for a hold. The cut was painting circles of blood on my knees.

I was stuck in the jungle and I had lost almost everything. I wanted to close my eyes and shrivel up in the bleaching sun. No help was going to come my way.

Diary of survival

I took stock of what I had managed to salvage: no tent or mosquito net or medicine, but two compasses, matches, fishing hooks and fishing line, an explosive flare, water-sterilising tablets, razor blades, four packets of dried soup, 12 packets of glucose tables, 20 aspirins and my money belt, with passport, air ticket and dollars. With my clothes were a leg-knife, my machete and my hat. I had also managed to rescue a cooking pan, water bottle, empty rucksack and a small strip of orange polythene. Plus two picture postcards of London, two pens and a notebook in which I sketched a map that I had memorised.

According to my calculations, the edge of the forest was at worst 110-130km (70-80 miles), as the crow flies, to the northeast. I thought I might manage 3km (2 miles) a day, 10km (6 miles) while I had the strength. (The true distance to the road would be double my estimate, avoiding gullies and cliffs. It would be triple this if I caught a fever.)

If I caught malaria, I might as well sit down and wait for a jaguar.

Before I left England I had attended a day course with Eddie McGee, a jungle survival expert. I could hear him now, his precise military tone positive and confident: 'Your will to survive counts for more than anything else.'

The next morning, **July 1**, I slung my rucksack over my shoulder, took hold of my machete in my right hand, placed the compass in the palm of my left hand and marched in a northeasterly direction, counting every pace through the bars of vines, leaf plates, snaking roots.

I notched every 100 paces up on a stick. I knew that 1,700 of my paces made a mile. My head worked like a clock, measuring time. 1 … 2 … 3 … 4 …

Every evening I wrote in my notebook.

July 5. I have been going five days. Feels like a month. 14 miles done of approx. 75 total. I must do more miles each day. The worst thing is not the gloom, the reeking moss, the ants in my eyes at night, monkeys taunting me and chucking sticks down, it is noise: the scraping of all the insects. I cannot escape from it. It's as if I've got earwigs in my ears.

Worse are the memories churning in my head. It is a battle between the weaker and stronger sides of my will. The stronger urges me on, the weaker side tells me to give up the struggle. Today I shaved for the first time since the accident. I took one razor blade and strapped it with fishing line to a strong thin twig. It also makes an effective knife.

My ration of seven glucose tablets a day is almost worse than nothing. I have promised myself I will stop to catch some fish at the next decent stream.

July 6. Crossed a 'decent stream'. Lost two hooks, didn't catch a thing. I imagine my stomach looks like a prune, withered and black. Did 5 miles today. I should be well over the Iratapuru ridge. But it is still just exhausting going up and down. The hills were only 300m. Must be over that height now.

July 9. Had a feast of Maraja berries, juicy purple berries, each one like a grape. But my stomach cannot take the diet. Crippling stomach pains. These helped by chewing charcoal from my campfire, a 'Jungle Eddie' trick. 35 miles total. Must be almost halfway, but my pace is getting slower.

July 12. 6.30am. Help in the form of Cashoe! He's with me again. Is it a dream? No, he really is warm in my arms.

Last night, as I stoked the fire, I heard a whimper. An emaciated Cashoe, with his white tail high, but his ribs jutting out so far they cast shadows in the fire glow. 12 days after the capsize he has found me.

5pm. Did 3 miles, Cashoe following. He is slow and easily exhausted. The stronger half of me is in the ascendant, I almost march through the greenery now, 1 … 2 … 3 … whisking my boots through the ground creepers, kicking off those that try to hold me back, swinging my machete through the lianas, carving the jungle up. For the first time I'm convinced I'm coming out of the hill range. But today I had not a dribble of water. Yet I'm sweating gallons. I suck pebbles to keep saliva in my mouth. I lick my arms for salt. I no longer wash my exposed skin. I have to fend off those mosquitoes somehow and sleeping in the wood smoke is the only way.

Sea of green *Benedict Allen makes his way through thick jungle on his journey from the Orinoco river to the mouth of the Amazon.*

July 13. My tongue swelled up in the night, and almost choked me. But later the rain came in torrents and I laid my head out from my shelter and let it splash in my eyes. Then I lapped it up from puddles like Cashoe. Only about 2 miles today, but Cashoe can't keep up. He is dying. The stronger half of me whispered in my ear, 'Of course, he's a walking refrigerator.' A thought I cannot dismiss. The meat on him could make all the difference. I have had no decent protein for two weeks. I cooked up my last packet soup, and did not share it. 43 miles total.

July 14. Continuing without deviation on a NE bearing. I'm sure this obstinacy will pay off. My rhythm is strong. 1 … 2 …3 … I can last 200 paces now, before notching them up on my stick. Today I came across a clearing. Daylight! The sun. A burning sphere, instead of putrid stuffy air. It is so good to feel my clothes baking, the water percolating away in steam.

There is a small patch of neck-high grassland only the size of a tree crown. I can't think why it's here. Not man-made. But there are locusts here. Big, juicy fat things. Clobbered 15 with a stick and netted 16 more with my shirt.

July 20. Only 3 miles, after my greatest of struggles of will. Just wanted to carry on lying in my shelter this morning. Cashoe came and licked my face. I really would have just lain there, but his continual nagging forced me to my feet. As we walked, I was dizzy. My eyeballs sank to the back of the sockets – they felt right up against my brain. The trees looked

If I don't get out of here I will be eaten up by one of the other animals. I can hear them competing around me. An ocelot. The shriek of a rat in the talons of an owl. Today I almost trod on a snake.

black. The river's the colour of Coca-Cola. Rain came in the afternoon. I haven't even reached the Cupixi River yet, and I have done 64½ miles. It makes no sense. Perhaps I am almost there.

July 22. Did 1 mile. With great effort. Shivering wildly with fever. I really feel like I've had it. If I don't get out of here I will be eaten up by one of the other animals. I can hear them competing around me. An ocelot. The shriek of a rat in the talons of an owl. Today I almost trod on a snake: a brown, ropy creature.

I have no inclination to keep writing this diary. I cannot see a use for it. I hardly have enough energy to move the pen.

My feet are rotting. My toes are cold and white. They cannot feel the forest floor. I'm brewing up *quina quina* bark for fever, after crushing it with my knife. My palms are sweaty, heavily creased and bright yellow like French Golden Delicious apples. Medicine first, then sleep.

July 23. 10am. The fever is bad. If only I could have ventilation. The jungle isn't like a cathedral, as some romantic said; it is like a stuffy room with everything in it sodden. All windows closed.

'The jungle will be your glory, the jungle will be your grave.' The weaker side of me is winning.

Found some snails in the stream, while cooling off. Will boil them. There are 25 of them, but only an inch long. I NEED VITAMINS AND PROTEIN.

4pm. Fever same or worse. It is so long since I have felt well that I find it hard to tell what condition my body is in.

Ate the snails. Also a mash of palm stems. I want only to close my eyes, but I've got to collect firewood. It is damp. I need medicine.

July 24. 11-ish am. I am racked by fever. Squalid dysentery. I cannot make a fire. Keep bathing to cool down, but just feel like curling up. Found a large, white grub in a fallen tree. Ate it alive, still wriggling.

4pm. I cannot last with much more of this. I cannot make a fire with wood wringing wet. I know that unless I move now and fight, I am finished.

July 25. 8am. Yesterday I killed my companion. Sharp blow with the machete butt to the back of skull. Then slit the throat. I waited until he wasn't looking. Afterwards, all bloody. I did make the fire. My adrenalin carried me through. Ate both kidneys and liver. Then bound body up with fishing line and palm leaves. There is so much meat. And it will be fresh for only days days. I stoked up the fire and smoked the legs as well as I could. Forced a broth of the meat down in the evening, though I had no hunger. I feel like a murderer. How silent it is without him.

July 27. 5.30pm. The great breakthrough. The stronger part of me is fighting back. Did 7 miles (79½ total) and camping by a river. Must be the Cupixi. A silver band of water as smooth as a mirror. A milky haze kisses the trees on the far bank, and I must be nearly out.

July 29. 6pm. My calculations say I have done 85 miles total. What has gone wrong? Where is the road? Where is daylight? I'm still on a northeast bearing, and fought oh so hard today. Over 6 miles through trees with snaky creepers up their trunks and bristly lianas.

July 31. I walked like clockwork, tick-tocking along: 4 … 5 … 6 … 7 … My loneliness was mixed with confusion. Why had I not reached the

Life-giver *A severed liana branch provides Benedict Allen with some much-needed moisture.*

outside world yet? It just didn't make sense. Too weak even to cry, I walked on and let my thoughts gently lift out of the forest and drift away. All the people I'd met in the jungle came and visited me, talked to me. *You are Mad White Giant. Mad White Giant.* Voices.

5pm. Collapsed today at about 11.30. Just felt faint and blood draining from my head. Blackness. Next I knew I was face-down in the leaves.

Fever is very severe, though better now. Did only 1½ miles. Barely able to make a shelter. I will sleep. Ants everywhere. Hate them. Nasty orange brutes that bite for no reason.

Later. Putting milky sap disinfectant of a tree on my cuts. Must rest. I can hardly see.

August 1. I've done it. Dabbling in a brook this morning, my mind suddenly cleared. I saw a cut branch. Not a torn one, a ripped one, but a cut one. A beautiful crisp, clean slice of a machete. And other cut branches are all around me. I want to remember them. Every one. Paths crisscross around me. I will choose one leading northeast. I must have done it. I hope I choose the right path.

The road to Macapá

Felled tree trunks were littered all the way along the track, but above their stumps the remaining forest canopy was as tightly shut as ever. Now the forest's stale reek was giving way to a dry, earthy smell: that of a newly ploughed field. I stepped in the direction of the smell, knowing I had lost the path, but not caring. The light, I had thought, would come all of a sudden. I would peel away a sheet of the creepers and there I would be, standing in it, blinking.

The light came at first in specks through the thicket of grey and black bamboo shoots, like stars in a clear night sky. The stars grew and grew, then coalesced into larger, irregular forms just in front of my eyes. The quality of the light was improving, too, increasing in brilliance.

Then I was on the verge of a cassava field. The spindly, shrubby plants looked meagre, in orderly rows. On the horizon was a primitive square hut.

A person came out of the hut; it was a man, with a back curved from too much field work. He stared at me. I stared at him. I scuffed and tripped through the cassava crop in his direction.

An arm's length away, I flipped off my hat and tried out a smile. He raised his eyebrows and his mouth fell wide open. I saw he had his hand out. I shook it, but the grip of this weak man was so tight on my twig fingers, I grimaced.

'The *senhor* has been out walking a long way today?'

'Yes,' I managed slowly, 'a long way.'

'Will the *senhor* stop for a second to have a coffee?'

I was unconscious when he pottered out of the hut and the next thing I remember was lying in a hammock.

For three days Jose brewed me rich coffee and a dozen herbal remedies, but he never did ask where I had come from. I was happy to be alive, but the happiness was mixed with uncertainty. I had entered the forest where the road had faded, and had crawled out where the same road had been abandoned five years before by construction workers beginning on it from

A person came out of the hut; it was a man, with a back curved from too much field work. He stared at me. I stared at him. I scuffed and tripped through the cassava crop in his direction.

this end. Somewhere in the 1,130km (700 mile) gap in the road, I had left part of myself behind.

On the third day I was on my feet again. A yellow government jeep came up the track to Jose's plantation, where the road stopped. The four surveyors explained that they were wondering whether it was worth starting work on the road project again, to open the forest right up.

I said that from what I'd seen of the forest, I wouldn't bother.

'Hah!' the men laughed. 'From what the foreigner has seen of the forest, we shouldn't bother!' They said they appreciated the joke very much and that they'd give me a lift back to wherever I'd come from. I laughed this time, far louder than the others had.

And then I was on the road to Macapá, and the mouth of the Amazon. ■

Where are they now?

AUTHOR, EXPLORER AND FILM-MAKER Benedict Allen has his own approach to exploration and presentation, which sees him travelling without such potentially life-saving aids as a satellite phone, GPS or even a film crew. He shuns sponsorship and goes it alone to some of the most hostile environments on earth, enduring loneliness, sickness and extreme discomfort for the sake of authenticity. In frequent, hair-raising situations, he relies on local resources, and he has at times been close to death, as in his Amazon adventure.

In the course of 'sinking into' remote communities, he has engaged in many rituals. Most notably in Papua New Guinea, with the Niowra people, at the age of 24, he participated in a male initiation ceremony where he was locked away for six weeks with other young men, force-fed, beaten several times a day and scarified over the back and chest, leaving him with permanent scars reminiscent of scales and marking him out as 'a man as strong as a crocodile'.

Allen made the first recorded crossing of the Central Mountain Range of Papua, continuing by canoe over the Torres Strait to Australia, was shipwrecked and, with his Papuan companions, reduced to living off limpets. He spent another seven months crossing the Amazon Basin at its widest, receiving training from the indigenous Matsés, the 'cat people' of Peru (so named because of the 'whiskers' and tattoos that adorn their faces). There he was shot at by hit men working for the infamous Colombian drug baron Pablo Escobar. On the same trip, Allen was abandoned by his guides, who walked off with his supplies.

He has travelled across the Namib Desert, the Mongolian steppe and the Gobi Desert, and trekked with dogs through Siberia. In the deserts of northwest Mexico, Allen ate peyote with the Huichol – a means of communing with the gods. He was writer and presenter of *Last of the Medicine Men*, an eight-part series on indigenous healers. A graduate in Environmental Science, he has never, he says, 'had a proper job'.

NEW ADVENTURES In 2008, Benedict Allen retraced the classic journey of traveller Eric Newby, made 50 years before, in the Hindu Kush mountain range of Afghanistan.

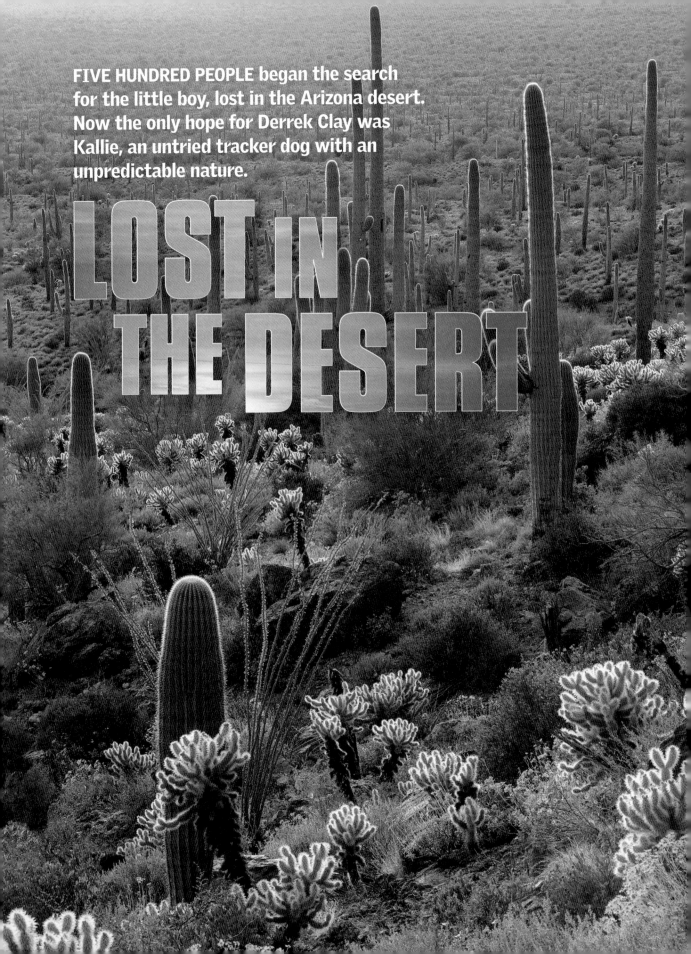

FIVE HUNDRED PEOPLE began the search
for the little boy, lost in the Arizona desert.
Now the only hope for Derrek Clay was
Kallie, an untried tracker dog with an
unpredictable nature.

LOST IN THE DESERT

Shelley Clay glanced out of her kitchen window to check on Damien, 4, and Derrek, 2. 'Hide and seek,' they chanted, crouching under shrubs in the yard of their trailer home in Maricopa, Arizona, a desert community southwest of Phoenix. Satisfied the boys were all right, Shelley turned her attention back to the roast she was preparing on that warm Saturday, April 27, 1991.

It wasn't until later, when her husband, Curtis Clay, a car mechanic, arrived home and Shelley went outside to greet him, that she noticed Derrek was no longer in the yard.

'Where's Derrek?' she asked her older son.

'That way,' Damien replied, pointing towards the desert.

'Derrek, Derrek!' the Clays called again and again as rising fear gripped them. They well knew the desert's dangers: scorpions, rattlesnakes, mountain lions and coyotes. Finally, their frantic calls unanswered, Shelley ran inside and called the police.

By the time Pinal County Deputy Gene Berry arrived, the desert was filled with neighbours looking for the youngster. In their zeal, they'd obliterated the boy's tracks. Help was summoned, and one of the biggest searches in the county's history was set in motion. Rescue teams were organised to cover sections of a 5km (3 mile) circle around the Clay home. That night, a helicopter swept the area, and early on Sunday morning volunteers on horseback scoured the shoulder-high web of vegetation for any sign of Derrek. Then a helicopter crew spotted a disposable nappy decorated with little elephants. From Shelley's description, the police knew it must be Derrek's. Spirits soared.

By Sunday night, National Guardsmen and the Border Patrol were on the scene, forming part of a human chain across the desert. Heading up the operation was James Langston, coordinator for the Maricopa County Sheriff's Office Search and Rescue team.

The searchers, more than 500 in total, found nothing. Even bloodhounds from the Arizona State Department of Corrections failed to find a single clue.

By early Monday morning, more than 36 hours had passed since Derrek was reported missing. Stepping outside the command post, Jim Langston watched the sun rise. 'How are we ever going to comb every inch of this terrain?' he wondered. Then an idea struck him.

Inside a tiny, windowless office at Utah's Department of Human Services in Salt Lake City, computer analyst Nancy Hachmeister, 35, was working at her keyboard when her beeper sounded. Reaching for the pager clipped to her waistband, she saw the number belonged to Don Hornecker, Arizona's emergency-services coordinator.

For ten years, Nancy had volunteered in searches for people lost in the wilderness – assisted by Utah's Rocky Mountain Rescue Dogs. 'Whatever it is, I can't go this time,' she thought. 'They will have to find someone else.'

Hidden dangers *Derrek Clay plays in the rock-strewn landscape that so nearly claimed his life. On the opposite page are some of the large spine-laden cacti that flourish in the desert where he disappeared.*

Harsh landscape *Much of southwest Arizona is covered in desert, a wild and hostile environment that bakes in sweltering heat by day and often cools down dramatically at night. For a 2-year-old to survive there for any length of time is remarkable.*

As the youngest of five daughters, Nancy had enjoyed endless hours with her dad when she was growing up. But on June 11, 1979, he was flying a DC-3 that crashed into a remote river. The bodies of the co-pilot and five passengers surfaced in the first week, but her father's corpse could not be located. Nancy agonised over his fate for 33 days, until searchers on rafts finally discovered his remains. Vowing to try to spare others such pain, she began to think about becoming a search-and-rescue volunteer.

Now, as she heard that a 2-year-old boy had been lost in the desert for two days, a chill swept over her. 'How long can a child live without water?' she thought. 'I've got to go.'

Lingering doubts

Until recently, Nancy had been assisted by Aja, her talented German shepherd. But Aja was injured, and Aja's daughter, Kallie, had replaced her. Nancy had begun to doubt that the daughter possessed her mother's fearless nature – a trait crucial for a search dog. Although Kallie had assisted in several live wilderness finds, there had been a few occasions when she had seemingly lost her nerve.

In one instance, when Nancy's pick-up truck was hit by a drunk driver, Kallie disappeared for several hours. Nancy found her in the brush, shaken and suffering from a massive chest wound. The dog's ordeal had left her unpredictable and fearful.

That Monday afternoon, Nancy and Kallie flew to Phoenix, then took a bus to the Clays' home. At the command post, she studied a map with coloured overlays denoting areas that were already being searched.

'Our deadline is 6pm tomorrow,' Jim Langston said. 'After that, the chances of finding the boy alive are bleak.' Nancy quickly decided that it would be pointless to allow Kallie out into the 30°C (85°F) temperatures. Dog and searchers would probably be quickly exhausted in such weather.

'We'll wait till sunset,' Nancy told Jackie Vernon, 31, an Eloy housewife whose first search-and-rescue assignment was to be Nancy's partner. 'Derrek's track should rejuvenate in the cooler air.'

When Nancy asked the Clays for something with their son's scent, Curtis handed her a pair of tiny white ankle socks retrieved from under the boy's bed. 'Find, Kallie!'

Nancy held out the socks for Kallie to sniff. 'This is Derrek. Wanna work?' Kallie could barely contain her excitement. Nancy clipped a chemical light-stick onto the dog's collar to make her visible, then called, 'Find, Kallie, find!'

Kallie bounded across the desert, looping around mesquite plants and cacti, her nose high. Here in the cool sands bleached by moonlight, Derrek's scent lingered.

'She's working well,' Nancy told Jackie. When they reached the area where the nappy had been found, a search helicopter suddenly swooped by so low Nancy swore she could touch it. Kallie froze, eyes glazed with fear.

'Let's get back to work, girl,' Nancy coaxed. The German shepherd cowered, her confidence shaken. 'Let's go, girl,' Nancy repeated forcefully. Slowly and cautiously, Kallie began tracking again.

Dangers of the desert

ARIZONA'S PARCHING DESERT country covers about a third of the state, and is home to a surprising wealth of flora and fauna, some of which poses a threat to human visitors.

Among the animals to fear are not just mountain lions, coyotes and rattlesnakes, but venomous sidewinder snakes and the rare black and yellow-patterned Gila monster, the only poisonous lizard in the USA. Small, thin scorpions can inflict a sting with the potential to kill a child, and some spiders and centipedes can also give you a painful bite.

Rattlesnakes are usually defensive, full of sound and fury signifying not a lot, but they will strike if stepped on, which is easily done because their camouflage is extremely effective. The only treatment for a rattlesnake bite is an 'antivenin', injected at a hospital. Mercifully, many rattlesnake bites are 'dry', delivering no venom.

Some 30 species of tarantula inhabit the Arizona deserts. Although they are not especially aggressive, these hairy spiders, measuring up to 13cm (5in), have two weapons in their armoury. They may rear up to bare their fangs, or perform a kind of 'handstand', using their rear legs to throw a puff of hair from the abdomen, which can be poisonous. They rarely bite human beings, and the hairs, though they cause irritation, can be removed with sticky tape.

The iconic cactus of the Arizona desert is the saguaro – the tall, weirdly anthropomorphic variety with upraised 'arms'. These can reach 15m (50ft) and live for 200 years, blooming for the first time after 50-75 years. Of the pernicious cholla that caused Kallie such distress there are some 20 species. The genus is closely related to the prickly pear, and is one of the most dangerous cacti in the desert. It reacts like a whip when brushed against, driving its spines into the skin. Efforts to pluck the spines out are in vain, as they transfer themselves to the fingers, and need to be removed with a comb.

One of the most endearing-looking of the genus is the teddy-bear cholla, which has a deceptively fluffy, cuddly appearance: it is not recommended that you hug it.

A poisonous Gila monster

With every passing hour, hopes of finding Derrek alive diminished. Nancy pictured the toddler wandering in the dark, stumbling, calling out to his mother. She removed Derrek's sock from her backpack and put it close to Kallie's nose. 'Check it out, Kallie. Is this Derrek?' The dog's eyes met hers as if to say, 'I'm doing my best.' She stroked the animal's coat. If Kallie sensed her handler doubted her, the dog's confidence would fade completely.

As the temperature dipped to around 12°C (about 55°F), the three returned to camp, exhausted. At 1am Jackie was sent home to get some rest. If necessary, she would return the next morning.

Nancy and Kallie woke at 5am and resumed the search. Vultures were circling in the distance, and Nancy feared they might be too late. Suddenly, Kallie yelped in pain. Cactus spines had pierced the padding on her paws.

'Roll over,' Nancy ordered. With a pair of surgical pliers she pulled out a dozen spines. Kallie's paw puffed up immediately. 'Come on, girl, let's work,' Nancy coached. Kallie rose slowly, determined to please her mistress.

By late morning, Kallie had become paralysed by the heat, and Nancy was feeling drained. The two returned to the command post to rest.

Faint cry

When the sun set, Nancy and Kallie resumed work, joined by Jackie. The deadline for finding Derrek had come and gone. Like the other volunteers, the women knew Derrek probably wouldn't be alive after 75 hours in the desert, but they all refused to give up hope.

About 9.45pm Kallie caught a scent in the still air and raced up a hillside. Again, she yelped in pain. A jumping cholla cactus had released an army of needles into the dog's legs and stomach. Nancy removed the

Utah's wonder dogs

THE SEARCH AND RESCUE (SAR) DOGS of the not-for-profit Rocky Mountain Rescue Dogs (RMRD) are highly trained to work off-leash to scent out casualties, even when a victim is buried in snow or under rubble, hidden in dense brush or swept away by water. They use 'air scent techniques' and track with their noses to the ground. When a dog picks up an airborne human scent, it will travel back and forth in a narrowing 'cone' until it locates the source, before returning to guide the handler to the find.

Much of their training, which includes mock searches, takes place in the extreme weather that dog and handler are likely to confront, such as blizzard conditions. And as no one can predict when an emergency may occur, the dogs are on constant standby.

The teams are also trained for search and rescue around water. Scents are forced by a compressor through underwater hoses, with bubbles on the surface identifying the scent source. The handler then gets the chance to observe and become acquainted with the dog's signal, be it a bark or a wag of the tail.

Since helicopters play an indispensable role in many rescues, the dogs – who may find the noise or the shadows of whirring propellers distressing – are introduced to them as part of the preparation for their vital work. They are first taken aboard a helicopter when it is still and silent, and only afterwards are they 'hot-loaded' onto one that is running. Eventually the dogs may even come to enjoy flying.

Like Kallie, these dedicated animals sometimes have to endure a degree of pain and suffering. For instance, crossing the sharp desert rock may hurt their paws and lame them, though dogs that are regularly walked on pavements can cope well with rocky deserts.

It's a serious business, but the bottom line of the advice to handlers from the RMRD is 'always, always to have fun with your dog'.

FINDING THE SCENT Handler Kellie Finch and her dog Sydney are trained in trailing techniques.

spines that she could see, but minutes later Kallie was struck again.

Exhausted, her paws sore and swollen, Kallie strained to keep going. 'How much longer can she push herself?' Nancy wondered.

Then an astonishing thing happened. As if propelled by an unseen force, Kallie raised her nose into the air and began to track furiously. She led the women to the base of a mountain more than 3 miles from camp, where they heard a faint cry – and another.

'Find Derrek!' Nancy shouted. But the dog, already racing ahead, had stopped at a paloverde tree and was on point.

'Got something to show me, Kallie?' Nancy shined a light into the tree branches. Nothing. She shifted the beam to the left. Was that just a branch? Or a leg? Yes! There, in a tangle of creosote bush, peeked a golden halo of hair. The small body was so dirty it blended into the earth.

Derrek lay with his eyes closed, wearing only a T-shirt and one sandal. His forehead was gouged and bleeding, his body scratched from head to toe. Nancy gently touched his arm. He didn't move.

Her heart sank. Were they too late? She leaned over and stroked Derrek's forehead, and the child looked up with beautiful blue eyes. Peering over Nancy's shoulder, Jackie fought back tears.

Desert saviours *Nancy, Kallie and Jackie relax at last on the night they found Derrek alive. Nancy has since left Rocky Mountain Rescue Dogs and formed her own search dog organisation – Utah Search Dogs.*

'Don't die on me!'

Nancy pulled Derrek into her arms and hugged him close. Knowing he was severely dehydrated, she rationed him a few drops from her water bottle. Too much too soon, she feared, could damage his brain.

A few feet away stood Kallie, her tail wagging a mile a minute. 'Did I do good?' she seemed to ask. Nancy patted the dog and gave her some water too.

By now Derrek was on the verge of delirium. Nancy radioed the base, but got no response. 'Don't die on me!' she cried, as she looked into the boy's sunken eyes.

The two women took turns carrying Derrek as they hurried towards base. Finally, at 10.32pm, Nancy made radio contact. 'I have a find. He's alive,' she reported, her voice shaking. Minutes later, a helicopter settled in the sand.

The rescue hadn't come a moment too soon. 'It's remarkable he survived,' said Dr David Tellez at Phoenix Children's Hospital. 'He couldn't have lasted much longer.'

Kallie herself was barely able to walk. A vet back in Salt Lake City removed more cactus spines, soaked her feet and treated her with antibiotics.

About a year after the rescue, Nancy and Kallie drove up to the Clays' home. Derrek's eyes lit up as he ran to the shepherd and threw his arms around her. Soon, the two were rolling around in the back of Nancy's truck.

Nancy will always cherish the memory of Derrek's rescue – and of Kallie's heroic effort. 'I doubted whether she had the temperament to be a good search dog,' she said. 'Now I know she does. We couldn't have found Derrek without her.' ∎

SWARM!

AS THE FAMILY explored the dense Florida swamp, there was one enemy they had not counted on – a swarm of angry yellow-jacket wasps was on the warpath.

Debbie Jacoby Walker lifted her gaze and smiled. Above the century-old cypress and water oaks of the Florida marsh, eagles glided across the afternoon sky. Here and there she caught sight of blue herons standing still and silent.

Having grown up in Maryland, the 41-year-old mother of two still felt a certain trepidation entering this wild jungle terrain. The steamy realm of alligators and water moccasin snakes was not her element. But high up on her husband Ben's home-built swamp buggy – a tank-like, open-air machine with 1.8m (6ft) tall tractor tyres – she felt safe.

That late October day in 1995 was the start of the hunting season, and 46-year-old Ben had left his nursery business in Naples, Florida, to scout for deer and wild boar. The native Floridian had brought Debbie and their boys, Matthew, four, and Mark, two, along.

Tired from their long day and lulled by the machine's rocking, the boys were napping in the back. Beneath their raised seats, Ben's two hunting dogs lay quietly in a cage.

'Shouldn't we head back?' Debbie asked.

'All we've got to do is follow our own tracks, and we'll be back before sunset,' Ben assured her.

The swamp buggy became entangled in branches, and Ben climbed onto one of the huge tyres to cut them away. A moment later, above the rumble of the idling engine, Debbie heard a high-pitched yelp from the dogs. Then Ben cried out, 'Oh, my God.'

'What's wrong?' she asked. Ben was clawing at his jeans. Debbie looked down and saw, from Ben's ankles to his thighs, a blanket of vibrating, probing yellow jackets.

Within seconds, thousands of wasps had engulfed the swamp buggy in a cloud of fury. Debbie felt the stiletto jab of scores of tiny stingers.

To the rescue *Phil Pelletier swung into action without hesitation when he was confronted by the sight of a badly injured Debbie Walker, who stumbled into him while seeking help for her family.*

The boys! She turned to see wasps swarming over her sleeping children. Matthew awoke screaming, helplessly waving his arms. She heard two-year-old Mark cry, 'Mommy, make it stop!'

Fighting his way back into his seat, Ben jammed the transmission into reverse, but the gears would not engage. 'We have to run,' he yelled. 'I'll go first. Throw the babies down to me.'

Ben leaped blindly into the tall subtropical grass. His right leg landed on something rock-hard, buckling beneath him. A searing pain shot through him. 'Debbie, wait!' He dragged himself to the rear of the vehicle. 'Drop Mark here! The ground's soft.'

Debbie hesitated. How could she toss her baby almost 4m (12ft) down? Then the great angry swirl slammed into her from behind. Debbie screamed and dropped Mark as she doubled over in agony.

The boy landed in the mud unhurt, and Ben dragged him away from the buggy. Debbie dropped Matthew, then tumbled down after him.

Still locked in their cage, the dogs howled forlornly. Debbie's heart broke. 'I can't help them now,' she thought. 'I've got to think of my family.'

She pulled Matthew away from the buggy.

Diverse environment *The Florida swamplands – the Everglades – is a subtropical wetland wilderness that encompasses many different ecosystems and allows a wide variety of species, including the yellow-jacket wasp, to flourish.*

'We've got to shield the kids,' she shouted. She and Ben began brushing the wasps off them and rolling the boys in the mud. But everything seemed vague and hazy. 'I've lost my glasses!' Debbie realised. Extremely short-sighted, she needed glasses even to find her way around the house.

Ben glanced at Debbie. Yellow jackets covered her face like a writhing mask. Already her cheeks, forehead and chin were starting to swell – the sign of an allergic reaction that could send her into fatal shock. 'Take Mark and move back down the trail, Deb,' Ben ordered. 'I'll send Matt after you.'

Picking up the boy, Debbie stumbled along the buggy tracks as far as she could from the yellow jackets. The swarm finally stopped pursuing her.

'Follow Mom,' Ben told Matthew hoarsely. 'She'll take care of you.'

The frightened four year old, still covered with yellow jackets, crawled away. When Debbie saw him coming alone, she realised Ben must be too injured to walk. 'Stay here,' she told the kids. Head down, arms flailing, she re-entered the yellow storm.

'Try to walk, Ben – I'll help you,' she said between gasping breaths. But Debbie couldn't lift the 1.85m (6ft 1in), 102kg (220lb) man. 'Oh, Ben,' she cried, 'what are we going to do?' Her speech was beginning to slur.

Anaphylactic shock

Ben knew they were in trouble. He was in terrible pain, and Debbie was going into shock – she'd been stung before, and had reacted so badly she'd had to seek hospital treatment. No one knew where they were, and night was coming on. 'Listen to me, Deb,' he said. 'You've got to run for help. Leave the babies.'

'I can't!' she said.

'They'll slow you down. Go while you still can. Follow the buggy tracks back to the camp we passed.'

Seeing her incapacitated husband and hearing her two small boys sobbing, Debbie knew she had no choice. 'I love you, Ben. I'll try my best.'

Ben watched her stumble out of sight. It seemed impossible she would make it in her condition. But the couple shared a deep Christian faith. He began to pray.

Debbie staggered through the muck, trying desperately to keep between the huge tyre tracks. Without her glasses, everything was a blur. Her mind was dull, her body lethargic.

The insect venom was doing its heinous, silent work. As anaphylactic shock sets in, the venom allergens first lower the blood pressure, reducing oxygen flow to the brain, heart and other vital organs. Then external body tissues, also short-changed of oxygen, open their cellular doors to fluids. These tissues swell, closing the throat and air passages. Some victims die quickly; others suffocate slowly.

Debbie was entering the early stages. And without knowing it, she had wandered off the buggy track.

Phil Pelletier had been looking forward to this hunting trip with his buddies for a long time. Yet the morning's hunt had been disappointing for the 45-year-old county recreation director. There had been plenty of game and his friends were in a festive mood, but something was tugging at him. He elected to stay behind to pack up their camp. He wasn't sure why.

It was 4.25pm before he headed his truck down the narrow, abandoned railroad bed they used for a road. Within 90m (100yd), a figure appeared. It was a woman, staggering and covered with mud, her face grotesquely swollen. 'Lord,' he thought, 'she's been beaten up bad!'

'Lady, are you all right?'

At the sound of his gentle voice, Debbie began screaming. 'My babies are dead! My husband broke his leg – attacked by yellow jackets. They were all over us!'

'I'll help you,' Pelletier said, trying to calm her. 'We'll look for them.'

'I can't,' she gasped. 'My throat is closing. I need medicine.' There was an unnatural look in her eyes, and her skin was a lifeless pale grey.

'I'll take you to Ortona,' Pelletier said. 'It's 5 minutes away. There's a store there. We can call for help.'

A sting in its tail

THE SOUTHERN YELLOW JACKET (*Vespula squamosa*) is the most common wasp species in Florida and one of the most aggressive stinging insects. Yellow jackets live in colonies of workers, queens and males, often in hollow logs, tree stumps, leaf piles and soil cavities. The workers, flying in their thousands, may be mistaken for honey bees, but can deliver multiple stings; for the honey bee, one sting is an act of suicide. Only females sting, and the necessary apparatus is contained in the abdomen. As a wasp prepares to sting, it curves its abdomen downwards and punctures the victim's skin with its stinging tube, which is connected to a venom sac. Barbs enable it to drive the sting deeper into flesh, as muscles pump out the chemical cocktail that causes sharp pain.

Yellow jackets are ferociously protective of the colony, posting 'guards' at the nest entrance. If a wasp flies near you or alights on you, don't flap at it, shoo it, swat it or run away, all of which may antagonise it. Rather, stay calm and still, and slowly raise your hands to cover your face. Never squash a wasp – this releases an alarm pheromone that can provoke an all-out attack. In summer, take precautions: rake up decaying, fallen fruit, secure your rubbish, keep food covered. If you are wasp-phobic, don't wear scented products.

Although we tend to think of wasps as a menace, they have a role to play in the ecosystem, providing a natural, biological control of agricultural and garden pests, of which they are voracious predators. They also contribute to pollination, and are a food source for numerous species of bird.

BEWARE THE FEMALE The yellow jacket's venom sac delivers venom via a valve to coat the insect's spear-like stinger at the rear.

Venom sac

Valve

Sting sheath

Stinger

Paramedics met them there and quickly gave Debbie an adrenaline injection. Her condition was listed as priority one: life-threatening.

As the paramedics worked, Debbie did not take her eyes off Pelletier, pleading with him to go back and look for her family. A father of two, he could only imagine her anguish.

'Don't worry,' he told the half-conscious mother, 'I'll find your family.'

Sweat trickled down Pelletier's back as he pushed his pick-up to nearly 100km/h (60mph) along the railroad bed into the swamp. Debbie had described to him the place where she came out of the woods. Suddenly Pelletier noticed an opening and slammed on the brakes. 'Maybe this is the spot,' he thought.

But the pick-up dipped low into the mushy, swollen marsh and began sinking. Quickly he backed up onto the railroad bed and drove on. Fifteen metres later, he found another narrow gap. He recalled there were old logging roads snaking through these woods. That must be the way she walked out.

Daylight was fading. Pelletier pushed ahead without finding a trail. The staccato sound of fan blades hitting water told him how deep his truck had sunk in the soggy terrain. A kilometre later a flash of colour caught his eye.

He idled the truck and looked again. There, sitting in a shallow waterhole, was a little boy! He was facing away, talking to himself. Not wanting to alarm him, Pelletier called from a distance, 'I've got your mama!'

At the sound of a voice, the child turned and started to cry. Pelletier was unprepared for the sight. Four-year-old Matthew's neck, arms and legs had swelled to grotesque proportions. His ears stuck straight out from his head. His skin – stretched tight and bloodlessly white – revealed hundreds of crimson-purple bites.

Lucky to be alive *Recovered from their ordeal, the Walker family stand beside the large swamp buggy they thought would keep them safe in the swamp.*

Scooping up the boy, Pelletier gently carried him to the truck. Matthew screamed and wriggled in pain. He began to shake, cold even in the 32°C (90°F) weather. Staring blankly, he put his head down. 'He's slipping away from me,' thought Pelletier. He had to get the child to a hospital. This was one life he could save.

Heading out, Pelletier tried to avoid waterholes. By the third one, his luck ran out. As water covered the pick-up's hood, its engine stalled. Picking up Matthew, now limp, Pelletier waded into the hip-deep pond.

Then, across a clearing, he spotted a man. It was Deputy Sheriff Carlin Coleman, who had followed Pelletier's tracks there.

'This boy needs help!'

Pelletier called. 'The only way we're going to bring the others out is with a swamp buggy.' He told Coleman about a friend's buggy at his camp.

The two men had driven only a short distance when they met Fire Chief Dennis Hollingsworth. The three decided Coleman would take the boy on to the store at Ortona, while Pelletier and Hollingsworth went back to the swamp in the borrowed buggy. It was 6.37pm. In an hour, their chances of finding Mark and Ben Walker would be virtually nil.

Back on the trail, Hollingsworth noticed a section of rutted mud. 'Hold it,' he commanded. 'There are two sets of buggy tracks, one big, one small. They cross right here.'

'The woman told me her husband has a big buggy,' Pelletier said. 'If she got mixed up here and followed the small tracks, it would account for her getting to my camp so fast. It was the luckiest thing she could have done.'

The two men followed the big ruts to a pond surrounded by thick palmetto grasses. Looking across, Pelletier caught the outline of a head.

Jumping into the pond, Hollingsworth furiously waded through the murky waters. There he saw the bloated, ashen face of Mark Walker. The fire chief choked back tears as he cradled the muddy toddler in his arms. 'We'll get you out of here, little buddy,' he promised.

He radioed his dispatcher. 'We've got him,' he said, his voice breaking. 'We'll bring him out, then go back in for his daddy.' It was agreed that Coleman would come and take the child to the Ortona store.

'We're coming, Ben'

Ben Walker hadn't moved since Debbie left. He had called to his boys and got no answer, so he feared they had wandered off after their mother and were lost. His only relief was that the yellow jackets had lost interest in him. They had targeted the swamp buggy, its engine still rumbling, as the enemy.

Ben was in great pain, drifting towards unconsciousness, when he heard the sound of another buggy. A man's voice rang out, 'Ben? You all right? We're coming, Ben.'

'Thank you, God,' Ben cried. 'Thank you.'

Shortly after, hunters went in to retrieve Ben's swamp buggy – and to free his dogs, who survived. The vehicle was moved, but wasps returned to it, even after being burned off. Finally, hunters burned the nest. Most yellow-jacket nests lie beneath the earth, but this one had expanded above ground to include a fallen tree. The nest was apparently disrupted when the Walkers' swamp buggy hit it with a tyre.

At Columbia East Pointe Hospital, Debbie was brought back from the edge of death. Compound fractures in Ben's right knee and upper leg required several operations, but he soon returned to work. The boys recovered quickly. To replace the family's memories of terror and pain, there was a heightened awareness of love, an emotion that moves people to acts of spontaneous courage and sacrifice.

Around the Ortona store they still talk about the inexplicable connections – the timely appearances of the right people at the right time; how every seemingly wrong turn ended up being right. They call it a miracle. ∎

Jumping into the pond, Hollingsworth furiously waded through the murky waters. There he saw the bloated, ashen face of Mark Walker. The fire chief choked back tears as he cradled the muddy toddler in his arms. 'We'll get you out of here, little buddy,' he promised.

RACE FOR HIS LIFE

TO RESCUE his fellow yachtsman in the Vendée Globe round-the-world race, Pete Goss would have to sail back into the eye of the storm – and forfeit his chance of winning. But Raphaël Dinelli was nowhere to be seen.

Pete Goss gasped in astonishment as the barometer aboard the 15m (50ft) *Aqua Quorum* dropped like a stone. The robust, 20 knot northerly wind he'd been riding suddenly veered to the southwest and began to shriek: 45, 50, 60 knots, with bursts of up to 70 – full hurricane weather.

Frantically, the 35-year-old Englishman lowered sail, leaving up only the storm jib, a triangular scrap of canvas in the bow. The *Aqua Quorum* bounced like a toy through breaking waves higher than a three-storey house.

Alone in icy waters between Australia and Antarctica, Goss was one of the 15 sailors entered in the Vendée Globe. The gruelling, nonstop race had begun nearly two months ago in the French port of Les Sables d'Olonne. He had sailed past the southern cape of Africa and Australia, and once he rounded Antarctica and Cape Horn in South America, the course would head back up the Atlantic.

Competitors take from three and a half to five months to complete the circuit – if they make it at all. On this Christmas night, 1996, Goss wondered if he would be the third life to be claimed by the Vendée since the race had begun seven years before, in 1989.

Bailing water from the cabin in the midst of the fury, Goss heard a bleep from the laptop computer on his chart table. It was an emergency call from the Australian Maritime Rescue Coordination Centre (MRCC): a boat named *Algimouss* had sent a mayday. 'Poor sods,' Goss thought. 'I wonder where they are.'

He hadn't recognised the name as a Vendée Globe boat. Minutes later, though, the computer bleeped again and spat out a fax from race headquarters: 'Hi, Pete. Raphaël is in trouble. Do you think you can help?'

Raphaël! The realisation hit Goss like a punch in the stomach.

Raphaël Dinelli and Pete Goss didn't know each other, but they might have been brothers, so similar were their stories. Professional sailors since their early years, they were penniless outsiders in a 'rich man's race'. Neither had the fame nor the huge budgets that corporate sponsors commonly throw at the sports stars and, in fact, Dinelli hadn't even qualified as an official entrant. Arriving at the last minute for departure, he discovered that he wasn't on the list of competitors. But he sailed off with the pack anyway as a 'pirate' entry.

Goss, a former Royal Marine commando, was a veteran of the shoestring approach. In one transatlantic race he had sailed in a catamaran so light that four men could pick it up and so short of space that he had had to sleep on deck. In another race his boat was so primitive that he navigated by following jetliners' vapour trails all the way to America. He came in second in his class – and the keel fell off his boat soon after a crane lifted it from the water.

'You're finished'

Goss had spent years planning for the Vendée. Begging and borrowing, he got a local shipyard to build the *Aqua Quorum* virtually at cost. Lead for the keel's 2 ton ballast bulb came entirely from public donations – everything from diving weights to leftover material from a church in his home town of Plymouth that was scrapping an old organ.

The *Aqua Quorum* was the smallest entry in the 1996 race, but she was thoroughly modern, built of carbon fibre and structured by Martyn Smith, who had worked on the nose section of the Concorde supersonic passenger jet.

As the race progressed, Dinelli and Goss made each other's acquaintance by radio with the help of fellow competitor Catherine Chabaud as interpreter (Goss spoke no French and Dinelli's English was rudimentary). They spoke of sailing conditions, exchanged wisecracks – and became friends.

He paused; with a wife and three children, did he have the right to take the risk? But he knew what his answer would be.

'Hell's teeth,' Goss muttered as he looked at a map. Dinelli was 160 nautical miles upwind. Getting to him would be suicidal madness. He banged out a message: was anyone closer to Dinelli who could help? The answer was negative. There were no nearby racers, no ships in the area, and at some 2,200km (1,350 miles) from the Australian coast, Dinelli was out of helicopter range. Goss was the only one.

He paused; with a wife and three children, did he have the right to take the risk? But he knew what his answer would be. So he crawled through the keyhole door of his cabin and put the helm hard over. Immediately *Aqua Quorum* was slapped down by the titanic power of the wind against the storm jib. I'm never going to make it, he thought, but the boat gamely righted herself and thudded off at an 80 degree angle into the teeth of the gale.

By now, the three central compartments of the *Algimouss* were waist-deep in water one degree above freezing. From an oilskin sack, Dinelli yanked his red survival suit over warm arctic clothes, grabbed the Argos radio beacons and tied them round his neck. All he could do now was wait. Watertight compartments fore and aft kept her afloat for the moment. But for how long?

For 3 hours *Algimouss* lay on her back in the storm with Dinelli trapped inside. When the ropes and cables that had been holding the broken mast to the boat finally parted, the boat righted itself and he scrambled on deck.

Nothing was left: no sails, no mast, no ropes, nothing. The life-raft was gone. 'Tu es cuit,' he said to himself. 'You're finished.'

But if Dinelli had to die, he was determined to die hard. He clambered to the roof of *Algimouss*'s cabin, held fast against being washed overboard by the nylon strap of his safety harness attached to a steel mooring eye. All through the afternoon he stood on the roof and bestrode *Algimouss* like a circus rider, knees bent, leaning into the wind and the waves to keep his circulation going.

In the darkness of night, he talked to his boat. 'We've got a pact. You don't give up and I won't give up, OK?' By the time Christmas night gave way to a cold, grey dawn he couldn't straighten up anymore and his eyes were nearly glued shut from hours of exposure to salt spray.

Hour after hour, Pete Goss tacked against the hurricane. His progress was maddeningly slow; reaching far out sideways, back and forth, back and forth, he sailed endless miles to gain a few precious miles of forward progress. Towering waves would knock the boat over, but the *Aqua Quorum* always came back. Gritting his teeth, Goss plugged on.

Finally, cold and exhausted, he set the autopilot and crawled below for a brief rest. Water covered the cabin floor, but he was too far gone to care. Pulling his sleeping bag around him he tied himself into his bunk and was

Two men against the sea *Pete Goss races to Dinelli's rescue in* Aqua Quorum *(main picture). Earlier the Frenchman clung desperately to his rapidly sinking yacht as it yielded to the ocean (inset).*

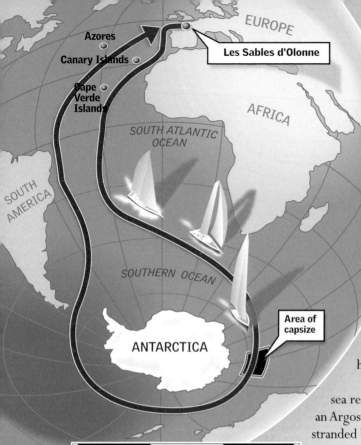

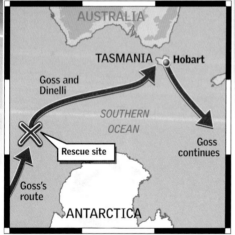

Vendée Globe challenge Les Sables
d'Olonne on the French west coast is the
starting point for the nonstop single-handed
yachting race (top) that covers a route of just
over 38,500km (24,000 miles). On Boxing
Day, 1996, 2,200km (1,350 miles) off the
coast of Australia, things went disastrously
wrong for Raphaël Dinelli when his yacht was
wrecked in the Southern Ocean (below).

out like a light – only to be jerked awake by
a thunderous crash and fireworks.

An aerosol bottle of highly flammable
lightweight lubricating oil had lodged
between terminals of the *Aqua Quorum*'s
generator, causing a short circuit. Frantically,
Goss wrested the bottle free before the
whole cabin exploded.

He went back on deck. The wind had
eased enough for him to set the mainsail.
Aqua Quorum leaped on like a thoroughbred.

Mayday

At 2am, Flight Lieutenant Ian Whyte, captain of
the Royal Australian Air Force Orion plane *Rescue
251* was awakened by his duty officer. There had
been a mayday in the Southern Ocean. Within hours
his four-engined turboprop was airborne.

The mission would be long and complicated. French
sea rescue services had taken the boats' positions from
an Argos satellite and fed it to Whyte. He had to locate the
stranded boat and if Dinelli was still alive, drop an Air-Sea
Rescue Kit, then find the rescue boat and guide it in.

Late in the afternoon of December 26, some 2,200km
(1,350 miles) from the Australian coast, the aircraft's sensor
operator picked up signals from Dinelli's Argos beacons.
Whyte descended through the clouds.

Throttled back at 180m (600ft), Whyte, copilot Nicholas
Platts and the rest of the crew scanned the horizon. The
visibility was poor, grey on grey. Suddenly, Whyte cried out.
'At 3 o'clock, object in the water.'

Platts released smoke canisters to mark the location. A steep
turn to come back, and there it was again. 'Oh, my God,' said
one of the crew. 'There's a guy standing there, waving!'

Flying at 90m (300ft), Whyte hit the release button and heard
the air-sea rescue kits tumbling from the open bomb-bay door.
Four containers connected by a long nylon cord headed for the
water. Inflating as it fell, the first container, a ten-man rubber
life-raft, hit in perfect position, 45m (50yd) upwind and abreast
of *Algimouss*. The second and third containers held food and
emergency supplies and the fourth, which hit the water behind
the target, was another ten-man raft. *Algimouss* was bracketed.

The two rafts with the food containers between them drifted
towards the stricken boat. With unsuspected new energy, Dinelli
grabbed the rope now nudging against *Algimouss* and began
reeling in the rafts. Then he fell headlong into the nearest one,
and cast off the rope. Moments later, the *Algimouss* disappeared
in a final flash. She had kept her side of the pact to the end.

Goss had sailed all night against the storm, so hard that the shackle fixing the sail to the mast snapped a shaft, tearing the sail. He jury-rigged a new shaft by filing down a screwdriver, but now his radar was out, his autopilot was flooded and his generator had ripped free of its mountings. He was on deck sewing up his ripped mainsail when a big grey aircraft swept overhead.

'Fantastic,' he said, putting down his tools. Going below, he acknowledged *Rescue 251*'s radio call that another Orion would be coming in the morning to guide him to Dinelli.

'I've had a bit of damage, but I've managed to fix it,' he told them. 'I'd best get back on deck now,' he said after enquiring once again about Raphaël's condition. 'Cheerio, and Merry Christmas.'

Platts and Whyte gazed at each other in amazement. In gale-force winds more than 2,000km (1,200 miles) from anywhere, Goss seemed about as concerned as if he were in a pedal boat in Hyde Park.

Pete's coming

The Orion swung back to *Algimouss* and dropped three hand-held radios in special boxes. To each was affixed a message: 'Pete Goss 10 hours in the south. Rescue tomorrow.' Then, with fuel running low, the Orion headed back.

Aboard *Aqua Quorum* Pete Goss stayed on deck, steering by hand. The temperature that night hovered near zero and the wind brought the chill factor close to minus 30. Fatigue invaded his body.

Before dawn, a new position update showed that Goss was only 10km (6 miles) from *Algimouss*. He began firing off flares and hallooing into the black night. Nothing. He fired blasts of a hand-held foghorn and, with a new burst of energy, he shinned up *Aqua Quorum*'s mast and peered into the gloom. Still nothing. 'Come on, Raphaël. You've got to help yourself!'

Goss's efforts were in vain. Inside his life-raft, Dinelli was bent double, wracked with cramps and shivering so hard he could not control his chattering teeth. But his eyes were wide open.

Don't sleep, he ordered himself. Pete's coming.

Dinelli thought of his childhood near Bordeaux, his happy-go-lucky youth as a surfboard champion, the warm years with his girlfriend Virginie and their 18-month-old daughter Philippine. He should be married. He would ask her. If he lived.

At dawn's first light, Goss radioed the Royal Australian Air Force. To his astonishment a reply came instantly: 'We have started our descent and should be with you in 4 minutes.'

They descended out of the clouds within a kilometre or so of *Aqua Quorum*. Flight Lieutenant Warren Hutchinson radioed the news: 'We have located the survivor and we'll lead you to him.' Goss had sailed right past Dinelli in the night, probably missing him by only a couple of hundred metres. He was just half an hour from his target.

The Orion now flew back and forth between the two boats like a sheepdog. 'Watch me,' Hutchinson told Goss. 'I'll flash our landing lights when we're on top of Dinelli.'

At last Goss saw a tiny speck of orange. Slowly, he brought

Dry land at last *Raphaël Dinelli (left) and friend Pete Goss (right) share a well-earned bottle of champagne after their terrifying ordeal at the mercy of the seas.*

Aqua Quorum alongside the raft. Dinelli stood, bent like an old man. Goss heaved him over the railing onto *Aqua Quorum*'s deck. Up in *Rescue 252*, the crew cheered.

But Dinelli now lay curled in a foetal position, unable to move, close to death. 'Come on, you're not going to croak on me now,' Goss said. Carrying the Frenchman forward to his cabin, he stripped off the man's survival suit and sodden clothes, pulled double layers of dry thermal clothing over him and hustled him into a sleeping bag. Then he poured a hot cup of tea with lots of sugar in it. Dinelli sipped greedily, then drifted off to sleep.

Goss had one more task. Back on the radio, he told Hutchinson and the crew of the Orion that he would make course for Hobart, on the Australian island of Tasmania. 'Thanks very much for your help,' he signed off. 'You guys have been great.' Hutchinson dipped his wings in farewell and headed home.

Under faxed instructions from the Vendée Globe's doctor, Goss nursed Dinelli back to health. After depositing him safely in Hobart in early January, he continued the race, finishing in fifth place.

In 1997 Raphaël Dinelli and Virginie were married. At their side was best man – now best friend too – Pete Goss. Two months before, Président Jacques Chirac had presented Goss with France's highest award, the *Légion d'honneur*. Two months later (in October), Goss's little boat was scudding across the ocean again in a transatlantic race from Le Havre to Cartagena, Colombia. But this time it carried a two-man crew: Goss and Dinelli. ■

Where are they now?

AS WELL AS THE *LÉGION D'HONNEUR* for his heroism, Pete Goss was awarded an MBE, and with unflagging enthusiasm he pursues his sailing career.

Under the inspirational banner of 'Dare to Dream', over five years Goss brought together sponsors and a team to build and sail *Team Philips*, a vast and innovative catamaran in which to race around the world. From the trials stage, though, it ran into trouble when a part of the port hull broke off, necessitating extensive repairs, and the craft had to be abandoned mid Atlantic in December 2000. *Team Philips* broke up days later.

In 2006, Pete competed in another two-hander, the Round Britain and Ireland Yacht Race, and in 2007, with *Team Philips* crewmates Paul Larsen and Andy Hindley, he took part in the biennial Rolex Fastnet challenge aboard the yacht *Cornwall Playing for Success* – the boat was named after the charity Pete founded to help to raise literacy, numeracy and IT skills in children with unrealised potential, through the motivation of sport. The three men set off from Cowes to sail for southern Ireland, around the Fastnet Rock Lighthouse and on to Plymouth. Once again, though, extreme weather was against him, and Pete's boat was one of 200 to retire.

Also in 2007 began a romantic project, the building of *Spirit of Mystery*. This replica of a 11m (37ft) long wooden lugger – a kind of fishing boat – put to sea on October 20, 2008, to re-create the journey made to Australia in 1854 by seven men from Newlyn, Cornwall – a distance of 11,800 nautical miles travelled in 116 days, with no engine and no modern navigational aids – steering by the stars alone.

JOURNEY'S END *Spirit of Mystery* arrives in Melbourne, her final destination, on March 9, 2009.

THE
KILLING FIELDS

THE COMMUNIST KHMER ROUGE GUERRILLAS who took over Cambodia in 1975 were a gang of brutal thugs who killed millions. In the midst of the horror emerged the love story of a young doctor, Haing Ngor, and his wife, Huoy. Enslaved and tortured, they vowed fidelity to their last breath.

'We don't have enough oxen,' one of the soldiers told us, 'but we have to plough the fields.' 'Oh no,' I said to myself. 'Are we going to use human beings to plough?'

Huoy and I had been on the move since the communists took over. From Phnom Penh to a refugee settlement. From there, we tried and failed to escape the country. Eventually we were herded to a remote part of Battambang Province.

The Khmer Rouge called a meeting. About 1,000 of us sat on the ground. To the west rose a mountain. On a plateau were two white dots, the smaller a *stupa* or funeral monument, the larger a Buddhist temple.

'Welcome to Phum Chhleav,' said Comrade Ik, a skinny, dark-skinned old fellow. 'Angka has let you come here to build a new society. You must work hard, but you must be patient. At the present time, Angka is poor. Angka will provide food, but sometimes it will not be enough.'

In the Khmer language, *angka* means 'organisation'. Comrade Ik talked about how important it was that we city people learn from the peasants, build our own houses and grow rice.

A few months before, my medical degree had been the culmination of seven years' effort. I was the main practitioner and part-owner of a gynaecological clinic. What good was my medical training now, when the Khmer Rouge wanted to kill doctors?

We were put to work. The Khmer Rouge gave hoes to the women to break up the topsoil. Two teenage soldiers took us men to paddies that had been hoed. There were eight wooden ploughs and four oxen by a hillock. 'We don't have enough oxen,' one of the soldiers told us, 'but we have to plough the fields.'

'Oh no,' I said to myself. 'Are we going to use *human beings* to plough? Is this what we have to do to build this advanced society they're talking about – go back to prehistoric times?'

The soldier's face combined limited intelligence with contempt for us city people. He held a long leather whip. 'You,' he said, pointing at me. 'Take this plough and get on the right side.'

The ground was still cracked from the dry season. I began to push forward against the crosspiece. Next to me, the ox walked forward in its harness. The soldier walked behind, guiding the plough. When we got to the field, he sunk the tip into the earth. The ox was stronger and the plough swerved to the right. I had to push with all my strength to keep it straight.

We ploughed down the field, early morning sun shining into my eyes. I looked around and saw men yoked with oxen and farther off the women with their hoes rising and falling. Above us rose the mountain with two white dots. 'Lord Buddha help me,' I thought. 'Help us all. Give us strength to make it through the day.'

Dysentery strikes

Life had been good in Phnom Penh, relaxed and prosperous. My patients spoke to me politely. Huoy and I were happy. We ate in restaurants nearly every night. But now we have no fried noodles. No fish with lemon and coriander. Every evening Huoy talks about favourite recipes and wishes we had more food.

SNAP! A searing pain across my back.

'Hey!' I yelled. 'How can I push if you're whipping me? Let me rest first.'

'Finish the field and then rest,' the soldier replied. But after a few more lengths of the field he stopped to roll a cigarette and I took a break too. Near sunset, the gong rang and we quit. We had not ploughed a single rice paddy.

In our hut, Huoy put a hot compress on my welts. She was crying. I was too tired to feel much. 'I don't know why we should go on, being treated like this. The Khmer Rouge should just kill us and get it over with.'

I didn't know what to say.

The rainy season arrived in Battambang. We ploughed in cold, nearly continuous rain. After a few hours my fingers were white and wrinkled, like staying in bath water too long. My normal weight of 64kg (140lb) dropped to 50kg (110lb). I began to have to excuse myself while ploughing to go to the bushes. I thought it was ordinary diarrhoea, then noticed white mucus on the ground and dark, purplish blood. And then I knew I was very sick.

I wasn't the only sick person. In Phum Chhleav more people were sick than healthy. The greatest single factor was malnutrition. The Khmer Rouge fed us a bowl of salty broth with a few spoonfuls of rice for lunch, and the same for dinner. That was all. They didn't allow us to gather wild foods.

There were other factors. We were unused to hard labour, hadn't built up natural immunities to the microorganisms of Battambang, didn't have proper latrines or bathing facilities. We didn't have much medicine, and the Khmer Rouge didn't let doctors like me practise.

The range of illnesses was amazing. There were fungal infections and malaria, pneumonia and tuberculosis. Almost everyone got diarrhoea, and many got amoebic dysentery, much more dangerous. That's what I had, dysentery, presumably from drinking contaminated water.

Taking the capital by force *Khmer Rouge guerrilla soldiers, wearing black uniforms, drive a jeep through the streets of Phnom Penh on April 17, 1975, the day Cambodia fell under Pol Pot's control.*

EXODUS AT GUNPOINT

Huoy went out to get medicine, but there was nothing to be had. Finally she traded some of our small hoard of gold, a *damleung*, or 34g (1.2oz), for 15 250mg tablets of a standard antibiotic.

I took one capsule twice a day as long as the supply lasted. In normal times I would have prescribed double the dosage, plus an antidiarrhoea medicine.

I shuttled back and forth from the reed mattress to a latrine she had dug near our tiny garden. My world shrunk to the hut and the garden. Every morning through cracks in the hut I saw burial processions. The dead were wrapped in plastic tarps and carried on boards suspended from a bamboo on the mourners' shoulders.

No way out *Khmer Rouge troops guard the Aranyaprathet Bridge at the frontier between Thailand and Cambodia.*

'Keep being strong'

By the 20th day I had to crawl on all fours. A perfect nurse, Huoy bathed me day and night. She cooked the little rice we had and fed me a spoonful at a time, with my head in her lap. After feeding me she kissed me and stroked my hair. I knew her thoughts: if I died, part of her would die too.

My weight was down to 32kg (70lb). Every rib showed.

My intestines were bubbling with liquids and gas and every few minutes more spurted out the back end. The poisons kept coming out, but inside the gurgling and mixing produced more.

On the morning of the 31st day, I decided to take my pulse, but my mind wandered. I turned my head and saw Huoy outside, taking clean sarongs from the line. 'What was I thinking? Oh yes, my pulse. If I tell my hand to move, it will obey.'

I watched my right arm swing over and the fingertips probe for the pulse in my left wrist. 'Not there. There. Yes. The beat is very slow.'

Huoy came in, put away the folded sarongs, and knelt and wiped my face with a damp cloth.

'I don't feel well,' I said. 'I think I am going to die.'

'You aren't going to die,' Huoy said firmly. She sat next to me. 'Keep being strong in your mind,' she said. 'Keep being strong and you will never die.' She cleaned my face and body with a damp towel. I lay on my side and waited.

In the early afternoon there was a sound of footsteps and a big loud voice.

'One person from every family, come to my house! We've got yams! Come get your rations!' It was the burly civilian leader of Phum Chhleav. With him were the section leaders and a crowd of excited followers, talking and waving.

I sent Huoy to get our ration.

Yams are basically carbohydrate. Put in a fire, they turn into charcoal. Eating carbon from burnt food reduces the symptoms of dysentery by trapping gases, and sometimes has a marginal effect on the infectious agent.

After a time Huoy returned. She showed me the ration: one yam the size of her fist.

Huoy was looking at the yam with a glazed, intent expression. I said, 'Sweet, please give me the food to eat. I think it will help. I know you are hungry, but we still have rice. You eat the rice.'

Huoy nodded with a sad smile. 'Whatever you want, I will do it. I want you to stay alive. As long as we both are alive we will be happy.'

I told her to burn the yam without cooking it. When it was burned, she cut it into pieces. The yam was black all through except for some yellow specks. She fed it to me one piece at a time.

My trips to the garden diminished from five times an hour to three. The next day they decreased to two an hour, and the day after that to once an hour. The yam had helped to turn the tide.

Within a few days, I could eat solid foods.

After another week, Huoy picked me up, draped my arm over her shoulder and gave me a stick as a cane. We took a few steps. The next day we walked around the hut.

It was 45m (50yd) to the railway track. It became my goal. When I finally made it, Huoy and I sat on the tracks, near a trestle with water underneath. I was tired but triumphant. Huoy was happy and smiling. We talked as we had in the old days, calling each other 'sweet.'

I said, 'Sweet, I'm going to live.'

The air was cool. We went underneath the trestle to bathe, and Huoy scrubbed the dust off me. I loved and respected Huoy more than ever. She had saved my life.

Early in 1976, Haing and Huoy were sent to the so-called 'front lines' to join a cooperative whose main task was digging irrigation canals. Denounced by the chhlop, *boy spies, for possession of some arrowroot, Haing was tortured, but he survived. Many others were killed for small offences, or for nothing. Before long, Haing was betrayed by an acquaintance and arrested again.*

A Cambodian mythological figure is the King of Death. The souls he sends to hell become *pret*, spirits of the damned, victims of everlasting tortures.

The Khmer Rouge who sat smiling at us was the King of Death. Well fed, he wore black clothes, a green Mao cap and an old green-and-white *krama* – the Cambodian all-purpose scarf – around his neck. He sat at a table and asked us to sit on the floor while he scanned the files. Several guards with holstered pistols stood at his side.

The King of Death was calm and sweet. 'Please tell Angka the truth,' he told us. 'If you do, you will not be punished. Angka never kills the innocent. Those who tell the truth will be re-educated.'

It was my turn. I sat in front of the judge with my *krama* folded on my knee. I could see only his legs and feet.

Working the land
Cambodia, formerly known as Kampuchea, is bordered by Thailand and Laos to the north, and Vietnam to the south and east. The mighty Mekong River, which crosses the country from north to south, provides fertile land for the production of rice. Although the country strives to modernise, with clothing now its largest export, three-quarters of the population still toil in the fields.

'Samnang, Angka knows who you are,' the King of Death began gently. 'You were a military doctor. You held the rank of captain. So please, tell Angka the truth. You will make it easier on yourself.'

The only thing they didn't know was my real name.

'If you tell the truth,' the King of Death said in his soothing voice, 'Angka will forget the past and let you operate and teach medicine. You will be a hero. But,' he said, 'if you don't tell the truth, you will be held responsible.'

'Comrade,' I said, 'I was not a captain, or a doctor. I was a taxi driver. I'm telling the truth. I work hard for Angka and never make trouble. This is the second time I've been to jail, and still Angka doesn't believe me.'

BAM! The kick came to my ribs. I fell over on my side. Then the other guard kicked me with his rubber-tyre sandals. The guards knew what they were doing. They kicked me in the ribcage, in the shoulders, the thighs and

A murderous regime

CAMBODIA'S LEADER, Prince Norodom Sihanouk, had attempted to stay neutral during the war in neighbouring Vietnam. But when the US-backed military government of Lon Nol took power in Cambodia, he backed the communist Khmer Rouge guerrillas, who ousted Lon Nol in 1975. The guerrillas were welcomed into Phnom Penh as saviours by citizens rejoicing at the prospect of peace. Just two days later the forced evacuation of the cities began.

The Khmer Rouge's leader from 1975 to 1979 was Pol Pot; he presided over the deaths of up to 1.7 million people by massacre, malnutrition and sickness. Not just doctors, but lawyers, students, journalists, harmful intellectual 'microbes', were eliminated in the interest of returning society to 'the simplicity of a single grain of rice'. The 'bourgeois mentality' was to be stamped out and 'Year Zero' was declared. Money, private property and religion were outlawed.

Born Saloth Sar in around 1925, into a landowning family, Pol Pot was a Maoist and a nationalist. According to one of the few Westerners to meet him while he was in power, he was softly spoken and well mannered. Behind the veneer was a man with a pathological fear and hatred of those he considered to be less than true Khmers (Cambodians) – Vietnamese, Chams, Thais and Laotians. In a campaign of 'purification', the Khmer Rouge moved against ethnic minorities.

After the 1979 invasion by the Vietnamese, Pol Pot and his forces retreated to the northern jungle from where they had emerged. Pol Pot officially stood down as Khmer Rouge leader in the late 1980s, and, following a violent power struggle within the organisation's ranks, in July 1997 he was charged with treason and tried before a 'people's tribunal', which sentenced him to life imprisonment.

In an interview after the trial, he was unrepentant, declaring 'my conscience is clear'. Talking later with the *Far Eastern Economic Review* he said, 'I do not reject responsibility. Our movement made mistakes, like every other movement in the world.' The 'mistakes' cost Cambodia one-fifth of its population and all but destroyed the country. Even now it remains one of the poorest, least-developed countries in Asia.

TAKING OVER Khmer Rouge leader Pol Pot heads a column of his Khmer Rouge guerrillas.

the back of my neck. Then the judge rapped on the table and the guards dragged me back to the line.

When all 18 prisoners had talked to the judge, the guards led us into an uncultivated field.

We saw a double line of wooden structures with uprights and crosspieces. In the middle of each was a pile of rice hulls and wood. In front lay a wooden cross with a length of rope. At the far end of the rows, prisoners were tied to the crosses, their bodies sagging against the ropes. The crosses were hanging from the crossbars. Smoke and flames rose around the prisoners' feet.

I thought, 'I hope Huoy never knows about this. Please, gods, keep Huoy away from this kind of punishment.'

The soldiers tied my arms to the cross, then my thighs and feet, then threw the rope over and hoisted me up. They lit each pile of rice hulls with cigarette lighters. Rice hulls give off thick, stinging smoke and burn slowly, for days.

My feet were about a metre above the wood and rice hulls. Smoke rose into my nostrils and eyes. My body dragged down on the ropes. My feet had no feeling. Iridescent green flies buzzed around my head.

There was a new smell. I looked down. The hair on my legs was shrivelled and burned. My feet must have been burning, but I could not feel them. To my right, a pregnant woman moaned, begging her mother to save her.

After four days and four nights with no food or water they let me down. The circulation returning to my arms and legs brought a pain hotter than the fire. They tried to make me kneel, but I fell over. They grabbed my hair and shook my head until I saw the plate in front of me. On the plate was fresh rice with two small fish.

'Are you a doctor?' a faraway voice asked. 'A captain?'

My mouth wouldn't work. In front of me was the plate heaped with rice.

'Just *shoot*,' I croaked. 'I can't bear it. Please, Angka, if you don't trust me, I will be happy to die. Just shoot.'

'Bigmouth!' the guard exclaimed. He shouted to other guards to come over. Before they put the plastic bag over my head, I glimpsed the pregnant lady. She had a bag over her head and was kicking convulsively. They tied the bag around my neck and I tried to breathe, but there was no air and I went wild, struggling to get the bag off, but I couldn't. Then they pulled the bag off and I took great gasping lungfuls of air.

They took the bag off the pregnant lady, but she had died. A guard picked up his rifle, which had a bayonet, and slashed her belly. He took the foetus out and threw it in a pile. The flies whooshed around the body of the poor woman. I lay on my side. They would disembowel me next, just for fun. It was nothing for them to cut someone open, just a whim.

Joyous news

Five minutes or 5 hours passed, I did not know the difference. At twilight, the guards untied us and helped us walk to jail. Of our group of 18, only five were alive. My feet and legs were covered with blisters, which popped as I walked.

They gave us watery rice; after four days with no food it was like a banquet. I expected to be killed but the next day they gave me rice again, and the next.

The kick came to my ribs. I fell over on my side. Then the other guard kicked me with his rubber-tyre sandals. The guards knew what they were doing.

They loaded me into an oxcart and drove me to another jail. After two months, soldiers escorted me and some other prisoners back to our cooperative, which was in a new location.

They took us to the common kitchen and told us to sit down. Huoy had seen us but hadn't recognised me. She was cutting vegetables.

The soldiers read the names. When she heard 'Samnang', Huoy froze, then stood up, shaking. She called out in a choked voice, 'My husband is here! My husband is here!'

We walked towards each other, afraid to embrace. I put my arm around her shoulders and took her aside. I whispered, 'I have survived. Don't worry. I will stay here with you.'

That night she snuggled next to me. She kissed me again and again. I was amazed that I had lived, that the gods had let me survive a second time, against the odds. To have my arm around my wife's soft female form, to feel her breathing. To hold her. She was so giving, so comforting. She was alive.

While Haing was in prison, his father, brother and sister-in-law had arrived at the cooperative, but all were taken and killed. While Haing was recovering from malaria, Haing and Huoy moved to a village called Phum Ra. Arrested and tortured for a third time, Haing Ngor miraculously returned alive to Phum Ra.

I loved watching Huoy in the mornings. When she slept, she hugged her little blue pillow to her chest, one she had brought with her from Phnom Penh. She rose before sunrise, brushed her hair, washed her face. As I got up groggily, she rolled the mosquito net, folded the nightclothes and the bedding. There was something about her – organised, clean, feminine, desirable – that attracted me on all levels.

I felt reborn. We watched the rice fields change from brown to green and to gold, and then there was joyous news: Huoy was pregnant.

We knew because of morning sickness. The only foods she could keep down were sweet. I hunted for papayas and jackfruits, traded gold for palm-tree sugar. But she didn't have much appetite.

I took my instruments out of hiding – stethoscope, blood-pressure cuff and thermometer – and gave her an exam, using spoons as an improvised speculum. Aside from the nausea, which caused a slight weight loss, she was healthy. She was 27.

By the third month Huoy's belly began to show. She was beginning to get over her morning sickness, and had that contented inner glow of a woman who is glad to be pregnant.

But the dry season of 1978 was a difficult time. The kitchen in Phum Ra began skipping meals. At first I stole food to make up for it. Angka's authority was breaking down. In April the common kitchen closed entirely.

Losing heart

Huoy became depressed. The unrelenting emptiness in her stomach was the greatest part of it. Draining her strength further were events like the purges. The latest was against 'Vietnamese'. The Khmer Rouge leaders decided that Cambodians of Vietnamese descent or who spoke Vietnamese were the cause of our problems. Yoeung, the adopted son of Uncle Phan, our village leader, was *chhlop*, a spy. He came around, trying to discover who spoke Vietnamese, and many were taken away. Huoy spoke fluent Vietnamese. The *chhlop* didn't find out, but still she became depressed.

I spent long hours consoling Huoy. She lay on the wooden bench in our tiny house, tired, hot, fanning herself. She was six months pregnant, with a swollen belly.

'If there is no food, how can I make milk in my breasts?' she whispered. 'How long can I go on like this? How long since Angka has given us food?'

'Don't worry,' I said. 'Your breasts will automatically have milk. This is my specialty. I know.'

'I know the milk comes automatically,' said Huoy. 'But maybe there won't be enough.'

I didn't know what to say. She was right. But for the moment, breast milk was the least of our problems. Even her malnourishment didn't worry me as much as the state of her mind. To Huoy, there was no use fighting any more. The hunger, the terror, the *chhlop*, the energy the baby drew from her – all these combined to break her will.

I took gold to buy rice, but there was only rice flour for sale. For a *damleung* of gold, I bought two small cans. I gave it all to Huoy but it wasn't enough.

Into labour

Huoy was seven months pregnant when she felt a pain like a menstrual cramp. A few hours later she had another.

'You're going into labour,' I told her.

Huoy turned her head to the wall. I heard her whisper, 'Help me, Mother. Please protect me.'

'Yes, please protect her,' I thought. 'A premature birth. No intensive-care unit, no operating room, no food. *Chhlop* hanging around, looking for trouble.'

It was forbidden for a man to deliver his wife's baby. If I delivered it the *chhlop* would find out. If I did anything that suggested I was a doctor, that would be the end.

Luckily a midwife named Seng Orn lived nearby. I knew her from Phnom Penh. If the birth was normal, Seng Orn and I could handle it. If there were complications, maybe we could handle it but maybe not. For one thing, I didn't have any equipment. For another, I was out of practice. The worst problem, though, was the *chhlop*.

Huoy's contractions were irregular and far apart, which is common for 'false' labour, before true labour begins. I held her hand as the contractions took her, and looked around. The thatched roof, the dirt floor. No running water or electricity. I would have given anything to be back in Phnom Penh.

Between contractions, Huoy asked me to help her to bathe. I washed her, tenderly. She lay clutching her small blue pillow. When the labour pains were 40 minutes apart, I summoned a neighbour, an old woman, to watch over her.

Soul destroying work *Forced labourers dig canals in Kampong Cham, Cambodia, at the height of the Khmer Rouge's control of the country.*

At 11 o'clock her waters broke.

That was normal. Seng Orn reported that the cervix was dilated to 3cm. The next interval was 10 minutes. Then 15. As the hands of my watch swept past 11.45 and the next contraction still hadn't come, we knew there was trouble.

I ran to where Seng Orn lived. We went to see her village leader, who let her go only after prolonged pleading. When we got to Phum Ra, we had to report to Uncle Phan. Yoeung, the *chhlop*, followed us into the yard.

By the time we returned to the house, it was nearly sunset. I timed the labour pains, which were half an hour apart. When Huoy went into contractions she looked at me and then her attention turned inwards. Frowning, contorting her face, she clenched my arms so tightly I thought my bones were going to break. Finally Huoy relaxed her hold. She became aware of her own tiredness, and then me sitting next to her. Her face was wet with perspiration, and I smoothed the wet strands of hair away from her forehead and tried to encourage her.

At 11 o'clock her waters broke. That was normal. Seng Orn reported that the cervix was dilated to 3cm.

The next interval was 10 minutes. Then 15.

As the hands of my watch swept past 11.45 and the next contraction still hadn't come, we knew there was trouble. The intervals should have gotten closer together, not further apart.

I had one ampoule of an antispasmodic medication. I drew it into a syringe and injected Huoy, to make it easier for the cervix to widen so the child could descend from the womb. I had one capsule of vitamins, and gave it to Huoy to make her feel as if she were getting medicine, to put her in a better frame of mind.

At midnight, her blood pressure was at the low end of the normal range. Her heartbeat was slower. 'Her cervix is still at 3cm,' Seng Orn said quietly.

I scraped some kernels of corn, cooked them with sugar and fed them to Huoy to give her energy.

Her contractions were strong but irregular. Her cervix was like a bottleneck, and it did not widen. One part of her was trying to expel the child and another was fighting to retain it. She wept. 'It hurts, sweet, it hurts,' she said. I pressed her belly downwards, trying to force the baby along. Seng Orn could see the top of the child's head but she didn't even have forceps. We lacked the most basic tools.

I rubbed Huoy's limbs again. She was wet from perspiration and from clenching. Even when she didn't have labour pains, she was crying.

Seng Orn pulled me aside for a conference. 'Caesarean?' she whispered.

'Cannot!' I hissed. 'The *chhlop's* outside. We will all die! We have no instruments!'

Huoy lay sunken and tired on the bench, clutching the pillow. Her arms and legs were thin as sticks. Her belly was still round, the child still inside.

I took up the stethoscope and the blood-pressure cuff. Her blood pressure had dropped. Her heartbeat was slow and very feeble.

'Do we have anything to eat?' said Huoy, in a whisper, like a child.

'The neighbours are looking for food for you,' I said.

'I need food! I need medicine. Sweet, please save my life. I'm too tired. I just need a spoonful of rice.' Before she died, she asked me to cradle her. I swung her onto my lap, held her in my arms. She asked me to let her kiss me.

I kissed her, and she kissed me. She looked at me with her great round eyes full of sorrow. She didn't want to leave. 'Take care of yourself, sweet,' she said.

People say I went crazy after Huoy died. I remember pounding my head against the wall, and people restraining me. When they dug the hole deep in the ground and put her in, I knelt and prayed and wept.

I thought about how I had been unable to save her. She had saved my life. But when it was my turn, I failed.

Huoy died in June 1978. Not long after that, village leaders were purged. Uncle Phan ran away before it could happen to him. In January 1979 civilians began to arrive, part of a disciplined retreat. Paranoia was everywhere. In our village, one wrong word and whole families were executed. The soldiers were in a frenzy. To them it was our fault that the 'enemy' was coming.

The Khmer Rouge leaders left secretly, at night. Twelve of us then set out for the Thai border. It was March 1979. We came upon uniformed men firing at some Khmer Rouge.

A soldier was alternately firing his rifle and beckoning us to come. A young man with pale yellow skin and slanting eyes, he wore a light green uniform. There was a red star on his plantation-style helmet.

He was Vietnamese. My time as a war slave was over. ∎

Where are they now?

ON FEBRUARY 25, 1996, at the age of 45, Dr Haing Ngor was shot and killed outside his apartment in the Chinatown district of Los Angeles. The man who had survived genocide, starvation, slave labour and heartbreak at the hands of the Khmer Rouge was victim to a mindless and abortive robbery, after parting with his $6,000 Rolex watch but refusing to relinquish a locket containing a photograph of his beloved wife, Huoy. Two days later, three members of the Oriental Lazy Boy Gang, Jason Chan, Indra Lim and Tak Sun Tan, were arrested and charged with first-degree murder.

Ngor was born on March 22, 1950, into a settled, happy family, and after medical school was able to set up his own practice. He met Huoy, a trainee teacher, in 1975, and they planned a rosy future together. The Khmer Rouge changed all that.

In his efforts to conceal his education and medical training

SCREEN DEBUT Haing Ngor received a Best Supporting Actor Oscar on March 25, 1985, for his role in *The Killing Fields*.

from his tormentors, and to maintain his posture as a 'simple taxi driver', Ngor even went without his spectacles, the mark of that most dangerous man, an 'intellectual', in their fanatical eyes.

After the 'liberation' of Cambodia by the North Vietnamese in 1979, slave labourers such as Ngor continued to endure terrible privations. He was able to escape to neighbouring Thailand, though, and in 1980 made his way to the USA.

There, because his qualifications were not recognised, he was unable to work as a doctor, but he was approached by Roland Joffé to play the lead role in a screen adaptation of Sydney Schanberg's book *The Death and Life of Dith Pran*. That film was *The Killing Fields*, a depiction of the bloody regime of Pol Pot, for which Ngor won an Oscar. He went on to co-star in several films, but did not let Hollywood turn his head, and set up a foundation to champion the cause of Cambodian refugees and to help to support the inhabitants of his abandoned homeland.

On the day that Ngor's killers were convicted, the world received final confirmation of the death from natural causes of the tyrant Pol Pot, at the age of 72.

PLANE DOWN IN THE ANDES

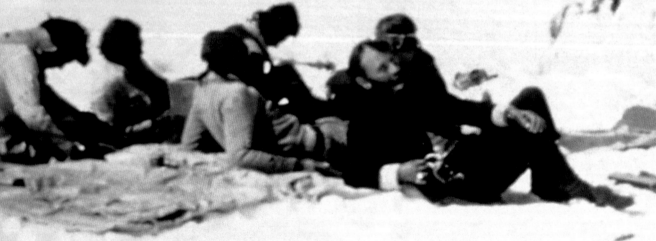

WHEN THE PLANE CARRYING a young Uruguayan rugby team crashed onto a freezing mountain slope, survival seemed unlikely for those left alive. A terrible decision would have to be made. Only then could Nando Parrado and two of his team-mates set off on an impossible trek to find help.

'Look at this, Nando. Should we be so close to the mountains?'

It was Friday the 13th, October 1972, and my friend Panchito was elbowing me from the window seat. I was sitting next to him as our twin-engine turboprop bounced and slid in the turbulence.

'Fasten your seat belts, please,' the steward told us.

We had joked about how we were flying over the Andes on such an unlucky day – Friday the 13th – but young men make those kinds of jokes so easily. Our championship rugby team had flown out of Montevideo, Uruguay, our home town, heading for Santiago, Chile, to play a top squad. There were 45 people aboard, including five crew members. Most of the passengers were my friends and team-mates, like Panchito, but family members were also with us, including my mother, Eugenia, and younger sister, Susy. I was 22 years old.

Since there was no way our little Fairchild, with its maximum cruising altitude of 6,860m (22,500ft), could fly an east-west route from low-lying Uruguay to Santiago, the pilots had gone about 320km (200 miles) south of Mendoza to Planchón Pass, a thin corridor through the Andes. Looking out of the window, I saw how the narrow glacial valleys gashed the steep slopes. In the Southern Hemisphere, winter had given way to early spring, but in the Andes temperatures still dipped to -37°C (-35° F).

I thought of my father, Seler. He'd dropped us off at the airport, saying, 'Have fun. I'll pick you up on Monday.' He kissed my mother and sister and embraced me.

While we were gone, he would do what he always did as head of a thriving hardware-store business: solve problems, work hard. Thanks to him, the Parrados would always be fortunate. He believed in this so firmly and our trust for him was so strong, how could we ever doubt him?

We were flying in thick cloud cover now, but through the breaks I saw a massive wall of rock and snow. Then, as the plane bobbed roughly, I noticed

Amid the wreckage *The 16 survivors from the Uruguayan Fairchild plane endured more than 70 days in the Andes. They were less than 160km (100 miles) from Santiago, but were stranded and helpless high in the mountains.*

that the swaying tip of the wing was no more than 8m (25ft) from the slopes of the mountain. The plane's engines screamed as the pilots tried to climb. The fuselage began to vibrate violently.

My mother and sister turned to look at me from one row up, and our eyes met. Then a powerful tremor rocked the plane. There was a terrible howl of metal grinding. I saw open sky above me and clouds swirling in the aisle; frigid air blasted my face. There was no time to make sense of it, no time to pray or to feel fear. As if some giant had scooped me up, I was hurled with incredible force from my seat to the front of the plane, where I descended into complete darkness and silence.

'Where is my mother?'

I lay unconscious, my face covered in blood and black bruises, my head swollen to the size of a basketball. Though my surviving team-mates took my pulse and were surprised my heart was still beating, my condition seemed so grave that they gave up on me.

The Fairchild's battered fuselage had come to rest at about 3,700m (12,000ft) on a snow-packed glacier flowing down the east slope of a massive, ice-crusted mountain. Thirteen passengers died. That left 32 of us still alive, some badly wounded. My team-mate Arturo had two broken legs; Enrique's stomach was impaled by a 15cm (6in) steel tube. Others had head injuries. Uninjured survivors became workers, helping to free trapped passengers.

On my third day lying in a black and perfect silence, a light appeared, a thin grey smear, and I rose out of the darkness like a diver slowly swimming to the surface. Gustavo, one of my team-mates, was crouching beside me, pressing snow to my lips. 'Here, Nando, are you thirsty?' he said.

The cold snow burned my throat as I swallowed, but my body was so parched I gobbled it in lumps and begged for more. I heard soft moans and cries of pain around me. Full of questions as my head cleared, I motioned Gustavo closer. 'Where is my mother?' I asked. 'Where is Susy?'

His face betrayed no emotion. 'Get some rest. You're very weak.'

I lay shivering on the plane's floor, listening for my sister's voice and glancing about for my mother, even as my head throbbed. When I reached up to touch the crown of my head, I felt rough ridges of broken bone beneath congealed blood and a spongy sense of give. My stomach heaved: it was shattered pieces of my skull against the surface of my brain.

When Gustavo came by again with more snow, I grabbed his sleeve. 'Where are they, Gustavo? Please.'

He looked into my eyes and must have seen I was ready. 'Nando, you must be strong. Your mother is dead.' Then he added gently, pointing to the rear of the plane, 'Your sister is over there. She's hurt very badly.'

Panic and grief exploded in my heart, but a lucid, detached voice said, 'Do not cry. Tears waste salt. You'll need salt to survive.'

I was astounded. Not cry for my mother, for the greatest loss of my life? I'm stranded, I'm freezing, my sister may be dying, my skull is in pieces. I should not cry? I heard the voice again, 'Do not cry.'

'There is more,' Gustavo said. 'Panchito is dead. Guido too.'

Sobs gathered in my throat, but before I could surrender, the voice spoke once more, 'They are gone. Look forward. Think clearly. You will survive.'

I now had an urgent desire to reach my sister. I rolled onto my stomach and started dragging myself on my elbows. When my strength gave out and my head slumped to the floor, someone lifted me.

And there, lying on her back, was Susy. Traces of blood were on her brow; her face had been washed. My friends helped me lie down beside her, and as I wrapped my arms around her, I whispered, 'I'm here, Susy. It's Nando.'

She turned and looked at me with her caramel-coloured eyes, but her gaze was so unfocused I couldn't be sure she knew it was me. I wrapped myself around her to protect her from the cold and lay with her for hours. In the chaos of that broken plane, stranded in the Andes, there was nothing

'Nando, you must be strong. Your mother is dead.' Then he added gently, pointing to the rear of the plane, 'Your sister is over there. She's hurt very badly.'

else I could do. I thought of my father's old advice to me: 'Be strong, Nando. Be smart. Make your own luck. Take care of the people you love.'

I told Susy, 'Don't worry. They will find us. They will bring us home.'

In those early days, all of us believed that rescue was our only chance of survival. We had to believe it. As the afternoon wore on, the frigid air took on an even sharper edge. The others found sleeping places in the fuselage and braced themselves for misery. Soon the darkness was absolute, and the cold closed in on us like the jaws of a vice. I suffered through the night, breath by frozen breath. When I felt I couldn't stand it any longer, I drew Susy closer. The thought that I was comforting her kept me sane.

Five days later, on our eighth day in the mountain, I was lying with my arm around my sister when I saw the worried look fade from her face. Her breathing grew shallow; then it stopped. 'Oh God, Susy. Please, no!' I cried.

My chest heaved with sobs. But I did not cry. Tears waste salt.

I made a silent vow to my father, who I knew was waiting for me. 'I will struggle. I will come home. I promise you, I will not die here!'

Staving off starvation

Twenty-seven survivors now remained of the original 45 aboard. For drinking water, we melted snow; to keep ourselves as warm as possible, we slept side by side at night, breathing each other's breath.

One morning around this time, after Marcelo, the captain of our rugby team, decisively led us to pool the little food we had – a few chocolate bars, some nuts and crackers, dried fruit, small jars of jam and a few bottles of liquor – I found myself standing outside the fuselage. I was looking down at the single chocolate-covered peanut in my palm.

The shattered fragments of my skull had been knitting themselves together; somehow, I was healing. Yet nothing was ordinary. The mountains were forcing me to change; my mind was growing colder and simpler. Our supplies had been exhausted. This peanut was the last bit of food I would be given, and I was determined to make it last. That day, I slowly sucked the chocolate off the peanut and then saved it in the pocket of my slacks.

The next day I separated the peanut halves, slipping one half back into my pocket and placing the other half in my mouth. I sucked gently on the peanut for hours, allowing myself only a nibble now and then. I did the same the day after that. When I'd finally nibbled the peanut down to nothing, there was no food left to eat at all.

At 3,700m (12,000ft) or higher, the body's caloric needs are astronomical. A climber scaling any of the mountains around the crash site would have required as many as 10,000 calories a day to maintain his current body weight. We weren't climbing, but still, our caloric requirements were much higher than usual. Even before our rations had run out, we'd never consumed more than a few hundred calories a day. Now, our intake was down to zero. Where once we'd been sturdy and vigorous young men, many of us in peak physical shape, I saw my friends growing thin and drawn.

In desperation we tried eating strips of leather from our luggage and ripped open seat cushions hoping for straw, but found only foam.

Extremes of temperature *Three of the men, from left to right, Eduardo Strauch, Pancho Delgado and Gustavo Zerbino, pose against the backdrop of the mountain range. Although the nights in December were still cold, it was warm enough during the day to cause sunburn.*

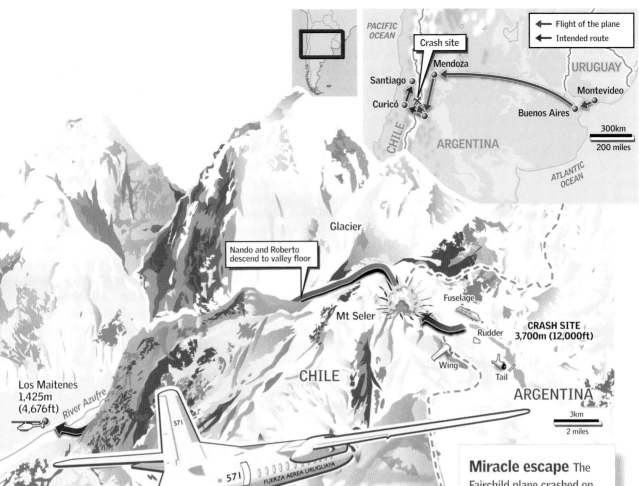

Flight of the plane
Intended route

Crash site

PACIFIC OCEAN

URUGUAY

Mendoza

Santiago

Montevideo

Curicó

Buenos Aires

CHILE

ARGENTINA

ATLANTIC OCEAN

300km
200 miles

Glacier

Nando and Roberto descend to valley floor

Fuselage

Mt Seler

Rudder

CRASH SITE 3,700m (12,000ft)

Wing

Tail

CHILE

ARGENTINA

Los Maitenes 1,425m (4,676ft)

River Azufre

571

571

FUERZA AEREA URUGUAYA

3km
2 miles

I kept coming to the same conclusion: until we were rescued, there was nothing here but aluminium, plastic, ice and rock. Sometimes I would rise and shout in frustration, 'There's nothing in this f— plane to eat!'

But of course there was food on the mountain. It was as near as the bodies of the dead lying outside the fuselage under a thin layer of frost. It puzzles me that despite my compulsive drive to find anything edible, I ignored for so long the obvious presence of the only edible objects within 160km (100 miles). Some lines, I suppose, the mind is slow to cross.

It was late afternoon when my gaze fell on the leg wound of a boy near me. I could not stop looking at it. Then I met the gaze of some others who had also been staring. In shame, we read each other's thoughts and glanced away. But something had happened. I'd recognised human flesh as food.

I knew those bodies represented our only hope of survival, but I was so horrified that I kept my feelings quiet. Finally I couldn't stay silent any longer. One night in the darkness, I confided in Carlitos, who was lying beside me. 'Are you awake?' I whispered to him.

'Yes,' he muttered. 'Who can sleep in this freezer?'

'Are you hungry?'

Carlitos cursed. 'What do you think? I haven't eaten in days.'

'We're going to starve here,' I said. 'I don't think the rescuers will find us in time. But I will not die here. I will make it home.'

Miracle escape The Fairchild plane crashed on October 13, about 320km (200 miles) south of Mendoza, Argentina (top). On December 12, Nando, Roberto and Tintin set out from the crash site (above), heading west, but sent Tintin back after three days when they reached the peak of the mountain that Nando named Mt Seler, after his father. The pair trekked on, spotting a herd of cows on December 19. On December 20 their route was barred by two rivers – it was on this day that they came upon Sergio Catalan, who brought back help. By December 22, all 16 survivors had been rescued.

'Nando, you are too weak.'

'I'm weak because I haven't eaten.'

'But what can you do? There's no food here.'

'There is food,' I answered. 'You know what I mean.'

Carlitos shifted in the darkness, but said nothing.

'I will cut meat from the pilot,' I whispered. 'He's the one who put us here; maybe he will help us get out.'

Carlitos cursed again.

'Our friends don't need their bodies any more,' I said.

A shocking pledge

In the following days, Carlitos shared our conversation with some of the others. A few admitted to having had the same thoughts. Roberto, Gustavo and Fito believed it was our only chance. We kept discussing it; then we decided to call a meeting and bring the issue out in the open. We all gathered in the fuselage on Sunday, October 22. Roberto began to speak.

'We're starving,' he said simply. 'Unless we eat some protein soon, we will die, and the only protein here is in the bodies of our friends.'

There was a heavy silence. Finally someone spoke. 'What are you saying? That we eat the dead?'

'We don't know how long we'll be trapped here,' Roberto continued. 'If we do not eat, we'll die. It's that simple. If you want to see your families again, this is what you must do.'

The faces of the others showed astonishment. 'But what will this do to our souls?' someone wondered. 'Could God forgive such a thing?'

'If you don't eat, you're choosing to die,' Roberto answered. 'Would God forgive that? I believe God wants us to do whatever we can to survive.'

The discussion continued for hours, but no one tried to talk us out of the idea. In the silence we realised we'd reached a consensus. Shortly after that, we all reached forward, joined hands, and pledged that if any of us died here, the rest would have permission to use his body for food.

After the pledge, the grisly logistics had to be faced. Roberto took charge. He rummaged around in the fuselage until he found some shards of glass; then he led three assistants out to the frosty graves. When they came back, they had small pieces of flesh in their hands.

Gustavo offered me a piece and I took it. It was greying-white, as hard as wood and very cold. I reminded myself that this was no longer part of a human being; this person's soul had left his body.

Out of the corners of my eyes I saw the others around me. Some were sitting with the meat in their hands, like me, summoning the strength to eat. Others worked their jaws grimly. Finally, I found my courage and slipped the food into my mouth. It had no taste. I chewed once or twice, then forced myself to swallow. I understood the magnitude of the taboo we had broken, but if I felt any strong emotion it was a sense of resentment that fate had forced us to choose between this horror and that of certain death.

That night, for the first time since we'd crashed, I felt a flicker of hope. We'd found the strength to face an unimaginable horror. There were no illusions now. We all knew our fight for survival would be uglier than we had imagined, but I felt that as a group we had made a declaration to the mountain that we would not surrender. For myself, I knew that in a small, sad way, I had taken my first step back towards my father.

Early the next morning, during our second week in the mountains, we learned from our primitive transistor radio that the search for survivors was being called off by the Chilean authorities. Search efforts in the Andes were simply too dangerous, the announcer said. After so much time in the frigid mountains, there was no chance anyone still survived.

After a stunned silence, several of us broke down. 'They've cancelled the search!' shouted Roy, one of our team-mates. 'They're abandoning us!'

Desperate hike

With a grim sense of resolve, I now accepted a simple truth: I would fight to leave this place, certain the effort would kill me, but frantic to start the climb nonetheless. I wanted the resourceful Roberto to come with me.

Finally, by the evening of December 11, our 60th night in the Andes, I found myself outside the plane, staring west at the mountains that blocked me from my home. As night fell, the largest of the mountains

The last taboo

IN JUNE 2008, A CESSNA 208 carrying nine passengers crashed into a mountainside in southern Chile. In freezing conditions, amid snow and sleet, the survivors huddled together in the crumpled fuselage. Two days later, the pilot died, having bled to death from a head wound, the passengers powerless to save him. In the five days that followed, the nine began to debate whether or not they might eat him. No agreement was reached and rescue came in time, but the case has distinct echoes of the Andes crash.

There is a powerful taboo against cannibalism, especially when it is an act of triumphalism in war, religious symbolism, insanity or deviance. In desperate circumstances the unthinkable becomes thinkable, especially in the face of starvation. After the Andes crash, the Vatican decreed that the 16 Catholics who had eaten human flesh were guilty of no sin: the souls of the dead were with God, their corpses mere husks.

Survival cannibalism has been practised on Polar expeditions, in cases of shipwreck, in concentration camps and in famine situations. In 1765 the crew of the stranded American ship *The Peggy*, having eaten their African slave, drew lots to determine who would be next. The sailor who drew the short straw was given a day to put his affairs in order, but he was reprieved when a ship loomed on the horizon.

In May 1845, Sir John Franklin led an expedition on his fourth search of the Northwest Passage, and when the party failed to return, three relief expeditions were mounted. The leader of one of these, Dr John Rae, reporting on the discovery of 30 corpses, related, without censure: 'From the mutilated state of many of the bodies and the contents of the kettles, it is evident that our wretched Countrymen had been driven to the last dread alternative – cannibalism – as a means of prolonging existence.'

PICTURE EXCLUSIVE
here 16 men took a terrible decision

THE DEAD SAVED OUR LIVES

I would have to climb grew darker and more forbidding. I saw no hostility in it, just power and cruel indifference. The moment I had feared had finally come.

'Please, God, don't let me fall,' I thought.

That was my greatest fear – to slide down some steep slope for hundreds of feet, knowing I was heading for a cliff and a long, hopeless drop to the rocks. But we were almost out of food. How long until we ran out completely, and began the horrific wait for someone to die? Who would go first? What would it be like for the last one alive? I knew that nothing the mountain could do to me would be worse than the future that waited here.

Soon night fell, and I went inside the Fairchild, lay down with my friends one last time, and tried to sleep. In the morning, I readied to go.

I'd dressed for the trek in a pair of slacks and three pairs of jeans. I wore three sweaters over a polo shirt and four pairs of socks. I covered the socks with plastic bags to keep them dry, stuffed my feet into my battered rugby shoes, and pulled a wool cap over my head, topping it with the hood I'd cut from Susy's coat. The others stood by, not sure what to say.

I grabbed an aluminium pole to use as a walking stick and took out my backpack. I would carry rations of raw meat, plus some odds and ends.

Roberto had finished dressing. Antonio, known as Tintin, was ready as well; he'd make the trek too. The three of us exchanged a nod; then I headed outside. Though there was a sharp chill in the air, the temperature was well above freezing. It was spring now in the Southern Hemisphere, and a perfect day for climbing: the wind was light, the sky brilliant blue.

'Let's hurry,' I said. 'I don't want to waste this weather.'

We ate breakfast and stood to say goodbye. Carlitos stepped forward and we embraced. 'You'll make it!' he said. 'God will protect you.'

The rescuer *Nando Parrado (left) and Roberto Canessa (right) walked for ten days through the mountains to get help. Between them sits Sergio Catalan, the shepherd who gave them bread and brought back help.*

I saw the wild hope in his eyes. He was so thin, weak, his eyes sunk deep into his skull. It broke my heart to think that our trek was my friend's only chance of survival. I wanted to let my tears flow, to scream at him, 'What am I doing, Carlitos? I'm so afraid!' But if I did that, my courage would crumble.

The others said goodbye with embraces and quiet encouragement. I was the one who had insisted it was possible to reach Chile on foot. I knew the others saw my behaviour as confident and optimistic; perhaps it gave them hope. But it was really nothing of the sort. It was panic. It was terror.

'Nando, are you ready?' That was Roberto, waiting for me, the mountains behind him. I trembled like a doomed man about to go to the gallows.

Finding signs of life

We crunched through the frozen snow in our crude clothing for three days. Most of the time I shivered uncontrollably from cold and fatigue. It was agonising; I was soon on the verge of complete collapse. 'I am a dead man! What am I doing in this place?' I yelled at one point.

Somehow the three of us reached the top of the first mountain. Then, assessing our progress before the descent, we decided to send Tintin back. We needed his food to reach Chile, and Roberto and I were the stronger climbers. We embraced Tintin as his eyes shone. 'Remember,' I told him, 'we'll always be heading west. If rescuers come, send them to find us!'

End in sight *The survivors who were left behind wave frantically as they are found at last by rescue helicopters, guided by Nando.*

On the morning of December 19, after we'd hiked for several hours, I waited for Roberto to catch up with me. The sole of my shoe flapped as I walked. I looked at the jagged rocks that littered the valley floor and wondered, 'Will my shoe fail first, or will I?' In the milder temperatures and at a lower altitude now, we were no longer at risk of freezing to death or of dying in a fall. It was a matter of simple endurance, of luck and time.

Later that day, we saw trees far ahead in the valley. Squinting at the horizon, Roberto said, 'Something's moving near the trees. I think I see cows.'

'It could be deer,' I told him. I was worried that Roberto, who was truly exhausted by now, might be hallucinating. 'Let's keep going.'

A few hours later, he bent over and picked something off the ground. It was a rusted soup can. 'People have been here,' he said.

'Let's keep walking,' I said. 'When we find a farmer, I'll get excited.'

As we trekked farther, we found more signs of human habitation: cow droppings, horse dung, tree stumps that showed the marks of an axe. Finally, as we rounded a bend, we saw, just a few hundred metres away, the small herd of cows Roberto had spotted earlier. 'There must be a farmhouse or something very close,' he said.

At camp that evening, Roberto's spirits were high, but I knew he could not stand many more hours in the mountains. 'My legs hurt badly,' he said. I told him to get some rest and that perhaps the next day we'd find help.

The next afternoon, I left Roberto on a soft turf of grass and followed a winding path of the river gorge. Again I saw cows grazing. But after walking about 270m (300yd), I saw another broad, swift river. We were cut off by the confluence of these two big streams. It didn't seem possible that we could cross either one. Barring a miracle, we had come to the end of our trail.

I told Roberto what I'd seen. We were both very hungry. What little meat we had left was going bad, and we considered trying to kill one of the cows. But Roberto pointed out that this would probably not incline the cow's owner to help us. In any event, we doubted we had the strength. Darkness was falling, and a chill was rising.

No time to lose

'I'm going to find some firewood,' I said, but when I had walked only a few yards across the meadow, I heard Roberto shout.

'Nando! A man on a horse! Look! A man on a horse!' He was pointing at the slope on the far side of the river gorge. 'Go! Run!' Roberto said.

Blindly I stumbled down the slope, but I saw nothing. I turned to see Roberto staggering down behind me. 'I swear I saw something,' he said.

I took Roberto's arm and was helping him back up when we heard a voice. This time I saw him, too, a rider on horseback, accompanied by two others. The man was shouting to us, but the noise of the river drowned out most of his words except for one: '*Mañana.*'

'We are saved,' Roberto said.

Back at the campsite, we lay down to sleep. My concern now shifted to the ones we'd left behind. Obsessed with trying to survive, I'd barely thought of them since leaving the crash site. I became frantic with worry.

'Don't worry,' Roberto told me. 'We'll make the man understand there's not a second to lose.'

The next morning, December 21, we awoke before dawn and glanced across the river. Sure enough, three men were sitting by a fire. I ran down to the lip of the gorge and climbed down to the river bank. On the other side, one of the men, wearing the clothes of a country peasant, did the same. I shouted to him, but the roar of the river drowned out my words.

The man took paper from his pocket, scribbled on it, then tied the paper around a rock with some string. He slipped a pencil under the string and threw it across the river to me. When I unfolded the paper, I read: 'There is a man coming later. Tell me what you want.'

My hands were shaking as I wrote: 'I come from a plane that fell into the mountains. I am Uruguayan. We have been walking for ten days. In the plane there are still 14 injured people. We don't have any food. We are weak. When are you going to come and fetch us? Please.'

I threw the note back with what little strength I had left. The rock barely made it over. When the man read the message, he raised his open palms in a gesture that said, 'Wait here. I understand.' Before leaving, he threw some bread to me. I took it to Roberto and we devoured it. Then we waited.

Mother and son *A heart-rending moment for survivor Roy Harley (left) as he is hugged by his mother just moments after he was rescued.*

Around 9am another man came and, after that, two Chilean policemen on horseback. The interest in us built from there. The next day, as soon as the fog lifted, I guided a helicopter rescue team to the crash site. My heart was pounding as I saw, even from a high altitude, a line of tiny figures coming out of the fuselage – Gustavo, Daniel, Pedro, Fito, Javier and others.

We were flown to a military base. Teams of doctors and nurses helped us into ambulances, which sped us to St John of God Hospital. As filthy clothing was peeled off my body and I was given a warm shower, my jaw dropped. The bones of my ribs and hips showed through the skin. My arms and legs had withered; my knees and elbows bulged like thick knots.

'Still,' I whispered to myself, 'I am alive. I am alive. I am alive.'

Suddenly I heard my older sister's voice shouting from the hallway, 'My brother is in there! I have to see him. Please!' In seconds she was in my arms, sobbing. Then I looked up.

In the hallway stood the slim, bowed figure of my father. I walked to him, embraced him, and hoisted him up in my arms until his feet left the ground. 'You see, Papa,' I said, setting him down again, 'I am still strong enough to lift you.' He touched me, held me – convincing himself that I was real.

And then, in the privacy of my hospital room, I shared with what was left of my family the miracle of being together again. ■

Where are they now?

WHEN NANDO PARRADO returned home after the crash, he was unnerved to find that all trace of himself had been removed from the family home, apart from a few photographs. His father, in his deep grief for his wife, his son and younger daughter, had begun to dismantle his life, purging the house of Nando's clothes and posters, selling his motorbike. With Nando's return his father's life began again, and he advised his son that he, too, must look forward. 'You will have a future. You will live a life.'

UNITED FOREVER
Roberto Canessa (left) and Nando Parrado (right) have both gone on to lead fulfilling lives since their ordeal.

And so it was to prove. Nando went on to enjoy great success in business, and to be a television producer and personality. He took up racing sports cars, motorcycles and stock cars, and in 1991 was one of a team of drivers to cross the Sahara – 8,500km (5,280 miles) from Morocco to Tunisia in 28 days.

He collaborated with author Piers Paul Reid on the book *Alive*, which told the story of the Andes survivors, and he served as technical adviser on the 1993 film version, in which the role of Nando was played by Ethan Hawkes. He then found himself in great demand internationally as a motivational speaker.

For all his success, though, he values family and friendship above everything. He lives in Montevideo with his wife, Veronique, and they have two grown-up daughters. Nando and Roberto Canessa have remained best friends.

Roberto is today one of the most highly respected paediatric cardiologists in Uruguay, twice awarded the National Prize for Medicine in his home land. He married Laura, his girlfriend at the time of the accident, and they have two sons and a daughter. In 1994, disaffected with the Uruguayan government, he formed his own political party and ran unsuccessfully for president. In *Alive* he was played by Josh Hamilton.

ACKNOWLEDGMENTS

Every effort has been made to trace and contact copyright holders prior to publication. If notified, the publisher undertakes to rectify any errors or omissions at the earliest opportunity.

Text credits
We are grateful for permission to include extracts from the following (in book order):

ON THE BACK OF THE BEAST **Stanley Williams**: *Surviving Galeras* (Little, Brown, 2001), copyright © Stanley Williams and Fen Montaigne 2001, reproduced by permission of the publishers, Little, Brown Book Group ▪ A LONG WAY TO FREEDOM **Nelson Mandela**: *Long Walk to Freedom* (Little, Brown, 1994), copyright © Nelson Rolihlahla Mandela 1994, reproduced by permission of the publishers, Little, Brown Book Group ▪ TERROR IN THE DARKNESS **Stephanie Slater** with Pat Lancaster: *Beyond Fear, My Will to Survive* (Fourth Estate, 1995), copyright © Stephanie Slater and Pat Lancaster 1995, reproduced by permission of Faith Evans Associates ▪ DISASTER IN IRAQ **John Simpson**: *The Wars Against Saddam* (Macmillan, 2003), copyright © John Simpson 2003, 2004, reproduced by permission of Pan Macmillan, London ▪ HE BEAT CANCER AND THE WORLD **Lance Armstrong**: *It's Not About the Bike* (Yellow Jersey Press, 2001), copyright © Lance Armstrong 2000 & 2001, reproduced by permission of The Random House Group Ltd ▪ LOST AT SEA **Tami Oldham Ashcraft** with Susea McGearhart: *Red Sky in Mourning* (Simon & Schuster, 2002), copyright © Tami Oldham Ashcraft 2002, reproduced by permission of Simon & Schuster UK Ltd ▪ ALONE ON THE MOUNTAIN **Joe Simpson**: *Touching the Void* (Jonathan Cape 1988), copyright © Joe Simpson 1988, reproduced by permission of The Random House Group Ltd ▪ ABOVE THE WORLD **David Scott** and **Alexei Leonov**: *Two Sides of the Moon* (Simon & Schuster, 2004), copyright © David Scott and Alexei Leonov 2004, reproduced by permission of Simon & Schuster UK Ltd ▪ ACROSS THE OUTBACK **Doris Pilkington**: *Rabbit-Proof Fence* (University of Queensland Press, 1996), copyright © Doris Pilkington-Nugi Garimara 1996, reproduced by permission of the publishers, Miramax Books c/o Hyperion. All rights reserved ▪ FUGITIVE IN THE DESERT **Chris Ryan**: *The One that Got Away* (Century, 1995), copyright © Chris Ryan 1995, reproduced by permission of The Random House Group Ltd ▪ BETWEEN A ROCK AND A HARD PLACE **Aron Ralston**: *Between a Rock and a Hard Place* (Simon & Schuster, 2004), copyright © Aron Ralson 2004, reproduced by permission of Simon & Schuster UK Ltd ▪ SARAJEVO DIARY **Zlata Filipovic**: *Zlata's Diary: A Child's Life in Sarajevo*, translated by Christine Pribischevich-Zoric (Viking, 1994, first published in France as *Le Journal de Zlata* by Fixot et editions Robert Laffont, 1993) copyright © Fixot et editions Robert Laffont 1993, reproduced by permission of Penguin Books Ltd ▪ BEYOND THE LAST OASIS **Ted Edwards**: *Beyond the Last Oasis* (John Murray, 1985), copyright © Ted Edwards 1985, reproduced by permission of Watson, Little Ltd for the author ▪ GROWING UP IN AUSCHWITZ **Eva Schloss** with Evelyn Julia Kent: *Eva's Story* (Castle-Kent, 2001, Eerdmans, 2009), copyright © Eva Schloss and Evelyn Julia Kent 1988, reproduced by permission of the authors ▪ KIDNAPPED IN THE JUNGLE **Matthew Scott** as told to Peter Foster and Caroline Davies: 'It was as if an angel had come down and whisked me away', *The Daily Telegraph*, October 14, 2003, copyright © The Daily Telegraph 2003, reproduced by permission of Telegraph Media Group Ltd ▪ IT'S STILL ME INSIDE **Simon Weston**: *Walking Tall* (Bloomsbury, 1989), copyright © Simon Weston 1989, reproduced by permission of Abingdon Management and Consulting on behalf of the author ▪ OUT OF THE BLUE **Bethany Hamilton**: *Soul Surfer* (Pocket Books, 2004), copyright © Bethany Hamilton 2004, reproduced by permission of Simon & Schuster UK Ltd ▪ TORTURE ON THE BURMA RAILWAY **Eric Lomax**: *The Railway Man* (Jonathan Cape, 1995), copyright © Eric Lomax 1995, reproduced by permission of The Random House Group Ltd ▪ THE LONG WAY DOWN **Brian Clark**: 'The Long Way Down', from an interview in Nova (WGBH Educational Foundation, 2006), copyright © WGBH/Boston 2006, reproduced by permission of WGBH Educational Foundation ▪ CAUGHT IN THE CROSSFIRE **Mary Quin**: *Kidnapped in the Yemen* (Mainstream, 2005), copyright © Mary Quin 2005, reproduced by permission of the publishers, Mainstream Publishing Co (Edinburgh) Ltd, Lyons Press/Globe Pequot Press, and Random House New Zealand Ltd ▪ DODGING TANKS AND GUNS **Kate Adie**: *The Kindness of Strangers* (Headline, 2002), copyright © Kate Adie 2002, reproduced by

permission of Headline Publishing Group Ltd ▪ I SURVIVED HIROSHIMA **Edward Sawyer**: 'I remember Hiroshima', *The Sunday Telegraph*, July 29, 1984, copyright © Noeline Tarrant 1984, reproduced by permission of Telegraph Media Group Ltd ▪ PERSECUTED FOR MY FAITH **Palden Gyatso**: *Fire Under the Snow* (Harvill Press, 1997), copyright © Palden Gyatso 1997, English translation copyright © Palden Gyatso and Tsering Shakya 1997, reproduced by permission of The Random House Group Ltd ▪ FLOWER FROM A CRUEL DESERT **Waris Dirie**: *Desert Flower* (Virago Press, 1998), copyright © Waris Dirie 1998, reproduced by permission of the publishers, Little, Brown Book Group ▪ BEHIND ENEMY LINES **George Millar**: *Maquis, the French Resistance at War* (Cassell Military, 2003), copyright © George Millar 1945, reproduced by permission of The Orion Publishing Group, London ▪ LAST PERSON RESCUED **Gill Hicks**: *One Unknown* (Pan Macmillan, 2008) copyright © Gill Hicks 2007, 2008, reproduced by permission of Pan Macmillan, London ▪ MAD WHITE GIANT **Benedict Allen**: *Mad White Giant: A Journey to the Heart of the Amazon Jungle* (Faber, 2002), copyright © Benedict Allen 1985 reproduced by permission of Faber & Faber Ltd ▪ THE KILLING FIELDS **Haing Ngor** with Roger Warner: *Survival in the Killing Fields* (Robinson, 2003), copyright © Sandwell Investment Ltd and Roger Warner 1987, reproduced by permission of the publishers, Constable and Robinson Ltd ▪ PLANE DOWN IN THE ANDES **Nando Parrado**: *Miracle in the Andes* (Orion, 2006), copyright © Nando Parrado 2006, reproduced by permission of The Orion Publishing Group, London

The following stories are copyright © Reader's Digest. All, except for THE LIONS OF TELEMARK, first appeared in the *Reader's Digest* magazine:

SURGERY AT 28,000 FEET (John Dyson) ▪ LOSING HEIGHT! (Tim Bouquet) ▪ THE FIGHT TO SAVE TENNEH (David Moller) ▪ STRUCK BY LIGHTNING (Ruaridh Pringle) ▪ THE LIONS OF TELEMARK (Jonathan Bastable) ▪ PLEASE DON'T LEAVE ME! (Jim Hutchison) ▪ LEOPARD ATTACK (John Dyson) ▪ I WILL CONFRONT MY FAMILY'S KILLER (David Gritten) ▪ HE'S DOWN THERE SOMEWHERE! (Tim Bouquet) ▪ CAVE OF DOOM (Tim Bouquet) ▪ MIRACLE OUT OF CHAOS (Lawrence Elliott) ▪ 65 HOURS IN A FROZEN TOMB (Louise Mills) ▪ THE DAY THE SKY FELL IN (John Dyson) ▪ THE SAND'S EATING ME ALIVE (John Dyson) ▪ IN THE JAWS OF DEATH (Jim Hutchison) ▪ MAYDAY! I DON'T KNOW HOW TO FLY (Robert Kiener) ▪ VOLCANO CHOPPER DOWN (Per Ola and Emily D'Aulaire) ▪ 'WE WON'T LET YOU DIE, DAD' (Kathy Cook) ▪ LOST IN THE DESERT (Donna Elizabeth Boetig) ▪ SWARM! (Gerry Johnson) ▪ RACE FOR HIS LIFE (Rudolph Chelminski)

Picture credits
All maps and diagrams are © Reader's Digest Association Ltd, except pp. 141 (bottom) and 161 (top). Story headings: all iStock, except pp. 78 and 196.
L=left, R=right, T=top, C=centre, B=bottom

Front Cover T Corbis/© Peace Memorial Museum/epa; Front Cover CR Getty Images/Kathleen Campbell/Stone; Front Cover B Getty Images/Anthony Correia; Front Cover CL Royal Geographical Society; **Back Cover** iStockphoto.com/© Thomas Pullicino; **1** Aron Ralston; **2-3** DPPI/Pete Goss; **4-5** iStockphoto.com/Zubin Li; **6-7** iStockphoto.com/Zubin Li; **8-9** iStockphoto.com/Clint Spencer; **10** INGEOMINAS; BL iStockphoto.com/Royce DeGrie; **10-11** INGEOMINAS; **12** Corbis/Roger Ressmeyer; **15** INGEOMINAS; **16** INGEOMINAS; **18-19** DigitalVision; **20** Corbis/Roger Ressmeyer; **23** Corbis/Kim Kulish; **25** T Getty Images/Luis Castaneda; B Corbis/© George Hall; **26** T Rex Features Ltd; B Getty Images/Keith Macgregor; **31** Rex Features Ltd; **32** T Corbis/© Gallo Images; BR Express Syndication; **33** Corbis/© Louise Gubb/SABA; **34** Express Syndication; **35** TL Corbis/© Gallo Images; **36** Getty Images; **39** Getty Images/AFP; **40** Getty Images; **42** Corbis/© Reuters; **43** T Rex Features Ltd/Stuart Clarke; B John Frost Historical Newspaper Service; **44** Thierry Boccon-Gibod; **48** Thierry Boccon-Gibod; **49** Thierry Boccon-Gibod; **50** T Mirrorpix; B Rex Features Ltd/News Group; **51** John Frost Historical Newspaper Service; **52** Mirrorpix; **53** L PA; R PA; **55** Mirrorpix; **57** Rex Features Ltd/News Group; **58** PA/Johnny Green/PA Archive; **61** ShutterStock, Inc/Digital N; **62** Rex Features Ltd/News Group; **63** Isle of Wight County Press; **64** T Corbis/Robert Patrick/Sygma; TL Rex Features Ltd/Assignments; B Corbis/Robert Patrick/Sygma; **67** Eastern Daily Press; **68** John Frost Historical Newspaper Service; **69** Rex Features Ltd/Greg

Williams; **70** Eastern Daily Press; **71** T Corbis/© Reuters; B BBC Photo Library; **72** Rex Features Ltd/Sipa Press; **74** Rex Features Ltd; **75** T Mirrorpix; B Abdullah Zaheeruddin; **76** BBC Photo Library; **77** BBC Wales; **78** © Ruaridh Pringle; (story heading: Science Photo Library/John A EY III); **79** © Ruaridh Pringle; **80** John Cleare/Mountain Camera; **81** © Ruaridh Pringle; **82** Science Photo Library/John A EY III; **83** © Ruaridh Pringle; **84** © Ruaridh Pringle; **85** © Ruaridh Pringle; **86** TL Getty Images/Linda Armstrong Kelly/Sports Illustrated; **86-87** Getty Images/Patrick Kovarik/AFP; **87** BR Getty Images/ Joel Saget/AFP; **88** Getty Images/Sports Illustrated; **89** Getty Images; **90-91** Getty Images/Doug Pensinger/Allsport; **93** Science Photo Library/ Mehau Kulyk; **94** Getty Images/Linda Armstrong Kelly/Sports Illustrated; **96** Getty Images/Doug Pensinger/Allsport; **97** PA/Laurent Rebours; **98** L PA/ Bernard Papon/AP Photo; R Getty Images; **99** T & B Getty Images/Mike Hill; C Courtesy of Tami Oldham Ashcraft; **100** Courtesy of Tami Oldham Ashcraft; **101** Courtesy of Tami Oldham Ashcraft; **102** Science Photo Library/NOAA; **107** Courtesy of Tami Oldham Ashcraft; **108** San Diego Union Tribune; **109** Simon Yates; TR Getty Images/Time Life Pictures; **111** Simon Yates; **112** Simon Yates; **115** Photolibrary.com/imagebroker.net; **117** The Kobal Collection/ Film Four/Pathe; **118** Simon Yates; **119** The Daily Telegraph/Martin Pope; **120** RIA Novosti; **121** John Frost Historical Newspaper Service; **122** T PA/AP; C PA/AP; B PA/AP; **123** RIA Novosti; **124** RIA Novosti; **125** Getty Images/AFP; **126-127** Photolibrary.com; **127** The Kobal Collection/Miramax/Dimension Films/Penny Tweedie; **129** National Library of Australia/F.H. Broomhall; **130** © Newspix/Colin Murty; **131** T Photoshot/ANT Photo Library; B Photoshot/ Imagebroker.net; **133** Photolibrary.com/Gillianne Tedder; **134** Louise Whelan Photography; **138** L © Newspix/Colin Murty; R © Newspix/Ross Swanborough; **139** T Courtesy of Chris Ryan; B Rex Features Ltd; **140** B Courtesy of Chris Ryan; **142** Imperial War Museum/E021338; **145** Courtesy of Chris Ryan; **147** T Getty Images/Corey Rich; B Aron Ralston; **148** Kristi Moore Curry; **150-151** iStockphoto.com/Zubin Li; **152** Aron Ralston; **153** Aron Ralston; **154** Corbis/© Kirk Mastin/Aurora Photos; **156** PA/E Pablo Kosmicki/AP; **157** T Norway's Resistance Museum; B PA/Erik Thorberg/Scanpix Norway; **159** The National Archives ref.HS 2-185-160; **160** The National Archives ref.HS 2-190-148; **161** T The National Archives ref.CAB126-171(1); **162** The National Archives ref.DEFE2-677#3; **167** The Kobal Collection/Columbia; **168** Collection Zlata Filipovic, Courtesy of Editions Robert Laffont.; L Rex Features Ltd/Sipa Press; **170** Corbis/© Patrick Robert/Sygma; **171** Reuters/Corinne Dufka; **172** Rex Features Ltd/Alexandra Boulat /Sipa; **173** Aidan Crawley Photography; **174** Alistair Macdonald; **174-175** Photolibrary.com/Photononstop; **176** Alistair Macdonald; **178-179** Alistair Macdonald; **181** T Photolibrary.com/age fotostock; B Corbis/Karen Kasmauski; **183** Ted Edwards; **184** Photolibrary. com/OSF; **187** Manchester Evening News; **188** T TVNZ Television Archive; B TVNZ Television Archive; **191** TVNZ Television Archive; **192** APN/New Zealand Herald; **193** TVNZ Television Archive; **195** Royd Kennedy; **196** Corbis/© Guenter Schindler/dpa; (story heading: Getty Images); L Courtesy of Eva Schloss; **197** Corbis/© dpa; **199** Getty Images; **200** T Corbis/© Bettmann; B Corbis/© Bettmann; **201** Corbis/© Michael St Maur Sheil; **203** Corbis/© epa; **205** TR Courtesy of Eva Schloss; BL PA/PA Archive; **206** Inset PA/PA Archive; Photolibrary.com/Jane O'Callaghan; BL Corbis/© William Parra/Stringer/ Reuters; **209** PA/Fernando Vergara/AP; **210** PA/Fernando Vergara/AP; **211** The Daily Telegraph; **212** PA/AP; **214** PA/PA Archive; **215** Getty Images/ AFP; **216** T iStockphoto.com/Stacey Newman; B ardea.com/Francois Gohier; **217** VII Photo Agency/Antonin Kratochvil; **218** VII Photo Agency/Antonin Kratochvil; **219** Photoshot/Andy Rouse; **220** VII Photo Agency/Antonin Kratochvil; **221** TL Courtesy of the Bogujevci Family; B PA/Dimitri Messinis/ AP; **222** PA/Tim Ockenden/PA Archive; **224** MaK (Manchester Aid for Kosovo); **225** Reuters/Stevan Lazarevic; **226** Courtesy of Saranda Bogujevci; **227** T iStockphoto.com/© Thomas Pullicino; TL Rex Features Ltd/Jeff Ross; BL Sheffield Newspapers; **228** Yorkshire Post Newspapers; **230** iStockphoto. com/© Mauro Scarone Vezzoso; **231** Guzelian Photography/Joan Russell; **232** Corbis/© Michael Freeman; **233** B PA/Martin Cleaver/PA Archive; **234** PA/Martin Cleaver/PA Archive; **237** Imperial War Museum/FKD 2028; **238** PA/PA Archive; **240** Touch Productions; **241** PA/Adam Butler/PA Archive; **242** PA/Malcolm Clarke/PA Archive; **243** T Rex Features Ltd/Sipa Press; B SeaPics.com, Inc; **244** Courtesy of Noah Hamilton and the Hamilton family; **245** Rex Features Ltd; **246** Courtesy of Noah Hamilton and the Hamilton family; **247** Photoshot/James Watt; **249** Courtesy of Noah Hamilton and the Hamilton family; **250** Courtesy of Noah Hamilton and the Hamilton family; **251** T Imperial War Museum HU 24392; TR Courtesy of Joe Payne; B Imperial War Museum HU 28599; **252** Imperial War Museum HU 4551; **255** R Imperial War Museum ART LD 6035, © Jacquie Mullender; **257** Imperial War Museum ART 15417 36, © Mrs Katie Grennan; **258** Getty Images/ Popperfoto; **261** Courtesy of Takashi Nagase; **262** PA/Carmen Taylor/AP;

262-263 Rex Features Ltd/Tamara Beckwith; **263** PA/Richard Drew/AP; **264** Janice Brooks; **265** PA/Amy Sancetta/AP; **266** PA/Amy Sancetta/AP; **268** PA/Suzanne Plunkett/AP; **269** PA/Chad Rachman/AP; **270** CR Rendering by Squared Design Lab, Courtesy National September 11 Memorial & Museum; B PA/Alex Fuchs/AP; **273** Piya Kochhar; **274** Getty Images/Terry O'Neill; **276** T Apex; B Apex; **277** CR by permission of Western Morning News/Photo, Tim Neale; B www.jasonhawkes.com; **278** Royal National Lifeboat Institution; **280** BL Getty Images/Roger Viollet; BR Courtesy of Mary Quin; **280-281** Courtesy of Mary Quin; **281** Courtesy of Mary Quin; **282** Getty Images/John Miles; **286** T Reuters/Aladin Abdel Naby; B Courtesy of Mary Quin; **289** Courtesy of Mary Quin; **290** Courtesy of Mary Quin; **291** T PA/Jeff Widener/ AP; B BBC Photo Library; **292** Rex Features Ltd/Sipa Press; **293** PA/Sadayuki Mikami/AP; **294** Rex Features Ltd/Sipa Press; **297** Getty Images/AFP; **299** Ken Lennox; **300-301** Getty Images/AFP; **301** TR ShutterStock, Inc/ Supri Suharjoto; **302** OnAsia/Hitoshi Katanoda; **303** OnAsia/Masao Endo; **304** T UNAVCO/GEON/USGS; **305** OnAsia/Greg Davis; **306** Corbis/© Patrick Robert/Sygma; **308** Corbis/© Michael S. Yamashita; **310** Corbis/© Karen Kasmauski; **313** PA/AP; **314** © Newspix/Brendan Esposito; TL © Newspix/ Chris Pavlich; **316** © Newspix; **317** © Newspix/David Crosling; **319** © Newspix/ Chris Pavlich; **320** © Newspix/Jeff Darmanin; **321** Apex/Mark Pearson; **322** Barry Marsden; **323** Apex/Emily Whitfield-Wicks; **325** Apex/Emily Whitfield-Wicks; **326** Getty Images; **327** PA/Barry Batchelor/PA Archive; **328** B The Visitor, Morecambe; **328-329** Collections/© Robert Estall; **329** Collections/ © David Askham; **331** Collections/Ashley Cooper; **332** Bay Search and Rescue; **333** The Visitor, Morecambe; **335** TR Courtesy of Sandra Prince; B Courtesy of Sandra Prince; **336** Courtesy of Sandra Prince; **337** Courtesy of Sandra Prince; **338** Photoshot/Jonathan & Angela Scott; **339** © Jim Hutchison; **341** Courtesy of Sandra Prince; **342-343** Royal Geographical Society; **343** Mirrorpix; **344** Royal Geographical Society; **345** Royal Geographical Society; **348** L Scott Polar Research Institute, University of Cambridge; R Royal Geographical Society; **349** Scott Polar Research Institute, University of Cambridge; **350** T Scott Polar Research Institute, University of Cambridge; B Scott Polar Research Institute, University of Cambridge; **352** Royal Geographical Society; **353** Royal Geographical Society; **354** Royal Geographical Society; **355** L Royal Geographical Society; R Science Photo Library/British Antarctic Survey; **356-357** Corbis/© Peace Memorial Museum/epa; **357** John Frost Historical Newspaper Service; **360** Corbis; **361** Getty Images/ AFP; **362** TR PA/AP; BL Reuters/Kyodo; **363** Getty Images/AFP; TL Corbis/ Anna Branthwaite; **364** Getty Images/AFP; **367** Corbis/Andy Rain/epa; **368** Getty Images/Daniel Berehulak; **369** T Austin J.Brown www.aviationpictures. com; BC Mirrorpix; B South Wales Echo; **370** Rex Features Ltd; **372** Mirrorpix; **374** Mirrorpix; **375** Mirrorpix; **376-377** Camera Press/Alexis Duclos/Gamma; **378** Corbis/© Kevin Fleming; **380-381** Corbis/© Liba Taylor; **382** Corbis/ © Kevin Fleming; **386** Corbis/Eric Robert/Sygma; **388** Corbis/Todd France; **389** Reuters/Leonhard Foeger; **390** C The National Archives ref.DEFE2-677 George Millar (1); **391** B Musée de la résistance et de la déportation, Besançon; **392** The National Archives ref.DEFE2-677 George Millar (2); **393** T Musée de la résistance et de la déportation, Besançon; C Musée de la résistance et de la déportation, Besançon; B Musée de la résistance et de la déportation, Besançon; **394** Getty Images; **397** Musée de la résistance et de la déportation, Besançon; **399** Musée de la résistance et de la déportation, Besançon; **400** Caroline Penn; **401** Corbis/© Douglas Peebles; **402** Agentur Bilderberg/ Peter Ginter; **403** © Per Ola D'Aulaire; **405** PA/David Jordan/AP; **407** The Kobal Collection/20th Century Fox/Ron Phillips; **408** T Rex Features Ltd; B © Gill Hicks; **411** Tim Anderson; **414** PA/PA Archive; **415** © Mike Prior; **416** Mirrorpix; **417** PA/PA Archive; **418** T Jean-Paul Boudreau; B Alamy Images/Bill Brooks; **421** Jean-Paul Boudreau; **422** Photolibrary.com/Radius Images; **424-425** Benedict Allen; **426** B Benedict Allen; **427** Benedict Allen; **429** Corbis/Colin McPherson; **430** Benedict Allen; **432** Benedict Allen; **433** Benedict Allen; **435** Benedict Allen; **436** Corbis/© George H.H. Huey; **437** Alvin Abrams; **439** Photolibrary.com; **440** Courtesy of Mindy Badovinatz; **441** © The Phoenix Gazette, May 1, 1991/(Photo David McIntyre); **442** TL Photoshot/James Carmichael Jr; **442-443** Photolibrary.com/Peter Lilja; **443** © Reader's Digest (photo Richard Bickel); **445** Photolibrary.com/Raymond Mendez; **446** © Reader's Digest (photo Richard Bickel); **448-449** DPPI/Pete Goss; **451** L PA/RAAF/AP; R PA/Tony MacDonough/AP; **453** DPPI/Pete Goss; **454** DPPI/Mark Lloyd; **455** T The Kobal Collection/Enigma/Goldcrest; B PA/D.Gray/AP; **457** Getty Images/AFP; TR Mirrorpix; **458** Rex Features Ltd/ Sipa Press; **460** PA/AP; **463** Getty Images/AFP; **465** Getty Images/AFP; **466-467** Corbis/© Group of Survivors; **468** Corbis/© Group of Survivors; **470** Corbis/© Group of Survivors; **473** John Frost Historical Newspaper Service; **474** Rex Features Ltd/Sipa Press; **475** Rex Features Ltd/Sipa Press; **476** PA/AP; **477** L Corbis/© KUBA; R Rex Features Ltd ■

They Lived to Tell the Tale is published by
The Reader's Digest Association Limited,
11 Westferry Circus, Canary Wharf, London E14 4HE

We are committed both to the quality of our products and the service we provide to our customers. We value your comments, so please do contact us on **08705 113366** or via our website at **www.readersdigest.co.uk**

If you have any comments or suggestions about the content of our books, email us at **gbeditorial@readersdigest.co.uk**

Concept code: UK2015/G
Book code: 400-265 UP0000-1
ISBN: 978 0 276 44539 2
Oracle Code: 250002305H.00.24

READER'S DIGEST PROJECT TEAM

Project Editor
John Andrews

Art Editor
Julie Bennett

Designer
Austin Taylor

Picture Researcher
Caroline Wood

Consultant Editor
Veronica Pratt

Editors
Mike Bailey
Tim Bouquet
Sally Cummings
Hugo de Klee
Steve Savage

Feature Writers
Jonathan Bastable
Rose Shepherd

Sub-editor
Ali Moore

Illustrators
Ian Moores
Lee Woodgate

Text Permissions Coordinator
Connie Robertson

Proofreader
Barry Gage

Origination by
Colour Systems
Limited, London

Printed and bound by
Neografia, Slovakia

READER'S DIGEST GENERAL BOOKS

Editorial Director
Julian Browne

Art Director
Anne-Marie Bulat

Head of Book Development
Sarah Bloxham

Managing Editor
Nina Hathway

Picture Resource Manager
Christine Hinze

Pre-press Account Manager
Dean Russell

Product Production Manager
Claudette Bramble

Senior Production Controller
Katherine Tibbals